Springer Texts in Business and Economics

Springer Texts in Business and Economics (STBE) delivers high-quality instructional content for undergraduates and graduates in all areas of Business/Management Science and Economics. The series is comprised of self-contained books with a broad and comprehensive coverage that are suitable for class as well as for individual self-study. All texts are authored by established experts in their fields and offer a solid methodological background, often accompanied by problems and exercises.

More information about this series at http://www.springer.com/series/10099

Jin Cao • Gerhard Illing

Money: Theory and Practice

Springer

Jin Cao
Research Department
Norges Bank
Oslo, Norway

Gerhard Illing
Department of Economics
LMU Munich
Munich, Germany

ISSN 2192-4333 ISSN 2192-4341 (electronic)
Springer Texts in Business and Economics
ISBN 978-3-030-19696-7 ISBN 978-3-030-19697-4 (eBook)
https://doi.org/10.1007/978-3-030-19697-4

This Springer imprint is published by the registered company Springer Nature Switzerland AG.
The registered company address is: Gewerbestrasse 11, 6330 Cham, Switzerland

Preface

Since the financial crisis, there have been dramatic innovations both in theoretical models of monetary policy and in actual policy as practiced by central banks in all advanced economies. Recent models emphasize the importance of financial frictions and of nonlinear effects in the context of system-wide failures of the banking system, fire sales, and liquidity crises. Central bank practice responded to current challenges with a wide range of unconventional monetary policy measures. Standard textbooks hardly address these issues, making it hard for students to judge the logic behind and the impact of these measures. This new textbook provides a thorough and detailed introduction into the new insights both in monetary theory and in policy, aimed at advanced undergraduate and master's education.

The textbook gives an introduction into modern monetary economics, emphasizing lessons from the recent financial crisis. The book focuses on intuition without going into technical details. A unique characteristic is the treatment of recent research on an intuitive level within simple models (most of them static and two-period), but also preparing for an extension to a truly dynamic analysis. We provide a systematic perspective on monetary policy, covering a wide range of models helping to better understand controversial issues.

Part I covers the long-run perspective, presenting traditional standard monetary policy models. We address classical issues such as neutrality of money, the natural rate of interest, determination of the price level, the role of seigniorage, and the interaction between monetary and fiscal policy in different regimes.

Part II introduces the core New Keynesian model. It characterizes optimal monetary policy for stabilizing short-term shocks. In that framework, we outline concepts such as the debate about rules vs. discretion, challenges arising from control errors, imperfect information, and robustness issues. Furthermore, we analyze the limits for traditional monetary policy at the effective lower bound and the challenges for optimal control presented by such a bound.

Finally, Part III focuses on the role of financial frictions. First, we present an overview on current monetary policy in practice. We characterize different monetary transmission mechanisms via banking, focusing on the key channels for unconventional monetary policy. We review models with incomplete markets, principal-agent problems, maturity mismatch, and leverage cycles. We show why the size of the stakes of investors and intermediaries plays a key role in lending with pro-cyclical features. We present a tractable model for handling liquidity management and show how the need to sell assets in crisis amplifies volatility of the real economy. In the final chapter, we discuss the relation between monetary policy and financial stability, addressing systemic risk and the role of macroprudential regulation.

This textbook is based on master's courses on money and banking taught at the LMU University of Munich and at the University of Oslo. It benefited enormously from many helpful comments from all our students. We would like to thank in particular Matthias Schlegl, Thomas Siemsen, Jiarui Zhang, Q. Farooq Akram and Norges Bank colleagues for constructive criticism and Bernhard Kassner for his assistance in preparing print design and figures for the book. We would also like to thank Kay Stoll at Springer for her assistance in preparing the book.

Oslo, Norway
Munich, Germany
February 2019

Jin Cao
Gerhard Illing

List of Chapters

Contents

Long-Run Growth: The Basic Framework

1

1.1 Introduction

Modern analysis of macroeconomics is done in complex models with dynamic stochastic general equilibrium (DSGE). The models characterize the general equilibrium of an economy in a dynamic and stochastic setting, with the behavior of all agents derived from explicit individual optimization. DSGE models study the equilibrium in a competitive economy, modified by various distortions, such as nominal and real rigidities like monopolistic competition.[1] During the last decade, there have been strong controversies about the usefulness and weakness of DSGE models. In this book, we provide an intuitive introduction into the structure and shortcomings of these models. In order to gain the basic intuition, we reduce the problem to a very simple case: In this chapter, we present a two-period non-stochastic model of the economy. In this dynamic base line scenario, we introduce important concepts for inter-temporal analysis which play a key role in modern monetary policy analysis. In Chap. 1, we look at a real economy, abstracting from monetary policy issues. Even though we introduce the notion of (fiat) money as additional good right from the beginning, money is just used only as unit of account (numeraire). Defining P_t as the price level (the price of goods of in terms of money), we take the evolution of the price level (the rate of inflation) as given. We derive the Fisher equation as arbitrage condition for portfolio allocation between real and nominal bonds. Later (in Part I), we study how central banks can control the price level in various monetary policy regimes when prices are perfectly flexible.

We start with an endowment economy with one representative agent. We illustrate the concepts of wealth constraint, inter-temporal optimization with time preferences, marginal rate of substitution (MRS), and the real rate interest. We derive optimality conditions for the inter-temporal path of consumption (the Euler

[1]Standard references are Christiano, Eichenbaum, and Evans (2005) and Smets and Wouters (2007). See also Christiano, Eichenbaum, and Trabandt (2018).

J. Cao, G. Illing, *Money: Theory and Practice*, Springer Texts in Business and Economics, https://doi.org/10.1007/978-3-030-19697-4_1

equation) and the natural rate of interest as key equilibrium condition. We show that our endowment can be interpreted as a base line model for a growing economy and that extending the setup to more than two periods is straightforward. Finally, we illustrate how to extend the model to allow for heterogeneity across households.

In Sect. 1.3, we introduce government spending and taxation in our two-period model and discuss conditions under which Ricardian equivalence holds. Section 1.4 extends our base line model by introducing the labor market, making production endogenous. We analyze the labor supply choice of households and the choice for optimal consumption bundle with preferences exhibiting elasticity of substitution between different heterogeneous goods. Since price setting behavior of firms will play a crucial role, we derive optimal price setting under monopolistic competition in an economy with heterogeneous firms.

Finally, we derive conditions for a general equilibrium in the economy for the case that all firms can adjust their prices optimally without cost. This provides an important reference point for later analysis: It characterizes the natural level of employment, potential output, and the corresponding natural real rate of interest in the absence of nominal rigidities—that is, the case that all prices are perfectly flexible. Due to monopolistic price setting and distortionary effects of taxation, the market equilibrium is distorted relative to the welfare maximizing first best level of production. The simple structure allows to solve explicitly for the equilibrium. We show that the level of economic activity and employment is inefficiently low as a result of the frictions. The structural inefficiency can be summarized by a simple markup factor.

1.2 Dynamic Macro in a Two-Period Model

Modern macro is about dynamic stochastic general equilibrium. The simplest setup is a model with just one representative agent, optimizing in an economy with imperfect competition and possibly incomplete asset markets. In order to gain the basic intuition, we reduce the problem to the easiest case: We consider a ***two-period economy*** with one consumption good per period and no uncertainty. To start with, initially we look at an ***endowment economy***. Resources of households are assumed to be exogenously given in each period; households can choose their consumption path across time: How much will they consume in the first period (the present), how much in the second (the future)? Later, we will allow for production being determined endogenously. The two-period setting allows us to characterize some key features of the inter-temporal allocation in the simplest way. Via inter-temporal trade, households can smooth consumption across time.

The two-period setting may look a bit artificial, since (hopefully) the future lasts much longer than the present. But it is straightforward to extend it to multiple periods—it will be just more cumbersome. Somewhat paradoxically, the simplest straightforward generalization is to extend our analysis to an infinite horizon.

The workhorse model of modern macro tries to capture all relevant choices on the macro level by analyzing the decision of one representative agent. This representative agent framework abstracts from all issues caused by heterogeneity, in particular distributional issues. A complete set of markets for each contingent state of the world allows for perfect insurance against idiosyncratic risks. In this chapter, we introduce the workhorse model and analyze inter-temporal trade via financial assets, abstracting from frictions in financial markets. First, we consider bonds paying a rate of interest and distinguish between nominal and real bonds. Later, we extend our basic model by introducing government bonds.

Assuming inter-temporal trade can be done via financial assets traded on perfect capital markets, the workhorse model characterizes a reference scenario in the absence of financial frictions. This approach has come under severe attack recently. After all, most challenges posed by the financial crisis cannot be captured within a single-agent framework. There is a heated debate about the currently fashionable way of doing macroeconomics. Capital market frictions are key for understanding the impact of disruption in financial intermediation. As we will see in later chapters, to motivate a role for money we need to introduce some trading frictions.

1.2.1 The Wealth Constraint

For many issues (like understanding long-run growth) it is useful to abstract from the monetary side of the economy. One strand of macro—the real business cycle theory—even tries to analyze determinants of short-run business cycle phenomena without reference to monetary policy. In this chapter we too are mainly concerned with the real side of the economy.

To simplify, we consider an economy with just one good and two periods (t, $t+1$). In each period, consumers receive some real endowment (income) Y_t and Y_{t+1} of a non-storable good.[2] Instead of consuming their endowment, individual consumers may prefer a different consumption path across both periods by trading claims on their endowment at an inter-temporal perfectly competitive capital market. We model inter-temporal trade as buying or selling nominal bonds—claims paying a fixed nominal interest rate i_t. How to characterize inter-temporal constraints in our economy and the optimal consumption path across time? Consumption of the same good next period is quite a different commodity, so it will have a different (relative) price. What is the price of future consumption in terms of consumption today? How is the interest rate determined in equilibrium?

Since there is just one good in this economy we might easily normalize the price of this good in the first period t to one.[3] But in order to provide a common

[2] That is, the good perishes completely if it is not consumed in the same period. Check to what extent the analysis must be modified when we allow for goods to be stored with some decay rate $\delta \in [0, 1]$.

[3] In standard microanalysis, consumers choose the optimal bundle, given their budget constraint. In general equilibrium, only relative prices are determined—the real rate of exchange between different commodities. The absolute price level is in determined and irrelevant. So the price of some arbitrary good can be normalized to one. In nearly all real economies, however, most prices are quoted in terms of a specific numeraire—the particular commodity which is used as money or medium of exchange. Modern economies use fiat money—a medium of exchange which has no intrinsic value. A key challenge for monetary economics is to provide a theory explaining how the price level is determined in a fiat money regime. We will come back to this issue in later chapters.

framework, we already introduce right from the beginning the nominal price level P_t. For that purpose, we use an extremely simplistic view of how P_t is determined. We assume that prices of all goods are quoted in terms of some unit of account. In an economy with fiat money, this will be the money stock M_t. The central bank is able to control the price level (and thus the rate of inflation). Assume that the price level is determined by the quantity of money.[4] Given the aggregate amount of real resources in each period, the nominal price level is $P_t = M_t/Y_t$ in period t and $P_{t+1} = M_{t+1}/Y_{t+1}$ in the following period with the rate of inflation $\pi_t = \frac{P_{t+1}}{P_t} - 1$ defined by $P_{t+1} = (1 + \pi_t)\, P_t$. In our simple setting, the central bank can control the rate of inflation simply by adjusting the growth rate of money supply relative to the growth rate of resources available: $\pi_t = \frac{M_{t+1}/Y_{t+1}}{M_t/Y_t} - 1 = \frac{M_{t+1}/M_t}{Y_{t+1}/Y_t} - 1$. For instance, $\pi_t = 0$ for $\frac{M_{t+1}}{M_t} = \frac{Y_{t+1}}{Y_t}$.

A consumer willing to save part of her resources from current income $P_t S_t = P_t(Y_t - C_t)$ can invest her savings in bonds with 1 year maturity. The nominal redemption value next period is $P_t S_t$. In addition, nominal bonds promise to pay a nominal interest rate i_t. So next year, the nominal payoff will be $P_t S_t(1 + i_t)$. In nominal terms, the per period budget constraints can be written as:

$$P_t C_t = P_t(Y_t - S_t),$$

$$P_{t+1} C_{t+1} = P_{t+1} Y_{t+1} + P_t S_t(1 + \pi_t). \tag{1.2.1}$$

But in real terms, the actual payoff at $t + 1$ strongly depends on the rate of inflation. The higher the rate of inflation, the lower is the real value of nominal bonds. Having invested $P_t S_t$ in nominal bonds, the consumer can afford next period in real terms the amount

$$C_{t+1} = Y_{t+1} + S_t(1 + i_t) \cdot P_t/P_{t+1}. \tag{1.2.2}$$

Alternatively, the consumer may invest in indexed bonds,[5] guaranteeing a real rate of return r_t —independent of the evolution of the price level. Indexed bonds allow next period the consumption $C_{t+1} = Y_{t+1} + S_t(1 + r_t)$. For indexed bonds,

[4]Nothing depends on this specific mechanism (the quantity theory of money). Crucial is that the price level (and thus the rate of inflation) is determined by the central bank. It may control the price level by other means, such as a strategy of inflation targeting. Later chapters discuss challenges to implement the target in different ways like a money growth rule or an interest rate rule.

[5]Indexed (inflation-linked) bonds are not frequently used. One reason may be that it is hard to specify all contingencies in detail, so such payments characterize an incomplete contract. It is not easy to specify exactly how to index payments to changes in the "true" rate of inflation. What commodity basket should be used? How to allow for adjustments in the way changes in the price level are calculated? Contractual arrangements with indexation are used mainly for long-term rent contracts. Governments also issue to some extent indexed bonds for financing debt (see the Focus Box on Inflation Linked Bonds).

interest payments are automatically adjusted according to the actual rate of inflation, paying out more in nominal terms with a higher increase in the price level.

At the time of saving, the future price level P_{t+1} is not yet known. Consumers form expectations about monetary policy and hence about the expected price level P^e_{t+1}. Arbitrage ensures that the effective real rate of return from indexed bonds cannot deviate from the expected real return of nominal bonds. The following condition (the **Fisher relation**) must hold:

$$1 + r_t = \frac{1 + i_t}{P^e_{t+1}/P_t} = \frac{1 + i_t}{1 + \pi^e_t}, \quad \text{or} \quad i_t = r_t + \pi^e_t + r_t \cdot \pi^e_t \approx r_t + \pi^e_t. \qquad (1.2.3)$$

To see this, let us allow the consumer to invest some share α in nominal and the rest (1–α) in indexed bonds promising the payoff $C_{t+1} = Y_{t+1} + S_t\left[\alpha \cdot (1 + i_t) \cdot \frac{P_t}{P_{t+1}} + (1 - \alpha) \cdot (1 + r_t)\right]$. If the Fisher relation does not hold, the consumer will prefer a corner solution, investing only in those bonds promising the superior return—either in indexed or in nominal bonds. So in equilibrium, arbitrage ensures that the return of both types of assets is equal.[6] Using this arbitrage condition, we can focus our analysis purely on the real side of the economy. Money is just a veil.

In this chapter, we abstract from any uncertainty about the evolution of the price level. We assume that agents correctly anticipate the future price level, so $P_{t+1} = P^e_{t+1}$. In general, when there is uncertainty about the future price level, this condition will hold only in expected value terms (see the following chapters).

Focus Box: The Fisher Relation

We need to distinguish between nominal and real interest rates. When prices are rising fast, the effective real rate of return of a bond may be rather low despite high nominal rates. Reversely, with falling prices (such as during periods of deflation), real interest rates can be quite high despite nominal rates being low or even close to zero. During the Great Depression (1929–1933) nominal rates have been very low by historical standards. Most observers interpreted this as a sign of a loose monetary policy. Nevertheless, real rates were rather high, suggesting monetary policy being too tight. So just looking at the nominal rate is neither helpful for judging the monetary policy stance nor a guide for investment purposes.

Obviously, when investing in nominal bonds, the expected rate of inflation plays a crucial role. Consumers can choose between buying real or nominal bonds. Nominal bonds pay some fixed interest rate, denominated in nominal terms. Real bonds are indexed bonds, with payments adjusted for the rate of

(continued)

[6]This has to be modified when the assets have different risk characteristics.

inflation. Therefore, the real rate of return is known in advance, whereas the nominal return varies with the rate of inflation realized over the life of the bond. When choosing between investing in real or nominal bonds, an investor is indifferent between both options only if the Fisher relation holds. So in equilibrium, this arbitrage condition must be fulfilled. It gives a straightforward relation between the real rate of interest r_t and the nominal rate of interest $i_t : i_t = r_t + \pi_t^e$. Irving Fisher (1896) emphasized this condition. It is called the Fisher relation, even though the relation was already known long time before Fisher's work.

In reality, P_{t+1} may be volatile due to inflation risk; so the Fisher relation holds only in expected terms. It can be used to extract market information about the expected rate of inflation. After all, according to the Fisher relation, the expected rate is just the spread—the difference between the return on nominal and indexed bonds $\pi_t^e = i_t - r_t$. The spread in the return of inflation-indexed bonds can be used to calculate a measure for the expected rate of inflation—the so called break-even inflation rate (BEIR). One attraction is that we can calculate the spreads for different maturities to compare how inflation expectations vary over different time horizons (for instance for bonds with 5 or 10 year maturity).

But changes in risk premiums may result in severe distortions of that information: With indexed bonds neither the purchaser nor the issuer faces any risk from unanticipated inflation. So indexed bonds insure against inflation risk; their price may contain an inflation risk premium. This may lead to a bias when estimating expected inflation via BEIR. But the direction of the bias is unclear. The premium may be positive or negative since ex ante both the issuer and the buyer of bonds benefit from reduced uncertainty. If both sides have the same degree of risk aversion, there is no bias. If buyers have a higher (smaller) degree of risk aversion, the return on the indexed bond will be biased upwards (downwards).

Furthermore, the market share of indexed bonds is fairly small in most economies. So they face a substantial liquidity risk: The risk that prices move significantly when many investors try to sell or buy at the same time. In contrast, the market for nominal bonds is extremely large and thus liquid. Buyers may be willing to pay a liquidity premium for bonds with high daily trading volume, particular in times when they are worried about liquidity risk. Distinguishing between the different types of risk premiums inherent in different bonds make it hard to extract reliable information about expected inflation. This is of particular concern in times of crisis unless the information provided has been adjusted for changes in risk premiums.

Focus Box: Inflation-Linked Bonds

Indexed bonds are mainly issued by governments. The world's first known inflation-indexed bonds were issued by the Commonwealth of Massachusetts in 1780 during the Revolutionary War. These bonds were invented to deal with severe wartime inflation and with angry discontent among soldiers in the USA. In modern times, the British government began to issue inflation-linked Gilts (gilt-edged securities) in 1981 after an extended period of high inflation. In 2008, the worldwide market for inflation-linked bonds comprised over $1.5 trillion. This sounds like an enormous sum, but it is only a small share of the total amount of outstanding bonds.

The US Treasury introduced inflation-indexed notes called TIPS (Treasury Inflation-Protected Securities) in January 1997. Economists had for quite some time urged the treasury to issue this instrument as a useful financial innovation. Many observers, however, had been rather skeptical whether there would be any demand for this kind of bonds. Many argued that hardly any investor will be interested in buying such bonds, fearing that the market will not be liquid. Some cynics even suggested, in order to save cost, that the treasury should send the ads for these new securities just to the members of the American Economic Association. Indeed, in 1999 these bonds accounted for less than 2% of the marketable federal government debt outstanding.

In Germany, the Bundesbank did not allow indexed bonds for a long time. The reason has been discussed in the weekly financial magazine *The Economist* (March 14, 2006):

> Some exhibits in Frankfurt's Money Museum ... help to explain why forbidding indexation was such a sacred cow in Germany. With a joystick that controls the money supply you can play being a central banker. The more money there is in circulation, represented by a tide of light rising up one column, the greater the velocity and price of goods and services, represented by light rising up another column, until inflation takes hold. Then you must race to dampen the money supply ahead of rising prices, without setting off a deflationary spiral (all too easy). ...
>
> During the Weimar Republic the Reichsbank, then Germany's central bank, played this game for real and sensationally lost control. The acceptance of constantly rising prices, known as inflationary expectations, seized the minds of the people and the entire world of commerce. Indexing prices to inflation only made things worse: It reached 1,024% in 1922, which was just about bearable, but galloped to 105,700,000,000% during 1923. Paper money became the cheapest form of heating fuel. By October 1923, 4.2 billion Reichsmarks could (or might) have bought you a dollar. Anyone who had supported Germany's effort in the first world war by buying government bonds got almost nothing in return when a new currency, the Rentenmark, was introduced in November. But inflation was halted.
>
> That is the background which prompted the 1948 currency law to forbid indexation clauses without the Bundesbank's permission. This permission was always refused, except for some long-term rental agreements. Due to the resistance of the Bundesbank, it took until March 2006 to introduce the first indexed government

(continued)

bonds. The issue of €5.5 billion of bonds was linked to the harmonized index of consumer prices in the euro zone (excluding tobacco). Not many German investors were interested: About 16% of the bonds were sold nationally; most were placed elsewhere in Europe, especially France.

Buttonwood Colum "Laying the ghost of 1923" (in: The Economist, March 14th 2006) Link: http://www.economist.com/agenda/displaystory.cfm?story_id=E1_VGNNRGP

Let us summarize the budget constraint for each period in real terms by the following equations:

$$C_t = Y_t - S_t, \tag{1.2.4}$$

$$C_{t+1} = Y_{t+1} + S_t(1 + r_t).$$

With perfect capital markets, we can merge the per-period budget constraints into one single wealth constraint by substituting for S_t. This wealth constraint tells us that the present discounted value of consumption cannot exceed present discounted value of income (the consumer's wealth)[7]:

$$C_t + \frac{1}{1 + r_t} C_{t+1} = Y_t + \frac{1}{1 + r_t} Y_{t+1}. \tag{1.2.5}$$

The wealth constraint defines all feasible inter-temporal allocations for the consumer (the line from $W_{t+1}(E, r_t)$ to $W_t(E, r_t)$ in Fig. 1.1). E characterizes the endowment point in Fig. 1.1. It is always feasible to consume the endowment point E with (Y_t, Y_{t+1}). As drawn in Fig. 1.1, endowment E is growing with $Y_{t+1} = (1 + g_t)Y_t > Y_t$ with g_t being the growth rate defined as $g_t = (Y_{t+1} - Y_t)/Y_t$. Obviously, on the aggregate level, aggregate consumption must be equal to aggregate endowment. So a representative agent has to be happy to consume exactly what is available in each period, and the interest rate needs to adjust accordingly. We will analyze general equilibrium in Sect. 1.2.4. Currently, we analyze the optimal choice for a consumer being able to save or borrow any amount at a given rate of interest.

The effective real price of future consumption in terms of consumption today is determined by the real rate of interest r_t. The higher r_t, the cheaper is future

[7]When the Fisher relation holds, we get the equivalent formulation merging the nominal budget constraints:

$$C_t + \frac{1}{(1 + i_t) \cdot P_t/P_{t+1}} C_{t+1} = Y_t + \frac{1}{(1 + i_t) \cdot P_t/P_{t+1}} Y_{t+1}.$$

Fig. 1.1 Wealth constraint

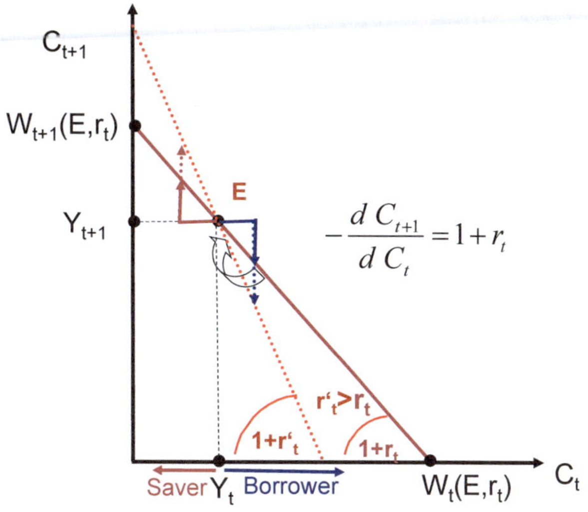

consumption relative to current consumption. Savings plus the real rate of interest earned between t and $t + 1$ adds to future income Y_{t+1}. It allows consumption next period: $C_{t+1} = Y_{t+1} + S_t(1 + r_t)$. Alternatively, if consumers prefer to borrow from future income streams by issuing real bonds, they want to consume more than their income in the current period ($S_t < 0$). But next period, they have to pay back the bond and, in addition, make interest payments. With $S_t < 0$, future consumption has to be lower than future income. When we wish to consume more than current income in one period, we need to consume less than current income in the other period. This is immediately evident when we rewrite the wealth constraint in the following way:

$$C_t - Y_t = -\frac{1}{1 + r_t}(C_{t+1} - Y_{t+1}). \qquad (1.2.6)$$

Saving one unit (giving up one unit of consumption today) raises future consumption by $1 + r_t$. Conversely, giving up $1 + r_t$ units of future consumption (borrowing) allows one unit more of consumption today. $1 + r_t$ is called the *gross* real interest rate, whereas r_t is the *net* rate. The real interest rate determines the slope of the wealth constraint. An increase in r_t rotates the wealth constraint around point E (see the steeper, dotted line in Fig. 1.1): A higher interest rate expands the set of feasible allocations for savers (making saving a more attractive option); at the same time it narrows the options for creditors (making borrowing more costly). Obviously, a change in the interest rate will have opposing wealth effects on savers and borrowers.

The optimal choice for the consumption path (with saving or borrowing) depends not only on the interest rate and the initial endowment, but also on inter-temporal preferences.

1.2.2 Inter-temporal Preferences

Preferences of the representative consumer are given by the time-separable utility function:

$$V(C_t, C_{t+1}) = U(C_t) + \beta U(C_{t+1}). \tag{1.2.7}$$

$U(C_t)$ is the utility function for period t. Usually, people are impatient—if they have the option to consume a given quantity either today or to wait for 1 year, they prefer to consume it right now. This impatience is captured by the discount factor $\beta \leq 1$. Alternatively, the degree of impatience can be characterized by the discount rate $\rho \geq 0$ at which future consumption is discounted relative to present consumption. β and ρ are linked by the relation $\beta = 1/(1+\rho) \leq 1$. Impatient people need to be rewarded for postponing consumption: Future consumption, measured in terms of present value, has to be "cheaper" than current consumption. Thus, postponing consumption needs to be rewarded by paying positive real interest rates.

Preferences can be represented by indifference curves, characterizing all consumption bundles (C_t, C_{t+1}) which give the same total utility $V(C_t, C_{t+1}) = \overline{V}$ (see the curve $\overline{V}$ in Fig. 1.2). People are—at least to some extent—willing to substitute current for future consumption. We can measure this willingness by the marginal rate of substitution (*MRS*)—the (absolute value of the) slope of the indifference curve. Mathematically,[8] it is the ratio of marginal utilities:

$$\text{MRS}: -\left.\frac{d\,C_{t+1}}{d\,C_t}\right|_{V=\overline{V}} = \frac{1}{\beta}\frac{U_{C_t}(C_t)}{U_{C_{t+1}}(C_{t+1})} = (1+\rho)\frac{U_{C_t}(C_t)}{U_{C_{t+1}}(C_{t+1})}. \tag{1.2.8}$$

In the second equation, we replace $1/\beta$ by $1+\rho$. We denote the marginal derivative of period utility with respect to consumption by $U_c(C) = \partial U/\partial C$.

In standard micro theory, the *MRS* between two goods tells us how much more consumption of the second good the consumer needs in order to be willing to give up one (marginal) unit of consumption of the first good. Here, the first good is current consumption C_t and the second good future consumption C_{t+1}. As you can see in Fig. 1.2, along a convex indifference curve, the willingness to give up current consumption in exchange for future consumption is increasing with C_t. To gain a better intuition, compare points *E* and *B* in Fig. 1.2. Current consumption is low in *E* relative to future consumption; the other way round in *B*. But both consumption bundles in Fig. 1.2 provide the same utility (just as point *A*).

[8]We can derive the *MRS* by total differentiation of inter-temporal preferences, holding overall utility constant:

$$dV = U_{C_t}(C_t)\,dC_t + \beta\,U_{C_{t+1}}(C_{t+1})\,dC_{t+1} = 0.$$

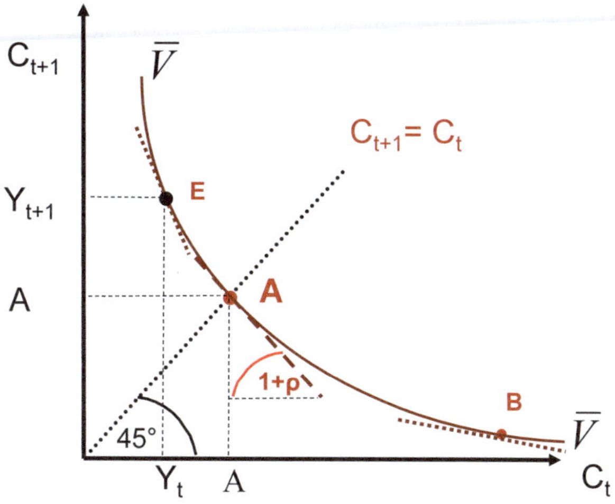

Fig. 1.2 Inter-temporal consumption: indifference curves

In *E*, you would need to gain a lot of additional consumption tomorrow in order to accept giving up some consumption today. Equivalently, that means that you would be willing to give up a lot from future consumption in order to gain a little bit more today. In *E*, the slope of the indifference curve is very steep, the **shadow price** (the consumer's evaluation) of current relative to future consumption being high. But the more consumption is available today relative to the future, the more eager you become to trade quite a bit of current consumption for a little bit more of future consumption—the slope gets flatter and flatter along the indifference curve when moving from point *E* to point *B* along the indifference curve.

Consumer's relative evaluation varies along the indifference curve. To define a consistent measure for the degree of impatience across heterogeneous agents, we use the slope (*MRS*) for the case that consumption is equal in both periods—such as at point *A*. All bundles with the same consumption level in both periods $(C_t = C_{t+1})$ lie on the 45° line. Since $U_{C_t}(C_t) = U_{C_{t+1}}(C_{t+1})$ for $C_t = C_{t+1}$, the absolute value of the slope along this line is always

$$-\left.\frac{d\,C_{t+1}}{d\,C_t}\right|_{V=\overline{V};\,C_t=C_{t+1}} = \frac{1}{\beta} = 1+\rho \tag{1.2.9}$$

Starting from a position of equal consumption in both periods, you need to gain at least $1+\rho$ units in the future in order to accept giving up one unit today.

As drawn in Fig. 1.2, indifference curves are convex, implying that a mix of consumption in both periods is preferred to consuming either today or tomorrow. The consumer prefers to smooth consumption across periods. Indifference curves are convex when the period utility function *U* is strictly concave.[9]

[9]That is, when the second derivative is negative $U_{C_t\,C_t}(C_t) < 0$.

1.2.3 Inter-temporal Demand: The Euler Equation

As in standard micro courses, we can derive the optimal inter-temporal choice for the consumer as the point of tangency of an indifference curve with the wealth constraint (as boundary of the set of feasible options). Mathematically, the household maximizes utility, subject to the wealth constraint.

$$V(C_t, C_{t+1}) = U(C_t) + \beta U(C_{t+1}), \tag{1.2.10}$$

$$s.t.\ C_t + \frac{1}{1+r_t} C_{t+1} \leq Y_t + \frac{1}{1+r_t} Y_{t+1}.$$

Inserting the wealth constraint into the utility function and differentiating lead to the following first order condition, frequently called the ***Euler equation***.[10]

$$\frac{U_{C_t}(C_t)}{\beta U_{C_{t+1}}(C_{t+1})} = 1 + r_t. \tag{1.2.11}$$

Euler Equation 1.2.11 is the key equation characterizing inter-temporal demand. Let us first give an intuitive interpretation of the Euler equation by rewriting the condition in a slightly more convenient way, replacing $\beta = 1/(1+\rho)$:

$$U_{C_t}(C_t) = \frac{1+r_t}{1+\rho} U_{C_{t+1}}(C_{t+1}). \tag{1.2.11a}$$

This condition says that marginal utility out of consumption, adjusted for the relevant rate of return, has to be equal across time. An increase in current consumption by one unit raises utility today marginally by $U_{C_t}(C_t)$. This, however, comes at the expense of reducing consumption in the future by $1 + r_t$, thus lowering future utility marginally by $(1 + r_t)\, U_{C_{t+1}}(C_{t+1})$. Since we discount future utility, the effective "cost" (in terms of foregone future utility) viewed from today is $U_{C_{t+1}}(C_{t+1}) \cdot (1 + r_t)/(1 + \rho)$. Since the period utility is concave $(U_{CC} = \partial^2 U(C)/\partial C^2 < 0)$, marginal utility $U_C(C)$ is decreasing in consumption. When the left-hand side exceeds the right-hand side overall utility increases if we

---

[10]Usually, the Euler equation is derived using complex dynamic techniques, such as dynamic programming, calculus of variation, or the maximum principle. For our purposes, however, it is sufficient to derive the Euler equation in the following straightforward way (For a more general case, we need to use the Lagrangian—see the Appendix A in the *Instructor's Manual for Money: Theory and Practice*). The wealth constraint defines a relation between consumption tomorrow and today:

$C_{t+1}(C_t) = Y_{t+1} + (1 + r_t)(Y_t - C_t)$ with $\partial C_{t+1}/\partial C_t = -(1 + r_t)$. Inserting this constraint into the utility function, allows us to state overall utility simply a function of current consumption C_t:

$\widehat{V}(C_t) = U(C_t) + \beta U(C_{t+1}(C_t)) = U(C_t) + \beta U(Y_{t+1} + (1 + r_t)(Y_t - C_t))$

Differentiating $\widehat{V}(C_t)$ with respect to C_t, the first-order condition for an interior optimum is:

$\frac{\partial \widehat{V}(C_t)}{\partial C_t} = \frac{\partial U(C_t)}{\partial C_t} + \beta \frac{\partial U(C_{t+1})}{\partial C_{t+1}} \frac{\partial C_{t+1}}{\partial C_t} = U_{C_t}(C_t) - (1 + r_t)\beta U_{C_{t+1}}(C_{t+1}) \overset{!}{=} 0$

Reformulating this first-order condition gives the Euler equation in the text.

raise current at the expense of future consumption. The opposite holds for the reverse case. The optimal mix between current and future consumption just balances marginal gains and losses. Agents prefer to smooth consumption across both periods.

As a thought experiment, assume that the left-hand side of the equation is smaller than the right-hand side. If so, it pays to increase future consumption at the expense of present consumption: Cutting C_t by a small amount Δ raises $U_{C_t}(C_t)$ just a little bit. At the margin, this will be offset by a marginal decrease in $U_{C_{t+1}}(C_{t+1})$, weighted with $(1+r_t)/(1+\rho)$. This takes into account the fact that (a) marginal utility $U_C(C_{t+1})$ falls next period with higher consumption; (b) future consumption can be increased by $\Delta(1+r_t)$ but (c) utility out of future consumption is discounted by $1/(1+\rho)$. The lower r_t and/or the higher ρ, the more will be consumed today relative to tomorrow.

When we consider preferences with a constant elasticity of substitution σ, we can derive an explicit closed-form mathematical solution E^* for inter-temporal demand from the Euler equation (see Focus Box on "Constant Elasticity of Inter-temporal Substitution"):

E^*: Euler Equation

$$\frac{C_{t+1}}{C_t} = \left(\frac{1+r_t}{1+\rho}\right)^{\sigma}. \tag{1.2.11b}$$

This Euler equation can be reformulated in a convenient way as a linear relation *Ln* E^{**} for the optimal growth rate of consumption (the change in consumption across time) as follows[11]

***Ln* E^{**}: Euler Equation**

$$\frac{\Delta C_t}{C_t} = c_{t+1} - c_t = \sigma(r_t - \rho). \tag{1.2.11c}$$

Euler Equation 1.2.11c is the basic relation which provides a micro-foundation for inter-temporal aggregate demand. It characterizes the factors determining consumption growth: The growth rate is a function of the real interest rate relative to the rate of time preference. Obviously, consumption growth is positive (negative) for $r_t > \rho$ ($r_t < \rho$). Furthermore, the consumption profile depends on the inter-temporal elasticity of substitution. There is an incentive to spread an increase in wealth across time for consumption purposes. The lower the elasticity σ, the less willing is the consumer to accept variations in the consumption path across time.

Whenever $r = \rho$, agents want to consume the same amount in each period. Since in that case marginal utility of consumption is equal across time, $U_{C_t}(C_t) = U_{C_t}(C_{t+1})$, the same quantity will be consumed in both periods (point A along the wealth constraint—see Fig. 1.3a).

[11]This is an approximation for discrete time analysis. It holds exactly for small time intervals. See the Focus Box on "Constant Elasticity of Inter-temporal Substitution."

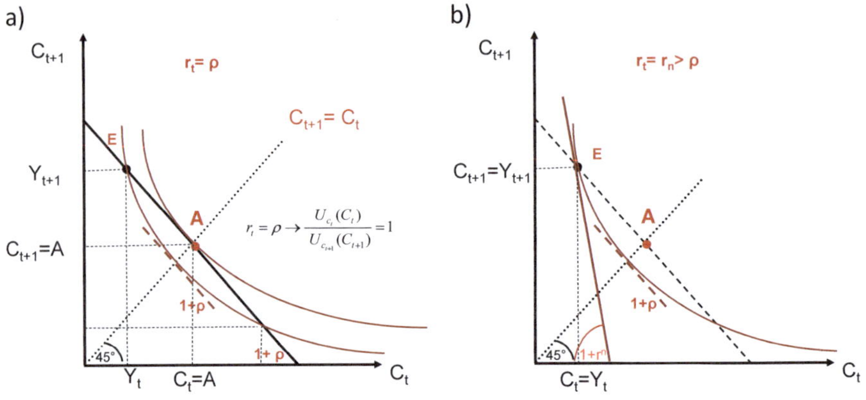

Fig. 1.3 Optimal consumption path. (**a**) Consumption smoothing for $r = \rho$. (**b**) Consumption tilting for $r > \rho$

If the interest rate exceeds the discount rate ($r > \rho$), it is optimal to consume more in the second period. We then get consumption tilting toward future consumption. Consider, as example, a rise in the interest rate such that the wealth constraint becomes just tangent to the indifference curve going through the endowment point E. At that interest rate the consumer is just happy to consume his/her endowment E (see Fig. 1.3b). In contrast, for $r < \rho$, he/she would like to consume more today than tomorrow. The point of tangency would be below the 45-degree line. Again, these results generalize for extensions to many, possibly infinite periods.

Focus Box: Constant Elasticity of Inter-temporal Substitution σ (CES) and the Optimal Consumption Path

The degree of concavity of the utility function is captured by the **elasticity of inter-temporal substitution σ**. An elasticity measures the percent change of some dependent variable when some independent variable changes by 1%. The elasticity of substitution σ gives us the following information: It tells us at what percentage rate the consumption ratio C_t/C_{t+1} will change (moving along the indifference curve) when the slope of the indifference curve (which—in equilibrium—is equal to the inter-temporal price, see next section) rises by 1%.

Frequently, we consider preferences with a Constant Elasticity of Substitution. They are represented by the CES payoff function:

$$U_t = \frac{1}{1 - 1/\sigma} C_t^{1-\frac{1}{\sigma}}, \ \sigma > 0; \quad \text{for } \sigma = 1 : U_t = \ln c_t.$$

σ is the elasticity of inter-temporal substitution: Consumption tomorrow relative to today C_{t+1}/C_t increases by σ% if the gross interest rate rises by 1%.

(continued)

When the elasticity of substitution is very high, the change in the consumption path will be substantial. In the extreme, if σ goes to infinity ($\sigma \to \infty$), preferences are $V = C_t + C_{t+1}/(1+\rho)$ with linear indifference curves $C_{t+1} = \overline{V} - (1+\rho)C_t$ with slope $1+\rho$ (in absolute value). A small change in the interest rate may lead to a dramatic change in the optimal consumption bundle. At the other extreme, with kinked indifference curves, there is no willingness to substitute across periods ($\sigma = 0$). If so, a change in the interest rate has no impact on the consumption profile (see Focus Box for Nerds "Some Extreme Cases").

For CES preferences, we can easily derive a closed form solution for the Euler equation. In that case $U_{C_t}(C_t) = (C_t)^{-\frac{1}{\sigma}}$ with first-order condition $\left(\frac{C_{t+1}}{C_t}\right)^{\frac{1}{\sigma}} = \left(\frac{C_t}{C_{t+1}}\right)^{-\frac{1}{\sigma}} = \frac{1+r_t}{1+\rho}$.

Taking both sides to the power of σ gives:

E*: Euler Equation**

$$\frac{C_{t+1}}{C_t} = \left(\frac{1+r_t}{1+\rho}\right)^{\sigma} \tag{1.2.11b}$$

A more convenient way is to write condition E* in log-linearized form:

Ln E**: Euler Equation**

$$\frac{\Delta C_t}{C_t} = c_{t+1} - c_t = \sigma\,(r_t - \rho). \tag{1.2.11c}$$

In order to derive Euler Equation 1.2.11c from Euler Equation 1.2.11b we take the natural log of equation E^*. For some readers, this may seem to be a quite scary exercise. But it pays to refresh some math, since we get straightforward, easy-to-interpret linear optimality conditions as reward. Simply recall that the natural log (ln) of a function $\left(\frac{X}{Y}\right)^{\alpha}$can be written as $\ln\left(\frac{X}{Y}\right)^{\alpha} = \alpha(\ln X - \ln Y) = \alpha(x - y)$. Here, for convenience we use for the log of any variable Z a small letter z instead of $\ln Z$:

$z = \ln Z$. Furthermore, the approximation $\ln(1+Z) \approx Z$ for small Z will be helpful. So let us take the natural log, *ln*, of both sides of the Euler equation E^* and use the notation $c_t = \ln C_t$ and $\ln(1+Z) \approx Z$.

$$\boldsymbol{Ln\ E^*} : \frac{1}{\sigma}(\ln C_{t+1} - \ln C_t) = \frac{1}{\sigma}(c_{t+1} - c_t) = [\ln(1+r_t) - \ln(1+\rho)]$$
$$\approx r_t - \rho.$$

$c_{t+1} - c_t$ is just the growth rate of consumption: $\Delta C_t / C_t$. To see this, define $\Delta C_t = C_{t+1} - C_t$. Obviously, $c_{t+1} - c_t = \ln\left(\frac{C_{t+1}}{C_t}\right) = \ln\left(1 + \frac{\Delta C_t}{C_t}\right) \approx \frac{\Delta C_t}{C_t}$.

(continued)

With preferences characterized by a constant elasticity of substitution, we get a linear wealth expansion path as drawn in Fig. 1.4. The wealth expansion path characterizes the optimal consumption bundle for different wealth levels at a constant interest rate. Micro-economic analysis calls this path the "Engel curve." With CES preferences, the ratio C_{t+1}/C_t of consumption tomorrow relative to today is constant for a given interest rate—independent of wealth. A parallel shift of the wealth constraint does not affect the optimal ratio. Such linear "Engel curves" allow for easy aggregation across agents with heterogeneous endowments, as long as they have the same preferences. In that case, aggregate demand is independent of the wealth distribution across agents.

1.2.4 The Natural Rate of Interest

Up to now we characterized the optimal choice of a representative consumer, given some arbitrary level of the real interest rate. Our key challenge, however, is to find out the driving forces determining the equilibrium interest rate. In our setting, the answer is simple enough: The real rate of interest has to be such that the representative consumer is happy to consume exactly what is available in each period. Nothing more, nothing less! On the aggregate level, the net wealth in a (closed) economy has to be zero. So rather than taking the interest rate as given we now reverse causality: The interest rate has to adjust in such a way that each period the representative consumer prefers to consume his/her endowment. Knowing this, we can use the Euler equation jointly with our resource constraints to determine the market equilibrium real rate. We call this the ***"natural" rate of interest***.

The natural real interest rate is determined by two equilibrium conditions:

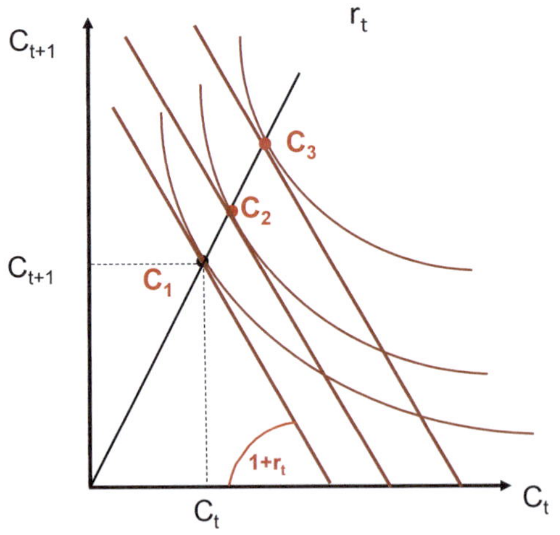

Fig. 1.4 Wealth expansion path for a given interest rate

1. The Euler equation E^* must hold for the representative consumer.

$$C_{t+1} = \left(\frac{1+r_t}{1+\rho}\right)^{\sigma} C_t \tag{1.2.11}$$

2. The resource constraints must hold in each period (aggregate consumption = endowment):

$$C_t = Y_t, \forall t. \tag{1.2.12}$$

This gives $\frac{Y_{t+1}}{Y_t} = \left(\frac{1+r_t}{1+\rho}\right)^{\sigma}$

Using the growth rate, defined as $\gamma_t = (Y_{t+1} - Y_t)/Y_t$ with $Y_{t+1} = (1+\gamma_t)\,Y_t$, we can rewrite the equilibrium condition as: $\frac{Y_{t+1}}{Y_t} = 1 + \frac{Y_{t+1}-Y_t}{Y_t} = 1 + \gamma_t = \left(\frac{1+r_t^n}{1+\rho}\right)^{\sigma}$ or $(1+\gamma_t)^{\frac{1}{\sigma}} = \frac{1+r_t^n}{1+\rho}$. This equation looks a bit complicated, but log-linearizing yields $\gamma_t = \sigma\left(r_t^n - \rho\right)$, using the approximation $\ln(1+Z) \approx Z$. Solving for the real interest rate, we get: $r_t^n = \rho + \frac{1}{\sigma}\gamma_t$.

Figure 1.5 shows how to determine the natural rate. In equilibrium, the representative household must be willing to consume exactly the resources available in each period (the endowment point *E*). So the interest rate has to adjust such that the wealth constraint becomes just tangent to the indifference curve going through that point. The gross natural interest rate (the net rate plus 1) has to be equal to the absolute value of the slope of indifference curve passing point *E*. Let us call that slope the inter-temporal shadow price—the interest rate which makes the representative consumer just happy to consume available resources. Only if the market rate is equal to

Fig. 1.5 The natural rate of interest

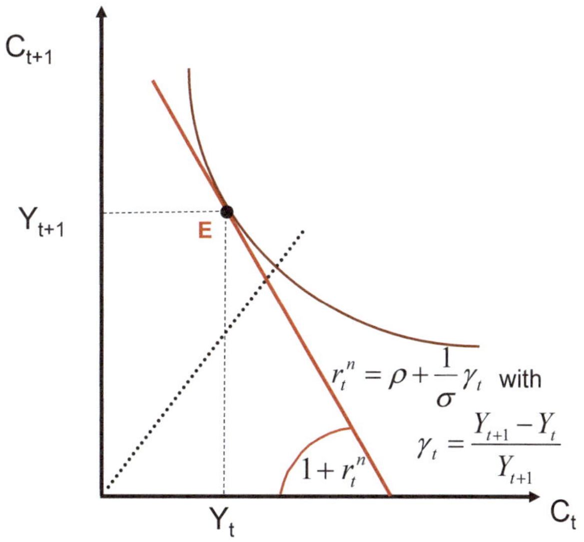

that shadow rate, the economy is in equilibrium. With higher growth the interest rate needs to rise to offset the incentive for smoothing consumption. The Focus Box for Nerds "Some Extreme Cases" illustrates how preferences (the inter-temporal willingness to substitute, determining the shape of the indifference curve) affect the natural interest rate r_t^n. The more concave preferences are the higher will be r_t^n.

Now we have a complete characterization of our simple "real business cycle" economy:

Aggregate Equilibrium:	For the whole economy, demand must be equal to supply (production; endowment). The equilibrium path depends on:
Preferences	(the discount rate and the inter-temporal elasticity of substitution)
Technology	(endowment; productivity growth $\gamma \rightarrow$ real inter-temporal exchange rate)

Summary for General Equilibrium

$$Y_t = C_t; Y_{t+1} = C_{t+1}; Y_{t+1} = (1+\gamma_t)\, Y_t; \Delta\, C_t/C_t = \gamma_t = \sigma(r_t - \rho) \rightarrow r_t^n = \rho + \frac{1}{\sigma}\gamma_t.$$

Using the resource constraints $Y_t = C_t, \forall t$ and defining $y_t = \log Y_t$, we see that the Euler equation characterizes the inter-temporal IS curve:

$$y_t = y_{t+1} - \sigma(r_t - \rho).$$

Focus Box for Nerds: Some Extreme Cases

To get a better intuition, let us consider two extreme cases. Assume first that we urgently want to consume in both periods in a fixed proportion. In that extreme case, there is no scope for inter-temporal substitution. Preferences are kinked—the elasticity of substitution is zero. This is captured by the case $\sigma = 0$ in Fig. 1.6a. With $\sigma = 0$, the consumer would like to consume the same amount in each period—independent of the interest rate. In that case, the indifference curves look like isoquants of a Leontief production function: There is no substitutability.

With an interest rate such that the wealth constraint is along the line *EA*, the consumer would choose point *A* in Fig. 1.6a, trying to borrow from future resources. But given aggregate endowment *E* with high future resources

(continued)

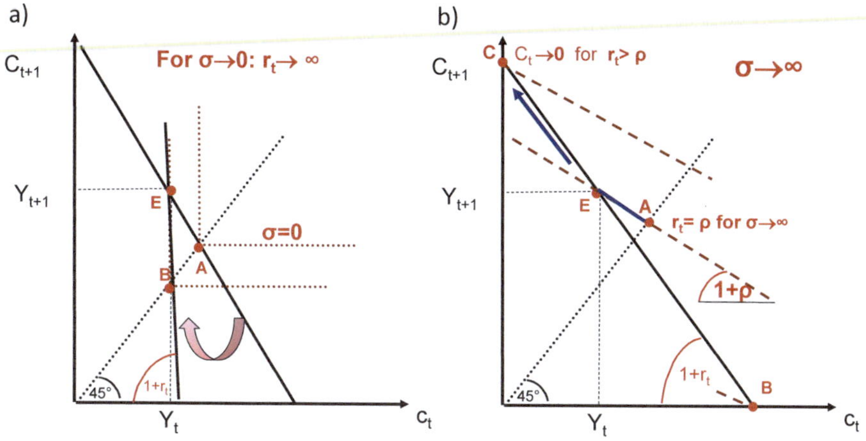

Fig. 1.6 Substitutability. (**a**) No substitutability $\sigma = 0$. (**b**) Perfect substitutability $\sigma \to \infty$

$Y_{t+1} > Y_t$, point A is simply not feasible. Only if the interest rate rises extremely high ($r_t \to \infty$), she will be deterred from borrowing. The equilibrium natural interest rate needs to make borrowing infinitely costly. Only at that rate the consumer is willing to accept the fact that future endowment exceeds resources available today. Effectively, she will not be better off at E than at point B.

Check yourself (by drawing a corresponding figure) that in the reverse case exceeds resources available today (with $Y_{t+1} < Y_t$, the interest rate would need to go infinitely negative ($r_t \to -\infty$)), in order to deter the consumer from trying to save. If storage (possibly with some decay rate δ) were feasible, the lower bound for the equilibrium natural interest rate would be the net storage rate $1 - \delta$.

In contrast Fig. 1.6b characterizes the opposite extreme with infinitely high elasticity of substitution ($\sigma \to \infty$), such as $V = C_t + C_{t+1}/(1+\rho)$. In that case, indifference curves are linear with the slope (in absolute value) $1+\rho$ (compare the dashed lines in Fig. 1.6b). Consumers are indifferent between consumption of one unit today or $1+\rho$ units tomorrow—consumption in both periods is perfectly substitutable at the gross rate $1+\rho$. As long as $r_t > \rho$ (as drawn with the line CB as wealth constraint), consumers would be better off postponing consumption toward the future. At $r_t > \rho$ they would like to choose point C with $C_t = 0$ rather than point E (Check yourself that they would be worst off at point B!). There is no incentive to smooth consumption. To make consumers happy to consume their initial endowment, the interest rate needs to be exactly equal to the time preference: $r_t = \rho$! In that case, being indifferent between E and A, they are willing to consume E.

Let us now draw some important conclusions from the insights we have derived up to now. The ***natural rate of interest*** r^n is higher

- The higher ρ: Impatience requires stronger incentives to save!
- The higher the growth rate γ_t: Because of incentives for consumption smoothing, high growth has to be balanced by a higher interest rate giving stronger incentives to save!
- The lower the elasticity of substitution: The more concave the utility, the stronger are the incentives to smooth consumption for a given positive growth rate. Therefore, a high interest rate is needed in order to provide sufficient incentives to be willing to consume more in the future!

Graphically, we can characterize these effects by modifying Fig. 1.5. With an increase in ρ indifference curves become steeper at all points. Thus the indifference curve will also be steeper at the endowment point E, raising the shadow price of current relative to future consumption and so driving up the natural rate. A higher growth rate γ_t is captured by an increase in Y_{t+1} relative to Y_t, shifting the point of endowment from E_1 toward E_2 in Fig. 1.7a, again with a steeper slope.

In principle, there is no reason why the equilibrium real rate of interest has to be positive. After all, the relative inter-temporal price is the gross rate $1 + r_t^n$. In a declining economy with negative growth rates, the equilibrium real rate is likely to be negative. But, as already pointed out by the Austrian economist Eugen von Böhm Bawerk in *Kapital und Kapitalzins* (1884), there are several reasons why in general we might have a positive natural rate of interest.

1. Impatience of consumers (consumers have a natural tendency toward a positive ρ)
2. Technological progress (generating a positive growth rate γ_t in the economy)
3. Productiveness of capital (accumulation via a higher capital stock allows to increase future productivity)

All these effects will cause the real rate of interest to be positive in normal times. But there may be shocks shifting the natural rate toward being negative, at least temporarily.

As a thought experiment, let us now ask what happens when some parameter values change. This is called comparative static analysis. It helps to gain some intuition for the impact on the equilibrium interest rate if specific shocks disturb the economy. Obviously, the answer depends strongly on whether such shocks are temporary or permanent.

(a) A permanent increase in productivity will shift the endowment point E^* in Fig. 1.5 proportionally in both periods. With CES preferences, such a shift has no impact on the slope, leaving the real interest rate unaffected (see Fig. 1.4).
(b) If future productivity rises (so g goes up), the natural rate has to increase to counter incentives to bring forward and consume already today (see Fig. 1.7a).

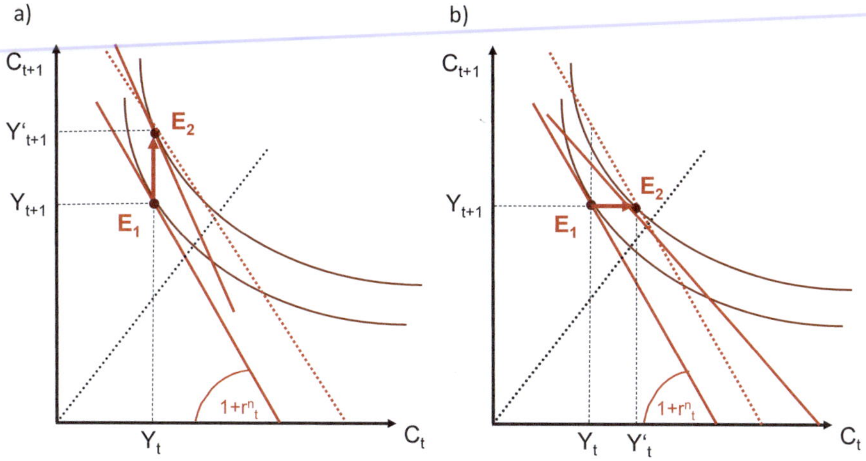

Fig. 1.7 Determinants of the natural rate. (**a**) An increase in future endowment raises the natural rate; (**b**) a temporary increase in current productivity reduces the natural rate

The gross rate needs to adjust such that the slope is equal to the new shadow price (the slope of the indifference curve at point E_2).

(c) In contrast, a temporary increase in productivity in the initial period 1 raises only Y_t. But as long as the interest rate stays constant, desired consumption tomorrow will rise as well today (see the dotted line in Fig. 1.7b). For the consumer, there is an incentive to postpone part of that gain to smooth consumption. This, however, is in conflict with resource constraints. To counter this incentive, the natural rate needs to be lower, giving incentives to consume all of the temporary increase in resources today (Note that we do not allow for capital accumulation in our simple setup).

Up to now, we ignored uncertainty in our economy. We simply assumed that Y_t and Y_{t+1} are perfectly known at the time when the consumer determines his consumption path. Unfortunately, in reality the future is not known. If we take that into account, the conditions derived will hold at best in expected value terms. So with $E(y_{t+1})$ as on average expected future endowment, we might rewrite our inter-temporal IS curve as:

$$y_t = E(y_{t+1}) - \sigma(r_t - \rho). \qquad (1.2.13)$$

A sound analysis, however, would require explicit stochastic optimization. If we do that, things get quite a bit more complicated. At that stage, let us just try to gain some intuition what we need to take into account. If future endowment is risky, there will be strong incentives for precautionary savings to insure against bad shocks. On the other hand, with future consumption being more risky than current consumption, giving up safe consumption today may require a compensating risk premium. Obviously, we need to distinguish between interest rates on safe assets (allowing us to insure against risks in future income) and interest rates on risky assets. To give incentives to hold risky assets, a risk premium has to be paid on these assets.

The extent to which agents can insure against risks is a key factor for determining the optimal allocation. When there are perfect markets for insurance idiosyncratic risks may be diversified away. In that case the correlation of assets with aggregate risk (affecting the whole economy) will be crucial. A high risk premium (a high real rate of return) will be needed for risky assets in times of high aggregate volatility. In contrast, assets which are negatively correlated with output are expensive. They are safe assets, promising to pay out a constant amount even in bad times, so holding them allows insuring against aggregate risk. In times of high aggregate volatility, they are in strong demand, giving a low return (a low interest rate).

Focus Box: Extension to Many (Infinite) Periods—No-Ponzi Games and Transversality Condition

The two-period model may seem pretty artificial. In reality, we do not have just to choose between today and tomorrow. Rather, the world extends into the future without definite time horizon, making our choice problem much more complicated. The best way to capture this is to consider a household optimizing from today on until infinity. Fortunately, our insights can easily be extended to such an infinite horizon economy. Surprisingly, we get exactly the same conditions. As simplest case, let us consider an economy growing at a constant rate of growth γ and a constant interest rate r. So the representative consumer maximizes:

$$\sum_{t=0}^{\infty} \frac{1}{(1+\rho)^t} U(c_t) \tag{1.2.14}$$

subject to the per period budget constraint: $W_{t+1} = (1+r)[W_t + (Y_t - C_t)]$ with $Y_{t+1} = (1+\gamma)Y_t$ and W_t as real wealth at period t. As shown below, the period budget constraints can be merged to a wealth constraint for life, when we impose $W_0 = 0$ and the No-Ponzi game condition. If so, the consumer is just subject to the wealth constraint:

$$\sum_{t=0}^{\infty} \left(\frac{1}{1+r}\right)^t Y_t = \sum_{t=0}^{\infty} \left(\frac{1}{1+r}\right)^t C_t \tag{1.2.15}$$

Using the Lagrangian parameter λ for the wealth constraint, the first-order condition in each period t is $\frac{1}{(1+\rho)^t} U_{C_t}(C_t) = \lambda \frac{1}{(1+r)^t}$ holds for all t, also for $t+1$: $\frac{1}{(1+\rho)^{t+1}} U_{C_{t+1}}(C_{t+1}) = \lambda \frac{1}{(1+r)^{t+1}}$.

Dividing both equations gives the familiar Euler equation $U_{C_t}(C_t) = \frac{1+r}{1+\rho} U_{C_{t+1}}(C_{t+1})$.

(continued)

Equilibrium

Using the resource constraints $Y_t = C_t$ for $t \geq 0$, and assuming that the growth rate is constant over time $\gamma_t = \gamma$ for $t \geq 0$, for CES preferences we again get as condition for the natural rate: $r^n = \rho + \frac{1}{\sigma}\gamma$ with r^n being constant over time.

No-Ponzi Game and Transversality Condition

Starting with some initial wealth, the budget constraints for each period can be merged into one single wealth constraint by reiterated substitution. As an exercise, let us do that for the first periods: Inserting $W_1 = (1+r)[W_0 + (Y_0 - C_0)]$ in $W_2 = (1+r)[W_1 + (Y_1 - C_1)]$, we get

$$W_2 = (1+r)(Y_1 - C_1) + (1+r)^2(Y_0 - C_0) + (1+r)^2 W_0.$$

If we reiterate the same procedure for T periods, this gives:

$$W_T = (1+r)(Y_{T-1} - C_{T-1}) + (1+r)^2(Y_{T-2} - C_{T-2}) + \ldots + (1+r)^T(Y_0 - C_0) + (1+r)^T W_0.$$

Dividing by $(1+r)^T$ and rearranging consumption terms to the other side of the equation, we get:

$$W_0 + \sum_{t=0}^{T-1}\left(\frac{1}{1+r}\right)^t Y_t = \sum_{t=0}^{T-1}\left(\frac{1}{1+r}\right)^t C_t + \left(\frac{1}{1+r}\right)^T W_t.$$

This equation generalizes the wealth constraint of our two-period setup at the beginning of this chapter. What about the unspecified terms W_0 and W_T? Since in our pure endowment economy, for the representative agent there cannot be positive wealth at the start of the world (more precisely, there cannot be positive aggregate wealth W_0), we now impose $W_0 = 0$. For wealth at the end of the world W_T, it makes sense to impose what is called the **No-Ponzi game condition** in dynamic optimization. The idea is first to rule out bubble solutions or "Ponzi games": Nobody will be allowed to accumulate so much debt during life such that the present value of debt still held at the end of the world will be positive. Mathematically, we impose

$$\left(\frac{1}{1+r}\right)^T W_T \geq 0, \text{or for } T \to \infty : \lim_{T\to\infty}\left(\frac{1}{1+r}\right)^T W_T \geq 0. \quad (1.2.16)$$

The No-Ponzi game condition states that the present value of the wealth held at the end of the world cannot be negative (Note that we ignore uncertainty in our analysis. If we allow for risk, an equivalent condition would hold in expected value terms.).

(continued)

As long as there is no satiation, you are always better off to consume at some stage rather than to leave positive wealth at the end of the world (at T). For that reason, the No-Ponzi game constraint will be strictly binding for the optimal solution, when solving the optimization problem for the representative consumer. Anticipating this fact, this justifies to impose the ***transversality condition***

$$\lim_{T\to\infty}\left(\frac{1}{1+r}\right)^T W_T = 0. \tag{1.2.17}$$

In general, the transversality condition is a necessary condition for optimality in dynamic optimization.

Our reasoning implies that the real rate of interest cannot be negative in long-run equilibrium. For $r < 0$, it would be optimal for all agents to incur unbounded debt and pay it back with income growing over time with interest payments on debt being negative. This is simply not feasible in the long run. More generally, in an economy growing at a constant rate $\gamma \geq 0$, the condition $r > \gamma$ must hold in the long run. Otherwise, the real burden of debt would steadily decrease across time. All agents would love to incur unbounded debt and pay it back with income growing faster than any interest payments on debt. The economy could grow out of any debt without problems. This cannot be an equilibrium.[12]

Imposing both $W_0 = 0$ and the transversality condition $\lim_{T\to\infty}\left(\frac{1}{1+r}\right)^T W_T = 0$, all per period budget constraints can be merged into one single wealth constraint such that the present value of consumption has to be equal to the present value of income:

$$\sum_{t=0}^{\infty}\left(\frac{1}{1+r}\right)^t Y_t = \sum_{t=0}^{\infty}\left(\frac{1}{1+r}\right)^t C_t. \tag{1.2.18}$$

[12]Note, however, that this reasoning no longer holds when financial frictions prevent smooth intertemporal trade. If so, we cannot rule out $r < \gamma$. The natural real rate of interest may even get negative as in OLG models as Eggertsson, Mehrotra, and Robbins (2017) or in infinitely lived agent models with non-satiation in wealth—see Illing, Ono, and Schlegl (2018).

1.2.5 Heterogeneous Agents

Up to now, we considered the optimization problem of a single household. She was able to trade bonds across time, taking the interest rate as given. But the individual plans of all households taken together must be compatible with aggregate resources available. If one household wants to postpone consumption, at least one other must be willing to borrow. Obviously, we need heterogeneity across households. The simplest case is that all households have the same preferences, but different endowments. To illustrate some issues involved, let us look at a simple extension with two types of agents A and B. To justify competitive behavior, there are many (possibly a continuum) consumers of both types (with equal weight) in the economy. We assume they have identical CES preferences, but allow for (possibly) heterogeneous endowments across time. The resource constraints can be represented in a standard Edgeworth box:

$$C_t^A + C_t^B = Y_t = Y_t^A + Y_t^B;\ C_{t+1}^A + C_{t+1}^B = Y_{t+1} = Y_{t+1}^A + Y_{t+1}^B. \tag{1.2.19}$$

To make it simple, we assume that the aggregate endowment is the same in both periods $Y_{t+1} = Y_t$, so the Edgeworth box is a square (see Fig. 1.8). With no aggregate growth, the indifference curves of both types of agents A and B are tangent along the 45° line, representing the linear wealth expansion path with slope $1 + \rho$ starting in point A for A and in point B for B.

Assume first that all agents have identical endowment: So both types of agents own exactly half of the aggregate income in both periods; the endowment point is E_1. In that case E_1 also characterizes the market equilibrium. The equilibrium interest rate needs to adjust such that all agents A and B are happy to consume just their endowment. The rate is determined by the slope of the indifference curve (the shadow price) in point E_1. We call this market clearing rate the **natural rate of interest**. With no aggregate growth, the equilibrium rate of interest is equal to the time preference $r_t^n = \rho$. With agents being identical, there will be no active trade of bonds (claims on future consumption) in equilibrium. Nevertheless, the natural rate is well defined. At any other rate, the market for bonds would not clear.

Let us now modify the income distribution. Assume now that agents of type A own more resources in period t (being more productive in the early period), whereas agents of type B own most of the resources in the following period $t + 1$ (being more productive late). So in Fig. 1.8 we start at point E_2 rather than at E_2. Now intertemporal trade is beneficial for both types of agents. Since all prefer to smooth consumption across time, they are all both better off swapping part of their endowment. In the first period, type A agents save whereas type B agents borrow. The market clearing equilibrium will be at point M_1. When agents are impatient, type B agents with low current income at t have lower wealth compared to type A; they cannot afford to consume as much resources as A. But aggregate consumption still has to be equal to aggregate endowment. Furthermore, the equilibrium rate of interest is still $r_t^n = \rho$. So the aggregate equilibrium can be represented by the choice problem of a single, representative agent owing all resources.

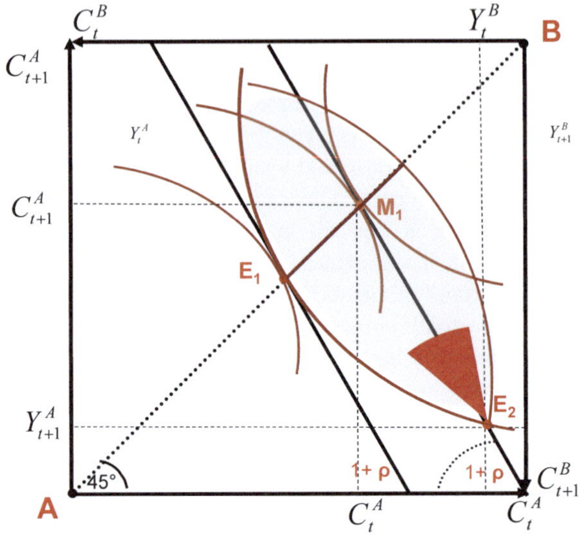

Fig. 1.8 Inter-temporal trade with heterogeneous endowments: The Edgeworth box

The workhorse model of modern macro usually abstracts from heterogeneity. It analyzes the market equilibrium with one representative agent in order to characterize the determinants of the natural interest rate.[13] Reducing the world to a single agent economy makes analysis extremely tractable. For that reason, it has become a popular tool in modern macroeconomics. It allows characterizing aggregate equilibrium in a straightforward way—by solving the optimal decision-making of one single agent, maximizing her utility subject to the aggregate resource constraints. Solving equilibrium in dynamic models with heterogeneous agents is much more challenging and complex. But the advantage of (relative) simplicity comes at a high cost. By construction, important features we may be interested in are blended out from the analysis.

When looking at just one representative agent, we obviously cannot address distributional effects. For some key questions in macro it makes perfect sense to abstract from such issues and focus on average aggregate behavior, rather than looking at diversity across individuals. It would be a great help if the analysis of a representative agent can represent the aggregate behavior of many agents in the economy in a robust way, each optimizing given the individual constraints. Unfortunately, conditions for aggregate behavior being the same as the behavior of a single representative agent turn out to be extremely restrictive (see Guvenen, 2011). In general, wealth and substitution effects across agents may lead to quite weird aggregate behavior. According to the Sonnenschein–Mantel–Debreu Theorem, we may generate nearly any arbitrary aggregate excess demand function by allowing for sufficiently diverse heterogeneous preferences. As shown by Gorman (1961), the

[13]In contrast, the overlapping generations model (OLG), by construction, has heterogeneous agents with limited trade across different generations.

key condition for aggregation is that individuals have linear wealth expansion paths (Engel curves) giving the same marginal propensity to consume out of wealth. So in the case of CES preferences, aggregate behavior can indeed be reduced to that of a representative agent. But we need to remember that this is truly a very special case.

Even in that special case, however, looking at just one representative agent runs the risk of ignoring central frictions which may be crucial for a monetary economy with intermediation and inter-temporal trade. Let us emphasize just one important point here: The aggregation sweeps a crucial incentive problem under the carpet. Agents of type A (the savers) need to hand over resources (their savings) to agents of type B in the first period, trusting to be paid back (including interest payments) next period. Having completed the first transaction, however, there is a risk that borrower B may renege on her promise to transfer resources at $t+1$. For instance, working effort at $t+1$ may be needed to generate a high income Y_{t+1}^{B} (see Sect. 1.4). Knowing that a substantial part of the reward for such hard work will need to be transferred to type A agents may hamper B's incentive to work as hard as promised.

Obviously, inter-temporal trade requires trust (enforcement of contracts). In the absence of trust, serious frictions may impede beneficial trade. In reality, however, such frictions are crucial for understanding the role of money. If trade against credit is not enforceable, agent A may ask for collateral when lending. If (modifying our simple setup) the good traded is a durable good (such as real estate), B may be able to offer A the right to hand the good back in case contractual payments are not honored next period. But such an arrangement cannot work in the case of perishable goods. In the absence of trust and collateral, agent A may ask for payment in cash instead and so the scope for inter-temporal trade may be rather limited.

The representative agent approach neglects such frictions. It assumes a legal regime with perfect enforceability. In such a regime, all points in the Edgeworth box are feasible contractual arrangements. Starting from point E_2 trading in the large (slightly shaded) area bounded by the intersection of indifference curves allows making both types of agents better off. In the absence of trust, the set of feasible contracts may shrink dramatically, as for example indicated by the shaded triangle in Fig. 1.8. So there are good reasons to doubt that the perfect world of frictionless inter-temporal trade is a good description of modern real world monetary economies.

1.3 Government Spending, Taxes, and Public Debt

1.3.1 The Role of Fiscal Policy

Let us now introduce fiscal policy. For a start, let us first consider an exogenously given path of government spending (public goods) (G_t, G_{t+1})in our two-period model. In order to finance spending, the government needs to raise taxes (T_t, T_{t+1}). Alternatively, it can issue bonds to finance spending via debt. Both spending and taxes are defined in real terms. Debt issued by the government is assumed to be in the form of nominal bonds B_t with one period maturity, paying gross interest $1 + i_t$ next year. Outstanding debt $(1 + i_{t-1})B_{t-1}$ issued in the past period needs to be paid back. The government budget constraint in period t and $t + 1$ is:

$$B_t - B_{t-1} = P_t G_t - P_t T_t + i_{t-1} B_{t-1}, \tag{1.3.1}$$

$$B_{t+1} - B_t = P_{t+1} G_{t+1} - P_{t+1} T_{t+1} + i_t B_t.$$

It is useful to distinguish between overall deficit (including interest rate payments on debt issued in the past) and the *primary deficit* (current public spending exceeding current tax revenues). For $P_t T_t > P_t G_t$ there is a *primary surplus*. Nominal debt increases whenever nominal interest payments exceed primary surplus.

Aggregating the per-period constraints into a single wealth constraint gives:

$$P_t G_t + \frac{1}{1+i_t} P_{t+1} G_{t+1} + (1+i_{t-1}) B_{t-1} = P_t T_t + \frac{1}{1+i_t} P_{t+1} T_{t+1} + \frac{1}{1+i_t} B_{t+1} \tag{1.3.2}$$

Let us divide both sides of the nominal constraint by the price index P_t and use the Fisher relation $\frac{P_{t+1}/P_t}{1+i_t} = \frac{1+\pi_t}{1+i_t} = \frac{1}{1+r_t}$ to reformulate the wealth constraint in real terms:

$$G_t + \frac{1}{1+r_t} G_{t+1} + (1+r_{t-1}) B_{t-1}/P_{t-1} = T_t + \frac{1}{1+r_t} T_{t+1} \left[+ \frac{1}{1+r_t} B_{t+1}/P_{t+1} \right] \tag{1.3.3}$$

The present value of tax revenues needs to cover the present value of government spending plus the initial debt. This condition would be relaxed if debt could be issued also in the final period (that is, if the last term is positive). But as shown in the footnote, there are good reasons to impose the transversality constraint[14]: $\frac{B_{t+1}/P_{t+1}}{1+r_t} = 0$.

Government spending requires real resources and so reduces available consumption. In general equilibrium, the aggregate resource constraint must hold in each period:

[14]No rational consumer is willing to buy any bonds in the final period $t + 1$ (compare the Focus Box on the No-Ponzi Game Constraint). After all, the world is ending at $t + 1$. So rather than buying bonds at that time, the representative consumer will always be better off by consuming her resources. Obviously, just as for private agents, we need to impose a No-Ponzi game constraint also for the government: Since public debt at the end of the world cannot be positive, the condition $B_{t+1} \leq 0$ must hold. With the government's No-Ponzi game condition being binding, we get the transversality condition $B_{t+1}/(1 + i_t) = \{B_{t+1}/P_{t+1}\} \cdot 1/(1 + r_t) = 0$. Of course, this condition needs to be modified if there is no definite final period. In that case, debt may indeed never be repaid. But nevertheless, we still get as feasibility condition that the present value of government spending plus the initial debt must be covered by the present value of revenues (see Sect. 3.4).

$$C_t = Y_t - G_t; C_{t+1} = Y_{t+1} - G_{t+1}. \tag{1.3.4}$$

Hence the natural real interest rate is now determined by:

$$\frac{U_c(Y_{t+1} - G_{t+1})}{U_c(Y_t - G_t)} = \frac{1+\rho}{1+r_t}. \tag{1.3.5}$$

To keep the aggregate structure simple, G_t is assumed to represent a bundle of goods having the same composition as the consumption basket C_t. Let us define $c_t = \log C_t$ and $y_t = \log Y_t$. With $g_t = G_t/Y_t$ as share of government spending to total production, we can reformulate $Y_t = C_t + G_t$ in log-linear terms as[15]:

$$y_t = c_t + g_t. \tag{1.3.6}$$

As long as taxes are not distortionary, the timing of taxation and deficit finance is irrelevant (see next section). When taxes are distortionary, optimal tax rates can be derived as those rates minimizing overall distortions, given the optimal path $\{G_t\}$. We will show this when characterizing endogenous production. In this chapter, we assume that fiscal policy chooses optimal government spending and tax rates minimizing distortions, given the government wealth constraint. The task of monetary policy instead is to control the price level respectively the rate of inflation (via money supply or interest rate policy). Seignorage revenue from printing money (potentially with inflationary impact) may be a way to mitigate the government's wealth constraint. In the same way, a surprise inflation triggering an increase in the current price level may reduce the real burden of nominal debt. In Chap. 3, we will discuss potential conflicts between monetary and fiscal authorities.

1.3.2 Ricardian Equivalence: The Irrelevance of Government Debt

The consumer's wealth constraint needs to be modified to take into account taxes and public debt. Obviously, taxes reduce current income. Government debt is held by private agents. The public debt B_{t-1} issued in the past represents initial wealth of those agents who bought those bonds in the past as a way to save for their future. With aggregating all households into just one representative consumer, net savings within the private sector itself need to be zero. In an endowment economy without private investment, the representative consumer can only save by holding public bonds. So her per-period budget constraints have to be modified as:

$$P_t C_t + B_t = P_t Y_t - P_t T_t + (1 + i_{t-1}) B_{t-1}, \tag{1.3.7}$$

[15]Write $\frac{C_t}{Y_t} = 1 - \frac{G}{Y_t} = 1 - g_t$. Taking logs on both sides and use $\log(1+Z) \approx Z$, we get $c_t - y_t = -g_t$ or $y_t = c_t + g_t$ (Note that g_t is here the share of government spending to real GDP, not the log of G!).

$$P_{t+1}C_{t+1} + B_{t+1} = P_{t+1}Y_{t+1} - P_{t+1}T_{t+1} + (1 + i_t)B_t.$$

Again, we can merge these constraints into the consumer's wealth constraint. Using the Fisher relation, this gives in real terms:

$$C_t + \frac{1}{1+r_t}C_{t+1} + \frac{B_{t+1}/P_{t+1}}{1+r_t} = Y_t - T_t + \frac{1}{1+r_t}(Y_{t+1} - T_{t+1}) + (1+r_t)B_{t-1}/P_{t-1} \tag{1.3.8}$$

The wealth constraint seems to suggest that public debt is private wealth. After all, private agents buy government bonds in order to save. But when we substitute the government's wealth constraint into the wealth constraint of the representative household, we realize that private wealth created from public bonds will be just cancelled out by corresponding tax obligations. In the aggregate, government debt cannot be net wealth for private agents! To see this, notice that the present value of tax revenues is given by:

$$T_t + \frac{1}{1+r_t}T_{t+1} = G_t + \frac{1}{1+r_t}G_{t+1} + (1+r_t)B_{t-1}/P_{t-1} - \frac{B_{t+1}/P_{t+1}}{1+r_t}. \tag{1.3.9}$$

Inserting this relation in the consumer's wealth constraint, replacing her tax burden, we see that her constraint effectively amounts to:

$$C_t + \frac{C_{t+1}}{1+r_t} = Y_t - G_t + \frac{Y_{t+1} - G_{t+1}}{1+r_t}. \tag{1.3.10}$$

This condition seems fairly intuitive: For the aggregate economy, the present value of aggregate consumption has to be equal to the present value of aggregate endowment, net of those resources used in the public sector. But the condition has a quite surprising implication: It says that the level of public debt is irrelevant in our simple representative agent economy. Since public debt is private wealth and at the same time imposes future tax obligations with the same present value, it is irrelevant how large the level of public debt is.

The timing of the taxes does not matter at all, since government debt is no net wealth for private agents. To gain a better understanding, assume the government finances current spending via debt rather than via imposing taxes. In that case, tax obligations for the private sector are shifted into the future. But anticipating that high taxes have to be paid in the future, the representative agent will increase her private savings right now in order to be able to cover these tax obligations later. This is called Ricardian equivalence.

This surprisingly strong result depends on some crucial assumptions:

First of all, we considered lump sum taxes. Imposing lump sum taxes does not reduce available resources, since they are not distortionary. This is a rather heroic assumption. When we allow for distortionary taxes, there are incentives for tax smoothing: The burden from financing high spending in one particular period should be smoothed across time in order to minimize overall distortions (see next section).

Furthermore, if there is some maximum sustainable level of taxation, the capacity to incur debt will be limited.

Second, the irrelevance of government debt relies strongly on the absence of imperfections in the bond market. If we allow for heterogeneity across agents, the inter-temporal relative price (the interest rate) may no longer be equal for all of them when future markets are imperfect. In an overlapping generation model, for example, agents born in the future are not able to participate in active trading today. Private and social discount rates may not be identical: When the government cares about the welfare of future agents, it may have a lower time preference than individual agents. Furthermore: Whenever the interest rate for borrowing and lending differs, the exact timing of taxes may have a significant impact. Credit or liquidity constrained agents may be better off if collection of taxes is deferred into the future. In that case, we need to take distributional issues into account.

Obviously, for a deeper understanding we need to consider an economy with heterogeneous agents, facing different inter-temporal prices. But in order to illustrate the key point in our simple framework, let us consider the case that government spending G_{t+1} is done only in the final period $t+1$. Resources available for the representative consumer are shifted down from point E toward point E_1 (see Fig. 1.9). The equilibrium natural rate is now determined by the slope of the indifference curve at E_1 with the wealth constraint along AC. When tax revenue $(T_{t+1} = G_{t+1})$ is also collected at $t+1$, point E_1 with $\{Y_t, Y_{t+1} - T_{t+1}\}$ characterizes the consumer's endowment point. In that case, she will neither borrow nor lend.

If, however, taxes $T_t = G_{t+1}/(1 + r_t^n)$ are already collected in period t, the endowment point is shifted toward E_2 with $\{Y_t - T_t, Y_{t+1}\}$. Now the consumer needs to borrow the amount T_t to be able to consume still at point E_1. This is no

Fig. 1.9 Failure of Ricardian equivalence with credit constraints

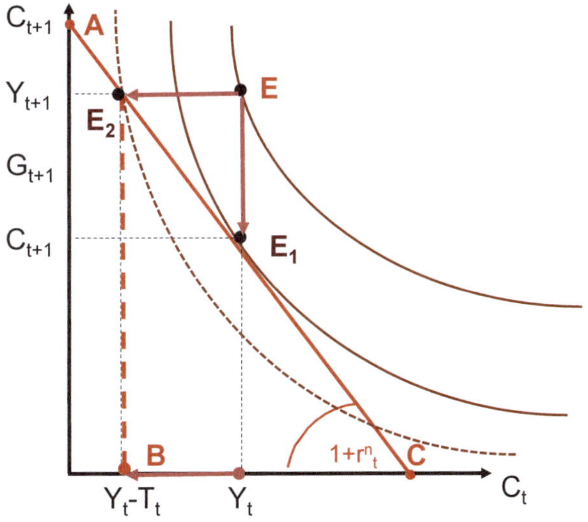

problem in the absence of credit restrictions. If, however, borrowing is not allowed, feasible consumption is now characterized by the line AB with a kink at E_2, representing the credit constraint. Being not able to borrow funds from future endowment to pay her tax obligations, the consumer ends up with an inferior payoff at E_2 as shown by the dotted indifference curve passing through that point.

Focus Box: The Optimal Provision of Public Goods

As in the text, economic analysis frequently takes the path of government spending $\{G_t\}$. as given exogenously without any micro-foundation. This does not imply that G_t represents just a waste of resources. It is straightforward to modify our model so as to discuss "optimal" public spending. For that purpose, we just have to specify the benefits provided by G_t. The natural way is to include public goods in the preference function of the representative agent:

$$V = U(C_1) + G(G_1) + \beta[U(C_2) + G(G_2)]. \tag{1.3.11}$$

The efficient allocation maximizes V subject to the constraints $C_t = Y_t - G_t; C_{t+1} = Y_{t+1} - G_{t+1}$. The optimal allocation strongly depends on the degree of substitutability between public and private goods. If G_t were a perfect substitute for private consumption, we would have $U(C_t) + G(G_t) = U(C_t + G_t)$. Any increase in G_t would simply crowd out private consumption (see Baxter & King, 1993). If G_t and C_t were instead perfect complements, any increase in private consumption would need to be matched by a corresponding increase in public goods. In general, government spending provides utility in the form of public, non-excludable goods. The easiest case to analyze is again to assume additive separability. The efficient allocation of the public good is characterized by the condition that the MRS between public and private consumption must be equal to one (as long as producing one unit of the public good requires the same input as producing one unit of the private good).

$$\frac{G_{G_t}(G_t)}{U_{C_t}(C_t)} = 1, \forall t. \tag{1.3.12}$$

General equilibrium requires $C_t + G_t = Y_t$. Most of the time, we abstract from these conditions for the optimal provision of public goods, and instead take the path of government spending $\{G_t\}$ as given. When we look at the role of fiscal policy for other purposes (like active stabilization), we should however check whether such policies may be in conflict with these conditions for efficient composition of aggregate production.

1.4 Endogenous Production: The Labor Market

Up to now, we considered a pure endowment economy. But the model can easily be reinterpreted as a production economy with a given amount of time N_t available for work. Again, let us focus on a two-period economy. Assume that output in each period can be produced using labor input N_t with the linear (constant returns to scale) technology

$$Y_t = A_t N_t; Y_{t+1} = A_{t+1} N_{t+1}. \tag{1.4.1}$$

We may interpret the endowment economy in the last sections simply as a production economy with fixed labor supply, producing the endowment $Y_t = A_t N_t$ and $Y_{t+1} = A_{t+1} N_{t+1}$. The parameter A_t represents labor productivity. Due to technological progress, productivity improves across time. So assume that A_t grows with some constant rate γ the growth rate of productivity: $A_{t+1} = (1+\gamma)A_t$. We do not analyze the driving forces for productivity growth, but take technological progress as exogenous.

All income produced will in the end be owned by the representative household—either as wage income $W_t N_t$ or as profits Π_t earned by those owning the firms. With a linear production technology, perfect competition and just one input (labor), competition eliminates profits ($\Pi = 0$), so all resources produced are paid out as income to workers. In equilibrium, the real wage will be equal to productivity

$$w_t = W_t / P_t = A_t. \tag{1.4.2}$$

Things get more interesting when we derive labor supply (the number of hours N worked) and thus aggregate production endogenously. Let us now characterize the general equilibrium in a representative agent economy with endogenous production and endogenous labor supply in a two-period setup. To simplify, we ignore government spending in this section.

The consumer has a given endowment of time which may be spent partly for leisure and partly as labor input N for production. Each consumer decides how to split the total amount of time available between work N and leisure. There is a trade-off between working more in order to afford a higher level of consumption C and the time spent on leisure by the representative consumer. Since hours worked reduce the time available for enjoying leisure, hours worked cause disutility. We assume that the period utility function is additively separable in consumption and work effort. Consumers decide about the path for consumption C_t and hours worked N_t.

Since we are also interested in the impact of monopolistic power and taxation on aggregate production, we have to use a model which is a bit more complex. First, in order to allow for incentive effects of taxation, we explicitly introduce tax rates. τ_t^C is the tax rate on consumption in period t; τ_t^N on wage income. Higher taxes on labor dampen the incentive to work; higher taxes on consumption may affect the intertemporal consumption path. Hence taxes will have distortionary effects.

Second, we are interested in the impact of monopolistic pricing power of firms. Thus we need to model imperfect competition, allowing for production of specific heterogeneous goods. At the same time, we want to stick to the convenient aggregate structure as far as possible. The simplest way to do that is to let the consumption good C_t represent the indirect utility out of consuming a consumption basket, which is composed of a large number of diverse goods produced in the economy.

This version of monopolistic competition based on Dixit–Stiglitz preferences has become the workhorse model for capturing price-setting strategies of firms. The most elegant way is to model a continuum of heterogeneous firms, each producing some specific good *i*. Each producer maximises his profits taking his market power into account. It is a result of limited substitutability, derived from preferences with constant elasticity of substitution θ between different products within the consumption basket.

1.4.1 The Consumer's Choice

Let us first define the choice problem of the representative consumer *j*. The optimization problem is to maximize utility

$$V(C_t, N_t, C_{t+1}, N_{t+1}) = U(C_t) - V(N_t) + \beta[U(C_{t+1}) - V(N_{t+1})]. \tag{1.4.3}$$

Subject to the period constraints

$$(1+\tau_t^C)P_tC_t + P_tS_t = P_tY_t = (1-\tau_t^N)W_tN_t + \Pi_t, \tag{1.4.4}$$

$$P_{t+1}C_{t+1} = P_{t+1}Y_{t+1} + (1+i_t)P_tS_t = (1-\tau_{t+1}^N)W_{t+1}N_{t+1} + \Pi_{t+1} + (1+i_t)P_tS_t.$$

In each period, the consumer chooses her consumption basket, consisting of a continuum of goods, taking the prices of all those goods as given. She also decides about her labor supply and her savings profile. We set up the preference structure in such a way that we can separate inter-temporal and intra-temporal choice. The optimal choices are characterized by three first-order conditions.

Let us first concentrate on the inter-temporal Euler equation. Again, we can merge budget constraints into a single wealth constraint:

$$\begin{aligned}(1+\tau_t^C)P_tC_t + \frac{1}{1+i_t}(1+\tau_t^C)P_{t+1}C_{t+1} &\leq (1-\tau_t^N)W_tN_t \\ + \Pi_t + \frac{1}{1+i_t}((1-\tau_{t+1}^N)W_{t+1}N_{t+1} + \Pi_{t+1}).\end{aligned} \tag{1.4.5}$$

The familiar wealth constraint has been adjusted for effects of taxes: The present value of spending on consumption goods including the taxes paid on consumption must be equal to present value of income, net of income taxes.

1. Euler Equation E^*

$$-\frac{dC_{t+1}}{dC_t} = \frac{U_C(C_t)}{U_C(C_{t+1})}(1+\rho) = (1+i_t)\frac{P_t}{P_{t+1}} \cdot \frac{1+\tau_t^C}{1+\tau_{t+1}^C} = (1+r_t) \cdot \frac{1+\tau_t^C}{1+\tau_{t+1}^C}. \tag{1.4.6}$$

Here, the Fisher relation is used to express the Euler equation in terms of the real interest rate. Let us now focus on the optimal trade-off between consumption and hours worked within each period.

2. Labor Supply (MRS Between Labor and Consumption)

$$\frac{V_N(N_t)}{U_C(C_t)} = \frac{W_t(1-\tau_t^N)}{P_t(1+\tau_t^C)} \text{ for } t, t+1. \tag{1.4.7}$$

Finally, we need to characterize the optimal consumption bundle. C_t^j now represents a consumption basket of a continuum of goods $C_t^j(i)$. The simplest way (even though technically still rather tricky—see Focus Box for Nerds) is to use the Dixit–Stiglitz model of monopolistic competition. It assumes that there is a continuum of goods. Consumers want to consume a bundle with all those goods with preferences characterized by constant elasticity of substitution θ between the different goods. Then, demand for each specific good depends on the relative price of that good compared to the aggregate price index for all goods and on θ. C_t^j gives the indirect utility derived from optimizing the consumption basket at given prices and for some fixed budget available. As derived in the Focus Box for Nerds, we get as additional first-order condition:

3. Optimal Consumption Basket

$$C_t^j(i) = \left(\frac{P_t(i)}{P_t}\right)^{-\theta} C_t^j. \tag{1.4.8}$$

1.4.2 Monopolistic Distortions: Market Power on the Product Market

Having characterized consumption choice, let us now turn our focus on firm's incentives for production. As a counter-factual thought experiment, let us first consider how the economy would look like if producers of all goods would behave competitively, not making use of their market power and all taxes could be collected in a lump sum fashion. Profits of the representative firm are $\Pi_t(i) = P_t(i)Y_t(i) - W_tN_t(i) = (P_t(i) - W_t/A)Y_t(i)$. With constant returns to scale and perfect competition, there cannot be any profits: $\Pi_t(i) = 0$. All firms will charge the same price $P_t(i) = P_t$. So in competitive equilibrium, $P_t(i) = P_t = W_t \cdot (1/A)$—the real wage will be equal to marginal productivity $w_t = W_t/P_t = A$. Finally, in equilibrium the sum of aggregate consumption and government spending has to be equal to aggregate production—so the condition $C_t + G_t = Y_t = AN_t$ must hold.

In reality, of course, there is neither perfect competition nor is it feasible to impose lump sum taxes. Therefore, as next step, we allow for imperfect competition and distortionary taxation. Both producers and workers have some monopoly power. Taxes have adverse incentive effects. Not surprisingly, as we will see, both monopoly power and taxation create distortions. With market power and distortionary taxes, potential output (the natural level of production realized in market equilibrium) is inefficiently low compared to the competitive case—the economy is plagued by structural inefficiency.

General equilibrium can be characterized graphically by the equilibrium level of hours worked and goods produced. In each period, this can be captured by the intersection of a price setting and a wage setting curve on the labor market. The price setting curve represents monopolistic power on the side of the firms. It leads to a downward shift of demand for labor. The wage setting curve captures market power on the worker's side. It will lead to an upward shift of the supply of labor.

For a start, let us focus on the monopolistic distortions from the producer's side. If firms have market power, they will charge a markup $\widehat{\mu}$ on marginal costs *W/A*, driving a wedge between marginal productivity and the real wage. Firm's monopoly power shifts labor demand downwards. With constant returns to scale the price will be $P(i) = \frac{1}{A}W(1+\widehat{\mu})$. Again, in equilibrium all firms will charge the same price $P_t(i) = P_t$. Monopolistic distortions drive up the price of the consumption good, reducing the effective real wage to

$$w = \frac{A}{1+\widehat{\mu}}. \tag{1.4.9}$$

This is captured in Fig. 1.10 by the fact that the price setting curve is below marginal productivity of labor. Given a competitive labor supply curve, the equilibrium level of employment N_n at point D is inefficiently low compared to the efficient outcome C. Note that this inefficiency is not a result of involuntary unemployment. Because of the real wage being lower, workers simply are no longer willing to work as much as under competitive conditions. They are still on their supply curve.

Obviously, monopoly power on the worker's side will also create distortions: It shifts effective labor supply (the wage curve) to the left. This way, employment will be reduced even further to N_n' in Fig. 1.10 with equilibrium at point E. With constant labor productivity, the bargaining power of workers cannot raise the real wage in equilibrium. In more general cases, real wage may even increase above the competitive level, but in any case, aggregate employment and production will be inefficiently low in the monopolistically distorted economy. Distortionary taxes will have the same effect: As long as leisure cannot be taxed, taxes (both income taxes and indirect consumption taxes) again drive a wedge between marginal rate of substitution and marginal productivity. Taxes have a similar impact on employment and production as monopoly power. As key insight, we can characterize the distortions in

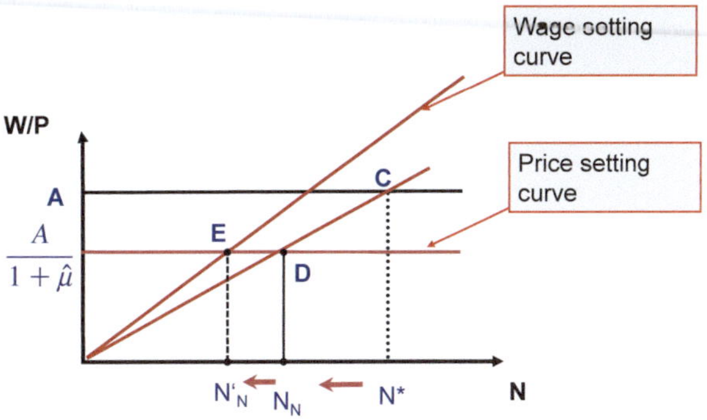

Fig. 1.10 The price and wage setting curve

our economy $(Y_n < Y^*; N_n < N^*)$ in a straightforward way: The structural inefficiency can be captured simply by the parameter $\Delta = Y^* - Y_n$.

Of course, monopoly power may have a significant distributional impact: The income of workers is reduced, whereas profits are positive. But nevertheless, aggregating across all households, aggregate private and public consumption still equals aggregate income which equals total production (this is just the same condition you have learned in basic macro: For a closed economy, $GDP = GNP$. Because in our simple economy, with no investment, we have $GDP = C + G$)! Abstracting from distributional issues, we take this relation into account by imposing the condition that the representative consumer earns all income.

Focus Box for Nerds: Monopolistic Competition a la Dixit/Stiglitz (Popular Among Central Bank Academics)—*Optional Material

Dixit and Stiglitz (1977) modelled preferences such that the elasticity of substitution θ between the different goods is constant by construction. Blanchard and Kiyotaki (1987) have been the first to introduce this approach in a modern, micro-founded macro model with sticky prices. The approach has quite a few attractions: First, it is able to model price setting behavior explicitly. Second, it allows for straightforward aggregation. The aggregate consumption demand can be represented by some composite bundle C_t. With constant elasticity for each good, there is a constant markup of prices over wages. Here, we consider the technically simplest case with a continuum of goods $i \in [0, \infty)$. Consumer j consumes a bundle of all goods i with total payoff from consuming defined as:

$$C_t^j = \left[\int_0^1 C_t^j(i)^{\frac{\theta-1}{\theta}} di \right]^{\frac{\theta-1}{\theta}} \quad (1.4.10)$$

(continued)

We want to characterize the optimal bundle for an arbitrary set of prices $P_t(i)$ for all goods i and some given budget $P_t Y_t^j$. Let us show that the optimal choice is characterized by the following intuitive condition:

$$C_t^j(i) = \left(\frac{P_t(i)}{P_t}\right)^{-\theta} C_t^j \tag{1.4.11}$$

We assume $\theta > 1$.When deciding about the quantity $C_t^j(i)$ consumed of some specific good i, consumer j will buy less of that good when the its price $P_t(i)$ is high relative to the prices of all other goods, measured by the price level P_t. Let us derive this condition in several steps. First, for a given nominal budget

$$P_t Y_t^j = \int_0^1 P_t(i) C_t^j(i) di \tag{1.4.12}$$

spent on the consumption basket C_t^j, consumer j chooses the optimal mix between all available goods based on their relative prices. Demand $C_t^j(i')$ for some specific product i' will be lower, the higher the price of this specific product $P_t(i')$ relative to the price $P_t(i)$ of good i. So indirect utility is maximised if the mix among all $C_t^j(i')$ in the consumption basket C_t^j is chosen optimally, given the prices of all these goods and given the available budget $P_t Y_t^j$. We maximize the Lagrangian:

$$\max_{\{C_t^j(i)\}} C_t^j = \left[\int_0^1 C_t^j(i)^{\frac{\theta-1}{\theta}} di\right]^{\frac{\theta-1}{\theta}} + \lambda\left[P_t Y_t^j - \int_0^1 P_t(i) C_t^j(i) di\right], \forall\, i \in [0,1] \tag{1.4.13}$$

For each specific good i, consumer j chooses the amount consumed optimally, given its price $P_t(i)$ and given some budget $P_t Y_t^j$. Let us determine the choice between two arbitrary goods i, i' in the basket. The first-order condition for good i' relative to good i is:

$$C_t^j(i') = \left(\frac{P_t(i')}{P_t}\right)^{-\theta} C_t^j(i) = P_t(i')^{-\theta} \frac{C_t^j(i)}{P_t(i)^{-\theta}}. \tag{1.4.14}$$

We use this condition to replace $C_t^j(i')$ in budget constraint Equation 1.4.12 for all goods i' in order to get

(continued)

$$\int_0^1 P_t(i')C_t^j(i')di' = \int_0^1 P_t(i')^{1-\theta}di' \frac{C_t^j(i)}{P_t(i)^{-\theta}} = P_tY_t^j. \tag{1.4.15}$$

Rearranging Equation 1.4.15 gives as demand for good i:

$$C_t^j(i) = P_t(i)^{-\theta}\frac{P_tY_t^j}{\int_0^1 P_t(i)^{1-\theta}di}. \tag{1.4.16}$$

Here, we have formulated demand for good i as a function of the price of this specific good $P_t(i)$, the aggregate price level P_t and some integral of all prices (Note that in that integral, we replaced the index i' by i: $\int_0^1 P_t(i')^{1-\theta}di' = \int_0^1 P_t(i)^{1-\theta}di$). Obviously, this integral is related to the aggregate price index, if we choose that price index appropriately. A sensible price index P_t has to satisfy the requirement $P_tY_t^j = P_tC_t^j$. For Equation 1.4.10 this gives the Dixit–Stiglitz price index:

$$P_t = \left[\int_0^1 P_t(i)^{1-\theta}di\right]^{\frac{1}{1-\theta}} \text{ with } P_t^{1-\theta} = \int (P_t(i))^{1-\theta}di. \tag{1.4.17}$$

Using the Dixit–Stiglitz price index, we can simplify our demand Equation 1.4.14 as:

$$C_t^j(i) = P_t(i)^{-\theta}\frac{P_tY_t^j}{\int_0^1 P_t(i)^{1-\theta}di} = \frac{P_t(i)^{-\theta}}{P_t^{-\theta}}\frac{P_tY_t^j}{P_t} = \left(\frac{P_t(i)}{P_t}\right)^{-\theta}C_t^j. \tag{1.4.18}$$

By construction $P_tC_t^j = \int_0^1 P_t(i)C_t^j(i)di$ since $C_t^j(i) = C_t^j\left(\frac{P_t(i)}{P_t}\right)^{-\theta}$ and $P_t^{1-\theta} = \int_0^1 (P_t(i))^{1-\theta}di$.

1.4.3 Example: Explicit Linearized Solution for Constant Elasticity of Substitution

For deriving explicit solutions it is again convenient to consider the case of constant elasticity of substitution for the preferences, that is we specify

$$U(C_t) = \frac{1}{1-1/\sigma}(C_t)^{1-1/\sigma}; V(N_t) = \frac{Z_t}{1+\varphi}(N_t)^{1+\varphi}. \tag{1.4.19}$$

The parameter σ represents the familiar elasticity of inter-temporal substitution, the parameter φ is the inverse of the (so called "Frisch") elasticity of labor supply (the larger φ the less elastic labor supply). The preference parameter Z_t captures temporary shifts in the willingness to work. The larger Z_t, the higher the current preference for leisure, so the higher the real wage needed to give incentives for working more hours.

Using this specification we can solve explicitly for Equations 1.4.6 and 1.4.7:

$$\left(\frac{C_t}{C_{t+1}}\right)^{-\frac{1}{\sigma}} = \frac{1}{1+\rho} \cdot \frac{1+i_t}{P_{t+1}/P_t} \cdot \frac{1+\tau_t^C}{1+\tau_{t+1}^C}, \tag{1.4.6a}$$

$$\frac{Z_t \cdot N_t^{\varphi}}{C_t^{-1/\sigma}} = \frac{W_t(1-\tau_t^N)}{P_t(1+\tau_t^C)}. \tag{1.4.7a}$$

In logarithmic form, the ***Euler Equation 1.4.6a*** gives the familiar inter-temporal consumption demand curve:

$$c_t = c_{t+1} - \sigma(r_t - \rho) - \sigma(\tau_t^C - \tau_{t+1}^C), \tag{1.4.6b}$$

$$\text{with } r_t = i_t - [E(p_{t+1}) - p_t] = i - E(\pi_t).$$

As long as the consumption tax rate τ_t^C is constant across time, the Euler equation (determining the inter-temporal choice) is the same as in the standard case. An increase in the consumption tax rate today relative to tomorrow induces the household to postpone consumption, encouraging her to save more. If, for some reason, policy wants to induce shifts in inter-temporal demand, this can be implemented either by a change in the real rate of interest (via interest rate policy) or by a temporary change in consumption tax.

From the log-linear condition $z_t + \varphi n_t + 1/\sigma \cdot c_t = w_t - p_t - \tau_t^N - \tau_t^C$ we get labor supply as:

$$n_t = \frac{1}{\varphi}(w_t - p_t - \tau_t^N - \tau_t^C) - \frac{1}{\varphi \cdot \sigma} c_t - \frac{z_t}{\varphi}. \tag{1.4.7b}$$

Labor supply is increasing in the effective real wage, net of taxes. Given the specification of additive separable preference between consumption and leisure, marginal utility of consumption is independent of hours worked. So by construction, for $\varphi > 0$ there is ceteris paribus complementarity between consumption and leisure in preferences: An increase in consumption has to go hand in hand with an increase in leisure and thus a reduction in hours worked unless the real wage rises sufficiently. The larger φ (the less elastic the labor supply), the stronger is this effect, and hence the stronger the increase in real wages net of taxes required to give incentives to work more. When preferences are quasi linear in leisure $(\varphi = 0)$ labor supply is elastic. In that case, the household is always willing to supply the amount of work needed to afford the consumption level $c_t = \sigma\left(w_t - p_t - \tau_t^N - \tau_t^C\right)$.

Note that effects on labor supply can be quite different with complementarity between consumption and work—see Monacelli and Perotti (2008) and Christiano, Eichenbaum, and Rebelo (2011).

1.4.4 Firms Pricing Strategy: Price Setting Under Monopolistic Competition

Each firm i produces a differentiated good i using labor with a constant returns technology

$$Y_t(i) = A_t L_t(i). \tag{1.4.20}$$

A_t is the level of technology at time t. We can think of movements in A_t as aggregate technological shocks. The firm's optimization problem in each period is to maximize profits:

$$\max \Pi_t(i) = P_t(i)Y_t(i) - W_t L_t(i),\ s.t.\ Y_t(i) = A_t L_t(i). \tag{1.4.21}$$

Due to limited substitutability θ, a generic producer i has some monopolistic market power, captured by the demand function derived for the representative consumer. The demand for his product depends on the price he charges relative to the prices of all other producers:

$$Y_t^d(i) = \left(\frac{P_t(i)}{P_t}\right)^{-\theta} Y_t = \left(\frac{P_t(i)}{P_t}\right)^{-\theta}(C_t + G_t). \tag{1.4.22}$$

We can calculate profits for firm i as follows (using $L(i) = Y(i)/A_t$):

$$\Pi_t(i) = P_t(i)Y_t^d(i) - W_t L_t(i) = \left[(P_t(i))^{1-\theta} - (P_t(i))^{-\theta}\frac{W_t}{A_t}\right]\frac{Y_t}{P_t^{-\theta}} \tag{1.4.23}$$

Independent of Y_t the optimal pricing strategy of firm i is characterized by the FOC:

$$\frac{\partial \Pi_t(i)}{\partial P_t(i)} = (1-\theta)\cdot(P_t(i))^{1-\theta} + \theta\cdot(P_t(i))^{-\theta-1}\frac{W_t}{A_t} = 0,\ \text{or},\ \theta - 1 = \theta\cdot P_t(i)^{-1}\frac{W_t}{A_t}$$

$$P_t(i) = \frac{\theta}{\theta-1}\cdot\frac{W_t}{A_t} = (1+\widehat{\mu})\cdot\frac{W_t}{A_t} \tag{1.4.24}$$

This gives Equation 1.4.25

$$\frac{W_t}{P_t(i)} = \left(1 - \frac{1}{\theta}\right)A_t = \frac{1}{1+\widehat{\mu}}A_t < A_t. \tag{1.4.25}$$

$\widehat{\mu} = \theta/(\theta-1) - 1 = 1/(\theta-1) > 0$ is the markup resulting from monopolistic price setting behavior. Since consumers exhibit imperfect elasticity of substitution θ between the different goods, each producer has some market power. The markup will be higher (markets will be less competitive) the smaller θ. To be well defined, we must have $\theta > 1$.

1.4.5 General Equilibrium: The Case of Flexible Prices

If firm i charges $P_t(i)$, we have

$$\frac{P_t(i)}{P_t} = \frac{\theta}{\theta - 1}\frac{1}{A_t}\frac{W_t}{P_t} = \frac{\theta}{\theta - 1}\frac{MC_t(i)}{P_t}. \tag{1.4.26}$$

As long as prices of all firms are fully flexible and productivity is the same across all firms, $P_t(i) = P_t$ and thus

$$\frac{W_t}{P_t} = \left(1 - \frac{1}{\theta}\right)A_t. \tag{1.4.27}$$

So we can easily calculate the general equilibrium in our economy by imposing labor market clearing in both periods:

$$\frac{V_N(N_t(i))}{U_c(C_t)} = \frac{1 - \tau_t^N}{1 + \tau_t^C}\frac{W_t}{P_t} = \frac{1 - \tau_t^N}{1 + \tau_t^C}\left(1 - \frac{1}{\theta}\right)A_t = \frac{1}{1 + \mu}A_t < A_t \tag{1.4.28}$$

with μ_t defined as

$$\mu_t = \frac{1 + \tau_t^C}{1 - \tau_t^N}(1 + \widehat{\mu_t}) - 1 > 0, \text{ or log linearized} : \mu_t = \tau_t^C + \tau_t^N + \widehat{\mu_t}. \tag{1.4.29}$$

Both market power (arising from monopolistic competition $\widehat{\mu} = \theta/(\theta - 1) - 1$) and distortionary tax rates on consumption τ_t^C and labor τ_t^N create a wedge compared to the first best outcome. The wedge is represented by the general markup factor μ_t which captures all these distortions. In the log-linear case, we can calculate a closed-form solution for general equilibrium. Using the equilibrium condition for the real wage $w_t - p_t = a_t - \widehat{\mu_t}$ or $w_t - p_t - \tau_t^N - \tau_t^C = a_t - \mu_t$, the market clearing for the labor market is:

$$\varphi n_t + \frac{1}{\sigma}c_t = a_t - z_t - \mu_t. \tag{1.4.30}$$

In equilibrium, the aggregate resource constraint $Y_t = C_t + G_t$ or $y_t = c_t + g_t$ in log-linear terms with $g_t = G_t/Y_t$ must hold in each period. Replacing $c_t = y_t - g_t$ (Equation 1.3.6) and $n_t = y_t - a_t$ (taking the log of $N_t = Y_t/A_t$) in Equation 1.4.30 we can solve analytically for the general equilibrium values y_{tn}, n_{tn}, and c_t. In our economy, y_{tn} is *potential output* or the *natural level of output* in period t. This is the level produced in the absence of nominal rigidities. It provides us with an important benchmark: If all prices and wages were flexible, the market outcome would always be y_{tn}. The corresponding labor input is n_{tn}. We can call this the *structural or natural level of employment*. c_{tn} is equilibrium consumption in the case of flexible prices.

$$y_{tn} = \frac{1}{\varphi + 1/\sigma}(a_t \cdot (1 + \varphi) - z_t + 1/\sigma \cdot g_t - \mu_t), \tag{1.4.31}$$

$$n_{tn} = \frac{1}{\varphi + 1/\sigma}(a_t \cdot (1 - 1/\sigma) - z_t + 1/\sigma \cdot g_t - \mu_t),$$

$$c_{tn} = \frac{1}{\varphi + 1/\sigma}(a_t \cdot (1 + \varphi) - z_t - \varphi \cdot g_t - \mu_t).$$

Finally, the natural real rate of interest is determined by the Euler equation which needs to be satisfied for inter-temporal consumption. In log-linearized version we have:

$$r_{tn} = i_t - E(\pi_t) = \rho + 1/\sigma \cdot (E(c_2) - c_1) - \sigma(\tau_2^C - \tau_1^C). \tag{1.4.32}$$

Note that for $\sigma = 1$ (logarithmic preferences in consumption: $U_c(C_t) = \ln C_t$), hours worked do not depend on the productivity level a_t in general equilibrium. The reason is that for logarithmic preferences, income and substitution effect for leisure cancel each other out: In equilibrium, higher productivity raises wages and thus the opportunity cost for leisure, dampening incentives to work. At the same time, higher wages allow for more consumption. As long as an increase in productivity leads to an equivalent increase in consumption, the representative agent is happy to consume the same level of leisure. To see this, note that for $\sigma = 1$ with a change in labor productivity Δa_t we have $\Delta n_t = 0$ and $\Delta c_t = \Delta y_t = \Delta a_t$ according to Equation 1.4.31. Hence logarithmic preferences in consumption provide a convenient motivation for the fact that empirically, hours worked do not necessarily decrease (or increase) with increasing productivity. Higher government spending, however, results in an increase in hours worked in order to offset the implied decrease in private consumption in the current period.

1.4.6 Structural Inefficiencies: Comparison with the First Best Level of Production

Due to monopolistic price setting and distortionary effects of taxation, the market equilibrium with flexible prices is characterized by an inefficiently low level of economic activity. We can derive the first best outcome by correcting for distortions. Assume that firms get paid a subsidy $s_t = \tau_t^C + \tau_t^N + \widehat{\mu}_t$ financed via lumps sum taxes such that all marginal distortions are eliminated. This way we can set $\mu_t = \tau_t^C + \tau_t^N + \widehat{\mu}_t - s_t = 0$. This gives as efficient outcome:

$$y_t^* = \frac{1}{\varphi + 1/\sigma}(a_t \cdot (1 + \varphi) - z_t + 1/\sigma \cdot g_t), \tag{1.4.33}$$

$$n_t^* = \frac{1}{\varphi + 1/\sigma}(a_t \cdot (1 - 1/\sigma) - z_t + 1/\sigma \cdot g_t),$$

$$c_t^* = \frac{1}{\varphi + 1/\sigma}(a_t \cdot (1 + \varphi) - z_t - \varphi \cdot g_t).$$

In the first best case, output, hours worked and consumption are all higher. As the result of structural inefficiencies, the market level of production, labor input, and consumption are all below the first best level (as shown in Fig. 1.10 for labor input). The distortions may be due to quite different reasons: Monopoly power of both firms and unions, negative incentive effects from taxation; finally (not modeled here), search frictions on the labor market causing search unemployment. The extent of the structural inefficiency is characterized by the markup factor μ_t. Alternatively, we may capture the structural inefficiency by the deviation of potential (the market outcome in the case of flexible prices) from first best level:

$$\Delta_t = y_t^* - y_{tn}, \text{with } \Delta_t = \frac{\mu_t}{\varphi + 1/\sigma} > 0 \text{ and } \frac{d\Delta_t}{d\mu} > 0; \ \frac{d\Delta_t}{d\sigma} > 0; \ \frac{d\Delta_t}{d\varphi} < 0. \quad (1.4.34)$$

Changes in most structural parameters will have an impact both on the equilibrium outcome and on the efficient solution. Consider, for instance, a shock increasing productivity a_t or a shock increasing the willingness to work (a decrease in the parameter z_t). Both shocks will boost actual and also efficient production. Production goes up if productivity rises and/or workers are willing to work harder. We can interpret these shocks as positive supply shocks. Effectively, only the combination of both type of "supply" shocks matters—the sum of productivity and labor supply shocks: $a_t \cdot (1 + \varphi) - z_t$.

As a further exercise, consider the impact of a temporary increase in government spending.

$$dy_t/dg_t = dn_t/dg_t = \frac{1}{1 + \varphi \cdot \sigma} < 1, \quad (1.4.35)$$

$$dc_t/dg_t = -\frac{\varphi \cdot \sigma}{1 + \varphi \cdot \sigma} < 0.$$

An increase in g_t will lead to a supply response. But the "supply side" multiplier from government spending is less than one for the following reason: If production were unchanged, private consumption would have to be cut one for one at the expense of higher public spending. Consumers, however, prefer to smooth consumption, so they are eager to work harder in order to partially offset the loss in current consumption. For $\sigma = 0$ or $\varphi = 0$ (inelastic, kinked inter-temporal preferences respectively perfectly elastic labor supply), they will keep up consumption at the initial level, driving the multiplier toward one. With $\sigma \to \infty$ or $\varphi \to \infty$ (linear inter-temporal preference respectively labor supply being inelastic), there is no reaction in output, driving the multiplier toward zero.

1.5 Summary

This chapter introduced important concepts for inter-temporal analysis which play a key role in modern monetary policy analysis. Here we focused on a real economy, using a simple two-period endowment economy with one representative agent. We derived optimality conditions for the inter-temporal path of consumption (the Euler equation) and the natural rate of interest as key equilibrium condition. We showed that our endowment can be interpreted as a base line model for a growing economy and illustrated how the setup can be extended to more than two periods in a straightforward way. We also showed how heterogeneity across households may be taken into account.

In Sect. 1.3, we introduced government spending and taxation in our two period model and discussed conditions under which Ricardian equivalence holds. Section 1.4 determined production endogenously. We derived optimal price setting under monopolistic competition in an economy with heterogeneous firms. The simple structure allowed to solve explicitly for the equilibrium. The general equilibrium conditions for output and labor market provide an important reference point for later analysis: They characterize potential output, the natural level of employment, and the corresponding natural real rate of interest in the absence of nominal rigidities. Due to monopolistic price setting and distortionary effects of taxation, the market equilibrium is distorted. As a result of the frictions, the level of economic activity and employment is inefficiently low relative to the welfare maximizing first best level of production. The structural inefficiency can be captured by a simple markup factor.

References

Baxter, M., & King, R. (1993). Fiscal policy in general equilibrium. *American Economic Review, 83*(3), 315–334.

Blanchard, O., & Kiyotaki, N. (1987). Monopolistic competition and the effects of aggregate demand. *American Economic Review, 77*, 647–666.

Christiano, L., Eichenbaum, M., & Evans, C. (2005). Nominal rigidities and the dynamic effects of a shock to monetary policy. *Journal of Political Economy, 113*(1), 1–45.

Christiano, L., Eichenbaum, M., & Rebelo, S. (2011). When is the government spending multiplier large? *Journal of Political Economy, 119*(1), 78–121.

Christiano, L., Eichenbaum, M., & Trabandt, M. (2018). On DSGE models? *Journal of Economic Perspectives, 32*(3), 113–140.

Dixit, A., & Stiglitz, J. (1977). Monopolistic competition and optimum product diversity. *American Economic Review, 67*(3), 297–308.

Eggertsson, G., Mehrotra, N., & Robbins, J. (2017). A model of secular stagnation: Theory and quantitative evaluation. *NBER working papers* 23093.

Fisher, I. (1896). Appreciation and interest. *Publications of the American Economic Association, First Series, 11*(4), 1–110.

Guvenen, F. (2011). Macroeconomics with heterogeneity: A practical guide. *Federal Reserve Bank of Richmond Economic Quarterly, 97*(3), 255–326.

Illing, G., Ono, Y., & Schlegl, M. (2018). Credit booms, debt overhang and secular stagnation. *European Economic Review, 108*, 78–104.

Monacelli, T., & Perotti, R. (2008). Fiscal policy, wealth effects, and markups. *NBER Working Papers* 14584.

Smets, F., & Wouters, R. (2007). Shocks and frictions in US business cycles: A Bayesian DSGE approach. *American Economic Review, 97*(3), 586–606.

Part I

Money and Equilibrium in the Long Run

2 Money and Long-Run Growth

2.1 Introduction

In Chap. 1, we presented a simple model of the real economy. Right at the start, we introduced the notion of (fiat) money as some additional good, being used as unit of account (numeraire) and as means of payment. We defined P_t as the price level (the price of goods of in terms of money) and M_t as the amount of money available at t. We derived optimality conditions for the inter-temporal path of consumption and also derived the Fisher equation as arbitrage condition for portfolio allocation between real and nominal bonds. We did not, however, analyze the motives for holding money. Instead, we simply assumed that there is a stable relation between real economic activity and money holding. But we have been rather vague about the reasons why people may be willing to hold money and to use nominal contracts and also about the way monetary policy might determine the price level.

In this chapter, we want to look into these issues in more detail. We try to answer some classical questions: Why do people hold cash even though it has no intrinsic value and is dominated in return since cash pays no interest? What fundamental economic forces determine the price level and the rate of inflation? What policy mistakes may cause periods of persistent high inflation or even hyperinflation? What could be responsible for triggering deflationary spirals?

To characterize equilibrium on the money market, we need some micro-foundation motivating both demand for and supply of money. Obviously, both depend on the specific institutions determining how transactions are organized in society—the financial system. In a pure barter economy, trading must be done via bilateral exchange of real goods without involving money. A barter economy requires double-coincidence of wants and thus imposes enormous frictions, limiting drastically the scope of feasible transactions. Using some socially accepted medium of transaction can increase the set of feasible transactions dramatically. Thus, introducing money allows a higher degree of specialization of production and so raises efficiency. To capture this idea, Robert Clower (1965) formulated the cash-in-advance constraint. It tries to model the notion that money buys goods and goods

J. Cao, G. Illing, *Money: Theory and Practice*, Springer Texts in Business and Economics, https://doi.org/10.1007/978-3-030-19697-4_2

buy money, but goods do not buy goods (see Sect. 2.4.1). Kiyotaki and Wright (1989) provide a detailed game-theoretic model demonstrating the efficiency gains from using money as medium of transaction.

But other institutional arrangements can also cope with the frictions imposed by barter trading. The problem of double-coincidence of wants can be addressed in different ways. Anthropologists present numerous historical examples for centralized ceremonial credit arrangements with trade organized neither via barter nor money. Complex credit systems (such as merchants and temple administrators offering loans to farmers) have been established long before standardized circulating units of metals like gold or silver were used as medium of exchange—for example, in the Mesopotamia area around 3200 BC. Such credit systems require enforcement mechanisms, limiting the degree of specialization: Trading may be restricted to take place within the own community (the local village) or it may require legal arrangements such as debt bondage, possibly forcing to sell one's own children into slavery.

As long as all inter-temporal trade can be done via perfectly enforceable contracts, there is no need to use money. The most sophisticated (and extreme) version of perfect credit markets is the modern work-horse model of microeconomic trade, the Arrow Debreu model. In that model, there is no role for money, since agents are assumed to be able to trade all future contingent claims at perfect, friction less markets with equilibrium prices already being determined in the initial period. All contracts will be enforced by the legal system.

Consider just one example: If you as a student invite your partner for dinner in a posh expensive restaurant, according to the standard micro model you are able to pay the waiter by promising him a claim on your future income, contingent on passing your exam with distinction. The waiter does not need to verify your promises since all contracts are assumed to be enforceable. There is even no need for him to worry about the risk of you failing the exams, since he is assumed to be able to hedge that risk via contingent future markets.

So you can just sign a piece of paper "IOU" (I owe you) specifying the amount owed and the time of repayment. Obviously, most waiters would refuse to bring the dishes you ordered and instead are likely to call the police rather than accepting your IOU. In contrast, when paying with cash, verifiability is no problem (other than making sure that the coins and notes offered are not faked). Introducing money (declaring some commodity or paper as legal tender) requires legal enforcement power of the payments made via that medium. If you pay via credit card, verifiability is taken care of by the issuing agency. In that sense, money saves on information costs, based on trust. By offering efficient payment systems (via checking account, credit cards or online banking), financial intermediaries reduce the information costs involved with monitoring contracts. Substantial economies of scale prevail by agreeing to use the same safe asset for payment—similar to communication being made much easier when all participants use the same language.

To understand the nature of money as liquid asset, frictions on contract enforcement are crucial. Agents are willing to be paid with money, because they trust that others will accept that medium later in exchange for goods they want to buy. So what determines the price of money? With metals like gold or silver used as medium of exchange, the price might be determined by some intrinsic fundamental value of the specific metal—such as the value when used as input in production. But the price of liquid assets as medium of exchange usually exceeds this "intrinsic" value—there is a liquidity premium. This is most obvious when we talk about fiat money—pieces of colored paper which have hardly any other use than as medium of exchange and unit of account (except, possibly being used for heating—as was the case during times of hyperinflation).

Why do people hold fiat money? It is intrinsically useless—there is no direct utility out of holding/consuming money. In Walt Disney's famous comics the rich uncle Scrooge likes to boast his own wealth by bathing in piles of cash. But usually, we do not enjoy storing piles of banknotes just to show off. Rather we are willing to hold money (cash) only because of its ability to buy goods. Money provides only indirect utility out of the consumption of real goods people can afford by paying cash. Agents need to pay with cash for transactions if it is too costly to verify the creditworthiness for anonymous counterparties. Money is a way to store information about the ability to pay—it saves on information costs. But why should we trust money more than other written promises (such as a piece of paper stating that I will transfer some commodities back to you in distant future)? Money is a social convention[1]: I am willing to accept and hold money today only if I can trust that other agents will accept it later on. So an inherent crucial feature of money is the self-fulfilling (and thus fragile) nature of its value: As soon as trust evaporates, agents will try to get rid of that medium, trying to pass it over to others before it loses any value.

In this chapter, we want to understand how the price level (the price of a commodity basket in terms of money) is determined in a fiat money economy. We want to understand how price stability may be implemented. What went wrong during hyperinflationary periods when people lost trust in the value of local money? What is the impact of deflation? To gain a better understanding, here we analyze the simplest case—an economy with perfectly flexible prices, focusing on long run issues. To simplify, we assume that output of the real economy will always be at its natural rate. Money is assumed to be super-neutral—it does not affect activity in the real economy. Price level and the stock of money change proportionally, leaving real money balances *M/P* and the real economy unchanged. As has already been observed by David Hume,[2] this will hold only in the long run. But currently we abstract from price stickiness which may cause short-run deviations. So by

[1]"Somehow the members of a society agree on what will be acceptable tender in making payments and settling debts among themselves (particular commodities or tokens as measures of value and media of exchange in economic transactions). General agreement to the convention, not the particular media agreed upon, is the source of money's immense value to the society. In this respect money is similar to language, standard time, or the convention designating the side of the road for passing." (Tobin, 1992).

[2]"To account, then, for this phenomenon, we must consider, that though the high price of commodities is a necessary consequence of the increase of gold and silver, yet it follows not

construction, we would not be able to analyze whether policy may stimulate real activity temporarily or why a deflationary spiral may risk the breakdown of the financial system with damage to economic activity. In a more realistic setting with at least some prices and wages being sticky, monetary policy can contribute to stabilize output fluctuations. This will be the topic of Chap. 4.

Focus Box: Gold Standard and Other Media of Exchange

For millennia, noble metals like gold, silver, or bronze bullion have been used as a main form of money. They served as unit of account, medium of exchange, and store of wealth. In medieval times, gold and silver coins minted by the sovereign were used as legal tender. But the specific medium chosen as money varies tremendously across human history. Not just standardized coins made of noble metals have been used as medium on exchange, but also salt, seashells, or cigarettes (in prisoner of war camps). On the island of Yap in the Pacific Ocean disks made of calcite stones were used as legal tender. It was difficult to transport these stones across islands with canoes. Thus, eventually debts were settled simply by changing the ownership of immovable stone wheels. This practice continued even after the sea flooded their sites and the stones were invisible at the bottom of a lagoon (Tobin, 1992).

A gold or silver specie standard involves the circulation of gold or silver coins to settle payments in transactions. In such a system the monetary unit is the value of a certain circulating coin. Rather than being shipped across regions, gold bullion may be stored in sealed lockers or in safe vaults such as Fort Knox. So as long as trust can be sustained, trades need not be settled by the physical transfer of the commodity used as unit of account.

We need to distinguish between two different regimes: *Gold specie standard (bullion)* (the circulation of specie to settle payments in transactions) and a *Gold exchange standard.* Here, the sovereign agrees to sell gold bullion on demand at a fixed price in exchange for circulating currency. The gold exchange standard usually does not involve the circulation of gold coins. Instead, the government guarantees a fixed price of domestic currency in terms of gold—or fixes the exchange rate with a country using the gold standard (specie or bullion), regardless of what type of notes or coins are used as a means of exchange. Unlike in a specie standard, however, the exchange rate may be (temporarily) suspended or adjusted to a new rate. So the sovereign (the government) can reset the face value to a specific quantity of gold any time.

At first sight, a strict specie standard seems to impose strict monetary discipline in the sense that the price level cannot be manipulated since the supply of money is exogenously given. As Fig. 2.1 plots the headline

(continued)

immediately upon that increase; but some time is required before the money circulates through the whole state, and makes its effect be felt on all ranks of people."

consumer price index (CPI) in the UK from 1250 till 2015. The price index measures the weighted prices of a commodity basket in terms of sterling (see Fig. 2.2 for variation in weights used between 1209 and 1869). It has been relatively stable in the UK before 1500 and then later in the period from 1650 till the beginning of the twentieth century. During the twentieth century, with fiat money dominating, we observe a dramatic increase in the price level (note that Fig. 2.1a has a logarithmic scale).

But a closer look demonstrates that things are more complex. First, there are good arguments to stabilize the price of a commodity basket rather than the price of a specific commodity. As shown in Fig. 2.1b, the overall price level exhibited much higher yearly fluctuations before the twentieth century. If the price of silver or gold is fixed, prices of all other commodities will fluctuate widely with random periods of inflation and deflation. So there may be high volatility for the purchasing power of the metal. As long as the supply of the specific metal used is fixed and there are no other shocks, there will be a gradual decline of the price index (deflation) in a growing economy. But exogenous increases in the supply lead to a drastic rise of the price level—the price of a basket of ordinary goods rises after discoveries of new resources, eroding the purchasing power. The strong increase in supply of gold and silver led to a (gradual) strong increase in the price level when Christopher Columbus discovered America in 1492 and plenty of the precious metals were shipped from South and Central America to Europe. Between 1500 and 1650, we observe a sharp rise in the UK consumer price index. For example, the sterling price of wheat increased sixfold during that period.

This drastic inflation was, however, only partly triggered by the increased supply of silver. The price of wheat relative to silver bullion increased only fourfold. At the same time, however, silver coins in addition also depreciated by 50% relative to silver for the following reason: During that period—in particular during the reign of Henry VIII—the Royal silver Mint reduced both the weight of its coins (an outright devaluation) and their fineness (debasement). Newly minted coins were debased regularly for the following reason: Over time, old worn out coins lost weight. By debasing, the weight of newly minted coins with same face value was made the same as the weight of averagely worn old ones.

By reducing the weight of the coins or their fineness, the sovereign can raise additional seigniorage revenue, with the face value being higher than production cost. Over six centuries the face value of sterling increased by a multiple of three times relative to its bullion weight.

Gresham's law: "Bad" money drives out "good" money. If coins with different weight are accepted as legal tender for economic transactions at a fixed rate even though the metal contained in the coins is of different value, people will use those coins with the lowest weight for payment, hoarding those

(continued)

coins with higher weight. Good money (coins with higher weight) disappears from transactions driven out by bad money. Such hoarding occurs regularly when a currency is debased, such as when the British monarchs Henry VIII and Edward VI reduced the metallic weight of English silver coins to a significantly smaller fraction of their former weight. Trying to persuade Queen Elizabeth I to restore an already debased currency, Sir Thomas Gresham pointed out in a letter to her written in 1558: "*If debased coin is attempted to be circulated with full valued coin, all of the latter will disappear from circulation, and the overvalued and debased coin will alone remain to the ruin of our commerce and business*".

Using specie as means of transaction absorbs real resources both for production and for transport which may be spent more efficiently otherwise. As an extreme example, the high transport costs incurred for moving stones across islands with canoes around Yap are clearly inefficient. The stones serve only a symbolic function. For that reason, Keynes denounced the gold standard as "a barbarous relic." From early on, financial innovation has introduced substitutes like fractional reserve banking trying to minimize wasting resources for symbolic purpose, culminating in modern regimes with fiat money (or, even more advanced, virtual electronic money). For modern central banks, official gold reserves represent only a small share of total assets held (see Fig. 2.3).

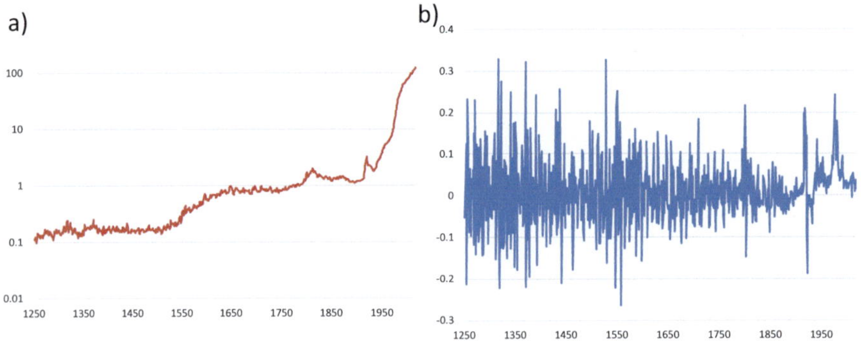

Fig. 2.1 UK Headline Consumer Price Index (CPI) 1250–2015. (**a**) Price level: Headline CPI (2010 = 100) log scale. (**b**) Change in price level: UK yearly CPI price fluctuations, 1250–2015 (Source: Bank of England, A millennium of macroeconomic data for the UK, Version 3, April 2017. https://www.bankofengland.co.uk/statistics/research-datasets)

The weights in the workers cost of living price index

Commodities	1840–69	1820–39	1730–1819	1375–1729	1280–1374	1245–79	1209–44
Food	0.620	0.670	0.720	0.720	0.720	0.750	0.800
Fuel	0.050	0.050	0.050	0.050	0.040	0.050	–
Lodging	0.100	0.075	0.045	0.045	0.075	–	–
Light	0.040	0.040	0.040	0.040	0.030	0.040	–
Soap	0.010	0.005	0.005	0.005	0.005	–	–
Clothing	0.120	0.120	0.120	0.120	0.120	0.150	0.180
Services	0.020	0.010	0.010	0.020	0.010	0.010	0.020
Tobacco	0.010	0.010	–	–	–	–	–
Books	0.015	0.010	–	–	–	–	–
Manufactures	0.015	0.010	0.010	–	–	–	–

Fig. 2.2 Weights in the cost of living price index (Source: Clark, 2009)

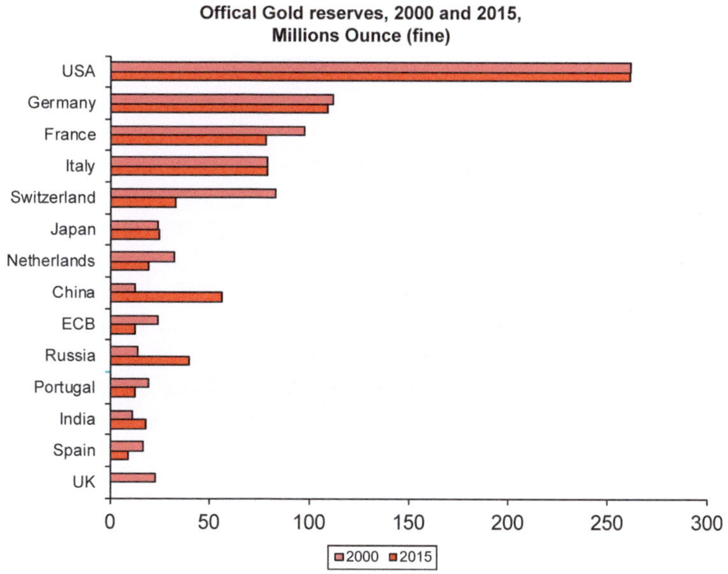

Fig. 2.3 Official Gold reserves of Central Banks (million troy ounces) (Source: IMF reserves template, Official Reserve Assets, Gold Volume)

2.2 Determinants of Price Level and Inflation

What factors determine the price level in a regime with fiat money? Obviously, central banks play a key role in preserving price stability. Those who are sceptic about incentives of policymakers to intervene in market mechanisms call for binding rules limiting the scope of discretionary leeway. Milton Friedman, for instance, propagated strict rules for the supply of money. In many countries the implementation of price stability has been assigned to a politically independent central bank with a clear mandate. Rather than fixing the price of a specific commodity (gold or silver), the mandate is to stabilize either the level or the growth rate (the rate of inflation) of an index of prices for a well-defined commodity basket.

In this chapter, we try to understand how central banks might implement price stability. This is a complex process. After all, the central bank cannot control the prices of specific goods—they are either set by the producer or negotiated between sellers and buyers. Some prices are fixed for a long period; others (like gasoline) change daily or even more frequently. We might expect that price stability can be achieved by limiting the supply of fiat money. Following Milton Friedman's famous quote *"Inflation is always and everywhere a monetary phenomenon"* (Friedman, 1963), limiting the growth rate of money supply for a long time has been seen as a key condition for ensuring a stable rate of inflation. But modern central banks use the interest rate (the opportunity cost for holding money) as a tool, with the supply of base money adjusting to demand—at least in the short run. Interest rate rules (such as the Taylor rule) have become the focus of modern monetary theory as an alternative commitment mechanism. We want to understand the implications of different rules.

2.2.1 Challenges for Simple Intuition

We start with a very simple model in order to understand why things turn out to be more complicated than simple intuition may suggest. The reason is that we face a complex dynamic problem. We have to take the reactions of private agents to central bank policy into account. Due to the key importance of trust, there may be indeterminacy with multiple, self-fulfilling equilibria. A sound analysis would require micro-foundations for the demand for money. As a first step, however, we simply take demand for money as given. We assume that money demand is a well-defined function of some key variables, in particular the nominal rate of interest. Given a stable money demand function, we ask how monetary policy can determine the current price level and the rate of inflation.

In order to focus on the issue of price level determination, we assume the classical dichotomy between the real and the monetary side of the economy. To simplify, we assume that the real economy is in long run steady state with constant endowment Y. This way, we can fully concentrate on the elements determining price level and inflation. Let us consider a standard, negatively sloped demand curve for money. We define money demand as a share of nominal GDP, $\frac{M_t^d}{P_t Y_t} i_t$ (with real activity Y being given). If the price level rises, nominal demand for money M_t^d increases proportionally, leaving real money balances unchanged. So the demand for nominal (real) money is homogeneous of degree one (zero) in prices. Given some initial money stock M_0, can we determine both the initial price level P_0 and the nominal rate of interest i_0? Will an increase in the money stock lead to a proportional increase in the initial price level, leaving everything else unchanged?

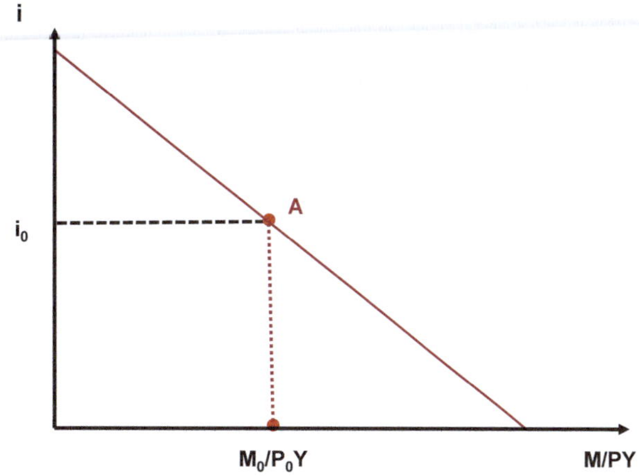

Fig. 2.4 Static equilibrium on the money market

How is the equilibrium nominal rate of interest determined? Figure 2.4 seems to suggest that the answer is pretty straightforward: The central bank as monopoly producer of money may simply fix either the money supply or the nominal interest rate. Equilibrium in the money market will then be realized at the intersection of supply and demand. But things are much more tricky, since want to determine not just i_t, but also the initial price level $P_{t.}$. With money demand being interest rate elastic, the initial price level and the nominal interest rate depend on the whole expected future path of monetary policy from now on until infinity. It is simply not sufficient just to set the current interest rate. Equilibrium is inherently forward looking. The reason is fairly intuitive: According to the Fisher relation, the nominal rate of interest is the sum of the real rate and expected inflation: $i_t = r_t + \pi_t^e$. But expectations about future inflation crucially depend on the expected path of future monetary policy.

So controlling the nominal rate boils down to pursue a credible inflation strategy: The higher the expected future rate of inflation, the higher the long-term nominal interest rate. In a forward-looking, non-stochastic rational expectations equilibrium, the expected rate of inflation has to be equal to the realized rate of inflation. In an economy with perfectly flexible prices, the central bank cannot affect the real rate of interest.[3] So it can only affect the long-term nominal rate via committing to some specific path for the rate of inflation in the future—by choosing some desired rate of inflation π^*.

Let us discuss different strategies to implement some target π^* as a steady-state policy. First, we look at a policy of controlling the money stock. Obviously, we cannot determine both P_0 and i_0 simultaneously by just setting the current money stock M_0. For a given nominal interest rate, P_0 is determined by M_0. But the interest

[3]Things get more complex when at least some prices are sticky. If so, the central bank can steer the short run real rate of interest by changing the nominal rate, as long as this policy has no adverse impact on inflationary expectations! We look at these issues in part II, starting with Chap. 4.

rate itself depends on expected inflation[4] and so on future monetary policy. Hence we need additional information about what is likely to happen in the future. With an increase in current money stock, the outcome will be quite different if agents expect monetary policy to be even looser in the future than if they expect a later reversal in policy. Consider the following thought experiment: The supply of money is fixed in the current period, but the expected rate of inflation in the future increases, driving up the nominal interest rate. If so, demand for money falls immediately, driving up the price level already today.

2.2.2 The Cagan Model: Money Supply, Price Level, and Interest Rates

We want to understand the reason why expectations about future monetary policy are a key driver for determining the price level in the current period. We cannot just look at current monetary policy (the current money supply or the current interest rate) in order to determine equilibrium. The intuition behind is fairly simple: Money demand depends on the nominal interest rate which—according to the Fisher equation—is determined by the expected rate of inflation. Therefore, forward-looking agents will take into account the expected future path of monetary policy when deciding about how much money to hold today. The higher the expected rate of inflation in the future (be it tomorrow, next year, or in ten years' time), the higher already the opportunity cost for holding money today and so the lower current demand for money.

As it turns out, there may be multiple self-fulfilling equilibria: When all agents expect higher rates of inflation, they will try to move out of money holding, triggering higher prices and so confirming their initial belief. Can we rule out self-fulfilling hyperinflationary bubbles, not caused by changes in fundamental policies? We will see that conditions to rule out such bubbles are not very plausible. The reason is simply that money (at least modern fiat money) is based purely on trust. If agents do no longer trust the stability of the monetary system, this system will no longer work. For that reason, credibility is a crucial condition for monetary economies. We might expect that strict rules (such as a Friedman rule with constant growth rate of money or—even more extreme—a fixing the money supply for ever or alternatively a Taylor rule responding with interest rate adjustments aggressively to deviations of actual inflation from target) might get around that credibility problem. As we will see later, this is not true in general. Additional assumptions are needed to rule out bubbles. Unfortunately, we face the same problem when we

[4]In a world with perfectly flexible prices, the nominal interest rate is determined by the sum of the natural real rate and expected inflation. With a share of prices being sticky and well-anchored expected inflation, monetary policy can a affect the real rate of interest by changing the nominal rate. This mechanism is the core transmission channel of modern monetary policy, analyzed in detail in Chap. 4. In this chapter, we rule this channel out by construction, focusing on the case of perfectly flexible prices.

implement interest rate rules (a strategy of inflation targeting) instead of money supply rules (see Cochrane, 2011).

Let us first start with a rather ad hoc log-linear money demand function introduced by Philip Cagan (1956) in his study of determinants of hyperinflation. Cagan simply assumed that the money demand function is isoelastic with constant elasticity of demand b : $\frac{M_t^d}{P_t Y_t} = C\,E(1+i_t)^{-b}$. Normalizing $Y_t = 1$ we get in log-linearized form with $m_t^d = \ln M_t^d, p_t = \ln P_t$ and $\ln Y_t = 0$:

$$m_t^d - p_t = c - b(E(i_t)). \tag{2.2.1}$$

The Fisher equation $i_t = r_t + E(\pi_t) = r_t + E(p_{t+1}) - p_t$ (formulated in log-linearized form) has to hold all the time as arbitrage condition. As already emphasized, we assume monetary policy does not affect the real economy and do take the natural real interest rate r as fixed. This gives

$$m_t^d - p_t = c - b[r_t + E(p_{t+1}) - p_t].$$

Let us normalize $c = br$ (so that all constant terms drop out). Then we can write money demand as a dynamic difference equation—purely a function of the evolution of the price level and the elasticity of money demand b:

$$m_t^d - p_t = -b[E(p_{t+1}) - p_t].$$

How is the price level determined for a given (possibly stochastic) money supply path $\{M_{t+s}\}$, $s = 0, \ldots, T$? In each period, equilibrium on the money market requires $m_t^d = m_t$, This gives the linear difference equation:

$$m_t - p_t = -b[E(p_{t+1}) - p_t]. \tag{2.2.2}$$

The price level is a forward-looking (non-predetermined) variable. To determine p_t, we need to calculate the forward-looking solution by iterated substitution of the difference equation:

$$p_t = \frac{1}{1+b} m_t + \frac{b}{1+b} E(p_{t+1}). \tag{2.2.3}$$

For the next period, we have $E(p_{t+1}) = \frac{1}{1+b} E_t(m_{t+1}) + \frac{b}{1+b} E_t[E_{t+1}(p_{t+2})]$. Using the law of iterated expectations $E_t[E_{t+1}(p_{t+2})] = E_t(p_{t+2})$ and substituting in Equation 2.2.3 we get

$$p_t = \frac{1}{1+b}\left(m_t + \frac{b}{1+b} m_{t+1}\right) + \left(\frac{b}{1+b}\right)^2 E(p_{t+2}).$$

Iterated substitution gives:

$$p_t = \frac{1}{1+b}\sum_{s=0}^{\infty}\left(\frac{b}{1+b}\right)^s E(m_{t+s}) + \lim_{s\to\infty}\left(\frac{b}{1+b}\right)^s E(p_{t+s}).$$

Assume (this is an assumption about monetary policy) that this sum converges

$$\left|\lim_{s\to\infty}\sum_{s=0}^{T-1}\left(\frac{b}{1+b}\right)^s E(m_{t+s})\right| < \infty$$

In order to rule out hyperinflationary bubbles, we need to impose the **"No bubbles"** restriction

$$\lim_{s\to\infty}\left(\frac{b}{1+b}\right)^s E(p_{t+s}) = 0. \tag{2.2.4}$$

So the **"fundamental" solution** is defined as:

$$p_t^F = \frac{1}{1+b}\sum\nolimits_{s=0}^{\infty}\left(\frac{b}{1+b}\right)^s E(m_{t+s}). \tag{2.2.5}$$

Only if condition Equation 2.2.4 holds, the price level is determined purely by "future monetary fundamentals."

2.2.3 Monetary Policy Experiments in the Cagan Model

To gain more intuition, let us solve for the current price level for some easy to solve examples, characterizing the future money supply process[5]:

(A) **Constant money supply**: $m_{t+s} = m_t = m$

In that case, we expect the price level to be constant and the rate of inflation to be zero all time. The nominal interest rate is just equal to the real rate. From Equation 2.2.5 we get

$$p_t = \frac{1}{1+b}\sum\nolimits_{s=0}^{\infty}\left(\frac{b}{1+b}\right)^s m_t = m_t. \tag{2.2.6}$$

[5]Note: $\sum_{s=0}^{\infty}\left(\frac{b}{1+b}\right)^s = 1+b$; $\sum_{s=0}^{\infty} s\left(\frac{b}{1+b}\right)^s = b(1+b)$.

(B) **Stochastic money supply with AR(1) process**:

$$m_{t+1} = \rho m_t + \varepsilon_{t+1};\ 0 \le \rho \le 1;\ E_t(\varepsilon_{t+1}) = 0.\ \text{So } E_t(m_{t+s}) = \rho^s m_t.$$

$$\text{Then } p_t = \frac{1}{1+b}\sum\nolimits_{s=0}^{\infty}\left(\frac{b}{1+b}\right)^s \rho^s m_t = \frac{1}{1+b}\sum\nolimits_{s=0}^{\infty}\left(\frac{b\rho}{1+b}\right)^s m_t,$$

$$p_t = \frac{1}{1+b}\frac{1}{1-\frac{b\rho}{1+b}} m_t = \frac{1}{1+(1-\rho)b} m_t. \quad (2.2.7)$$

(B1) m_t follows a random walk ($\rho = 1$): $p_t = m_t$;
(B2) m_t serially uncorrelated: ($\rho = 0$): $p_t = \frac{1}{1+b} m_t = \frac{1}{1+b}\varepsilon_t$.

Case (B1) generalizes case (A), demonstrating that random shocks to a fixed money supply do not affect the solution. Case (B2) is of pure theoretical curiosity.

(C) **Money supply growing at a constant rate**: $m_{t+s} = m_t + \mu s$

$$p_t = \frac{1}{1+b}\sum\nolimits_{s=0}^{\infty}\left(\frac{b}{1+b}\right)^s m_t + \frac{1}{1+b}\sum\nolimits_{s=0}^{\infty} s\left(\frac{b}{1+b}\right)^s \mu = m_t + b\mu. \quad (2.2.8)$$

In this case, the price level will rise rate at a constant rate, resulting in a constant rate of inflation $\pi = \mu$. The higher the rate of future money growth, the higher will be the current price level even when the current stock of money stays constant. An increase in the expected rate of inflation raises immediately the nominal interest rate. This makes money holding less attractive, dampening already current demand. The impact on the current price level will be stronger the higher the elasticity of money demand.

(D) **A change in the growth rate of money implemented immediately at t_0**:

Suppose the economy has been in steady-state equilibrium in the past with money supply growing at a constant rate μ_0. At t_0 the central bank announces and implements an immediate change in the growth rate to μ_1. If μ increases, expected inflation and so the nominal rate of interest rises, dampening money demand immediately. As long as money supply is fixed, an immediate upward jump in the price level is needed for clearing on the money market. Consider now instead a slower growth rate of money as shown in Fig. 2.5, aiming to dampen inflation. When credible, both expected rate of inflation and the interest rate fall immediately, stimulating demand for real money balances already today. At $t_0, k(i)$ jumps due to lower future expected interest rates. Assuming again no jump in the money supply, the immediate additional demand would now require a downward jump in the price level (see Fig. 2.6).

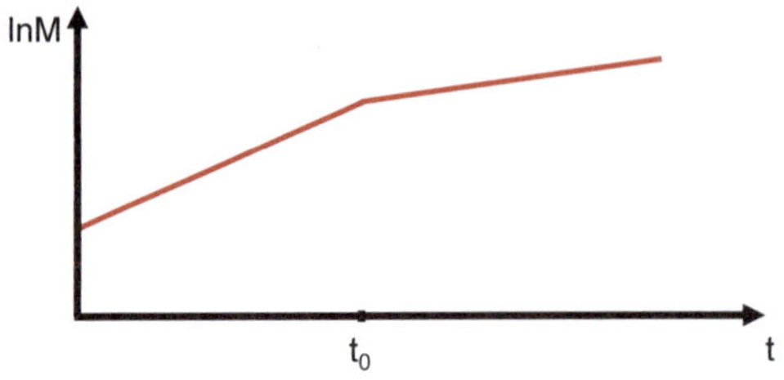

Fig. 2.5 Reduction in the rate of money growth

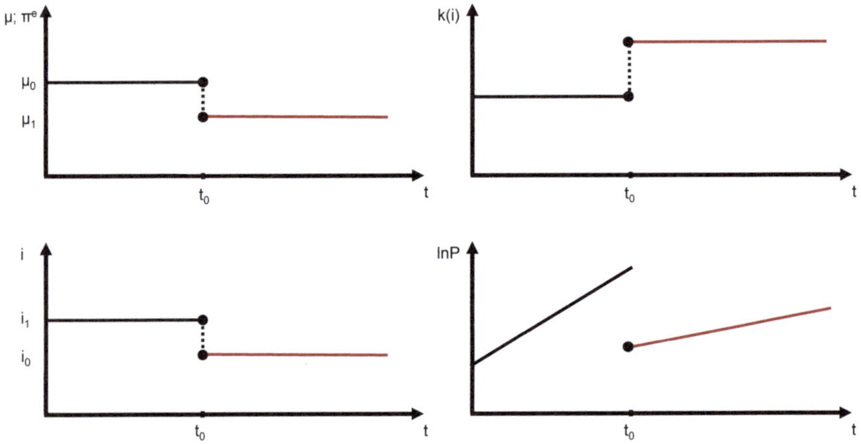

Fig. 2.6 Interest rate, money balances, and price level after a change to a lower rate of money growth

With perfectly flexible prices, the implemented change in monetary policy has no real effects. But when prices are downward sticky, the intended policy change of disinflation might cause serious real frictions, triggering a recession (see Chap. 4). Aiming to avoid a downward jump in the price level, equilibrium might alternatively be achieved by an immediate upward jump in the money supply, trying to accommodate the immediate increase in money demand. The disinflationary process, however, may not be credible if it starts with a discrete increase in the money supply.

(E) **An anticipated increase in the money supply at some future date T:**

As a final exercise, let us now consider a policy change (an increase in money supply) announced already at time t_0 but to be implemented with some delay at $t_0 + T$ with $T \geq 1$.

$$m_{t_0+s} = \begin{cases} m_1 & t_0 \leq s \leq t_0 + T \\ m_2 > m_1 & s \geq t_0 + T \end{cases}$$

With rational expectations, agents will react to the anticipated increase at T immediately as soon as it is announced for the following reason: They know that after the increase in money supply at day $t_0 + T$, the price level will be permanently higher at $p_t = m_2$, $\forall t \geq t_0 + T$. Assume there is a discrete jump in the price level from m_1 to m_2 at $t_0 + T$. Anticipating that jump, agents would expect a drastic increase in the rate of inflation already the day before, that is between $t_0 + T - 1$ and $t_0 + T$. So they will rush out of money holding the day before. Thus, with rational expectations, the price level will need to rise already at that day. Otherwise there would be enormous arbitrage opportunities. Equilibrium on the money market requires that:

$$m_{t_0+T-1} - p_{t_0+T-1} = -b[E_{t_0+T-1}(p_{t_0+T}) - p_{t_0+T-1}]. \tag{2.2.9}$$

Inserting $m_{t_0+T-1} = m_1$ and $E_{t_0+T-1}(p_{t_0+T}) = m_2$, we can solve for the price level as:

$$p_{t_0+T-1} = \frac{1}{1+b}m_1 + \frac{b}{1+b}m_2 = m_1 + \frac{b}{1+b}(m_2 - m_1). \tag{2.2.10}$$

Of course, we can apply the same reasoning also for day $t_0 + T - 2$. This gives[6]

$$p_{t_0+T-2} = m_1 + \left(\frac{b}{1+b}\right)^2 (m_2 - m_1).$$

Reiterated substitution gives the price path starting from time t_0

$$p_{t_0+T-j} = m_1 + \left(\frac{b}{1+b}\right)^j (m_2 - m_1), \quad 0 \leq j \leq T. \tag{2.2.11}$$

So there will already be a discrete jump in the price level at the day of announcement with the price level slowly rising such that it will reach m_2 smoothly at T without jump any more. Note that we get $p_{t_0+T} = m_1 + (m_2 - m_1) = m_2$ at T (that is, for $j = 0$) according to Equation 2.2.11.

2.3 Optimal Monetary Policy: The Long-Run View

In the last section, we looked at the implication of various, fairly arbitrary paths for the money supply. Of course, the actual path will be determined by the central bank. The specific policy chosen depends on its objective. So let us briefly discuss different policy objectives.[7] We ask: How can we define price stability? Should we target the price level or the rate of inflation? There have been several hyperinflationary

[6]Insert $m_{t_0+T-2} = m_1$ and Equation 2.2.10 for $E(p_{t_0+T-1})$ to solve for $m_{t_0+T-2} - p_{t_0+T-2} = -b[E_{t_0+T-1}(p_{t_0+T-1}) - p_{t_0+T-2}]$.

[7]Note, however, that in this chapter, we only consider long-run issues, neglecting stabilization policy.

episodes. The reason behind these episodes may have been the motive to generate higher seigniorage revenue for the government—just like in periods of debasing in medieval times. How can we characterize the policy which maximizes seigniorage? Will it really lead to hyperinflation? Philip Cagan (1956) was interested in studying determinants of these episodes in detail.

2.3.1 Price Level Versus Inflation Targeting

Does it make a difference whether the central banks follow a price level target or an inflation target? If the central bank were able to implement its job impeccable, both tasks would be equivalent, since $P_{t+1} = (1 + \pi_t)P_t$. To see this, consider the following case: Starting at P_0, we assign the central bank the task to let the price level grow at the constant rate π^*. So at T, the price level should be $P_T = P_T^* = (1 + \pi^*)^T P_0$. With perfect control, it does not make any difference whether we impose targets for the level P_t or for its growth rate π^*.

Things will be quite different, however, when there are control errors. Let us do analysis in continuous time, using the approximation $(1 + \pi)^t \rightarrow e^{\pi t}$. So we have $P_t = P_0 e^{\pi t}$ or $\ln P_t = p_t = p_0 + \pi t$ in logarithmic form. Realistically, all the time random shocks drive actual inflation temporarily above or below the target: Control errors ξ_t with $E(\xi_t) = 0$ and $E(\xi_t^2) = \sigma_\xi^2$ disturb current inflation such that

$$p_{t+1} - p_t = \pi_t = \pi^* + \xi_t. \tag{2.3.1}$$

Assume our target is $p_t = p^*$ or $\pi^* = 0$. In that case, under inflation targeting we have $\pi_t = \xi_t$. So the price level follows a random walk:

$$p_t = p_{t-1} + \xi_t. \tag{2.3.1a}$$

For illustration, consider what happens when a shock occurs at T shifting p_t upward from p^* toward $p_T = p^* + \xi_t$ in Fig. 2.7. Inflation targeting ignores past errors; it just tries to keep the price level at the new current level p_T, whatever happened in the past. The price level stays at the dark (red) line. Past errors are forgiven. If no new shocks occur, there will be no inflation after T. So volatility of the current rate of inflation will be low at all times.

In contrast, price level targeting forces to correct past mistakes. With some speed of adjustment, the price level must be brought back to the initial target $p_t = p^*$ (see the dashed [blue] line in Fig. 2.7). Of course, this triggers a period of deflation (persistent negative rates of inflation) after a positive shock. Temporary price shocks will not be treated as bygones; they have to be absorbed through deflation or inflation in periods ahead. Obviously, inflation volatility will be higher under price level targeting. When the correction is done with speed λ, we have

$$p_t = p_{t-1} + \lambda(p^* - p_{t-1}) + \xi_t. \tag{2.3.1b}$$

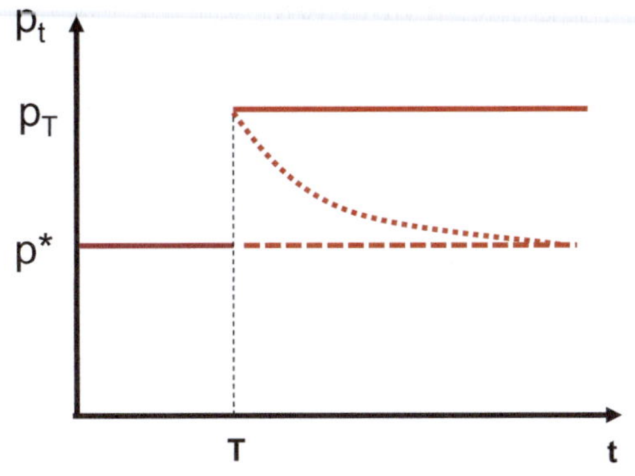

Fig. 2.7 Price level vs. inflation targeting: control error at T

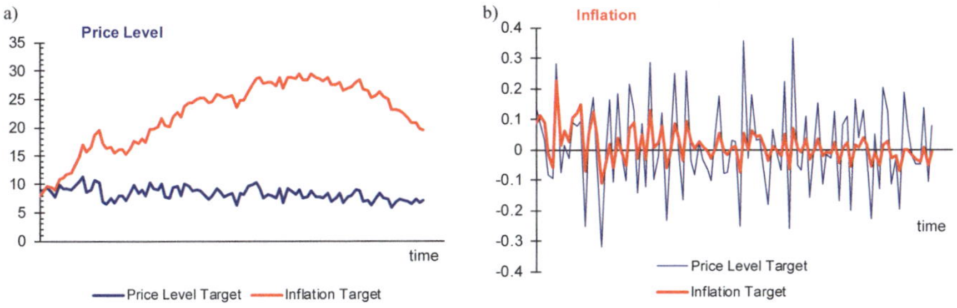

Fig. 2.8 Price level vs. inflation targeting. (**a**) Price level follows random walk under inflation targeting. (**b**) High inflation volatility under price level targeting

Figure 2.8 illustrates the volatility of price level and inflation for both strategies [the (red) dark lines represent the case of inflation targeting].

So the seemingly similar targets have quite different implications for volatility. Which one should we prefer? The answer depends on costs and benefits. If the key concern is long-run price stability, level targeting is superior. But one may doubt why long-run price stability of fiat money should be an important policy objective. After all, money is used mainly in order to have access to short-run liquidity. There are plenty of other assets (like inflation-indexed bonds or stocks paying dividends) which can be used as long-term store of value. Indexation of long-term contracts is a feasible option. So it may be more important for fiat money to be a safe medium of transaction insuring against short-term fluctuations in purchasing power. In this view, low volatility of inflation is essential. Furthermore, high volatility of the rate of inflation may lead to high fluctuations of real economic activity in the presence of price stickiness with negative welfare implications. Mainly for that reason, most central banks currently aim to target inflation rather than the price level.[8]

[8]There are, however, strong debates about the best strategy. In particular when monetary policy is impeded by the fact that interest rates cannot be reduced below some effective lower bound, a level-

2.3.2 The Optimal Rate of Inflation

What target should we set for the rate of inflation? In many industrialized countries, central banks target an inflation rate of around 2% (see Table 2.1). In most countries, the specific target is set by the central bank's monetary policy committee. In some countries (such as New Zealand or the UK), the target is specified by the government in policy target agreements. Historically, the 2% rate has frequently been motivated by an upward bias in measurement (measures of consumer price inflation overestimate the true rate when they do not adjust for substitution bias) and by the argument that downward nominal price and wage rigidity may impede price adjustments when the rate is too low. But what is the optimal rate of inflation? Should central banks raise the target rate above 2%, should they try to keep inflation at a rate of zero, or should they instead aim even at a deflationary policy? There are heated controversies about the optimal rate of inflation.

Again, the answer to this question requires careful analysis of the welfare effects of different rates. The answer strongly depends on the way costs and benefits are modeled. For example, if price adjustment costs are assumed to be the key frictions (as in New Keynesian models discussed in Chap. 4), it seems best to minimize the need for price adjustments—so the optimal policy is most likely a policy keeping the rate of inflation at zero. With any other rate (positive or negative), there is a constant need for adjusting all prices.

In contrast, in theoretical models with perfectly flexible prices, frequently the optimal rate turns out to be negative: The best policy is to make sure that the nominal interest rate is zero—this is the so-called **Friedman rule** propagated by Milton Friedman. According to this rule, it is optimal to implement a rate of deflation equal to the real rate of interest. With prices falling steadily, money earns the same rate of return as real bonds, driving the opportunity costs of holding money toward zero. This way, trading frictions motivating the need to hold money are minimized.

Rather than calling for deflation, instead a rate higher than 2% may be justified for the following reason: The zero lower bound on interest rates imposes severe constraints on monetary policy creating serious real distortions. Since the lower the average target rate, the higher the probability of hitting the zero bound, a robust design may try to minimize that risk by aiming at a higher rate such as say 4%. Chapter 7 looks at this issue in detail. Finally, if enforcement of tax revenue creates severe distortions, it may be optimal to implement a higher rate of inflation in order to generate seigniorage income. Inflation acts as a tax on money holding.

Usually, monetary policy is assumed to be neutral and super-neutral in the long run in the sense that it will not affect the real rate of growth of production. It does

---

based targeting approach may be preferable in order to credibly prevent deflationary spirals. Targeting the price level could be a credible commitment to allow for higher rates of inflation until the intended path has been reached without undermining central bank credibility in the long run (see Chap. 7).

Table 2.1 Inflation targets in selected countries

Country	Indicator	Numerical value Definition/Target	Ex ante horizon
Australia http://www.rba.gov.au/inflation/inflation-target.html	CPI	2–3%, on average, over the cycle	Medium-term average
Canada http://www.bankofcanada.ca/core-functions/monetary-policy/inflation/	CPI	2% midpoint of a inflation control target range of 1–3%	Over the medium term: achieve the target typically within a horizon of 6–8 quarters
Euro area https://www.ecb.europa.eu/mopo/strategy/pricestab/html/index.en.html	Harmonised Index of Consumer Prices (HICP)—focus on the euro area as a whole	Below, but close to 2% since May 2003; [From 1999 till May 2003: Below 2%]	Over the medium term
Japan https://www.boj.or.jp/en/mopo/outline/qqe.htm/	CPI	2% since January 2013 [before: goal of 1% set in February 2012]	At the earliest possible time
New Zealand http://www.rbnz.govt.nz/-/media/ReserveBank/Files/Publications/Factsheets%20and%20Guides/factsheet-what-is-inflation.pdf	CPI	Within 1–3% a year as specified in a Policy Target Agreement (initially in 1990 range 0–2%; later revised several times	On average over the medium term (in practice 6–8 quarters)
Norway http://www.norges-bank.no/en/Statistics/Inflation/	CPI	2% (adjusted from 2.5% since March 2018)	Flexible inflation targeting regime (weight is given to both variability in inflation and variability in output and employment)
Sweden http://www.riksbank.se/en/Monetary-policy/Inflation/Adoption-of-the-inflation-target/	CPI	2% since January 1993	Normally 4–8 quarters
UK http://www.bankofengland.co.uk/monetarypolicy/Pages/framework/framework.aspx	CPI	Price stability specified by the Government's inflation target of 2% since 2004; [Until December 2003: 2.5% for RPIX Inflation]	If CPI inflation is more than 3% or less than 1%, the Governor of the Bank must write an open letter to the Chancellor explaining the reasons

(continued)

Table 2.1 (continued)

Country	Indicator	Numerical value Definition/Target	Ex ante horizon
USA Fed Source: https://www.federalreserve.gov/faqs/economy_14400.htm	Price index for personal consumption expenditures (PCE)	2% (since January 2012)	Rate most consistent over the longer run with the Fed's mandate for price stability and maximum employment
Inflation targets for other Countries http://www.centralbanknews.info/p/inflation-targets.html			

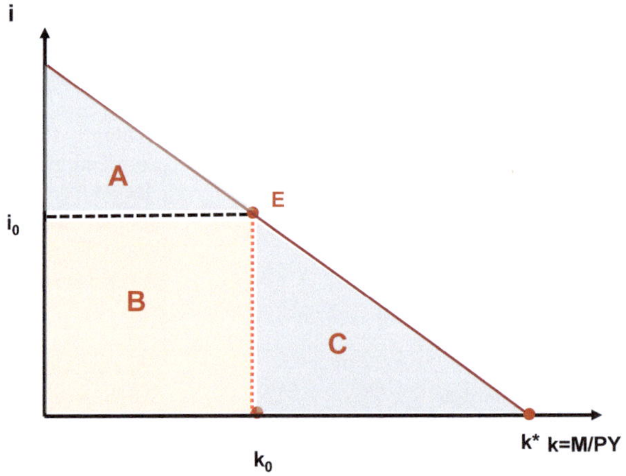

Fig. 2.9 Friedman's optimal quantity of money

affect, however, the well-being of consumers: A higher nominal rate of interest forces consumers to economize on money balances; so it will raise transaction cost for shopping (see Focus Box for Nerds on "Cash goods in a cash-in-advance model" in Sect. 2.3). A positive nominal rate of interest works like a tax on money holding, introducing inefficiencies into the economy. Figure 2.9 characterizes steady-state equilibrium in the following sense: The central bank follows a policy implementing the same steady-state rate of inflation in each period which is perfectly expected by private agents, leading to the equilibrium nominal interest rate i_0. At that rate, private agents are willing to hold the amount k_0 as the share of money to nominal GDP. The demand curve represents their marginal willingness to pay for holding money. Let $k = M/PY$ be the amount of non-interest earning money held by the private sector as share of nominal GDP. The opportunity cost for holding money is the rectangular area B (i_0k_0). The benefit for consumers is represented by triangle A—the aggregate willingness to pay (the integral below the demand curve) minus aggregate cost B.

By picking some target rate of inflation π^* the central bank as monopoly producer determines the steady-state outcome. What policy would maximize consumer benefit? A policy trying to minimize inefficiencies would try to equalize marginal cost with marginal benefit. Production of fiat money is nearly costless; the marginal cost of producing more fiat money is close to zero. At k^*, aggregate consumer surplus (the sum of the areas $A+B+C$) minus cost (0) is maximized. So the efficient policy would try to implement a nominal interest close to 0—it would satiate consumers with money holding. This policy has been propagated by Milton Friedman (1969) as "Optimal Quantity of Money."

Equivalently, the central bank could pay nominal interest on money balances at a rate equal to the market nominal interest rate. Paying interest on reserves held by commercial banks is nowadays standard for many central banks. But it would be administratively extremely cumbersome to pay interest on cash.

In the same way, it is difficult to implement a negative interest rate on cash as has been suggested by Silvio Gesell in his proposal of "Schwundgeld," taken up in the discussion of zero bound on nominal interest by Goodfriend (2000) and Buiter and Panigirtzoglou (2003).

2.3.3 Seigniorage

At times when metals were used as media of exchange, the revenue for the government generated from issuing coins was the difference between the value of the metal and its production costs. This revenue is called seigniorage. Since the cost of printing paper money (banknotes) is close to zero (apart from costs to prevent counterfeiting), issuing cash generates revenue for the central bank at negligible costs. For modern central banks, cash plays only a minor role; they mainly provide bank reserves to private banks. In return, they receive interest bearing bonds as assets. As long as reserves (as the central banks liability) do not pay interest, this again creates seigniorage revenue. Thus, seigniorage revenue provided for the government is generated by a positive nominal rate of interest (or, more generally, the interest rate on money being lower compared to bonds): $S = i\,k$ (see Sect. 3.3 for details).

Since money demand depends negatively on interest rates, we have

$$S = i\,k(i) \text{ with } \partial k/\partial i < 0. \tag{2.3.2}$$

Demand for real money balances declines with the rate of inflation. Seigniorage is zero for $i = 0$. But there will also be no revenue from seigniorage when agents are no longer willing to hold money because the rate of inflation is too high, driving up the nominal interest rate as $i_t = r_t + E(\pi_t)$. Obviously, there is some maximum level of steady-state revenue. How can we determine the maximum steady-state government revenue from money creation?

Fig. 2.10 Seigniorage revenue in steady-state equilibrium

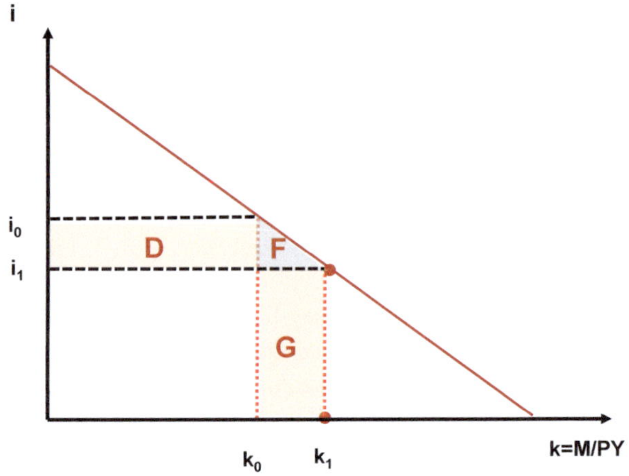

At i_0, people are willing to hold k_0, creating seigniorage income $i_0 k_0$ (the area B in Fig. 2.9). With a lower interest rate i_I people increase money balances up to k_1 generating seigniorage $i_1 k_1$ (see Fig. 2.10). On the one hand, seigniorage revenue will be reduced by $(i_0 - i_1)k_0$—the light shaded rectangular D. On the other hand, the increase in money holding raises seigniorage by the rectangular G, $i_1(k_1 - k_0)$. Since a lower interest rate raises consumer's welfare by the area $D+F$, aggregate welfare (as the sum of surplus of consumers, producers, and government) is definitely higher with decreasing interest rate i. If the central bank as monopoly producer is interested in maximizing steady-state seigniorage revenue, it will choose the steady-state inflation rate maximizing the revenue B. A higher price (an increase in inflation and thus in i) will dampen demand, but raise revenue for given demand. So the monopoly producer has to trade-off area D against G. The profit maximizing condition for a monopolist with zero cost is to charge the price at which marginal revenue is equal to zero (marginal cost).

The answer is straightforward. If printing money incurs no cost (a useful benchmark), steady-state revenue is simply $S = i\,k(i)$. Maximising S gives the condition

$$\frac{\partial S}{\partial i} = k(i) + i\frac{\partial k}{\partial i} = 1 + \eta_k = 0 \tag{2.3.3}$$

with $\eta_k = \frac{\partial k}{\partial i}\frac{i}{k}$ as interest elasticity of money demand.

The revenue maximizing strategy is to choose money growth rate (or inflation) such that elasticity of money demand is equal to minus one. This is the standard condition for a monopoly producer maximizing revenue: $\eta_k = \frac{\partial k}{\partial i}\frac{i}{k} = -1$.

$$S = i \cdot k(i);\ \frac{\partial S}{\partial i} = k(i) + i\frac{\partial k}{\partial i} = 0;\ \eta_k = \frac{\partial k}{\partial i}\frac{i}{k} = -1.$$

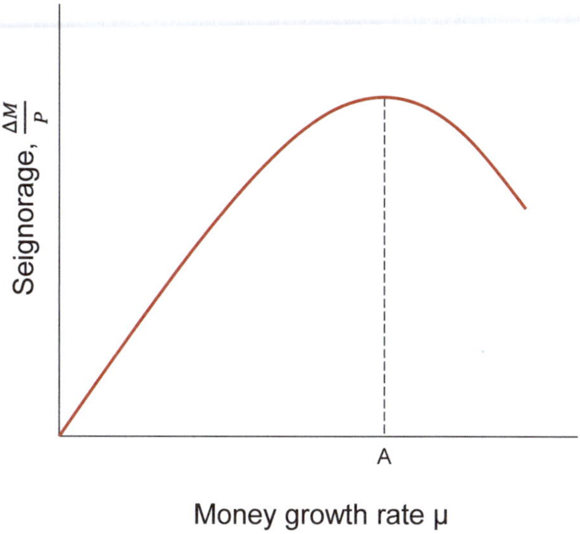

Fig. 2.11 Laffer Curve for seigniorage revenue

For $i = 0$, seigniorage revenue $S = i\,k(i)$ is zero. With i rising (as a result of increasing inflation, triggered by money growth), revenue first increases even though demand for real money balances declines. But above some point A (when absolute value of elasticity of money demand gets smaller than 1), revenue goes down. The higher the rate of inflation (and thus, in a rational expectation equilibrium, the interest rate), the more people try to move out of money holding. With elasticity of money demand being higher than one, the decline in demand more than offsets the price increase. So revenue declines above some price A as shown in Fig. 2.11. This curve is the familiar revenue effect for a monopolist selling his product with price elastic demand. It does not pay to raise his price further when absolute elasticity of demand gets higher than 1. If so, additional revenue from the higher price is more than offset by reduced demand. In public finance with tax rate as price, this effect is called Laffer curve.

Since tax revenue is essential for financing government activities, for general welfare analysis the deadweight loss created from interest rates has to be traded off against the deadweight loss caused by other, traditional distortionary taxes. Following the theory on "optimal taxation" Edmund Phelps argued that it is optimal to use a mix of inflation tax and traditional taxes when the latter are distortionary as well. So he argued that the Friedman rule does not hold. As the theory of optimal taxation suggests, to minimize overall distortions it is usually optimal to use all tax rates including the inflation tax. The less elastic the demand for a specific commodity, the lower the distortion, so the higher should the tax rate be. This result, however, does not apply to intermediate inputs. If money is viewed just as an intermediate input for producing final outputs like consumption goods, it will not be optimal to tax money (see Correia & Teles, 1996).

2.4 Micro-Foundations for the Demand for Money

Up to now, following Cagan, we simply imposed an ad hoc demand function for money balances and imposed the condition that real money balances are homogeneous of degree 0 in prices. Furthermore, we arbitrarily imposed the "No bubbles" restriction formulated in Equation 2.2.4. In order to do a sound welfare analysis, we need to provide a deeper motivation for money demand from first principles. In the following, we try to provide some micro-foundation. We will see that real money balances are indeed homogeneous of degree 0. But we will also see that there is hardly a justification for the "No bubbles" restriction.

2.4.1 The Cash-in-Advance Constraint

A natural (even though rather ad hoc) way to give money a role in this economy is to impose the so-called "cash-in-advance constraint." Let us assume that for some subset of goods X_t (the so called "cash goods"), cash is needed if you want to buy them. In contrast, other goods (let us call them "credit goods" C_t) may be bought without money (such as using credit card).

So we now have to take into account the constraint $P_tX_t \leq M_t$: Cash goods X_t bought at the end of the current period cannot be purchased unless paid via money. In a representative agent economy, to impose such a condition seems to be pretty silly—if the representative agent consumes just what she produces, there is definitely no need to use money. But we should not take the single agent model literally. Rather, it is a stylized way to represent a production economy with many heterogeneous agents consuming an enormous variety of goods which are all produced by specialized firm using specialized inputs. All goods can be produced using the same linear technology $C_t + X_t = N_t$. It is straightforward to model this explicitly (The most elegant approach is the setup of Blanchard–Kiyotaki, with Dixit–Stiglitz preferences—see the Focus Box in Chap. 1). Here, we simply use X_t as composite aggregate good, consisting of a huge (possibly infinite) variety of different types of cash goods. Each single household produces just one specific type, but consumes the whole spectrum of all types. In order to buy these types, she needs to pay with cash. At the end of each period, the representative agent wants to consume both cash and credit goods according to her preferences: $U(C_t, X_t)$.

What is the impact of the cash-in-advance constraint on the economy? We have to be precise about the exact timing conventions. Let us impose the following timing sequence: At the beginning of period t, agents hold initial wealth $W_t = (1 + i_{t-1})B_{t-1} + M_{t-1}$ accumulated during the last period. Wealth can be held either in form of bonds or as cash. Storing cash has an opportunity cost: It does not earn interest, but it allows buying cash goods at the end of the current period according to the cash-in-advance constraint $P_tX_t \leq M_t$. In contrast, all wealth invested in interest bearing bonds with nominal yield i_t give the gross return $(1 + i_t)B_t$ at the start of next period. At the beginning of period t, the agent decides about how much money to hold. Obviously, money is dominated as a store of wealth by bonds as long as i_t

>0. For that reason, households try to economize on holding cash: They will not store more than the amount needed for the transactions to buy the cash goods X_t desired in period t. Mathematically, the inequality constraint will be strictly binding: $P_t X_t = M_t$. Thus, we can rewrite the utility function as an indirect function of real money balances:

$$U(C_t, X_t) = U\left(C_t, \frac{M_t}{P_t}\right). \tag{2.4.1}$$

Note that real money balances M_t/P_t now show up in the (indirect) utility function, even though money does not provide utility itself. The indirect utility of money holding has been derived here from consuming cash goods purchased by holding money.

2.4.2 Money in the Utility Function

Putting "money in the utility function" is, however, a much more general approach which can be motivated in different ways. An alternative story, for instance, yielding the same formalization, is the following: Money saves on transaction costs (the shopping time required to purchase goods). In this approach, money serves as an intermediate input for producing consumption, captured by a transaction technology. The Focus Box "Shopping time model" shows how to derive an indirect utility function for real money balances from the shopping time model.

The higher the nominal price level P_t, the lower are the real money balances, so the lower the benefit from holding a nominal amount of money M_t. In this book, we will assume that preferences per period can be represented by an additive separable payoff function:

$$U(C_t, M_t/P_t) = U(C_t) + V(M_t/P_t). \tag{2.4.2}$$

$V(M_t/P_t)$ represents the indirect utility of money holding.

Given wealth W_t, the agent decides how much credit goods to consume during period t. At the same time, he decides how much wealth to accumulate for the next period either in form of cash or bonds (see Fig. 2.12). So his per period budget constraint is:

$$P_t C_t + B_t + M_t = P_t Y_t + W_t, \text{ with wealth } W_t = (1 + i_{t-1})\, B_{t-1} + M_{t-1}. \tag{2.4.3}$$

It is instructive to rewrite the budget constraint in terms of wealth, eliminating bond holding B_t: Since wealth accumulated for the next period is $W_{t+1} = (1 + i_t)\, B_t + M_t$, solving for B_t gives $B_t = \frac{1}{1+i_t}(W_{t+1} - M_t)$. Inserting this relation, we can formulate the per period budget constraint as the following difference equation:

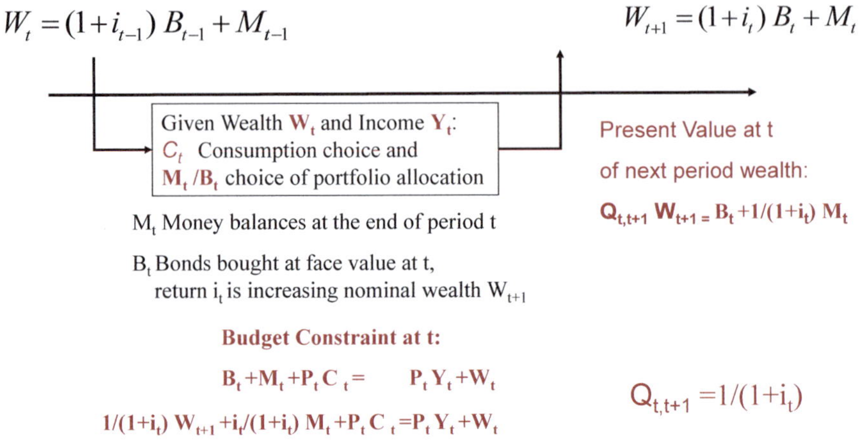

Fig. 2.12 Timing convention

$$P_t C_t + \frac{i_t}{1+i_t} M_t + \frac{W_{t+1}}{1+i_t} = P_t Y_t + W_t. \tag{2.4.3a}$$

Solving for W_t, the evolution of wealth across two consecutive periods is characterised by:

$$W_t = P_t C_t + \frac{i_t}{1+i_t} M_t - P_t Y_t + \frac{W_{t+1}}{1+i_t}.$$

Via iterated substitution, we can merge the evolution of wealth across periods into one single wealth constraint. Starting in period 0, iterated substitution gives:

$$W_0 + \sum_{t=0}^{\infty} Q_t (P_t Y_t) = \sum_{t=0}^{\infty} Q_t \left(P_t C_t + \frac{i_t}{1+i_t} M_t \right) + \lim_{t \to \infty} Q_t W_t \tag{2.4.4}$$

with

$$Q_t = \prod_{j=0}^{t-1} \frac{1}{1+i_j}, \quad \text{for } t \geq 1 \text{ and } Q_0 = 1 \tag{2.4.5}$$

as the compound nominal discount factor for the time between period t and period 0. Note that $Q_{t+1}/Q_t = \frac{1}{1+i_t}$. The term Q_t looks a bit frightening, but it is just a generalisation of the standard discount factor allowing for variable interest rates. For a constant interest rate i, we have $Q_t = \left(\frac{1}{1+i}\right)^{t-1}$ with $Q_0 = \left(\frac{1}{1+i}\right)^0 = 1$.

Ruling out bubbles, we impose the No-Ponzi Game condition

$$\lim_{t\to\infty} Q_t W_t \geq 0. \tag{2.4.6}$$

In our dynamic optimization problem, this condition will be binding, resulting in the transversality condition: $\lim_{t\to\infty} Q_t W_t = 0$.

Using the transversality condition, the wealth constraint is captured by the following intuitive equation:

$$W_0 + \sum\nolimits_{t=0}^{\infty} Q_t P_t Y_t = \sum\nolimits_{t=0}^{\infty} Q_t \left(P_t C_t + \frac{i_t}{1+i_t} M_t \right). \tag{2.4.4a}$$

The sum of initial wealth inherited from the past and the present value of income must cover total spending, which is the present value of consumption, including the expenditures from money holding. Holding money affects the agent's wealth constraint in a straightforward way: For the amount of wealth held in the form money, the agent foregoes nominal interest payments. The opportunity cost of holding money[9] instead of bonds is $\frac{i_t}{1+i_t}$. In a world without inflation, the cost comes from the fact that money provides no real return. With inflation, the *real* return on money will be even negative, since the rate of inflation erodes purchasing power of money.

Summary: The Money-in-the-Utility Approach (MIU)

Let M_t/P_t denote real money balances at the beginning of period t (money held before consumption and production). Then, the optimization problem is:

$$\text{Max} \sum\nolimits_{t=0}^{\infty} \frac{1}{(1+\rho)^t} U(C_t, M_t/P_t), \tag{2.4.1a}$$

$$s.t. \qquad W_t = (1 + i_{t-1})\, B_{t-1} + M_{t-1}, \tag{2.4.3a}$$

$$P_t C_t + B_t + M_t = P_t Y_t + W_t. \tag{2.4.3b}$$

Using iterated substitution of Equations 2.4.3a and 2.4.3b the inter-temporal budget constraints for each t collapse to the single wealth constraint:

$$W_0 + \sum\nolimits_{t=0}^{\infty} Q_t (P_t Y_t) = \sum\nolimits_{t=0}^{\infty} Q_t \left(P_t C_t + \frac{i_t}{1+i_t} M_t \right) + \lim_{t\to\infty} Q_t W_t \tag{2.4.4}$$

with nominal discount factor Equation 2.4.5 $Q_t = \prod_{j=0}^{t} \frac{1}{1+i_j}$ and $Q_0 = 1$.

(continued)

[9] When interest i_t^M is paid on money, the opportunity cost reduces to $\left(i_t - i_t^M\right)/(1 + i_t)$.

Imposing the transversality condition $\lim_{t\to\infty} Q_t W_t = 0$, the wealth constraint boils down to:

$$W_0 + \sum\nolimits_{t=0}^{\infty} Q_t P_t Y_t = \sum\nolimits_{t=0}^{\infty} Q_t \left(P_t C_t + \frac{i_t}{1+i_t} M_t \right). \qquad (2.4.4a)$$

Maximizing Equation 2.4.1 subject to Equation 2.4.3a gives as optimality conditions:

Euler Equation

$$\frac{U_c(C_t)}{U_c(C_{t+1})} = \frac{P_t}{P_{t+1}} \cdot \frac{1+i_t}{1+\rho} = \frac{1+i_t}{(1+\rho)(1+\pi_t)}, \text{ with } \frac{P_{t+1}}{P_t} = 1+\pi_t. \qquad (2.4.7)$$

The Euler equation characterizes the familiar inter-temporal optimality condition.

Money Demand Equation

$$\frac{U_m(M_t/P_t)}{U_c(C_t)} = \frac{i_t}{1+i_t}. \qquad (2.4.8)$$

According to the money demand equation, money will be held such that the ratio of marginal utilities between money and credit goods is equal to the opportunity cost of holding money—the nominal rate of interest! The higher i (the higher the rate of interest), the less money is held.

To gain deeper intuition, let us illustrate the explicit solution first for the utility function with constant elasticity of substitution:

$$U\left(C, \frac{M}{P}\right) = \left[\alpha^{\frac{1}{\sigma}} C^{1-\frac{1}{\sigma}} + (1-\alpha)^{\frac{1}{\sigma}} \left(\frac{M}{P}\right)^{1-\frac{1}{\sigma}}\right]^{\frac{\sigma}{\sigma-1}}. \qquad (2.4.1b)$$

The first-order conditions give as Euler Equation $\frac{C_{t+1}}{C_t} = \left(\frac{1+r_t}{1+\rho}\right)^{\sigma}$ (2.4.7b) and the micro-based version of the Money Demand Equation $\frac{M_t}{P_t} = \frac{1-\alpha}{\alpha}\left(\frac{i_t}{1+i_t}\right)^{-\sigma} C_t$ (2.4.8b).

With logarithmic preferences $(\sigma = 1)$, $U(C_t, X_t) = \alpha \ln(C_t) + (1-\alpha)\ln(M_t/P_t)$, we get as money demand function: $\frac{M_t}{P_t} = \frac{1-\alpha}{\alpha}\left(\frac{i_t}{1+i_t}\right)^{-1} C_t$.

Let us use the specification $\frac{M_t}{P_t} = \left(\frac{i_t}{1+i_t}\right)^{-\sigma} C_t$ (with $\alpha = 1/2$) to try to understand how monetary policy affects the equilibrium outcome. In this

(continued)

chapter, we assume that all prices are perfectly flexible even in the short run. To make it simple, consider the case that real endowment Y_t in the economy is growing at a constant rate γ. If so, in a steady state, real consumption will also grow at the same rate γ. From the Euler equation we know that, for all t, $\Delta C_t/C_t = \gamma = \sigma(r^n - \rho)$. Obviously, in this economy the natural rate of interest is constant across time: $r^n = \rho + \frac{1}{\sigma}\gamma$.

Focus Box for Nerds: Cash goods in a Cash-in-Advance Model (*Optional Material)

Formally, the cash-in-advance model and the shopping time model can be seen as special cases of the MIU approach. Take the CIA model:

$$\text{Max} \sum_{t=0}^{\infty} \frac{1}{(1+\rho)^t} U(X_t, N_t),$$

s.t.

1. $W_t = (1 + i_{t-1})\, B_{t-1} + M_{t-1}$,
2. $P_t X_t + B_t + M_t = P_t N_t + W_t$,
3. $P_t X_t \leq M_t$.

Transversality condition $\lim_{t\to\infty} Q_t W_t = 0$.

$$W_0 + \sum_{t=0}^{\infty} Q_t P_t N_t = \sum_{t=0}^{\infty} Q_t \left(P_t X_t + \frac{i_t}{1+i_t} M_t \right).$$

X_t is a "cash good" which can be purchased only via cash. In contrast, leisure (the time not spent on working N_t) can be consumed without cash (it represents a credit good). The CIA constraint drives a wedge between consumption of cash and credit goods:

$-\frac{\partial U/\partial X_t}{\partial U/\partial N_t} = 1 + \frac{i_t}{1+i_t}$. For $i_t > 0$, the constraint $P_t X_t \leq M_t$ becomes binding (giving a positive demand for money). So in the objective function, we can substitute $X_t = m_t = M_t/P_t$. Thus, the optimization problem is formally equivalent to maximizing utility out of real money balances and consumption of credit goods.

Similarly, the shopping time model can be transformed as a problem of maximizing the indirect utility function $V(X_t, N_t) = U(f(X_t, N_t))$.

(continued)

Formally, as in the MIU approach, via iterated substitution the intertemporal budget constraints (1) and (2) can be reduced to a single wealth constraint. We get:

$$\sum_{t=0}^{\infty} \frac{1}{(1+\rho)^t} U(X_t, N_t) + \mu \left[W_0 + \sum_{t=0}^{\infty} Q_t P_t N_t - \sum_{t=0}^{\infty} Q_t \left(P_t X_t + \frac{i_t}{1+i_t} M_t \right) \right]$$
$$+ \sum_{t=0}^{\infty} \lambda_t (M_t - P_t X_t).$$

This gives the Euler equation above and the equivalence of a money demand function.

The demand for money is decreasing with the interest rate: With increasing *i*, less cash goods relative to credit goods are consumed. The requirement to pay via cash forces people to hold money one period in advance, so the effective price of consumption for cash goods increases to $1 + i_t/(1 + i_t)$. Obviously, the cash-in-advance constraint introduces a distortion between the effective price of consumption and for cash goods (see Fig. 2.13).

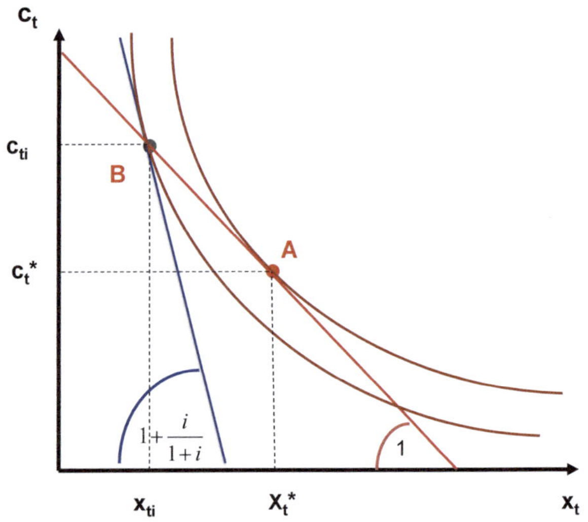

Fig. 2.13 Distortion between cash and credit goods

Focus Box for Nerds: Shopping Time Model (*Optional Material)

A representative agent has standard preferences defined on real consumption:

$$\text{Max} \sum_{t=0}^{\infty} \frac{1}{(1+\rho)^t} U(X_t, N_t).$$

The basic idea of the shopping time model is that money reduces transaction costs (the shopping time required for purchasing goods). In a sense, money serves as an intermediate input for producing consumption. This can be captured by a transaction technology $T(C_t, m_t)$ with $T_{C_t} > 0$; $T_{m_t} < 0$.

$T(C_t, m_t)$ represents the real resources used up when C_t is consumed and m_t are real money balances available. The higher the stock of real money balances, the lower these resources (money allows savings on transaction costs). So the per period budget constraint has to be modified according to:

$$\frac{W_{t+1}}{1+i_t} + \frac{i_t}{1+i_t} M_t + P_t(C_t - N_t) + P_t T(C_t, m_t) = W_t.$$

Now, redefine gross consumption as: $X_t = C_t + T(C_t, m_t)$. Since X_t is increasing in C_t, this function can be inverted to $C_t = f(X_t, m_t)$. Thus, we can reformulate the optimization problem via the indirect utility function:

$$\sum_{t=0}^{\infty} \frac{1}{(1+\rho)^t} U(f(X_t, m_t), N_t)$$

$s.t.\ W_0 + \sum_{t=0}^{\infty} Q_t P_t N_t = \sum_{t=0}^{\infty} Q_t (P_t X_t + \frac{i_t}{1+i_t} M_t)$.

This is formally equivalent to the MIU approach. In particular, the special case with exogenous labor supply $N_t = Y_t$ (with N_t constant) gives a MIU function $V(X_t, m_t) = U(f(X_t, m_t))$ except that now, the structure of the indirect utility function $V(X_t, m_t)$ is well specified by the transaction technology: $X_t = C_t + T(C_t, m_t)$.

The FOC for consumption path and real money balances are:

$$\frac{U_c(c_t)\frac{\partial C_t}{\partial X_t}}{U_c(c_{t+1})\frac{\partial C_{t+1}}{\partial X_{t+1}}} = \frac{1+i_t}{(1+\rho)(1+\pi_t)},$$

$$\frac{U_c(c_t)\frac{\partial C_t}{\partial m_t}}{U_c(c_t)\frac{\partial C_t}{\partial X_t}} = \frac{\frac{\partial C_t}{\partial m_t}}{\frac{\partial C_t}{\partial X_t}} = \frac{i_t}{1+i_t}.$$

2.5 Bubbles and Self-Fulfilling Inflationary Expectations (In-) Determinacy of the Price Level

2.5.1 The No-Bubble Condition: Relevance of a Transversality Constraint

When we introduced the Cagan model to determine the price level—given some expected path of money supply—we showed that the forward-looking solution is characterized by the first-order difference Equation 2.2.3:

$$p_t = \frac{1}{1+b} m_t + \frac{b}{1+b} E\, p_{t+1}.$$

In that section we focused on one specific solution for this difference equation which we called the "fundamental solution":

$$p_t^F = \frac{1}{1+b} \sum\nolimits_{s=0}^{\infty} \left(\frac{b}{1+b}\right)^s E(m_{t+s}). \tag{2.2.5}$$

We derived Equation 2.2.5 simply by imposing a "No-Bubble" condition (Equation 2.2.4) without providing economic motivation. Having now outlined a micro-founded theory for the demand for money, in this section we want to check the plausibility of the No-Bubble condition. Without that additional condition the difference equation has also many other (bubble) solutions:

$$p_t = p_t^F + b_t = \frac{1}{1+b} m_t + \frac{b}{1+b} E\left(p_{t+1}^F + b_{t+1}\right) \tag{2.5.1}$$

as long as b_t follows the stochastic process $\{b_t\}$[10]: $b_{t+1} = \frac{b+1}{b} b_t + v_{t+1}$ with $E_t v_{t+1} = 0$.

Since $b_t = \frac{b}{1+b} E_t b_{t+1}$, we just added the same number on both sides of the equation, so $p_t = p_t^F + b_t$ is also a solution to the difference equation.

By construction, for any s and so also for $s \to \infty$ the present value of $E(b_{t+1})$, will be b_t:

$$\lim_{s\to\infty} \left(\frac{b}{1+b}\right)^s E_t b_{t+s} = \lim_{s\to\infty} \left(\frac{b}{1+b}\right)^s E_t \left(\frac{b+1}{b}\right)^s b_t = b_t \tag{2.5.2}$$

[10]More generally: A stochastic bursting bubble can also be a solution, if

$$b_{t+1} = \begin{cases} \dfrac{b+1}{b}\dfrac{1}{p} b_t + v_{t+1}, & \text{with prob } p, \\ v_{t+1}, & \text{with prob } 1-p, \end{cases} \qquad \text{and } E_t(v_{t+1}) = 0.$$

b_t is a bubble, with b_{t+s} exploding at the rate $1+\frac{1}{b}$. Since the present value is constant, it is a solution to the difference equation. $p_t = p_t^F$ will be the unique solution only if the no-bubble condition holds: $b_t = 0$ if

$$\lim_{s\to\infty}\left(\frac{b}{1+b}\right)^{s} E\, p_{t+s} = 0. \qquad (2.2.4)$$

So the solution to the difference equation is not specified without imposing some additional endpoint constraint. In real growth models, usually the transversality constraint is imposed as one equilibrium condition (making the No-Ponzi Game condition binding). The economic motivation for the No-Ponzi Game condition is that since real resources are limited (bounded), violating the constraint would be in contradiction with feasibility constraints. But unlike the No-Ponzi Game condition, there is no resource constraint ruling out nominal explosions: Transversality conditions can rule out real explosions but not nominal explosions. Self-fulfilling inflationary expectations ("speculative hyperinflation") may make money useless as a medium of exchange without violating any aggregate resource constraints! Along that path, money simply ceases to play a useful role, and we converge to a pure barter economy. If pure barter is a feasible solution (after all, people living in the stone age were able to survive), then we cannot rule out real money balances going to zero as an equilibrium.

Money has to be essential to rule out such a price path. We need to have a closer look at the microeconomic foundations for the money demand function in order to understand what that implies! Based on the Brock–Sidrauski model (the Money-in-the-Utility approach), we will now try to get a better understanding of that issue. Under what conditions can we rule out bubbles? As derived in the last chapter, the optimality conditions for the representative consumer require

(a) Euler equation: $\frac{U_C(C_t)}{U_C(C_{t+1})} = \frac{1+r_t}{1+\rho}$,
(b) Fisher equation $1+i_t = (1+r)\cdot(1+\pi_t) = (1+r)\cdot\frac{P_{t+1}}{P_t}$,
(c) FOC for money demand $\frac{U_m(m_t)}{U_C(C_t)} = \frac{i_t}{1+i_t}$ with $m_t = \frac{M_t}{P_t}$ as real money balances.

To focus on the key issues, we analyze the case of additive separable utility: $u(C,m) = u(C) + V(m)$. In addition, we assume that the real economy is in a steady state with $C_{t+1} = C_t = Y$. In this case, according to the Euler equation we have $r_t = r = \rho$. We can normalize $u_c(C) = 1$ and simplify the first-order condition for the money demand equation as:

$$V_m(m_t) = \frac{i_t}{1+i_t} = \frac{i_t}{(1+\rho)(1+\pi_t)}. \qquad (2.5.3)$$

Let us now try to determine the evolution of the price level. If $\{P_t, P_{t+1}, \ldots\}$ with $P_{t+1} = (1+\pi_t) \cdot P_t$ is the equilibrium path for some arbitrary path of money supply$\{M_t, M_{t+1}, \ldots\}$ with $M_{t+1} = (1+\mu_t) \cdot M_t$, real money balances $\{m_t, m_{t+1}, \ldots\}$ evolve across time according to the following difference equation:

$$\frac{m_{t+1}}{m_t} = \frac{M_{t+1}/M_t}{P_{t+1}/P_t} = \frac{1+\mu_t}{1+\pi_t} = \frac{(1+\mu_t)(1+\rho)}{1+i_t}. \tag{2.5.4}$$

In the last part of Equation 2.5.4 using the Fisher equation we substituted $1+\pi_t = (1+i_t)/(1+\rho)$ so as to reformulate the dynamic evolution of real money balances across time (the difference equation) in terms of the equilibrium interest rate at each date. According to the optimality condition Equation 2.5.3 we have $V_m(m_t) = \frac{i_t}{1+i_t} = 1 - \frac{1}{1+i_t}$. So we can substitute $\frac{1}{1+i_t} = 1 - V_m(m_t)$ to characterize the evolution of real money balances along any equilibrium path by the following nonlinear difference equation:

$$m_{t+1} = (1+\mu_t)(1+\rho)[1 - V_m(m_t)]m_t. \tag{2.5.4b}$$

Let us now characterize monetary equilibria for a simple policy with constant money growth:

$$M_{t+1} = M_t(1+\mu). \tag{2.5.5}$$

As one solution for this policy, we expect real money balances being in a steady state m^* with the rate of inflation being determined by the rate of money growth $\pi = \mu$ and the nominal interest rate being equal to $1+i = (1+\rho)(1+\mu)$. Let us check that this is indeed a steady state. If $m_{t+1} = m_t = m^* > 0,\ \forall t$ is a steady state with positive real balances, Equation 2.5.4b must hold at any time and so we get:

$$1 = (1+\mu)(1+\rho)[1 - V_m(m)], \text{ or } \frac{1}{1 - V_m(m)} = 1 + i$$
$$= (1+\mu)(1+\rho). \tag{2.5.4c}$$

In this steady state, both real money balances and the nominal interest rate i stay constant across time. The price level rises at the rate equal to the money growth rate $P_{t+1} = P_t(1+\mu)$ such that $\frac{M_t}{P_t} = m^*, \forall t$. The initial price level is determined by$P_0 = M_0/m^*$. The larger μ, the lower will be steady-state real balances and so the higher the initial price level. The reason is obvious—just as discussed above for the case of equilibrium with a Cagan money demand: The higher the rate of inflation, the lower the willingness to hold money. The Friedman rule would be implemented with $\mu = -\rho$ (a constant reduction in money balances at a rate equal to the negative real interest rate. Such a policy drives nominal interest rate to zero, making sure that

Fig. 2.14 m^* as steady state

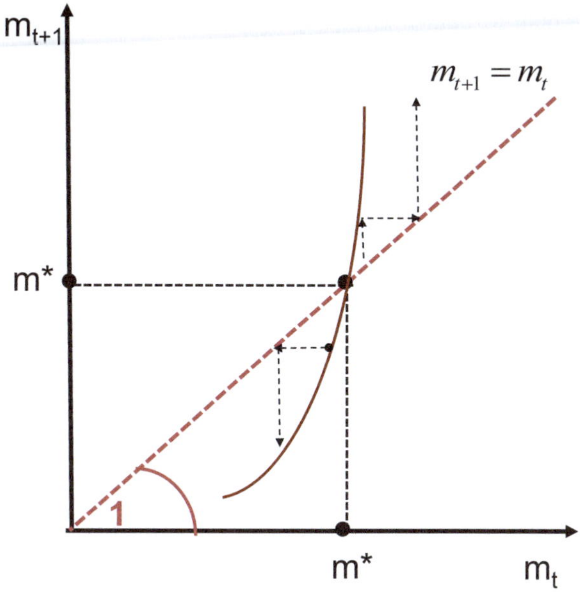

the real rate of return on money balances is equal to the real rate of interest r. m^* is highest for $\mu = -\rho$.

So it seems that a central bank trying to implement some stable target rate of inflation π^* simply needs to let money supply grow at the rate[11] $\mu = \pi^*$. This would be true if m^* is the only unique solution for the difference Equation 2.5.4b. Unfortunately, this may not be the only feasible equilibrium path. There may be other steady states, and there may be self-fulfilling price paths resulting in real money balances decreasing across time. In order to check possible equilibria paths, we need to characterize the path for the difference equation outside the steady state m^*.

The key is to figure out what happens if we move away from m^*. Locally around m^*, the function is steeper than 1. We know that at m^*, $m_{t+1} = m_t$ and thus$(1+\mu)(1+\rho)[1 - V_m(m^*)] = 1$. But with concave preferences, marginal utility of real money balances $V_m(m_t)$ is decreasing in m—the second derivative is negative: $V_{mm}(m) < 0$. So $V_m(m > m^*) < V_m(m^*)$. If we start from a level m_0 slightly above m^* in Fig. 2.14 we have$(1+\mu)(1+\rho)[1 - V_m(m > m^*)] > 1$, so $m_{t+1} > m_t$. The other way round for $m < m^*$, since $(1+\mu)(1+\rho)[1 - V_m(m < m^*)] < 1$.

Starting with some arbitrary $m_0 > m^*$, we will move even further away from m^* to the right since $m_{t+1} > m_t$. In a similar vein, if we start from a level m slightly below m^*, we will move further away to the left ($m_{t+1} < m_t$). In that sense, the steady state m^* is unstable. At the same time, however, it is locally unique. In a positive range around m^*, it is the only resting point. With forward-looking behavior (rational expectations), the price level P_0 and the price path $P(t) = P_0\,(1+\mu)^t$

[11]More generally, in an economy growing with rate γ, we have $1 + \mu = (1+\gamma)(1+\pi)$.

would be pinned down uniquely if all other paths could be ruled out as violating some reasonable constraints. Lack of stability would be of no concern at all if we could show that there is no other feasible dynamic path possibly converging to some other steady state. If so, the locally unique steady state m^* would be the only global solution. In that case, with forward-looking rational agents, the economy would immediately reach the steady-state equilibrium m^* as soon as some policy μ is announced. Unfortunately, this turns out to require fairly special conditions. Let us see why.

2.5.2 Can We Rule Out Divergent Paths?

First, we look at some $m_0 > m^*$ as starting point. Since $\Delta(m_t) > 0$ for all $m > m^*$, we get a deflationary price path. Real money balances are rising across time, since prices fall.

For $m^* < m_0 < m_1 < \ldots,$ real balances are exploding for $T \to \infty: \lim_{T\to\infty} P_T = 0; \lim_{T\to\infty} m_T = \infty$. This cannot be an equilibrium, if m is bounded from above as a consequence of resource constraints! Otherwise, the transversality constraint would be violated. This argument rules out deflationary price paths.

But note the implicit assumption here is that the inter-temporal wealth constraint for the government is not assumed to hold even out of equilibrium—there is no Ricardian fiscal regime imposed. In a Ricardian fiscal regime, the real value of nominal government debt must be equal to the present value of future real primary government surplus even out of equilibrium. If—along some deflationary path—the real value of nominal debt doubles, the government would need to double real taxes imposed to pay off that debt. This way, the positive wealth effect from rising real money balances would be offset by equivalent tax increases. In such a regime, the economy may end up in a deflationary trap (See Woodford, 2003, Chap. 2.4).

2.5.3 Hyperinflationary Paths

Now let us look at some $m_0 < m^*$ as starting point, so $m_{t+1} < m_t$. In that case, we move along a hyperinflationary path: The price level will be exploding for $T \to \infty: \lim_{T\to\infty} P_T = \infty$. Whether such a path may be an equilibrium depends on the behavior of m close to 0. So we need to check what happens to

$$\lim_{m_t \to 0} (1+\mu)(1+\rho)[1 - V_m(m_t)]m_t. \tag{2.5.6}$$

Note that m_t can never become negative as drawn in Fig. 2.15a. If that would happen with P_t rising, we can rule out such paths easily. However, if m_t converges toward 0 as drawn in Fig. 2.15b, such an inflationary path cannot be ruled out. Under

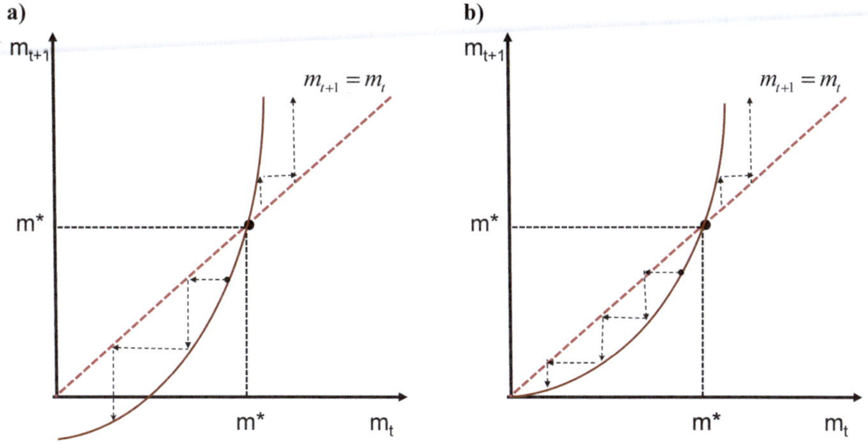

Fig. 2.15 Self-fulfilling bubbles. (**a**) Unique steady state ($\lim_{m_t \to 0} m_t \cdot V_m(m_t) > 0$). (**b**) two steady states ($\lim_{m_t \to 0} m_t \cdot V_m(m_t) = 0$)

what conditions is a hyperinflationary path not feasible? Obviously the first part of the Equation 2.5.6 will always converge to 0 for $m_t \to 0$: $(1+\mu)(1+\rho)\ m_t \to 0$. Hence we can focus on the limit of $\lim_{m_t \to 0} \{-(1+\mu)(1+\rho)V_m(m_t) \cdot m_t\} = \lim_{m_t \to 0} \{-V_m(m_t) \cdot m_t\}$.

m_t would need to become negative at some stage if

$$\lim_{m_t \to 0} m_t \cdot V_m(m_t) > 0, \quad \text{for } m_t \to 0. \tag{2.5.7}$$

Since negative real money balances are not feasible, condition Equation 2.5.7 is the condition to rule out such a path as solution. For $\lim_{m_t \to 0} m_t \cdot V_m(m_t) > 0$ there exists a unique steady state at m^*. In contrast, if $\lim_{m_t \to 0} m_t \cdot V_m(m_t) = 0$, $m_t = 0$ will always be a feasible second steady state. If people do not expect that others accept fiat money, money will be useless—the price for money will be zero; that is, the level for real goods in terms money will be infinite. But even worse: In that case, we do not only have $m_t = 0$ as a second steady state solution, any path leading to $\lim_{t \to \infty} m_t = 0$ will be also an equilibrium—there exist a number of paths with rational expectations all of them converging toward the self-fulfilling hyperinflationary equilibrium. This seems fairly counterintuitive. But can we really rule out these type of equilibria by imposing the condition Equation 2.5.7 $\lim_{m_t \to 0} m_t \cdot V_m(m_t) > 0$? That condition says that money has to be essential in the following sense: If real money balances are close to zero, marginal utility out of money balances rises faster than the rate at which money goes to zero. Money must be essential in the following sense: People cannot survive without at least a small amount of money. Such a condition is, however, quite implausible. If money is not crucial, the economy can easily converge to a barter equilibrium: $\lim_{t \to \infty} m(t) = 0$. There are good reasons not to rule out barter trade as equilibrium: People used to survive in ancient time before the invention of fiat money.

2.5.4 Example: CES Payoff Function

As an example, let us now consider a specific payoff function with constant elasticity of substitution for real money balances: $V(m) = \frac{1}{1-1/\sigma} m^{1-1/\sigma}$.

For that function, condition Equation 2.5.7 is fulfilled if

$$\lim_{m \to 0} mV'(m) = \lim_{m \to 0} m^{1-1/\sigma} > 0, \quad \text{for } \sigma < 1. \tag{2.5.7b}$$

For $m \to 0$, marginal utility of real money balances must go faster to infinity than m goes to 0. Intuition in terms of indifference curves: The indifference curves between C and M/P are not allowed to cross the $m = 0$ line. It must not be possible to substitute real money balances against real consumption. Money must be essential in the following sense: Any bounded finite consumption bundle of real goods cannot be a substitute even for a tiny amount of real money balances. Corner solutions as point B in Fig. 2.16 are ruled out.

If we accept that pure barter economies (those not using any fiat money) are feasible, this strong assumption does not seem to be plausible. History documents quite a few examples how economies switch to barter trade after the breakdown of the financial system (after/during hyperinflationary episodes, or after the breakdown of the Soviet Union). Of course, such periods usually are characterized by severe

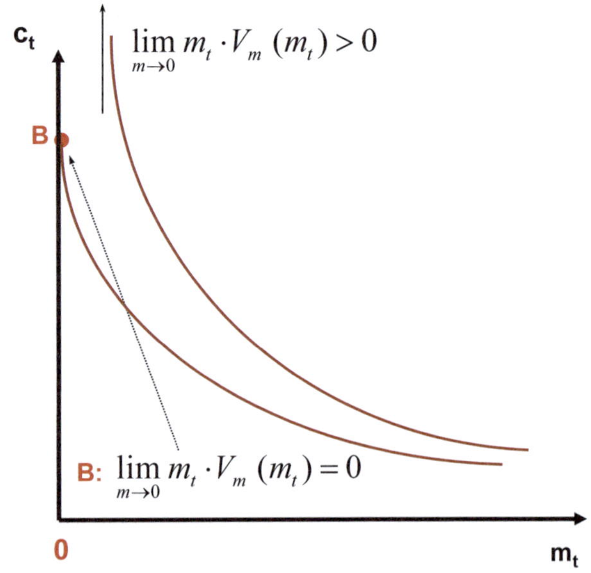

Fig. 2.16 Real money balances as essential good

damage to the real economy, so the convenient technical assumption of dichotomy between the real and the nominal side of economy (the real endowment path not being affected by movements of the nominal price level) is not justified in that case. Obviously, the breakdown of financial intermediation during periods of hyperinflation is bound to have a damaging impact on the real side of the economy. But our argument still holds if we allow for such effects as long as we do not require money to be essential in the sense discussed here.

We can try to infer the indirect utility for the log-linear Cagan demand function:

$$\ln m = \ln M - \ln p = c - bi,$$

$$V'(m) = \frac{c - \ln m}{b} = i > 0, \quad \text{for } c > \ln m,$$

$$V(m) = m \; \frac{c - \ln m + 1}{b}, \quad \text{with } V''(m) = -\frac{1}{bm} < 0,$$

$$\lim_{m \to 0} mV'(m) = -m \ln m = 0.$$

So self-fulfilling explosive price paths might not be ruled out for that case (this is just the border case).

We need additional assumptions in order to rule out purely hyperinflationary paths. Different routes have been taken: A simple route was to select the steady state $m^* > 0$ as only plausible solution. This may be justified if the high-inflation steady state is not stable under adaptive learning behavior and thus can be ruled out as implausible. Alternatively, we may impose some mechanism like a government promise to move to a commodity standard when the price level threatens to go beyond some maximum limit (Obstfeld & Rogoff, 1983).

2.6 Interest Rate Feedback Rules

Can we rule out the indeterminacy of self-fulfilling inflation expectation equilibria if central banks control interest rates instead of the money supply in order to target the inflation rate? Let us assume that the central bank targets the inflation rate π^* in the following way:

$$i_t = r + \pi^* + \varphi \cdot (\pi_t - \pi^*) \tag{2.6.1}$$

Equation 2.6.1 says that the central bank responds to deviations of the actual rate from target by adjusting the nominal interest rate by $\varphi \cdot (\pi_t - \pi^*)$ with φ as a measure of the strength of the response. Such a rule is a variant of the so-called Taylor rules (see Chap. 6). Again, we simplify assuming that the real interest rate r is constant across time. As we will see, the stability of the system crucially depends on the strength of the response—the parameter φ and on the way expected inflation is formed. According to the Fisher equation (as arbitrage condition) the interest rate varies with expected inflation.

$$i_t = r + \pi_t^e. \tag{2.6.2}$$

Under what conditions do we get a locally determinate solution with an interest rate feedback-rule? The dynamics crucially depend on the way inflationary expectations are formed. At the time when Milton Friedman propagated money growth targeting instead of interest rate targeting, economic models focused on the case of adaptive expectations—that is expectations depend only on past experience. So let us first start with that case and simply assume that $\pi_t^e = \pi_{t-1}$. Inserting these adaptive expectations in Equation 2.6.2, together with Equation 2.6.1 yields: $\pi_{t-1} = \pi^* + \varphi \cdot (\pi_t - \pi^*)$.

This gives the following difference equation:

$$\pi_t = \pi^* + \frac{1}{\varphi} \cdot (\pi_{t-1} - \pi^*). \tag{2.6.3}$$

Starting with any arbitrary π_0, we have inflation evolving across time according to

$$\pi_T = \pi^* + \frac{1}{\varphi^T} \cdot (\pi_0 - \pi^*). \tag{2.6.4}$$

If the response to deviations from target is weak ($\varphi < 1$), we get an exploding path. So with adaptive expectations, interest rate targeting turns out to be unstable for $\varphi < 1$. Using the concept of adaptive expectations in his analysis, Milton Friedman concluded that pure interest rate targeting (with $\varphi = 0$) is bound to be unstable. Our analysis illustrates, however, that we can get a stable inflation path if the central bank—rather than fixing the interest rate permanently—uses a feedback rule, responding aggressively enough (with $\varphi > 1$) to deviations of inflation from target. For a strong feedback ($\varphi > 1$), the stability properties of the difference equation reverse. Such a strong response $\varphi > 1$ is now called the "Taylor principle" according to John Taylor (1993) who propagated such feedback rules. Nevertheless, despite the system being stable, there is indeterminacy about the actual path: The difference Equation 2.6.3 has many solutions. All multiple equilibria can be indexed by an arbitrary level of initial inflation π_0 in Equation 2.6.4. The Taylor principle suggests that an interest rate rule with strong enough feedback response can ensure a stable, even though not unique inflation path.

Adaptive expectations result in a backward-looking solution of the difference equation. In the model with adaptive expectations, expected inflation always turns out to be wrong: Expectations are constantly proved to be false, even though the structure is completely deterministic. Private agents learning from past mistakes are likely to revise the way they form their expectations. Starting with Lucas (1972), it has become standard to look at rational expectations solutions (see Chap. 4), imposing the condition that the specific expectations assumed in the model should be in line with the predictions of that model. With rational expectations, we have to solve the difference equation in a forward-looking way. Stability and determinacy properties completely reverse compared to the case of adaptive expectations. It is straightforward to see this in our simple model. With forward-looking expectations, we have

$$\pi_t^e = E(\pi_{t+1}).$$

Inserting these expectations in Equation 2.6.2, and merging with Equation 2.6.1, we now get a forward-looking difference equation for arbitrary φ:

$$\pi_{t+1} = \pi^* + \varphi \cdot (\pi_t - \pi^*). \tag{2.6.5}$$

In a perfect foresight equilibrium (in the absence of control errors), for any given π_0 we can solve forward the future inflation rate path as rational expectation equilibrium. Now we get

$$\pi_T = \pi^* + \varphi^T(\pi_0 - \pi^*).$$

With $\varphi < 1$, for any π_0 , the inflation rate across time uniquely converges toward $\lim_{T\to\infty} \pi^T = \pi^*$. So now the inflation rate path is stable for $\varphi < 1$, but again there are multiple solutions, characterized by the initial value π_0 (see Fig. 2.17a). This result is the base of the classic doctrine (Sargent and Wallace (1975) that inflation is indeterminate with an interest rate target under rational expectations. There is indeterminacy with multiple equilibria. Just as in the case of monetary targeting, the difference equation has many solutions for $\varphi > 0$, indexed by an arbitrary initial rate π_0 and arbitrary sunspot variables. Sargent and Wallace show that even though a strict peg (fixing $i_t = i = r + \pi^*$ with $\varphi = 0$) can determine uniquely the future expected path (with $\pi_t^e = \pi^*$), such a peg leaves the current price level indeterminate: Actual inflation is unpredictable, not pinned down by the equilibrium conditions. So arbitrary shocks like sunspots can result in a shift of the price level.

With $\varphi > 1$ things get more interesting: If the central bank reacts sufficiently strong to inflation deviating from target ($\varphi > 1$) there is still an infinite number of

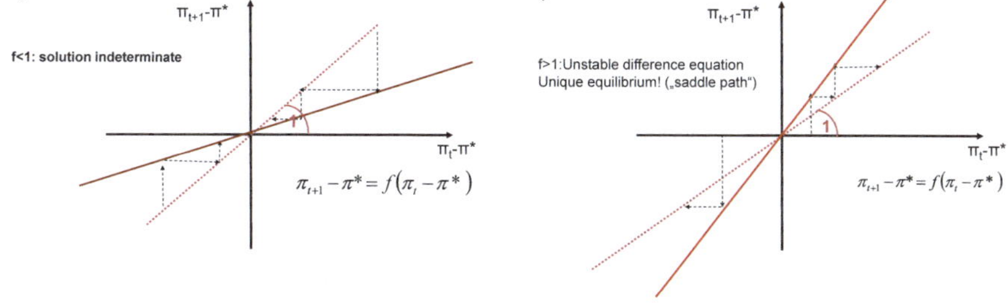

Fig. 2.17 Locally (in-) determinate solutions

non-local equilibria. But all of the feasible equilibria except one eventually explode with π_t^e growing without bound, resulting either in self-fulfilling inflation or self-fulfilling deflation (see Fig. 2.17). Just as in the case of money supply targeting, these exploding paths seem fairly implausible. Additional assumptions are needed in order to rule out these paths. If we can plausibly rule out such solutions, then $\pi_0 = \pi^*$ remains as the unique locally bounded solution (see Woodford, 2001, 2003). This way, the inflation rate is determined by a pure interest rate target. A promising way to select among different equilibria is to analyze specific learning procedures. It is quite unrealistic to assume perfect foresight, implying that all agents are able to calculate the future (possibly stochastic) policy path. With learning, past experience will play a role, resulting in a mix between forward- and backward-looking solutions. But as extensively discussed in Cochrane (2011), it is hard to justify ruling out non-local solutions using standard assumptions about fundamentals. Obviously, even the Taylor principle still cannot rule out global indeterminacy unless we impose additional restrictions (for details see Cochrane, 2011). The fiscal theory of the price level, discussed in the next chapter, suggests one mechanism to determine the price level.

2.7 Summary

In this chapter we considered monetary policy in a dynamic growth model with flexible prices. Monetary policy was assumed to be neutral or super-neutral in the sense that it does not affect real variables in the economy. This way, we tried to understand monetary policy design from a long-run perspective. To motivate a demand for money, we introduced various ways to provide a micro-foundation for money holding: Frictions such as the cash-in-advance constraint and the shopping time model make it costly for agents to trade without money. We show that, formally, the role for money generated by these frictions can be captured in a quite general way by the "money in the utility function" approach. Characterizing the dynamic optimality conditions, the demand for money is determined by the opportunity cost of holding money—the nominal rate of interest.

By construction, the role of monetary policy is fairly limited in that context and straightforward to characterize: Central banks should aim to achieve price stability (low inflation) to minimize distortions arising from holding money balances. Since the inflation tax creates inefficiencies in models with money holding, optimal policy is characterized by the Friedman rule: Money balances should give the same return as safe bonds. One way to implement that goal is to set the nominal rate of interest equal to zero. An alternative way would be to pay interest on money at a nominal return equal to the rate for bonds.

Price level and inflation are determined not just by current monetary policy, but also by the expected future path of monetary policy. Thus we need additional information about what is likely to happen in the future. Solving in a forward-looking way for price level and inflation, it turns out that neither a policy holding money supply fixed forever nor feedback interest rate rules may be sufficient to pin down a unique path for the price level. To rule out indeterminacy with equilibria characterized by bubbles and self-fulfilling inflationary expectations, additional elements are needed (such as money being essential or institutional arrangements guaranteeing a floor for the price level). The intuition behind is a key feature of fiat money giving it quite different characteristics compared to standard commodities: You accept money as medium of exchange if you trust that others are willing to accept that money in the future. If that trust fades, the willingness to hold money evaporates. Neither money supply rules nor interest rate feedback rules on their own can rule out such a process.

In this chapter, we abstracted from fiscal policy. But the current price level will be influenced not just by the expected future path of monetary but also of fiscal policy. Empirically, real money balances are a very small share of GDP, so the revenue impact for fiscal policy seems to be rather small. But with government debt usually being denominated in nominal terms, movements in the price level may have substantial impact on the real value of debt. The real value erodes in periods of hyperinflation; it increases in periods of deflationary spirals. The next chapter analyzes the interaction between monetary and fiscal policy in detail.

In models with flexible prices, welfare costs from monetary distortions (the welfare triangle under the money demand function) turn out to be rather small for low rates of inflation. A key reason for that result is that the economy is assumed to be always in long-run equilibrium. As we will see in Part II, this is no longer true when prices are sticky. In that case, shocks are likely to shift the economy far away from equilibrium and the target rate of inflation. By stabilizing prices and output, monetary policy may contribute substantially to raising welfare. Part III considers the challenges in periods when stabilization policy is impeded.

References

Buiter, W., & Panigirtzoglou, N. (2003). Overcoming the zero bound on nominal interest rates with negative interest on currency: Gesell's solution. *Economic Journal, 113*(490), 723–746.

Cagan, P. (1956). The monetary dynamics of hyperinflation. In M. Friedman (Ed.), *Studies in the quantity theory of money*. Chicago, IL: University of Chicago Press.

Clark, G. (2009). The macroeconomic aggregates for England, 1209-2008. *University of California Davis, Economics* WP 09-19, October 2009.

Clower, R. (1965). The Keynesian counter-revolution: A theoretical appraisal. In F. H. Hahn & F. P. R. Brechling (Eds.), *The theory of interest rates*. London: Macmillan.

Cochrane, J. (2011). Determinacy and identification with Taylor rules. *Journal of Political Economy, 119*(3), 565–615.

Correia, I., & Teles, P. (1996). Is the Friedman rule optimal when money is an intermediate good? *Journal of Monetary Economics, 38*(2), 223–244.

Friedman, M. (1963). *Inflation: Causes and consequences*. New York: Asia Publishing House.

Friedman, M. (1969). The optimum quantity of money. In *The optimal quantity of money and other essays* (pp. 1–50). Chicago, IL: Aldine.

Goodfriend, M. (2000). Overcoming the zero bound on interest rate policy. *Journal of Money, Credit, and Banking, 4*(32), 1007–1035.

Kiyotaki, N., & Wright, R. (1989). On money as a medium of exchange. *Journal of Political Economy, 97*(4), 927–954.

Lucas, R. (1972). Expectations and the neutrality of money. *Journal of Economic Theory, 4*, 103–124.

Obstfeld, M., & Rogoff, K. (1983). Speculative hyperinflations in maximizing models: Can we rule them out? *Journal of Political Economy, 91*(4), 675–687.

Sargent, T., & Wallace, N. (1975). Rational expectations, the optimal monetary instrument, and the optimal money supply rule. *Journal of Political Economy, 83*, 241–254.

Taylor, J. (1993). Discretion versus policy rules in practice. *Carnegie-Rochester Conference Series in Public Policy, 39*(1), 195–214.

Tobin, J. (1992). Money. In Macmillan Publishers Ltd (Ed.), *The new Palgrave dictionary of economics*. London: Palgrave Macmillan.

Woodford, M. (2001). The Taylor rule and optimal monetary policy. *American Economic Review: Papers and Proceedings, 91*, 232–237.

Woodford, M. (2003). *Interest and prices*. Princeton, NJ: Princeton University Press.

3 Interaction Between Monetary and Fiscal Policy: Active and Passive Monetary Regimes

3.1 Introduction

Up to now, we looked at a very stylized theoretical model, trying to understand mechanisms behind the determination of price level and rate of inflation. We studied the possibility of self-fulfilling hyperinflationary (or deflationary) equilibria even when central banks try to implement some steady-state target rate of inflation π^*. Looking at historical episodes, however, suggests that periods of hyperinflation usually arise during times of distress for public finance. The intuition behind this mechanism is fairly straightforward: If government spending (or public debt) gets out of control, there is a need to resort to other means for generating revenues, and usually the printing press seems to provide an easy way out. Any analysis ignoring fiscal–monetary interactions is likely to reach misleading conclusions about how inflation is determined during these episodes.

Financing government spending via money printing is a standard trigger for high and possibly hyperinflation. Obviously, there is a link between public debt and incentives to print money, so we need to study closer the link between fiscal and monetary policy. Printing money creates seigniorage revenue for the government. It is one source of revenue just like taxation. Usually, seigniorage is just a small part of government revenue. But if public debt is high, there is a strong temptation to ease the government budget constraint by "activating the printing press". High marginal tax rates cause allocative distortions. By issuing government bonds, the tax burden is shifted into the future instead, but at the cost of imposing an additional burden from interest rate payments.

Printing money alleviates the interest burden, but it triggers distortions out of higher inflation. When anticipated, the increase in inflation drives interest rates up at the same time, corroding the demand for money. Hence, effective seigniorage in real terms is likely to decline dramatically. Can the need to create seigniorage income for the government really be a convincing explanation for monetary policies ending in hyperinflation? Have such policies been motivated by the attempt to maximize some steady-state seigniorage revenue or are they instead the result of a loss of control in

J. Cao, G. Illing, *Money: Theory and Practice*, Springer Texts in Business and Economics, https://doi.org/10.1007/978-3-030-19697-4_3

government? Philip Cagan (1956) studied these questions in his analysis of hyperinflationary periods. However, we will see that frequently, high debt does not trigger inflation at all.

This chapter analyzes the interaction between monetary and fiscal policy in detail. We want to understand why there is no clear relation between debt and inflation. As we have seen in Chap. 2, inflation is not just strongly determined by current monetary policy. Expectations about how monetary policy evolves in the near and distant future also play a crucial role. Since monetary policy actions frequently have some fiscal impact, the effectiveness of monetary policy also depends on the response of fiscal policy. For that reason, we first study different notions of central bank's seigniorage. Then, we work out how seigniorage revenue modifies the government budget inter-temporal constraint and provide a sustainability analysis of debt. We show under what conditions the debt to GDP ratio converges to a stable long-run steady state, emphasizing the role of primary surplus and seigniorage revenue. The condition for debt sustainability helps to understand why the reactions both of fiscal and monetary policy to shocks are crucial for determining the rate of inflation. We distinguish between different regimes, depending on who is the active player. In one regime, fiscal policy automatically adjusts such that monetary policy is allowed to control inflation. Here monetary policy is active, free to pursue its objectives, with fiscal policy assumed to be passive, being constrained by central bank actions. However, there can also be an alternative regime, with active fiscal and passive monetary policy. In that regime, the price level is determined by fiscal behavior with debt being stabilized by the central bank adjusting either seignorage revenue or simply the price level. We analyze both regimes. In the regime with active monetary policy, sometimes called Ricardian regime, inflation and price level are determined as in the quantity theory of money outlined. Our analysis in Chap. 2 was based on this case. With active fiscal policy, the outcome can be quite different. Following Sargent and Wallace, we show that an adjustment of seignorage may result in "unpleasant monetarist arithmetic": A temporary tightening of monetary policy may even lead to an increase even in the current price level. With government debt issued in nominal terms, fluctuations in the price level may adjust the real value of debt, bringing expected future revenues in line with the current nominal value of debt. This mechanism is called the fiscal theory of the price level. Proponents of that theory argue that price level adjustments are a suitable way to eliminate the possible indeterminacy of the price level in a Ricardian regime.

3.2 A Brief Look at History

Is there a direct link between the level of government debt (or the debt to GDP ratio) and the rate of inflation? Obviously not. If we look at the data, we get quite a diverse picture. The experience during the Weimar republic and in Serbia after the break down of the Soviet Union are classical examples of hyperinflation being caused by the need to finance government spending. Figure 3.1a suggests that the increase in the debt to GDP ratio in Argentina and Brazil during the 1980s might have triggered

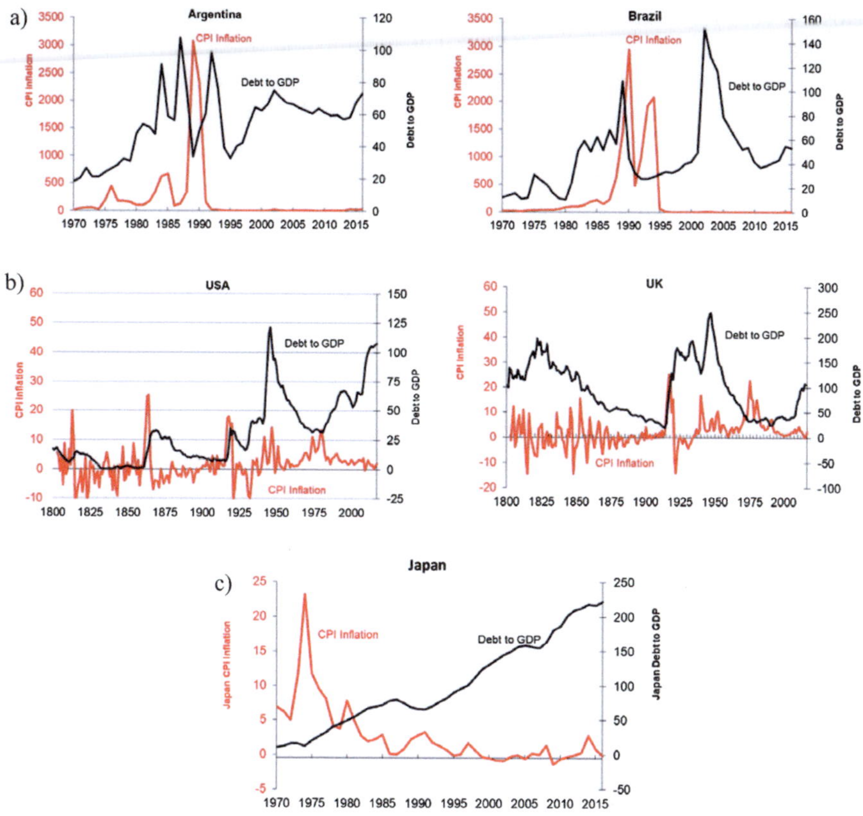

Fig. 3.1 Debt to GDP and inflation. (**a**) Debt to GDP and inflation, Argentina and Brazil 1975–2015 (Source: IMF Global Debt Database, OECD Economic Outlook). (**b**) Debt to GDP and inflation, the UK and the US 1800–2015 (Source: Bank of England A millennium of macroeconomic data for the UK, Version 3, April 2017, Rogoff and Reinhart, http://www.reinhartandrogoff.com/data/, OECD Economic Outlook). (**c**) Debt to GDP and inflation, Japan 1975–2015 (Source: OECD Economic Outlook)

high rates of inflation up to 3000% per year. After the collapse of the currency board in Argentina in January 2002, inflation went up to 26% following several years of deflation, but the spike in the debt to GDP ratio during that period triggered a real default on international, dollar denominated bonds.

The experience in the UK and the USA (Fig. 3.1b) shows that even when debt to GDP ratios shoot up above 120% or even 200%, this explosion need not automatically be followed by a debasement of currency. Instead, frequently they have been followed by a period of repression for the financial sector—imposing an effective tax on asset holders with real interest rates being below the rate of real growth: Nominal rates for government bonds have been lower than nominal growth rates for an extended period. Under such conditions, high nominal growth rates allowed to "grow out of debt" (see Reinhart & Sbrancia, 2015). In Japan, with nominal growth close to zero for more than two decades and debt to GDP shooting above 200%, again there is no link between debt to GDP and inflation (Fig. 3.1c). In contrast, in quite a few other countries hyperinflation started already at much lower debt to GDP levels even lower compared to those in Argentina and Brazil.

Obviously, things are much more complex. The key issue is how both monetary and fiscal authorities are expected to react with their future policy actions to current shocks in the economy. What is the optimal policy design? Usually, we look at the optimal solution of a social planner. But for some issues, it is more realistic to analyze assignments of different tasks to different agencies. So it may make sense to delegate the task of price stability to an independent central bank and assign fiscal policy (the task to decide about the path of government spending and taxation) to the treasury. Obviously, since both tasks are interdependent, at least some times there are bound to be inherent conflicts.

It is useful to distinguish between regimes with either monetary or fiscal authority being active or passive (Leeper & Walker, 2012). If, after some increase in debt, fiscal policy is expected to respond with tough measures reducing the level of debt either by raising taxes or cutting government spending, the treasury (the fiscal authority) is called passive. It takes the inter-temporal government wealth constraint serious and makes sure that this constraint holds all the time (without forcing the central bank to take actions). Such a regime is called "Ricardian regime". In that case, the central bank is called the active part (it is committed to push its own agenda, such as implementing price stability), whereas the treasury is acting passively. Note that the treasury is not meant to be passive in deciding about the optimal path for government spending. Quite the contrary. But when adjusting the spending path following shocks, it takes the inter-temporal wealth constraint seriously for a given price level. So it does not try to interfere with price level determination. In contrast, if the central bank follows a passive policy, it responds endogenously to movements by the treasury, the latter being committed to some predetermined path of taxes and spending, not adjusting that path passively as a response to exogenous shocks.

Usually, standard analysis simply assumes that the path of fiscal policy automatically adjusts such that monetary policy is allowed to control inflation. In our terminology, fiscal policy is assumed to be passive. Obviously, this is not always a correct description of history. Frequently, the treasury tries to impose constraints on central bank options, and things may end up pretty bad. Exactly for that reason, specific institutional arrangements (like the independence of central banks) have been established to force fiscal policy to be passive.

In order to understand these issues better, we first have to get a clear understanding of the link between central bank's seigniorage and the government budget constraint.

3.3 Seigniorage

The government (the treasury) raises taxes and issues bonds in order to finance government spending. However, it is also the monopoly producer of base money. Even though central banks in many countries all over the world acquired a status of independence for day-to-day operations, effectively they are part of the government. Revenue from seigniorage directly flows to the treasury. Central banks may have the power to decide how much seigniorage income is distributed to the treasury per period, but in the end the central bank's balance sheet is part of government's assets. Hence, in this section, we will treat seigniorage as government revenue.

Since costs for printing money are nearly negligible, issuing additional base money is one way for the government to generate revenues in order to get access to real resources. This revenue is called seigniorage. Keep in mind that we here are talking about base money provided by the central bank, not about deposits offered by private banks! In former days, before the use of fiat money (banknotes), seigniorage was evident: It was the difference between the revenue generated by denominating coins with some nominal value and the cost of the metals like gold and silver used as medium of transaction. Frequently, coins were gradually debased as currency. That is, the quantity of gold, silver, copper, or nickel contained in a coin was reduced. The purpose was to create more coins out of a given amount of specie and so to raise additional revenue for the sovereign at the expense of his citizens. This allowed building more fancy palaces, but of course it reduced the purchasing power of the coins (triggered inflation). With modern fiat money, the mechanism to generate revenue is essentially the same, except that production costs for fiat money (colored pieces of paper) are close to zero.

What are the gains for the treasury? Effectively, printing money enables the government to save on interest payments for government bonds. The higher the stock of base money, the lower the stock of (interest bearing) government bonds needed to finance a given path of spending and taxes. So essentially, seigniorage per period from issuing some stock of base money M is nothing else but the interest payments saved by being able to reduce net issuance of bonds exactly by that amount M. Of course, the nominal amount is irrelevant; what counts are the real resources obtained. So we should look at real money balances M/P. Frequently, it is even more useful to measure M/P as a share of real GDP, Y. Writing $k = M/PY$ for the ratio of money to nominal GDP we get:

$$S = i\ k. \tag{3.3.1}$$

By issuing base money, the government saves on interest payments for bonds. These savings (revenue from seigniorage) are due to the fact that private agents are willing to hold at least part of their assets in the form of noninterest-bearing central bank money instead of interest-bearing government bonds. Since private agents are willing to hold part of their wealth in the form of noninterest-bearing assets called money, the treasury does not need to issue interest-bearing bonds exactly equal to the amount of outstanding base money. Nowadays, most central banks pay some positive interest $0 \leq i_M \leq i$ at least on part of the base money such as bank reserves. If interest i_M is paid on money, seigniorage arises only from the difference between interest on money and interest on bonds, that is

$$S = (i - i_M)\ k. \tag{3.3.1a}$$

In the following sections, we analyze the case $i_M = 0$. It is straightforward to extend the analysis to more general conditions. Frequently, an alternative concept is used for measuring seigniorage, namely the additional amount of money printed in each period. This definition has strong intuitive appeal. The revenue from creating additional base money is equal to the increase in the money base ΔM. To measure this revenue as a share of GDP, we again have to divide ΔM by nominal GDP. This way, the real resources the government is able to extract as part of GDP from printing new money can be written as:

$$S_M = \frac{\Delta M}{PY} = \frac{\Delta M}{M}\frac{M}{PY} = \mu \cdot k. \tag{3.3.2}$$

S_M captures current revenue from printing new base money as share of GDP. As shown in the equation, we can reformulate that term using the definition of money growth rate $\mu = \Delta M / M$. S_M is equal to the growth rate of money times the money base k. What is the difference between S and S_M; how do they fit together? We will see that S_M is just a part of total seigniorage. The correct measure is S. Both concepts relate to each other in the following way. Use the Fisher equation $i = r + \pi^e$ and assume rational expectations, $\pi^e = E(\pi)$. Now let us do steady state analysis. In steady state, k—the money stock relative to GDP—will be constant across time. With a constant nominal interest rate, money demand as share of GDP will stay constant. So in equilibrium, the money stock grows proportional with nominal GDP. That is, the rate of money growth is the sum of the rate of real growth γ and inflation: $\mu = \gamma + \pi$. For given γ, the higher μ, the higher the rate of inflation $\pi = \mu - \gamma$. With rational expectations, the nominal rate of interest rises with μ proportionally, giving the relation $i = r + \mu - \gamma$. Using that relation, the difference between the two concepts can be seen as:

$$S = i \cdot k = \mu \cdot k + (r - \gamma) \cdot k = S_M + (r - \gamma) \cdot k. \tag{3.3.3}$$

In a dynamically efficient steady state the condition $r > \gamma$ must hold (see the focus box "*No-Ponzi Games and Transversality Condition*" in Sect. 1.2.4). Thus, S_M is lower than S by the factor $(r - \gamma) \cdot k$. The difference is that S_M only captures the revenue from printing new money. In order to derive the correct measure, we have to take into account that effective total net debt of government is lower the higher the assets held by the central bank (the higher the stock of money). In the central bank's balance sheet, noninterest-bearing liabilities (the stock of money) are equal to the central bank's assets which earn positive interest i. Here, we assume complete markets. If so, the risk-adjusted return on all assets held will be equal—there is no difference in return on government bonds, privately issued bonds, foreign reserves, or even gold. Arbitrage takes care that the risk-adjusted return will be the same for all assets in equilibrium. Take the case of gold as noninterest-bearing asset, for example. According to the Hotelling rule, the real price of gold (relative to other goods) is supposed to rise such that real return on gold is equal to the return of other assets.

▶ **Note** If we take risk into account, the effective return may differ across asset classes, but here we abstract from that issue. In particular, the risk tolerance of the central bank (as part of government) may differ from the willingness to hold risk by those private agents able to bear risk. By buying more risky assets in unconventional monetary operations (quantitative easing), the central bank may change the risk structure of assets held in the private sector. We ignore this possibility. In a representative agent economy, there would be no effect if the central bank buys risky assets the private sector is not willing to hold for the following reason: The representative agent will take into account that his tax obligations are getting more risky by this operation and so will take off-setting actions. After all, the overall risk does not disappear in the economy. So obviously, unconventional monetary operations can have real effects only if there are distortions in the market (like missing insurance markets against macro risks) which are not captured by a representative agent model. In an economy with distortions and heterogeneous agents, the central bank may be able to remove some of these distortions by buying risky assets. Providing social insurance mechanisms not offered in private markets may reduce overall risk in the private sector of the economy (see Chaps. 9 and 10).

Why is the effective real return of the money base k equal to $r - \gamma$? The nominal return of the assets held by the central bank is i. If nominal GDP grows at the rate $\pi + \gamma$, the assets must earn this rate just in order to keep the ratio of assets to GDP constant: The return must at least compensate for inflation and real growth to keep money as share of GDP constant. Hence, the effective real return is just $i - \pi - \gamma = r - \gamma$. Thus, the real savings from issuing money balances compared to issuing nominal government bonds with interest payments i is $(r - \gamma) \cdot k$. This term has to be added to the seigniorage from printing fresh money to calculate total seigniorage in steady state.

Up to now, when measuring $S = i\,k$, we simply took k as given, independent of central bank policy. But when the central bank increases the growth rate of money, this may cause a higher rate of inflation and so a higher nominal rate of interest. k will stay constant only as long as money demand does not respond to interest rates. When we analyze periods of hyperinflation, this is certainly no sensible assumption.

Philip Cagan studied periods of hyperinflation in history. Using a log-linear money demand function, he tried to estimate the money growth rate which

Table 3.1 Hyperinflation and Seigniorage

	Period	Highest inflation per month (%)	Average inflation per month (%)	Average rate of money growth per month (%)	Seigniorage maximizing growth rate of money
Hungary	Aug. 1945–Jul. 1946	1.295×10^{16} Jul. 1946	19,800	12,200	32
Poland	Jan. 1923–Jan. 1924	275 Oct. 1923	50	72	54
Germany	Aug. 1922–Nov. 1923	29,525 Oct. 1923	322	314	20
Greece	Nov. 1943–Nov. 1944	13,800 Oct. 1944	365	220	28
Republic of Serbia	Apr. 1992–Jan. 1994	309,000,000 Jan. 1994	10,700		

Source: Philip Cagan (1956), Table 1; Michael Bruno (1991)

maximizes seigniorage in steady state. As shown in Table 3.1, during hyperinflationary periods the actual growth rate of money was far above the rate maximizing steady state seigniorage. With money growth and inflation being so high—driving up nominal interest rates—real money demand declines such that we move to the wrong side of the Laffer curve. With a lower rate of money growth (inflation), money demand and thus revenue would have increased. This result is called Cagan's paradox and suggests that hyperinflation cannot be explained as an attempt to generate high steady-state revenue.

Cagan did not use the concept of rational expectations, but instead assumed adaptive expectations. That is, when forming their expectations agents do not try to fully anticipate the future path of the price level; instead they rely on past experience. With adaptive expectations, interest rates lag behind actual inflation. So the decline in money demand occurs at a slower rate, allowing the treasury to generate higher revenue at least for some intermediate time interval. When agents are slow to learn an increase in the rate of inflation may help to generate higher revenues at least for some time. Hyperinflations usually start at fairly low rates, but then they tend to accelerate pretty fast. Average monthly data may give a misleading picture. Even worse: Hyperinflations are short-lived episodes lasting around 20 months.

Due to lack of data, empirical analysis using monthly data usually include some period preceding hyperinflation (with lower rates), hence, monthly studies of money demand may give misleading results. Mladenovic and Petrovic (2010) used daily data for the last 6–7 months with most severe hyperinflation in Serbia in 1991–1992 (a period with one of the highest rates worldwide: The average monthly currency depreciation rate was 10,700% compared to 322% during German hyperinflation). They show that the public adjusts money demand at daily frequency in these extreme conditions, but the estimates for the demand elasticity are far lower than those obtained with monthly data. They conclude that the economy has been on the correct, increasing side of the Laffer curve most of the time during Serbian hyperinflation.

Overall, historical experience is hard to reconcile with some rational motivation for creating seigniorage as a long-term, steady-state outcome. Obviously, during such periods institutional arrangements required for generating sustainable tax revenues have broken down, forcing authorities to resort to other ways of financing. Alternatively, hyperinflationary episodes may be seen as a way to adjust the price level after some serious shock, wiping out a substantial part of past nominal debt obligations. This explanation is in line with the so-called fiscal theory of the price level.

3.4 The Government's Inter-temporal Budget Constraint

In Sect. 1.3, we introduced the government's budget constraint in a two-period model without seigniorage. It is straightforward to extend the analysis to (infinitely) many periods. If B_{t-1} is the level of (bond financed) nominal debt incurred at last period $t-1$, in nominal terms government debt evolves across time for some path of spending, tax revenue, and seigniorage according to the equation:

$$\Delta B_t = B_t - B_{t-1} = D_t = G_t - T_t - \Delta M_t + i_t B_{t-1} \tag{3.4.1}$$

Nominal debt increases $\Delta B > 0$ when a current deficit D has to be financed by issuing additional bond-financed debt. The bond-financed deficit D consists of (1) the primary deficit $PD = G_t - T_t$—the excess of government spending G over revenue from taxation T; and (2) the interest burden arising from debt issued in the past $i_t B_{t-1}$. The higher the seigniorage from printing money ΔM, the lower the need to issue new bonds. In general, ΔM is fairly small and so it is usually ignored when discussing debt sustainability. Here, we include it as part of revenue.

Whenever the interest burden from debt issued in the past exceeds current net revenue $i_t B_{t-1} > T_t - G_t + \Delta M_t$, total debt issued will increase. The higher the debt level and the higher the interest rate, the more likely debt rises even despite a primary surplus and positive seigniorage. But nominal values are rather uninformative. Why should we care if nominal debt increases simply because of inflation, as long as both nominal revenues increase at the same or even a faster rate? What really matters is the real deficit (imposing a real burden on the private sector), so we need to divide by the price level P. Growing debt will be of limited concern whenever real GDP is growing at the same rate or even faster than the real interest rate. To correct for these effects, we need to look at the ratio of nominal debt to nominal GDP $b_t = \frac{B_t}{P_t Y_t}$. How does the debt to GDP ratio evolve across time? The real burden of debt as share of GDP is the real interest (net of the real growth rate) to paid on the debt ratio b_t. What determines changes $\Delta b_t = b_t - b_{t-1}$ in that ratio? To find out, we simply rewrite Equation 3.4.1 as a ratio of current nominal GDP. As a first step, reformulate Equation 3.4.1 as a difference equation between B_t and B_{t-1}:

$$B_t = G_t - T_t - \Delta M_t + (1 + i_t) \cdot B_{t-1}.$$

The debt next year is the gross debt (including interest payments) inherited from last year plus the primary deficit. After dividing all terms by current nominal GDP, we get

$$\frac{B_t}{P_t Y_t} = \frac{G_t}{P_t Y_t} - \frac{T_t}{P_t Y_t} - \frac{\Delta M_t}{P_t Y_t} + (1 + i_t) \cdot \frac{B_{t-1}}{P_t Y_t}.$$

As shown in the focus box, this can be rewritten as the following simple and key difference equation for the debt to GDP ratio:

$$b_t - b_{t-1} = g_t - \tau_t - \mu \cdot k_t + \frac{1 + r_t}{1 + \gamma_t} \cdot b_{t-1}. \tag{3.4.2}$$

Focus Box: How to Derive Equation 3.4.2 from Equation 3.4.1

First, we normalize all terms in Equation 3.4.1 by current nominal GDP, using the following definitions:

$b_t = B_t / P_t Y_t$ is the debt to GDP ratio at time t;
$g_t = G_t / P_t Y_t$ is government spending relative to GDP;
$\tau_t = T_t / P_t Y_t$ is taxes relative to GDP.

The increase in money printed relative to GDP (seigniorage from money printing) can be expressed as: $\frac{\Delta M_t}{P_t\ Y_t} = \frac{\Delta M_t}{M_t} \cdot \frac{M_t}{P_t\ Y_t} = \mu \cdot k_t$ with μ as growth rate of money and k_t as money held as share of GDP. Using these ratios, we get from Equation 3.4.1 $b_t = g_t - \tau_t - \mu \cdot k_t + (1 + i_t) \cdot \frac{B_{t-1}}{P_t Y_t}$.

Finally, using the definition $P_t = (1 + \pi_t) P_{t-1}$; $Y_t = (1 + \gamma_t) Y_{t-1}$ and the Fisher equation $\frac{1 + i_t}{1 + \pi_t} = 1 + r_t$ we can simplify the last term as follows:

$$\frac{B_{t-1}}{P_t Y_t} \cdot (1 + i_t) = \frac{B_{t-1}}{P_{t-1} Y_{t-1}} \frac{1 + i_t}{(1 + \pi_t)(1 + \gamma_t)} = b_{t-1} \cdot \frac{1 + r_t}{1 + \gamma_t}.$$

The debt ratio depends on: (1) Primary deficit $g_t - \tau_t$—the difference between public spending as share of GDP and the tax rate (part of both spending and taxes are just transfers across agents; for dynamic effects, the net between spending and tax rate is crucial), (2) seigniorage as share of GDP $\mu \cdot k_t$ and (3) the real debt burden—the real interest to be paid on debt accumulated in the past, corrected for the growth rate in the economy: $\frac{1+r_t}{1+\gamma_t} b_{t-1}$. This burden is higher (a) the larger the debt accumulated in the past and (b) the larger the real rate of interest compared to the growth rate in the economy. This is fairly intuitive: Strong real growth dampens the debt to GDP ratio, easing the debt burden.

Given some initial debt to GDP ratio b_0, the inter-temporal government budget constraint imposes constraints on the feasible future path of the primary deficit $g - \tau$. To gain a better intuition, let us conduct a steady-state analysis with constant growth rates. Consider an economy with constant real rate of growth γ and constant real rate of interest r (this simplifies calculations and notation, but can easily be generalized). Let us also assume a constant money growth rate μ. If γ, μ, r stay constant across time, how will b_t evolve across time? To answer that question, we simply iterate Equation 3.4.2.

Starting with b_0, via iterated substitution we get for, say, three periods:

$$b_3 = (g_3 - \tau_3 - \mu \cdot k) + \left(\frac{1+r}{1+\gamma}\right)(g_2 - \tau_2 - \mu \cdot k) + \left(\frac{1+r}{1+\gamma}\right)^2 (g_1 - \tau_1 - \mu \cdot k) + \left(\frac{1+r}{1+\gamma}\right)^3 b_0.$$

Extending this to T periods gives:

$$b_T = \sum\nolimits_{\tau=1}^{\infty} \left(\frac{1+r}{1+\gamma}\right)^{T-\tau} (g_\tau - \tau_\tau - \mu \cdot k) + \left(\frac{1+r}{1+\gamma}\right)^T b_0.$$

Solving the equation for b_0 and extending $T \to \infty$ gives:

$$b_0 = \sum\nolimits_{\tau=1}^{\infty} \left(\frac{1+\gamma}{1+r}\right)^{\tau} (\tau_\tau - g_\tau + \mu \cdot k_t) + \lim_{T\to\infty} \left(\frac{1+\gamma}{1+r}\right)^T b_T. \tag{3.4.3}$$

Unless debt can be rolled over infinitely, outstanding initial debt needs to be covered by the present value of the primary surplus (the surplus of tax revenues over government spending) plus seigniorage. Since $r > \gamma$, the discount factor $((1+\gamma)/(1+r))^T$ converges to zero for $T \to \infty$. So in an infinite horizon context, the stock of debt issued as share of GDP needs never to be fully repaid. But it cannot grow at a rate faster than the rate at which the discount factor goes to zero. Nevertheless, the government operating within its long-term budget has to take the No-Ponzi-Game condition into account: Private agents are not willing to hold public debt unless the present value of the future debt level is non-positive (see Chap. 1). This imposes the transversality condition that the last term in Equation 3.4.3 cannot be positive:

$$\lim_{T\to\infty} \left(\frac{1+\gamma}{1+r}\right)^T b_T = 0. \tag{3.4.4}$$

So we get

$$b_0 = \sum_{\tau=1}^{\infty} \left(\frac{1+\gamma}{1+r}\right)^{\tau} (\tau_\tau + \mu \cdot k_t - g_\tau). \tag{3.4.3b}$$

The initial debt to GDP ratio must be covered by a future primary surplus including seigniorage revenue in present value terms, discounted by the effective net real interest rate $r - \gamma$—the real rate corrected for the growth rate in the economy. Just as the value of a firm being the present value of all future dividends, the value of current government debt has to be backed by the present value of future surplus of tax revenues over government spending and seigniorage revenue.

Of course, τ_t and g_t may vary substantially over time. To gain a better intuition, let us introduce the notion of the permanent tax ratio $\overline{\tau}$ and spending ratio $\overline{g}$ which give the same present value as the expected, possibly fluctuating stream of tax revenues respectively government spending for $T \to \infty$:

$$\sum_{\tau=1}^{\infty} \left(\frac{1+\gamma}{1+r}\right)^{\tau} \tau_t = \sum_{\tau=1}^{\infty} \left(\frac{1+\gamma}{1+r}\right)^{\tau} \overline{\tau} \approx \frac{\overline{\tau}}{r-\gamma},$$

$$\sum_{\tau=1}^{\infty} \left(\frac{1+\gamma}{1+r}\right)^{\tau} g_t = \sum_{\tau=1}^{\infty} \left(\frac{1+\gamma}{1+r}\right)^{\tau} \overline{g} \approx \frac{\overline{g}}{r-\gamma}$$

using the approximation $\sum_{\tau=1}^{\infty} \left(\frac{1+\gamma}{1+r}\right)^{\tau} \approx \frac{1}{r-\gamma}$

Substituting $\overline{\tau}$ and $\overline{g}$ (and $\overline{k}$ as steady-state base money to GDP) in Equation 3.4.3b gives:

$$b_0 = \sum_{\tau=1}^{\infty} \left(\frac{1+\gamma}{1+r}\right)^{\tau} (\overline{\tau} - \overline{g} + \mu \cdot \overline{k}\,) \approx \frac{\overline{\tau} - \overline{g} + \mu \cdot \overline{k}}{r-\gamma}. \tag{3.4.5}$$

This condition has a straightforward intuitive interpretation: The current level of debt to GDP has to be equal to the present value of future permanent revenue from primary surplus (as ratio to GDP) plus seigniorage—discounted by the effective real interest rate[1] $(1+r)/(1+\gamma) - 1 \approx r - \gamma$.

Key Assumptions

1. The real interest rate exceeds the growth rate: $r > \gamma$ (otherwise, there would be no need to care about wealth constraints—any debt could be paid back in finite time if the real growth rate exceeds the real rate of interest (note that the right hand side in Equation 3.4.5 would switch signs with $r - \gamma < 0$).
2. The transversality condition holds: $\lim_{T\to\infty} \left(\frac{1+\gamma}{1+r}\right)^{T} b_T = 0$.

[1] This approximation is strictly true only for continuous time analysis. But it holds also for discrete time analysis as long as time intervals are small.

Relation Between Different Seigniorage Concepts and the Government Wealth Constraint

If we analyze the government's balance sheet, we need to distinguish between the gross debt $\widetilde{b}$ issued by the treasury (as share of nominal GDP), and the assets b held by the private sector. Since part of the gross debt is held by the central bank, it should not count as net debt for the consolidated public sector. Even though independent central banks can decide on their own what share of profits to pay out to the treasury each year, they are part of the public sector. The central bank's assets are equal to the money base k. The central bank may hold quite different asset classes other than government bonds. These assets may differ in their risk characteristics. During the financial crisis, some of the assets bought by central banks have been considered to be rather toxic—with highly uncertain recovery value. They bought bonds issued by private firms, by private banks, or mortgage asset-backed securities. However, using market values for proper accounting, if we consolidate the balance sheets of treasury and central bank, in the end the real burden of government debt is just the net debt held by private sector.

If we consolidate the assets held by the central bank, net government debt is $b_t = \widetilde{b}_t - k_t$. In Equations 3.4.3 and 3.4.3b we defined the government wealth constraint in terms of net debt b_t. We assumed that revenue generate by future money printing flows directly to the government. As a thought experiment, let us now first separate the balance sheets of the treasury and the central bank and assume seigniorage from printing money accrues to the central bank. Excluding central bank's current assets and the present value of her future revenue from money printing, the government's total gross debt burden would need to be financed by excess of future tax revenues over government spending such as:

$$\widetilde{b}_0 = \sum\nolimits_{t=1}^{\infty} \left(\frac{1+\gamma}{1+r}\right)^t (\tau_t - g_t) \approx \frac{\overline{\tau} - \overline{g}}{r - \gamma}.$$

At the end of each year, however, the central bank distributes profits (revenues minus cost) to the treasury. To simplify, assume that operating costs are zero, so profits equal revenue—that is they equal seigniorage as defined in Equation 3.3.1 respectively Equation 3.3.2:

$$S_t = i \cdot k_t = \mu \cdot k_t + (r - \gamma) \cdot k_t.$$

(continued)

In real terms, the present value of central bank's steady-state seigniorage is

$$\frac{i \cdot k_0}{r - \gamma} = \frac{S_M}{r - \gamma} + \frac{(r - \gamma) \cdot k_0}{r - \gamma} = \frac{\mu}{r - \gamma} \cdot k_0 + k_0.$$

This term can be split in two parts: (a) the present value of the revenue accruing from future money printing and (b) the present value of the assets currently held by the central bank. The latter just amounts to the initial stock of base money k_0—the sum of all the central bank money issued already in the past.

Let us now take into account that the central bank is part of the government. Thus the government's gross debt is partly covered by the present value of seigniorage revenue. Only the remaining part needs to be financed—in present value terms—by an excess of future tax revenues over government spending. Measured in terms of gross debt $\widetilde{b}_0$, the effective government's wealth constraint is

$$\widetilde{b}_0 = \frac{\tau - g}{r - \gamma} + \frac{S_0}{r - \gamma} = \frac{\tau - g + i\,k_0}{r - \gamma} = \frac{\tau - g + \mu\,k}{r - \gamma} + k_0 = b_0 + k_0.$$

Obviously, the government's gross debt $\widetilde{b}_0$ is equal to net debt b_0 held by the private sector as defined in Equation 3.4.3b plus the central bank's assets k_0.The intuition behind is that the interest burden for the government is alleviated by the fact that no interest has to be paid on base money.

Of course, payments of interest on base money reduces seigniorage: $S_t = (i - i_M) \cdot k_t$. Suppose the central bank pays interest on reserves i_M at the same rate as the rate for short-term treasury bonds. Obviously, $S_t = 0$ for $i = i_M$. In that case, the Friedman rule holds—there are no longer opportunity costs for holding money. At the same time, there will be no seigniorage income. Evidently, $i = 0$ is just a special implementation of such a policy.

3.5 Sustainability of Debt

What limits does the government wealth constraint impose for the debt ratio? Under what conditions will the debt ratio explode, with risk to move on the verge to bankruptcy? The debt ratio will explode unless current debt obligations are covered by a future primary surplus which, in present value terms, makes sure that the wealth constraint holds. But frequently, governments run persistent deficits. Will a government with a constant deficit necessarily run into solvency problems? Does it make sense to impose some upper limit to the deficit ratio d or should we even impose conditions requiring a positive primary surplus?

We have to distinguish between primary deficit and total deficit. The latter also includes interest payments on debt issued in the past. How will the debt ratio evolve when the deficit ratio for the overall budget (including debt service) stays constant? Will the debt ratio explode? Under what conditions does the debt to GDP ratio b_t converge to some stable steady-state level? b_t stays constant whenever effective real net interest payments on outstanding debt are just offset by a corresponding primary surplus plus seigniorage revenue. The surplus does not have to cover all nominal interest payments, since part of the nominal burden will be alleviated by a rising nominal GDP (due to inflation and real growth), so the debt-to-GDP ratio can be stable even when the overall deficit is positive. Let us assume the government tries to keep the long-run ratio of nominal deficit to GDP constant. That is, it aims to stabilize the sum of primary deficit and interest payments on debt outstanding relative to GDP: $d_t = g_t - \tau_t - \mu \cdot k_t + i \cdot b_{t-1} = d$.

Will the real debt ratio explode with such a policy or instead converge toward some stable, sustainable level? Using the Fisher equation in Equation 3.4.2, the debt ratio evolves according to[2]:

$$b_t = g_t - \tau_t - \mu \cdot k + \frac{1+i}{(1+\pi)(1+\gamma)} \cdot b_{t-1}$$
$$\approx g_t - \tau_t - \mu \cdot k + (1 + i - \pi - \gamma) \cdot b_{t-1} = b_{t-1} + d - (\pi + \gamma) \cdot b_{t-1}.$$

Hence, the debt ratio evolves according to the difference equation:

$$b_t - b_{t-1} = d - (\pi + \gamma) \cdot b_{t-1}. \tag{3.5.1}$$

As shown in Fig. 3.2 this difference equation converges toward some steady-state debt ratio $\lim_{T\to\infty} b_T \approx b^* = \frac{d}{\pi+\gamma}$ independent of the initial ratio. The steady-state debt to GDP ratio will be higher the higher the deficit ratio and the lower the growth rate of nominal GDP. Assume, for example,[3] the expected real rate of growth is $\gamma = 0.03 = 3\%$ and the target rate of inflation is $\pi = 0.02 = 2\%$. Imposing a limit of $d = 0.03$ for the overall deficit, b is then expected to converge to $b^* = 0,03/0,05 = 0.6 = 60\%$ independent of the starting point. Of course, the lower γ and π, the higher will be the steady state ratio b^*.

[2]As long as i, π, g are all small, we can use the approximation $\frac{1+i}{(1+\pi)(1+\gamma)} = 1 + i - \pi - \gamma$. This way, we get a very tractable solution, even though it strictly holds only for continuous time analysis.

[3]These numbers characterize the average rates for the European economy at the time when the Maastricht criteria have been designed.

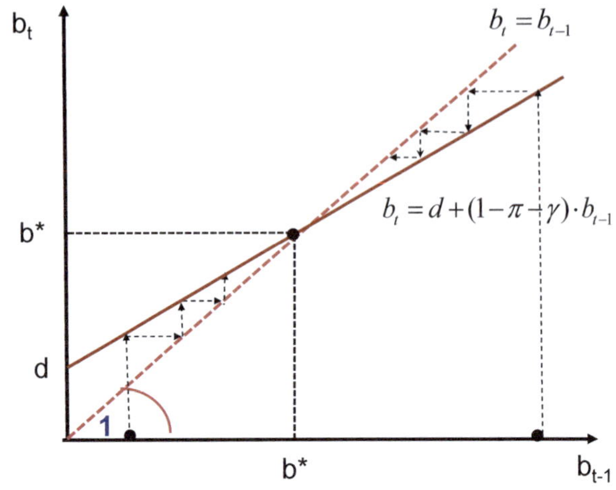

Fig. 3.2 Debt sustainability: convergence toward a steady state

Sustaining b^* as steady state requires to enforce the permanent primary surplus[4] $ps^* = (r - \gamma) \cdot b^*$. The higher the steady state b^*, the higher the tax burden imposed on the economy (the larger the primary surplus needed) for a given net real interest rate $r - \gamma$. b^* is sustainable as long as $ps^* = (r - \gamma) \cdot b^*$ can be implemented in the economy. Along the adjustment path toward the steady state, the primary surplus adjusts such that the total deficit ratio d is kept constant. The higher the initial debt ratio, the higher the interest rate burden, and therefore, the higher the surplus ps_t needed to keep d constant.

$ps^* = (r - \gamma) \cdot b^*$ is the key equation for understanding the inter-temporal government budget constraint and its implication for the path of fiscal sustainability. In any economy, there is some upper bound $\tau_{\max} < 1$ (the maximum enforceable tax rate: Nobody would be willing to work and produce voluntary for $\tau = 1$) and some lower bound $g_{\min} > 0$—the minimum level of government spending needed to make sure that the economy keeps going. An economy without any public goods ($g = 0$) guaranteeing enforcement of property rights by legal authorities and police, providing basic education, etc., cannot be sustainable. Hence there is some maximum level of public debt ratio beyond which bankruptcy sets in:

$$b_t \leq b_{\max} = (\overline{\tau}_{\max} - \overline{g}_{\min} + \mu \cdot \overline{k}_{\max}) \sum\nolimits_{t=1}^{\infty} \left(\frac{1 + y}{1 + r}\right)^t$$
$$\approx \frac{\overline{\tau}_{\max} - \overline{g}_{\min} + \mu \cdot \overline{k}_{\max}}{r - y}. \tag{3.5.2}$$

One may debate strongly about how to calculate the exact bounds for the critical $b_{\max}$. Note that this critical bound very much depends on the expected long-term

[4]Note that $(\pi + \gamma) \cdot b^* = d = g - \tau - \mu \cdot k + i \cdot b^*$. With $i = r + \pi$ this implies $\tau - g + \mu \cdot k = (r - \gamma) \cdot b^*$.

growth rate and on the expected long-term interest rate. But whatever the exact critical boundary may be, it is evident that a fiscal policy path implying b_t to increase steadily over time runs the risk of exceeding that critical boundary—it runs the risk of being not sustainable. Given that negative shocks (such as an increase in the real rate $r - y$) may adversely affect $b_{\max}$ and that serious shocks to the economy (like a financial crisis) may result in a drastic sudden increase in b_t, it seems reasonable to impose some prudent cushion for the steady-state level $b_t \leq b^* << b_{\max}$. A prudent policy should provide fiscal space for absorbing shocks by targeting a sufficiently low b^*.

Since it is rather arbitrary to estimate the rates $\overline{\tau}_{max}$ and $\overline{g}_{min}$, sustainability analysis in practice usually tries, as pragmatic approach, to calculate the adjustment in primary surplus required for stabilizing the current debt ratio, given reasonable assumptions about long-term growth and interest rates. Alternatively, one may aim to lower b_t to some desired target rate b^*_{t+T} within a given time horizon T. Frequently, policy makers are reluctant to enforce adjustment hoping to postpone tough, unpopular measures and betting that some positive shock in the future may alleviate the pressure. If so, the debt ratio is likely to increase further, forcing a stricter adjustment in the future.

In this section, we assumed that all adjustment will be done by fiscal policy by changing the path of public spending and taxation. In reality, usually there is also pressure on monetary authorities to help to ease the burden of adjustment. The debt burden can be alleviated by raising seigniorage revenue (implying a higher rate of inflation) or by lowering the real value of nominal debt: An immediate increase in the current price level reduces the real value of outstanding debt. Obviously, both ways conflict with the objective to control the price level and/or the rate of inflation. We will discuss potential conflicts between monetary and fiscal authorities in the next section.

3.6 Adjustment Mechanisms: Monetary Versus Fiscal Adjustment

If some shock shifts the initial debt to GDP ratio b_0 upwards, which adjustment mechanisms for government budget and monetary policy may be required? Does the government need to cut future spending and raise taxes? Will it try to bring down the debt to GDP ratio aggressively or will it try to stabilize it at a higher level? Will seigniorage be raised to finance the gap or will the price level rise, eroding the real value of initial debt? Obviously there is a huge variety of adjustment mechanisms with quite different policy implications. The impact on inflation and the price level strongly depends on which of these measures financial markets expect to be taken in the future. As Fig. 3.1 has illustrated impressively, inflation responds quite differently to increases in b_0 in different settings. Let us have a closer look at the government wealth constraint. It is straightforward to see that there is a need to coordinate fiscal and monetary policy.

$$b_0 = \frac{B_0}{P_0 \cdot Y_0} = \sum\nolimits_{\tau=1}^{\infty} \left(\frac{1+\gamma}{1+r}\right)^{\tau} (\tau_\tau + \mu \cdot k_t - g_\tau). \tag{3.4.3b}$$

In Equation 3.4.3b, the initial level of nominal debt B_0 is given from promises made in the past. We also take the real level of GDP Y_0 as given. The current price level P_0 is determined as a forward-looking variable, determined by the expected path of monetary policy. If (net) government debt is close to maximum sustainable level, some adjustment has to take place. Since there are quite different options to cope with looming solvency problems, there is an evident link between public debt and the pressure on the central bank to change its policy course. Effectively, there are four different ways how to adjust when the debt ratio is too high. Current and future policies are interlinked, and there is some indeterminacy about what is going to happen. In order to illustrate the issues involved with different options, let us consider a simple example. Assume that initially the economy is in a steady-state equilibrium with some mix of $\overline{\tau}, \overline{g}, \mu$ ensuring solvency and price stability with inflation equal to the target rate. Then, a shock triggers an increase in current government spending ΔG_0, initially financed via deficit, pushing the initial debt level up by $\Delta G_0 = \Delta B_0$. The impact on the economy depends crucially on the type of adjustment to that shock private agents are expecting both by the government (the treasury) and the central bank.

(A) The treasury may be expected to react to the increase in nominal debt obligations by cutting spending or raising taxes sometime in the future as described in Sect. 3.6.1 or (B) the central bank may be expected to react by loosening monetary policy in order to raise future seigniorage (via higher money growth or less aggressive response of interest rates to inflation as analyzed in Sect. 3.6.2). In both scenarios, the government's wealth constraint will be strictly obeyed whatever the price level P_0 is. The only question is which agency moves. The effects of monetary policy actions strongly depend on the fiscal policy actions they stimulate. If they stimulate none, monetary policy cannot control price level and inflation. Alternatively, (C) the initial price level may jump (as suggested by the "fiscal theory of the price level"—see Sect. 3.6.3). This way, adjustment of the nominal price level brings the real burden of debt in line with future revenue. Finally (D), there can be a real default on government debt outstanding (take, as just one of many cases, the default on Argentinian bonds in 2002).

3.6.1 Fiscal Adjustment

In regime A, the central bank actively and aggressively pursues its objective (to implement some target rate of inflation π^*). In contrast, the treasury responds passively. It is expected to always adjust future taxes to the state of government debt—that is, present value of future primary surplus will be increased in order to satisfy the wealth constraint for any given price level P_0. Similarly, it will also adjust ex post taxes or spending to any change in P_0. With deflation raising the real value of debt, policy needs to be tightened. Following Eric Leeper, regime (A) is called **active monetary and passive fiscal policy**.

In this regime, monetary policy is able to target inflation—it can actively implement its inflation target. In contrast, fiscal policy as passive player ensures the validity of the wealth constraint. The tax authority must be willing and able to raise taxes in the face of rising government debt in order to stabilize the debt to GDP ratio.

$$\sum_{\tau=1}^{\infty}\left(\frac{1+\gamma}{1+r}\right)^{\tau}\Delta(\tau_t - g_t) = \frac{\Delta B_0}{P_0 \cdot Y_0}.$$

In this regime, fiscal policy is passive in the sense that the treasury commits to raise the future primary surplus by increasing taxes and/or cutting future spending whenever real debt increases. This strategy takes both the central bank path $\mu \cdot k_t$ and also the real debt ratio $b_0 = B_0/P_0$ as given. The reaction analyzed in the real model outlined in Chap. 1 describes such an adjustment process. The treasury adjusts its future plans for spending and taxes for any given path of monetary policy. It is committed to raise the future surplus so as to finance a current deficit. Adjustment to the real value of the debt occurs via changes in the future primary surplus. The response to spending shocks may be delayed, but it must be unbounded: There is a commitment that the primary surplus will increase in proportion to real debt b, no matter how large real debt may get.

In this regime, there is no risk that the central bank may be forced to deviate from own targets such as maintaining price stability. In such a regime, the treasury takes the inter-temporal wealth constraint as given even out of equilibrium. Sometimes this is called **Ricardian regime**.

3.6.2 Adjustment of Seigniorage Revenue (Sargent–Wallace)

In scenario B, the treasury actively commits to some future path of primary surplus, and the central bank has to adjust passively to make sure that the government wealth constraint holds after the shock. The "active" tax policy sets the tax rate independently of government debt. It makes realized transfers equal to promised transfers. In contrast, monetary policy now "passively" adjusts the nominal interest rate so as to ensure that the wealth constraint holds. Following Eric Leeper, regime (B) is called **passive monetary and active fiscal policy**.

The central bank needs to raise the rate of money growth (and so inflation), taking the path of government spending and taxes as given. Of course, raising μ, by increasing inflation and interest rates, will negatively affect real money demand $k(i)$. As long as the economy is on the increasing side of the Laffer curve, nevertheless, an increase in μ will generate more revenue from seigniorage.

$$\sum_{\tau=1}^{\infty}\left(\frac{1+\gamma}{1+r}\right)^{\tau}\Delta\mu_t\cdot k_t=\frac{\Delta B_0}{P_0\cdot Y_0}.$$

In a famous paper called "Some unpleasant monetarist arithmetic", Sargent and Wallace (1975) showed that if the treasury is not willing to move (to consolidate its budget, committing to a higher primary surplus in the future after an increase in current deficits) and the central bank tries to play tough as well, the following paradox may arise: A temporary tight monetary policy may lead to an increase even in the current price level $P_{0.}$ The reason is that because of the delay in policy adjustment, private agents rationally anticipate that in the future, the rate of inflation needs to be even higher in order to satisfy the government wealth constraint Equation 3.4.3b. As seen in Chap. 2, anticipated higher expected future inflation can raise current price level. This will be true whenever money demand is sufficiently elastic. In principle, tight money today tends to dampen the price level. But given that the treasury is not willing to adjust primary surplus, a policy of tight money right now is bound to trigger even higher rates of inflation in the future. The anticipation of that effect even far in the future dampens current real money demand already today. With elastic demand, the second effect dominates.

If treasury and central bank have different objectives (policy being not determined by a unique—possibly welfare maximizing—government agency), the interaction between the two players can be modelled as a chicken game: Who will blink first—fiscal or monetary authority? Who imposes discipline on whom? Sargent and Wallace (1975) argue that the natural assumption is that the fiscal authority moves first (by committing to some path of primary surplus), and monetary policy must be determined in a way consistent to that path. If so, the central bank can make money tighter now only by making it looser in the future. They suggest that changes in mechanism design may help to bind monetary authority by committing to an announced fixed rule (such as a Taylor rule). Imposing strict rules may be seen as attempts to change the rules of the game such that the central bank can commit not to adjust.

Focus Box: Chicken Game and the Role of Commitment

Let us analyze a stylized game between fiscal and monetary authority on the verge of bankruptcy, limiting each actor to just two strategies. The fiscal authority can choose between (1) a high deficit with excessive spending ($d = 1$) or (2) debt consolidation (fiscal reform) ($d = 0$).

(continued)

The monetary authority can choose between

1. Price stability ($\pi = 0$) or
2. Using the printing press to avoid bankruptcy, triggering high inflation ($\pi = 1$). So the payoff matrix of a game with actions chosen independently is captured in Fig. 3.3.

The first number in each payoff matrix represents the central bank's payoff, the second number the treasury's payoff. Both authorities have different objectives; so their payoffs differ with the strategies implemented. ($\pi = 0$, $d = 1$) is not sustainable for long. It is bound to end up in bankruptcy, giving both authorities the worst payoff (which is normalized to 0). Fiscal consolidation ($d = 0$) is preferred by the central bank (allowing her to achieve price stability $\pi = 0$). With this combination, the central bank achieves the highest payoff (4). For the treasury, however, implementing spending cuts and raising taxes is unpopular, so its payoff is higher when the central bank gives in and resorts to the printing press. The combination ($\pi = 1$, $d = 1$) is the preferred outcome from the treasury's point of view, but it gives a low payoff of two to the central bank. The other way round with ($\pi = 0$, $d = 0$). When both authorities change their course ($\pi = 1$, $d = 0$), bankruptcy is avoided and budget surplus achieved, giving both a payoff normalized to three.

With simultaneous moves, there are two **Nash-equilibria** in pure strategies: Both (1) ($\pi = 1$, $d = 1$) and (2) ($\pi = 0$, $d = 0$) are best response equilibria.

If treasury trusts that the central bank will give in first, it is best not to blink but rather continue with excessive spending. If the central bank expects the treasury not to blink, it is best for her to give in, giving the outcome (1). Symmetrically, (2) is also an equilibrium. But there is a high risk that neither of these equilibria will occur, but instead rather the equilibrium in randomized strategies with a high risk of realizing the worst outcome.

With sequential moves, the possibility of commitment is crucial. In the game tree below, again both ($d = 0$, $\pi = 0$) and ($d = 1$, $\pi = 1$) are Nash equilibria. But if the treasury moves first as in Fig. 3.4, ($\pi = 0$, $d = 0$) is not subgame perfect. ($\pi = 1$, $d = 1$) is the only subgame perfect outcome.

If, in contrast to the game tree shown below, the central bank would have the power to commit to a no-bailout strategy right from the start, the sequencing of moves would reverse, ($\pi = 0$, $d = 0$) as subgame perfect solution.

Fig. 3.3 Chicken game between fiscal and monetary authority

		Monetary authority	
		$\pi = 1$	$\pi = 0$
Fiscal authority	$d = 0$	3,3	2,4
	$d = 1$	4,2	0

Fig. 3.4 Sequential game between fiscal and monetary authority

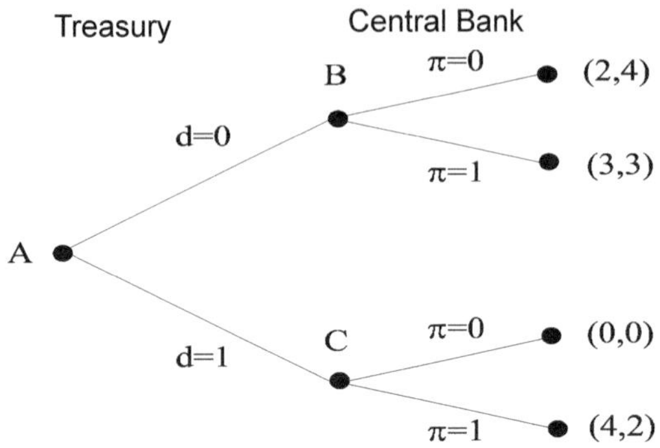

3.6.3 Adjustment of the Price Level: The Fiscal Theory of the Price Level

Both regime A and regime B look at fairly conventional policy measures, both taking the initial price level P_0 and thus the initial real value of debt as given. Implicitly, in both regimes debt is assumed to be denominated in real terms (inflation-indexed) and will always be honored. In reality, however, most debt is denominated in nominal terms. In that case, fiscal shocks can be dampened simply by letting the price level adjust:

$$\Delta P_0 = \Delta B_0.$$

The initial price level P_0 adjusts such that the right-hand side of Equation 3.4.3b stays unchanged. In that case, a change in the price level is the adjustment mechanism to bring the real market value of nominal debt in line with the expected real backing of debt as defined by the right-hand side of the equation. This mechanism is called the "**fiscal theory of the price level**."

The fiscal theory of the price level, first propagated by Leeper (1991) and Sims (1994) (see also Cochrane, 2011; Leeper, 2013; Leeper & Walker, 2012; Woodford, 2003), suggests a quite a different adjustment mechanism for the price level. After a shock to B_0 the price level P_0 simply jumps such that, in equilibrium, the wealth constraint holds again. Initially, the fiscal theory of the price level was seen as an esoteric, rather arcane special case. But it illustrates a fairly simple important point: Suppose both the treasury and the central bank want to be active players, not willing to adjust in the future. If the treasury is committed to some path for government spending and taxation and the central bank to some inflation target, independent of the shocks occurring, such shocks are likely to trigger strong fluctuations in the price level.

This shows that some form of fiscal backing is essential for the determinacy of the price level. If fiscal policy forces the central bank to monetize debt, monetary policy may lose control of the price level, with monetary backing replacing fiscal backing. Independent central banks with clear mandates to target price stability can help to prevent such monetary backing, but some form of fiscal backing is essential for effective control of inflation. Fiat money equilibria must have fiscal backing (see Sims, 2013). Such a fiscal backing may be a commitment of fiscal policy to switch to generating a stable primary surplus if the price level gets too high. This places a lower bound on the real value of government debt and so guarantees a floor for the value of nominal debt liabilities, eliminating unstable solutions (exploding price level) as equilibria. In a symmetric way, fiscal policy needs to commit to running primary deficits when inflation is below target to eliminate price level imploding.

As pointed out by Sims (2013), some fluctuations in the price level may be an efficient insurance mechanism against severe shocks. Nominal long term government debt can act as a fiscal cushion—a buffer to dampen severe shocks, helping to implement an optimal state dependent tax policy. When taxes are distorting, it is efficient to smooth tax rates across time. Fluctuations in the price level can provide such a tax smoothing, holding interest rates and taxes constant. Sims (2013) shows that unexpected inflations and deflations tend to roughly offset surprise fiscal stresses in "well-managed economies", producing non trivial effects on the government budget constraint. Effectively, price fluctuations work as insurance mechanism by making the real value of long-term debt state contingent. So for some shocks inflation may act as a welfare improving cushion. The fiscal theory of the price level provides a foundation for that idea and illustrates the challenges involved.

The absence of such insurance may be quite costly in welfare terms. On the other hand, in not so well-managed economies there may be strong incentives to misuse such an insurance mechanism. If financial markets fear that spikes in the price level may simply be triggered to avoid unpleasant fiscal adjustment, they are likely to charge high risk premiums. This creates the possibility of multiple, Pareto ranked equilibria (see Sect. 10.1), illustrating the need for commitment devices to not abuse such an insurance mechanism: If financial markets regard the probability for a spike in the price level as high, they charge a high risk premium, raising the burden of debt and so making it more likely to trigger the spike. In contrast, if so risk premiums are low with the risk of such a spike considered to be small, the debt burden stays low so there is no reason to trigger the spike.

How should mechanisms be designed to rule out the problem of multiple equilibria? If financing excessive government spending via money risks triggering hyperinflation, how can we cut the link between government debt and central bank financing? Based on the devastating experience with hyperinflation during the Weimar republic, the newly created Deutsche Bundesbank in Germany was explicitly prohibited to buy government bonds on the primary market. Following that role model, the ECB constitution (as written in the Maastricht treaty adopted in Maastricht on 10 December 1991) rules out direct lending to euro area governments. Fiscal rules in the Maastricht treaty try to impose fiscal discipline on government debt (such as the limit of 60% for debt to GDP ratio and 3% for deficit to GDP ratio).

The rules in the Maastricht treaty for the design of the ECB are a good (or, as it turns out, rather badly designed) example for such a mechanism design. Historical experience taught that fiscal-monetary interaction often consists of attempts by the fiscal authorities to get the central bank to buy more government debt than is consistent with stable inflation. If the treasury pursues its own interest for political economy reasons, this can result in a pretty bad outcome and may justify a design forcing the treasury to be passive. An institutional design in the euro area with a single, large central bank and fractured fiscal authorities of many small national treasuries was seen as less likely to be subject to this inflationary pressure from the fiscal side than in the usual single-country fiscal-monetary pair of institutions. For that reason, it seemed to be a great idea to assign the task of price stability as a clear mandate to an independent central bank without a central fiscal counterpart.

This design is based on the idea that a determined central bank can always control inflation by controlling money growth. But a central bank can actively (independently) determine the time path of prices only if its policy actions trigger a validating response from the fiscal authorities. There is no automatic mechanism by which fiscal discipline can be compelled by a central bank that controls money growth. Unfortunately, the Euro crisis demonstrated the fault lines in this design—There are serious gaps in the institutional structure of the Euro Area for the following reason: The inflexible design ignores that central banks controlling fiat money may play a crucial welfare improving role as lender of last resort.

For such central bank activities, there is a crucial need for fiscal backing, since by nature these actions are subject to considerable fiscal risks that have to be borne by the treasury (or rather, in the end, by the taxpayer). Without central fiscal counterpart, however, it is hardly feasible to undertake such actions without risking some impact on price stability. As argued above, under some conditions, movements in the price level may be the optimal response to severe shocks.

Such adjustment mechanisms are not feasible if debt is denominated in foreign currency or if the acting government has no control over central bank policy (as is the case for countries in the EMU or for US states, which do not have their own currencies). Debt issued in foreign currency is real debt, indexed to local inflation by exchange rate adjustments. In that case, an explicit real default on the debt issued is required in order to achieve a corresponding reduction in the real debt burden. From an economic point of view, an increase in the price level seems to be nothing but an implicit default, effectively lowering the real burden of debt just as with an explicit legal default. But legally, nominal and real government debt are quite different, as are inflation and outright default. Unanticipated high inflation does impose losses on investors in nominal sovereign debt, but it does not involve renegotiation or court proceedings. Contracted payments are made and the securities remain tradable (Sims, 2013).

3.7 Summary

In this chapter we studied the interaction between monetary and fiscal policy in detail. Frequently, monetary policy actions have some fiscal impact, hence, the effectiveness of monetary policy strongly depends on the response of fiscal policy. We showed how central bank's seigniorage revenue modifies the government budget inter-temporal constraint. In a sustainability analysis of debt, we characterized conditions for the debt to GDP ratio converging to a stable long run steady state. The condition for debt sustainability helps to understand why the reaction both of fiscal and monetary policy (primary surplus and seigniorage revenue) to shocks are crucial for determining the rate of inflation.

In some periods in history, hyperinflation seems to have been triggered by exploding government debt. But there is no clear relation between debt and inflation. Other episodes are characterized by high debt and deflation. Obviously, the result strongly depends on the responses both of monetary and fiscal agencies. We distinguished between different regimes, depending on who is the active player. In one regime, fiscal policy automatically adjusts such that monetary policy is allowed to control inflation. Here monetary policy is active, free to pursue its objectives, with fiscal policy assumed to be passive, being constrained by central bank actions. But there can also be an alternative regime, with active fiscal and passive monetary policy. In that regime, the price level is determined by fiscal behavior with debt being stabilized by the central bank adjusting either seignorage revenue or simply the price level. We analyzed both regimes. In the regime with active monetary policy, sometimes called Ricardian regime, inflation and price level are determined as in the quantity theory of money. With active fiscal policy, the outcome can be quite different. Following Sargent and Wallace, we showed that adjustment of seignorage may result in "unpleasant monetarist arithmetic": A temporary tightening of monetary policy may even lead to an increase even in the current price level. With government debt issued in nominal terms, fluctuations in the price level may adjust the real value of debt, bringing expected future revenues in line with the current nominal value of debt. Some fluctuations in the price level may provide an efficient insurance mechanism against aggregate shocks. We analyzed the fiscal theory of the price level and characterized the challenges involved for designing credible mechanism to prevent misuse of such an insurance scheme.

References

Bruno, M. (1991). High inflation and the nominal anchors of an open economy. In *Princeton essays in international finance* (Vol. 183). Princeton, NJ: International Economic Section.

Cagan, P. (1956). The monetary dynamics of hyperinflation. In M. Friedman (Ed.), *Studies in the quantity theory of money*. Chicago, IL: University of Chicago Press.

Cochrane, J. (2011). Determinacy and identification with Taylor rules. *Journal of Political Economy, 119*(3), 565–615.

Leeper, E. (1991). Equilibria under 'active' and 'passive' monetary and fiscal policies. *Journal of Monetary Economics, 27*(1), 129–147.

Leeper, E. M. (2013). Fiscal limits and monetary policy. *NBER Working Paper* 18877.

Leeper, E. M., & Walker, T. B. (2012). Perceptions and misperceptions of fiscal inflation. In A. Alesina & F. Giavazzi (Eds.), *Fiscal policy after the financial crisis* (pp. 255–299). Chicago, IL: The University of Chicago Press.

Mladenovic, Z., & Petrovic, P. (2010). Cagan's paradox and money demand in hyperinflation: Revisited at daily frequency. *Journal of International Money and Finance, 29*, 1369–1384.

Reinhart, C. M., & Sbrancia, B. (2015). The liquidation of government debt. *Economic Policy, 30* (82), 291–333.

Sargent, T., & Wallace, N. (1975). Rational expectations, the optimal monetary instrument, and the optimal money supply rule. *Journal of Political Economy, 83*, 241–254.

Sims, C. (1994). A simple model for study of the determination of the price level and the interaction of monetary and fiscal policy. *Economic Theory, 4*(3), 381–399.

Sims, C. (2013). Paper money. *American Economic Review, 103*(2), 563–584.

Woodford, M. (2003). *Interest and prices*. Princeton, NJ: Princeton University Press.

Part II

Monetary Policy in the Short Run

4 New Keynesian Macroeconomics

4.1 Introduction

Up to now we considered monetary policy in a dynamic growth model with flexible prices. Monetary policy was assumed to be neutral or super-neutral in the sense that it does not affect real variables in the economy. This way, we tried to understand monetary policy design from a long-run perspective. By construction, the role of monetary policy is fairly limited in that context and straightforward to characterize: Central banks should aim to achieve price stability (low inflation) to minimize distortions arising from holding money balances. Since the inflation tax creates inefficiencies in models with money holding, optimal policy is characterized by the *Friedman rule*: Money balances should give the same return as safe bonds. One way to implement that goal is to set the nominal rate of interest equal to zero. An alternative way would be to pay interest on money at a nominal return equal to the rate for bonds. In any case, in these models, welfare cost from monetary distortions (the welfare triangle under the money demand function) turns out to be rather small. Empirically, real money balances are a very small share of GDP.

Modern monetary policy, however, is not just about implementing long-run price stability. A key issue is to what extent policy instruments may be used for stabilizing short-run fluctuations.

4.1.1 The Rational Expectation Equilibrium Revolution

For a long time, the Keynesian IS/LM model used to be the standard framework for analyzing stabilization policy. According to that model, both monetary and fiscal policy can be useful instruments for stabilizing short-run fluctuations in the economy. But that framework did not address the feedback between policy and the behavior of private agents. Frequently, it was simply assumed that private agents form expectations adaptively, learning from past experience without trying to infer future policy actions. In such a world, policy can influence real variables persistently

J. Cao, G. Illing, *Money: Theory and Practice*, Springer Texts in Business and Economics, https://doi.org/10.1007/978-3-030-19697-4_4

by surprise changes in nominal variables, as long as private agents do not learn from past mistakes. This, however, seems fairly implausible. Milton Friedman attacked this view by quoting Abraham Lincoln's famous statement: "*You may fool all of the people some time, and you can fool some people all of the time, but you can't fool all of the people all of the time.*"

The view that monetary policy may help to stabilize came under attack with the rational expectation revolution by the work of Lucas (1972) and Sargent and Wallace (1975): In the island model of Lucas (1972), systematic stabilization policy is bound to be ineffective. For example, anticipated increases in the money supply will be neutral, having no real effects. In contrast, unanticipated policy changes may indeed have an impact on real variables. But a policy relying on surprises is likely to be welfare reducing, interfering with private choices based on individually optimal actions. If people get confused because they misinterpret nominal price changes for changes in real prices, they are likely to be worse off.

This line of research stimulated real business cycle analysis. It focuses on the real side of the economy—abstracting from nominal variables. In that view, business cycle fluctuations are seen as efficient responses to real shocks. There is no point in stabilizing such shocks. As an illustrative example, consider seasonal fluctuations. It makes no sense to stabilize production of strawberries over the whole year. If low temperature prevents them from growing in winter, it would be extremely costly (require an enormous waste of energy for heating greenhouses) to keep output of strawberries stable each month. Any attempt to stabilize seasonal shocks seems to be patently inefficient.

4.1.2 Lucas' Critique of Keynesian Approach

In the 1970s a wave of drastic increases in the oil price caused severe disruptions in production all over the world. As response to these supply side shocks, many central banks tried to stimulate production by looser monetary policy—relying on a stable Phillips curve (a positive short-run relation between output and inflation). Even though that helped to dampen a fall output in the short run, in the end it led to significantly higher rates of inflation in most Western countries. With an increase in the expected rate of inflation the Phillips curve turned out to be unstable—it shifted upwards. This experiment provided a powerful support for the critique by Robert Lucas and others of Keynesian stabilization policy suggesting that in the end, such a policy is bound to fail.

A central argument is that rational private agents will react consciously to changes in policy. So after a policy change, seemingly stable relations may break down.[1] A reduced form analysis based on past data collected during times of quite

[1]Robert Lucas was not the only one to notice this phenomenon. An interesting illustration is the so-called "Goodhart's law" formulated by Charles Goodhart (1975). His "law" refers to the experience that money demand in the UK became fairly unstable as soon as the central tried to

different policy regime can lead to completely wrong conclusions. Basing forecasts about the impact of policy changes on relations which used to be stable in the past may be seriously misleading. A change in policy may trigger changes in expectations of private agents and so lead to a change in their behavior which results in quite different outcomes. A proper modeling of economic policy has to take the endogenous response of private agents into account. Doing that properly requires sound microeconomic foundations.

4.1.3 Policy Conclusions in Lucas-Type Models

As emphasized by Lucas and Sargent (1978): "[Models with rational expectations equilibria] *will focus attention on the need to think of policy as the choice of stable rules of the game, well understood by economic agents. Only in such a setting will economic theory help predict the actions agents will choose to take.*" The idea of the rational expectations theory is an appealing starting point for welfare analysis. After all, if the need for stabilization policy is based on agents being myopic or suffering from bounded rationality or other behavioral elements, welfare analysis is based on rather shaky grounds. But the rational expectations revolution made far too strong claims: Lucas and Sargent argued that a policy of systematic stabilization is bound to be ineffective, since monetary policy can have real effects only if the central bank surprises (is trying to fool people): "*The government countercyclical policy must itself be unforeseeable by private agents*. . .*while at the same time be systematically related to the state of the economy. Effectiveness, then, rests on the inability of private agents to recognize systematic patterns in monetary and fiscal policy*" (Lucas & Sargent, 1978).

Furthermore, according to that view, a systematic policy is welfare reducing, since it distorts individually optimal rational choices. But in the controversy between the Keynesian and the real business cycle view, it soon became evident that the radical policy conclusions depend on much stronger implicit assumptions. Modern Keynesians have been quick to point out that these conclusions do not follow simply from the rational expectation revolution. Rather, they are based on two additional very special assumptions:

(A) *In the absence of intervention, market will reach equilibrium with flexible prices: There are no price rigidities and so there is no role for demand shocks causing deviations of output from the level reached as equilibrium with flexible prices.*

target money supply. More generally, previously statistically estimated stable regularities tend to collapse once they are used as instruments of control by policymakers: When the government tries to control particular financial assets, these may become unreliable as indicators. When investors try to anticipate the effects of policy changes in order to make profit, the relationship between instruments and targets may break down.

(B) *The market equilibrium is socially efficient. There are no externalities resulting in inefficiently low activity.*

4.1.4 Rational Expectation Equilibrium with Sticky Prices: The New Keynesian Model

The real business cycle theory is based on the view that any imbalances are quickly self-correcting with prices adjusting so fast that equilibrium will be reached most of the time. In such an inherently stable, self-equilibrating economy, monetary policy would indeed have no positive real effects. Econometric evidence, however, is hard to reconcile with many predictions of this approach. Evidence that changes in monetary policy have significant impact on the real economy indicates that distortions, such as sticky prices and wages, prevent the economy from moving to the flexible price outcome in reasonable time. The New Keynesian model incorporates such rigidities. It allows us to integrate them in the real business cycle framework. It turns out that there is a prominent role for monetary policy in the presence of coordination failures/sticky prices in models with rational expectations.

(1) Stanley Fischer (1977) and John Taylor (1980) already emphasized that (A) does not hold in the presence of wage or price rigidities. If nominal contracts are set before observing shocks, systematic monetary policy can act as a public good in the presence of coordination failure: After the realization of shocks, monetary policy allows—as central coordination mechanism—for a smoother reversion to the flexible price outcome, saving on private adjustment and coordination costs. In that case, central bank policy can be seen as a public good—in analogy to daylight savings time as pointed out by Milton Friedman (see the box below).

> Milton Friedman presented a related argument in favor of flexible exchange rate policy:
>
> *The argument for a flexible exchange rate is, strange to say, very nearly identical with the argument for daylight savings time. Isn't it absurd to change the clock in summer when exactly the same result could be achieved by having each individual change his habits? All that is required is that everyone decides to come to his office an hour earlier, have lunch an hour earlier, etc. But obviously it is much simpler to change the clock that guides all than to have each individual separately change his pattern of reaction to the clock, even though all want to do so. The situation is exactly the same in the exchange market. It is far simpler to allow one price to change, namely, the price of foreign exchange, than to rely upon changes in the multitude of prices that together constitute the internal price structure.* Source: Friedman (1953, page 173)

(2) In the presence of structural inefficiencies, market equilibrium is inefficiently low. As shown in Sect. 1.4.5, output and labor input are too low relative to the efficient outcome in the presence of wage and price setting. If externalities distort market outcome, there is a need to think about second best policy. Market equilibrium at best may be constrained efficient.

In order to try to understand the role of price rigidities, we need a model which allows for explicit price setting. The first generation of models to introduce monopolistic competition was the static model of Blanchard and Kiyotaki (1987). Much of macro research during the last 20 years has integrated key elements of these Keynesian features into dynamic models, with explicit modeling choices for consumption, saving, money holding, and leisure in a dynamic stochastic environment with sticky price setting.

Modern dynamic versions of the current workhorse model, which incorporates most of these aspects, are known as the "New Keynesian" model or the "**New Neoclassical Synthesis**."[2] This approach tries to provide explicit micro-foundations with dynamic optimization. The models used are fairly sophisticated with forward-looking behavior. At the same time, however, they are drastically simplified to allow for explicit closed-form solutions. For instance, usually preferences are assumed to have constant elasticity of substitution. Most versions abstract from capital formation. The models focus on specific price setting assumptions (in particular, the Calvo price setting mechanism) in order to generate tractable steady state solutions. The structure is designed such that aggregate behavior can be derived in a representative agent type model (despite heterogeneity).[3] So it is a "general equilibrium" analysis with quite specific preferences, designed to give explicit solutions (allowing for approximation to linear functions). Many recent extensions relax these strong assumptions—unfortunately at the cost of increasing complexity.

In this chapter, we present a very simple stylized version of this model with the following key features: monopolistic competition (price setting); heterogeneous goods; representative agent models with structural inefficiencies. The basic framework with just two periods (which we call period 1 and 2 in this chapter) has already been presented in Chap. 1. But now, we allow for some prices to be sticky. The first period characterizes the "short run" with some prices having been fixed in advance. Following Benigno (2015), we assume that in the first period (the short run), a share α of firms has already set their prices in the past (say in period 0) before observing the realization of shocks in period 1. When setting their price, they have rational expectations p_i^e about the price level prevailing in period 1. Using all information available at the time of price setting, their forecast is consistent with the price level

[2]First surveys have been presented by Clarida, Gali, and Gertler (1999) and Goodfriend and King (1997). "Classic" textbooks of the the "New Keynesian" approach are Woodford (2003) and Gali (2015).

[3]Modern extensions introducing heterogeneity usually require calibrating/estimating large and complex quantitative models with computer simulations (as a survey see, for example, Guvenen, 2011).

realized on average $E(p_1)$. So the following condition must hold with rational expectations:

$$p_i^e = E(p_1). \quad (4.1.1)$$

The second period captures the long run, with all prices being flexible, so the economy moves to the flexible price outcome characterized in Chap. 1. When prices are sticky, price adjustment is costly and creates distortions. We assume that the central bank targets some price level P^* with the target rate of inflation π^* being $\pi^* = 0$. This is a drastic simplification both of reality and of the dynamic "New Keynesian" model. But it helps to gain a better intuition about the underlying mechanisms driving the results.

We show how imperfect competition creates aggregate demand externalities on the macro level. By introducing sticky prices, we can analyze the short-run effects of monetary policy and shocks. In particular, a micro-founded model helps to understand the effects on output and welfare. If firms have monopoly power, they are willing to accommodate shifts in demand as long as price exceeds marginal cost. So movements in demand—both positive and negative—will have an impact on output, at least within some range (as long as marginal costs are below prices). We look at how monetary policy should respond to shocks in this simple stylized setup and discuss designs for credible monetary policy. In line with the modern New Keynesian approach, we focus on interest rate policy rather than money supply. In order to concentrate on the key mechanisms, we abstract from incentives for real money balances. So we analyze a "cashless" economy. The role of money can be modeled in a simple extension by including real money balances in the utility function along the lines presented in part 2.

Some key features of the new generation dynamic models can easily be captured in this setup. We gain intuition for some important general insights:

(A) Forward-looking behavior allows analyzing the impact of a change in policy.
(B) Systematic, anticipated stabilization policy can be quite effective in the presence of price rigidities.
(C) When market equilibrium is inefficient, a surprise in monetary policy may be welfare improving (due to the nature of aggregate demand externalities).
(D) It is, however, not possible to implement a policy of systematic surprise → problem of dynamic inconsistency, calling for credible commitment mechanisms. This feature helps to understand the crucial role of institutions (the need for independent, credible central banks)
(E) The setting captures some realistic features of current monetary policy. It provides a framework to analyze the design of interest rate rules and to compare performance of different institutional designs aiming to implement a second best outcome.
(F) Explicit micro-foundations allow for detailed welfare analysis.
(G) Dynamic New Keynesian economics allows confronting theory with data. Obviously, our two-period shortcut is not sufficient for empirical analysis.

Nevertheless it helps to convey key mechanisms prevailing also in the more sophisticated dynamic versions.

4.2 Sticky Prices: Short-Run Aggregate Supply and Aggregate Demand

4.2.1 Price Adjustment Costs and Monopolistic Competition

The flexible price equilibrium characterized in Chap. 1 is a useful benchmark case, but in reality a substantial part both of prices and wages are not adjusted daily, but rather set for some fixed period. As pointed out by Mankiw (1985) and Akerlof and Yellen (1985), for price setting firms with monopolistic power it may be the optimal response not to adjust prices, if the firm is facing price adjustment costs. The intuition behind that argument is the following: After some shock, the marginal gain for monopoly producer to adjust price is fairly small (of second order). After all, the price has been set optimally in the first place. If adjusting the price is costly, it is quite likely that for small shocks the gains from readjusting the price is lower than the adjustment cost. This may be true even more if the other firms do not adjust either. If so, firms will respond to shocks not with a change in pricing, but instead with a larger change in quantity. Let us illustrate that argument for unexpected increase in demand for the good produced. Assume initially, demand is characterized by the line D_0 in Fig. 4.1a. With constant marginal cost MC, the optimal monopoly price is determined by the condition that marginal revenue equals marginal cost (resulting in price p_0 with output y_0 and profits $(p_0 - MC) \cdot y_0$ characterized by the dotted rectangular A). The efficient output level would be at y^* when demand (marginal willingness to pay) is equal to marginal cost.

Now consider a purely nominal increase shifting demand outwards toward the line D_1. A purely nominal shock will, however, leave the optimal real variables unchanged. So the nominal shock will also raise both marginal revenue MR_1 and marginal cost MC_1 proportionally such that they are still equal at y_0 as drawn in Fig. 4.1b. For the monopolist, it would be optimal to raise his own price proportionally to the level p_1, leaving quantity at y_0. With a pure nominal shock, real profits would be unchanged.

But let us now analyze what happens if price adjustment is costly. If the price stays at p_0, higher demand will be accommodated up to y_1 instead of y_0. Not adjusting price reduces profits by the dotted rectangular area B. Since initially price has been above marginal cost anyway, increased sales will nevertheless lead to additional profits represented by rectangular E. Obviously E is smaller than B (otherwise p_1 would not be the profit maximizing price), but for small shocks the difference will be fairly small. After all, prices have been set optimally initially. If so, adjustment after small shocks can only have second-order effects on profits according to the envelope theorem. Even small menu costs can easily outweigh the loss in profits from not adjusting prices (the area B minus E).

Fig. 4.1 Menu costs: second-order effects of sticky prices on profits

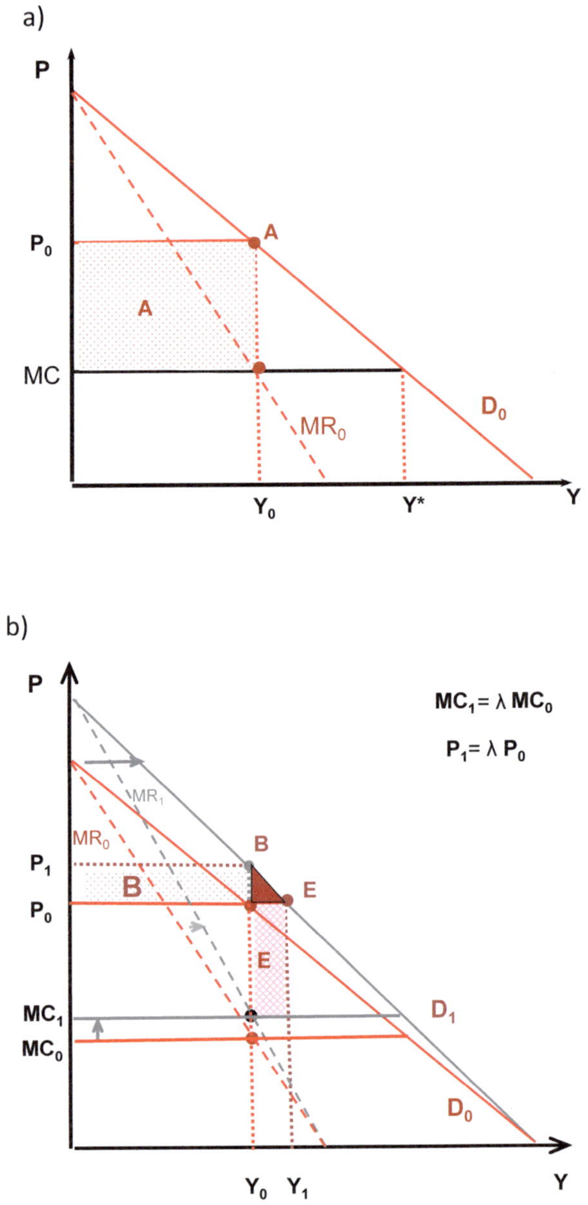

If firms have monopoly power and price adjustment is costly, they are willing to accommodate shifts in demand as long as price exceeds marginal cost. Prices will be sticky. Thus, movements in demand, either positive or negative, will have an effect on output, at least within some range (as long as marginal cost is below price). This has serious implications for the design of monetary policy: Since monetary policy can affect aggregate demand via its influence on the real rate of interest, it may be optimal to let aggregate demand adjust via central bank action in such a way that costly price adjustment for individual firms is no longer needed. In that case, monetary policy provides a public good in analogy with the daylight savings time Milton Friedman alluded to.

Focus Box: Aggregate Demand Externalities

Monopolistic distortions cause the aggregate price level to be inefficiently high, driving the real wage below the first-best level. There would be welfare gains if each firm agreed to lower the own price. Cutting its own price i, however, would not benefit the owners of firm i. Instead, the benefit would go to the whole economy. So lowering the own price cannot be a Nash-equilibrium. Seen in this way, monopolistic competition causes negative aggregate externalities.

Let us modify our model slightly to see this more clearly. Think about agent i as being the owner of some firm i producing the specific good i. He earns all revenue from selling his own production. Higher revenue of firm i allows him to consume more and so raise his utility. As consumer he wants to consume the bundle of all goods. So his interest is to charge a high price $P(i)$ for his own product, but he would prefer to buy all other products at rather low prices. Since we have a continuum of agents, each agent has measure zero for the aggregate economy. His own actions (the price he charges) have no impact on the aggregate price level P. Each agent takes P as given. But with all agents behaving in the same way, in equilibrium the individual price charged must be equal to the aggregate price level: $P(i) = P$.

In Fig. 4.2, $V_i(P, P(i))$ is the utility of agent i charging price $P(i)$ when the aggregate price level is P. At a given aggregate price level P, i's optimal pricing strategy can be characterized by the optimal response $P(i) = P_i(P)$. The dotted curves $V_i(P(i)/P;M/P)$ indicate how individual utility changes for different P by adjusting the price $P(i)$ of the own product, taking the aggregate price level P as given. The thick dashed curve $V_i(P(i) = P;M/P)$ represents utility in case all agents would charge the same price. Utility for all agents would be highest at point A with competitive price $P(i) = P = P^*$. But at P^*, the owner of each single agents individually would be better off by charging a higher price $P(i) = P_i(P^*) > P^*$. So $P(i) = P = P^*$ cannot be a Nash-equilibrium. With rising aggregate price level, the incentive to increase the own price further gets smaller and smaller. At some point M (at the monopolistic price level $(P = P_m)$, there is no longer an incentive to deviate. The price $P_m > P^*$ is the equilibrium price level with monopolistic competition.

(continued)

Figure 4.3 illustrates that there may be multiple equilibria in the presence of price adjustment costs. $V_i\left(\frac{M_k}{P}\right)$ gives the real payoff for firm i when all firms charge the same price P and money supply is given by M_k (corresponding to the thick dashed curve in Fig. 4.2). $V_i\left(\frac{p_i}{p_j}, \frac{M_k}{p_j}\right)$ is agent's i payoff when all other firms charge P_j whereas firm i charges P_i with money supply given by M_k. P_0 is the monopolistic competitive outcome for money supply M_0 with flexible prices: At point A, no single firm has an incentive to deviate if all others charge P_0. If money supply is now increased to $M_1 = \lambda M_0$, all prices would be raised proportionally to $P_1 = \lambda P_0$ in the absence of price stickiness, leaving the real payoff unchanged (point C). If, however, prices of all other firms are fixed at P_0, firm i finds himself at point B with the benefit of adjusting its own price being fairly small. As soon as price adjustment costs *pac* exceed k_0, firm i has no incentive to raise its own price. So leaving prices unchanged at point B is an equilibrium outcome, yielding higher payoff for all agents.

But there may be a another second equilibrium in pure strategies: If all other firms adjust their price to P_1 (point C), firm i finds himself at point D when charging price P_0. As long as price adjustment costs *pac* do not exceed k_1, it will benefit from raising its own price as well up to P_1. So for the range of price adjustment costs *pac* between $k_0 < pac < k_1$, we have 2 monopolistic competitive pricing equilibria: Either all firms leave prices sticky at P_0 or all firms adjust their prices to P_1. The reason for multiple equilibria is that price setting are strategic complements: It benefits to follow competitor's price strategies.

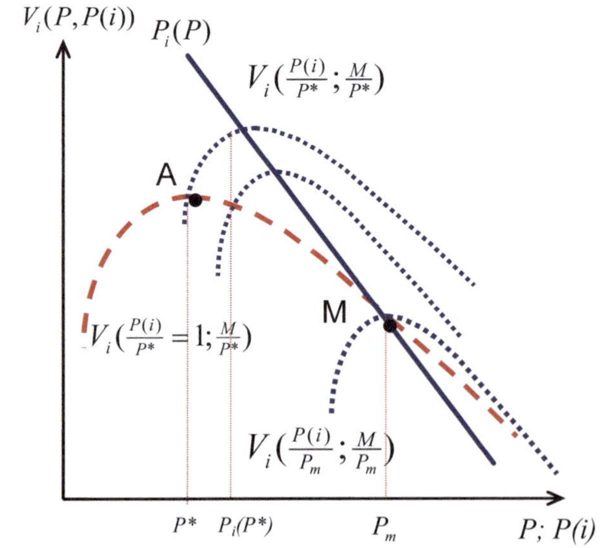

Fig. 4.2 Negative aggregate externalities from monopolistic price setting

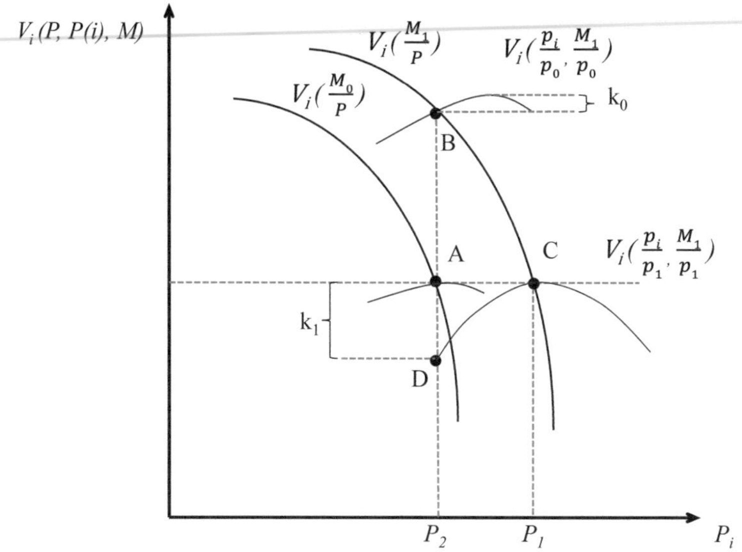

Fig. 4.3 Multiple equilibria with price adjustment costs: Prices as strategic complements

4.2.2 Aggregate Supply and Aggregate Demand

In Chap. 1, we have already introduced monopolistic pricing power of firms and distortionary effects of taxation. Since in the long run (period 2) all prices are assumed to be flexible, the long-run equilibrium is again characterized by the conditions derived in Chap. 1. But in the first period (the short run), a share α of firms has already fixed prices ex ante (say at period 0) before observing the shocks hitting the economy in that period. Those firms need to base their pricing decision on expected demand for their specific product, given the information available at that time. Obviously, demand depends—among other factors—on expected aggregate conditions and on what monetary policy is expected to be implemented in period 1.

Having set their prices, a variety of shocks may occur: Productivity may change; consumers may change their willingness to work; they may become more patient. Government spending may increase or fall, tax rates may change and monopolistic markup may turn out to be higher or smaller than expected. Finally, the central bank may act in a different way than anticipated. As it turns out, we need to distinguish between different types of shock: Demand shocks, supply shocks and markup shocks have quite different implications.

Since prices have been set optimally ex ante, individual gains from adjusting after small shocks will be rather small (see the previous section). So it may not be worthwhile to readjust prices in the presence of menu costs. Even small costs of price adjustment can easily exceed individual gains. But on the aggregate level, aggregate welfare losses may be quite large because of demand externalities. In

Fig. 4.4 AD AS model

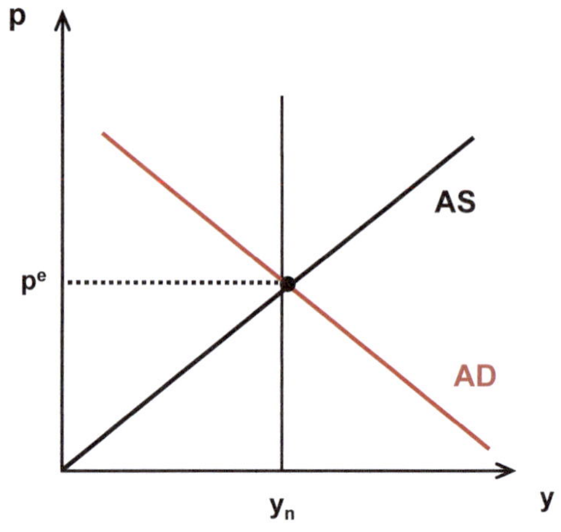

contrast, the central bank is able to respond to these shocks by adjusting the rate of interest (or the money supply).

The remaining share $1 - \alpha$ of firms with flexible prices will adjust prices optimally once shocks are realized. The higher the aggregate demand, the larger the prices they charge. But those firms with prices fixed in advance are not able to adjust their prices. Instead, they will accommodate demand at unchanged prices. If aggregate demand turns out to be higher than expected, they are willing to produce more at the same price. In the opposite case, they cut down on production. This way, shifts in demand will result in output gaps—deviations from potential output. Actual production may be larger or smaller than potential: $y_1 \neq y_{1n}$. So in the short run, output supplied is not fixed at potential. Instead we have a positively sloped aggregate supply curve as drawn in Fig. 4.4. The larger the share α of firms with sticky prices, the flatter short run aggregate supply, as prices change less in response to changes in y.

4.2.3 Short-Run General Equilibrium with Sticky Prices

In this section, we explicitly derive both the AS and the AD curve within our two-period model. Based on the setup presented in Chap. 1, we characterize the general equilibrium in a representative agent economy with endogenous production and endogenous labor supply in a two period setup with a share α of prices being sticky in period 1.

4.2.3.1 The AD Curve

For a start, let us recall the behavior of our representative consumer in Chap. 1. We focus on the case of constant elasticity of substitution for the utility function. We consider the log-linearized equations for demand and supply. In each period, consumers decide about the path for consumption C_t and of hours worked N_t.

The representative consumer has Dixit–Stiglitz preferences with constant elasticity of substitution θ among a continuum of heterogeneous goods $C_t(i)$ within the consumption basket C_t. Each good $C_t(i)$ is produced by some firm i with market power derived from limited substitutability across goods. Taking prices as given, the optimality conditions apply irrespective of whether firms have flexible of fixed prices. For CES preferences, they can be summarized in log-linearized version as follows:

We recall three key equations.[4] Demand for some specific good i is

$$c_t(i) = -\theta(\, p_t(i) - p_t)\, c_t, \quad t = 1, 2. \tag{4.2.1}$$

Euler Equation *ln E**

$$c_1 = c_2 - \sigma(i - (\, p_2 - p_1) - \rho) - \sigma(\tau_1^C - \tau_2^C), \text{ with } \pi = p_2 - p_1 \text{ and}$$
$$r = i - \pi. \tag{4.2.2}$$

The implicit condition for labor supply is given by:

$$w_t - p_t = \varphi\, n_t + \frac{1}{\sigma} \cdot c_t + z_t + \tau_t^N + \tau_t^C, \quad t = 1, 2. \tag{4.2.3}$$

The Euler equation 4.2.2 is our key equation for deriving a downward sloping aggregate demand function (AD curve). For a given interest rate and given the expected price level in period 2, the real interest rate rises with an increase in the current price level p_1. Since consumers dampen current relative to future consumption at a higher interest rate, current aggregate demand will fall with a rising price level p_1. The Euler equation provides the micro-foundation for the New Keynesian IS curve. In order to get the New Keynesian version of aggregate demand, we need to combine the Euler equation 4.2.2 with the general equilibrium condition $y_1 = c_1 + g_1$.

AD Curve

$$y_1 = y_2^e - \sigma(i - (p_2^e - p_1) - \rho) - \sigma(\tau_1^C - \tau_2^C) + (\, g_1 - g_2). \tag{4.2.4}$$

Current demand in period 1 depends on the real rate of interest. The higher the real rate interest, the stronger are incentives for consumers to postpone consumption into the future. Anticipated inter-temporal changes in consumption taxes will also affect current consumption. From now on, we make the following simplifying assumptions: We consider a stationary economy without growth, that is $y_2^e = y_1^e = \overline{y}_n$. Furthermore we assume $\tau_1^C = \tau_2^C; g_1 = g_2$. Demand shocks are captured by the shock parameter $\eta \sim F(E(\eta) = 0, \mathrm{Var}(\eta) = \sigma_\eta^2)$. Finally we assume $p_2^e = p^e$. So the AD curve simplifies to:

[4]Note that here lower case letters denote the log variable: $z = \ln z$.

AD Curve

$$y_1 = \overline{y}_n - \sigma(i - (p^e - p_1) - \rho) + \eta. \tag{4.2.4a}$$

The AD (aggregate demand) curve has been derived from general equilibrium conditions, given specific assumption about monetary policy. Obviously, current aggregate demand strongly depends on the expected actions of the central bank next period and on the current interest rate policy. So essentially, the AD curve is a function of central bank behavior. For now, we take the interest rate and given the expected price level next period p_2^e as given. We assume that in period 2, the central bank targets some long-term steady-state price level p^*. So $p_2^e = p^*$.

Evidently, aggregate demand depends on current monetary policy and in particular on the way the central bank reacts to current shocks. In the next sections, we will analyze optimal monetary policy. As a thought experiment, however, we first assume that in period 1, the central bank keeps the nominal interest rate i constant. As long as the central bank keeps the nominal interest rate i constant, aggregate demand decreases with a rise in the current price level p_1. The real interest rate $r_1 = i - (p^e - p_1)$ is higher (inflation between period 1 and 2 lower), the higher the current price level.

4.2.3.2 The AS Curve

To get a better understanding of implications of sticky prices for the impact of short-run monetary policy on output and welfare, we model sticky prices in the simplest setting: We assume that a share α of firms has to fix their prices already at an initial stage (period 0) before the realization of shocks occurs in period 1 (the short run). Those firms have rational expectations. In period 1, they expect the economy to reach on average potential output with the corresponding price level p_1^*. Basing their own pricing decision on average wages and prices expected to prevail in period 1,[5] they will set their prices exactly at $p_1^e(i) = p_1^*$. When shocks realize later in period 1, price adjustment costs prevent these firms from updating their prices. Instead, they will accommodate shifts in demand by producing more or less than the level initially planned (as long as marginal cost is below price).

The remaining firms (the share $1 - \alpha$ of firms) will adjust their prices optimally in period 1 after observing the realization of shocks. In case aggregate demand is higher, they will charge a higher price $\widetilde{p_t}(i)$. To characterize general equilibrium with the share $1 - \alpha$ of prices being sticky is a bit more complex than the case of perfectly prices.

---

[5]Being aware that they will be able to adjust their prices freely in the following period, firms do not need to take into account what might happen later in period 2. Otherwise, the price setting strategy would be more complex. Firms would need to form expectations about future demand for the whole time interval during which they might not be able to adjust prices, requiring dynamic optimisation techniques. The popular Calvo mechanism allows a steady-state analysis of such forward-looking price setting behaviour, but the qualitative results are similar to those derived in the simple setting here. The two-period model captures the essence of price setting under rational expectations.

Firms Pricing Strategy: Price Setting Under Monopolistic Competition
The optimal pricing strategy of firm i with constant returns technology is characterized by the FOC

$$\widetilde{p_t}(i) - p_t = w_t - p_t - a_t + \widehat{\mu_t}. \tag{4.2.5}$$

The effective aggregate price level p_1 prevailing in period 1 is a mix of fixed and flexible prices. The price of those firms which have been set already in advance ex ante (before the realization of shocks) equals the expected price p_1^e. Let $\widetilde{p_t}(i)$ be the price set optimally by firm i with prices adjusted flexibly ex post, once shocks have been realized. Their price setting strategy is characterized by Equation 4.2.5. The aggregate price level p_1 is $p_1 = \alpha p_1^e + (1-\alpha)\widetilde{p_t}(i)$ as first-order approximation. When prices of all firms were flexible $\widetilde{p_t}(i) = p_t$, output would be at potential. In that case, in equilibrium the real wage is simply be determined by labor productivity corrected for monopolistic markup: $w_t - p_t = a_t - \widehat{\mu_t}$.

If there is price dispersion, however, aggregate output may be higher or lower than potential. Yet workers are willing to work more (less) only if real wages rise (fall)—they are assumed to move always along their labor supply curve. In equilibrium, the labor supply condition Equation 4.2.3 must always hold (note that we do not consider involuntary unemployment). So real wages must rise when the output gap is positive, and they fall with a negative output gap. Combining Equations 4.2.3 and 4.2.5, we have

$$\widetilde{p_t}(i) - p_t = \mu_t + z_t - a_t + \varphi \cdot n_t + \frac{1}{\sigma} \cdot c_t. \tag{4.2.8}$$

We can substitute the equilibrium conditions $n_t = y_t - a_t, c_t = y_t - g_t$, in Equation 4.2.8 so as to write flexible prices as a function of y_t:

$$\widetilde{p_t}(i) - p_t = \left[\varphi + \frac{1}{\sigma}\right] \cdot y_t + \mu_t + z_t - a_t \cdot [1+\varphi] - \frac{1}{\sigma} \cdot g_t. \tag{4.2.8b}$$

For all firms adjusting their prices to shocks it will optimal to charge the same price $\widetilde{p_t} = \widetilde{p_t}(i)$. From Equation 4.2.6a we know that when output is at potential ($y_t = y_{tn}$), Equation 4.2.6a $\left(\varphi + \frac{1}{\sigma}\right) \cdot y_{tn} = a_t \cdot (1+\varphi) - z_t - \frac{1}{\sigma} \cdot g_t - \mu_t$ will hold. So we can replace the structural parameters in Equation 4.2.8b by the term $\left(\varphi + \frac{1}{\sigma}\right) \cdot y_{tn}$ in order to write the optimal pricing Equation 4.2.8b as a function of the output gap (with p_1 as the price level prevailing at y_1). Those firms who adjust prices do it in the following way:

$$\widetilde{p_1} - p_1 = \left(\frac{1}{\sigma} + \varphi\right) \cdot (y_{tn} - y_{1n}). \tag{4.2.8c}$$

The general price level is a weighted average of sticky and flexible prices:

$$p_1 = \alpha \cdot p_1^e + (1-\alpha) \cdot \widetilde{p_1}, \text{ so } \widetilde{p_1} = \frac{1}{1-\alpha} p_1 - \frac{\alpha}{1-\alpha} p_1^e, \text{ with}$$
$$p_1^e = E_0(p_1). \tag{4.2.9}$$

Substituting $\widetilde{p_1}$ in Equation 4.2.8c gives the New Keynesian Phillips curve or AS (aggregate supply) curve.

AS Curve

$$p_1 - p_1^e = k\,(y_1 - y_{1n}), \text{ with } k = \frac{1-\alpha}{\alpha}\left(\frac{1}{\sigma} + \varphi\right). \tag{4.2.10}$$

The AS curve is upward sloping in the price level. For $p_1 = p_1^e$ output is at potential. The slope k of the AS curve depends on the share of sticky prices. If all prices were flexible, all firms would adjust their prices such that the economy automatically reaches potential output. With $\alpha \to 0$, all firms will adjust, so there will be no output gap: $y_1 \to y_{1n}$. With a share α of sticky prices, production will deviate from potential in general equilibrium. For a positive output gap $(y_1 > y_{1n})$, there is upward pressure on prices, but those firms having sticky prices are willing to produce more at p_1^e, the price set initially. Obviously, those goods being cheaper goods will now have a larger share in the consumption basket. The larger α, the flatter the AS curve. For $\alpha \to 1$, no firm will adjust, so $p_1 = p_1^e$ and the AS curve is perfectly elastic. Similarly, the AS curve will be steeper the larger φ and/or the smaller σ. The reason is that effective labor supply becomes less elastic, so marginal cost will rise faster with rising production.

Summary: Potential Output—The Log-Linearized Version

General Equilibrium with Flexible Prices as Point of Reference

When prices of all firms are fully flexible, the economy will reach potential output. This reference point has already been analyzed in Chap. 1. Here, we briefly recall the closed-form solution for the log-linearized version. If $p_t(i) = p_t$ for all i, according to the optimal pricing strategy (Equation 4.2.5) the equilibrium real wage will be $w_t - p_t = a_t - \widehat{\mu_t}$. Together with Equation 4.2.3—the implicit condition for labor supply—and the definition $\mu_t = \tau_t^N + \tau_t^C + \widehat{\mu_t}$ in general equilibrium the following condition must hold: $a_t - \widehat{\mu_t} = \varphi \cdot n_t + \frac{1}{\sigma} \cdot c_t + z_t$. Using equilibrium conditions $c_t = y_t - g_t$ and

(continued)

$n_t = y_t - a_t$, we can solve for the flexible price (natural rate) solution y_{tn}, n_{tn} and (via the Euler equation) r_{tn}.

$$y_{tn} = \frac{1}{\varphi + \frac{1}{\sigma}} \left(a_t - (1+\varphi) - z_t + \frac{1}{\sigma} \cdot g_t - \mu_t \right), \tag{4.2.6a}$$

$$n_{tn} = \frac{1}{\varphi + \frac{1}{\sigma}} \left(a_t \cdot \left(1 - \frac{1}{\sigma}\right) - z_t + \frac{1}{\sigma} \cdot g_t - \mu_t \right), \tag{4.2.6b}$$

$$r_{tn} = i_t - \pi_t = \rho + \frac{1}{\sigma}[(y_{t+1n} - g_{t+1n}) - (y_{tn} - g_{tn})] + (\tau^C_{t+1} - \tau^C_t). \tag{4.2.6c}$$

To solve for the first best levels $y_t^*; n_t^*$ simply set $\mu_t = 0$. The structural inefficiency is

$$\Delta = y_t^* - \overline{y}_{1n}, \text{ with } \Delta = \frac{\mu}{\varphi + \frac{1}{\sigma}} > 0. \tag{4.2.7}$$

The potential may be disturbed by different types of shocks—aggregate supply shocks and markup shocks. $y_{1n} = \overline{y}_{1n} + \varepsilon_t - u_t$ with $\varepsilon_t \sim F(E(\varepsilon) = 0, \text{Var}(\varepsilon) = \sigma^2_\varepsilon)$ and $u_t \sim F(E(u) = 0, \text{Var}(u) = \sigma^2_u)$. The nature of these shocks will be discussed in the next sections.

Ex ante, when the share α of firms with sticky prices decide about their pricing strategy, they know only the mean value$\overline{y}_{1n} = E(y_{1n})$.

4.3 Shocks to Short-Run Equilibrium and Interest Rate Policy

We can summarize equilibrium conditions by two key equations:

AD Curve

$$y_1 = \overline{y}_{1n} - \sigma(i - (p^e - p_1) - \rho) + \eta, \tag{4.2.4a}$$

AS Curve

$$p_1 - p_1^e = k\,(y_1 - y_{1n}), \text{ with } k = \frac{1-\alpha}{\alpha}\left(\frac{1}{\sigma} + \varphi\right), \tag{4.2.10}$$

and $y_{1n} = \overline{y}_{1n} + \varepsilon - u; \overline{y}_{1n} = E(y_{1n}); y_1^* = y_{1n} + \Delta + u = \overline{y}_{1n} + \Delta + \varepsilon.$

$$\eta \sim F(E(\eta) = 0, \mathrm{Var}(\eta) = \sigma_\eta^2); \varepsilon \sim F(E(\varepsilon) = 0, \mathrm{Var}(\varepsilon) = \sigma_\varepsilon^2);$$
$$u \sim F(E(u) = 0, \mathrm{Var}(u) = \sigma_u^2).$$

$\Delta = y_t^* - \overline{y}_{1n}$ measures the structural inefficiency in the absence of shocks. Both supply and markup shocks shift natural output. Since supply shocks shift both natural and efficient output, they do not affect the gap between both—in contrast to markup shocks.

In order to solve for general equilibrium, the only information needed in addition is about central bank's policy. Assume current policy can be summarized by some interest rate rule:

$$i = f(y_1 - y_n, p_1 - p^*).$$

We will then derive optimal policy analytically in the next chapter. Here, in the last part of this chapter, let us discuss informally (graphically) what might be the adequate response by the central bank.

4.3.1 Demand Shocks

Let us now analyze the general equilibrium and the impact of interest rate policy, using the AS/AD model. By adjusting the nominal rate i the central bank can influence aggregate demand and thus has a direct impact on the current price level. First we discuss the equilibrium in case the central bank does not adjust the interest rate to demand shocks. With a constant nominal interest rate, demand shocks shift the AD curve upward or downward. In Fig. 4.5, $AD + \eta_1; \eta_1 < 0$ represents a negative demand shock; $AD + \eta_2; \eta_2 > 0$ a positive one. Since some prices are sticky, a negative demand shock will drive output below *potential*, causing pressure

Fig. 4.5 Demand shocks

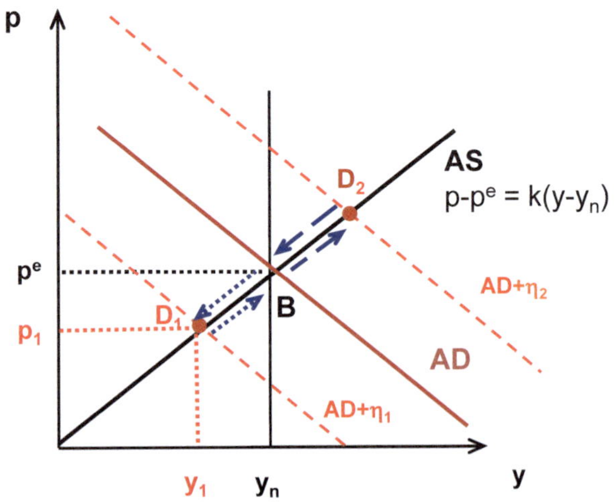

to lower prices for those firms with flexible prices. Both output and price level fall (point D_1 with p_1, y_1). With a positive shock, we get the opposite response (point D_2). So as long as monetary policy stays passive, the price level will deviate from the target rate. In the case of sticky prices, monetary policy needs to act countercyclical in order to stabilize the price level. With a negative demand shock, the central bank needs to cut interest rates in order to stimulate current demand. It must cut the nominal rate sufficiently (more than the decrease in the price level) so as to lower the real rate in order to stimulate demand. Optimally, a lower real rate of interest will shift demand back to the initial level. The reverse holds for positive shocks. In the presence of demand shocks, an active countercyclical interest rate policy shifting demand such that the price level is brought back to $p = p^e$ at B ensures at the same time that $y = \overline{y}_n$.

4.3.2 Supply Shocks: Divine Coincidence

Next, let us look at negative supply and positive markup shocks. Both type of shocks shift the AS curve to the left—see Figs. 4.6 and 4.7. But the optimal policy response will be quite different. To get a better understanding, let us start with the case that initially, there is no gap between *potential* output and the *efficient* (first-best) level of output—so $\Delta = 0$ or $\overline{y}_{1n} = y^*$.

In this section, we consider a negative supply shock $\varepsilon < 0$—such as a temporary drop in productivity or an increase in the preference for leisure, making it attractive to cut down the number of hours worked. These shocks shift potential output y_{tn} to the left. But at the same time, they also shift the efficient level y^* proportionally: $y_t^* = y_{tn} = y^* + \varepsilon$. In Fig. 4.6 the new efficient level y^* has now been shifted toward point A with $\{p^e, y^* + \varepsilon\}$. Note that the AS curve is also shifted: As long as prices correspond to expected prices, production will stay now at the new lower potential output y_{tn}. So the new AS curve intersects p^e at y_{tn}.

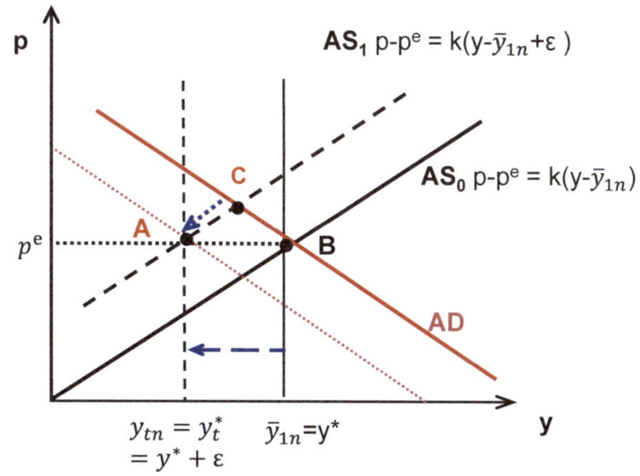

Fig. 4.6 Supply shocks

Fig. 4.7 Markup shocks

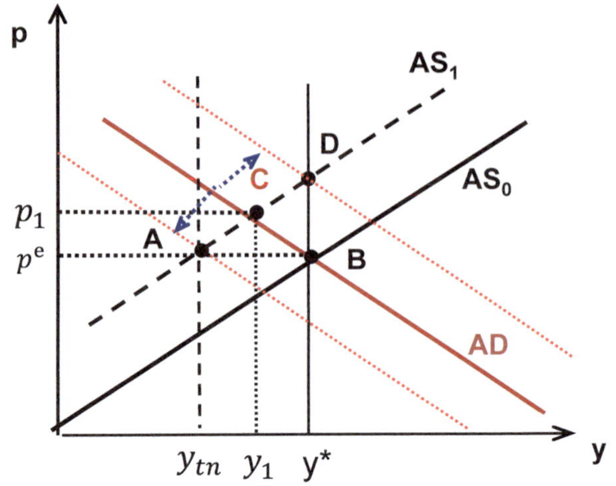

Preventing output from falling to the new potential would require prices rising above p^e. But in the case of supply shocks, this cannot be optimal. The optimal strategy is to stabilize prices at p^e. Such a policy makes sure that output reaches the new target level $y^* + \varepsilon$. In contrast, the optimal policy is to accommodate the shock such that the economy reaches y_{tn}. Note that this requires active monetary policy: An increase in the interest rate needs to dampen aggregate demand, shifting it to the left (the dotted line) in order bring it back to the lower supply to make sure that the price level keeps stable. This way, monetary policy ensures that all prices are the same and output is equal to the new potential output after realization of shocks, eliminating any output gap. Thus, no firm has to incur adjustment costs; and the representative agent consumes exactly the same bundle as in the case of flexible prices. Again, stabilizing prices and output are complementary objectives.

An obvious example are seasonal fluctuations of production. In winter time, it would require an extremely costly technology in Northern countries to stabilize local output of specific agricultural products (like strawberries or lettuce), whereas at that time Christmas trees may be offered at low cost according to seasonal demand. In former days, when the share of agricultural sector in total output was large, seasonal factors contributed substantially to total output fluctuations. Obviously, it makes no sense to try to stabilize seasonal fluctuations.

Up to now, we looked at the simple case $\Delta = 0$. It is evident that the allocation will be optimal in the absence of structural distortions. Obviously, things get more complicated in general—given all the distortions (represented by the markup factor μ), we can reach only a second-best outcome. But it turns out that our informal insight still holds: Given that monetary policy cannot affect structural distortions, stabilizing the price level (which is equivalent to stabilizing *potential* output) is second-best optimal in the face of supply shock even for $\Delta > 0$ as long as temporary changes in structural parameters (productivity a_t or willingness to work z_t) affect both *potential* y_{tn} and efficient output y_t^* in a very specific way: They leave the structural wedge between both and thus also $\Delta = y_t^* - \overline{y}_{tn} = \frac{\mu}{\varphi+1/\sigma}$ unaffected.

As long as the gap Δ between *potential* and the *efficient* (first-best) level of output is constant and invariant to demand and supply shocks, stabilizing the price level (or a target rate of inflation) is equivalent to eliminating the output gap in the presence both of supply and demand shocks. There is no trade-off between stabilization of prices or inflation and the stabilization of the welfare-relevant output gap. So in the face of supply shocks (like shocks to technology or the leisure parameter) there is no need for intervention. A policy stabilizing prices stabilizes output and so also the welfare-relevant (log) distance of output from first best. Blanchard and Gali (2010) call this fact *divine coincidence*.

Of course, such a policy cannot address the structural inefficiencies $\Delta = y_t^* - \overline{y}_{tn}$. Output is too low relative to the first best outcome. Facing structural rigidities, the key challenge is to implement reforms removing these distortions (reducing the elements driving the markup). But monetary policy cannot improve on the market outcome. As long as supply shocks shift both y_{tn} and y_t^* in the same way, central bank policy is not able to stabilize y_t at a level above y_{tn}. In that case, monetary policy can at best steer the economy back toward *potential* output y_{tn}. Other instruments ("structural reforms") are needed to address structural inefficiencies. They should be directly targeted toward the underlying distortions. Things are quite different for markup or cost-push shocks u. We will gain a better understanding of the difference in the next section.

4.3.3 Markup Shocks: Trade-Off Between Stabilizing Output and Prices

Policy conclusions are quite different in the presence of other shocks. Consider a shock u leaving the first best outcome unchanged at y^*, but moving only natural output downwards such that we now have $y_{tn} = y^* - u$. Such a shock may be due to an increase in the markup charged by monopolistic firms or due to higher distortionary tax rates. In the terminology of New Keynesian macroeconomics those shocks are called markup or cost-push shocks. Just as in the case of supply shocks, adverse markup shocks shift both y_{tn} and the AS curve toward the left (see Fig. 4.7). Now, however, y^* stays unchanged. Quite in contrast to the case of supply shocks, it is no longer optimal to accommodate the shock, trying to stabilize the price level at point *A*.

There are good arguments to stabilize markup shocks: Allowing prices to rise above p^e helps to bring y_t closer to the target y^*. At the same time, however, that comes at the cost of deviating from the price target. Evidently, we are now facing a trade-off between stabilizing prices and stabilizing output. It is now longer straightforward to talk about optimal monetary policy. What should be the policy objective? Note that all feasible combinations are along the new AS curve. Should we try to steer the economy toward point *A* or *D* or some other point? If we leave the interest rate unchanged, we end up at point C with (p_1, y_1)—the intersection between the new AS curve and the AD curve. We need to do thorough analysis, carefully looking at the relevant trade-off. This will be the task of Chap. 5.

Obviously, the "divine coincidence" outlined in the case of supply shocks (the absence of a trade-off between stabilization of prices and output) is fairly artificial—it is due to a rather special feature of the model: The lack of nontrivial real imperfections. If we allow for additional frictions, this coincidence no longer holds; a trade-off between inflation and output gap stabilization arises. All shocks affecting $\mu_t = \tau_t^N + \tau_t^C + \widehat{\mu_t}$ have an impact on $y_t^* - y_{tn}$. Consider, as example, exogenous temporary "distortion shocks" like variations in tax changes, or changes in desired markups by firms. They leave first-best output unchanged, but disturb the second-best outcome. So by definition these shocks affect the output gap $y_t^* - y_{tn}$! We call them cost push shocks u_t. A trade-off between stabilizing the price level and efficient output arises also if we allow for sticky wages rather than sticky price setting. As shown by Erceg, Henderson, and Levin (2000), in that case stabilizing a weighted average of wage and price inflation is equivalent to stabilizing the gap Δ! They show that stabilization of a composite inflation index is nearly optimal for a large range of parameter values.

Blanchard and Gali (2010) introduce additional real wage imperfections. They introduce an index of real wage rigidities, modeling a slow adjustment of wages to labor market conditions. They show that this creates a trade-off even for supply shocks. They use a rather ad hoc modeling strategy, trying to capture search frictions in the labor market. Endogenous variations in wage markups result from the sluggish adjustment of real wages. In the presence of such real wage imperfections, the second-best output fluctuates in response to supply shocks. Since movements in second-best output are the result of distortions, not of preferences or technology, first-best output is unchanged. Consequently, the gap between the first- and second-best levels of output is no longer constant.

4.4 Conclusions

Extending the baseline model presented in Chap. 1 by allowing a share of prices to be sticky, in this chapter we have set up a stylized New Keynesian model. We derived two core equations of the New Keynesian model from individual optimization. The Euler equation provides a micro-foundation for the New Keynesian IS curve or aggregate demand curve. Price setting behavior of individual firms generates a traditional upward sloping aggregate supply curve when some share of firms is not able to adjust prices. Once prices have been set, shocks disturb the economy, shifting it away from long-run equilibrium.

The model allowed us to analyze the impact of various shocks on all variables determining general equilibrium. We considered shocks to aggregate demand—shifting only the AD curve (pure demand shocks, like a change in the time preference parameter), aggregate supply (like shocks on technology and leisure) and so-called markup or cost-push shocks. Whereas supply shocks affect both potential and efficient level of production in the same way, markup shocks shift the AS curve, but do not affect the efficient level of production.

We showed that these shocks will shift the economy away from natural output and the target price level if the central bank does not respond to shocks, keeping the nominal interest rate unchanged. Active interest rate policy, trying to stabilize the real interest rate at its natural rate, is needed in order to stabilize the economy. The appropriate response crucially depends on the specific nature of underlying shock. The following chapter derives the optimal monetary policy response depending on the type of shocks.

References

Akerlof, G., & Yellen, J. (1985). Can small deviations from rationality make significant differences to economic equilibria? *American Economic Review, 75*, 708–720.

Benigno, P. (2015). New-Keynesian economics: An AS-AD view. *Research in Economics, 69*, 503–524.

Blanchard, O., & Gali, J. (2010). Labor markets and monetary policy: A new Keynesian model with unemployment. *American Economic Journal: Macroeconomics, 2*(2), 1–30.

Blanchard, O., & Kiyotaki, N. (1987). Monopolistic competition and the effects of aggregate demand. *American Economic Review, 77*, 647–666.

Clarida, R., Gali, J., & Gertler, M. (1999). The science of monetary policy: A new Keynesian perspective. *Journal of Economic Literature, 37*, 1661–1707.

Erceg, C. J., Henderson, D. W., & Levin, A. T. (2000). Optimal monetary policy with staggered wage and price contracts. *Journal of Monetary Economics, 46*(2), 281–313.

Fischer, S. (1977). Long-term contracts, rational expectations, and the optimal money supply rule. *Journal of Political Economy, 85*, 191–205.

Friedman, M. (1953). *The case for flexible exchange rates, published in Friedman, M. essays in positive economics*. Chicago, IL: University of Chicago Press.

Gali, J. (2015). *Monetary policy, inflation, and the business cycle: An introduction to the new Keynesian framework and its applications* (2nd ed.). Princeton, NJ: Princeton University Press.

Goodfriend, M., & King, R. (1997). The new neoclassical synthesis and the role of nonetary policy. In B. Bernanke & J. Rotemberg (Eds.), *NBER macroeconomics annual 1997* (pp. 231–282). Cambridge, MA: MIT Press.

Goodhart, C. (1975). Problems of monetary management: The UK experience. In *Papers in monetary economics* (Vol. I). Sydney, NSW: Reserve Bank of Australia.

Guvenen, F. (2011). Macroeconomics with heterogeneity: A practical guide. *Federal Reserve Bank of Richmond Economic Quarterly, 97*(3), 255–326.

Lucas, R. (1972). Expectations and the neutrality of money. *Journal of Economic Theory, 4*, 103–124.

Lucas, R., & Sargent, T. (1978). After Keynesian macroeconomics. In After the Phillips curve: Persistence of high inflation and high unemployment. Federal Reserve Bank of Boston, Conference Series No. 19, pp. 49–72.

Mankiw, G. (1985). Small menu costs and large business cycles: A macroeconomic model of monopoly. *Quarterly Journal of Economics, 100*, 529–537.

Sargent, T., & Wallace, N. (1975). Rational expectations, the optimal monetary instrument, and the optimal money supply rule. *Journal of Political Economy, 83*, 241–254.

Taylor, J. (1980). Aggregate dynamics and staggered contracts. *Journal of Political Economy, 88* (l), 1–23.

Woodford, M. (2003). *Interest and prices*. Princeton, NJ: Princeton University Press.

Optimal Monetary Policy

5

5.1 Introduction

In Chap. 4, we analyzed the impact of different shocks on general equilibrium in the presence of price stickiness. If the central bank keeps the nominal interest rate unchanged, these shocks will shift short-run equilibrium away from potential output and from the target price level. Active monetary policy can try to steer the economy back to potential by adjusting the nominal rate of interest. In this chapter, we derive optimal monetary policy when the central bank minimizes welfare losses arising from price dispersion among different goods. With sticky prices, the price dispersion induces consumers to choose an inefficient mix (with the marginal rate of substitution across goods being equal to relative prices). We characterize these welfare losses intuitively and show that they can be captured by a quadratic loss function as second-order Taylor approximation.

Optimal policy can be characterized by an optimal stabilization curve for output and price level, independent of the policy instrument. We show that the optimal policy response crucially depends on the specific nature of underlying shock. Both for demand and supply shocks it is optimal to stabilize the price level, thus minimizing price distortions. Keeping price stable, output will stay at its potential. In the presence of markup shocks, however, there is a trade-off between implementing price stability and bringing output close to the efficient level.

Due to monopolistic competition, distortions cause structural inefficiency: Output and employment in market equilibrium are inefficiently low relative to their first-best level. So a welfare maximizing central bank might try to stimulate the economy by raising the price level above expected level. But as soon as private agents anticipate this incentive, they will form higher price expectations right from the start. In the end, it is not feasible in equilibrium to stimulate the economy above potential output. As first shown by Barro and Gorden (1983), the attempt to stimulate will fail, the central bank cannot systematically raise output above market equilibrium. In Sect. 5.3 we characterize the outcome of the Barro–Gordon model using game theoretic concepts: A strategy to bring the economy closer to the first-best level by monetary

J. Cao, G. Illing, *Money: Theory and Practice*, Springer Texts in Business and Economics, https://doi.org/10.1007/978-3-030-19697-4_5

policy is—in game theoretic terms—not subgame perfect or time consistent. The attempt to raise welfare results just in an inefficiently high price level. The discretionary solution imposes even stronger welfare losses for society. We analyze the problem of dynamic inconsistency in detail and derive the discretionary, dynamic consistent equilibrium. We show that the outcome is inferior relative to a policy committing not to raise price level on average above expectation—we call that outcome the commitment solution.

By committing itself to a binding rule, the central bank will be able to implement a superior policy outcome. The optimal targeting rule allows the central bank flexibility to respond to shocks in the economy. The adequate response, however, depends on the nature of specific shocks. This insight raises the issue about feasible commitment mechanisms. In Sect. 5.4 we analyze various strict rules (such as price level targeting, nominal GDP targeting, the delegation of monetary policy toward conservative central bankers or simple instrument rules such as strict interest rate or money growth targeting) as second-best policies to implement a policy getting close to optimal outcome. We show that a mechanical commitment to simple instrument rules, with the instrument being only a function of a small subset of all information available to the central bank is likely to be sub-optimal. A more adequate institutional design committing the central bank to solve the dynamic consistency problem is to specify targeting rules (defining explicit objectives for monetary policy, providing a criterion for (the forecasts of) the target variables to be fulfilled).

In this chapter, the problem of dynamic consistency is due to an inflation bias arising from structural inefficiency. As we will see in Chap. 7, monetary policy is instead likely to be subject to a deflation bias when the interest rate hits the effective lower bound. In Chap. 7, we will see that the formal structure behind that bias is very similar to the model presented here in Sect. 5.3.

5.2 The Social Welfare Function

A systematic policy, adjusting the interest rate to shocks, may be able to raise welfare by stabilizing the economy. Let us now derive the optimal policy rule. As shown in the focus box for nerds "*The quadratic loss function as second order welfare approximation*," welfare losses arising from output gaps in the presence of sticky prices can be captured approximately by the quadratic loss function:

$$L = \frac{1}{2}(y_t - y_t^*)^2 + \frac{1}{2}\cdot\frac{\theta}{k}\cdot(p_t - p_t^e)^2. \tag{5.2.1}$$

Here y_t^* represents efficient production at period t. The first term in the loss function captures aggregate distortions arising both from the output gap and from persistent structural inefficiencies. Since $y_t^* = y_{tn} + \Delta + u$ and $y_{tn} = \overline{y}_{tn} + \varepsilon - u$, we can write that term as

$$y_t - y_t^* = y_t - y_{tn} - \Delta - u = y_1 - \overline{y}_{1n} - \varepsilon - \Delta. \qquad (5.2.2)$$

The second term $p_t - p_t^e$ arises from deviations of the price level from target (the difference being the current rate of inflation). It captures distortions from price dispersion among the different goods in the consumption bundle.

In the loss function, these losses are weighted with the factor θ/k. If the aggregate price level deviates from the price set by those firms with sticky prices, this causes relative distortions between different goods produced. For obvious reasons, these distortions increase with the share α of firms with predetermined prices. They also increase with the elasticity of substitution θ across goods (for details see Sect. 5.2.1 and the focus box for nerds).

We assume that the central bank minimizes social losses, represented by the loss function above. In doing so, it has to take into account the conditions characterizing general equilibrium in our simple New Keynesian economy as derived in Chap. 4. They are summarized by the AS and AD curves:

AS Curve:

$$p_1 - p_1^e = k(y_1 - y_{1n}), \text{ with } k = \frac{1-\alpha}{\alpha} \cdot (1/\sigma + \varphi) \text{ and}$$
$$y_{1n} = \overline{y}_{1n} + \varepsilon_1 - u_1; \overline{y}_{1n} = E(y_{1n}).$$

AD Curve:

$$y_1 - \overline{y}_1 = -\sigma(i_1 - \rho) + \sigma(p^e - p_1) + \eta_1.$$

Again, all shocks are assumed to have mean zero and some constant variance. Compared to the more general AD curve derived in the last section from the Euler equation, we make (without loss of generality) the following simplifying assumptions here: We consider a stationary economy without growth, that is $y_2^e = y_1^e = \overline{y}_1$. We assume that initially $\tau_1^C = \tau_2^C$; $g_1 = g_2$. All demand shocks in period 1 are captured by η. So in the absence of shocks, the natural real rate of return is $r_n = i_1 - (p^e - p_1) = \rho$. If we allowed for growth or for anticipated changes in fiscal policy, the natural real rate of return would need to be modified accordingly. Finally, we assume that the expected price level in the second period is $p_2^e = p^*$. Ex ante, the average expected real interest rate will be $E(r) = \rho$.

In the AS curve, ε characterizes a supply shock affecting both potential and efficient level of production in the same way, whereas u is a markup shock disturbing just potential output. So $y_{1n} = \overline{y}_{1n} + \varepsilon_1 - u_1$, whereas $y_1^* = \overline{y}_1^* + \varepsilon_1$; with $\overline{y}_{1n} = E(y_{1n})$; $\overline{y}_1^* = E(y_1^*)$; $y_1^* = y_{1n} + \Delta + u_1 = \overline{y}_{1n} + \Delta + \varepsilon_1$.

When deriving the optimal policy, minimizing welfare losses subject to general equilibrium constraints, we need to distinguish between target rules and instrument rules. The optimal policy defined in terms of the targets affecting welfare can be characterized as a function $p_1 = p_1(\varepsilon_1, u_1, \eta_1)$ and $y_1 = y_1(\varepsilon_1, u_1, \eta_1)$. Notice that when deriving the target rule, AD is not really a constraint. After all, the central bank's policy variable i can affect AD directly. So, as long as i itself is unconstrained, by adjusting i the central bank is able to steer AD such as to implement the optimal policy. The role of condition AD is just to calculate the appropriate instrument—an instrument rule characterizes how the instrument (such as the interest rate policy $i_1 = i_1\ (\varepsilon_1, u_1, \eta_1)$ needs to adjust to implement the optimal solution.

More generally, for any given interest rate, we can calculate the resulting outcome in terms of output and prices in a straightforward way. Just insert the AS curve: $p_1 - p_1^e = k\ (y_1 - \overline{y}_{1n} - \varepsilon_1 + u_1)$ in the AD curve $y_1 - \overline{y}_1 + \sigma(p_1 - p_1^e) = \eta_1 - \sigma(i_1 - \rho)$.

This gives as general equilibrium for the AS–AD model as: $(y_1 - \overline{y}_1\ ) \times (1 + \sigma \cdot k) = \eta_1 + \sigma \cdot k(\varepsilon_1 - u_1) - \sigma(i_1 - \rho)$ or

$$y_1 - \overline{y}_1 = \frac{1}{1 + k \cdot \sigma}[\eta_1 + \sigma \cdot k(\varepsilon_1 - u_1) - \sigma \cdot (i_1 - \rho)], \text{ and} \tag{5.2.3}$$

$$p_1 - p_1^e = \frac{k}{1 + k \cdot \sigma}(\eta_1 - \varepsilon_1 + u_1) - \frac{k \cdot \sigma}{1 + k \cdot \sigma}(i_1 - \rho). \tag{5.2.4}$$

In the New Keynesian framework, following standard central bank practice, we assume that the interest rate is used as policy instrument. Of course, if the policy parameter i hits some boundary, conventional interest rate policy may no longer be effective. As we will see later in Chap. 7 on liquidity trap, in that case the central bank may be subject to a zero-bound constraint. Another constraint may arise from the fact that monetary policy cannot respond to regional shocks (see the box on currency union).

Alternatively, we might think about money supply as the policy instrument. In order to model that, we need to supplement our setup with an equation characterizing equilibrium on the money market. This way, we could reformulate AD as a function of money supply and derive the conditions for the appropriate level of money supply. If money demand is, however, unstable relative to shocks affecting the real side of the economy, interest rate targeting turns out to be superior to money targeting (see Sect. 5.4.4).

5.2.1 Welfare Losses from Price Dispersion

Sticky prices create price dispersion, causing welfare losses. When productivity is the same for all goods $Y(i) = A \cdot N(i)$, the marginal rate of transformation between different goods is minus 1. For an efficient mix of heterogeneous goods the marginal rate of substitution has to be equal to the marginal rate of transformation. Since consumers decide about their mix by setting the marginal rate of substitution equal to relative prices, they will choose an inefficient mix whenever prices are dispersed. This inefficiency can be captured by the fact that labor input needed is inefficiently high. Aggregate labor supply $N = \int_0^1 N(i)di$ required to produce some given aggregate level of production Y is higher the larger the price dispersion. We have the simple relation:[1]

$$N = \int N(i)di = \frac{1}{A} \cdot \int Y(i)di = \frac{Y}{A} \int \left(\frac{P(i)}{P}\right)^{-\theta} di = \frac{Y}{A} \cdot D.$$

$D = \int \left(\frac{P(i)}{P}\right)^{-\theta} di$ is the dispersion index. $D = 1$ for $Y = Y_n$. As shown in the focus box for nerds, the second-order Taylor approximation for $d = \ln D$ is a function of the variance of prices:

$$d \approx \frac{1}{2}\theta \operatorname{Var}(p(i)) = \frac{1}{2}\theta \frac{\alpha}{1-\alpha}(p - p^e)^2.$$

To gain a better intuition about the welfare loss from dispersion, let us consider a simple graphical example with firms producing just two heterogeneous goods $Y(i), Y(j)$. Since both firms use the same technology, the transformation curve between these goods $Y(i)$ and $Y(j)$ has slope -1. Assume the firm j producing $Y(j)$ has sticky prices $p(j)$, whereas firm i is able to adjust prices to shocks. We consider the case that aggregate production stays constant at Y_n. With Y_n being produced, the transformation curve with slope -1 characterizes all feasible allocations between the two types of goods. When prices for both goods are equal, the consumer will choose the symmetric consumption bundle Y_n with $Y_n(i) = Y_n(j) = \frac{1}{2}Y_n$ as drawn in Fig. 5.1.

Now let us consider a shock raising the markup u, driving the equilibrium price above expected price p^e. As long as all prices are flexible, prices for both goods rise proportionally. So even after the shock, prices will still be equal: $p(i) = p(j)$. As long as Y_n is produced,[2] the consumption bundle stays unchanged, maximizing utility for the representative consumer at the given aggregate level Y_n. But with $p(j)$ being sticky, good $Y(j)$ with sticky prices has now become cheaper relative to $Y(i)$. So the representative consumer will now[3] choose Y_0 instead of Y_n (Fig. 5.1). Demand for $Y(j)$ goods increases, stimulating production of these goods. In contrast, demand for good $Y(i)$ with higher price is dampened. The consumer is worse off,

[1]We get the link between labor input $N(i)$ for a specific product $Y(i)$ and aggregate output using $N(i) = Y(i)/A$ and $Y(i) = \left(\frac{P(i)}{P}\right)^{-\theta} Y$.

[2]The increased markup depresses real wages, so both aggregate labor supply and output will fall in equilibrium. This general equilibrium effect causes additional distortions, captured by the term $y - y^*$. Focusing on the impact of price dispersion, we keep Y_n constant in our analysis.

[3]With a negative markup shock, firm i with flexible prices will lower its price. The flexible price good becoming cheaper, now X_0 instead of Y_n will be chosen in Fig. 5.1. The analysis is symmetric.

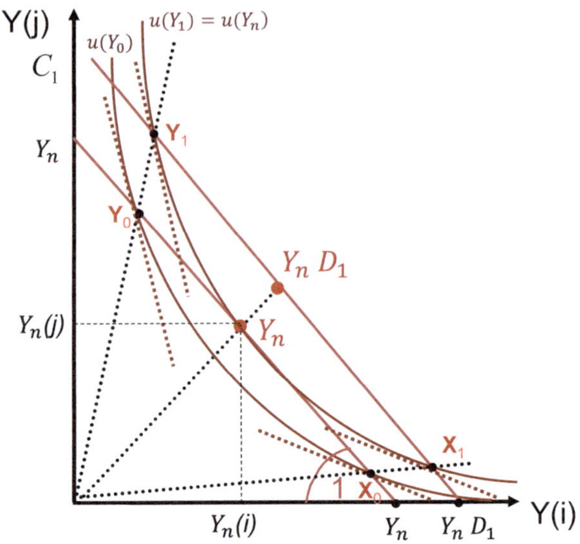

Fig. 5.1 Welfare loss from dispersion

ending up with utility $u(Y_0) < u(Y_n)$. Thus, price dispersion leads to an inefficient choice of the consumption bundle. In order to compensate for the loss from price dispersion, a higher output level Y_1 (requiring more labor effort N_1) needs to be produced such that $u(Y_1) = u(Y_n)$ (see Fig. 5.1).

Figure 5.2 shows how the implied welfare loss from price dispersion is captured by higher labor effort $N_1 = \frac{Y_n D_1}{A}$ required to produce $Y_1 = Y_n D_1 > Y_n$ with $D_1 > 1$ instead of Y_n. In the lower part of Fig. 5.2, we characterize the degree of price dispersion between $p(i)$ and $p(j)$. The price charged by type i firm is represented along the ray $p(i)$, the price by type i firm along the ray $p(j)$. As long as both firms charge the same price (such as P_0 in point A), there is no price dispersion ($D = 1$). Thus, aggregate input $N_n = Y_n/A$ is needed to produce Y_n. This implies a disutility of labor $V(N_n)$.

Now consider a shock hitting the economy such that the optimal price rises from P_0 to P_1. If all prices were fully flexible, all firms would charge $P(i) = P_1$ (point B). But if some firms j do not adjust their price, leaving it fixed at $P_0(j) < P_1(i)$, there is now price dispersion $\overline{D}$ (point C). Producing the consumption bundle Y_1 providing the same utility as in Y_n requires higher labor input $N_1 = Y_1/A = Y_n D_1/A$, ending up with higher disutility of work. It is easy to see from Fig. 5.2 that the larger the price dispersion, the larger the welfare loss.

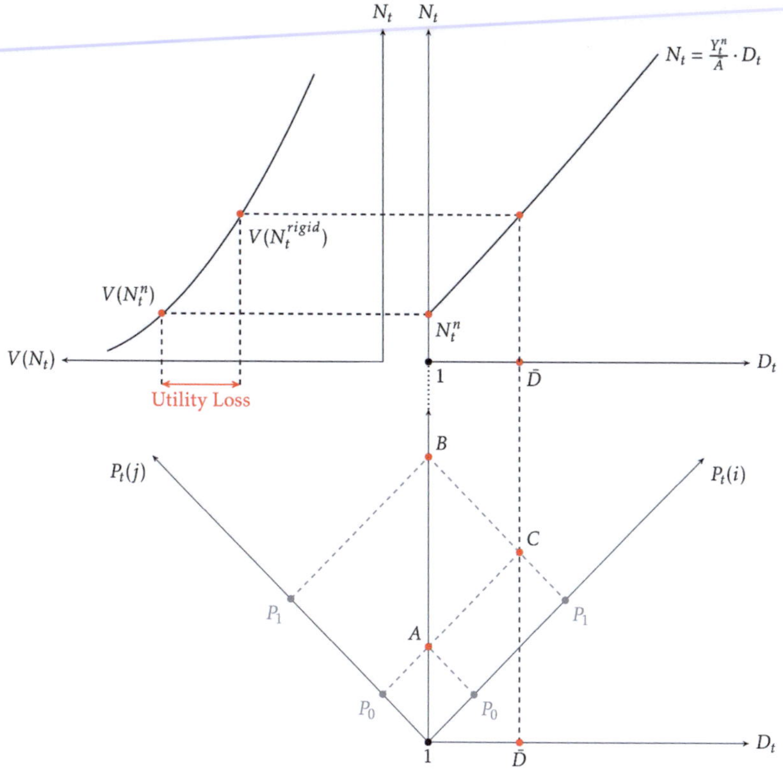

Fig. 5.2 Welfare loss from dispersion in terms of labor input

Focus Box for Nerds: The Quadratic Loss Function as Second-Order Welfare Approximation

The aggregate welfare loss arising from distortions in an economy with monopolistic competition and sticky prices can be approximated (as second-order Taylor approximation) by the quadratic loss function used in this section:

$$L = \frac{1}{2}(y_t - y_t^*)^2 + \frac{1}{2} \cdot \frac{\theta}{k} \cdot (p_t - p_t^e)^2. \qquad (5.2.1.1)$$

If you simply trust that statement, you may skip this focus box. Here, we want to provide an intuitive proof for that result. Unfortunately, such a proof is fairly technical—only real nerds may enjoy reading the following paragraphs.

(continued)

In public finance, it is popular to use quadratic loss functions to capture welfare losses (the loss in rents for consumers and producers) from distortionary taxation. Similarly, in monetary policy analysis, for a long time a quadratic loss function has been used to characterize optimal monetary policy. But rather than using an ad hoc criterion, a welfare analysis truly based on microeconomic principles should motivate optimal policy as the policy which maximizes the welfare of the representative agent. As has been shown by Woodford (2003), using the quadratic loss function can indeed be justified as second-order approximation. This analysis allows us to characterize precisely what weights should be attached: The weights depend on preference parameters (the elasticity of substitution) and on the share of firm with sticky prices.

In this focus box, we want to show how the losses arising from deviations of output from potential output (or rather from the efficient level) can be linked to preference parameters. To have a closed system, let us abstract from government spending (otherwise we would need to characterize also optimal spending). So in general equilibrium, consumption has to equal output $c = \ln C = \ln Y = y$. Employment will equal the amount of work needed to produce aggregate output. Let us first express actual levels in terms of the aggregate output gap—that is we look at the percentage deviation of the actual from potential output:

$$\widehat{y} = y - y_n \approx (Y - Y_n)/Y_n. \tag{5.2.1.2}$$

More precisely, we use the following second-order approximation $\frac{Y}{Y_n} = e^{\widehat{y}} = 1 + \widehat{y} + \frac{1}{2}\widehat{y}^2 + \|\xi^3\|$. We drop all terms of third or higher order $\|\xi^3\|$. Since all these terms are fairly small (close to zero $\|\xi^3\| \approx 0$), we can neglect them. So we have

$$\frac{Y}{Y_n} - 1 \approx \widehat{y} + \frac{1}{2}\widehat{y}^2;\ \frac{C}{C_n} - 1 \approx \widehat{c} + \frac{1}{2}\widehat{c}^2;\ \frac{N}{N_n} - 1 \approx \widehat{n} + \frac{1}{2}\widehat{n}^2. \tag{5.2.1.3}$$

Let us now start the second-order approximation of utility

$$V(C, N) = U(C) - V(N). \tag{5.2.1.4}$$

Since preferences are additive separable, the quadratic approximation can be done separately with $U(C)$ and $V(N)$, respectively ($V_{CN} = 0$). A Taylor expansion around potential output $C = C_n = Y_n$ gives:

(continued)

$$U(C) = U(C_n) + U_C(C_n) \cdot (C - C_n) + \frac{1}{2} U_C(C_n) \cdot (C - C_n)^2 + \|\xi^3\|$$
$$= U(C_n) + C_n \cdot U_C(C_n) \cdot \left(\frac{C - C_n}{C_n}\right)$$
$$+ \frac{1}{2} C_n^2 \cdot U_C(C_n) \cdot \left(\frac{C - C_n}{C_n}\right)^2 + \|\xi^3\|. \qquad (5.2.1.5)$$

The second line is simply a reformulation in terms of percentage deviation of the actual from potential output. Using $\|\xi^3\| \approx 0$ and substituting the approximation $\frac{C - C_n}{C_n} \approx \widehat{c} + \frac{1}{2}\widehat{c}^2$ into Equation 5.2.1.5, (for the second bracket with square operator, use $\frac{C - C_n}{C_n} \approx \widehat{c}$) gives:

$$U(C) = U(C_n) + C_n \cdot U_C(C_n) \cdot \left[\hat{c} + \frac{1}{2}\hat{c}^2\right] + \frac{1}{2} C_n^2 \cdot U_{CC}(C_n) \cdot \hat{c}^2 + \|\xi^3\|$$
$$= U(C_n) + C_n \cdot U_C(C_n) \cdot \hat{c}$$
$$+ \frac{1}{2}\left[C_n \cdot U_C(C_n) + C_n \cdot U_C(C_n) \cdot \frac{C_n \cdot U_{CC}(C_n)}{U_C(C_n)}\right] \cdot \hat{c}^2 + \|\xi^3\|.$$

Using the definition of elasticity of substitution[4] $\sigma(C) = -\frac{U_C(C)}{C \cdot U_{CC}(C)}$ we can simplify to

$$U(C) = U(C_n) + C_n \cdot U_C(C_n) \cdot \left[\hat{c} + \frac{1}{2}\left(1 - \frac{1}{\sigma}\right) \cdot \hat{c}^2\right] + \|\xi^3\|, \quad \text{or :}$$

$$U(C) - U(C_n) = C_n \cdot U_C(C_n) \cdot \left[\hat{c} + \frac{1}{2}\left(1 - \frac{1}{\sigma}\right) \cdot \hat{c}^2\right] + \|\xi^3\|. \qquad (5.2.1.5a)$$

Using the aggregate equilibrium condition $C = Y$ and $\widehat{c} = c - c^n = y - y^n \equiv \widehat{y}$ we can write Equation 5.2.1.5a in terms of the output gap:

$$U(C) - U(C_n) = Y_n \cdot U_C(Y_n) \cdot \left[\hat{y} + \frac{1}{2}\left(1 - \frac{1}{\sigma}\right) \cdot \hat{y}^2\right] + \|\xi^3\|. \qquad (5.2.1.5b)$$

In exactly the same way as deriving Equation 5.2.1.5a, we also get a quadratic approximation for disutility of labor:

(continued)

[4]For CES preferences $U = \frac{1}{1-1/\sigma} C^{1-\frac{1}{\sigma}}$, the elasticity is constant—independent of consumption level C. $\sigma(C) = -\frac{U_C(C)}{C \cdot U_{CC}(C)} = \sigma$ since $U_C = C^{-\frac{1}{\sigma}}$ and $U_{CC} = -\frac{1}{\sigma} \cdot C^{-\frac{1}{\sigma}-1} = -\frac{1}{\sigma} \cdot U_C / C$.

$$V(N) - V(N_n) = N_n \cdot V_N(N_n) \cdot \left[\hat{n} + \frac{1}{2}(1+\varphi) \cdot \hat{n}^2\right] + \|\xi^3\|, \text{ with } \hat{n} = \ln \frac{N}{N_n}. \quad (5.2.1.6)$$

(Note that $\varphi(N) = \frac{N \cdot V_{NN}(N)}{V_N(N)}$ is the inverse (!) of the elasticity of labor supply).

It is quite a bit more complicated to reformulate this expression for the labor market in terms of the output gap. First, let us use the optimality condition for labor supply to define the relation between $V_N(N_n)$ and $U_C(C_n)$:

$$V_N(N_n) = \frac{W}{P} \cdot U_C(C_n). \quad (5.2.1.7)$$

Optimal pricing for firm i, $\frac{P(i)}{P} = \frac{\theta}{\theta - 1} \frac{W}{AP}$ with θ as the elasticity of substitution between two goods i, j gives:

$$\frac{W}{P} = A \frac{P(i)}{P} \frac{\theta - 1}{\theta}. \quad (5.2.1.8)$$

Output is at potential when all prices are flexible and thus $P(i) = P$. So we have:

$$V_N(N_n) = A \cdot \frac{\theta - 1}{\theta} \cdot U_C(C_n). \quad (5.2.1.7a)$$

Using the production function $Y_n = N_n \cdot A$, we can now rewrite equation (Equation 5.2.1.6) as:

$$V(N) - V(N_n) = Y_n \cdot U_C(Y_n) \cdot \left(\frac{\theta - 1}{\theta} \cdot \hat{n} + \frac{1}{2}(1+\varphi) \cdot \hat{n}^2\right) + \|\xi^3\|. \quad (5.2.1.6a)$$

In order to rewrite the term $\hat{n}$ finally in Equation 5.2.1.6a in terms of the aggregate output gap $\widehat{y}$, there is still some work to do. $N = \int_0^1 N(i)\, di$ denotes aggregate labor supply. We get the link to aggregate output using $N(i) = \frac{Y(i)}{A}$ and $Y(i) = \left(\frac{P(i)}{P}\right)^{-\theta} Y$ such that:

$$N = \int_0^1 N(i) di = \frac{1}{A} \cdot \int_0^1 Y(i) di = \frac{Y}{A} \int_0^1 \left(\frac{P(i)}{P}\right)^{-\theta} di = \frac{Y}{A} \cdot D$$

(continued)

with $D = \int_0^1 \left(\frac{P(i)}{P}\right)^{-\theta} di$ as dispersion index. $D = 1$ for $Y = Y_n$. A second-order Taylor approximation for $d = \ln D$ gives:

$$d \approx \frac{1}{2}\theta \operatorname{Var}(p(i)) = \frac{1}{2}\theta \frac{\alpha}{1-\alpha}(p - p^e)^2.$$

Using $n = y - a + d$ and $n_n = y_n - a$, we can now formulate in terms of the output gap

$$\hat{n} = n - n_n = y - y_n + d = \hat{y} + d.$$

Calculating Equation 5.2.1.4 from Equation 5.2.1.5b and Equation 5.2.1.6a gives

$$\begin{aligned} L(C,N) &= V(C,N) - V(C_n,N_n) \\ &= Y_n \cdot U_C(Y_n) \cdot \left(\frac{1}{\theta}\hat{y} - \frac{1}{2}\left(\varphi + \frac{1}{\sigma}\right) \cdot \hat{y}^2 + \frac{1}{2}\left(\frac{\theta - 1}{\theta}\right)d\right) + \|\xi^3\|. \end{aligned}$$

Being interested in $V(C,N) - V(C^*,N^*)$ rather than $V(C,N) - V(C_n,N_n)$, we need to reformulate this expression, using the definition of log level of potential and efficient level of output

$$y^n = \frac{1+\varphi}{\varphi + \tilde{\sigma}^{-1}}a - \frac{1}{\varphi + \tilde{\sigma}^{-1}}\mu,$$

$$y^* = \frac{1+\varphi}{\varphi + \tilde{\sigma}^{-1}}a.$$

We have:

$$y^* - y^n = \frac{1}{\varphi + \tilde{\sigma}^{-1}}\mu = \frac{1}{\theta \cdot \Gamma}.$$

With $\varphi + \tilde{\sigma}^{-1} = \Gamma$ rewrite:

$$(y - y^n - y^* + y^n) - \frac{1}{\theta \cdot \Gamma^2} = \hat{y}^2 - \frac{2}{\theta \cdot \Gamma}\hat{y} + \frac{1}{\theta \cdot \Gamma^2} - \frac{1}{\theta \cdot \Gamma^2} = (\hat{y} - y^*)^2.$$

(continued)

Substitute back and use $\widehat{y} = y - y^n$:

$$U = -\frac{Y^n \cdot U_C(Y^n)}{2}\left\{\Gamma(y - y^n - y^* + y^n)^2 + \left(\varphi + \frac{1}{\theta}\right)\mathrm{Var}[p(i)]\right\} + \|\xi^3\|$$

$$= -\frac{Y^n U_C(Y^n)}{2}\left\{\Gamma(y - y^*)^2 + \left(\varphi + \frac{1}{\theta}\right)\mathrm{Var}[p(i)]\right\} + \|\xi^3\|, \quad (5.2.1.9)$$

$$\mathrm{Var}[p(j)] = \frac{\alpha}{1-\alpha}(p - p^e)^2. \quad (5.2.1.10)$$

Taking Equation (5.2.1.10) back into Equation (5.2.1.9), we have:

$$L = \frac{Y^n U_C(Y^n)}{2}\left\{\Gamma(y - y^*)^2 + \left(\varphi + \frac{1}{\theta}\right)\theta^2 \frac{\alpha}{1-\alpha}(p - p^e)^2\right\} + \|\xi^3\|.$$

Define the loss function: $L(C, N) = V(C, N) - V(C^*, N^*)$

$$L = \frac{1}{2}\left\{(y - y^*)^2 + (\theta \cdot \varphi + 1)\frac{\alpha}{1-\alpha}\frac{\theta}{\Gamma}(p - p^e)^2\right\}. \quad (5.2.1.11)$$

Equation (5.2.1.11) is the loss function consistent with the quadratic loss function

5.2.2 Game Theoretic Analysis of Optimal Monetary Policy

Let us now calculate the optimal central bank policy in period 1. Since we want to capture the interaction between central bank and private agents forming rational expectations, we have to distinguish between the policy announced ex ante and the optimal reaction ex post as a response to the shocks observed. We can model that as a game between central bank and public in the following three stages:

- **Stage 1:** Before the start of period 1, the central bank announces some policy rule. We can characterize it in terms of the price level intended in response to the shocks realized in each period $p_t{}^a = f_p(\varepsilon_t, u_t, \eta_t)$ or as an interest rate rule $i_t{}^a = f_i(\varepsilon_t, u_t, \eta_t)$.
- **Stage 2:** Private agents (the share α of firms) sign nominal contracts (fix their prices), based on the expectations about the price level prevailing in period 1 (and possibly in period 2). After the contracts have been arranged, shocks occur, disturbing the economy.
- **Stage 3:** Observing the shocks $(\varepsilon_t, u_t, \eta_t)$, the central bank responds with some policy $i_t = f_i(\varepsilon_t, u_t, \eta_t)$ in order to implement $p_t = f_p(\varepsilon_t, u_t, \eta_t)$

We assume that the central bank tries to minimize losses of the representative agent, represented by the quadratic loss function:

$$L = \frac{1}{2}E(y_1 - y_1^*)^2 + \frac{1}{2}\cdot\frac{\theta}{k}\cdot E(p_1 - p^*)^2 \qquad (5.2.2.1)$$

subject to the short run supply function: $p_1 - p_1^e = k(y_1 - y_{1n})$ with $y_{1n} = y_1^* - \Delta - u_1$. We can write the constraint as:

$$p_1 - p_1^e = k(y_1 - y_1^* + \Delta + u_1). \qquad (5.2.2.2)$$

We need to solve the game backwards. Ex post at stage 3, once shocks $\varepsilon_1, u_1, \eta_1$ are realized, the central bank observes the realized values. Taking the AS curve Equation 5.2.2.2 as constraint the central bank reacts to the shocks by influencing output and price level so as to minimize welfare losses. At that stage, there is no longer uncertainty. Thus, we can solve the optimization problem by simply setting up the Lagrangian (adding the AS constraint with weight λ to the loss function).

$$\Lambda = \frac{1}{2}(y_1 - y_1^*)^2 + \frac{1}{2}\cdot\frac{\theta}{k}\cdot(p_1 - p^*)^2 + \lambda\cdot[p_1 - p_1^e - k\,(y_1 - y_1^*) - k(\Delta + u_1)]. \qquad (5.2.2.3)$$

As first-order conditions for an interior minimum, we get:

$$\frac{\partial\Lambda}{\partial y_1} = (y_1 - y_1^*) - \lambda\cdot k = 0, \qquad (5.2.2.3a)$$

$$\frac{\partial\Lambda}{\partial p_1} = \frac{\theta}{k}(p_1 - p^*) + \lambda = 0, \qquad (5.2.2.3b)$$

$$\frac{\partial\Lambda}{\partial\lambda} = p_1 - p_1^e - k\;(y_1 - y_1^*) - k(\Delta + u_1) = 0. \qquad (5.2.2.3c)$$

Combining Equations 5.2.2.3a and 5.2.2.3b gives a negatively sloped relation between p_1 and y_1:

$$p_1 - p^* = -\frac{1}{\theta}(y_1 - y_1^*). \qquad (5.2.2.3d)$$

We call that relation the ***optimal stabilization curve***. It has slope $-1/\theta$. Note that this curve always passes through the point (p^*, y^*). Since neither η_1 nor u_1 affect y^*, these shocks have no impact on the optimal stabilization curve. In contrast, supply shocks ε_1 shifts y^* and so also the optimal stabilization curve.

Inserting Equation 5.2.2.3d in the AS curve Equation 5.2.2.2 solves for the optimal level:

$$p_1 = p^* + \frac{1}{1+k\theta}(p_1^e - p^*) + \frac{k}{1+k\theta}(\Delta + u_1). \tag{5.2.2.4}$$

Equation 5.2.2.4 characterizes the optimal response of the central bank (in terms of the price level) at stage 3 for any arbitrary expected price level p_1^e, once shocks are realized. So it is the central bank's reaction function. At stage 2, when setting their price, firms want to predict the price level as best as possible. Of course, at the time when firms fix their prices, they do not yet know the realization of the shocks. But they are able to anticipate the central bank's reaction in the next stage. They know that given $E_0(p_1)$ the price level at stage 3 will be:

$$p_1 = p^* + \frac{1}{1+k\theta}(E_0(p_1) - p^*) + \frac{k}{1+k\theta}(\Delta + u_1).$$

In order to minimize prediction errors, they will pick their best forecast based on all information available at stage 2 (period 0). So we need to impose Equation 4.1.1: $p_1^e = E_0(p_1)$. Since $E(u_1) = 1$, we have $E_0(p_1) = p^* + \frac{1}{1+k\theta}(E_0(p_1) - p^*) + \frac{k}{1+k\theta}\Delta$, or

$$p_1^e = E_0(p_1) = p^* + \frac{\Delta}{\theta}. \tag{5.2.2.5}$$

Equation 5.2.2.5 characterizes the equilibrium for the case of rational expectations of private agents about central bank policy. It is a bit tricky to interpret the general case $\Delta > 0$. We will do that in detail in Sect. 5.3.

Here, to gain better intuition, let us first consider the straightforward case $\Delta = 0$. That is, we assume there are no persistent markup distortions. Nevertheless temporary markup shocks u_t may cause deviations of potential output from the optimal level ex post. In that case, the optimal policy is straightforward. For $\Delta = 0$ we have $p_1^e = p^*$. Inserting in Equation 5.2.2.4 we get the central bank's reaction function as:

$$p_1 - p^* = \frac{k}{1+\theta \cdot k}u_1. \tag{5.2.2.6a}$$

Inserting p_t in the AS curve and using $y_1^* = y_{1n} + \Delta + u_1$ and $y_{1n} = \overline{y}_{1n} + \varepsilon_1 - u_1$ gives:

$$y_1 - y_{1n} = \frac{1}{1+\theta \cdot k}u_1; y_1 - \overline{y}_{1n} = \varepsilon_1 - \frac{\theta \cdot k}{1+\theta \cdot k}u_1, \text{ or } y_1 - y^* = -\Delta - \frac{\theta \cdot k}{1+\theta \cdot k}u_1. \tag{5.2.2.6b}$$

So Equations 5.2.2.6a and 5.2.2.6b characterize the optimal policy in terms of the key variables affecting welfare, output, and price level. To calculate the appropriate interest rate to implement the solution characterized by these conditions let us first characterize i as a function of output gap and price deviations. So simply invert the AD curve, solving for i:

$$i = \rho + \frac{1}{\sigma}\eta_1 - \frac{1}{\sigma}(y_1 - \overline{y}_1) - (p_1 - p^e).$$

To implement policy Equations 5.2.2.6a and 5.2.2.6b, the interest rate must respond to shocks as follows:

$$i = \rho + \frac{1}{\sigma}\left(\eta_1 - \varepsilon_1 - \frac{(\sigma - \theta)\cdot k}{1 + k\cdot\theta}u_1\right). \tag{5.2.2.6c}$$

The intuition is fairly straightforward: In the face of both demand and supply shocks, the optimal policy is to stabilize output at potential. This coincides with price stability.

5.2.3 Graphical Analysis of Optimal Monetary Policy

Let us now analyze the outcome graphically. Again, to simplify exposition, in this section we only consider the case $\Delta = 0$ (The general case $\Delta > 0$ will be analyzed in Sect. 5.3). Indifference curves can be represented by ellipses around the bliss point B with (p^*, y^*). Ellipses further away from the bliss point represent larger losses—see Fig. 5.3. A central bank targeting p^* will set the interest rate such that in the absence of shocks, point B will be realized. Given some interest rate i, the AD curve is $p_1 - p_1^e = -\frac{1}{\sigma}(y_1 - \overline{y}_1) + \frac{1}{\sigma}\eta_1 - (i_1 - \rho)$ with slope $-1/\sigma$. Shocks shift either AS or AD curve around the bliss point B.

Fig. 5.3 Demand shocks

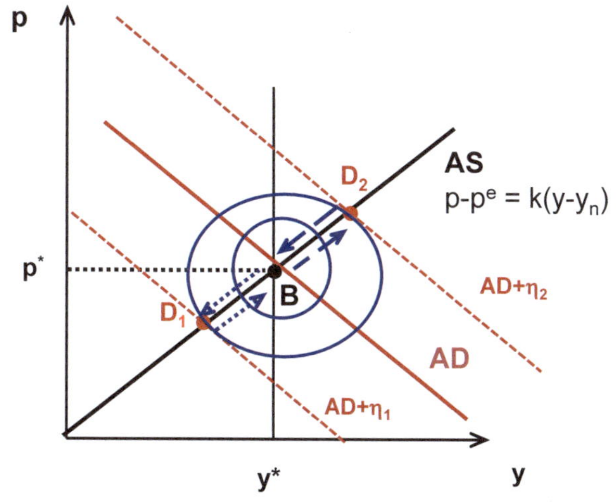

Let us first consider a ***demand shock*** shifting the AD curve upwards or downwards in Fig. 5.3. With a negative (positive) demand shock η_1 (η_2), there is downward (upward) pressure both on output and the price level. As long as the interest rate stays constant, the economy will move toward point D_1 (D_2). So in the absence of active monetary policy, both output and prices shift away from target in the same direction. The central bank can offset that deviation by cutting (raising) interest rate sufficiently to bring AD back to the original level. This requires active intervention. But in the case of AD shocks, stabilizing prices and output are complementary objectives. There is no trade-off between these two targets.

Next, let us look at ***negative supply*** or ***positive markup shocks***. Both shocks shift the AS curve to the left—see Figs. 5.4 and 5.5. With no change in the interest rate,

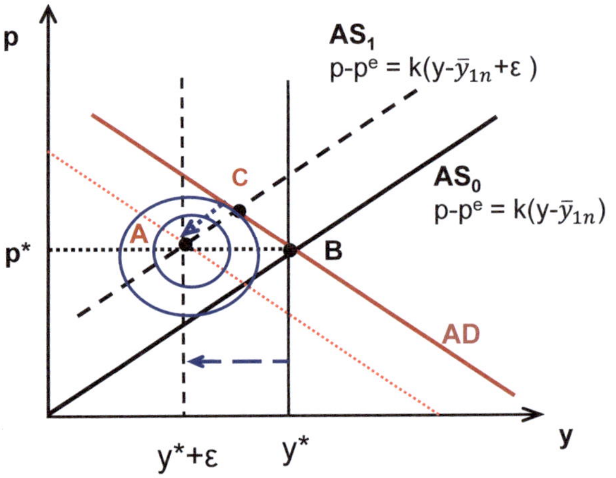

Fig. 5.4 Negative supply shock

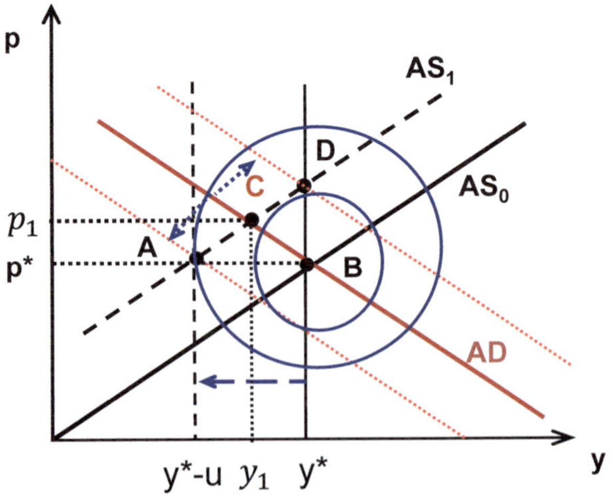

Fig. 5.5 Markup shock

the new equilibrium is at the intersection between the AD curve and the new short-run AS curve (point *C*). Prices will rise; at the same time, output will be above the new shocked potential output, but below the initial level y^*. In the case of a supply shock, the optimal level y^* at the same time has also been shifted to the left. The new bliss point for the indifference curves is now shifted to point *A* with $\{p^*, y^* + \varepsilon\}$. Thus, the optimal policy is to accommodate the shock such that the economy reaches that point. This requires an increase in the interest rate, dampening aggregate demand to the left (the dotted line) in order bring it back to the lower supply such as to keep the price level stable. Stabilizing prices at p^* is the optimal policy. At the same time, this policy makes sure that output reaches the new target level $y^* + \varepsilon$ at point *A*. Again, stabilizing prices and output are complementary objectives.

In contrast, however, a markup shock has quite different implications: Again, it shifts the potential output to the left toward $y^* - u_1$. But in contrast, optimal output is still unchanged at the initial level y^* with a markup shock. So the bliss point stays at *B* (see Fig. 5.5). Thus, it is no longer optimal to accommodate the shock, trying to stabilize the price level at point *A*. One may conjecture that instead the central bank should try to stabilize output at y^* (resulting in point *D*). We, however, now face a trade-off between stabilizing prices and stabilizing output. Any attempt to stimulate y toward y^* drives p further away from the target rate p^*. Any attempt to dampen the economy in order to achieve price stability at p^* drives y further below y^*. We need to be aware of the trade-off involved, arising from the positively sloped AS curve. We have to weigh costs and gains from policy. As long as policy stays unchanged (leaving i constant), point *C* with $\{y_1, p_1\}$ will be realized—the intersection between the initial AD curve and the shocked AS curve.

In the presence of markup shocks, the optimal response depends on the shape of the loss function. The optimal mix between price and output stabilization is characterized by the point of tangency between the shifted short run AS curve and the indifference curves characterizing the loss function. As drawn in Fig. 5.5, the optimal point *D* is closer to y^* than the market outcome, so the central bank should stimulate the economy in the face of markup shocks driving potential output below the target rate. The opposite reaction is optimal with negative markup shocks, driving potential output above target.

In Fig. 5.6 the optimal stabilization curve is drawn as the line of all points of tangency between indifference curves and the short-run AS curve. Markup shocks u_1 shift the short-run AS curve. Optimal stabilization policy requires that the central bank adjusts the interest rate in such a way that—independent of the specific shock—aggregate demand will be at the intersection between the short-run AS curve and the optimal stabilization line. As drawn in Fig. 5.6 the stabilization line is steeper than the AD curve at constant interest rate i. If a markup shock u_1 shifts the economy below y_1^*, at unchanged policy with constant interest rate i, the economy moves toward point C''. For optimal policy, the central bank should allow the price level to rise in order to move output closer to the target rate y_1^*

Fig. 5.6 Optimal stabilization line

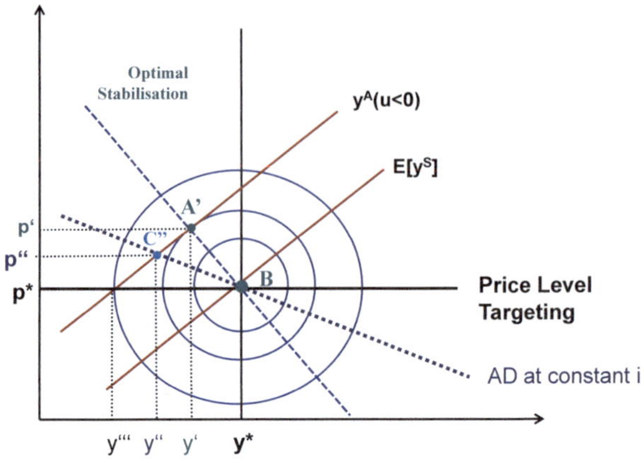

(point A'). The interest rate needs to be cut in order to stimulate aggregate demand. The welfare gain from stabilizing output (stimulating y) dominates the loss arising from the fact that prices increase even further above the target p^*. This is the case whenever the stabilization curve is steeper than the AD curve, that is for $\sigma > \theta$.

We get the opposite result for $\sigma < \theta$. In that case, the stabilization line will be flatter than the AD curve, and so the optimal response to shocks shifting the economy below y_1^* is to dampen price rather than output movements. As an extreme case, for $\theta \to \infty$ iso-loss curves are parallel to p^*; stabilizing the price level at p^* is the optimal policy independent of output fluctuations. For the opposite extreme ($\theta \to 0$), iso-loss curves are parallel to y^*; so stabilizing y^* is optimal. Finally, for $\sigma = \theta$, the AD curve coincides with the optimal stabilization line. If so, leaving the interest rate constant (doing nothing) is the optimal response to the markup shock.

In general the central bank should react actively by adjusting interest rates to shocks. Note that according to the optimal interest rule, the adequate response strongly depends on the nature of the shock. Identifying the underlying shock properly is a key challenge for the central bank. Stabilizing nominal GDP is equivalent to stabilizing the log of prices and output: $p + y = const$. This will be the optimal policy for markup shocks if the green line has the slope -1. This is a very special case. Even if we assume $\sigma = \theta$, leaving interest rates unchanged would be the optimal response only for markup shocks. For other shocks, stabilizing potential output (equivalent to stabilizing the price level) is superior. For $\theta = 1$, the slope of the optimal stabilization line is -1. In that case, stabilizing nominal GDP is the optimal policy both for demand shocks and for markup shocks. Nevertheless even for $\theta = 1$ the central bank should aim to stabilize the price level rather than nominal GDP after supply shocks.

5.3 The Problem of Dynamic Inconsistency

5.3.1 Barro–Gordon Model: The Discretionary Solution

In the last section, when we derived the optimal policy in period 1, we sketched the intuition for the case $\Delta = 0$ so $y_{t\,n} = y_t^* - u_t$ with $E(u_t) = 0$. But we need to take into account also persistent structural distortions in the economy. After all, in reality economies are facing many distortions, arising from monopoly power, tax rates, and many other elements. A welfare maximizing central bank might try to stimulate the economy by raising the price level above expected level. But as soon as private agents anticipate this incentive, they will form higher price expectations right from the start. In the end, it is not feasible in equilibrium to stimulate the economy above potential. As first shown by Barro and Gordon (1983), the attempt to stimulate will fail, the central bank cannot systematically raise output above market equilibrium. In Sect. 5.3 we characterize the outcome of the Barro–Gordon model using game theoretic concepts.

Sometimes, the literature focuses on the simple case $\Delta = 0$ by assuming that these distortions can be corrected via paying subsidies to firms. If a subsidy is chosen appropriately, it might offset the effective markup μ. But paying such subsidies would require additional taxes, possibly creating even more distortions. $\Delta = 0$ could be implemented only when subsidies can be financed via lump-sum taxes. But it is seems a bit odd to allow imposing lump-sum taxes to finance subsidies which are used to correct distortionary taxation.

The case $\Delta = 0$ gives a straightforward yet somewhat misleading reference point. As long as $\Delta = 0$, the policy the central bank implements at stage 3 is exactly the policy announced at the initial stage 1:[5] After all, as shown in the last section, it is optimal to implement the policy Equation 5.2.2.6a $p_t = p^* + \frac{k}{1+\theta} u_t$ with $E(p_t) = p^*$. Announcing this policy rule at stage 1 will be credible. This is no longer the case when we analyze the general case $\Delta > 0$. The reason is that the central bank has strong incentives to deviate from such an announcement at stage 3, once shocks have been realized. As shown in the previous section, the central bank's reaction function is

$$p_1 = p^* + \frac{1}{1+k\theta}(p_1^e - p^*) + \frac{k}{1+k\theta}(\Delta + u_1). \tag{5.2.2.4}$$

[5]This statement needs to be qualified in a dynamic context. If we can spread the costs from stabilising shocks across time, there may be a stabilization bias in the following sense: It would be better to commit to spread the burden of adjustment across time rather than to incur all costs in the current period. But once the shock fades out in the next period, it would be optimal to renege on that promise. After all, announcements made in the past may no longer be seen as binding. We analyze this inconsistency problem in detail in the presence of the zero lower bound in Chap. 7.

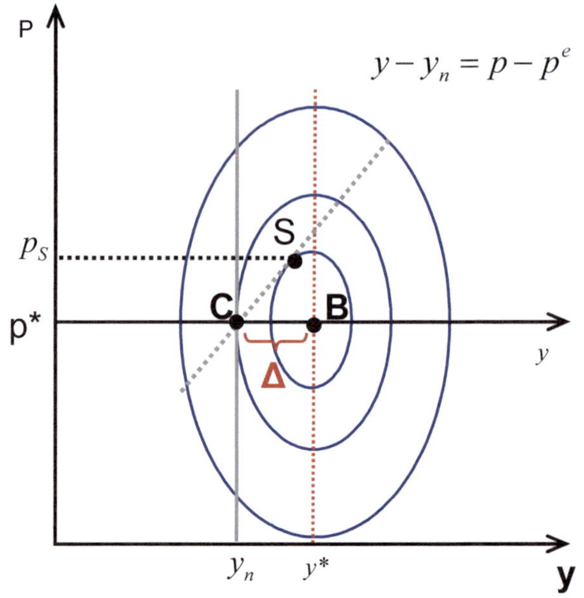

Fig. 5.7 Incentives for surprise inflation

In a rational expectation equilibrium this gives expected price level

$$p_1^e = E_0(p_1) = p^* + \frac{\Delta}{\theta} > p^*. \tag{5.2.2.5}$$

To gain a better intuition about the underlying mechanism, let us look at Fig. 5.7. Again, indifference curves are represented by ellipses around the bliss point B. To make it simple, let us ignore shocks for a moment. Let us make the following thought experiment: At stage 1, the central bank announces the policy Equation 5.2.2.6a promising to implement the target level p^*. If all firms believe her announcement ($p^e = p^*$), the real constraint for the central bank at stage 3 is the AS curve as drawn in Fig. 5.7, intersecting potential output at point C with $p = p^*$ and $y = y_n$. But the target rate y^* is above potential by $\Delta = y_1^* - y_{1\,n}$. Thus, triggering a surprise inflation to raise output above y_n driving production closer to y^* will reduce losses (raise welfare) as long as the marginal costs of such a policy (creating price distortions by driving the price level above the target p^*) are smaller than the marginal gains out of getting closer to target output. Obviously, at point C with $p = p^*$, marginal costs of a small increase in the price level are close to zero, whereas marginal gains from reducing distortions Δ are strictly positive. So it definitely pays to raise p a little bit above p^*. At the optimum, the marginal costs of raising the price level further will be just equal to the marginal gain. This condition holds at the point of tangency between an iso-loss curve and the policy constraint defined by the relevant AS curve—point S in C.

Given $p^e = p^*$, the constraint AS is the dotted curve CS. Along that curve, point S is the best feasible combination, minimizing losses along the line CS. So at stage 3, the central bank has an incentive to raise the price level up to p_S in order to stimulate output above potential, aiming to steer the economy closer to the first-best level y^*.

The larger the structural distortions Δ, the stronger is this incentive. It also depends on the slope of the AS curve (here normalized to $k = 1$) and on the relative weight θ of price distortions compared to deviations of output from target level. θ determines the shape of the iso-loss curves. The smaller θ, the steeper these curves. The larger θ, the closer point S will be to C—with strong preferences against price dispersion, stabilizing prices is considered to be more important than stimulating output.

Obviously, S cannot be an equilibrium outcome. The price-setting firms will anticipate already at stage 2 the bank's incentive to trigger a surprise inflation later. Knowing the structure of the economy and the bank's objective, they are able to figure out her reaction function. Expectations are consistent only if $p_t^e = E_{t-1}(p_t)$. For equilibrium, we impose the condition that the expected price level is equal to the price level realized on average in that period as a result from actual central bank's actions, given the information available at that point in time. This outcome can be seen as a Nash-equilibrium: Given that outcome, no agent (neither price setting firms nor the central bank) has an incentive to deviate. Following Robert Lucas (1972), this consistency requirement is called rational expectations equilibrium in the macro literature. In the next section, we will derive this equilibrium.

5.3.1.1 Discretionary Equilibrium with Rational Expectations

How do we solve for the consistent equilibrium with rational expectations? The answer is fairly straightforward: In equilibrium, both the central bank's reaction function and Equation 4.1.1: $p_t^e = E_{t-1}(p_t)$ must hold. Graphically, both conditions can be characterized as in Fig. 5.8. The consistency requirement for price setting firms $p_1^e = E_0(p_1)$ has slope 1. The central bank's reaction function is given by Equation 5.2.2.4. At stage 2, u_1 is not yet known, but using $E(u_1) = 0$ firms are able to calculate the average price level, $E(p_1) = E_0(p_1) = p^* + \frac{1}{1+k\theta}(E_0(p_1) - p^*) + \frac{k}{1+k\theta}\Delta$.

For $p_1^e = p^*$ the curve will be above C at point S with $p_t = p^* + \frac{\Delta}{1+\theta} > p^*$. The reaction curve is less steep with slope $\frac{1}{1+k\theta} < 1$. To calculate equilibrium, just insert

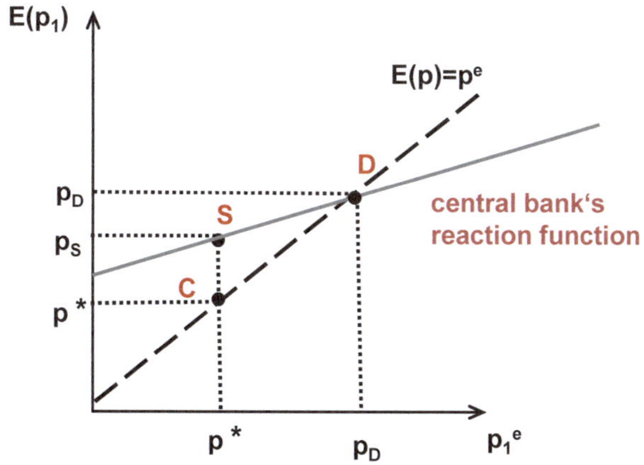

Fig. 5.8 Central bank's reaction function

p_1^e for $E_0(p_1)$ in the reaction function and solve for p_1^e. The intersection of both curves characterizes the ***discretionary, dynamic consistent equilibrium***

$$p_D^e = E(p_t) = p^* + \frac{\Delta}{\theta}. \tag{5.2.2.5}$$

So at stage 3, the central bank's response to shocks will be:

$$p_{1D} = p^* + \frac{\Delta}{\theta} + \frac{1}{1+\theta} u = p_1^e + \frac{1}{1+\theta} u_1, \tag{5.3.1.1.1}$$

$$p_1^d = p^* + \frac{\Delta}{\theta} + \frac{k}{1+\theta \cdot k} u_1, \tag{5.3.1.1.2}$$

$$y_1^d = \overline{y}_{1n} + \varepsilon_1 - \frac{\theta \cdot k}{1+\theta \cdot k} \cdot u_1 = y_1^* - \Delta - \frac{\theta \cdot k}{1+\theta \cdot k} \cdot u_1. \tag{5.3.1.1.3}$$

The corresponding interest rate policy implementing this allocation is:

$$i = \rho + \frac{1}{\sigma}\left(\eta - \varepsilon - \frac{\sigma \ - \theta}{1+\theta} u_t\right). \tag{5.3.1.1.4}$$

Since $p_t^e = p_D^e = p^* + \frac{\Delta}{\theta} > p^*$ (see Equation 5.3.1.1.2), policy is now characterized by an inflation bias. The bias is stronger the larger the persistent structural inefficiencies Δ and the smaller the weight θ of price distortions relative to those coming from deviations of output from target output y^*.

In equilibrium, the price level is inefficiently high. The central bank, however, is not able to steer the economy away from potential output. This is evident from

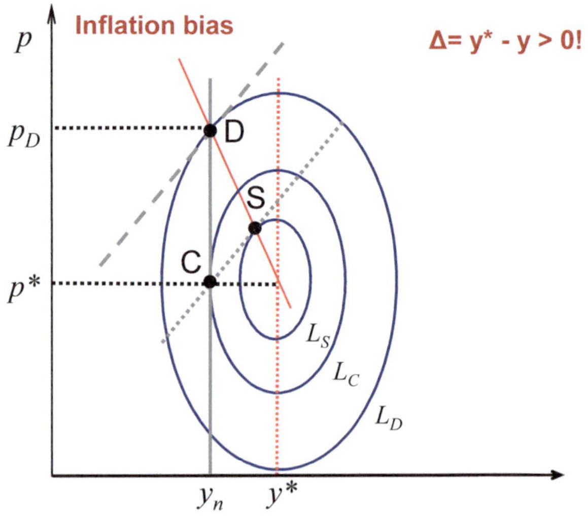

Fig. 5.9 Dynamic consistent equilibrium

Fig. 5.9. Point D is the discretionary outcome with rational expectations of price setting firms. In equilibrium, the expected price level deviates so much from the target p^* that it is no longer optimal for the central bank to raise p even further. In D, marginal cost from price distortions $p_D - p^*$ is just equal to marginal gain from stimulating the economy above potential. In the end, in equilibrium it is not feasible to stimulate the economy above potential. The attempt to raise welfare results just in an inefficiently high price level and imposes even stronger welfare losses for society.

5.3.1.2 Welfare Analysis

Inserting Equations 5.3.1.1.2 and 5.3.1.1.3 in the expected loss function, we can calculate the unconditional expected welfare loss ex ante—before knowing the realization of shocks:

$$\begin{aligned} E(L_D) &= \frac{1}{2}E(y_t - y_t^*)^2 + \frac{1}{2}\frac{\theta}{k} \cdot E(p_t - p^*)^2 \\ &= \frac{1}{2}E\left(-\Delta - \frac{\theta \cdot k}{1+\theta \cdot k}u_1\right)^2 + \frac{1}{2}\frac{\theta}{k} \cdot E\left(\frac{\Delta}{\theta} + \frac{k}{1+\theta \cdot k}u_1\right)^2 \\ &= \frac{1}{2}\left[\Delta^2 + \left(\frac{\theta \cdot k}{1+\theta \cdot k}\right)^2 E(u)^2 + \frac{\theta}{k} \cdot \frac{\Delta^2}{\theta^2} + \frac{\theta}{k}\frac{k^2}{(1+\theta \cdot k)^2}E(u)^2\right], \end{aligned}$$

$$\begin{aligned} E(L_D) &= \frac{1}{2}\Delta^2 + \frac{1}{2}\frac{\Delta^2}{\theta \cdot k} + \frac{1}{2}\left(\frac{\theta \cdot k}{1+\theta \cdot k}\right)^2 \sigma_u^2 + \frac{1}{2}\frac{\theta \cdot k}{(1+\theta \cdot k)^2}\sigma_u^2 \\ &= \frac{1}{2}\left[\Delta^2\left(\frac{1+\theta \cdot k}{\theta \cdot k}\right) + \frac{\theta \cdot k}{1+\theta \cdot k}\sigma_u^2\right]. \end{aligned} \tag{5.3.1.2.1}$$

The welfare loss of discretionary policy consists of four parts. The first part $\frac{1}{2}\Delta^2$ is the loss arising from structural inefficiency Δ. Monetary policy is not the adequate tool to solve these distortions. But the second part $\Delta^2/2\theta k$ is the loss arising from the inflationary bias, driving the target rate toward p^D, exceeding p^* by $\frac{\Delta}{\theta}$. The other parts arise from variations due to stochastic markup shocks. In the absence of flexible stabilization, the loss from markup shocks would be larger. But even though they are stabilized optimally, perfect stabilization is not feasible—in contrast to demand shocks (note that supply shocks do not cause welfare losses due to divine coincidence). First, markup shocks shift output away from the target level, resulting in the expected welfare loss $\frac{1}{2}\left(\frac{\theta \cdot k}{1+\theta \cdot k}\right)^2\sigma_u^2$. Second, they distort price away from the target p^* creating expected loss $\frac{1}{2}\frac{\theta \cdot k}{(1+\theta \cdot k)^2}\sigma_u^2$. Adding both effects gives $\frac{1}{2}\frac{\theta \cdot k \cdot (1+\theta \cdot k)}{(1+\theta \cdot k)^2}\sigma_u^2$.

5.3.2 The Commitment Solution

An adequate institutional design committing the central bank not to give in to the temptation may to eliminate the inflation bias and so solve the dynamic consistency problem. What is the optimal strategy when the central bank can commit at stage 1 to implement later at stage 3 the policy rule announced earlier? The central bank is now able to bind itself to the initial announcement $p_t^C = p_t^a$. So the announcement made at stage 1 will have a direct impact on the price level expected by those firms fixing their prices at stage 2. Thus, when designing its policy, the central bank will not only take into account the AS condition at stage 3, but also the fact that her announced rule will have a direct impact on the price level expected by those firms fixing their prices at stage 2. So the rational expectation Equation 4.1.1: $p_t^e = E(p_t)$ has to be taken into account as additional constraint for policy design at stage 1.

Under commitment, the central bank tries to minimize losses by designing a policy rule, taking both constraints into consideration. It minimizes the loss function Equation 5.2.2.1 subject to Equation 5.2.2.2 and to Equation 4.1.1. We insert the AS constraint directly in the policy function and add the rational expectation condition as additional constraint, using the Lagrangian parameter λ. Under commitment, when choosing its policy, the central bank can directly determine p_1^e. So she will not only choose the optimal response $p_1(u_1)$ for each realization of the shock u_1, but can also choose p_1^e. Knowing that raising the price level later will have an adverse effect on p_1^e constrains her incentive to stimulate the economy at stage 3. This shows up by the fact that the Lagrangian parameter λ plays a role in all first-order conditions.

$$\underset{p_1^e;p_1(u)}{\Lambda} = \frac{1}{2}E\left(\frac{1}{k}\cdot(p_1 - p_1^e) - \Delta - u\right)^2 + \frac{1}{2}\cdot\frac{\theta}{k}\cdot E(p_1 - p^*)^2 + \lambda[E(p_1) - p_1^e], \text{ or}$$

$$\underset{p_1^e;p_1(u)}{\Lambda} = \frac{1}{2}\int\left\{\left(\frac{1}{k}\cdot(p_1(u) - p_1^e) - \Delta - u\right)^2 + \frac{1}{2}\cdot\frac{\theta}{k}\cdot(p_1(u) - p^*)^2 + \lambda[p_1(u) - p_1^e]\right\}f(u)du.$$

First-Order Conditions for Commitment Solution:

(A) Taking the first derivative with respect to the expected price level p_1^e, we need to set $\partial\Lambda/\partial p_1^e = 0$. This looks rather messy, since p_1^e shows up in the first and last term of the integrals. But we can use the Leibniz rule $\frac{d}{dx}\int f(x,u)du = \int\frac{\partial}{\partial x}f(x,u)du$. This gives
FOC for p_1^e: $\int\{-1/k(1/k(p_1 - p_1^e) - \Delta - u) - \lambda\}f(u)du = 0$.
Using $\int uf(u)du = E(u) = 0$ and $\int p_1(u)f(u)du = E(p_1)$ gives $p_{1C}^e = E(p_1) + k^2\cdot\lambda - k\cdot\Delta$.
Since $p_{1C}^e = E(p_1)$ we get $\lambda = \Delta/k$.

(B) After observing state u_1, the FOC condition for the optimal price level $p_1(u_1)$ is: $\partial\Lambda/\partial p(u_1) = 0$.
This gives $1/k(1/k(p_1 - p_1^e) - \Delta - u_1) + \theta/k \cdot (p_1 - p^*) + \lambda = 0$, or:
FOC for $p_1(u_1)$: $p_1(1 + \theta \cdot k) = p_1^e + \theta \cdot k \cdot p^* + k(\Delta + u_1) - k^2 \cdot \lambda$ for all u_1.
Using condition $\lambda = \Delta/k$ from A), we have $p_1(1 + \theta \cdot k) = p_1^e + \theta \cdot k \cdot p^* + ku_1$, so in particular: $E(p_1)\ (1 + \theta \cdot k) = p_1^e + \theta \cdot k \cdot p^* + kE(u)$. Imposing $p_1^e = E(p_1)$ gives $p_{1C}^e = p^*$. Thus $p_1^C(u) = p^* + \frac{k}{1+\theta \cdot k} u_1$.

So under commitment the optimal policy is Equation 5.2.2.6a with $p_1 = p^* + \frac{1}{1+\theta \cdot k} u_1$. On average the economy will end up at point C in Fig. 5.9—the commitment solution. Using the AS curve Equation 5.2.2.2, output fluctuations are characterized by Equation 5.2.2.6b. Again, we can calculate the expected loss ex ante before knowing the realization of shocks. For the commitment solution we get:

$$\begin{aligned} E(L_C) &= \frac{1}{2} E\left(-\Delta - \frac{\theta \cdot k}{1 + \theta \cdot k} u_1\right)^2 + \frac{1}{2} \cdot \frac{\theta}{k} \cdot E\left(\frac{k}{1 + \theta \cdot k} u_1\right)^2 \\ &= \frac{1}{2}\left[\frac{\theta \cdot k}{1 + \theta \cdot k} \sigma_u^2 + \Delta^2\right]. \end{aligned} \tag{5.3.2.1}$$

$E(L_C) < E(L_D)$ The difference $E(L_D) - E(L_C) = \frac{1}{2} \frac{\Delta^2}{\theta \cdot k}$ is the result of the inflation bias $\frac{\Delta}{\theta}$ in case of discretion, causing a systematic additional loss $\frac{1}{2} \frac{\Delta^2}{\theta^2}$, weighted with θ/k. The commitment solution avoids this loss and so implements the constrained-efficient second-best outcome. It minimizes expected ex ante losses, given that monetary policy cannot cope with structural distortions.

Of course, expected losses would be even lower if the central bank could persuade all price setters to expect the price level p^* on average, but later at stage 3 renege on her promises. As shown in the next section $E(L_S) < E(L_C) < E(L_D)$ with $E(L_S)$ as expected loss under surprise inflation. A systematic surprise inflation, if feasible, would drive output closer to y^* and thus reduce the distortions Δ arising from structural inefficiency. Obviously, a systematic surprise is a contradiction in itself: *You can't fool all of the people all of the time.* At stage 2, price setting firms will anticipate the incentive. According to the Lucas critique, private agents will respond to policy. That is, they will raise their price expectation, trying to prevent losses from setting their prices too far away from the expected mean. As pointed out above, in the end this will result in the inferior outcome $E(L_D)$.

5.3.3 The Incentive for a Surprise Inflation

As shown in Fig. 5.9, point C is no Nash equilibrium. It is not dynamically consistent. Assume that private agents expect $p_t^e = p^*$. According to the central banks reaction function Equation 5.2.2.4 the optimal response ex post is to set prices at

$$p_S = p^* + \frac{k}{1+\theta \cdot k}(\Delta + u_1). \tag{5.3.3.1a}$$

In the absence of commitment power, the central bank has a strong incentive for a surprise inflation, driving output up above potential in order to bring it closer to y^*. We get

$$y_S - y_{1n} = p_S - p_1^e = \frac{1}{1+\theta \cdot k}(\Delta + u_1).$$

Thus

$$y_S - y^* = y_S - y_{1n} - \Delta - u = -\frac{\theta \cdot k}{1+\theta \cdot k}(\Delta + u_1). \tag{5.3.3.1b}$$

If such a policy would be feasible, the expected loss ex ante would be even lower than in the case of commitment:

$$\begin{aligned} E(L_S) &= \frac{1}{2}E\left(\frac{\theta \cdot k}{1+\theta \cdot k}(\Delta + u_1)\right)^2 + \frac{1}{2}\cdot\frac{\theta}{k}\cdot E\left(\frac{k(\Delta + u_1)}{\theta \cdot k}\right)^2 \\ &= \frac{1}{2}\cdot\frac{\theta \cdot k}{1+\theta \cdot k}(\Delta^2 + \sigma_u^2). \end{aligned} \tag{5.3.3.1c}$$

Of course, the average price level of such a policy is $E(p_S|p^*)| = \frac{k}{1+\theta \cdot k}\Delta$. So clever agents anticipating that response would never expect $p_t^e = p^*$ from the beginning. Instead, we end up at the discretionary solution.

Summary
Discretionary Solution:

$$p_{1D} - p^* = \frac{\Delta}{\theta} + \frac{k}{1+\theta \cdot k}u_1, \quad \text{with} \quad p_{1D}^e = p^* + \frac{\Delta}{\theta}, \tag{5.3.1.1.2}$$

$$y_1^d = \overline{y}_{1n} + \varepsilon_1 - \frac{\theta \cdot k}{1+\theta \cdot k}\cdot u_1 = y_1^* - \Delta - \frac{\theta \cdot k}{1+\theta \cdot k}\cdot u_1, \tag{5.3.1.1.3}$$

$$E(L_D) = \frac{1}{2}\left[\Delta^2\left(\frac{1+\theta \cdot k}{\theta \cdot k}\right) + \frac{\theta \cdot k}{1+\theta \cdot k}\sigma_u^2\right]. \tag{5.3.1.2.1}$$

(continued)

Commitment Solution:

$$p_{1C} - p^* = \frac{k}{1 + \theta \cdot k} u_1, \quad \text{with} \quad p^e_{1C} = p^*, \tag{5.2.2.6a}$$

$$y_{1C} = \overline{y}_{1n} + \varepsilon_1 - \frac{\theta \cdot k}{1 + \theta \cdot k} \cdot u_1 = y_1^* - \Delta - \frac{\theta \cdot k}{1 + \theta \cdot k} \cdot u_1, \tag{5.2.2.6b}$$

$$i = \rho + \frac{1}{\sigma}\left(\eta_1 - \varepsilon_1 - \frac{\sigma - \theta}{1 + \theta} u_1\right), \tag{5.2.2.6c}$$

$$E(L_C) = \frac{1}{2} \frac{\theta \cdot k}{1 + \theta \cdot k} \sigma_u^2 + \frac{1}{2} \Delta^2. \tag{5.3.2.1}$$

Surprise Solution:

$$p_{1S} - p^* = \frac{k}{1 + \theta \cdot k} (\Delta + u_1), \quad \text{given} \quad p^e_{1C} = p^*, \tag{5.3.3.1a}$$

$$y_{1S} - y^* = \frac{\theta \cdot k}{1 + \theta \cdot k} \cdot (\Delta + u_1), \tag{5.3.3.1b}$$

$$E(L_S) = \frac{1}{2} \frac{\theta \cdot k}{1 + \theta \cdot k} (\sigma_u^2 + \Delta^2). \tag{5.3.3.1c}$$

5.4 Strict Rules as Second-Best Commitment Mechanisms for Implementing Optimal Policy

Bob Lucas argues that structural models should take the response of private agents to changes in policy into account. His argument triggered the rational expectation revolution in macroeconomic modeling. The Lucas critique provides a justification for a policy based on rules in monetary economics. If the central bank can commit to a rule, the scope for discretionary actions may be limited, resulting in a superior commitment outcome. Since $E(L_S)$ is not feasible, there are strong arguments to design monetary policy in such a way that the central bank can acquire reputation not to give in the temptation to abuse her policy instruments. If some mechanism design can provide commitment power, the central bank may be able to implement the second-best outcome with expected losses $E(L_C)$. Unfortunately, as we will see in this section, it is not evident how to design strict rules which are robust.

As just shown, the optimal policy is characterized by Equations 5.2.2.6a and 5.2.2.6b. They describe how price level and output (the pair (p,y)) should respond to specific shocks in the economy. Since optimal policy should respond to markup shocks, these distortions pose a key challenge for inflexible rules. Obviously, the optimal policy could be implemented via flexible price targeting. If the central bank can commit to stabilize prices on average at p^*, but to respond flexibly to markup shocks, it would commit to achieve condition Equation 5.2.2.6a). Naturally, also Equation 5.2.2.6b) will hold. But the central bank can implement its policy only via some transmission mechanism. Just stating that she intends to steer the price level as in Equation 5.2.2.6a) is not enough. The central bank has to actively respond to shocks with changes in her policy instrument in order to steer the economy toward the desired outcome.

The standard transmission mechanism for monetary policy is the impact on the real interest rate. By adjusting the nominal interest rate i (at given expected prices) as policy instrument, the central bank can influence demand via the interest rate channel. By inserting Equations 5.2.2.6a and 5.2.2.6b in the AD curve we can calculate the interest rate required to implement the optimal policy Equation 5.2.2.6c. Note, however, that the interest rate rule for the discretionary solution looks exactly the same. The reason is that under a pure interest rate rule the price level is indetermined (see Sect. 2.6). So ex ante, the central banks needs also to commit to some limit on money supply to determine p.

Alternatively, the optimal rule may also be characterized as money supply. In order to determine money supply, we need to introduce a money demand function and the additional equilibrium condition: "demand of money equals supply." Assume the money demand function is given by the log-linearized equation:

$$m_1 - p_1 = y_1 - \varsigma i_1 + \xi. \tag{5.4.1}$$

Here ξ is a monetary shock disturbing the demand for base money with $E[\xi] = 0$, $\mathrm{Var}(\xi) = \sigma_\xi^2$. We can solve for the optimal money supply targeting rule by inserting the solution Equations 5.2.2.6a, 5.2.2.6b and 5.2.2.6c. This gives

$$m_1 = p^* + \frac{1}{1+\theta}u + \overline{y}_1^n + \varepsilon - \frac{\theta}{1+\theta}u - \varsigma\left[\rho + \frac{1}{\sigma}\left(\eta - \varepsilon + \frac{\theta - \sigma}{1+\theta}u\right)\right] + \xi, \quad \text{or}$$

$$m_1 = p^* + \overline{y}_1^n - \varsigma\rho + \frac{(1-\theta)\ (1+\varsigma)}{1+\theta}u + (1+\varsigma)\,\varepsilon - \varsigma\eta + \xi. \tag{5.4.1a}$$

In the absence of control errors and as long as the central bank is able to identify the specific type of shocks, it is easy to characterize optimal rule in terms of the policy instrument—be it the interest rate or money supply. The optimal interest rate rule is Equation 5.2.2.6c), the optimal money supply rule Equation 5.4.1a. The response strongly depends on the type of shocks[6]. As long as (1) all shocks can be identified, (2) the target pair (p, y) can be controlled perfectly, and (3) the central bank is able to commit to such rules, all these policies are equivalent. In central bank practice, none of these strong assumptions is satisfied. In the next sections, we will

[6]Note that we do not characterize the optimal rule as a Taylor rule, responding to deviations of output and price level from target in the past. When shocks are persistent, a forward-looking Taylor rule (predicting output and prices at unchanged policy) may be used as instrument rule.

discuss implications for policy when we relax the assumptions. First, we analyze alternatives if the central bank cannot commit to follow complex rules.

It may not be possible to commit to a policy rule as in Equation 5.2.2.6a. Alternatives may be inflexible rules binding the central bank to some restrictions. One option could be to impose a price level target p^*. Alternatively, the central bank may commit not to react at all to shocks, but rather commit to fix the interest rate in a such way that the economy reaches p^* on average. Such inflexible rules are bound to be inferior compared to the commitment rule outlined above.

As exercise, let us calculate expected losses from a strict price level target and from targeting nominal GDP. To simplify exposition, in Sect. 5.4, we focus on the case $k = 1$ and $\sigma = 1$. This normalizes the slope of AS curve equal to 1 and the AD curve equal to -1. A price level target stabilizes both demand and supply shocks optimally by construction. Instead, markup shocks will not be stabilized at all by offsetting adjustments. So a price level target implies higher output fluctuations for markup shocks. In contrast, a policy targeting nominal GDP may result in the optimal response for markup shocks: For the special case $\theta = \sigma(=1)$, doing nothing is the optimal response for markup shocks. At the same time, demand shocks will be stabilized perfectly. But targeting nominal GDP will not stabilize prices in the face of supply shocks. It is a useful exercise to calculate expected losses for both cases. In contrast to NGDP or price targeting (both aimed at stabilizing policy targets), a policy committing to keep instruments fixed (such as targeting interest rate or money supply) is strictly inferior. In particular, targeting money is likely to lead to additional volatility as will be shown below.

5.4.1 Strict Price Level Targeting

With strict price level targeting, $p_{t\ PT} = p^*$, output shocks will never be dampened. So output always stays at potential: $y_{t\ PT} = y_{t\,n} = \overline{y}_{t\,n} + \varepsilon_t - u_t$. Since $y_t^* = y_{t\,n} + \Delta + u_t$ we have $y_{t\ IT} - y_t^* = -(\Delta + u_t)$. With $k = 1$ and $\sigma = 1$, expected losses are: $E(L_{PT}) = \frac{1}{2}E(-(\Delta + u_t)^2) = \frac{1}{2}(\Delta^2 + \sigma_u^2)$. Price level targeting helps to implement the optimal response to demand and supply shocks, but does not stabilize markup shocks when there is a conflict between price and output stability. So losses are larger compared to the commitment solution, but smaller compared to the discretionary case.

5.4.2 Nominal GDP Targeting

Recently, nominal GDP targeting (NGDP) has become a popular strategy. In our model, trying to fix nominal GDP is equivalent to steering the economy toward the line $p_1 + y_1 = p^* + \overline{y}_n = const.$ This is a stabilization line with the slope being equal to -1. The central bank commits to bring the economy back to that line after shocks. We get:

$$y_1 - \overline{y}_n = \frac{1}{2}(\varepsilon_1 - u_1), \text{ and } p_1 - p^* = \frac{1}{2}(u_1 - \varepsilon_1).$$

A demand shock (shifting both output and prices in the same direction) will be stabilized perfectly. When a supply shock increases potential output, under NGDP targeting prices fall to keep nominal GDP constant. With a markup decreasing potential output, prices rise.

Since $y_1{}^* = \overline{y}_n + \Delta + \varepsilon_1$, we get $y_1 - y_1{}^* = -\frac{1}{2}(\varepsilon_1 - u_1 + \Delta)$. So overall expected losses are

$$E(L_{NGDP}) = \frac{1}{2}E\left(-\frac{1}{2}(\varepsilon_1 - u_1 + \Delta)\right)^2 + \frac{1}{2}\theta\, E\left(\frac{1}{2}(u_1 - \varepsilon_1)\right)^2$$

$$E(L_{NGDP}) = \frac{1}{2}\Delta^2 + \frac{1}{2}\frac{1+\theta}{4}(\sigma_\varepsilon^2 + \sigma_u^2) > \frac{1}{2}\Delta^2 + \frac{1}{2}\frac{\theta}{1+\theta}\sigma_u^2.$$

For $\theta = 1$, nominal GDP targeting coincides with the optimal stabilization line for markup shocks (we normalized $\sigma = 1$). So markup shocks are stabilized optimally for the case $\theta = 1$. Demand shocks are also stabilized optimally. In contrast, the response to supply shocks is sub-optimal, since in that case, prices rather than nominal GDP should be kept stable. Thus, the response of NGDP is sub-optimal for supply shocks.

5.4.3 Strict Interest Rate Targeting

An inflexible interest rate rule binding the central bank to a policy not responding to shocks at all is equivalent to fixing $i = \rho$. This rule ensures that $E(p_1) = p^*$. So the AD curve is $y_1 - \overline{y}_n = -(p_1 - p^*) + \eta_1$.

With the AS curve as $p_1 - p^* = (y_1 - y_n)$ and $y_n = \overline{y}_n + \varepsilon_1 + u_1$, we can solve for $\{y_1, p_1\}$ as:

$$y_1 - \overline{y}_n = \frac{1}{2}(\eta_1 + \varepsilon_1 - u_1),$$

$$p_1 - p^* = \frac{1}{2}(\eta_1 - \varepsilon_1 + u_1).$$

Since $y_1{}^* = \overline{y}_n + \Delta + u_1$, we have $y_1 - y_1{}^* = \frac{1}{2}(\eta_1 + \varepsilon_1 + u_1) + \Delta$. Thus, expected losses from setting $i = \overline{i} = \rho$ amount to:

$$E(L_{i=\bar{\imath}}) = \frac{1}{2}E\left(\frac{1}{2}(\eta_1 + \varepsilon_1 + u_1) + \Delta\right)^2 + \frac{1}{2}\theta E\left(\frac{1}{2}(\eta_1 - \varepsilon_1 + u_1)\right)^2$$

$$E(L_{i=\bar{\imath}}) = \frac{1}{2}\Delta^2 + \frac{1}{2}\frac{1+\theta}{4}\left(\sigma_\eta^2 + \sigma_\varepsilon^2 + \sigma_u^2\right) > \frac{1}{2}\Delta^2 + \frac{1}{2}\frac{\theta}{1+\theta}\sigma_u^2.$$

Not surprisingly, fixing the interest rate at $\bar{\imath}$ without reacting to any shock at all is bound to create huge volatility. In particular, neither demand nor supply shocks are dampened. Obviously, the central bank needs to respond to shocks by adjusting its policy instrument (the interest rate) carefully.

5.4.4 Strict Money Supply Targeting (Poole Analysis)

Another strict instrument rule which does not respond to the shocks is a rule of strict money supply. In this case, the best the central bank can do rather than Equation 5.4.1a is

$$m_1 = p^* + \overline{y}_1^n - \varsigma\rho. \tag{5.4.1b}$$

Before we solve for the welfare loss of such a strategy, let us compare the strict money supply with a strict interest rate rule $i = \rho$. Both are inflexible rules which do not respond to shocks. The money supply rule targets potential output and the efficient price. But money demand introduces an additional shock term ξ. This term captures exogenous shifts in the money demand due to temporary movements between holding money and holding other, interest bearing financial assets. Shifts due to flight to safety in times of increased uncertainty are one key reason for such volatility (see Chap. 8 for details). If the money supply rule does respond to these shocks, this shock term adds additional volatility relative to a strict interest rate rule.

Let us consider the impact in Fig. 5.10a. $m_{d1}(i, y_1)$ characterizes the average money demand. Given that money supply is fixed at m_1, the interest rate is determined by the intersection of money demand and inelastic money supply. The equilibrium rate at the average money demand $m_{d1}(i, y_1)$ is i_1. If money demand falls (shifts downwards), the interest rate will fall in order to clear the market. Inversely with an increase in money demand. The induced change in the interest rate will have a direct effect on aggregate demand.

For example, let us look at a flight to safe assets like money, inducing an increase (upward shift) in money demand such as $m_{d3}(i, y_1)$. As long as the central bank does not accommodate the increased demand for safe money by providing additional liquidity, the interest rate will rise toward i_3 (point B). The higher interest rate dampens aggregate demand and will lead to a decline in economic activity. In the opposite case (a shift out of money as safe asset toward other more risky assets), the downward shift in money demand will lead to a fall in nominal interest rate i_2 (point C), stimulating aggregate demand.

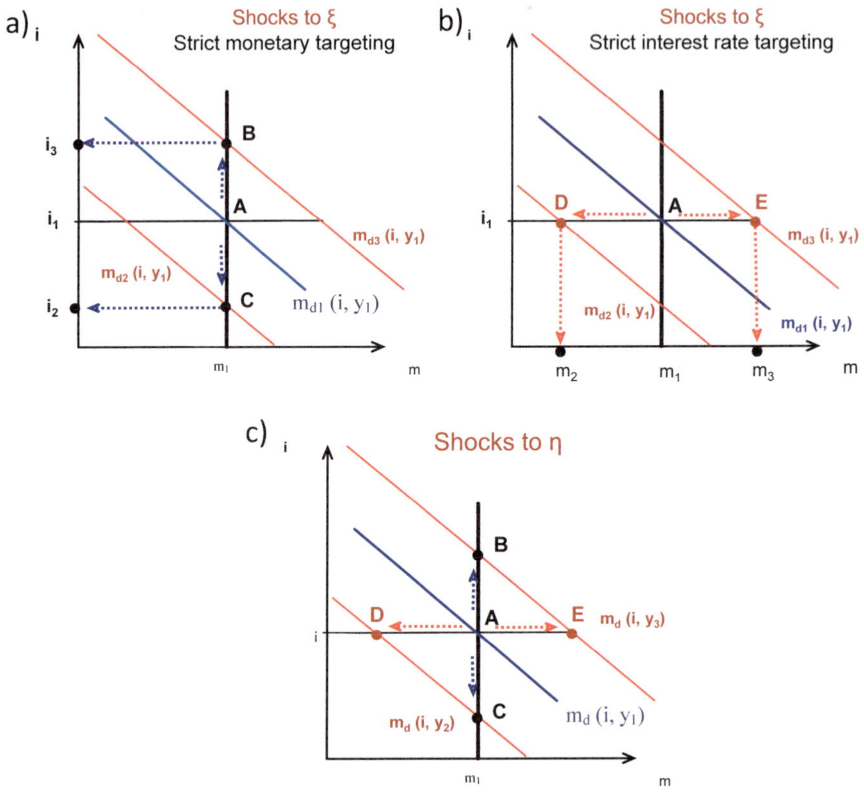

Fig. 5.10 (**a**, **b**) Shocks to ξ: monetary vs. interest rate targeting, (**c**) Shocks to η

As long as the shift in money demand is due to financial disturbances ξ, these interest rate changes induce inefficient responses of aggregate demand. They result in higher volatility both of real activity and prices. To prevent these effects, it would be optimal to stabilize demand by keeping the interest rate constant. That is exactly what a strategy of strict interest rate targeting does. At the given interest rate, money supply will be determined endogenously. It will always be equal to the quantity of money demanded at the rate determined by the central bank. At the rate i_1 money supply will be m_1 when demand is $m_{d1}(i, y_1)$. With an upward shift in demand to $m_{d3}(i, y_1)$, the central bank accommodates additional demand at unchanged rate, so point E will be realized. In the opposite case, the central bank responds to a lower money demand with a reduction in liquidity provided, reaching point D.

The higher the substitutability between money and close substitutes, the higher the volatility of ξ. During the last decades, financial innovation reduced transaction costs for shifting between different asset classes. High substitutability raises the volatility of money demand: Money demand has become highly unstable compared to the period before 1980. This suggests that strict monetary targeting may cause high real volatility. On the other hand, however, money demand may also be shifted by shocks to the real economy. After all, demand for money depends both on output and interest rate: $m_d(i, y)$. In the face of shocks affecting real demand y, fixing money supply instead of interest rates can work as automatic stabilizer in contrast to fixing the interest rate. With fixed money supply, the interest rate adjusts to ensure equilibrium on the money market. In the case of real demand shocks, these adjustments—instead of causing additional volatility, rather help to dampen the shocks. This is illustrated in Fig. 5.10c which repeats nearly exactly the same analysis as in Fig. 5.10a, b, except that now the shifts in money demand arise from positive or negative shocks in real demand. Just as in the analysis above, strict monetary targeting results in fluctuations in the nominal interest rate. But in the face of demand shocks this may be just what the doctor ordered. To be more precise: With a positive real demand shock, shifting money demand upward $(m_d(i, y_3))$ higher interest rates (as in point B) will help to dampen the shocks, stabilizing rather than destabilizing the economy. The nominal interest rate will adjust automatically. In contrast, if the central bank keeps the interest rate fixed (accommodating money demand as in point E), there is no mechanism to mitigate the demand shock. As long as the automatic interest rate adjustment under money targeting is not too strong, real volatility will be higher under strict interest rate targeting.

Let us compare this argument with a shock ξ. Such a shock, again, shifts the money demand curve and will result in high fluctuations of interest rate under money targeting. But now, these fluctuations do not help to dampen real shocks, quite the contrary, they induce fluctuations in real demand and prices, reducing overall welfare.

Let us now figure out under what conditions monetary targeting may be superior to strict interest rate rule. William Poole (1970) analyzed this issue already in an old Keynesian model with sticky prices. He pointed out that the optimal choice between the two instruments depends on the relative volatility of the financial sector relative to real demand. Let us figure out whether Poole's argument still holds in the New Keynesian framework. After all, we now have to take into account quite a variety of shocks—in addition to financial and demand shocks we also need to address the response in the face of supply and markup shocks. Furthermore, with a positively sloped (rather than perfectly elastic) AS curve and rational expectations, things may be much more complex than in traditional models. As it turns, however, we get nearly exactly the same result as in Poole (1970). To derive that, we just need to calculate expected losses from strict monetary targeting and compare them with the outcome of strict interest rate targeting. To make our analysis tractable, we consider the case $\sigma = 1$.

Under the rule Equation 5.4.1b the nominal interest rate will be:

$$i_1 = \frac{1}{\varsigma}(p_1 - p^*) + \frac{1}{\varsigma}(y_1 - \overline{y}_1^n) + \rho + \frac{1}{\varsigma}\xi.$$

Substituting into AD curve gives

$$y_1 - \overline{y}_1^n = \eta - (p_1 - p^*) - \left(\frac{1}{\varsigma}(p_1 - p^*) + \frac{1}{\varsigma}(y_1 - \overline{y}_1^n) + \frac{1}{\varsigma}\xi\right),$$

$$y_1 - \overline{y}_1^n = \frac{\varsigma}{1+\varsigma}\eta - (p_1 - p^*) - \frac{1}{1+\varsigma}\xi. \qquad (5.4.4.1)$$

In equilibrium, AS will be equal AD, so we can insert the AS curve in (5.4.4.1)

$$p_1 - p^* = y_1 - \overline{y}_1^n - \varepsilon + u. \qquad (5.4.4.2)$$

Solve for equilibrium, we get:

$$y_1 - \overline{y}_1^n = \frac{1}{2}\left[\frac{\varsigma}{1+\varsigma}\eta + \varepsilon - u - \frac{1}{1+\varsigma}\xi\right], \qquad (5.4.4.3)$$

$$p_1 - p^* = \frac{1}{2}\left[\frac{\varsigma}{1+\varsigma}\eta - \varepsilon + u - \frac{1}{1+\varsigma}\xi\right]. \qquad (5.4.4.4)$$

Using the relation $y_1^* = y_1^n + \Delta + u = \overline{y}_1^n + \varepsilon + \Delta$ (5.4.4.3) can be written as:

$$y_1 - y_1^* = \frac{1}{2}\left[\frac{\varsigma}{1+\varsigma}\eta - \varepsilon - u - \frac{1}{1+\varsigma}\xi\right] - \Delta. \qquad (5.4.4.5)$$

Hence, the welfare loss under a strict money supply rule can be calculated as:

$$\begin{aligned}
E[L]_m &= \frac{1}{2}\left[\text{Var}\,(y_1 - y_1^*) + (E(y_1 - y_1^*))^2\right] \\
&\quad + \frac{\theta}{2}\left[\text{Var}\,(p_1 - p^*) + (E(p_1 - p^*))^2\right] \qquad (5.4.4.6) \\
&= \frac{1}{2}\left\{\frac{1}{4}\left[\left(\frac{\varsigma}{1+\varsigma}\right)^2\sigma_\eta^2 + \sigma_\varepsilon^2 + \sigma_u^2 + \left(\frac{1}{1+\varsigma}\right)^2\sigma_\xi^2\right] + \Delta^2\right\} \\
&\quad + \frac{\theta}{2}\left\{\frac{1}{4}\left[\left(\frac{\varsigma}{1+\varsigma}\right)^2\sigma_\eta^2 + \sigma_\varepsilon^2 + \sigma_u^2 + \left(\frac{1}{1+\varsigma}\right)^2\sigma_\xi^2\right]\right\} \\
&= \frac{1+\theta}{8}\left[\left(\frac{\varsigma}{1+\varsigma}\right)^2\sigma_\eta^2 + \sigma_\varepsilon^2 + \sigma_u^2 + \left(\frac{1}{1+\varsigma}\right)^2\sigma_\xi^2\right] + \frac{1}{2}\Delta^2.
\end{aligned}$$

Compared to the welfare loss under strict interest rate rule:

$$E(L)_i = \frac{1+\theta}{8}\left(\sigma_\eta^2 + \sigma_\varepsilon^2 + \sigma_u^2\right) + \frac{1}{2}\Delta^2$$

we have:

$$E(L)_i - E(L)_m = \frac{1+\theta}{8}\left\{\left[1 - \left(\frac{\varsigma}{1+\varsigma}\right)^2\right]\sigma_\eta^2 - \left(\frac{1}{1+\varsigma}\right)^2\sigma_\xi^2\right\}.$$

So $E(L)_i - E(L)_m > 0$ if and only if:[7]

$$\left[1 - \left(\frac{\varsigma}{1+\varsigma}\right)^2\right]\sigma_\eta^2 > \left(\frac{1}{1+\varsigma}\right)^2\sigma_\xi^2,$$

$$\text{or} \quad \varsigma > \frac{1}{2}\left(\frac{\sigma_\xi^2}{\sigma_\eta^2} - 1\right). \qquad (5.4.4.7)$$

For $\sigma_\eta^2 > \sigma_\xi^2$ condition in Equation 5.4.4.7 will always hold, since $\varsigma \geq 0$. If the variance of the demand shock exceeds the variance of the monetary shock, an inflexible monetary targeting rule is always superior to an inflexible interest rate rule. The intuition behind this result is the fact that targeting money supply works as automatic stabilizer for shocks affecting real demand: If money is held fixed, interest rate movements partly offset real demand shocks. On the other hand, when money demand is highly volatile, it will be costly (in terms of expected welfare) to choose such a rule. If $\sigma_\xi^2 > \sigma_\eta^2$, the interest elasticity of money demand must be sufficiently high to offset the negative impact of volatile financial shocks. The larger the elasticity of money demand ς with respect to interest rate changes, the more likely Equation 5.4.4.7 is to hold even with highly volatile financial shocks.

5.4.5 Delegation of Monetary Policy to a Conservative Central Banker

Assume that the central bank is not able to commit to policy Equation 5.2.2.6a with p_{tC}. Preferences about price relative to output losses differ across society, with agents having different weights θ_i. Preferences of the median voter are θ_m.

[7]Note that the term $(1+\varsigma)^2$ cancels out on both sides. This gives: $(1+\varsigma)^2 - \varsigma^2 = 1 + 2\varsigma > \frac{\sigma_\xi^2}{\sigma_\eta^2}$ and thus Equation 5.4.4.7.

$$L = \frac{1}{2} E(y_t - y_t^*)^2 + \frac{1}{2} \cdot \theta_m \cdot E(p_t - p^*)^2. \tag{5.4.5.1}$$

The median voter m is not able to commit to follow a specific policy himself, but he could commit to delegate monetary policy to some other type with higher or lower preferences for price stability. Ken Rogoff (1985) showed that the median voter will appoint a conservative person (with a higher weight $\theta_{CB} > \theta_m$ attached to price stability) as the central banker. To see this, note that delegating monetary policy to some agent θ_{CB} with loss function

$$L_{CB} = \frac{1}{2} E(y_1 - y_1^*)^2 + \frac{1}{2} \theta_{CB} E(p_1 - p_1^*)^2 \tag{5.4.5.1b}$$

will result in the policy

$$\begin{aligned} p_{CB} - p^* &= \frac{\Delta}{\theta_{CB}} + \frac{1}{1+\theta_{CB}} u; \ y_{CB} = \overline{y}_n + \varepsilon - \frac{\theta_{CB}}{1+\theta_{CB}} \cdot u; \ p_{CB}^e \\ &= p^* + \frac{\Delta}{\theta_{CB}}. \end{aligned} \tag{5.4.5.1c}$$

The median voter will judge policy outcome according to his preferences θ_m. Obviously, delegating policy to some progressive agent with a lower weight $\theta_{CB} < \theta_m$ does not make any sense: It would not only distort stabilization of markup shocks, but also result in a higher inflation bias to appoint someone as central banker with a low preference for price stability. Instead, delegating policy to a more conservative agent $\theta_{CB} > \theta_m$ may improve welfare of the median voter (it may result in lower expected losses ex ante) for the following reason: On the one hand, θ_{CB} will stabilize shocks less than optimally (from the point of view of θ_m). But on the other hand, delegated policy to him can work as a commitment mechanism in order to dampen the inflation bias: $\frac{\Delta}{\theta_{CB}} < \frac{\Delta}{\theta_m}$ for $\theta_{CB} > \theta_m$. Obviously, there is a trade-off: The more conservative the agent, the lower the inflation bias, but the stronger distortions from inefficient stabilization. Will it be optimal to appoint an inflation nutter? That is somebody caring only about price stability, not at all being concerned about output losses—a person with a very high value $\theta_{CB} \to \infty$. The median voter will pick an agent with preferences θ_{CB} such that CB's policy minimizes m's own losses, so we have to weigh the losses from policy θ_{CB} with the preference θ_m of the representative agent.

That is, we need to determine θ_{CB} so as to minimize expected losses:

$$\begin{aligned} \underset{\theta_{CB}}{\text{Min}} \ E(L_{CB}) &= \frac{1}{2} E\left(-\Delta - \frac{\theta_{CB}}{1+\theta_{CB}} u\right)^2 + \frac{1}{2} \theta_m E\left(\frac{1}{\theta_{CB}} \Delta + \frac{1}{1+\theta_{CB}} u\right)^2 \\ &= \frac{1}{2} \Delta^2 + \frac{1}{2} \theta_m \frac{1}{\theta_{CB}{}^2} \Delta^2 + \frac{1}{2} \left[\frac{\theta_{CB}^2}{(1+\theta_{CB})^2} + \frac{\theta_m}{(1+\theta_{CB})^2} \right] \sigma_u^2. \end{aligned}$$

The first-order condition (the derivative wrt θ_{CB}) can be written[8] as

$$-\theta_m \frac{1}{\theta_{CB}^3}\Delta^2 + \frac{\theta_{CB}-\theta_m}{(1+\theta_{CB})^3}\sigma_u^2 = 0, \quad \text{or}$$

$$\frac{\theta_{CB}-\theta_m}{\theta_m}\left[\frac{1}{1+1/\theta_{CB}}\right]^3 = \frac{\Delta^2}{\sigma_u^2} > 0. \tag{5.4.5.2}$$

This gives an implicit function determining the optimal $\theta_{CB} = F\left(\theta_m, \Delta, \sigma_u^2\right)$. θ_{CB} is increasing in θ_m and in Δ, it is decreasing in σ_u^2. Obviously, it is optimal to delegate policy to a conservative agent with $\theta_{CB} > \theta_m$ unless there are either no structural distortions ($\Delta = 0$), that is, there would be no inflation bias; or volatility $\sigma_u^2 \to \infty$ is so large that gains from stabilizing shocks are bound to outweigh losses from the inflation bias of the median voter. It does, however, not make sense to appoint an extreme conservative – an inflation nutter $\theta_{CB} \to \infty$ unless structural distortions are really large ($\Delta \to \infty$) or volatility is extremely low $\sigma_u^2 \to 0$.

The model may be seen as a motivation for delegating monetary policy to an independent central bank. A conservative central banker implements a policy more oriented toward price stability. Empirically, there seems to be evidence that central banks with a higher degree of independence implement a policy with lower average rates of inflation. In Rogoff's model, the conservative central banker has not just independence concerning the instruments used, but also when defining the objective function. According to the model, the reduced inflation bias comes at a cost: Output needs to be more volatile in order to keep inflation stable. Empirical research, however, finds no evidence that central bank independence is associated with higher real fluctuations (Alesina and Summers 1993).

5.4.6 Targeting Versus Instrument Rules

In this section, we showed that simple mechanical rules are likely to result in sub-optimal outcome relative to the optimal commitment policy characterized in Sect. 5.3. This holds in particular for a commitment to instrument rules such as interest rate or money growth targeting, since in mechanical rules the instrument is only a function of a small subset of all information available to the central bank. As example, we considered the extreme case of interest rate or money growth targeting, but as shown in Chap. 6, the argument still holds for more complex instrument rules such as a Taylor rule, specifying the interest rate as a function of output and price deviations. The optimal policy response, however, should crucially depend on the

---

[8]For differentiating $\frac{\theta_{CB}^2}{(1+\theta_{CB})^2}$ use the rule $\left[\frac{f(x)}{g(x)}\right]' = \frac{f'g - fg'}{g^2}$. So we get $\frac{2b_{CB}(1+b_{CB})^2 - {b_{CB}}^2 2(1+b_{CB})}{(1+b_{CB})^4} = 2\frac{b_{CB}(1+b_{CB}) - {b_{CB}}^2}{(1+b_{CB})^3} = 2\frac{b_{CB}}{(1+b_{CB})^3}$.

specific type of shocks. A more adequate institutional design for committing the central bank to solve the dynamic consistency problem would be to specify targeting rules—that is, it should define explicit objectives for monetary policy, providing a criterion for (the forecasts of) the target variables to be fulfilled.

As argued by Svensson (2003), a commitment to targeting rules has a number of advantages. It allows to use all relevant information and the use of judgment. So it is more robust to both disturbances and model variation than instrument rules, and is likely to lead to better monetary-policy outcomes than instrument rules. Svensson suggests that an optimal targeting rule should express the equality of the marginal rates of transformation and the marginal rates of substitution between the target variables (such as derived in Sect. 5.3 in a simple form) in an operational way.

In practice, monetary policy avoids a strict commitment to instrument rules. Successful monetary policy reforms have frequently formulated explicit and increasingly precise objectives for monetary policy. They created an institutional setting where the central bank is strongly committed to achieving those objectives. Specific targeting rule specify conditions for the target variables (or better for the forecasts of these target variables), leaving the instruments at the discretion of the central bank. As long as targets will be reached, the central bank is allowed to use very elaborate and complex decision-making processes, collecting, processing, and analyzing large amounts of information are, and to exercise considerable judgment. Chapter 6 analyzed in detail the challenges involved in the presence of uncertainty and limited information. Usually, interest rate will be adjusted such that the resulting inflation forecast is on target at an appropriate horizon (usually about 2-years ahead). Such arrangements can be viewed as a type of optimal contract between society and the central bank to which monetary policy decisions have been delegated. As shown by Walsh (1995), properly specified optimal contracts can implement the commitment solution.

5.5 Conclusions

In this chapter, we derived optimal monetary policy when the central bank minimizes welfare losses arising from price dispersion among different goods. We characterized these welfare losses and showed that they can be captured by a quadratic loss function as second-order Taylor approximation. The optimal policy response crucially depends on the specific nature of the underlying shock. Both for demand and supply shocks it is optimal to stabilize the price level, thus minimizing price distortions. Keeping price stable, output will stay at potential. In the presence of markup shocks, however, there is a trade-off between implementing price stability and bringing output close to the efficient level.

Since market equilibrium is inefficiently low due to distortions, there is an incentive for a welfare maximizing central bank to trigger a surprise inflation. Following Barro and Gordon (1983), we characterized the problem of dynamic consistency using game theoretic concepts. In Sect. 5.3 we characterize the outcome of the Barro–Gordon model: A strategy to bring the economy closer to the first-best level by monetary policy is—in game theoretic terms—not subgame perfect or time consistent. The attempt to raise welfare results just in an inefficiently high price level since the central bank cannot systematically raise output above market equilibrium.

We showed that the discretionary, dynamic consistent equilibrium is inferior relative to the commitment solution and discussed various mechanisms how to impose binding rules as commitment mechanism. Since the adequate response depends on the nature of specific shocks, mechanical simple instrument rules are bound to be sub-optimal. Targeting rules specify conditions for the (forecasts of) target variables, leaving the instruments at the discretion of the central bank. Being more robust to disturbances and model variation, they allow the use of all relevant information and the use of judgment.

In this chapter, we used a very stylized two-period model to address crucial issues in the simplest way. Modern DSGE models exhibit many features which allow for a much more detailed analysis, in particular matching empirical dynamics. But some key features of the new generation of dynamic models can be captured in our setup in a straightforward way. We gained intuition for some important general insights:

(A) Forward-looking behavior allows analyzing the impact of a change in policy.
(B) Systematic, anticipated stabilization policy can be quite effective in the presence of price rigidities.
(C) When market equilibrium is inefficient, a surprise in monetary policy may be welfare improving (due to the nature of aggregate demand externalities).
(D) But it is not possible to implement a policy of systematic surprise. The problem of dynamic inconsistency calls for credible commitment mechanisms. This feature helps to understand the crucial role of institutions (the need for independent, credible central banks)
(E) The setting captures some realistic features of current monetary policy. It provides a framework to analyze the design of interest rate rules and to compare performance of different institutional designs aiming to implement a second-best outcome.
(F) Explicit micro-foundations allow for detailed welfare analysis.

In addition, dynamic New Keynesian economics allows confronting theory with data. Obviously, our two-period shortcut is not sufficient for empirical analysis. Nevertheless it helps to convey key mechanisms prevailing also in the more sophisticated dynamic versions.

References

Alesina, A., & Summers, L. H. (1993). Central bank independence and macroeconomic performance: Some comparative evidence. *Journal of Money, Credit and Banking, 25*(May), 151–162.

Barro, R. J., & Gorden, D. B. (1983). Rules, discretion, and reputation in a model of monetary policy. *Journal of Monetary Economics, 12*, 101–120.
Lucas, R. (1972). Expectations and the neutrality of money. *Journal of Economic Theory, 4*, 103–124.
Poole, W. (1970). Optimal choice of monetary policy instruments in a simple stochastic macro model. *Quarterly Journal of Economics, 84*, 197–216.
Rogoff, K. (1985). The optimal degree of commitment to an intermediate monetary target. *Quarterly Journal of Economics, 100*, 1169–1190.
Svensson, L. (2003). What is wrong with Taylor rules? Using judgment in monetary policy through targeting rules. *Journal of Economic Literature, 41*, 426–277.
Walsh, C. (1995). Optimal contracts for independent central bankers. *American Economic Review, 85*, 150–167.
Woodford, M. (2003). *Interest and prices*. Princeton, NJ: Princeton University Press.

Monetary Policy Under Uncertainty

6

6.1 Introduction

In Chap. 5, we characterized optimal monetary policy for the case that the central bank can exactly identify the nature and size of shocks and that it has perfect control about the instruments used. In reality, most central banks have a huge staff collecting and analyzing large amounts of information, but information in real time is rather noisy. Many data sets are frequently revised, providing contradictory signals. Policymaker need to exercise considerable judgment about the reliability of all signals received. But there are even quite a few more challenges for implementing policy objectives: There exists enormous uncertainty about the exact transmission mechanism between central bank instruments and its objectives. No central bank has perfect control about the price level. Even more worrying: Central bankers face uncertainty about the true model of the economy. In our simple setting, we assumed that we know exactly how the economy works, having perfect knowledge about all relevant fundamental data and the underlying processes. But in reality, the models used for the analysis may be far off from the correct model. If small changes in the model would lead to drastic deviations from the policy derived as the optimal one, there is not much point in pursuing such a policy. Instead, we would rather prefer policies whose outcomes are fairly robust to such changes. In Sect. 6.2, we analyze how our results need to be modified to take into account control errors, imperfect information and robustness issues. Intuition suggests that central bankers facing these challenges should act more cautiously. On the other hand, robustness may require knowledge about how the economy might respond outside of traditional standards, suggesting the need for brave experiments.

In the New Keynesian DSGE framework, monetary policy is supposed to adjust the nominal rate interest such that the real rate is in line with the natural rate of interest. In Sect. 6.3, we illustrate the difficulties central banks face in practice in following that advice. This requires reliable estimates of potential output, the natural rate of interest, and of expected inflation. For illustration, we look at the challenges involved in formulating a reliable Taylor rule.

J. Cao, G. Illing, *Money: Theory and Practice*, Springer Texts in Business and Economics, https://doi.org/10.1007/978-3-030-19697-4_6

Due to the forward looking nature of monetary policy, not only current actions but also expected actions in the future play a crucial role. Since effectiveness strongly depends on private agents correctly understanding central bank actions, transparent communication is an essential ingredient of modern policy. But there may be reasons why too much transparency might be harmful. Section 6.4 focuses on this issue.

6.2 Control Errors, Imperfect Information, and Robustness

6.2.1 Uncertainty About Instruments/Precision of Information Variable

Up to now, most of the time we took it for granted that the central bank can easily identify the type of shocks and that it has perfect control about the instruments such that it is able to implement the policy objective however defined. However, in practice, this is definitely not the case. First of all, real-time data are usually fairly ambiguous. Most of the time, they provide contradictory signals. A lot of data are subject to frequent revisions. So it is no surprise that an enormous amount of research activity at central banks tries to filter out the relevant information. Furthermore, there exists quite a lot of uncertainty about how monetary policy instruments (be it short-term interest rate, money supply, or other additional tools like minimum reserve requirements or tools for quantitative easing) affect both real activity and/or nominal prices. In technical terms, there is huge uncertainty about the transmission mechanism between policy instruments, intermediate targets, and final objectives. In stark contrast to the models we used, central bankers cannot be sure that the way they interpret the world (the model they use) is the correct one. In other words, there is uncertainty about the correct model.

How will these different types of uncertainty affect our results? Should the central bank respond by acting more cautiously or should they instead be more aggressive? William Brainard (1967) was one of the first to address this issue formally. He showed that if the central bank is uncertain about how effective actions are, it should moderate the response to new information. This result has become quite popular among central bankers. After all, the intuition seems fairly obvious: Being risk averse, one should avoid introducing additional noise in the economy by using policy instruments which run the risk of creating higher volatility. The argument for less intervention seems to conform to the natural tendency of being conservative as central banker. But recently, this argument has been challenged by a couple of papers suggesting that a robust policy design may justify—at least in some cases—an even more aggressive response to new information, compared to the optimal policy in the absence of uncertainty. In this chapter, we try to shed some light on this debate. As we will see, the optimal response depends very much on the specific type of uncertainty. A more extensive treatment can be found in the instructive survey by Barlevy (2011).

In order to analyze the impact of uncertainty in a tractable way, we focus on a simplified example: For now, let us ignore the trade-off between conflicting targets and assume that the central bank as single objective is just interested in minimizing deviations from the target price level. When we concentrate on demand shocks, this simplification is not really without loss of generality. After all, in that case there is no trade-off between price and output stability. So let us assume the central banks objective is:

$$\operatorname{Min} E(L) = \frac{1}{2} E(p - p^*)^2. \tag{6.2.1.1}$$

Now assume a demand shocks η puts upward or downward pressure on the economy (the price level). Using instrument Z, the central bank tries to stabilize p at p^*. Obviously just announcing that it wants to do that is of no use. It needs to be aware of the transmission mechanism between the instrument Z and the target price level target p. Assume this is given by the equation:

$$p - p^* = \eta - zZ. \tag{6.2.1.2}$$

η is the demand shock. The policy instrument Z could be the nominal interest rate. An increase in the interest rate (a larger Z) is supposed to dampen the price level. The parameter z measures to what extent this is effective—it captures the transmission mechanism: $\frac{\partial p}{\partial Z} = -z$.

Inserting this relation, we can write expected losses as a function of the policy instrument Z:

$$\operatorname*{Min}_{Z} E(L) = \frac{1}{2} E(\eta - zZ)^2. \tag{6.2.1.1b}$$

Since we consider a quadratic loss function, the expected payoff depends only on the mean and the variance of the stochastic terms—there is certainty equivalence. So we can characterize the optimal strategy for fairly general stochastic processes, without imposing specific assumptions on the distribution. We just need to specify mean and variance. Later on, however, for the case of Bayesian updating, we will consider normal distributions.

6.2.1.1 Reference Point: Perfect Control and Complete Information

We know already that in the absence of any uncertainty such as control errors or incomplete information about the true type of shock, the optimal strategy is to stabilize demand shocks perfectly. This is confirmed by deriving the first order condition: $z(\eta - zZ) = 0$ which gives

$$Z = \frac{\eta}{z}. \tag{6.2.1.1.1}$$

So we have the familiar standard result that in the face of demand shocks policy should stabilize the price level perfectly by completely off-setting the shock. The central bank can do so without problem as long as it (a) has perfect control about z—the transmission mechanism between interest rate changes and the price level—and (b) is able to identify the shock η. Let us now make the model more realistic by modifying these assumptions in turn.

6.2.1.2 Uncertainty About the Transmission Mechanism

In reality, no central bank has perfect control about the price level. There is high uncertainty about the transmission mechanism—the impact of a change in the interest rate on the price level. The uncertainty about the impact of the policy instrument on the target is even more challenging for unconventional policies, required in times of financial crises. Formally, we may model this type of uncertainty in different ways. A natural route is to allow the parameter z to be a stochastic variable. z amplifies the policy instrument Z by multiplying its impact. So when z is a random variable, there is multiplicative uncertainty. In addition, there may also be some linear uncertainty in the sense that a random term ς introduces additional linear noise between the instrument and the target, disturbing the target. If we characterize random terms by z and ς, we have the stochastic transmission mechanism:

$$p - p^* = \eta - zZ + \varsigma. \tag{6.2.1.2a}$$

Without loss of generalization, we assume that z is a random variable with positive mean $E(z) = \bar{z}$ and variance σ_z^2. Furthermore, $E(\varsigma) = 0$ and variance σ_ς^2. Inserting the equation in the loss function and calculating expected losses, we easily see that linear uncertainty has no effect[1] on the optimal strategy, whereas multiplicative uncertainty leads to a dampened response:

$$E(L) = \frac{1}{2}E(\eta - zZ + \varsigma)^2 = \frac{1}{2}\left(E(\eta^2) - 2ZE(z)\eta + Z^2E(z^2) + E(\zeta^2)\right).$$

Differentiating with respect to variable Z gives as first order condition:

$$-E(z)\eta + ZE(z^2) = 0, \quad \text{or} \quad Z = \frac{\bar{z}}{E(z^2)}\eta.$$

Since $\text{Var}(z) = \sigma_z^2 = E(z^2) - (E(z))^2 = E(z^2) - \bar{z}^2$, we have $E(z^2) = \sigma_z^2 + \bar{z}^2$. Thus $Z = \frac{\bar{z}}{\sigma_z^2 + \bar{z}^2}\eta$.

With multiplicative uncertainty about the transmission mechanism, the central bank will react more cautiously compared to the case of perfect control, i.e., the response is dampened:

---

[1]Note that $E(L) = \frac{1}{2}E(\eta - zZ + \varsigma)^2 = \frac{1}{2}E(\eta - zZ)^2 + E(\eta - zZ) \cdot E(\varsigma) + \frac{1}{2}E(\varsigma^2)$. Since $E(\zeta) = 0$ the intermediate multiplicative terms with $E(\zeta)$ cancel out.

$$Z = \frac{\bar{z}}{\sigma_z^2 + \bar{z}^2}\eta < \frac{1}{\bar{z}}\eta. \qquad (6.2.1.1.1a)$$

The intuition behind this result is straightforward: Due to the uncertainty about the transmission mechanism, a more aggressive response Z may induce larger fluctuations of p. The larger the variance σ_z^2, the more cautious should be the reaction. Being risk averse, the central bank will try to avoid a policy that leads to higher volatility of the price level. An important additional insight of our analysis is that the optimal response crucially depends on the nature of the underlying uncertainty. Whereas the optimal response Z is strongly affected by multiplicative uncertainty, linear uncertainty is irrelevant: Independent of its variance, the parameter ς plays no role in the optimality condition. The reason is that the additional noise arising from the term ς cannot be affected by varying the scale of the instrument used (the level Z).

Obviously, the specific details matter. The key issue is whether a more aggressive policy adds or lowers volatility of social losses. As has been shown in the literature, sometimes policy should respond even more aggressively to information about missing a target. That will be the case if such an aggressive response helps to limit losses—at least for the worst case scenario. We will discuss this in Sect. 6.2.2 when we look at robust rules.

6.2.1.3 Imperfect Observability of Shocks

In the last section, we assumed that the central bank does not have perfect control, i.e., there is uncertainty about the transmission mechanism. To focus on that aspect, we still assumed that the central bank has perfect knowledge about the shock η at the time of action. In this section, we analyze exactly the opposite problem: Now, the central bank receives only a noisy signal about the shock η. How should it respond to imperfect, possibly distorted information? To concentrate on that issue, in this section we abstract from uncertainty about transmission mechanism. Obviously, the response should depend on the precision of the signal received. The more precise the signal, the more active should be the response. So our intuition is that this type of uncertainty will again lead to a more cautious reaction. Let us confirm that this is indeed the case.

Formally, we can model the revision of information as a Bayesian updating process. The demand shock (the parameter η) is a stochastic variable. Initially, the central bank has some a priori information about the distribution of η. New information will lead to a revision of this distribution. In the best case, with perfect precision of the signal, the true parameter η can be observed without control errors ex post, once the shock has realized. More realistically, however, incoming new information is usually not perfect even after realization of the shock. Rather than the true value η, the central bank can observe only the noisy signal $\psi = \xi + \eta$. The signal is distorted by a random process ξ. Given the signal ψ, the central bank has to draw conclusions about the true value η, revising the underlying probability distribution $\eta|\psi$, given available ex post information. The larger the noise, the less reliable will be the signal.

The precision of signal ψ is inversely related to the variance of the noise term ξ. We have:

$$E(L) = \frac{1}{2}E(\eta|\,\psi - zZ + \varsigma)^2 = \frac{1}{2}\left(E(\eta|\,\psi)^2 - 2\cdot Z\cdot z\cdot E(\eta|\,\psi) + Z^2 z^2 + E(\zeta^2)\right).$$

Again differentiating with respect to the policy variable Z, the first-order condition for optimal policy is $-z\cdot E(\eta|\psi) + Z\cdot z^2 = 0$. So only the expected mean of the shock is relevant and we can rewrite the condition as:

$$Z = \frac{1}{z}E(\eta|\,\psi). \tag{6.2.1.1.1b}$$

To solve the Bayesian updating problem, we have to specify the underlying probability distribution. We can do the updating in a straightforward way if we assume that both η and ξ are normally distributed random variables: $\eta \sim N\left(E(\eta), \sigma_\eta^2\right)$, $\xi \sim N\left(E(\xi), \sigma_\xi^2\right)$.

We need to understand some basics about probability distributions. For our purposes, it is sufficient to note the following facts: If both η and ξ are independent normally distributed random variables, then ψ is normally distributed according to $\psi \sim N\ \left(\overline{\eta} + \overline{\xi}, \sigma_\eta^2 + \sigma_\xi^2\right)$. In order to update our belief about the true value of η after having observed the noisy signal ψ, we need to calculate the conditional expectation $E(\eta|\,\psi)$. Given ψ, we want to infer the parameter η taking into account that noise ξ may have distorted the signal. We can do this inference using Bayes' rule. For $\overline{\eta} = \overline{\xi} = 0$, the conditional expectation is simply $E(\eta|\,\psi) = \frac{\sigma_\eta^2}{\sigma_\eta^2 + \sigma_\xi^2}\,\psi$.

Substituting this term in the FOC gives as optimal policy:

$$Z = \frac{\sigma_\eta^2}{\sigma_\eta^2 + \sigma_\xi^2}\,\frac{1}{z}\,\psi. \tag{6.2.1.1.1c}$$

Again, policy response Z is muted relative to the optimal policy $\frac{1}{z}\Psi$ with perfect control. If the noise is small (the variance σ_ξ^2 low), the signal ψ is highly reliable. For $\sigma_\xi^2 \to 0$, the central bank has perfect information and acts accordingly with policy being close to perfect control. On the other hand, when the signal ψ is very unreliable $(\sigma_\xi^2 \to \infty)$ the central bank should not react at all to the noisy signal ψ.

6.2.2 Robustness (Robust Control)

The last section confirmed Brainard's (1967) intuition that the central bank will act less aggressively as a response to uncertainty. This result has been challenged in more recent research. Some papers have shown that the central bank should act more forcefully when facing uncertainty under some conditions—at least as long as the policy goal is to avoid disaster. This result has been derived in models doing robustness analysis. The key idea of robustness is the following: Usually, policymakers are not sure which model of the economy is the correct one. For example, there are many competing ways to model the transmission mechanism. Some policy which might perform extremely well in some specific model may lead to a quite disastrous outcome if a different model turns out to be the correct one. Academics doing pure research may be convinced that the model they use is the proper one, but central bankers should be more careful. They have to be aware that reality may be much more complex than elegant models seem to suggest. Hence, policymakers may prefer to pursue policies that are "robust" in the sense that they perform well against a broad range of models.

One way to handle model uncertainty could be to assign specific probabilities to all feasible models. This way, we may try to judge how likely it is that each specific model represents the correct one. One would then pick the strategy which minimizes expected losses across all relevant models, each weighted with the probability attached. But it may seem rather arbitrary for policymaker to attach specific probabilities to specific models. Instead, as strategy of robust optimal control, frequently the minimax rule is used (see, for instance, Hansen & Sargent, 2008). This rule tries to avoid disastrous outcomes by picking the strategy, which minimizes the maximum feasible loss out of all relevant models.

Early applications of robustness usually found that policymakers should respond more aggressively to information than they would otherwise. However, as Barlevy (2011) shows, this is not an inherent feature of robustness; rather it is a specific feature of the models explored in the literature. He shows that in other setups robustness can lead to the same dampening principle as outlined by Brainard (1967). Somewhat provocatively he argues "results concerning robustness that arise in particular environment are not necessarily robust to changes in the underlying environment."

To illustrate these arguments, let us rephrase the problem of this chapter so as to interpret it as modeling uncertainty in an extremely simple setting. The policymaker may have some benchmark model z for describing the transmission mechanism between the instrument and the target (price level stability): $p - p^* = \eta - zZ$. But it also needs to take into account a class of other models that potentially may be a better description of the mechanism. We model this as a set of perturbations ε around the benchmark model z. So let the range of feasible models be

$$p - p^* = \eta - (z + \varepsilon) Z$$

with ε being restricted to some interval around zero, i.e., $\underline{\varepsilon} < 0 < \overline{\varepsilon}$. The policy Z is robust if the worst performance under Z (across all models the policymaker takes into account) is better than the worst performance of all other policies.

Following Barlevy (2011), we consider different cases for the feasible range $[\underline{\varepsilon};\overline{\varepsilon}]$ to demonstrate that we will reach quite different solutions for the robust control strategy, depending on the specific problem. To solve for the robust strategy, we need to calculate the maximum potential loss (the worst performance) for each policy value Z across all feasible models $\varepsilon \in [\underline{\varepsilon};\overline{\varepsilon}]$. Then, we pick the policy Z which ensures the lowest maximum potential loss. This is called minimax strategy. Let us consider different cases.

First, let us assume that the absolute value of the minimum parameter is smaller than z: $|\underline{\varepsilon}| < z$ or $\underline{\varepsilon} > -z$. Economically, it means that we can rule out that an increase in the policy instrument, instead of dampening the impact on the price level may lead to perverse effects, driving prices up even more. That is, we can be sure that $\frac{\partial p}{\partial Z} < 0$.

In that case, the optimal robust strategy turns out to be:

$$Z = \frac{1}{z + (\underline{\varepsilon} + \overline{\varepsilon})/2}\eta.$$

Obviously, the optimal intensity of the response strongly depends on the asymmetry of the endpoints of the distribution. To see this, we need to understand how the loss $L_\varepsilon = \frac{1}{2}(\eta - (z + \varepsilon)Z)^2$ changes as a function of ε for some given response Z. It is straightforward to see that for the quadratic loss function, the largest losses occur at the endpoints (see Fig. 6.1). Since we want to minimize the maximum feasible loss, it is optimal to pick the level Z which equalizes losses at both endpoints.

If the support—the region of uncertainty—is symmetric around z (that is, $|\underline{\varepsilon}| = \overline{\varepsilon}$), losses at both endpoints are equal by construction. The best we can do in that case is to pick $Z = \eta/z$. Obviously, for symmetric uncertainty, the optimal response under model uncertainty is to be neither more cautious nor more aggressive than in the absence of model uncertainty. After all, $Z = \eta/z$ is also the best policy if we are absolutely certain that the true model parameter is z—that is, if $|\underline{\varepsilon}| = \overline{\varepsilon} = 0$. If the support is asymmetric, however, things get more interesting. First note that the response will be dampened compared to the case of certainty if $|\underline{\varepsilon}| < \overline{\varepsilon}$. In that case,

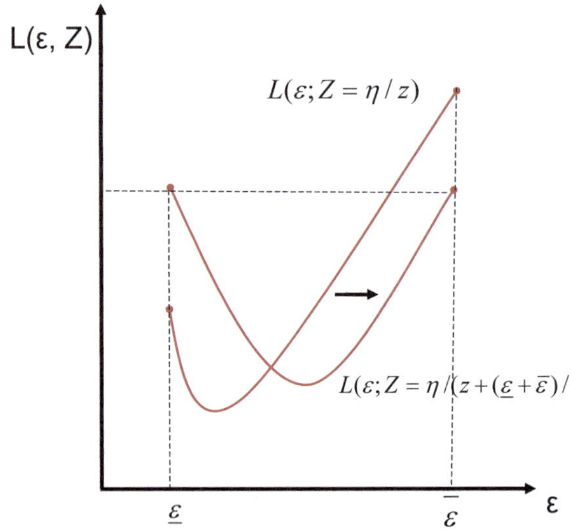

Fig. 6.1 Optimal robust strategy under model uncertainty

raising the instrument may rather result in a too strong than a too weak response of the price level. The risk that the policy may be too effective is higher than the opposite risk. So it is natural to be inclined to be more cautious. This case is shown in Fig. 6.1. For $Z = \eta/z$, the loss at $\underline{\varepsilon}$ is smaller than the loss at $\overline{\varepsilon}$. Lowering Z shifts the loss function to the right. This reduces losses at the higher end $\overline{\varepsilon}$ but raises them at the lower end $\underline{\varepsilon}$. Since the robust strategy is to balance losses at both extreme points, it is optimal to dampen the response Z until that condition holds.

For the case $|\underline{\varepsilon}| > \overline{\varepsilon}$, we get exactly the opposite result. Now $(\underline{\varepsilon} + \overline{\varepsilon})/2 < 0$, so policy should respond more aggressively compared to the case of certainty. The intuition is straightforward. When the region of uncertainty is higher for negative values of ε, there is a strong risk that the impact of the policy instrument may turn out to be quite ineffective. So the obvious response is to act more aggressively. Now, with a response $Z = \eta/z$ losses are highest at the lower end $\underline{\varepsilon}$. By behaving more aggressively, the maximum loss in case the policy turns out to be fairly ineffective is reduced. Of course, this comes at the expense of raising the maximum loss in case policy turns out to be extremely effective. But again, the robust strategy is exactly to try to balance the outcome for both extreme points.

Hence, the results of our robustness analysis conform nicely to our intuition: In order to avoid extreme losses, we should either be more aggressive or more cautious, depending on what strategy helps to better limit losses impending under the relevant extreme case scenario. However, we do not get a simple, clear-cut result. Rather, the optimal response strongly depends on specific circumstances. To see this even more starkly, let us now modify our initial assumption that $|\underline{\varepsilon}| < z$. If we allow instead for the case $|\underline{\varepsilon}| > z$, there is some risk of a perverse reaction of our policy instrument. For some parameter values (ε being strongly negative—even though that range may be rather small), an increase in our instrument may drive prices up even more, instead of the intended dampening effect. So we cannot rule out that—at least in some unfortunate cases—despite all good intentions, rather than offsetting the underlying demand shock in the economy, we may make things even worse by raising interest rates.

If so, the optimal response changes dramatically. Now, the best we can do is to do nothing—that is, to set $Z = 0$. Hence, we will be much more cautious than in the absence of model uncertainty. It is easy to see why: $Z = 0$ gives the loss $L_\varepsilon = \frac{1}{2}(\eta)^2$ independent of ε. As long as we can be sure that raising the policy instrument dampens the price level (that is, as long as $|\underline{\varepsilon}| < z$), a positive Z will always result in lower losses compared to doing nothing. But now, if we cannot rule out that a positive Z may lead to a perverse reaction, the maximum feasible losses for positive values of Z will always be higher than if we do not act at all. Again, this result seems to make perfect sense—the argument is fairly intuitive. But there are several problems: First of all, a policy of "doing nothing" may not be well defined. As we discussed extensively in former sections, it makes quite a substantial difference whether we keep money supply constant instead of keeping the interest rate fixed. Even worse: Since communication plays an important role for modern central banking practice, "doing nothing" might alternatively be seen as a policy recommendation for issuing no statements by the central bank any more.

Finally, and most important, the range for possible perverse effects may be quite tiny. The likelihood of such an event may be seen to be extremely small. If so, in order to avoid a highly unlikely worst-case scenario, robustness analysis forces a policy which will result in substantial losses in most cases. To demonstrate this within our example, let us initially start from a range such that $|\underline{\varepsilon}| < z$ with $|\underline{\varepsilon}|$ being close to z. Furthermore assume the parameter range is asymmetric with $|\underline{\varepsilon}| > \overline{\varepsilon}$. As we know, in that case an aggressive response is called for: The closer $|\underline{\varepsilon}|$ is to z, the more aggressive the policy should be. Assume now that, for some reason, the lower range is slightly extended such that the worst outlier $|\underline{\varepsilon}|$ now exceeds z just a little bit. If so, robustness calls for a discontinuous, quite dramatic shift from a highly aggressive policy toward doing to nothing at all—just because there may be perverse effects for a very small parameter range.

The example illustrates an important weakness of robustness analysis. A robust strategy is chosen because it performs best in the worst-case scenario, even if that scenario is quite unlikely and even if the same strategy performs much worse than alternative strategies in most, if not all, remaining scenarios. Svensson (2007) phrases this criticism as follows: "*If a Bayesian prior probability measure were to be assigned to the feasible set of models, one might find that the probability assigned to the models on the boundary are exceedingly small. Thus, highly unlikely models can come to dominate the outcome of robust control.*" Svensson and others suggests that policymakers instead should proceed as Bayesians; that is, they should assign subjective beliefs to the various scenarios they contemplate and then choose the strategy that minimizes the expected loss according to their subjective beliefs. Even if we modify our robustness analysis in that way, however, the intuition derived in our setting here concerning reasons for the response being more aggressive or more cautious will still hold.

6.3 Data Uncertainty

> The natural rate is not fixed or unalterable in magnitude. . .In general, we may say, it depends on the efficiency of production, on the available amount of fixed and liquid capital, on the supply of labor and land, in short on all the thousand and one things which determine the current economic position of a community; and with them it constantly fluctuates.—Knut Wicksell, *Interest and Prices*, 1898, p. 106

> Unfortunately, we have as yet devised no method to estimate accurately and readily the natural rate of either interest or unemployment. And the "natural" rate itself will change from time to time.—Milton Friedman, American Economic Association Presidential Address, 1968.

6.3.1 Introduction

Optimal policy as outlined in Chap. 5 suggests the central bank should aim to bring the real rate of interest close to the equilibrium real rate of interest, or the natural rate. The equilibrium natural rate is time varying, shifted by shocks such as time preference or technology shocks. In a New Keynesian DSGE model, the natural rate of interest is the rate that keeps the economy's output at the level that would prevail if all wages and prices were flexible. This hypothetical reference point, the market equilibrium in the absence of nominal rigidities, corresponds to the notion of potential output. The difference between actual and potential output, the output gap, is a measure of inflation pressure. Frequently potential output is calculated using some method to decompose actual output into a trend and a cyclical component. Techniques range from simple time series filter methods to more complex structural model based decompositions. But not only actual, but also potential output can be time varying, so econometric estimates may be seriously misleading. Being a purely theoretical concept, potential output is simply not observable in reality. In the same vein, the true value of long-run equilibrium values for the real interest rate is not observable.

Even if it was easy to identify the nature of shocks and the current output gap clearly, there is enormous uncertainty about the degree of persistence of shocks. Shocks may be temporary, but they may also last rather long, some of them being permanent. It is hard to distinguish between highly persistent and truly permanent trends. Even worse, if hysteresis effects prevail, with the wrong policy response, temporary shocks may trigger permanent effects. So the challenge is to provide reliable estimates of all relevant variables. In real time, reliable information is scarce. Available data are noisy; most macroeconomic data are subject to mismeasurement and frequent revision. Policy decisions cannot wait until there is a clear picture.

Central banks usually have a large professional staff, observing the relevant data and trying to make reliable forecast about key variables. To get robust results, they usually estimate different models, using all available information, including market forecasts such as surveys of professional forecasters. Even with the best use of available expertise, policy decisions need to take into account the underlying uncertainty due to large noise in crucial data. The following sections briefly illustrate the challenges involved.

6.3.2 Uncertainty and Taylor Rules

John Taylor suggested a simple rule as a benchmark for how monetary policy should be conducted. According to the so-called Taylor rule, monetary policy should adjust the policy rate as a function of both inflation and the output gap, i.e., the gap between output and its long-run potential, noninflationary, level. Algebraically, this rule can be written as:

$$i_t = r_t^* + \pi^* + \alpha_\pi(\pi_t - \pi^*) + \alpha_y(y_t - y_t^*).$$

Here i_t is the short-term interest rate, π_t is the inflation rate and π^* is the target rate of inflation, y_t is GDP and y_t^* is potential output. r_t^* is the real interest rate prevailing when output and inflation are at target levels. The interest rate should be adjusted according to the difference between current and target rate of inflation (the "inflation gap") and the difference between actual and "natural" rate of output (the "output gap"). The coefficients determine how aggressive the central bank reacts to deviations from target. They reflect either preferences of central bankers or the legal mandate. The higher the aversion to output volatility, the larger the weight on the second term.

If inflation is at the target rate $(\pi_t = \pi^*)$ (with π^* usually 2%) and output is at potential $(y_t = y_t^*)$, then the Taylor rule prescribes setting the nominal policy rate at $r_t^* + \pi^*$. Hence, the intercept term strongly depends on the equilibrium real rate r_t^*. In a Taylor rule, knowing the natural real rate r_t^* is key to evaluate the degree of policy accommodation. A real policy rate below r_t^* can be seen as accommodative; a rate above r_t^* as tight.

In Taylor's original rule $i_t = 2 + 1.5(\pi_t - \pi^*) + 0.5(y_t - y_t^*)$, feedback parameters were set at 1.5 for inflation, 0.5 for output, and r^* at 2%, in line with historic averages. For the period between 1987 and 1992, the value predicted by his rule fitted remarkably well to the actual rate set by the Fed as illustrated in Fig. 6.2. During that period, under chairman Paul Volcker the Fed had fundamentally changed its policy framework, responding more vigorously to inflation. That change resulted in disinflation, followed by a long period of low inflation and low output volatility (the so-called period of Great Moderation) from 1984 to 2007.

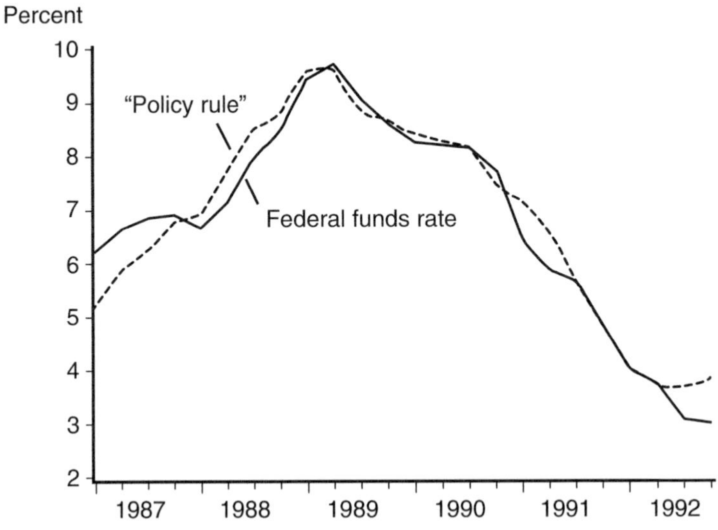

Figure 1. Federal funds rate and example policy rule.

Fig. 6.2 The original Taylor rule (1993)

Estimating the coefficients of a Taylor-type rule for that period econometrically, the Fed's rule obeyed the Taylor principle, reacting to inflation with a weight stronger than 1. According to Clarida, Gali, and Gertler (2000), starting in 1979 there has been a regime change with the Fed following sensible policy rules and thus ensuring macroeconomic stability. In contrast, in the pre-Volcker area in the 1970s, actual policy was looser than suggested by Taylor's rule. According to estimates based on ex post data as published after final revisions, during the 1970s the Fed did not seem to obey the Taylor principle. Violating that principle has been interpreted as the reason why inflation was strongly increasing at that time.

But final data were not yet available at the time when actual decisions about policy rates had to be taken. Using historic real-time data as available at the time of each policy decision, Orphanides (2001) found that the Taylor principle holds even in the pre-Volcker area with policy responding to inflation forecasts four quarter ahead stronger than one to one. He argues that the problem was that the Fed responded too strongly to perceived output gaps in the pre-Volcker area. When central bankers observed a decline in real growth in the 1970s, they believed that output was falling far below potential. Later, estimates of growth rates for potential output were revised down substantially. When measured properly using ex post data, the actual output gap turned out to be rather small. Hence, policymakers proved to be too optimistic about the economy's ability to sustain rapid growth without inflation at a time when inflationary pressure should have been the focus.

The debate about proper Fed policy before 2007 provides valuable insights on the sensitivity of simple rules to different specifications. Taylor (2009) argues that Fed policy was too easy during the period 2002–2005 and so contributed to the housing boom, excessive risk taking, and thereby to the financial crisis. Sticking to his original rule, in those years the Fed set its funds rate far too low (by about 2% points on average) (see Fig. 6.3).

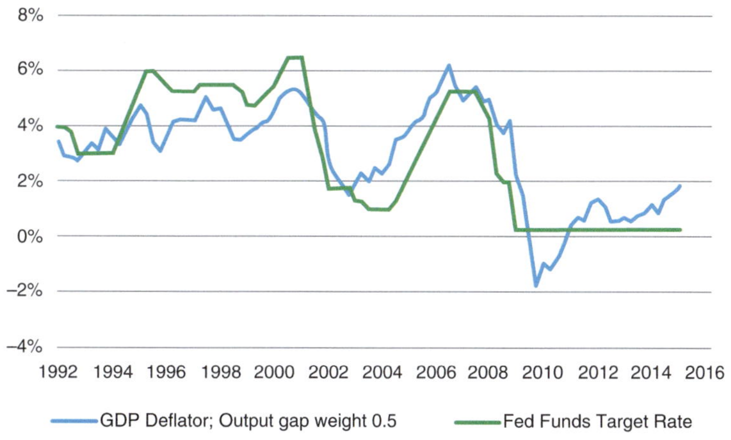

Fig. 6.3 Fed funds target rate vs. the original Taylor rule 1992–2015 (Source: Bernanke, 2015)

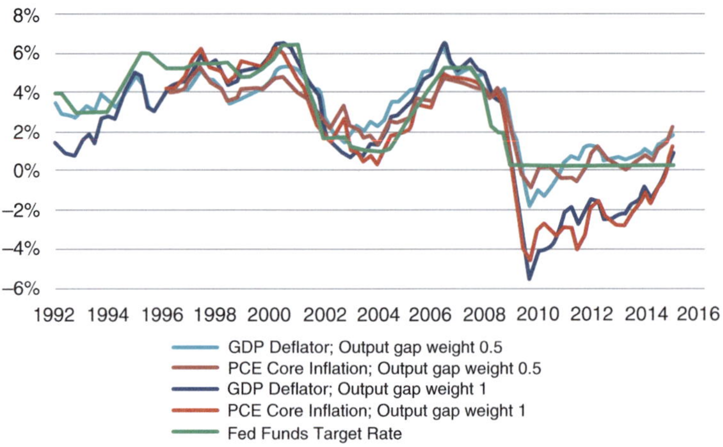

Fig. 6.4 Fed funds target rate vs. different Taylor rules 1992–2015 (Source: Bernanke, 2015)

Following the original Taylor rule (Taylor, 1993), in Fig. 6.3 the currently observed GDP deflator is used as information variable for the rate of inflation. Bernanke (2010) argues that the Fed instead follows a forward-looking rule. Given the lags involved, forward-looking monetary policy tries to avoid overreacting to volatile temporary movements and instead focuses on forecast values of the target variables.

$$i_t = \alpha_t + \gamma_1(E(\pi_{t+1}|I_t)) - \pi^*) + \gamma_2(E(y_{t+1}|I_t)) - y^*).$$

Internal real-time FOMC forecasts are published only with delay. To calculate alternative rules, Fig. 6.4 instead uses core inflation as a proxy measure for predicted future inflation. Core inflation, excluding volatile components such as energy and food, is a more efficient predictor for future inflation compared to overall (headline) inflation. The alternative Taylor-type rules drawn in Fig. 6.4 modify the original Taylor version in two other ways. Since 2000, the Fed focuses on the Personal Consumption Expenditures price index (PCE) as the measure for inflation rather than focusing on GDP deflator or CPI data. Data for the core PCE deflator are available from 1995 on. All three measures follow broadly similar trends, but differ in detail.[2]

[2]The GDP deflator, calculating the prices of domestically produced consumer goods and services (including imputed prices of government spending), excludes the prices of imported consumer goods. The CPI is based on a survey of what households are buying; the PCE is based on surveys of what businesses are selling. The CPI puts a large weight on housing costs. The PCE includes expenditures consumers do not pay directly for, such as medical care. It also tries to correct for substitution effects between goods when some get more expensive.

On average, the PCE has been about half a percentage point lower than the Consumer Price Index (CPI). The PCE forecasts around 2003/2004 indicated a threat of deflation, whereas CPI data released at the same time showed core inflation at target. Later data revisions raised the estimates of PCE inflation for that period.

Second, the alternative rules presented also differ in the weight attached to the output gap. In Taylor's original rule, the coefficient on the output gap was set equal to 0.5. The modified Taylor rules presented in Fig. 6.4 use a larger weight equal to 1 on the output gap, in line with actual behavior being more aggressive to output shocks (see Taylor, 1999). The predictions of the modified Taylor rule based on core PCE with a weight 1 on output gap is generally quite close to actual Fed policy. From 2009 on, benchmark rules suggest to set the policy rate negative. Reference rates get more negative, the stronger weight attached to the output gap. The rules provide no guidance about what to do in that case. The next chapter analyzes this problem in detail.

Evidently, the benchmark scenario provided by any Taylor-type rule strongly depends both on the weight put on the feedback parameters and on the nature and quality of the data used as input. The appropriate weights depend on preferences of policymakers, but also on changes in the structure of the economy and the policy transmission mechanism. It is a straightforward and instructive exercise to check how sensitive the benchmark rule is using different data and weights as input. Orphanides and Wieland (2008) and Nikolsko-Rzhevskyy and Papell (2013) provide instructive reference.

All rules presented in Fig. 6.4 simply impose various coefficients. Alternatively, Taylor rules can be estimated using real-time data, trying to characterize actual Fed actions: Which rule provides the best fit for the central bank rate among the class of all estimated rules with constant coefficients and inflation and output gap as exogenous variables? In those estimations, usually the fit is strongly improved by allowing for interest rate smoothing. So the actual policy rate is allowed to be a mix between the rate in the previous period and the rate suggested by the Taylor rule:

$$i_t = \rho\, i_{t-1} + (1-\rho)\, i_{i_t}^{T*} + \eta_t.$$

The estimated coefficient for ρ is usually quite high (up to close to 1), suggesting there is a lot of inertia in policy decisions.

6.3.3 Estimating Potential Output and the Natural Rate

Potential output is frequently measured as the trend value of output such as the fitted value from regressing real GDP on a time trend. Actual output is assumed to fluctuate around a given, smoothly evolving trend. Standard time series methods for de-trending apply some filter to real-time data. They use some weighted average of the past (usually either a linear, quadratic, or Hodrick–Prescott filter) as an estimate of what is normal. Instead of output measures, studies often use the estimated gap between unemployment and the natural unemployment rate instead. Both measures are closely related via Okun's law. The latter variable poses the same estimation challenges as potential output. Both in theory and practice, potential output does not evolve smoothly. As the discussion on policy during the pre-Volcker area in the 1970s indicated, the noise inherent in such estimates may lead to large policy errors.

Figure 6.5 illustrates challenges for actual policy facing uncertainty about potential output.

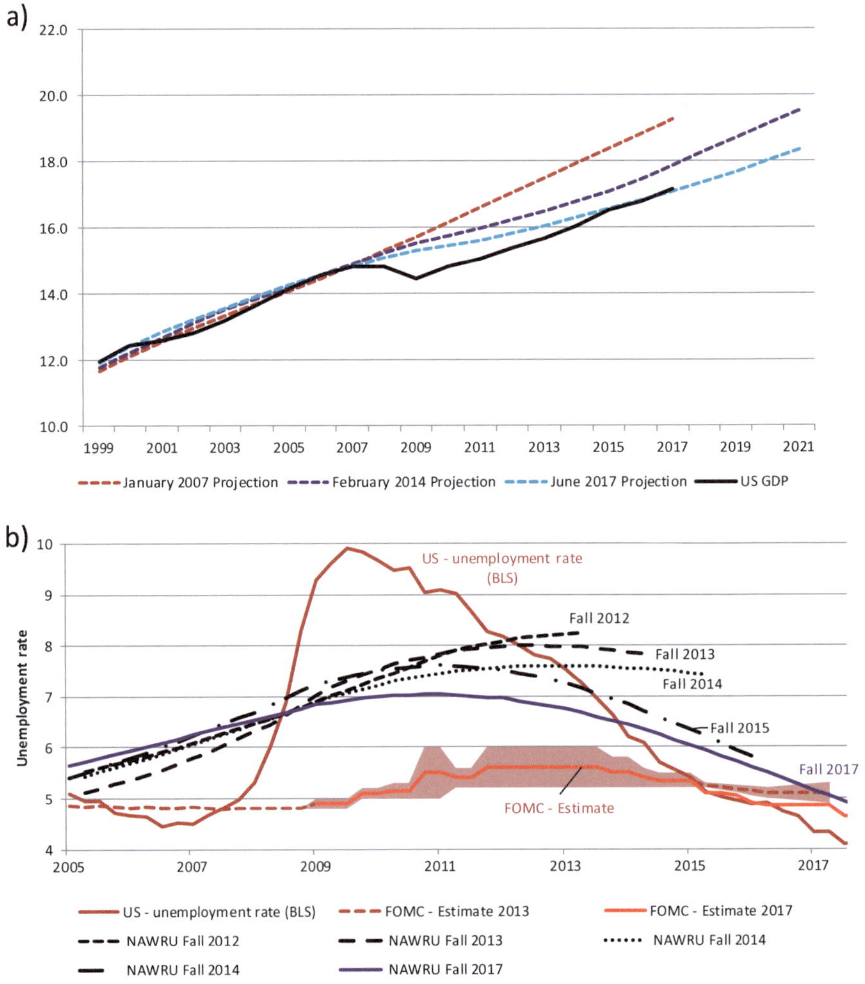

Fig. 6.5 (**a**) Revisions to CBO Estimate of Potential Output vs. actual US GDP. (**b**) Estimates of US natural rate of unemployment (FOMC and European Commission [NAWRU in AMECO database]) vs. actual US unemployment rate (BLS)

In the USA, the Congressional Budget Office (CBO) as nonpartisan organization produces regularly independent estimates. Figure 6.5a compares CBO estimates for potential GDP as calculated in 2007, 2014, and 2017 with the actual evolution of real GDP. After the financial crisis, estimates of potential GDP have been revised severely downwards, suggesting less slack (a smaller output gap) and so the risk of inflationary potential if policy stays accommodative.

Similarly, Fig. 6.5b illustrates ambiguity about US unemployment data. It compares real unemployment data with estimates of different vintage for the natural (structural) rate in the USA for the same period. Just as the CBO, the Federal Open Market Committee (FOMC)—the policy board of the FED—regularly reviews economic and financial conditions, producing—among others—economic projections for the civilian unemployment rate. Even though the actual rate of unemployment more than doubled in the USA within 2 years to nearly 10% during the financial crisis, the FOMC—in line with CBO forecasts—hardly raised its projections for the "natural rate of unemployment"—the rate of unemployment arising from all sources except fluctuations in aggregate demand. From 1948 to 2004, both CBO and FOMC based their estimates on the concept of the nonaccelerating inflation rate of unemployment (NAIRU)—the rate that can be sustained while maintaining a stable inflation rate. For more recent years, however, they use a different approach to estimate the natural rate, as the relation described by the Phillips curve became much less clear in the aggregate data during the 1990s and early 2000s (see Shackleton, 2018).

Figure 6.5b contrasts those estimates with estimates from the European Commission (Ecofin) for the USA, based on the concept of "non-accelerating wage rate of unemployment" (NAWRU). In contrast to the FOMC method, this methodology strongly relies on the Phillips curve. It identifies a rate of unemployment as structural when the rate of wage inflation stays unchanged at that rate. However, when the Phillips curve is very flat with expectations of inflation being well anchored, wages will adjust slowly with any changes in employment, so the current actual rate of unemployment is likely to be identified as being close to natural. Ecofin's forecast for the natural rate in the USA were initially much higher than the FOMC forecast. With unemployment falling, they have been substantially revised downwards later. Since macro-experiments, being extremely costly, are hardly feasible, it is difficult to guess the evolution of the actual rate of unemployment if the Fed would have relied on Ecofin forecasts rather than FOMC estimates and raised rates early on. But if hysteresis effects prevail, it seems likely that the actual rate would have stayed higher.

Blanchard, Cerutti, and Summers (2015) find strong evidence that, since the 1960s, recessions in advanced economies have often been followed by lower growth 5–10 years afterwards than any prerecession forecast or trend would have predicted. Hence, lower frequency fluctuations seem to have long-term consequences. The causality, however, is not obvious: According to hysteresis effects, recessions dampen potential growth if policy does not respond aggressively enough. But there may also be reverse causality: Bad news about future potential growth, triggering lower investment, lead to a recession.

The measurement of the natural real rate of interest r^*—the level of the short-term real rate that is consistent with full employment and stable inflation in the medium term—faces conceptually similar challenges as the measurement of potential output or the natural rate of unemployment. As Wicksell (1898) and Friedman (1968) already emphasized, the "natural" rate itself constantly fluctuates; there is no method to estimate it accurately. The natural real rate crucially determines the constant term in Taylor-type rules. Frequently, the average value in the past across some time range is used as raw estimate. Based on historical data, Taylor (1993) assumed r^* to be constant at 2% in his original rule. If the natural rate were constant over time, the sample mean of actual real interest rates would be a reasonable estimate.

There is, however, some evidence that the equilibrium real interest rate has trended downwards over the past 30 years. Not adjusting for that trend risks to introduce an upward bias in the traditional Taylor rule, the implied policy being too tight, pushing the nominal interest rate towards a too high level. To estimate changes in the trend, one might look at the 10-year moving average of ex post real rates or use more sophisticated econometric time series filtering techniques.

Laubach and Williams (2015) use a multivariate model that takes into account movements in inflation, output, and interest rates. Using the Kalman filter they partially adjust their estimate of the unobserved variables (natural rate and natural output) based on the distance between the model's predictions for real GDP and inflation and the actual outcomes. According to Laubach and Williams (2015), the 50-year average for the short-term rate in the USA is about 2%. However, they find a gradual descent from 1980 followed by a precipitous drop during the Great Recession. Figure 6.6a presents one-sided estimates (based only on current and past observations). The 10-year averages shown illustrate the decline. Figure 6.6b presents corresponding estimates from Holston, Laubach, and Williams (2017) for Canada, the Euro Area, USA, and UK. All these estimates of the natural rate are subject to great uncertainty (see also Taylor & Wieland, 2016).

Hamilton, Harris, Hatzius, and West (2016) come to similar conclusions, calculating the equilibrium real interest rate across time in a quite different way. They collected a data set on 21 countries, with annual data in some cases going back to 1858 and quarterly data since 1970. To calculate the ex ante real rate, they use the discount rate set by the central bank (or close substitute) along with inflation estimates. To calculate annual series for the ex ante real interest rate, they constructed a proxy for expected inflation using auto-regressions estimated over rolling windows.

As shown in Fig. 6.7, Hamilton et al. (2016) find that the natural rate of interest varies significantly over time. There are prolonged periods when it is high and others when it is low, making the natural rate extremely difficult to predict. The equilibrium

Fig. 6.6 One-sided estimates of the natural rate by Holston, Laubach and Williams. (**a**) US since 1960. (**b**) Canada, Euro Area, USA, and UK since 1980

rate cannot be estimated using long historical averages. The range of forecast error is so large as to make the projections of little use as a guide for monetary policy. Theory suggests that the natural rate of interest should be closely linked to the economy's trend growth rate. But in practice, that link appears to be quite loose. The real equilibrium rate is affected by other factors such as stringency of financial market regulation, uncertainty and risk aversion, trends in inflation, fiscal policy, and asset price movements.

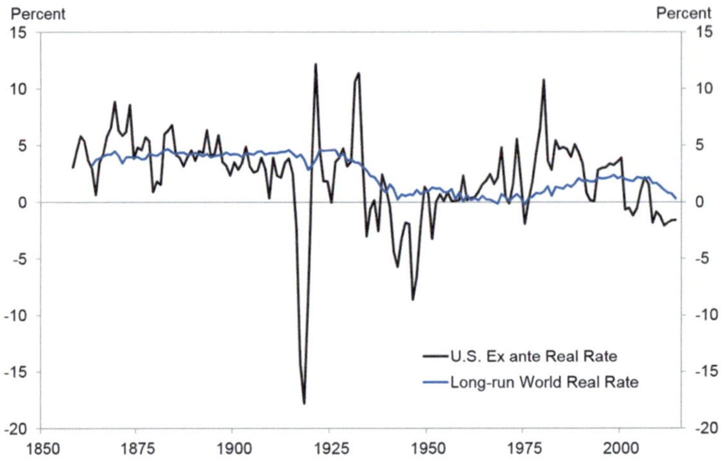

Fig. 6.7 Hamilton et al. (2016), Ex ante real rate estimates

6.3.4 Measures for Inflation Expectations

Market-based measures like inflation indexed long-term bonds seem to provide an ideal way to measure real yields. Market-based expectations are easily calculated from the prices of financial assets. They are available at high frequency without the need to rely on statistical models, surveys, or the judgment of forecasters. Treasury Inflation-Protected Securities, or TIPS, provide protection against potential increases in inflation. The return is automatically adjusted with inflation, as measured by the Consumer Price Index. The U.S. Treasury started issuing TIPS in 1997. The difference between the yield of non-indexed and indexed bonds of the same maturity is called breakeven inflation rate (BEIR). According to the Fisher equation, BEIR should be a straightforward measure of expected inflation. The 10-year BEIR is a measure of expected inflation during the next 10 years, on average. A popular measure of long-term inflation expectations is the 5-year break even inflation, 5 years forward—the difference between BEIR of 10- and 5-year maturity. Figure 6.8 illustrates how these measures for expected inflation evolve in the USA since 1998.

$$\begin{aligned} BEIR\ Yield &= Yield\ on\ Nominal\ Bonds - Yield\ of\ TIPS \\ &= Expected\ Inflation + Inflation\ Risk\ Premium \\ &\quad - Liquidity\ Risk\ Premium. \end{aligned}$$

In practice, things are more complex. Various risk premiums may contaminate the information in market data. Since the real return of nominal bonds decline with inflation, these bonds also contain a risk premium for inflation risk in addition to the real yield and expected inflation. Investors demand an extra yield for bearing the inflation risk embedded in holding nominal bonds. Reverse, the market for indexed

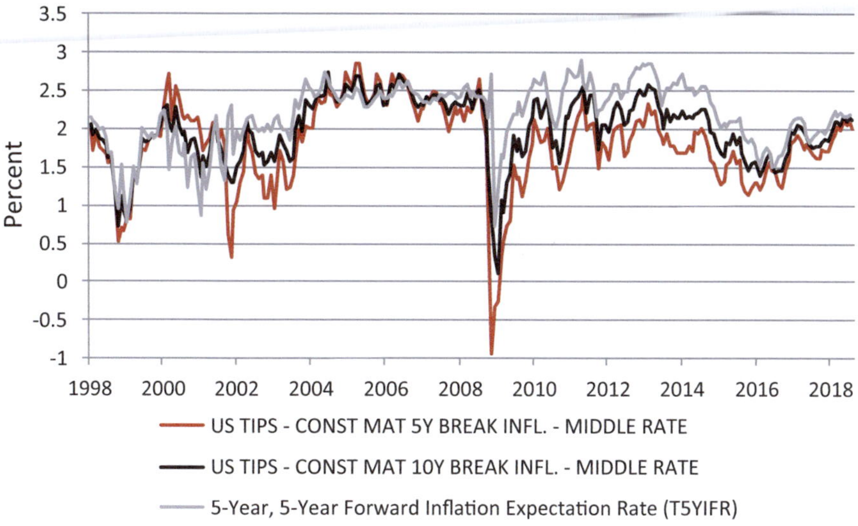

Fig. 6.8 US BEIR (5 years, 10 years, and 5 years, 5 year forward) (Source: FRED)

bonds is thinner than the market for nominal bonds. Holding less liquid bonds will contain a premium for liquidity risk. Changes in these rates may simply reflect fluctuations in the relevant risk premiums due to time-varying volatility. For that reason, frequently BEIR measures are called "inflation compensation" rather than "inflation expectation."

Market-based expectations of inflation can alternatively be calculated from prices on inflation swaps. These market derivatives (based on payments investors receive to compensate for inflation over the relevant horizon) are not affected by liquidity factors. Haubrich et al. (2012) from the Cleveland Fed estimate different risk premiums from a term structure model based on inflation swaps and calculate the real yield corrected according to that model. Fluctuations in risk premiums are rather small (see Fig. 6.9a). Estimates based on inflation swaps are less volatile compared to yields derived from TIPS (Fig. 6.9b). Both measures reflect market-based expectations for future headline CPI inflation including food and energy prices.

According to Crump, Eusepi, and Moench (2018), variations in term premiums account for the bulk of the cross-sectional and time series variation along the yield curve. They also largely explain the yield curve's reaction to structural economic shocks, emphasizing the importance of term premiums for monetary transmission mechanism.

From 2014 till 2016, inflation expectations as measured either by BEIR or via inflation swaps declined substantially worldwide. This is in striking contrast with other measures based on surveys of predictions made by professional forecasters such as the Survey of Professional Forecasters (SPF). Forecasts based on surveys are more stable such as the mean point estimates for SPF. Figure 6.10a compares forecasts for *long-term CPI inflation expectations* 5 years ahead in the USA based

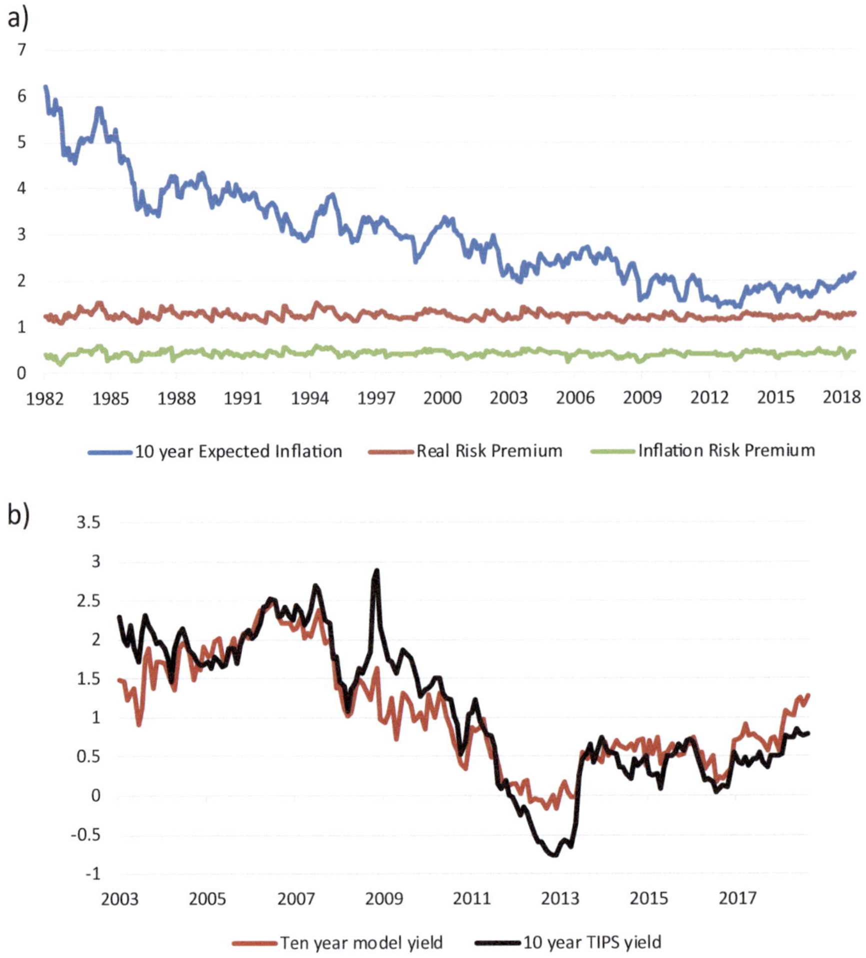

Fig. 6.9 Risk premiums and market-based expectations of inflation. (**a**) 10 year Expected Inflation and Real and Inflation Risk Premium. (**b**) 10 year yield: Model vs. TIPS (Source: Haubrich, Pennacchi, and Ritchken, 2012, Cleveland Fed, https://www.clevelandfed.org/en/our-research/indicators-and-data/inflation-expectations/inflation-expectations-archives/ie-20161018.aspx)

on SPF from the FRB Philadelphia with those derived from BEIR. The same holds for the Euro area: Fig. 6.10 contrasts expected inflation derived from inflation swaps in the Euro Area for 1 and 5 years (available since August 2008) with those from the Survey of Professional Forecasters (SPF) as carried out by the ECB (available since 1999).

Term structure models allow estimating expected inflation for different time horizons as a function of the maturity of bonds. Figure 6.11 shows the average expected rate of inflation (as annual rate) between today and n years from today, plotted as a function of the time horizon n. Again, different methods of measurement

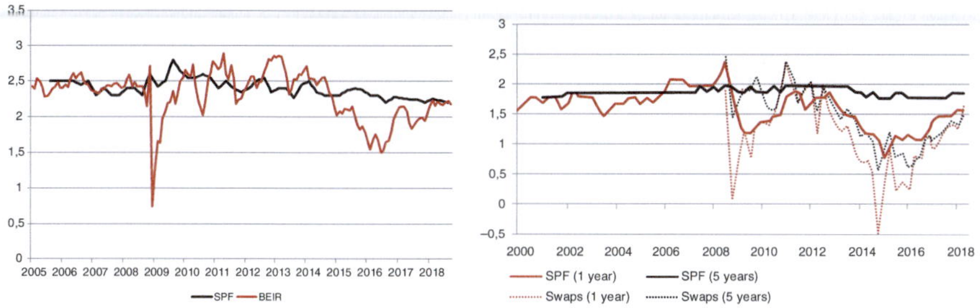

a) USA

b) Euro Area

Fig. 6.10 Expected Inflation: Survey of Professional Forecasters vs. BEIR resp. Inflation Swaps. (**a**) USA 5-Year, 5-Year Forward. (**b**) Euro area (Source: FRB Philadelphia, FRED, ECB)

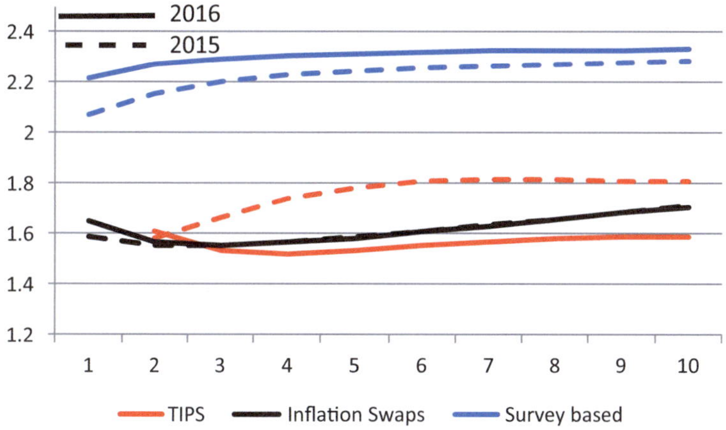

Fig. 6.11 Conflicting signals from various measures for expected inflation

yield contradictory conclusions. All dark lines plot rates starting in April 1, 2016. All broken lines give the same rates starting one year earlier April 1, 2015. The red lines represent expected inflation derived from TIPS according to Gürkaynak, Sack, and Wright (2010). Black lines represent expected inflation derived from inflation swaps as calculated in Haubrich et al. (2012). Finally, the blue lines represent information derived from SPF and the Blue Chip forecasts according to Aruoba (2018).

Relying on the TIPS measure, expected inflation declined between 2015 and 2016. On the other hand, relying on inflation swaps, expected inflation hardly changed. In contrast, expected inflation increased from 2015 to 2016 based on survey-based forecasts. Survey-based forecasts suggested that CPI inflation was expected to rise within 3 years from April 2016 on and then stay slightly above 2.3%. Given that the average spread between PCE and CPI inflation over recent years was around 0.3% points, this was in line with the Fed successfully targeting PCE inflation at 2%. In contrast, according to market-based estimates, the Fed was expected to miss its target for a long-time horizon. After 2017, BEIR measures for *long-term expectations* 5 years ahead in the USA came again in line with SPF data

(See Fig. 6.10a). Obviously, a sound policy analysis requires a careful analysis of the reasons underlying contradictory signals.

Given the uncertainty involved in measuring "natural rates" one may argue that policy minimizing the risk of errors should try to de-emphasize the weight put on stabilizing output. The larger the weight attached to the output gap in the feedback rule, the more serious the measurement issue. Even if optimal control policy might call for putting a rather large value to the output gap, the uncertainty about the proper model specification may suggest a more cautious response. Optimal policies may perform rather poorly if the central bank's information set is mis-specified. In contrast, simpler policy rules may be more robust in the sense that they perform well in a wide variety of models.

Should robust policy instead choose a rule simply focusing on keeping expected inflation on target? Unfortunately, the issue of noisy signals cannot be ignored even with such a simple strategy. As just illustrated, different information variables for inflation expectations can easily give contradictory signals. The correct size of the output gap is usually a key determinant of inflationary pressure. Policy inertia to prevent huge mistakes from misperceptions is no answer to these challenges. A strategy of doing nothing (wait and see) is not well defined for monetary policy: Should the central bank leave interest rates constant or follow a policy of constant rate of money growth as suggested by Friedman with his *k*-percent rule? Should it follow a simple rule like a standard Taylor rule responding to measures of inflation and output gap in exactly the same way as in former episodes? Such simple rules ignore the complexity involved in making good policy decisions. This is obvious when the central bank faces asymmetric risks. In a liquidity trap, the costs involved in overshooting of inflation may be substantially lower than the cost of triggering a deflationary spiral leading to secular stagnation.

Focus Box: Optimal Policy and Market-Based Expectations

Assume the central bank only cares about inflation. It aims to minimize deviations from the target inflation level. Hence, it intends to keep expected inflation—measured with real-world expectations—close to its target. In principle, it would need to carefully estimate real-world expectations of future inflation. If financial investors were representative of all agents, the optimal strategy would instead be fairly simple: Ideally it would adjust monetary policy so that *market-based* expectations of future inflation—such as measured by BEIR—over the medium term are equal to the inflation target, possibly adjusted for a constant risk premium. Accordingly, there would be no need to use any other information in setting policy than market-based expectations. Since participation in financial markets is, however, limited, the investors who determine asset prices and market-based probabilities may not be representative of all agents. Furthermore, changes in the rate measured could also reflect changes in market assessment of other risks such as liquidity or inflation risk.

6.4 Central Bank Transparency

6.4.1 Inflation Targeting: The Move Toward Increased Transparency

Focus Box: Trend Toward Independence and Transparency

In a detailed study, Dincer and Eichengreen (2014) estimate the extent of independence and transparency of more than 100 central banks for the period from 1998 to 2010. Building on preceding studies such as Eijffinger and Geraats (2006), they construct indices trying to measure various aspects of independence and transparency. They find a steady trend toward greater transparency and independence over time not only in advanced countries, but also in emerging markets and in developing economies (see Fig. 6.12). Transparency has tended to rise in particular in countries with deeper financial markets and with strong political institutions. Both the level and the variability of inflation seem to be significantly affected by both central bank transparency and independence, even though it is difficult to disentangle the impact of each single factor. Earlier studies find considerable evidence that central banks with policy independence in the pursuit of their mandated objectives deliver better economic outcomes (see Alesina & Summers, 1993).

The degree of independence is measured by looking at indicators for independence in policy formulation, its objective or mandate, limits on lending to the public sector, governing rules for the appointment and dismissal of the chief executive officer (CEO), and other board members.

Dincer and Eichengreen (2014) look at various measures of transparency, mainly collected from central bank's webpages. They try to capture different aspects such as political, economic, procedural, and operational transparency. Political transparency refers to openness about policy objectives. Economic transparency focuses on the economic information that is used for monetary policy, including economic data, the model of the economy that the central bank employs to construct forecasts or evaluate the impact of its decisions, and the internal forecasts (model based or judgmental) that the central bank relies on. Procedural transparency is about the way monetary policy decisions are taken. Policy transparency captures prompt disclosure of policy decisions, together with an explanation of the decision, and an explicit policy inclination or indication of likely future policy actions. Operational transparency concerns the implementation of the central bank's policy actions. Geraats (2002) provides a taxonomy of different types of transparency.

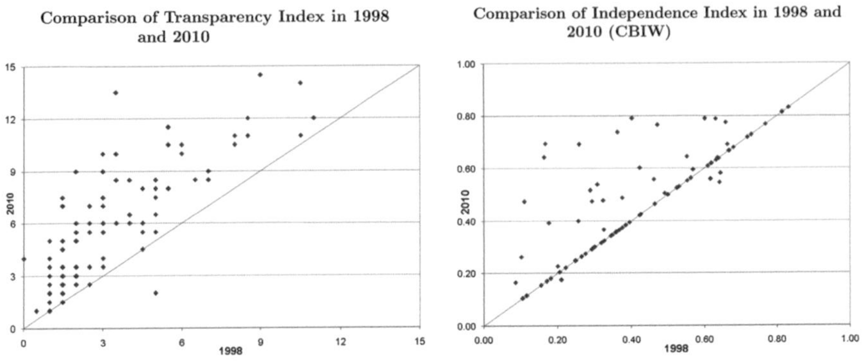

Fig. 6.12 Transparency and Independence Indices, Dincer and Eichengreen (2014)

During the last decades, central banks worldwide became both more independent and more transparent (see Focus Box). Central bank independence can be an effective way to insulate monetary policy from short-term political pressures, helping to address the time-consistency problems discussed in Chap. 5. Some central banks can even specify the objectives of monetary policy themselves (such as the target range of inflation). In most countries, parliament or government define these objectives, but central banks are independent in the sense that they are free to choose the instruments needed to implement the given policy objectives.

Independent central banks enjoy considerable discretion. So taking decisions in a transparent way and being accountable are crucial conditions for establishing and maintaining the democratic legitimacy of central banks as a public institution. In New Keynesian models, management of expectations is key for effective monetary policy, calling for transparent communication about policy objectives (such as specifying the numerical target for the rate of inflation) and about the intended policy path. Expectations about the future path of nominal interest rates are the key determinant for current aggregate demand. Reliable information about the precise nature of shocks and their persistence helps private agents to take better informed actions. To set prices optimally, firms need to have precise insights into the central bank's reaction function. So monetary policy seems most effective if the central bank conveys all relevant information to the public in the most transparent way. There have been heated debates whether central banks should publish not only their forecasts about relevant economic variables (or the underlying forecasting model), but also internal forecasts of future policy decisions or even specify explicitly the loss function behind their actions. More precise, a transparent central bank may state publicly its objectives as well as the constraints it sees itself facing as it pursues those objectives.

Central banks changed their communication policy dramatically during the last 30 years. In former days, many central banks were extremely secretive. Before February 1994, the Fed even did not publicly announce the target for the federal funds rate after taking decisions at its meetings. They thought the ability to take markets by surprise was important for influencing financial conditions. Over time the statement was expanded to include more detailed information. Not before May 1999 the Fed began publishing statements with explicit guidance about the future stance of policy. After the financial crisis 2008, explicit forward guidance became an essential component of its policy.

Other central banks became more transparent as well. Actual practice, however, differs in various ways. Some central banks give press conferences immediately after meetings, trying to clarify policy decisions to the public. Others publish the minutes of their meetings with some delay, revealing differences in opinion either anonymously or clearly indicating dissenting views. For example, the Fed releases minutes three weeks after every policymaking meeting, offering details on the heterogeneity of perspectives expressed. As part of implementing inflation targeting, many central banks now publish detailed forecasts of relevant economic variables. In inflation reports, they make projections of the likely path of inflation and output growth some years ahead. These projections are published two to four times a year, in documents explaining the central bank's view of the current state of the economy and of the reasoning behind its current policy actions. Inflation targeting reports can be seen as a way to credibly establish the central bank's commitment to maintaining price stability.

A communication challenge is to properly convey the uncertainty involved in making forecasts. Real-time data are unreliable, leading to frequent revisions following updates. Both the uncertainty connected to data revisions and the uncertainty about future shocks make the confidence band for any predictions usually fairly wide—the longer the time horizon, the wider. Furthermore, different members of the policy committee may consider different forecasting models as being more appropriate, leading to divergent views even given the same data. In the committee, there may be no unique preferred path for future policy decisions. So for various reasons, publishing just a mean forecast can be seriously misleading. Some central banks (like the Bank of England, the Swedish Riksbank, and Norges Bank in Norway) use fan-charts to convey the uncertainty involved in predictions. Darker (lighter) shaded areas represent stronger (weaker) confidence bands for the predicted path. Since future changes in monetary policy are heavily dependent on data, which are not yet known, forecast accuracy is decreasing with the length of time, reflected by the band getting larger.

For illustration, consider the fan chart in Fig. 6.13, reproduced from the Bank of England's Inflation Report from February 2016. It indicates the probability of various outcomes for CPI inflation in the UK for its forecast period (3 years ahead). The report explains: *If economic circumstances identical to today's were to prevail on 100 occasions, the MPC's best collective judgement is that inflation in any particular quarter would lie within the darkest central band on 30 of those occasions. The fan charts are constructed so that outturns of inflation are also expected to lie within each pair of the lighter red areas on 30 occasions. In any particular quarter of the forecast period, inflation is therefore expected to lie somewhere within the fans on 90 out of 100 occasions.* Only with 10% probability inflation can fall anywhere outside the red area of the fan chart.

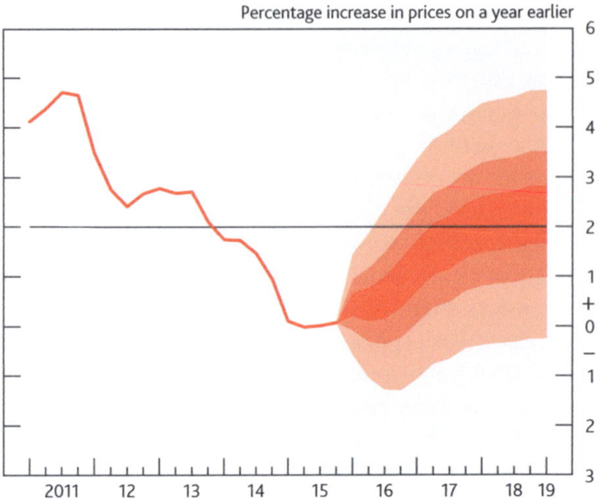

Fig. 6.13 UK CPI inflation projection based on market interest rate expectations and £375 billion purchased assets (Source: Bank of England, 2016)

Since the future path of the economy will crucially be shaped by the policy decisions taken, forecasts of future output and inflation strongly depend on the underlying future interest rate path. Forecasts may differ widely depending on whether they are based on (1) assuming the interest rate to stay constant from now on, (2) using market expectations for the interest rate path, or (3) using the own forecast of optimal policy. In its inflation report, the Bank of England bases its CPI inflation projections on market interest rate expectations. Apart from the future interest rate path, the expected length of unconventional policy measures as discussed in Chap. 7 has also an impact on expected future inflation and output. In its fan chart, the Bank of England assumes that the stock of assets purchased remains unchanged at £375 billion throughout the forecast period.

Some central banks, like the Reserve Bank of New Zealand since 1997 and Norges Bank in Norway since 2005, display and discuss estimates of future settings of the policy rate, indicating the intended optimal policy. Figure 6.14 reproduces Norges Bank's interest rate forecast, published on December 13, 2018. The forecast is based on a system of averaging models (SAM), a Bayesian average of the outcomes from more than 200 models. Norges Bank publishes such forecasts after each monetary policy decision, together with consistent forecasts for output gap and inflation. Aiming to help the public to better understand the central bank's view on its path of monetary policy rate, it also publishes the decomposition of change in the interest rate path, i.e., how the change in the interest rate forecast between two monetary policy decisions can be decomposed into contributions from exogenous disturbances. In addition, it publishes the interest rate forecast under various hypothetical scenarios to reflect how the central bank reacts to uncertainties. According to

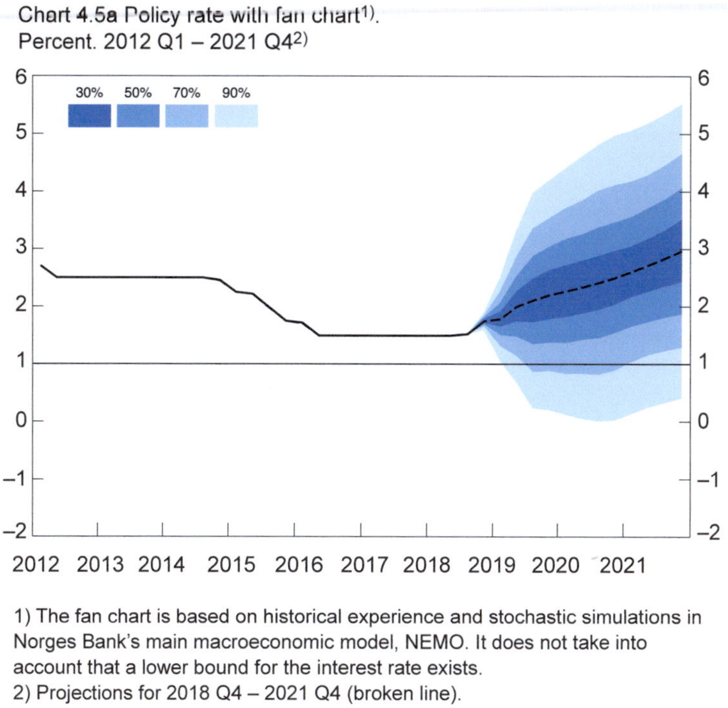

Fig. 6.14 Norges Bank projections for the key policy rate (Source: Norges Bank December 13, 2018)

Norges Bank, "... *Transparency is necessary for accountability. With accountability the central bank can build credibility and trust, both by showing that the objectives are actually attained in the longer run, and by explaining deviations from targets. . . . (The communication instruments), understood as information about future policy intentions, may be viewed as a natural extension of this accountability framework.*"

Since 2011, the Fed started to publish so called "dot plots": Each FOMC member projects what he or she thinks should happen to the Fed Funds Rates during the following years. Each dot in Fig. 6.15 summarizes the projection of a member of the policymaking Federal Open Market Committee as made in March 2016 for the Fed's short-term target interest rate under the assumption that she or he has complete control of monetary policy. So projections of each member are not based on actual expected policy, but based on the own preferred policy, given the own assessment about the state of the economy. The degree of heterogeneity of the dots published is an indication of the extent of disagreement among policymakers.

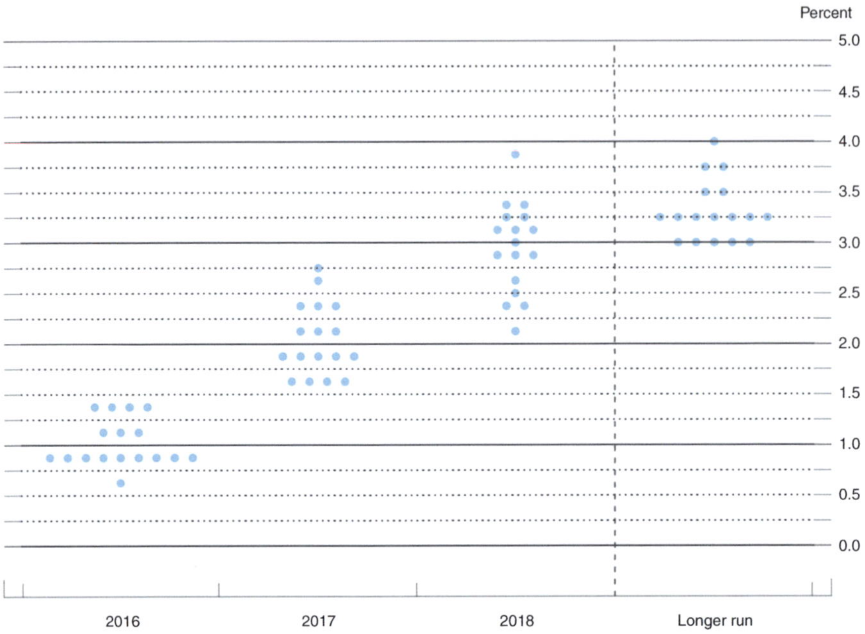

Fig. 6.15 Dot plot (US Fed), March 16, 2016

6.4.2 Multiplier Effects of Public Information: Can Transparency Be Harmful?

When the central bank provides precise information, we would expect market prices to be more informationally efficient. Providing more precise information will result in a closer alignment between market participants' expectations about the course of future short-term rates and the central bank's own views. Central bank communication actively influences long-term rates and financial market prices. However, it not only conveys authoritative information about fundamentals, it also plays a coordinating role. Private agents, anticipating that their return depends not just on their own information about true fundamentals, but also on being close to average opinion, tend to overemphasize public signals. Keynes described this phenomenon when he compared the stock market with a beauty contest: In that contest participants are asked to choose the top 6 "most beautiful" faces out of 100 women. The winner is the person closest to the consensus judgement of all participants. Keynes pointed out this generates strategic complementarity: "*It is not a case of choosing those [faces] which, to the best of one's judgment, are really the prettiest, nor even those which average opinion genuinely thinks the prettiest. We have reached the third degree where we devote our intelligences to anticipating what average opinion expects the average opinion to be. And there are some, I believe, who practice the fourth, fifth and higher degrees*" (Keynes, *General Theory of Employment Interest and Money*, 1936).

Due to the coordination externality caused by strategic complementarity, financial markets tend to overreact to public information. As shown by Morris and Shin (2002), in that case more transparency may be detrimental. In their model, public statements convey information on the underlying fundamentals, but they also serve as a focal point for the beliefs of the group as a whole. Public signals serve as a coordination device. When consensus views influence people's decision-making process, public information may be overweighted in individual decisions to the detriment of private information. There is a multiplier effect of public information, with private agents being too much focused on signals observable also by all others. Morris and Shin (2002) show that the welfare effect of increased public disclosures is ambiguous. So it may not be optimal to disclose information at all. The central bank may face a trade-off between welfare gains that result from being able to steer the future beliefs of economic agents, and the impaired signal value that results from disclosures of its forecasts.

This argument stirred strong controversies. Should the central bank really withhold information? What is the optimal degree of transparency? Research stimulated by that work showed that the scepticisms about transparency is valid only under special conditions but is not justified in general.

The model of Morris and Shin (2002) assumes that the beauty contest element of individuals' decisions is socially wasteful. It enters only as a zero sum component in the agents' payoffs. That is, in the end the better informed will gain at the expense of those paying less attention to the public information provided. This assumption is crucial for their results. If by signalling its own intentions, the central bank helps all agents to take better informed choices, the zero sum issue is of no relevance. If coordination has some social value, then the effect of greater precision of public information on welfare is unambiguously positive.

Nevertheless, limits to transparency due to the beauty contest nature of public information may be a relevant concern. As shown below, however, it turns out that welfare is locally decreasing in the precision of public information only under empirically very restrictive conditions: The precision of public signal has to be small relative to the precision of private signals. When the public signal has precision no lower than the precision of the private signal, welfare is higher with the public signal than without even in a beauty contest context.

We present a simple stylized model, based on Morris and Shin (2005) to illustrate the issues involved. There is a continuum of small investors with unit mass. They try to infer the true value V of the underlying fundamental state. Investor i's chooses his/her own evaluation a_i. a is the evaluation profile over all investors.

Investor i's payoff function is

$$U_i(a,V) = -(1-r)(a_i - V)^2 - r\gamma\left(L_i - \overline{L}\right)$$

$$\text{with } L_i = \int_0^1 (a_j - a_i)^2 dj;\ \overline{L} = \int_0^1 L_j dj.$$

L_i is a measure for how far the own evaluation deviates from average market evaluation $\overline{L}$.

The term $(a_i - V)^2$ in the utility function says that the further away my own evaluation from fundamentals V, the higher the losses. It represents the standard loss component related to fundamentals: The payoff is higher the closer my own evaluation is to the true state of the economy.

But the payoff for each investor depends not only on the fundamental value, but also on how close the own evaluation comes to the average opinion in the market. The second term represents the zero-sum component of the coordination game as described in Keynes's beauty contest example. With asset prices being strongly dependent on average judgement in the community, it does not pay to be too far from average opinion. There is an incentive to go with the market, guessing other agents' evaluations. This creates an information externality. It is not sufficient to judge market value just based on my own signals; it is also crucial to judge best the actions of all other agents. The term r characterizes the strength of that externality.

Each investor observes a noisy private signal $x_i = V + \varepsilon_i$ with ε_i as noise term $(E(\varepsilon_i) = 0; \sigma_\varepsilon^2)$. The precision of private information is inversely related to the signal's variance. Precision is $\beta = \frac{1}{\sigma_\varepsilon^2}$.

The central bank observes a public signal $y = V + \eta$ which is also noisy with η as noise term $(\eta \sim (E(\eta) = 0, \sigma_\eta^2))$. The precision of public information is $\alpha = \frac{1}{\sigma_\eta^2}$.

All signals (both private and public) are assumed to be conditionally independent given the true state.

If the central bank discloses its information, y will be a public signal observable by all investors. Since both private and public information about fundamental V are noisy, a rational investor tries to update information according to Bayesian rules. Given the information set $I_i = \{x_i, y\}$, investors face a standard signal extraction problem. With Bayesian updating, each signal is weighted with its precision, so the expected value V from i's point of view is: $E(V) = \frac{\alpha\, y + \beta\, x_i}{\alpha + \beta}$. This is individual i's best prediction of V, relying purely on the information set I_i. But with $r > 0$, for each investor it will also be crucial to guess the behaviour of all other investors. Let us assume that estimates of all investors are formed as a linear combination between private and public information with k as the weight for the private signal, so we have $a_j(I_j) = kx_i + (1 - k)y$.

If so, my own estimate about the average prediction of the market is now:

$$E_i(a) = k\frac{\alpha\, y + \beta\, x_i}{\alpha + \beta} + (1 - k)\, y = k\,\frac{\beta}{\alpha + \beta}x_i + \left(1 - k\,\frac{\beta}{\alpha + \beta}\right)\, y.$$

After receiving the signals $I_i = \{x_i, y\}$, each investor chooses $a_i(I_i)$ so as to minimize expected losses. The individually optimal prediction, derived as first-order condition, is:

$$a_i(I_i) = [(1 - r)E_i(V) + rE_i(a)].$$

So we have

$$a_i(I_i) = \frac{\alpha}{\alpha + \beta(1-r)} y + \frac{\beta(1-r)}{\alpha + \beta(1-r)} x_i = V + \frac{\alpha}{\alpha + \beta(1-r)} \eta + \frac{\beta(1-r)}{\alpha + \beta(1-r)} \varepsilon_i.$$

In the absence of the externality ($r = 0$) the individual prediction corresponds to the individually best prediction of V when relying only on the own information set. But for $r > 1$, public information y being common knowledge is overweighted relative to the private information; the externality creates a multiplier effect. Each investor giving extra weight to the public signal, any noise in that signal will be amplified. One can show that this linear equilibrium is the unique equilibrium of the coordination game with a beauty contest element.

Social welfare, $W(a|V)$ as average utility of all investors depends only on the fundamentals-based payoff. Normalized by $1 - r$, social welfare is:

$$W(a|V) = \frac{1}{1-r} \int_0^1 U_i(a|V)\, di = -\int_0^1 (a_i - V)^2 di.$$

Using $a_i(I_i)$, we get

$$E\left[W(a|V)\right] = -\frac{\alpha + \beta(1-r)^2}{\left[\alpha + \beta(1-r)\right]^2},$$

$$\text{with } \frac{\partial E\left[W(a|V)\right]}{\partial \alpha} = \frac{\alpha - \beta\ (2r-1)(1-r)}{\left[\alpha + \beta(1-r)\right]^3}.$$

Taking the precision of the public signal as a measure of transparency, the main result of Morris and Shin (2005) is that social welfare may be decreasing in transparency (in α)—see Fig. 6.16. If so, all investors might be better off if the central bank does not disseminate the public signal at all. Withholding the public signal is equivalent to effectively setting $\alpha = 0$ with $E\,W(a|\,V, \alpha = 0) = -\frac{1}{\beta}$. The condition for $\frac{\partial E[W(a|V)]}{\partial \alpha} < 0$ is $\alpha < \beta(2r-1)(1-r)$.

As Svensson (2007) argues, this condition is unlikely to hold for reasonable parameter values. In particular since $(2r-1)(1-r) < 1$, more transparency unambiguously increases welfare whenever the public signal is more precise than private signals (that is if $\alpha > \beta$).

Furthermore, if coordination itself has social value, there is no longer an ambiguous effect of α. If we allow for a social value of coordinated action, welfare is globally increasing in α. In that case, expected welfare is given by the equation

$$E\left[W(a|V)\right] = -\frac{\alpha + \beta(1-r^2)}{\left[\alpha + \beta(1-r)\right]^2}.$$

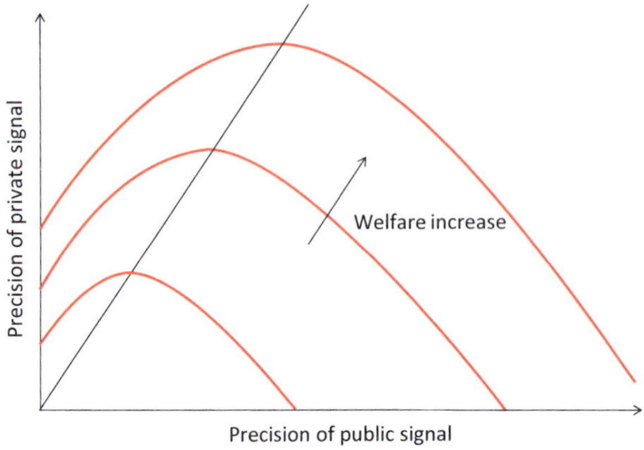

Fig. 6.16 Welfare from precision of public and private signals. Source: Morris and Shin (2002, p. 1529)

6.5 Summary

In this chapter, we analyzed how our results about optimal monetary policy have to be modified if we take into account that real decision-making has to cope with control errors, imperfect information and robustness issues. Intuition suggests that central banks facing these challenges should act less aggressively as a response to uncertainty. Brainard (1967) already formalized this notion. But we learned that specific details matter. The key issue is whether a more aggressive policy adds or lowers volatility of social losses. Policy response should depend on the precision of the signal received when information is noisy. The more precise the signal, the more active should be the response with Bayesian updating in case of a quadratic loss function. Similarly, actions should be dampened if there is multiplicative uncertainty about the transmission mechanism. Robust control theory, however, using minimax rules, suggests that under some conditions central banks might act more aggressively, aiming to avoid really bad outcomes (limit losses impending under extreme case scenarios).

A key challenge for the optimal policy derived in a New Keynesian framework is that it depends on quite a few variables which are hard to observe in reality: Monetary policy is supposed to adjust the nominal rate interest such that the real rate is in line with the natural rate of interest. Rehearsing the debate about optimal policy after the financial crisis 2008, we illustrated that simple rules like the Taylor principle may lead to quite ambiguous predictions if we take that issue seriously into account. We showed the challenges involved in estimating potential output, the natural rate of interest and measuring expected inflation.

There has been a steady trend toward more transparency and independence for central banks across the world. Most impact of monetary policy is created by influencing the expected future path of actions. With agents being forward looking, effectiveness strongly depends on private agents correctly understanding central bank actions. Hence, transparent communication is an essential ingredient of modern policy. However, there may be conditions when too much transparency might be harmful: Since public information plays also a coordinating role, private agents might overemphasize public signals. In that case, social welfare may be locally decreasing in transparency. We have shown, however, that more transparency unambiguously raises welfare whenever the public signal is more precise than private signals.

References

Alesina, A., & Summers, L. H. (1993). Central bank independence and macroeconomic performance: Some comparative evidence. *Journal of Money, Credit and Banking, 25*(May), 151–162.

Aruoba, B. (2018). Term structures of inflation expectations and real interest rates. *Journal of Business and Economic Statistics*. https://doi.org/10.1080/07350015.2018.1529599.

Bank of England. (2016). *Inflation Report*, February 2016.

Barlevy, G. (2011). Robustness and macroeconomic policy. *Annual Review of Economics, 3*, 1–24.

Bernanke, B. (2015). The Taylor rule: A benchmark for monetary policy? *Brookings Blog*. http://www.brookings.edu/blogs/ben-bernanke/posts/2015/04/28-taylor-rule-monetary-policy.

Blanchard, O., Cerutti, E., & Summers, L. (2015). Inflation and activity, two explorations and their monetary policy implications. *ECB Forum on Central Banking*, May 2015.

Brainard, W. (1967). Uncertainty and the effectiveness of policy. *American Economic Review, 57* (2), 411–425.

Clarida, R., Gali, J., & Gertler, M. (2000). Monetary policy rules and macroeconomic stability: Evidence and some theory. *Quarterly Journal of Economics, 115*(1), 147–180.

Crump, R., Eusepi, S., & Moench, E. (2018). The term structure of expectations and bond yields, revised staff reports 775. Federal Reserve Bank of New York.

Dincer, N., & Eichengreen, B. (2014). Central Bank transparency and independence: Updates and new measures. *International Journal of Central Banking, 10*(1), 189–253.

Eijffinger, S., & Geraats, P. (2006). How transparent are Central Banks? *European Journal of Political Economy, 22*(1), 1–22.

Friedman, M. (1968). The role of monetary policy. *American Economic Review, 58*(1), 1–17.

Geraats, P. M. (2002). Central Bank transparency. *The Economic Journal, 112*(483), 532–565.

Gürkaynak, R., Sack, B., & Wright, J. (2010). The TIPS yield curve and inflation compensation. *American Economic Journal: Macroeconomics, 2*, 70–92.

Hamilton, J. D., Harris, E. S., Hatzius, J., & West, K. D. (2016). The equilibrium real funds rate: Past, present and future. *IMF Economic Review, 64*(4), 660–707.

Hansen, L., & Sargent, T. (2008). *Robustness*. Princeton, NJ: Princeton University Press.

Haubrich, J., Pennacchi, G., & Ritchken, P. (2012). Inflation expectations, real rates, and risk premia: Evidence from inflation swaps. *Review of Financial Studies, 25*(5), 1588–1629.

Holston, K., Laubach, T., & Williams, J. (2017). Measuring the natural rate of interest: International trends and determinants. *Journal of International Economics, 108*(1), S59–S75.

Laubach, T., & Williams, J. (2015). Measuring the natural rate of interest redux. *Federal Reserve Bank of San Francisco Working Paper* 2015-16.

Morris, S., & Shin, H. S. (2002). Social value of public information. *American Economic Review, 92*(5), 1521–1534.

Morris, S., & Shin, H. S. (2005). Central Bank transparency and the signal value of prices. *Brookings Papers on Economic Activity, 2*, 1–43.

Nikolsko-Rzhevskyy, A., & Papell, D. H. (2013). Taylor's rule versus Taylor rules. *International Finance, 16*(1), S71–S93.

Orphanides, A. (2001). Monetary policy rules based on real-time data. *American Economic Review, 91*(4), 964–985.

Orphanides, A., & Wieland, V. (2008). Economic projections and rules of thumb for monetary policy. *Federal Reserve Bank of St. Louis Review*, July/August, pp. 307–324.
Shackleton, R. (2018). Estimating and projecting potential output using CBO's forecasting growth model. *Congressional Budget Office Working Paper* 2018-03, Washington, DC.
Svensson, L. (2007). Robust control made simple: Lecture notes. Princeton University, Lecture notes.
Taylor, J. (1993). Discretion versus policy rules in practice. *Carnegie-Rochester Conference Series in Public Policy, 39*(1), 195–214.
Taylor, J., & Wieland, V. (2016). Finding the equilibrium real interest rate in a fog of policy deviations. *Business Economics, 51*, 147–154.
Wicksell, K. (1898). *Geldzins und Güterpreise*. Jena: Gustav Fischer Verlag.

The Liquidity Trap: Limits for Monetary Policy at the Effective Lower Bound

7

7.1 Introduction: The Effective Lower Bound

According to the New Keynesian model outlined in the previous chapters, monetary policy works mainly by adjusting the short-term nominal interest rate. By responding properly to different kinds of shocks with an increase or decrease of the rate, the central bank can achieve two goals at the same time: It can both implement price stability and dampen output fluctuations. The adequate interest rate reaction under optimal policy depends on the specific kind of shock. Uncertainty about the nature of shocks and the exact transmission mechanism poses challenges for optimal policy. Nevertheless, interest rate rules such as the Taylor rule provide a simple policy guideline capturing the essence of optimal monetary policy. For at least two decades, it seemed that central banks could solve all challenges of monetary policy design perfectly by adapting this abstract framework: Inflation rates came down worldwide; at the same time, fluctuations of output and employment were at a historic low. Many economists viewed problems of the business cycle as solved. It was the age of the "Great Moderation." It seemed like the fulfillment of John Maynard Keynes's dream that central bankers as economists would be humble technicians like dentists: boring practitioners of an uncontroversial and undeniably helpful science.

Starting in August 2007, when markets for commercial bonds and the interbank market began to dry out and short-term interest rates were sharply rising for many assets, suddenly these calm and quiet times were gone. At first, some central banks reacted quite reluctantly, being afraid of the risk of high inflation driven by high oil prices. Most of them, however, cut their interest rates worldwide aggressively down to zero during 2008 and 2009. Nevertheless, in many countries output declined strongly; unemployment was rising dramatically. Obviously, with rates hitting a lower bound, conventional interest rate policy came to its limits.

The great financial crisis posed severe challenges. In response, central bankers tried a huge range of unconventional monetary policy measures. They used a variety of quite different options, starting from forward guidance to expanding the balance

J. Cao, G. Illing, *Money: Theory and Practice*, Springer Texts in Business and Economics, https://doi.org/10.1007/978-3-030-19697-4_7

sheet dramatically with quantitative and qualitative easing. The standard New Keynesian model cannot address some of these measures. In a framework with a complete set of frictionless future markets, the size and composition of the central bank's balance sheet should be irrelevant: As long as all assets can be traded perfectly, there is no need to intervene in these markets. We need to introduce frictions in financial markets to get a more realistic picture. The following chapters will show in detail how that may lead to quite different conclusions.

In this chapter, we keep strictly within the standard interest rate setting framework, still abstracting from problems in financial intermediation. We will study optimal interest rate policy in the New Keynesian framework, explicitly taking into account the constraint imposed by the effective lower bound. As we will see, the key lesson from the theoretical analysis is the idea that under this constraint the central bank should aim to keep interest rates low for a long period, in order to stimulate current demand by committing to low long-term rates. We illustrate this feature in a highly stylized three-period framework, characterizing explicitly the optimality conditions involved, and show that there is a problem of dynamic inconsistency, creating a deflation bias. This lesson had a strong impact on actual policy design. The notion of forward guidance, which played a key role in unconventional policies, follows naturally from commitment to optimal interest rate policy at the zero lower bound. The attempt to communicate and commit in a transparent way to keep the path of short-term interest rates low for an extended period far into the future is a key element of optimal policy.

Focus: The Zero Lower Bound During Financial Crisis

In 2009, most central banks cut their short-term rate down to zero. Nevertheless, the recession deepened and inflation slowed even further. Standard rules of thumb indicated that the target rate should be cut even further. Interest rates, however, cannot fall much below zero, since people will instead just try to hoard currency, which pays zero interest. The economy is stuck at the Zero Lower Bound. Later, as some central banks experimented with negative rates, it turned out that rates can indeed be set slightly negative without triggering hoarding; nevertheless, there is an effective lower bound (see Sect. 7.4).

Figure 7.1, taken from Rudebusch (2010), plots the Fed's target rate since 2002 and compares it with a simple policy rule similar to a Taylor-type rule. Rudebusch obtained this rule by running a statistical regression of the funds' rate on the inflation rate and the unemployment gap, using data from the past two decades. According to his estimate, the interest rate response is best described by the following rule:

$$i = 2.1 + 1.3\,\pi - 2.0\,(u - u_n).$$

Here, π is the year-over-year inflation rate, measured by core consumer price inflation. $u - u^*$ is the gap between the actual unemployment rate and the "natural rate" u^*. The predicted value for i depends not only on current

(continued)

inflation and unemployment, but also on the natural rate u_n. Obviously, u_n is time varying; it cannot be observed without noise. As already emphasized in Chap. 6, there is substantial uncertainty about the extent to which variations in the actual rate of unemployment are cyclical or structural. Rudebusch used the Congressional Budget Office's estimate of the natural rate of unemployment as a proxy for u_n. The estimated policy rule provides a simple guideline. It recommends lowering the funds rate by 1.3 percentage points if inflation falls by 1 percentage point and by 2 percentage points if the unemployment rate rises by 1 percentage point. As shown in Fig. 7.1, this rule of thumb corresponds fairly well to the actual target funds rate during late 2007 and 2008. At that time, as the economy slowed, the Fed lowered its target by over 5 percentage points to essentially zero. In 2009, the rule of thumb suggests that—if possible—the funds rate should be reduced by another 5 percentage points in line with the Fed's historical policy response. Rudebusch's estimate was first published in 2009; Fig. 7.1 is an update from June 2010.

The dashed line also provided a prediction on the Fed policy for the following years, based on the information available in June 2010. To predict the future path, Rudebusch used the median economic forecasts of the Federal Open Market Committee (FOMC 2010) for π, u, and u_n as input. In June 2010, these forecasts predicted slowly falling unemployment and continued low inflation. Based on these forecasts and the historical rule—ignoring the zero lower bound—the funds rate would stay negative until late 2012. In fact, the Fed held the rate near zero for more than 5 years until December 2015.

We need to be aware, however, that the numbers presented as suggested target rate in Fig. 7.1 are not to be carved in stone as some kind of optimal rule. Rudebusch calculated that rule of thumb based on the Fed's actual policy during past decades. Nevertheless, the exact data obtained as target interest rate path strongly depend on some key parameters used as input for the calculation. (1) The weight put on output relative to inflation, (2) the way output or unemployment gap are estimated, and (3) the specification of the rate of inflation used. As input for inflation, Rudebusch looked at core CPI inflation. Since the core rate excludes volatile food and energy prices, it can be seen as a more reliable measure of the medium-term inflation trend and thus as a better predictor of future inflation than current overall or headline inflation. Since 2000, the Fed focuses on the Personal Consumption Expenditures price index (PCE) as measure for inflation. On average, the PCE has been about half a percentage point lower than the Consumer Price Index (CPI).[1] The

(continued)

[1]The CPI is based on a survey of what households are buying; the PCE is based on surveys of what businesses are selling. The CPI puts a large weight on housing costs. The PCE includes expenditures consumers do not pay directly for, such as medical care. It also tries to correct for substitution effects between goods when some get more expensive.

original Taylor rule (1993) used the GDP deflator as measure for inflation. All three measures follow broadly similar trends, but differ in detail.

Using different specifications can lead to dramatically different conclusions. In fact, at that time John Taylor heavily criticized the unconventional policy of the Fed as "highly interventionist and discretionary" monetary policy, deviating from a rules-based approach. He argued that if sticking to the original version of his rule as initially proposed by himself (Taylor 1993), there would be no need to act aggressively. For illustration, Fig. 7.2 shows two target rules calculated by Nikolsko-Rzhevskyy and Papell (2013). Using overall headline CPI inflation and the CBO output gap as input, they calculate a rule using the weights such as in the original version of Taylor (1993):

$$i = 1 + 1.5\pi + 0.5\,(y - y_n).$$

For comparison, they alternatively calculate the same rule with a weight of one for the output gap

$$i = 1 + 1.5\pi + (y - y_n).$$

Figure 7.2 clearly illustrates that the stronger the weight attached to the output gap (the red line), the stronger the call for a more aggressive response. With a weight of 0.5 on the output gap, the rates prescribed for the period 2009–2011 are not as strongly negative as calculated by the rule used by Rudebusch (2010).[2] Focusing on current overall inflation, both rules presented suggest that the Fed should have raised rates in 2008. Following such an advice (to raise interest rates at the height of the financial crisis) might have made the crisis worse with potentially disastrous effects.

One reason for this striking difference is that according to the original Taylor Rule (1993) interest rates should respond to headline inflation. At that time, inflation was high due to a spike in oil prices. By focusing on core inflation, the Fed instead took a forward-looking approach, responding to forecasts of future inflation. It was determined to cut interest rates fast, facing the prospect of deflation at the zero lower bound. Apart from such differences in the measures used as input, another key reason for the ambiguity of rules of thumb is the inherent uncertainty about the true natural real rate of interest and the true output gap resp. the natural rate u^* as discussed in the previous chapter. These variables are purely theoretical concepts, not observable in reality. Given the uncertainty about the true values, some ambiguity is unavoidable. As shown in Chap. 1, the natural real rate of interest r is a crucial

(continued)

[2]Rudebusch used the unemployment gap. If according to Okuns's law, $u - u_n = 2\,(y - y_n)$, a weight of 2 for the unemployment gap is equivalent to a weight of 1 for the output gap.

determinant of the long-run value of the nominal rate with $i = r + \pi^e$. Using $\pi = \pi^e = \pi^*$ and $y = y_n$, the average value in the Taylor rule varies directly with r. Therefore, the nominal rate has to be lower on average when the natural real rate of interest decreases.

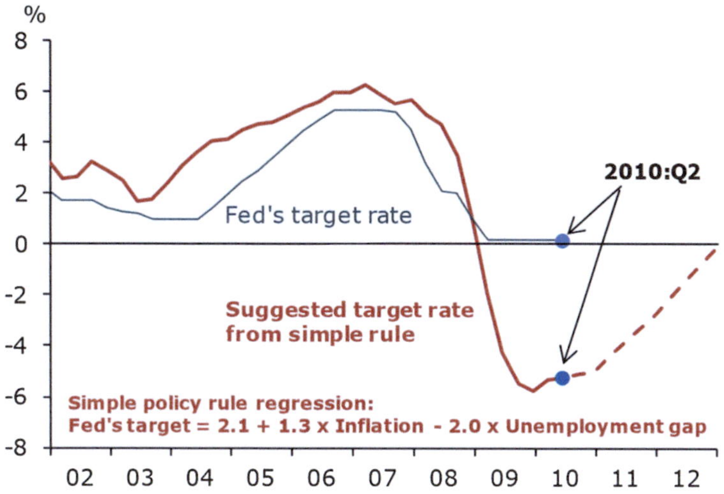

Fig. 7.1 The zero lower bound [Source: Rudebusch (2010)]

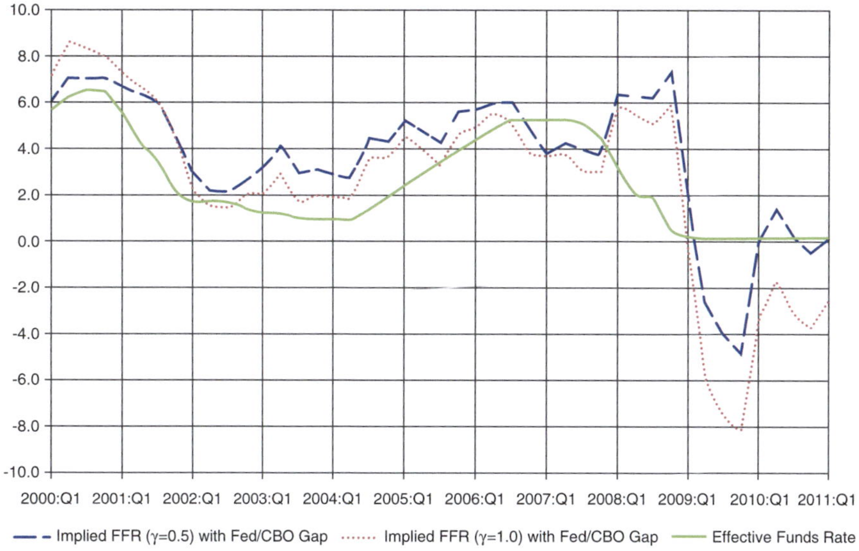

Fig. 7.2 Debate about Taylor rules [Source: Nikolsko-Rzhevskyy and Papell (2013)]

7.2 Interest Rate Policy at the Effective Lower Bound

For quite some time, theorists focused on the challenges posed by the fact that nominal interest rates cannot become negative. To be more precise, the effective lower bound for interest rates may be slightly negative rather than exactly zero. Even though the effective bound may be lower, for convenience we will still call this constraint the zero lower bound.

Stimulated by the experience of Japan since 1990, the zero lower bound has been analyzed within the New Keynesian framework for quite some time. For a long time, however, these studies have been seen as a pure academic exercise, carried out more for intellectual curiosity interested in exotic outliers such as Japan seemed to be at that time. The mainstream view among empirical research was that the episodes at the ZLB would be relatively infrequent and generally short-lived, typically lasting not more than 1 year. This research was mainly based on the experience of the tranquil Great Moderation period of the 1980s and 1990s.

The study of the zero lower bound (ZLB) on nominal interest rates provides an impressive example how insights obtained from theoretical models can have a strong impact on policy in practice. The research led to a number of concrete policy prescriptions that influenced policymaking during and after the global financial crisis. Key lessons have been that short-term rates (1) should be cut aggressively when deflation or a severe downturn threatens and (2) should also be kept "lower for longer" as the economy recovers. The intuition underlying this insight is that the expectation of an extended low level of short-term interest rates reduces longer term yields and eases financial conditions more broadly.

Brayton, Laubach and Reifschneider (2014) compare the optimal control path to the outcome of a simple feedback rule such as a Taylor-type rule. The interest rate paths constructed use the Federal Reserve Board's FRB/US model in conjunction with baseline forecasts of real activity, inflation and interest rates that are consistent with the FOMC's Summary of Economic Projections (SEP). The red lines in Fig. 7.3 show the optimal commitment path relative to standard rules and the corresponding predictions for long-term real interest rate, unemployment, and inflation for the USA, using data from September 2012.

Brayton et al. (2014) calculate the optimal control policy that minimizes the intertemporal loss function of the central bank with dynamics of the macro economy as described by a New Keynesian model. They derive the optimal path such that it satisfies the zero lower bound on nominal interest rates. The path calculated assumes that the central bank can commit to its plan and its intended effects on real activity and inflation, thereby constraining their future policy actions. The optimal path for Fed policy is calculated using data from September 2012. As shown in Fig. 7.3, according to the optimal path the interest rate should stay at zero much longer (until end of 2015) compared to a standard rule. This policy would lead to lower real bond yields and result in a faster recovery (lower unemployment) and higher inflation.

As pointed out by Brayton et al. (2014), calculating the optimal control policy requires the explicit specification both of the central bank's loss function and of the modeling structure of the economy. The rule derived is sensitive to these

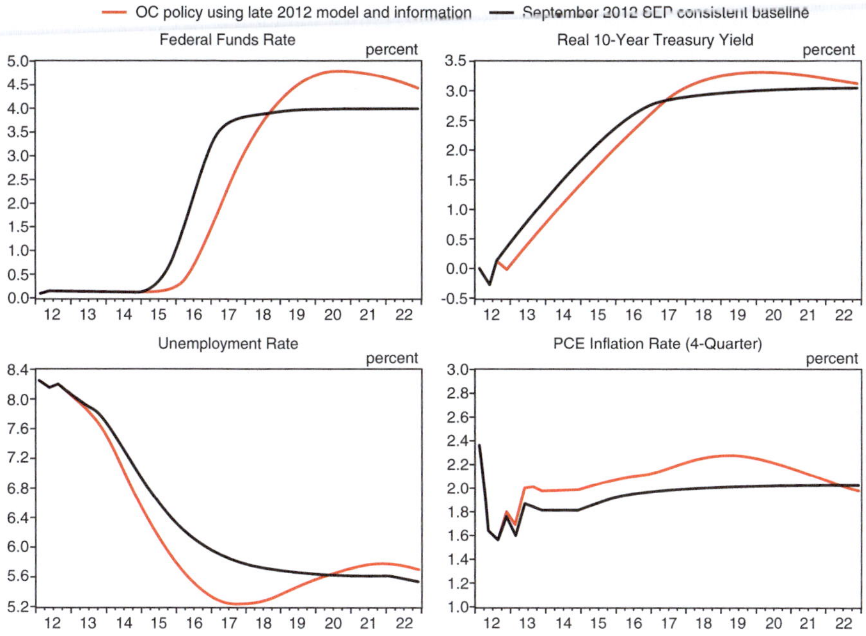

Fig. 7.3 Optimal control policy vs. standard rule [Source: Brayton et al. (2014)]

specifications and so may not be robust to uncertainty about the structure of the macro economy. As discussed above, Taylor-type rules suffer from similar ambiguities.

An interesting feature of the optimal control policy is that—once the ZLB is no longer binding—it would be optimal to raise inflation for some time above the target of 2% and lower unemployment below 5.5%, the level which at that time was considered to be the natural rate. When a severe shock hits the economy, interest rates should be cut aggressively. However, due to the ZLB, the initial policy response is restricted and bound to be too weak, leaving inflation, and output inefficiently low. In order to compensate for the lack of immediate response, the optimal policy should commit to keep both inflation and output later above the target rate, even long after the shocks have gone. Therefore, the optimal path requires a commitment to overshoot the target later, when the economy is back to normal. This way, positive long-run inflationary expectations can be induced, lowering the effective real rate of interest already today.

This, however, poses a serious credibility problem: Later, at the time the economy returns back to normal, there is no incentive any longer to stick to the promise to stimulate above normal, just because of such a promise made at the time of crisis. So the promised policy is not time consistent.

Frequently, it is argued that price level or nominal GDP targeting can solve the credibility problem. Nevertheless, in such a regime, similar issues arise as under inflation targeting: It is optimal to commit to a higher price level for some time once the ZLB will no longer be binding. However, unlike inflation targeting, a price-level target constrains the credible amount of overshooting, by inducing deflationary expectations when returning back to the target in later periods. It will be optimal to commit to holding nominal rates at zero for an extended period even after the shock has abated.

7.3 Model Analysis: Dynamic Inconsistency of Optimal Control

In previous chapters, we assumed that there is no limit in adjusting the interest rate i. In reality, however, the zero lower bound may be a serious constraint. In this section, we provide a theoretical analysis of optimal policy when the zero lower bound is binding in a stylized simple three-period setting. We derive an explicit analytical solution with price level targeting. We show that optimal policy turns out not to be time consistent. The model is taken from Illing and Siemsen (2016). In line with the analysis of previous chapters, we analyze the case that price level targeting emerges endogenously as welfare optimal policy. To this end, we deviate from the Calvo assumption and assume that firms are ex ante heterogeneous: A share of firms exhibits long-run price stickiness over the whole model horizon.

A negative demand shock drives the economy to the zero lower bound. Following Eggertsson and Woodford (2013), a straightforward way of modeling such a shock is to allow for temporary shifts in the time preference parameter ρ. Remember from Chap. 4 (Sect. 4.2.3.1) that current aggregate demand $y_1 = y_n - \sigma\ \left(i - \left(p_2^e - p_1\right) - \rho\right)$ is increasing in ρ. Assume $y_n = y^*$ and $\rho = \overline{\rho} + \eta$ with $\overline{\rho} = E(\rho)$. η is a time preference shock with $E(\eta) = 0$. The central bank is expected to target the future price level at p^*, so $p_2^e = p^*$. For a given time preference ρ and for any given price level in the current period, an increase in the nominal rate i raises the real rate and thus desired savings, so dampening demand for current consumption.

The line $S(\overline{\rho})$ in Fig. 7.4 represents aggregate savings as a function of the nominal interest rate for $\rho = \overline{\rho}$. In our economy without capital formation, aggregate desired savings have to be zero in equilibrium. So the equilibrium real rate is $r = \rho$. With $p_1^e = p_2^e = p^*$ and $E(\rho) = \overline{\rho}$, ex ante the equilibrium nominal rate will be $i = \overline{\rho}$. An increase in time preference to $\rho = \overline{\rho} + \widetilde{\eta}$, $(\widetilde{\eta} > 0)$ raises current demand (dampens aggregate savings) at a given interest rate. It shifts both the savings schedule (Fig. 7.4) and the AD curve (Fig. 7.5) upwards.

At the rate $i = \overline{\rho}$, there will be excess demand, driving prices, and output up (see point E in Figs. 7.4 and 7.5). The optimal interest rate policy is to counteract the decrease in the willingness to save by adjusting the nominal interest rate one for one: $i = \overline{\rho} + \widetilde{\eta}$. This counter cyclical policy dampens demand to bring the economy back toward the bliss point A with p^*, y^*. There is no problem with stabilizing positive demand shocks. In principle, monetary policy can also cope with negative demand shocks by cutting the interest rate as long as these shocks are not too large. When $\eta = -\overline{\rho}$, however, the economy hits the zero lower bound. With even stronger shocks $(\eta < -\overline{\rho})$, time preference becomes negative $(\rho_1 < 0)$, requiring to

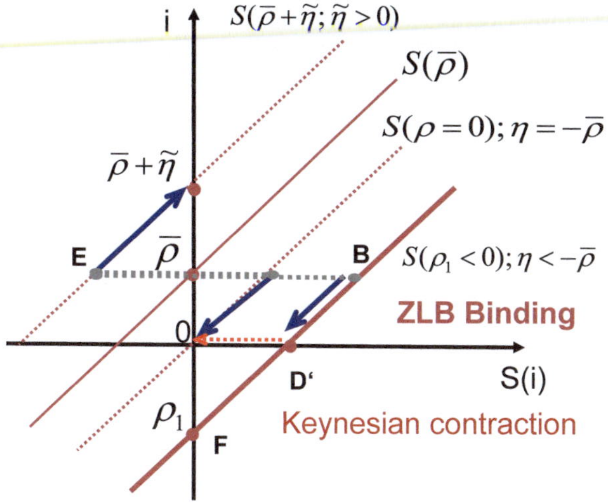

Fig. 7.4 Zero lower bound

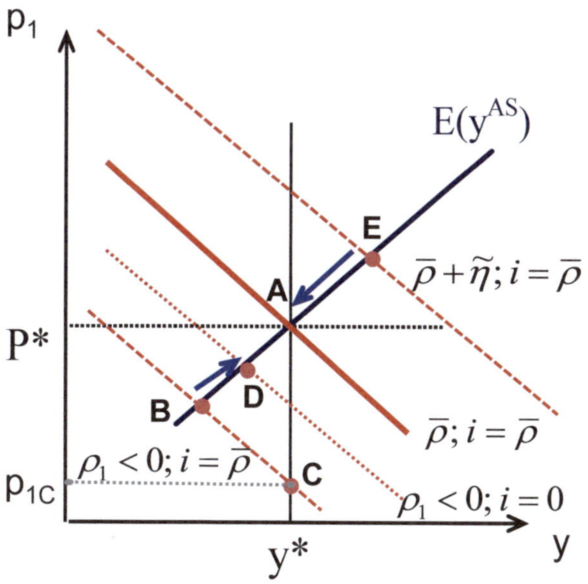

Fig. 7.5 AD AS model with Zero Lower Bound

implement a negative real rate of interest. As long as the central bank cannot enforce negative nominal rates on money holding, the zero lower bound will now be a serious constraint for monetary policy. In that case, a negative nominal rate (see point *F* in Fig. 7.4) would be required in order to shift AD back to the original level. This, however, is not feasible. There is a "savings glut," resulting in a lack of demand in the current period. Conventional interest rate policy no longer works. Traditional monetary policy can shift the economy at best from point B to point D (Fig. 7.5). The economy gets stuck at an inefficiently low output level. Obviously, standard interest rate policy can stabilize shocks properly only as long as they are not too large.

In the absence of price rigidities p_1 would fall sufficiently so that—at constant interest rate $i = \rho$—the economy turns back to the natural rate despite the downward shift in demand (see point C Fig. 7.5). With prices being sticky, however, this deflationary process cannot work. Quite the contrary, in the presence of nominal debt contracts, deflation may trigger a further reduction in demand, causing a deflationary spiral—the economy gets stuck in the liquidity trap.

When the zero lower bound is binding, the only way to implement a negative real rate of interest with prices being sticky is to raise the price level p_2 in period 2 above p^*. Announcing a higher $p_2 > p^*$ for the next period would raise expected inflation, driving down the real rate of interest even though the nominal rate cannot be lowered any more. Such a policy, suggested by Paul Krugman (1998), can help to raise output and get around the liquidity trap.

Krugman (1998) called such an unconventional policy a commitment to being irresponsible. He argued that such an announcement is not really credible. We are now facing exactly the reverse credibility problem as in the case of the inflation bias: Private agents will anticipate the central bank's incentive to renege on its promise and instead try to implement price stability as soon as the shock is gone. Characterizing the optimal price-setting strategies for firms and the optimal monetary policy in different periods will be quite tricky and requires sophisticated skills in dynamic optimization. Here we illustrate the issue by a fairly simple example, extending the setup of our model from Chap. 4 in a straightforward way. Rather than just looking at the short run and the long run, let us now extend the short run to 2 periods. The long run (with most prices being flexible) does not begin before period 3.

Consider an economy that extends to 3 periods, $t = 1, 2, 3$. At $t = 1$, a representative household maximizes its expected utility over the entire horizon

$$\max_{\{C_t, N_t\}_{t=1}^{3}} E_1 \left[\sum_{t=1}^{3} \left(\prod_{j=1}^{t-1} \frac{1}{1+\rho_j} \right) \left(\frac{C_t^{1-\frac{1}{\sigma}}}{1-\frac{1}{\sigma}} + \frac{N_t^{1+\varphi}}{1+\varphi} \right) \right], s.t.$$

$$P_1 C_1 + B_1 = W_1 N_1 + T_1,$$

$$P_2 C_2 + B_2 = W_2 N_2 + (1 + i_1^S) B_1 + T_2,$$

$$P_3 C_3 = W_3 N_3 + \left(1 + i_2^S\right) B_2 + T_3$$

in which ρ_j is the stochastic discount rate in $t = j$, σ is the elasticity of intertemporal substitution, φ is the elasticity of labor supply. The household consumes real goods C_t at price level P_t in t, supplies labor N_t for wage W_t, saves in each period through purchasing short-term nominal bonds B_t with maturity for one period, and gets paid interest rate i_t^S for the bonds one period later. The household gets a nominal lump-sum transfer T_t in each period.

The household's optimization problem leads to the standard New Keynesian AD curve:

$$y_t - y^* = E_t\left[y_{t+1} - y^*\right] - \sigma\left(i_t^S - \left(E_t\left[p_{t+1}\right] - p_t\right) - \rho_t\right)$$

in which $y_t = \ln Y_t$ with Y_t being the aggregate output in t, $p_t = \ln P_t$, and y^* is the log natural output level.

To capture the price stickiness as in the standard new Keynesian framework, assume that all firms start at the optimal price level p^*, but they are ex ante heterogeneous in their price setting behavior. A share α_1 of the firms have long-term price rigidity: They have to stick to p^* in $t = 1, 2$. In order to vary the degree of long-run rigidity independent of rigidities in the previous periods, we allow a share λ of α_1 types to change their prices in period $t = 3$. The share α_2 of firms have short-term price rigidity: They fix their short-run price for the next period at the end of the previous period. So they have to stick to p^* in $t = 1$, but they can adjust prices for the following period afterwards. The rest of firms are free to set prices in all three periods.

In contrast to Calvo pricing, where both short-run and long-run stickiness are controlled by the Calvo-parameter only, this pricing scheme allows us to elaborate on the (potentially asymmetric) effects of short-run and long-run price stickiness on optimal monetary policy commitment. Using a three-period model keeps this price scheme analytically traceable, as it limits the accumulation of price dispersion over time.

Similar as in the standard New Keynesian framework, monopolistically competitive firms follow the production function $Y_t = AN_t$, and the productivity A is constant over time. The standard New Keynesian Phillips curve is then defined by

$$p_t - p^* = \kappa_t(y_t - y^*), t = 1, 2, 3$$

in which $\kappa_1 = \frac{1-\alpha_1-\alpha_2}{\alpha_1+\alpha_2}\left(\frac{1}{\sigma} + \varphi\right)$, $\kappa_2 = \frac{1-\alpha_1}{\alpha_1}\left(\frac{1}{\sigma} + \varphi\right)$, and $\kappa_3 = \frac{1-\alpha_1\lambda}{\alpha_1\lambda}\left(\frac{1}{\sigma} + \varphi\right)$. Note that without long-term price rigidity there would be no output gap in $t = 2, 3$, as $\lim_{\alpha_1 \to 0}\kappa_2 = \lim_{\alpha_1 \to 0}\kappa_3 = +\infty$, but there would still be an output gap in $t = 1$, as $\lim_{\alpha_1 \to 0}\kappa_1 \neq +\infty$. α_2-type firms fix their prices for just one period ahead. Therefore, unlike under a Calvo mechanism, when optimizing, firms do not need to internalize that they may not be allowed to re-optimize in the future. Thus, the aggregate supply curve is determined by the nominal anchor p^*, from which some firms will never deviate.

The optimal monetary policy that targets the price level $\{p_t\}_{t=1}^3$ minimizes the quadratic loss function

$$L_1 = \frac{1}{2}E_1\left[\sum_{t=1}^{3}\left(\prod_{j=1}^{t-1}\frac{1}{1+\rho_j}\right)\left\{(y_t - y^*)^2 + \frac{\theta}{\kappa_t}(p_t - p^*)^2\right\}\right]$$

with constraints from the AD curve, the AS curve and the ZLB. There always exists an optimal policy rate i_t^S that minimizes the social loss, as long as the rate is above the zero lower bound.

Initially, the economy is in steady state with a natural rate $\overline{\rho} > 0$. Now, in period 1, a negative time preference shock hits the economy, making the zero lower bound binding. There is no persistence, so the economy reverts back to normal next period: $\rho_2 = \rho_3 = \overline{\rho} > 0$. The central bank cannot prevent a recession in period 1 even by cutting the interest rate down to zero. It could, however, announce to raise the price level p_2 in the following period 2 above p^* in order to lower the current real interest rate and so prevent p_1 and y_1 from falling too far.

The idea behind a promise to raise the price level in period 2 is the intention to increase the expected rate of inflation. This helps to drive down the effective real rate of interest in period 1 so as to stimulate current consumption even at the zero lower bound $i = 0$ despite p_1 being sticky. To stabilize the price level in period 1 at target $p_1 = p^*$, the condition $i - (p_2^e - p^*) - \rho_1 = 0$ must hold. With the zero lower bound $i = 0$ binding and $\rho_1 < 0$ being negative, the price level in period 2 would need to rise by $|\rho_1|$ to $p_2 = p^* - \rho = p^* + |\rho_1|$. Such a policy (stabilizing the economy fully in period 1), however, cannot be the optimal commitment strategy: Raising p_2 above p^* causes inefficiencies next period (see the next paragraph). The optimal commitment strategy is to promise to raise p_2 only so much that the marginal loss in period 2 (from accepting a price above target $p_2 > p^*$) will be just equal to the marginal loss in period 1 (from accepting a price below target $p_1 < p^*$). Along the commitment path, the real interest rate in period 2 must stay below the natural rate at that time (being $\overline{\rho}$) (see the Focus Box for the derivation of discretionary and commitment policy). So the central bank needs to commit to keep the nominal rate below the rate which would be appropriate at that time (again being $\overline{\rho}$) (see Fig. 7.6). In period 2, both price level and output will be above target (Fig. 7.6). The focus box at the end of this section provides details of the analytical solution.

The problem, however, is that a promise to implement the commitment solution is hardly credible. As soon as the shock has gone and time preference reverts back to $\overline{\rho}$ in period 2, the central bank has a strong incentive to renege on its promises. After all, at that stage, aggregate demand reverts to normal, so there is no longer any reason to stimulate the economy. The promise to raise the price level anyway implies that the central bank is nevertheless willing to trigger a boom, shifting both output and prices beyond the optimal level p^*, y^*. To see this, consider the case that the central bank promises to raise next period's price level to p_2 . α_2-type firms will fix their prices for period 2 after the central bank announcing her strategy in period 1, but before the central bank acts in period 2. At the time of commitment, the relevant AS curve is $AS^{ex\ ante}$ with slope k_2. If α_2-type firms trust the central bank's promise to raise price level to $p_2^* > p^*$, they will fix their prices at p_2^* already before period 2 starts. Therefore, the relevant AS curve ex post—once α_2-type firms have fixed their prices as well—is now flatter than $AS^{ex\ ante}$ due to higher price rigidities: $y_2 - y^* = \frac{1}{k_1}\left(p_2 - \frac{1}{\alpha_1+\alpha_2} \cdot (\alpha_1 p^* + \alpha_2 p_2^*)\right)$. The average price level next period will be $\widehat{p}_2 = \frac{\alpha_1}{\alpha_1+\alpha_2} \cdot p^* + \frac{\alpha_2}{\alpha_1+\alpha_2} \cdot p_2^*$, shifting the AS curve upwards to $AS^{ex\ post}$ as in Fig. 7.7.

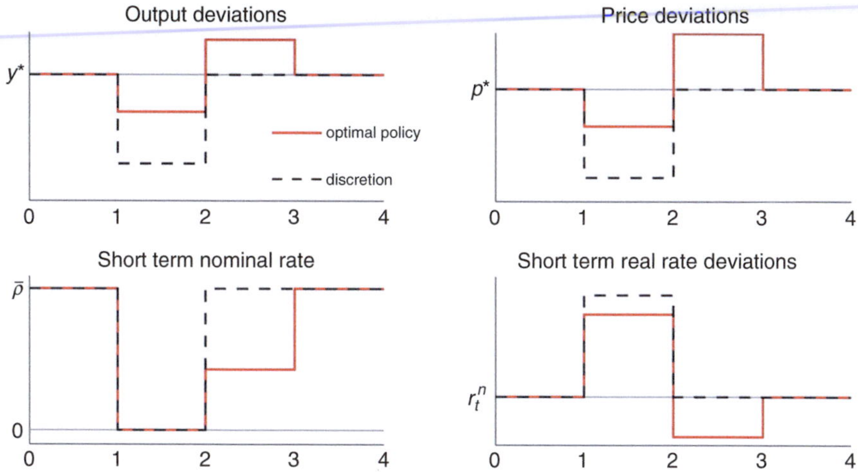

Fig. 7.6 Commitment path vs. discretion [Source: Illing and Siemsen (2016)]

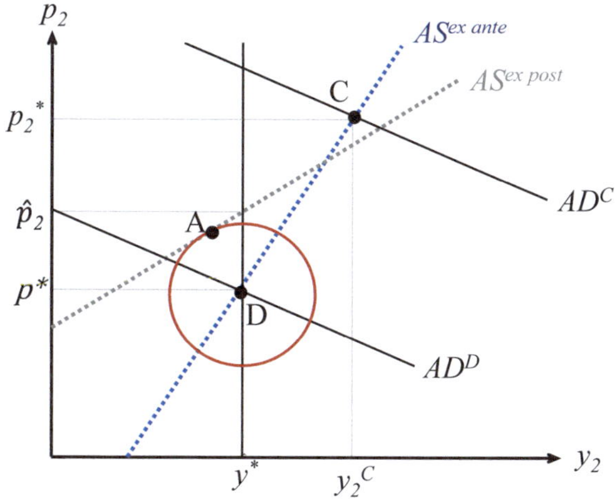

Fig. 7.7 Dynamic inconsistency

Sticking to the promise would steer the economy toward point C. Given the inefficient boom $\{p_{2C}, y_{2C}\}$ created by such a stimulus, there is a strong incentive for the central bank to ignore past statements and instead try to calm down the overheated economy. When private agents trust the announcement in period 1, ex post the relevant AS curve is $AS^{ex\ post}$. But then the optimal policy ex post is to choose point A rather than C in Fig. 7.7. Private firms of type α_2 doubting the central bank's commitment to stick to its promises will anticipate that incentive already in period 1 and so will charge a price below p_2^*. Neither will private consumers in period 1 trust that the central bank is willing to implement a high rate of inflation. Being afraid that instead the real rate of interest will stay high, they prefer to save rather than to spend in period 1. But that means the strategy unravels; in the end the unique discretionary equilibrium is to implement p^*, y^* at point D. The announcement is not dynamically consistent: Once period 2 has been reached, the central bank has a strong incentive not to follow its promises of being irresponsible. Being not credible in the first place, the strategy is bound to fail.

Again, this credibility problem is not just a theoretical curiosity. As discussed in more detail later in Sect. 7.5, during the last decade, central banks refined their communications policy, making forward guidance about the future path of the funds rate a central part of policy. The promise "to keep rates at an exceptionally low level for an extended period" may be seen as a commitment device to stick to the policy of optimal control as outlined above and not reverse course later on when times get better. Just as Odysseus bound himself to his ship's mast so he could enjoy the pleasure of the Sirens' song without giving into the temptation to swim toward them, so drowning himself, central bankers' statements may be viewed as a commitment to bind them to future courses of action even though they are not time consistent.

With the interest rate as the only policy instrument being stuck at zero, forward guidance works solely by altering the public's expectations of future central bank policies. The New Keynesian model suggests that announcing a commitment to holding the policy rate at zero for longer, if credible, will have powerful effects: Inflation expectations rise immediately when future monetary policy is expected to be more expansionary. News about lower future real interest rates at any horizon—even far into the future—have the same effect on current consumption (consumption being a function of the expected real rate reaching far into the future).

Given the strong impact on inflation expectations predicted by the New Keynesian model, it is, however, remarkable that measured rates of expected inflation stayed fairly low during the great financial crisis, despite the use of forward guidance and other policy measures. One reason may be that central banks worldwide have been amazingly reluctant to commit to a temporarily overshooting of the inflation rate above 2%, much less so to revert to the initial price level path as before crisis. Having been an academic at Princeton, Bernanke (2002) criticized the Bank of Japan for not being aggressive enough, advocating policies such as raising the inflation target to 3–4%; and using helicopter money to allow for a money-financed fiscal expansion. After becoming chairman of the Fed, he avoided to address such proposals. When he was chairman, the Fed explicitly committed, on January 25, 2012, to target the rate of 2%. "*The Committee judges that inflation at the rate of 2%, as measured by the annual change in the price index for personal consumption expenditures, is most consistent over the longer run with the Federal Reserve's statutory mandate.*"

Just as other central banks, Fed members were extremely reluctant to emphasize that "optimal control" should promise more inflation in the future. One reason may be the fear that reversion to price stability after overshooting may be hard to control. Some see this lack of commitment as the main reason why forward guidance may have been less successful than hoped for. They suggest that level targeting such as targeting nominal GDP (NGDP) would help to make potential overshooting be anticipated, controlled, and credible. Given a commitment to some price level path, the risk of de-anchoring inflationary expectations after a period of temporarily higher rates may be less serious. As the analysis in this chapter demonstrates, the credibility problem is, however, pervasive even under level targeting, in particular taking into account the need to deflate after overshooting.

Hence, making such a commitment credible poses serious challenges. After all, current decision makers can easily be replaced later in the future. It is hard to commit to some policy path beyond your own term of office. The problem of dynamic consistency may be one reason why central banks worldwide used a huge variety of other unconventional policy measures such as quantitative and qualitative easing as well. According to the New Keynesian model with a complete set of future markets, such policies can work only via the expectation channel as commitment mechanism for not raising interest rates. Otherwise, they will be ineffective according to the Wallace theorem (as discussed in Sect. 8.3). Chapter 8 analyses why unconventional measures may be effective once financial frictions are taken into account.

Our analysis clearly demonstrated that in the presence of the ZLB, the scope for effective interest rate policy is limited. Under such conditions, it is easy to see that countercyclical fiscal policy may help to stabilize the economy. As shown in Illing and Siemsen (2016), it will be optimal to shift the path of fiscal policy relative to the first best path by raising government spending (lowering taxes) in the first period (during the liquidity trap) relative to the second period. During times when the real rate is too high (staying above the natural rate), additional government spending can help to bring the market rate closer to the shadow (natural) rate. Since even under commitment, monetary policy will never succeed to bring the real rate down to the natural rate during the liquidity trap, additional instruments can improve upon pure monetary policy. Fiscal policy will be even more powerful when it can commit to cut spending below the first best path in later periods. Such a countercyclical policy would allow private agents to consume more in the future; the incentive to smooth consumption will also induce additional demand during the liquidity trap, giving rise to a powerful fiscal multiplier.

Focus: Commitment Under the Zero Lower Bound: The Analytical Solution

The central bank minimizes the quadratic loss function

$$L_1 = \frac{1}{2}E_1\left[\sum_{t=1}^{3}\left(\prod_{j=1}^{t-1}\frac{1}{1+\rho_j}\right)\left\{(y_t - y^*)^2 + \frac{\theta}{\kappa_t}(p_t - p^*)^2\right\}\right]$$

subject to the constraints imposed by the AD curve, the AS curve, and the ZLB.

Before the time preference shock sets in at the beginning of period 1, private agents expect the central bank to stabilize perfectly, so $p_1^e = p_2^e = p_3^e = p^*$. Initially all firms have set their prices equal to p^*.

(continued)

Let us first characterize discretionary policy. Since at t = 2, the economy reverts back to normal with $\rho_2 = \rho_3 = \overline{\rho} > 0$, the optimal policy at that time is to set $i_2 = \overline{\rho}$. Once the ZLB stops being binding, the central bank implements $E(p_2) = E(p_3) = p^*$ and $E(y_2) = E(y_3) = y^*$. At $t = 1$, the central bank will cut down rates to zero: $i_1 = 0$.

Inserting $i_1 = 0$, $E(p_2) = p^*$ and $E(y_2) = y^*$ in the AD curve between periods 1 and 2 gives $y_1 - y^* = \sigma\,[\rho_1 - (p_1 - p^*)]$.

Using $p_1 - p^* = \kappa_1[y_1 - y^*]$ we have $p_1 - p^* = \frac{\kappa_1\sigma}{1+\kappa_1\sigma}\rho_1 < 0$ and $y_1 - y^* = \frac{\sigma}{1+\kappa_1\sigma}\rho_1 < 0$.

At $t = 1$, the economy is stuck in a liquidity trap: Deflation (the price level falling) triggers a fall in output below normal. Note, however, that—in contrast to inflation targeting—price-level targeting provides an automatic stabilization mechanism: Knowing that the central bank will revert to p^* once the ZLB stops being binding, private agents can rely on inflation occurring between periods 1 and 2. The stronger the deflation (undershooting) during the liquidity trap period, the higher is the rationally anticipated inflation that leads the economy back to target. This helps to dampen the real interest rate and hence also output shortfalls.

The central bank, however, can do better than discretion by committing herself to raising the price level in period 2 above target. This way, losses in the initial period can be contained, shifting part of the burden into the future. By spreading losses across time, overall welfare losses can be limited. The central bank announces a price path $\{p_2, p_3\}$ to forward guide expectations and thus influence the current real rate.

Solving the analytical solution for optimal commitment solution can be quite tricky. To simplify, we assume in the following that it will be optimal to revert to p^* in period 3.[3] Knowing that $p_3^e = p^*$ and $y_3^e = y^*$, there are no welfare losses in the final (long-run) period, so we can focus on the optimal trade-off between periods 1 and 2, minimizing

$$L_{CB} = \tfrac{1}{2}E(y_1 - y^*)^2 + \tfrac{1}{2}\tfrac{\theta_{CB}}{k_1}E(p_1 - p^*)^2 + \beta\left\{\tfrac{1}{2}E(y_2 - y^*)^2 + \tfrac{1}{2}\tfrac{\theta_{CB}}{k_2}E(p_2 - p^*)^2\right\}$$

subject to the following constraints:

(A) The AS curves in both periods: $y_t - y^* = \frac{1}{k_t}(p_t - p^*)$ $t = 1, 2$

(B) The AD curves in both periods: $y_1 - y^* = y_2 - y^* - \sigma(i_1 - (p_2^e - p_1) - \rho)$; $y_2 - y^* = -\sigma\,(i_2 - [p^* - p_2^e] - \overline{\rho})$

(C) The ZLB: $i_t \geq 0$

(continued)

[3]As shown in Illing and Siemsen (2016), this may not be the case if the current shock is too severe. In that case, it would be optimal to raise p_2 so much that the deflation required for reverting to p^* in the final period would too costly. Here, however, we abstract from that complication.

In the absence of the ZLB, the AD curves just give the optimal value for the interest rates in each period. Now, however, the constraint $i_1 = 0$ has to be taken into account in period 1. The AD curve in period 2 gives the optimal rate i_2. Again, we need to take the ZLB as serious constraint $i_2 \geq 0$. Imposing $i_1 = 0$ we get as first-order conditions:

(A)

$$-(p_1 - p^*) = \frac{1}{1+\rho_1} \frac{k_1}{k_2} \frac{(1+\theta\ k_2)}{(1+\theta\ k_1)} \frac{(1+\sigma\ k_1)}{(1+\sigma\ k_2)} (p_2 - p^*)$$

(B)

$$p_1 - p^* = \frac{k_1}{k_2} \frac{(1+\sigma\ k_2)}{(1+\sigma\ k_1)} (p_2 - p^*) + \frac{\sigma\ k_1}{1+\sigma\ k_1} \rho_1$$

(C)

$$i_2 = \overline{\rho} - \frac{1+\sigma\ k_2}{\sigma\ k_2} (p_2 - p^*) \geq 0$$

Condition (A) states that marginal losses should be equal across time. With the ZLB binding, constraint (B) bites. This induces co-movements between p_1 and p_2: Raising p_2 will lower the real rate of interest in the first period, stimulating demand and so raising p_1. The commitment solution requires that p_2 (and y_2) are above target, so as to raise below target levels for p_1 and y_1. Spreading the loss across time helps to raise overall welfare. Condition (C) indicates that the ZLB may also be binding if p_2 needs to rise strongly above p^*. This will be the case for large shocks. If so, it will be optimal to set also $i_2 = 0$ and to raise the price level in period 3 as well: $p_3 > p^*$. This helps to prevent the need for strong deflation when getting back to the target after the stimulus in period 2. More generally (in a model with more than 3 periods), it will be optimal to keep interest rates at zero for longer. The system of equations (A)–(C) is a system of three equations for three unknowns (p_1, p_2, i_2) and can thus be solved easily. See Illing and Siemsen (2016) for details.

7.4 Negative Nominal Rates

Since 2008, central banks worldwide have cut their policy rates close to zero, following the experience in Japan in the mid-1990s. Some central banks shied away from going all the way down to zero: The Bank of England viewed 0.25 as the lower limit. Constrained by zero lower bound (ZLB), central banks faced a great challenge for standard interest rate policy. Given the perceived inability to push short-term nominal rates below zero, central banks felt forced to experiment with unconventional policies—including large-scale asset purchases and forward guidance—in order to try to achieve their targets for inflation and economic activity.

The zero lower bound has fascinated economists for a long time at least since the Great Depression. With central banks charging negative rates, people would rather prefer to withdraw all money from bank accounts and hoard it in cash. John Hicks (1937) phrased this argument in the following way: "*If the costs of holding money can be neglected, it will always be profitable to hold money rather than lend it out, if the rate of interest is not greater than zero. Consequently the rate of interest must always be positive.*"

Due to costs of holding cash, however, the value of the lower bound on nominal interest rates is not precisely zero. Recently, starting in 2014, central banks in some European countries have even experimented with negative policy rates such as −0.50% in Sweden or even −0.75% in Switzerland. They implemented slightly negative nominal yields for part of bank deposits without triggering a flight onto hoarding cash. Obviously, costs prevent people from withdrawing all their funds from bank deposits even at slightly negative rates. There is the risk of being robbed when putting paper money at home under the pillow; there are costs of renting, maintaining, and securing storage facilities such as vaults to store piles of bank notes; there are costs of shipping cash around—be it by mail or by horse—in a safe and timely manner. Settling payments electronically definitely provides substantial convenience. An ECB study by Schmiedel, Kostova and Ruttenberg (2012) estimates the private cost of cash payments to be around 1.1% of GDP in Euro Area countries.

Nevertheless, unless supported by other instruments, the policy rate cannot be too negative without risking hoarding of money. The effective lower bound depends on a variety of institutional factors. Key is the size of costs associated with storing, transferring, and spending large amounts of currency. If all central bank liabilities were electronic, paying a negative interest on reserves (charging a fee) would be trivial. Yet as long as central banks are willing to convert electronic deposits into zero-interest paper currency in unlimited amounts, it is hard to push interest rates below slightly negative levels. Hoarding cash is inconvenient and risky, but if rates become too negative, it becomes worth it. It may be inconvenient to hold large amounts of currency, but at a sufficiently negative interest rate, banks or other institutions could profit from holding cash, for a fee, on behalf of their customers.

Some even argue that by clever policy design (such as abolishing banknotes with large denomination or even more drastically, abolishing all physical cash and replacing it with pure electronic money, so enforcing a cashless society) the effective lower bound can be made arbitrary low. Paper currency creates a zero lower bound only as long as banks or private agents can withdraw unlimited quantities of paper currency and redeposit it later on at par at the central bank. Silvio Gesell (1916), in April 1919 briefly Minister of Finance in Bavaria, already suggested a simple way to get around that constraint. Gesell suggested imposing a stamp duty in order to tax holding paper money. Thus, the money issued by the central bank loses its value over time, thereby encouraging people to spend and invest in real assets instead of hoarding money. During the depression in the beginning of the 1930s last century, Wörgl, a small town in Austria, tried to adapt his proposal. In Chap. 23 of his *General Theory of Employment, Interest and Money*, Keynes summarized Gesell's idea as follows:

> Currency . . . would only retain their value by being stamped each month, like an insurance card, with stamps purchased at a post office. The cost of the stamps . . . should be roughly equal to the excess of the money-rate of interest (apart from the stamps) over the marginal efficiency of capital corresponding to a rate of new investment compatible with full employment. The actual charge suggested by Gesell was 1 per mil. per week, equivalent to 5.2 per cent per annum . . . . (Keynes 1936).

The modern equivalent of such a stamp duty would be to let paper currency gradually depreciate against electronic money to ensure that paper money carries also effectively a negative rate of return. In some regions, local community currencies like the Chiemgauer in Upper Bavaria in 2003 are designed to lose 2% of its value every quarter: The Chiemgauer has to be "topped up" every 3 months by purchasing a coupon of 2% (a stamp duty). In its electronic version, the Chiemgauer can be held for 30 days without depreciation, then following a daily depreciation of 0.022% per day. Such local currencies are, however, mainly a marketing instrument designed for promoting local business. After all, people in these regions still have always the option to switch to central bank currency as substitute as long as there is no stamp duty enforced on that currency. With a stamp duty on national currency, it is an open issue to what extent that currency would be replaced by other substitutes (like international currency).

Some prominent economists have strongly argued in favor of abolishing paper money (Rogoff 2014) or implementing gradual depreciation of paper money against electronic money (Agarwal and Kimball 2015). A key issue with abolishing paper money is the anonymous nature of cash. Historically, an essential property of money is that neither buyer nor seller requires knowledge of its history, preserving anonymity. In contrast, electronic money leaves electronic footprints and can be traced by authorities. The anonymity of cash facilitates tax evasion and illegal activity; at the same time, it allows to preserve privacy. Rogoff argues that there is significant evidence that in most countries a large share (more than 50%) of currency is used to hide transactions. He argues that abolishing cash could help both to reduce black market activities and to eliminate the zero lower bound on the nominal interest rate. In many countries (such as Sweden and Norway), the convenience of electronic payments has already resulted in nearly crowding out old-fashioned paper money completely. Obviously, people do not consider the lack of privacy as a serious concern. In contrast, proposals to abolish the 500 € banknote stirred strong controversies in the Euro area, with defenders of the paper money citing Dostoyevsky with the quote: "*Money is coined liberty and so it is ten times dearer to a man who is deprived of freedom*" in his novel "The House of the Dead." Dostoyevsky wrote that novel after having stayed 4 years in a prison camp in Siberia.

Rognlie (2015) studies optimal monetary policy with negative rates for the case that it is not feasible to impose negative rates on holding cash. In that case, the following trade-off arises: Negative rates can help to stabilize the economy, but at the same time, they imply an inefficient subsidy to paper currency. Just as—following

Friedman—money holding is inefficiently low when interest on cash is lower than on short-term government debt ($i_d > i_m$), the reverse is true in the opposite case $i_d < i_m$: Implementing negative rates $i_d < 0$ gives agents incentives to hold too much cash as long as there is no negative return to cash $i_m = 0$. Effectively, the central bank subsidizes cash holding, generating negative seigniorage revenue. When rates become modestly negative, however, there need not necessarily be an abrupt change in the effectiveness of monetary policy, provided banks and their customers will not hoard paper currency, urgently seeking to avoid the levy from negative rates, making money demand infinitely elastic at zero. As long as there is no stampede into paper currency, there is no clear discontinuity, so negative rates can be beneficial in stabilizing shocks. Rognlie (2015) argues that close to 0%, the positive stabilizing effect always dominates. Negative rates are generically optimal whenever output averages below its efficient level. In a benchmark scenario, breaking the ZLB with negative rates is sufficient to undo most welfare losses relative to the first best. More generally, the gains from negative rates depend inversely on the level and elasticity of currency demand. Abolishing paper currency will only be optimal when currency demand is highly elastic. Obviously, the option to set negative nominal rates reduces the risk to hit the effective lower bound and so lowers the optimal long-run inflation target.

One concern is that negative policy rates may not necessarily translate into cheaper bank lending. If banks are not able to maintain their interest margins by paying negative rates on deposits, bank profitability and resilience may be damaged. The markup that banks add to the cost of obtaining funding from the central bank compensates for credit risk, term premia and the cost of originating, screening, and monitoring loans. If banks are unable or unwilling to pass negative rates on to their depositors, spreads and so bank's profit may be squeezed, preventing them from lending normally. Instead, the search for yield may encourage risk taking and so contribute to the instability of the financial sector.

7.5 Forward Guidance

With the fed funds rate near zero, central banks turned to *forward guidance*. They tried to convince market participants that short-term rates will stay low for some time, trying to "talk down" longer term rates, such as mortgage rates. There are different variants of forward guidance. It can be qualitative, without specifying details (such as a promise to keep short-term rates low "for a considerable period"). Quantitative forward guidance gives numerically explicit conditions that might lead to a policy change. It can be time-dependent (promising to hold rates low "at least through" some explicitly specified date) or data-dependent, tying future policy actions to specific conditions in the economy, such as quantifying some threshold for the rate of inflation or the rate of unemployment, allowing to adjust as new information arrives. All these efforts are "open-mouth operations."

In the context of the textbook New Keynesian model, forward guidance can be seen as signaling some commitment for keeping the interest rate low. Since "open-mouth" talk is cheap, however, the problem of dynamic consistency may prevent markets and the public to trust these announcements. Empirical evidence taken from event studies, however, suggests that forward guidance can indeed be powerful. Using survey data from professional forecasters—the Blue Chip Economic Indicators—Engen, Laubach und Reifschneider (2015) find that initial actions of the Fed in 2008 led to only modest changes in policy expectations of professional analysts, being quite optimistic about a fast pace of recovery.

In March 2009, the Fed promised for the first time to keep "exceptionally low levels of the federal funds rate for an extended period." In August 2011, the Fed set a date (mid-2013) for how long it expected to maintain "exceptionally low levels for the federal funds rate." In December 2012, it replaced the date threshold with a quantitative threshold: It pledged to maintain the "exceptionally low" federal funds target at least as long as unemployment is above 6.5% and inflation is low.

Figure 7.8 taken from Swanson and Williams (2014) plots the number of quarters until the private sector expected the funds rate to rise above 37.5 basis points, as measured by the median, "consensus" response to the monthly Blue Chip survey of professional forecasters. Prior to December 2008, the FOMC was not expected to set the funds rate below 37.5 basis points. After the FOMC cut the target funds rate close to zero in December 2008, the Blue Chip consensus expectation of the length of time until the first funds rate increase fluctuated between two and five quarters until August 2011. On August 9, 2011, the FOMC announced that it expected to keep the funds rate near zero "at least through mid-2013." Private sector expectations of the time until liftoff jumped immediately to the maximum length of seven or more quarters (the Blue Chip forecast horizon extends forward only six quarters).

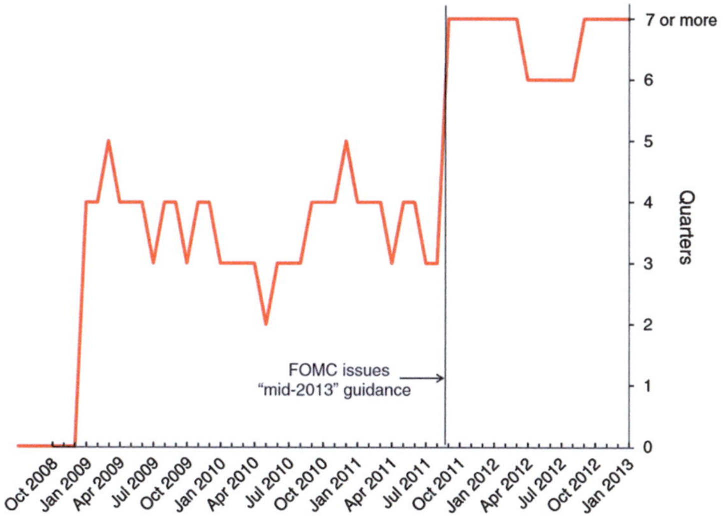

Fig. 7.8 Number of quarters until federal funds rate is expected to rise above 37.5 basis points, from the monthly Blue Chip survey of forecasters [Source: Swanson and Williams (2014)]

One must, however, be careful in interpreting such event studies as successful commitment. Campbell et al. (2012) distinguish between two kinds of forward guidance. "Odyssean" forward guidance changes private expectations by publicly committing the central bank to deviate from its usual policy reaction function. In contrast, "Delphic" forward guidance merely provides a forecast of future policy, confirming public's expectations that the central bank follows its typical policy reaction function. It is challenging to distinguish between these two, in particular if the path announced involves a conditional commitment, reserving the right to change course if the data on which the forecast is based change. After all, the optimal length of commitment depends on how the economy evolves, complicating transparent communication. More pronounced statements might simply be interpreted as bad news of the economy weakening even further, triggering a contractionary rather than an expansionary effect.

In standard New Keynesian models, central bank communication about the current state has no impact on demand, since the current state is assumed to be common knowledge for all. In reality, private agents have less than perfect information; each agent has a different information set. Inflation expectations are heterogeneous and adjust only slowly. Wiederholt (2015) shows that with sluggish and dispersed inflation expectations forward guidance has smaller effects on current consumption than under perfect information. First, those households that do not update their inflation expectations do not change their consumption. Second, announcing a commitment to forward guidance reveals that the economy is in a bad state. This dampens inflation expectations for those who update, potentially offsetting the more expansionary effect of future monetary policy.

7.6 Raising the Inflation Target

One way to relax the constraint imposed by the effective lower bound is to raise the inflation target π^*. If private agents trust the announcement that the central bank aims for a higher target inflation rate in normal times, they will expect inflation to be higher on average and thus also raise their expected rate of inflation. The Fisher equation suggests that the nominal rate of interest adjusts one for one to changes in the expected rate of inflation. Therefore, a higher inflation target would raise nominal rates on average, thus reducing the risk that the zero lower bound will be binding for policy in the future.

Blanchard et al. (2010) suggest that raising the inflation target from 2% to 4% might be welfare improving. A careful evaluation requires a careful analysis of the trade-off between costs and benefits of such a policy. Quantitative conclusions about the optimal rate of inflation are fairly sensitive to the choice of the model used to assess the costs and benefits of inflation (or deflation) in the steady state. As shown in Chap. 2, the standard welfare cost is the distortion created by the inflation tax, lowering holdings of real money balances. To eliminate distortions, according to the Friedman rule, a zero nominal interest (setting $\pi^* = -r_n < 0$) is the optimal policy.

Paying interest on reserves and cash would be an equivalent policy. New Keynesian models focus on the costs arising from the need for price adjustments. In the model characterized in Sect. 7.3, these costs can be captured by the resulting price dispersion, distorting the allocative role of prices. The higher the average rate of inflation, the larger these distortions will be, provided the share of firms with sticky prices is not decreasing in the target rate of inflation. So in these models the optimal target rate is $\pi^* = 0$. According to Nakamura, Steinsson, Sun, and Villar (2018), however, analyzing data on price dispersion for the USA since 1977, there is no evidence that prices deviated more from their optimal level during periods with inflation higher than 10% per year, compared to more recent episodes when inflation was close to 2% per year. This finding suggests that price stickiness may indeed be decreasing with a higher target, de-emphasizing the relevance of the costs of inflation in standard New Keynesian models.

The benefit of a higher inflation target is to reduce the occurrence of zero lower bound (ZLB) episodes. Therefore, it is crucial to evaluate the likelihood and the welfare costs of such episodes. There would be hardly any costs if tools from unconventional monetary policy could help to get rid of the ZLB constraints. New Keynesian models incorporating the ZLB, calibrated prior to the Great Recession concluded that episodes when the constraint will be binding are likely to be both very rare and short-lived. Taking into account both the arguments for the Friedman rule and the role of sticky prices, Schmidt-Grohé and Uribe (2010) found the optimal target rate to be a small amount of deflation. In their calibration, the ZLB was binding only if the nominal interest rate falls more than 4 standard deviations below its target level. Obviously, such calibrations can be quite sensitive to the historical episodes included. The experience after the Great Recession suggests that ZLB episodes may be quite costly and more frequently. They may also last much longer than most estimates in the past predict. According to Kiley and Roberts (2017), the ZLB is likely to be binding in the USA around 20–40% with a target rate of 2%, if the Fed cannot commit to deliver substantial accommodation even long after the ZLB would otherwise be binding.

According to studies discussed in Sect. 6.3.3, the natural real rate has been declining over the last decades. Such a trend reduces the normal nominal rate at unchanged expected inflation and so makes it more likely that the ZLB will be binding. This argument calls for an increase in the target rate π^* in order to ensure that policy effectiveness for fighting future recessions will not be impaired. This argument is even stronger if the economy is likely to exhibit higher volatility compared to the episode of the great moderation.

7.7 Multiple Equilibria at the ZLB Under Taylor Rules

In this chapter, we have modelled the ZLB as a serious negative demand (time preference) shock hitting the economy. There is, however, an alternative, quite different view of the ZLB problem. Benhabib, Schmitt-Grohé, and Uribe (2001) have argued that the ZLB may be just one of multiple self-fulfilling rational expectations equilibria if the central bank follows a Taylor-type rule. As shown in Chap. 2, if the central bank follows the Taylor principle (an active policy rule adjusting nominal interest rates more than one for one when inflation deviates from a given target π^*), there will be only one unique locally bounded solution in standard models. Hence, active Taylor-type rules help to stabilize inflation at the target rate. However, Benhabib, Schmitt-Grohé and Uribe (2001) show that in the presence of the ZLB, a strict adherence to this rule may produce two steady states, one of which involves ending up in an inferior steady state with interest rates being trapped at the zero bound. In the presence of a zero bound on nominal interest rates, a Taylor rule creates a second steady state for the economy with deflation and nominal interest rates staying at zero. The reason is simply that at the ZLB, the Taylor principle (with a strong response $\alpha > 1$ more than one for one) is no longer feasible.

Figure 7.9 illustrates the basic mechanism. It plots two relations between the policy rate (the nominal interest rate) and the rate of inflation. The policy rate is on the vertical axis, the inflation rate on the horizontal axis. π^* is the target rate. The solid line around the target rate π^* represents an active linear Taylor rule $i = r + \pi^* + \alpha(\pi - \pi^*)$ with slope $\alpha > 1$. Along the dashed line, the policy rate is always equal to the real rate plus inflation $i = r + \pi$. In a steady state, $\pi^e = \pi$. So all steady-state equilibria will be along the dashed line with $i = r + \pi^e$, representing the Fisher relation for safe assets. The "active" policy rule intends to keep inflation near the target. To implement the target rate π^* as steady-state equilibrium requires that the central bank reacts strongly to deviations of inflation from target with an active Taylor rule: The nominal rate is raised more than one for one when inflation is above target (for $\pi > \pi^*$). When inflation is below target (for $\pi < \pi^*$), the nominal rate needs to be lowered, again more than one for one.

In Fig. 7.9, the short-term nominal rate is adjusted linearly in response to current inflation. The slope of the line $\alpha > 1$ indicates the strength of the reaction. Since the Taylor policy rule is steeper than one, the line cuts the Fisher equation from below in the neighborhood of the target rate. At $\pi = \pi^*$, the solid line crosses the dashed line. At π^* there is no need to change the policy rate. Private agents expect the current rate of inflation to prevail in the future. The Fisher relation holds: $\pi = \pi^e = \pi^*$. As long as there are no further shocks to the economy, nothing will change with respect to inflation or the nominal interest rate. The economy stays at an equilibrium.

Nevertheless, as can be seen from Fig. 7.9, the solid line crosses the dashed line a second time, creating another steady state. In Fig. 7.9, this second steady state occurs at the rate of $-r$ at the Zero lower bound with $i = 0$ and $\pi = \pi^e = -r$. At this steady state, private agents expect a steady deflation at the rate of $-r$. In the presence of the zero lower bound, the Taylor rule can no longer be active (responding with a slope steeper than one) for all negative rates of inflation. Once the policy rate hits the zero lower bound, active interest rate policy is no longer feasible: The central bank cannot lower the rate even further. Policy has switched to being passive. Evidently, the Taylor rule is flat in that region.

When inflation decreases further, there is no way to cut the policy rate. When inflation increases, the policy rate also cannot increase more than one for one. Even

Fig. 7.9 Multiple equilibria under Taylor rules

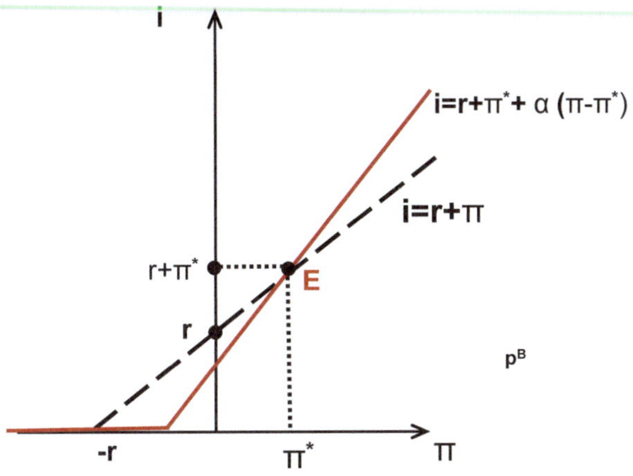

though inflation is well below target, fluctuations in inflation do not lead to a policy response at all in the neighborhood of the unintended steady state. The zero lower bound introduces a nonlinearity in the response function, forcing the central bank to switch to a passive regime. Even if we would consider nonlinear rules instead, the slope of such a nonlinear rule would be forced to become less than one and finally close to zero as the lower bound $i = 0$ is reached.

In our analysis, we assumed a positive target rate of inflation $\pi^* > 0$. Therefore, the second equilibrium with deflation is an unintended, inferior steady state. According to the Friedman rule, the second steady state with $i = 0$ with $\pi = -r$ is optimal, satiating all agents with money balances. If so, there would be no reason to worry about that outcome—quite the contrary: Deflation would be desirable minimizing the opportunity cost of holding money. The question whether deflation is harmful or beneficial to the economy is controversial. In a world with pervasive downward nominal rigidities, however, deflation is likely to create persistent disequilibrium in markets for goods and employment. It causes the economy to stay in a low activity level below potential output, so there are good reasons to fight deflationary pressures and target a positive rate π^*.

Bullard (2010) argues that the Benhabib et al. (2001) model captures reasonably well the experience of Japan getting stuck at a "too low" rate of inflation. In Fig. 7.10, Bullard (2010) draws a nonlinear Taylor-type rule quite similar to the linear rule discussed in Fig. 7.9. He plots nominal interest rates and inflation for both the USA and Japan during the period from January 2002 through June 2015 with monthly frequency. The Japanese data are the circles in the figure, and the US data are the squares. All data are taken from the main economic indicators of the OECD. Inflation is the core CPI rate. As short-term nominal interest rate he uses the relevant policy rate in both countries—in the USA, the federal funds rate and in Japan the overnight call rate. The real rate is assumed to be constant and the same for both countries at $r = 0.5$. In the figure, the "targeted" steady state occurs at an inflation

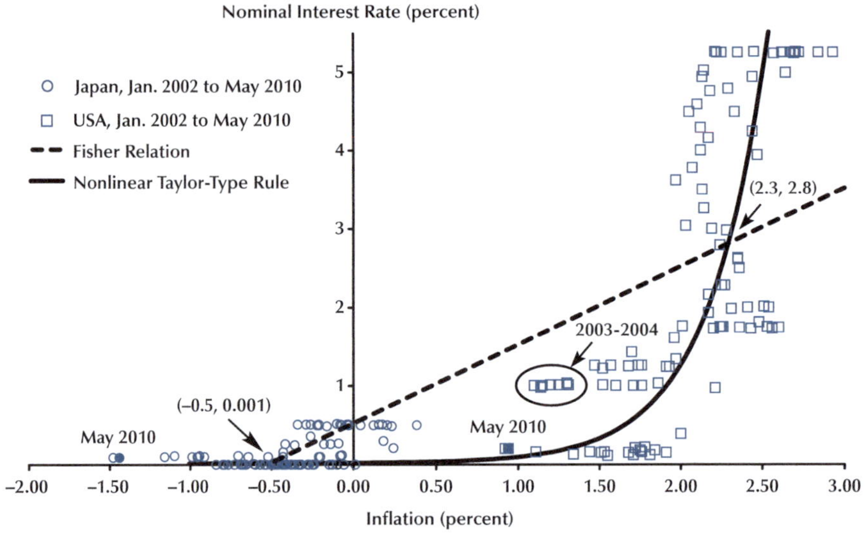

Fig. 7.10 Interest rates and inflation: Japan vs. USA [Source: Bullard (2010)]

rate of 2.3% and a nominal interest rate of 2.8% (denoted by the arrow on the right side of the figure).

The data in Fig. 7.10 hardly mix during this time period: All US data always lie to the northeast, and the Japanese data usually lie to the southwest. According to Bullard (2010), Japan has been locked into the unintended steady state with low nominal interest rate, suffering through more than one "lost decade." Promises to keep the policy rate near zero may increase the risk of falling into the unintended Japanese-style steady state of Fig. 7.10 by pulling inflation and inflation expectations lower. By keeping nominal rates low, monetary policy may itself create disinflationary expectations, causing inflation to stay low. Rather than curing disinflationary slumps, such a policy may prolong them.

Following Schmitt-Grohé and Uribe (2010), the central bank might instead commit to setting a higher lower bound strictly above zero in order to eliminate the bad equilibrium. If the deflation trap is just one of several equilibria—one of them to be realized by arbitrary changes in beliefs—a strict commitment never to lower the interest rate below—say—2% might be sufficient to rule out such an event. If all agents immediately jump to a higher expected rate of inflation, there might be a smooth transition to the desired equilibrium with the intended rate of inflation. If the economy instead falls into the liquidity trap as the result of shocks such as modelled in Sect. 7.3, a policy raising the nominal interest rate, by raising the real rate one for one, would aggravate problems of a deflationary spiral. It seems weird to argue that the commitment not to use stabilization tools in the range below target would be a credible mechanism to prevent the economy from falling into the liquidity trap.[4]

A key feature of the analysis of Benhabib et al. (2001) is that the central bank is assumed to rigidly follow strictly a Taylor-type policy. It is committed to use interest rate adjustment as the only tool, even long after it ceases to make sense (long after policy becomes passive). This strict adherence creates the second steady state for the economy. Many of the responses described in the next chapters attempt to remedy the situation by recommending a switch instead to some other policy when inflation is far below target. If policymakers commit to a sharp and credible regime switch, it may be possible to rule out the unintended equilibrium. If communicated transparently, unconventional policy measures such as quantitative easing may implement such a regime shift. We analyze these measures in the following chapter.

7.8 Summary

During the great recession, standard Taylor rules suggested the nominal interest rate should be lowered quite far into negative territory. When interest rates get negative, however, it would make sense to withdraw cash from bank accounts and hoard it instead. Therefore, central banks are facing a lower bound for the interest rate as policy instrument. For a long time, that bound has been assumed to be exactly at zero. As recent experience in some countries illustrates, inconvenience and storage costs allow the rate to become slightly negative before hoarding sets in. Nevertheless, there is an effective lower bound on interest rates (for convenience, we still call it zero lower bound—ZLB) limiting the scope for active interest rate policy.

In this chapter, we analyzed how optimal policy needs to be modified in the New Keynesian model—as outlined in Part II—taking that constraint explicitly into account. In line with the New Keynesian framework, here we focused purely on characterizing the interest path, abstracting from other unconventional tools (such as quantitative or credit easing) aiming to mitigate frictions in financial intermediation. They will be covered in the following chapters.

[4]In models with multiple rational expectations equilibria, the adequate policy response crucially depends on the stability properties of these equilibria. It is reasonable to assume that agents learn at least partly from observing past history. Howitt (1992) demonstrated in a traditional monetary model that an interest rate peg is unstable under adaptive learning. A peg has explosive dynamics if expectations are based on extrapolation from past data.

Recently, García-Schmidt and Woodford (2019) and Evans and McGough (2018) introduce different learning mechanisms in New Keynesian models. They show that setting interest rates according to a peg that is maintained forever will cause instability. Pegging the interest rate peg at a high level triggers a gradual deterioration in inflation expectations. The decline in inflation expectations leads to higher ex ante real interest rates and declining output. According to Evans and McGough (2018), a policy of temporarily low interest rates followed by an explicit return to normal rates later guided by a standard Taylor rule can avoid this outcome. Such a policy brings inflation back to target and the economy back to steady state.

We learned that, given the ZLB constraint, the central bank should aim to keep interest rates low for a long period, in order to stimulate current demand by committing to low long-term rates. The study of the zero lower bound (ZLB) on nominal interest rates provides an impressive example how insights obtained from theoretical models can have a strong impact on policy in practice. The research led to a number of concrete policy prescriptions that influenced policymaking during and after the global financial crisis. Key lessons have been that short-term rates (1) should be cut aggressively when deflation or a severe downturn threatens and (2) they should also be kept "lower for longer" as the economy recovers. The intuition underlying this insight is that the expectation of an extended low level of short-term interest rates reduces longer term yields and eases financial conditions more broadly. We have seen that the notion of forward guidance, which played a key role in unconventional policies, follows naturally from optimal interest rate policy at the zero lower bound. The attempt to communicate and commit in a transparent way to keep the path of short-term interest rates low for an extended period far into the future is a key element of optimal policy.

But we also learned that—quite similar to the issue discussed in Sect. 5.3—optimal policy is facing a problem of dynamic inconsistency: The optimal control path requires a commitment to overshoot the target later, when the economy is back to normal. At that stage, however, there is a strong incentive for policy to renege on the promised path. This created a deflation bias, resulting in suboptimal outcome. We illustrated this feature in a highly stylized three-period framework, characterizing explicitly the optimality conditions involved. We also studied alternative ways to overcome the ZLB such as a policy abolishing cash (to eliminate the option for hoarding) or raising the inflation target, aiming to reduce the probability of getting constrained by the ZLB.

References

Agarwal, R., & Kimball, M. (2015). Breaking through the Zero Lower Bound. *IMF Working Paper* WP/15/224. Washington, DC.

Benhabib, J., Schmitt-Grohé, S., & Uribe, M. (2001). The perils of Taylor rules. *Journal of Economic Theory, 96*(1), 40–69.

Bernanke, B. (2002). *Deflation: Making sure "it" doesn't happen here*. Remarks before the National Economists Club, Washington, DC. https://www.federalreserve.gov/boarddocs/speeches/2002/20021121/

Blanchard, O., Dell'Ariccia, G., & Mauro, P. (2010). Rethinking macroeconomic policy. *IMF Staff Position Note*.

Brayton, F., Laubach, T., & Reifschneider, D. (2014). Optimal-control monetary policy in the FRB/US model. *FEDS Notes*, Washington, 21 November 2014.

Bullard, J. (2010). Seven faces of "the peril". *Federal Reserve Bank of St. Louis Review*, September 2010, pp. 339–352.

Campbell, J. R. C., Evans, L., Fisher, J. D. M., & Justiniano, A. (2012). Macroeconomic effects of FOMC forward guidance. *Brookings Papers on Economic Activity*, pp. 1–54.

Eggertsson, G., & Woodford, M. (2013). The zero interest-rate bound and optimal monetary policy. *Brookings Papers on Economic Activity, 2003*, 1.

Engen, E., Laubach, T., & Reifschneider, D. (2015). The macroeconomic effects of the Federal Reserve's unconventional monetary policies. *Finance and Economic Discussion Series* 2015-005, Federal Reserve Board, Washington.

Evans, G., & McGough, B. (2018). Interest rate pegs in new Keynesian models. *Journal of Money, Credit and Banking, 50*(5), 939–965.

García-Schmidt, M., & Woodford, M. (2019). Are low interest rates deflationary? A paradox of perfect-foresight analysis. *American Economic Review, 109*(1), 86–120.

Hicks, J. R. (1937). Mr. Keynes and the "classics"; A suggested interpretation. *Econometrica, 5*(2), 147–159.

Howitt, P. (1992). Interest rate control and nonconvergence to rational expectations. *Journal of Political Economy, 100*, 776–800.

Illing, G., & Siemsen, T. (2016). Forward guidance in a model with price-level targeting. *CESifo Economic Studies, 62*(1), 47–67.

Keynes, J. M. (1936). *The general theory of employment, interest and money*. London: Macmillan.

Kiley, M. T., & Roberts, J. (2017). Monetary policy in a low interest rate world. *Brookings Papers on Economic Activity, 48*, 317–396.

Krugman, P. R. (1998). It's Baaack: Japan's slump and the return of the liquidity trap. *Brookings Papers on Economic Activity, 1998*(2), 137–205.

Nakamura, E., Steinsson, J., Sun, P., & Villar, D. (2018). The elusive costs of inflation: Price dispersion during the U.S. great inflation. *The Quarterly Journal of Economics, 133*(4), 1933–1980.

Nikolsko-Rzhevskyy, A., & Papell, D. H. (2013). Taylor's rule versus Taylor rules. *International Finance, 16*(1), S71–S93.

Rognlie, M. (2015). *What lower bound? Monetary policy with negative interest rates*. Boston, MA: Mimeo, MIT.

Rogoff, K. (2014). Costs and benefits of phasing out paper currency. *NBER Macroeconomics Annual, 29*, 445–456.

Rudebusch, G. D. (2010). The Fed's exit strategy for monetary policy. *FRBSF Economic Letter, Federal Reserve Bank of San Francisco*, Issue June 14.

Schmiedel, H., Kostova, G., & Ruttenberg, W. (2012). The social and private costs of retail payment instruments: A European perspective. *ECB Occasional Papers Series*, No. 137.

Schmitt-Grohé, S., & Uribe, M. (2010). The optimal rate of inflation. In B. M. Friedman & M. Woodford (Eds.), *Handbook of monetary economics* (Vol. 3, 1st ed., pp. 653–722).

Swanson, E., & Williams, J. (2014). Measuring the effect of the zero lower bound on medium- and longer-term interest rates. *American Economic Review, 104*(10), 3154–3185.

Taylor, J. (1993). Discretion versus policy rules in practice. *Carnegie-Rochester Conference Series in Public Policy, 39*(1), 195–214.

Wiederholt, M. (2015). Empirical properties of inflation expectations and the zero lower bound. Goethe University Frankfurt.

Part III

Unconventional Monetary Policy, Financial Frictions and Crises

In Part II, our analysis of monetary policy stayed strictly within the standard New Keynesian framework, abstracting from financial frictions. Nominal and real rigidities such as stickiness in price setting or rigidities in labor market prevent price and output from reaching their efficient levels. In that framework, by using the short-term interest rate, or, monetary policy rate, as the main instrument and steering peoples' expectations on the future path of monetary policy, the central bank can dampen fluctuations effectively. It may even be able to stabilize price level and employment at the same time—in the best case of a "divine coincidence" (Blanchard and Galí 2007).

The conventional analytical framework for monetary policy characterizes a rather tranquil, "near steady state" scenario in which volatility in the macro economy is relatively low. However, when large adverse shocks hit the economy, in similar scale as in the Great Recession, this tranquil scenario is unlikely to prevail. In order to stimulate the economy, the central bank may need to cut the policy rate aggressively all the way down not just towards the zero lower bound but even into negative territory. Optimal monetary policy may no longer be implementable if restrictions of the (effective) zero lower bound are binding, as discussed in Chap. 7. Conventional monetary policy gets to its limit in reviving the economy during recessions. In that case, the economy may react to monetary policy quite differently compared to tranquil times. Central banks may need to explore other unconventional tools to achieve their mandate.

The previous chapters focused on the effects of monetary policy on macro economy. After the central bank announces its policy rate, however, its impact follows a long, thorny way to reach the real economy. In our analysis so far, problems in the so-called "transmission mechanism" via the banking sector have been blended out. There seems to be need to care about the details of the intermediation process. We assumed that financial markets are running smoothly without disruptions. In reality, however, large shocks are likely to cause severe disruptions of financial intermediation. For that reason, we need to study the transmission via the banking sector carefully. This will be our focus in the next chapters. First of all, the central bank implements its monetary policy through open market operations to move the money market rate to its target. This shifts banks' funding cost as well as liquidity positions in their balance sheets, inducing them to adjust credit supply to households and firms, leading to further changes in the macro economy level, such as investments, output and consumption. Chapter 8 analyzes in detail such bank lending channel through which monetary policy affects the real economy.

In the "near steady state" scenario, banks function smoothly as they are supposed to do; therefore, in conventional New Keynesian framework a frictionless transmission mechanism is taken as granted, treating banks as black box or rather neglecting them completely. However, in reality, banks are never static black boxes; instead, they evolve and react actively to various shocks from real economy, financial market, monetary policy, as well as regulatory rules. Frictions in financial markets and financial intermediation prevent banks from optimally raising funding and allocating credits. These frictions may be aggravated by economic shocks, forcing banks to reallocate resources, generating a feedback to the real economy and amplifying the initial shocks. As a result, monetary policy needs to respond to these frictions, trying to reduce the excess volatilities. Chapter 9 provides an overview of financial frictions and their implications for monetary policy.

An even more important consequence of monetary transmission through the banking sector is that monetary policy does not only alter the volume of the banks' credit supply, but also shifts the risk components in the banks' balance sheets. Through active open market operation, the central bank is itself an active player in the financial market, and the almost unlimited size of its balance sheet gives the central bank infinite power of ammunition. The conduct of monetary policy moves liquidity in the market, which affects the likelihood of systemic market stress; therefore, monetary policy has profound implications for financial stability. On the other hand, banks also actively react to monetary policy in their liquidity and risk management practice, frictions in financial market may encourage them to take excess risks—so-called "risk taking channel"—which may bring down the entire world economy. Chapter 10 discusses the relation between monetary policy and financial stability.

Reference

Blanchard, O., & Galí, J. (2007). Real wage rigidities and the New Keynesian model. *Journal of Money, Credit, and Banking, 39*(S1), 35–65.

Monetary Policy in Practice 8

8.1 Introduction

In the New Keynesian model, central banks use the short-term interest rate as their main instrument (as policy rate). In reality, policy-induced changes affect real variables such as aggregate output and employment via quite different mechanisms. A central bank needs to implement monetary policy using a combination of various tools. This chapter gives an informal survey of different channels of monetary transmission mechanisms. Most of these channels work via various tools affecting intermediation in the banking sector. Well-functioning monetary policy relies on a well-functioning banking sector, transmitting monetary policy targets into supply of credits that further affects real activities in the macro economy.

However, if the banking sector fails and conduits of credits are clogged, typically in financial crises, conventional monetary policy tools and instruments will not be able to reach firms and households that are hungry for credits any more. Under such situation, the central bank must be decisive to step in with unconventional measures, clean up and restart the entire banking system, or even try to act as a market maker itself, and directly reach the lenders and borrowers in the real economy.

In the following chapters, we will analyze monetary transmission mechanisms both in normal and in crisis times and present a variety of detailed models of financial intermediation. For introduction, the next section focuses on the link between the central bank's balance sheet management and the transmission into the banking sector. Section 8.3 illustrates the failure of standard monetary transmission mechanisms during the financial crisis and various policy responses, in particular the policy of qualitative and quantitative easing. At the end of this chapter, we emphasize different channels of monetary policy transmission. Apart from the traditional interest rate channel, we need a better understanding of two credit channels: The balance sheet channel and the bank-lending channel. The following chapters present various theoretical foundations for these channels.

J. Cao, G. Illing, *Money: Theory and Practice*, Springer Texts in Business and Economics, https://doi.org/10.1007/978-3-030-19697-4_8

8.2 Monetary Policy Transmission

The central bank's balance sheet management is crucial for the conduct of monetary policy. Being the bank of all banks, it affects the balance sheets of all private banks in the economy, these adjusting their credit supply to firms and households, leading to an expansion or a contraction in real activities. Along this way, monetary policy makes its impact on the macro economy via different channels. These channels are the so-called transmission mechanisms of monetary policy.

8.2.1 The Central Bank's Balance Sheet

Table 8.1 presents a stylized balance sheet of a central bank. Its liabilities include cash in circulation—the legal tender as medium for transaction as well as for value storage—and bank reserves. Bank reserves are the deposit accounts where banks deposit electronic cash at the central bank. In many countries, banks are required to hold a certain amount of reserves to meet the cash demand from depositors. The central bank may pay interest on banks' reserves. A central bank can adjust its money supply through both cash in circulation and banks' reserve accounts. Thus, total liabilities constitute the money base (*MB*) of the economy.

The central bank assets include:

- Loans to banks. Banks can raise reserves by borrowing from the central bank via its discount window, paying a discount rate on these loans. Usually these loans are overnight loans, but the maturity can be longer under certain circumstances. A central bank has the commitment to lending to banks without limit, especially when banks are not able to borrow from elsewhere, i.e., the central bank is the lender-of-last-resort in a banking system. Bank reserves obtained from the discount window are called borrowed reserves (*BR*).
- Securities purchased by the central bank. These securities are mostly, but not restricted to, government securities. When the central bank buys securities in open market operation, no matter whether from banks or from nonbank institutions / individuals, the cash that central bank pays eventually ends up either as cash held by individuals or as bank reserves, increasing the level of reserves in the banking sector. With the reverse operation, when the central bank sells securities, it drains reserves from banks. Bank reserves obtained from security purchases are called nonborrowed reserves (*NBR*).

Table 8.1 A stylized central bank's balance sheet

Assets	*Liabilities (MB)*
• Loans to banks (*BR*) • Government securities (*NBR*) • Other securities (*NBR*)	• Cash in circulation • Bank reserves

Aggregating across the entire central bank's balance sheet, the money base is equal to the sum of two types of bank reserves, i.e., $MB = BR + NBR$.

It is worth noting that institutional details differ slightly from country to country. Some central banks, such as the European Central Bank, do not directly purchase securities from the primary market; instead, they adjust bank reserves in market operations using reverse repurchase agreements (repo). In a reverse repo agreement, the central bank increases bank reserves by lending cash to the banks, say the amount X, against eligible collateral. The private bank has to post securities (usually these are highly liquid securities such as government securities or corporate bonds, but other assets may also be accepted) with face value Z as collateral, with a promise to repurchase the securities after a certain period at the price of Y, as shown in Fig. 8.1. In this way, the central bank provides the amount X of bank reserves over the agreement period. The interest rate the central bank charges on the agreement, $\frac{Y-X}{X} \times 100\%$, is called "repo rate." The discount on collateral value, $\frac{Z-X}{X} \times 100\%$, is called "haircut."

At maturity, the private bank is due to pay money to the central bank to redeem her obligations. However, in order to do so, the counterparties typically need to borrow new funds from the central bank. This way, the central bank provides the necessary reserves once more, at the official repo rate. If, at maturity, the central bank issues less new repos to the banking sector than the amount it has terminated, overall bank reserves will decrease, tightening overall monetary policy.

A repo (collateralized borrowing) is equivalent to a secured loan, with private banks as borrower. The central bank receives securities as collateral to protect herself against default by the bank. In addition, the haircut insures against default of the security. The riskier the asset, the higher the haircut. During the financial crisis, the ECB (similar to other central banks) extended the range of assets accepted as collateral; it even accepted nonmarketable securities (see Fig. 8.2). At the same time, it raised the haircuts on collateral to protect against default risk.

The central bank can loosen monetary policy not only by extending the list of securities that banks can pledge as collateral, but also by extending the average maturity (the agreement period) for repo transactions. Whereas during normal times, standard repo operations had a length of just 2 weeks, during crisis the ECB extended the average maturity initially to 6 months and later even to 1–3 years. This reduced banks' uncertainty about reserves provided in the future. The central bank, however, could adjust the repo rate at any time before maturity. Furthermore,

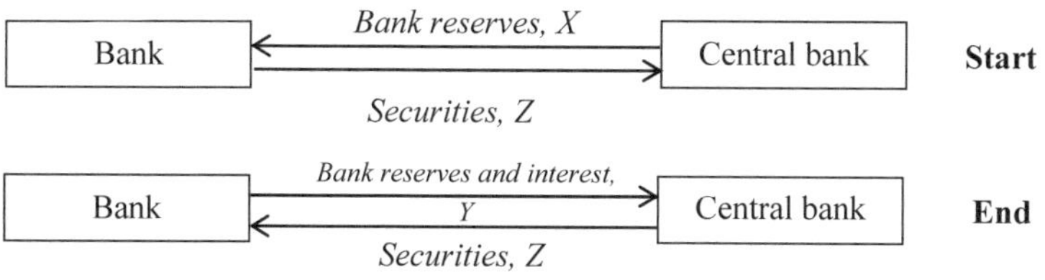

Fig. 8.1 The start and the end of a repo agreement

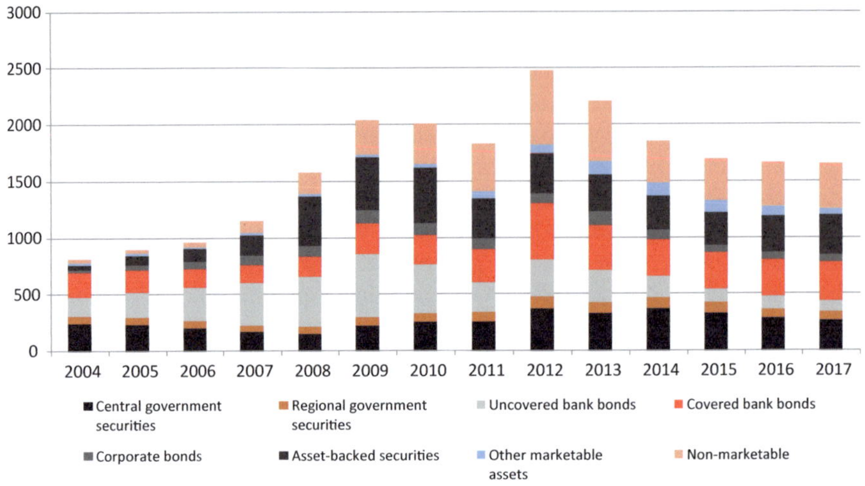

Fig. 8.2 The use of collateral (source: ECB). Since the crisis, the ECB has accepted significantly more nonmarketable securities

banks had the right to terminate repos earlier in case they would prefer to hold lower reserves.

8.2.2 Links Between the Central Bank and the Banking Sector

Changes in the central bank's balance sheet have an impact on the banks' balance sheets through several linkages. Table 8.2 presents a stylized bank's balance sheet. On the liability side, the bank gets funding through equity, bonds issuance, and importantly, through deposits from firms and households—including term deposits that stay in the deposit accounts for a fixed period—and on call deposits that depositors can withdraw anytime. To meet the cash demand for depositors, the bank needs to hold cash reserves—usually deposited in the central bank's deposit account. In some countries, reserve requirements are imposed: Banks must hold cash reserves no less than a certain proportion to the checkable deposits; however, even

Table 8.2 A stylized bank's balance sheet

Assets	*Liabilities*
• Loans • Government securities and other liquid assets • Bank reserves	• On call deposits • Term deposits • Loans from the central bank • Loans from other banks • Bonds • Equity

for countries (such as Norway) with no reserve requirements, banks do have an incentive to hold reserve buffers.

Bank reserves are crucial links between the central bank and the banking sector. When the central bank purchases securities (or accepts securities as repo) in open market operation, bank reserves will rise. This allows banks to take more checkable deposits. At the same time, it can issue more loans on the asset side (see later more details in Sect. 9.5 on Bianchi-Bigio model). So, increasing bank reserves implies an expansionary monetary policy, leading to an increase in aggregate credit supply. The opposite happens when the central bank sells securities under a contractionary monetary policy.

Holding reserves is costly for banks. Although frequently the central bank pays interest on (part of) bank reserves, the interest return from reserves is much lower than other assets such as loans. Therefore, banks usually hold required reserves, but they try to minimize holdings of excess reserves. However, due to daily fluctuations in bank liabilities, at the end of the day there are always some banks short of reserves, as well as other banks with excess reserves. Therefore, banks can trade with each other in the interbank market for reserves (in the USA, this is called federal funds market), so that banks can raise reserves via overnight interbank loans at the market interest rate (it is called federal funds rate in the USA). As an alternative, banks can also borrow reserves from the central bank's discount window. Interbank loans and discount loans are usually collateralized; therefore, banks also hold safe assets such as government securities on their balance sheets. The interest rate in the market for reserves is usually the one that monetary policy targets. The central bank intervenes in the market to keep the rate close to its target.

Briefly speaking, monetary policy is conducted via central bank's balance sheet management—namely, through open market operations, accounts for bank reserves, and discount window—which directly affects elements in the banks' balance sheets: bank reserves, securities, discount loans, etc., shifting the equilibrium in the market for reserves. This leads to a change in the interbank lending rate for reserves, and supply of bank lending. In the next sections, we will see how the interbank lending rate is determined by the implementation of monetary policy, and how it is translated into shifts in bank lending.

8.2.3 Equilibrium on the Money Market

Supply of and demand for bank reserves determine the equilibrium rate in the market for reserves. First, banks' demand for reserves is a decreasing function of the market rate for reserves: The lower the rate, the cheaper it is for banks to borrow, so the higher the demand for reserves. However, the rate cannot fall below the interest rate that the central bank pays on bank reserves, as banks can deposit in the central bank at this rate as much as they want. Therefore, as Fig. 8.3 shows, the demand curve R_D for reserves is a decreasing function of the market rate for reserves, and bounded below by the interest rate paid on central bank's reserve accounts, i_r.

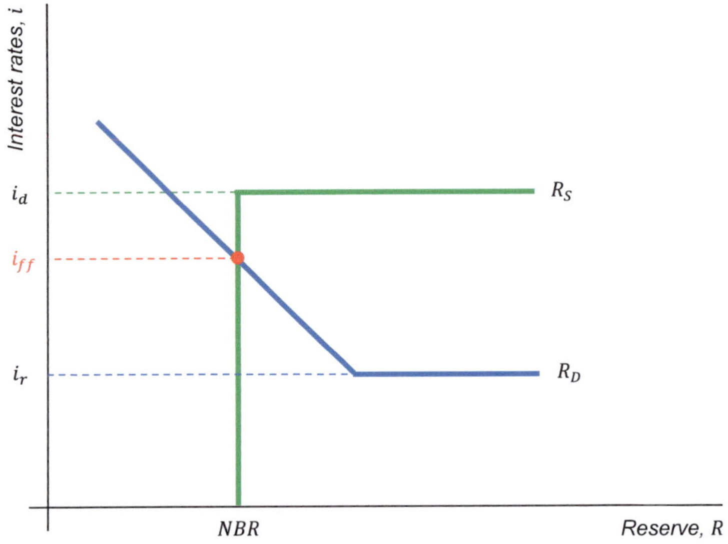

Fig. 8.3 The equilibrium rate in the market for reserves

The central bank's supply of bank reserves comes from two sources: open market operation (non-borrowed reserves, *NBR*) and discount loans (borrowed reserves, *BR*). During the period between two open market operations, the supply of *NBR* is fixed by the previous open market operation, therefore, its supply curve is a vertical line as R_S curve in Fig. 8.3. Beyond *NBR*, banks can borrow as much as they want from the discount window at the discount rate i_d, therefore, the supply curve of bank reserves is bounded above by i_d.

In equilibrium, the market rate for reserves, i_{ff}, is determined by the intersection of supply and demand curves. The equilibrium rate can only move within the corridor that is bounded by the floor i_r and the ceiling i_d. In practice, by simply narrowing the corridor around its target policy rate via changing i_r and i_d, the central bank can reduce the volatility of i_{ff} and keep it close to the monetary policy rate.

Shifting the corridor does not only restrict the volatility in i_{ff}, but also may change the level of bank reserves in the system, depending how drastic the shift of the corridor is. Figure 8.4 shows what happens after a small cut in discount rate i_d: It simply narrows the corridor, but does not change the equilibrium bank reserves. However, if the cut is drastic enough so that the demand curve crosses the horizontal part of the supply curve (as in Fig. 8.5), the discount rate is so low that banks are indifferent between borrowing from other banks and from discount window ($i_{ff} = i_d$). In equilibrium, bank reserves will be increased by the discount loans (*BR*). A further cut in the discount rate (i_d to i'_d) will further increase borrowed reserves from discount loans (*BR* to *BR′*—see Fig. 8.5).

A more direct way to change bank reserves and move market equilibrium is open market operation, by the central bank purchasing or selling securities. Suppose the

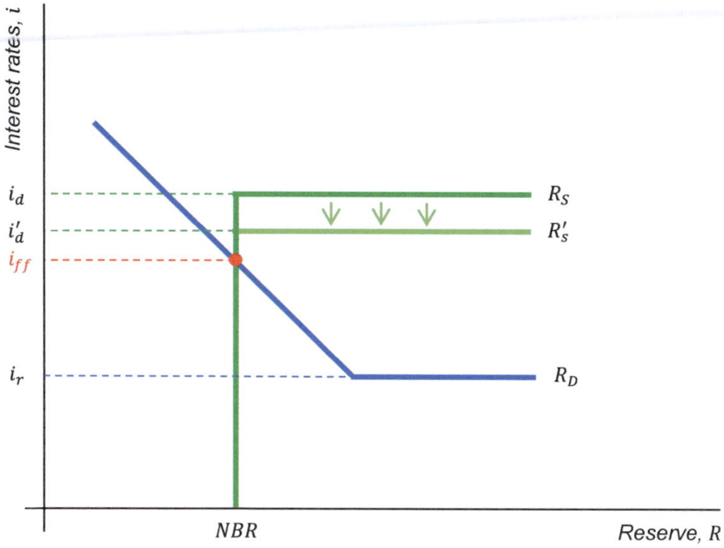

Fig. 8.4 Cutting discount rate without changing bank reserves

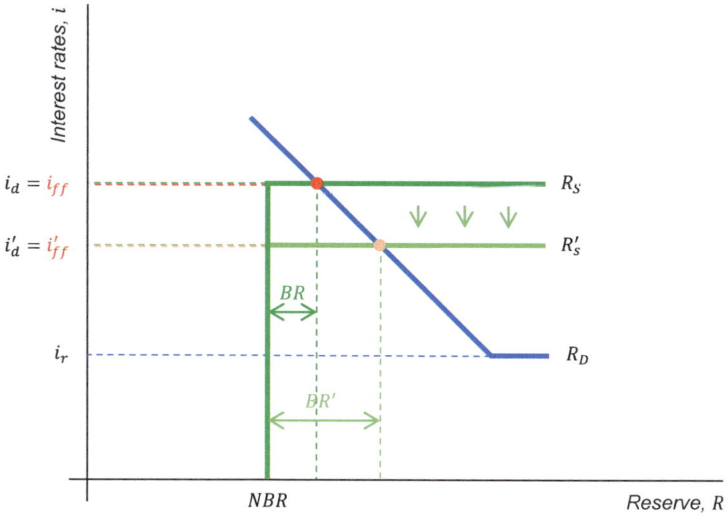

Fig. 8.5 Borrowed reserves from the discount window

central bank conducts expansionary monetary policy through security purchase, which increases aggregate bank reserves as in Fig. 8.6: If the securities are purchased from banks, there will be direct rise in bank reserves; if the securities are purchased from nonbank institutions or individuals, the cash that the central bank pays will end up in their bank accounts, which eventually increases bank reserves. With more

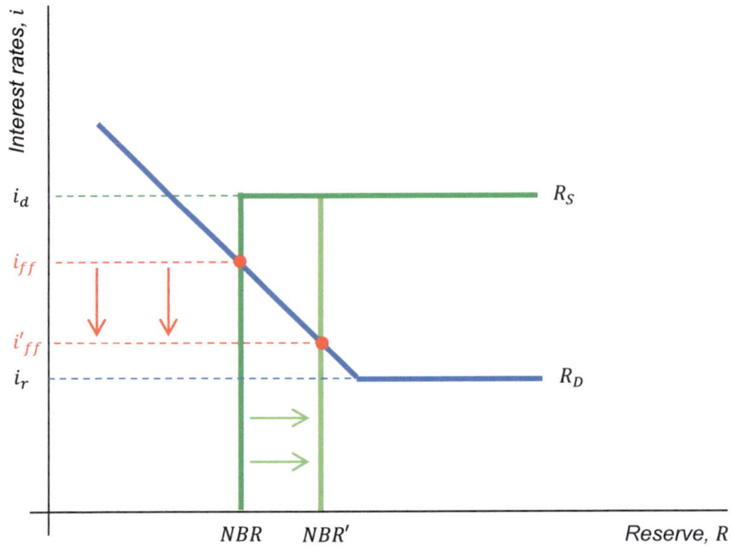

Fig. 8.6 The effect of open market security purchase

reserves, banks are less likely to fall short of reserves, or, reserves are less scarce in the interbank market. This leads to a fall in the market rate for reserves. Figure 8.6 shows the shift in market equilibrium: Open market security purchases increase non-borrowed reserves in the banking system, shifting the supply curve to the right (*NBR* to *NBR′*), and i_{ff} falls as a result.

In many countries, another powerful tool to shift the interbank market equilibrium is the adjustment of reserve requirements. Suppose that the central bank raises the required reserve ratio such that more banks are likely to fall short of reserves; therefore, there will be higher demand in the market for reserves, shifting the demand curve to the right (R_D to R'_D in Fig. 8.7). Such rising scarcity of reserves increases the market rate for interbank lending (i_{ff} to i'_{ff}); if the shift in reserve requirement is too high that makes the demand curve cross the horizontal part of the supply curve, banks will eventually have to borrow from the central bank's discount window to fulfill the new requirement. Thus, raising required reserves is a contractionary monetary policy measure.

8.3 Failures of Monetary Transmission Mechanism

In normal times, the bank reserves determine the equilibrium rate in the interbank-market which follows the target rate set by the central bank closely. Central bank policy actions smoothly transmit into the banking sector and in the end reach the real economy. The interest rates of other, riskier assets move fairly closely with the target rate, with the spreads between different risk classes hardly affected. Figure 8.8

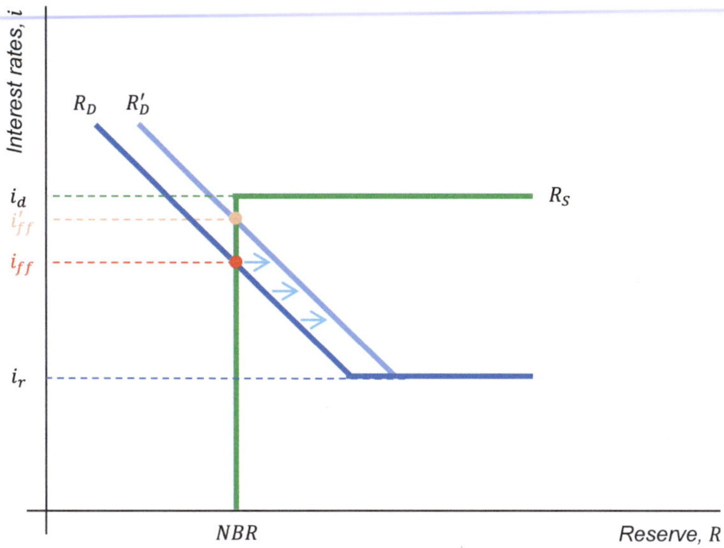

Fig. 8.7 The effect of higher reserve requirement

shows that the rate for overnight loans on the interbank market follows the corridor set by central banks closely. After the start of 2007–2009 crisis, most central banks worldwide, from America to Australia, lowered their policy rates fairly quickly to close to zero, as shown in Fig. 8.8.

8.3.1 The Financial Crisis: Spikes in Risk Spreads

Before the crisis, the rates for unsecured lending over slightly longer periods (over 1–3 months) also followed the target rate set by the central bank very closely (see Fig. 8.9 for the USA). But starting in August 2007 and aggravated in September 2008, things changed dramatically. During the financial crisis, short-term rates spiked dramatically on the interbank market and even stronger for other, more risky assets. Even the rates for highly (AA) rated Asset-backed Commercial Papers with short maturity of 30 days shot up during that period. Traditionally, bank runs were triggered by withdrawals from retail depositors. In contrast, the financial crisis that started in 2007 centered on the interbank market: Spreads on unsecured interbank lending which had been at extremely low levels for several years suddenly sparked up significantly with doubts rising about the exposure of banks to risky subprime securities. Those banks that relied heavily on interbank funding suffered a severe liquidity shock to the liability side of their balance sheet. At the same time, there was a sharp increase in the use of outstanding credit lines by borrowers, fearing tighter credit restrictions in the near future. Nonfinancial firms asked for more liquidity precisely at the time when funding liquidity for banks was drying up.

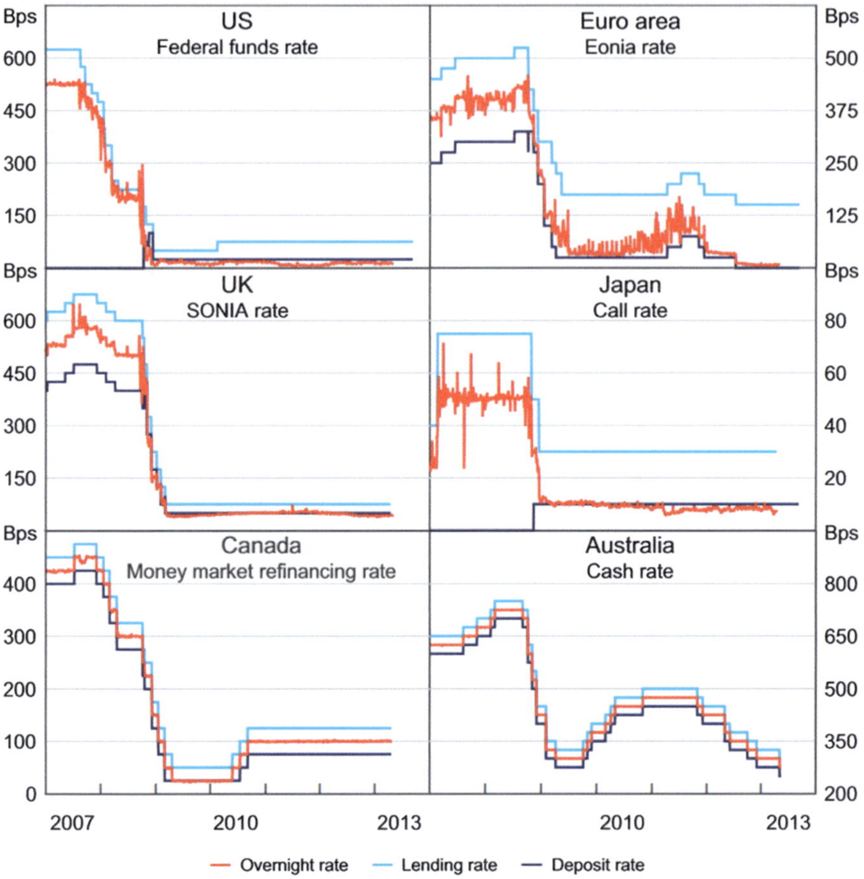

Fig. 8.8 Monetary policy rates (in basis points, 1 basis point = 1/100 of 1%) in the USA, Euro Area, UK, Japan, Canada, and Australia before, during and after the crisis. In each of the charts, the upper line shows the evolution of the discount rate, the bottom line is the interest rate paid on bank reserves, and in between is the market rate for reserves (note that the Fed started to pay interest on reserves from October 2008) (Source: Bech & Monnet, 2013)

Those who paid attention only to bank-based lending and traditional money supply figures missed the evolving problems in credit markets. Whereas market-based providers of credit (such as financial commercial papers and overnight repos) contracted rapidly, commercial bank lending, and money supply M2 was initially even rising, with banks playing their role as buffer for their borrowers in the face of deteriorating market conditions (see Fig. 8.10 and Adrian & Shin, 2009). Brunnermeier (2009) provides a good reference for the causes of the financial crises. Here, we focus on the challenges that central banks faced during the crises and recessions that follow, as well as the unconventional policy measures to address these challenges.

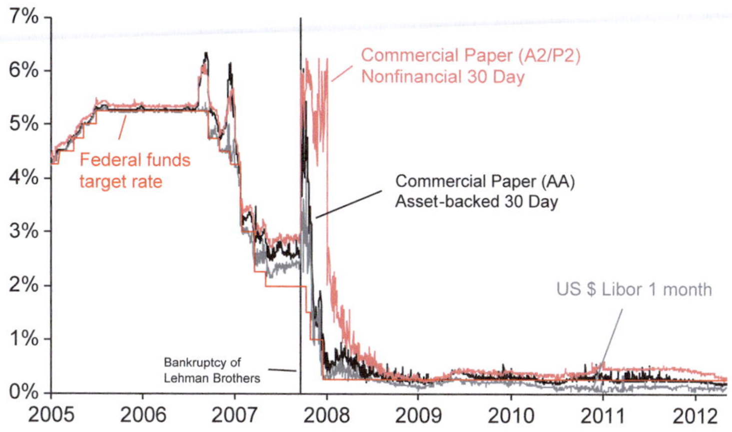

Fig. 8.9 Federal funds target rate, short-term rates on the interbank market (Libor 1 month); rates for Commercial Papers with short maturity of 30 days (Commercial Paper (A2/P2) Nonfinancial 30 Day: Short-term, unsecured promissory notes issued by nonfinancial corporations with a maturity of 30 days. A2/P2 denotes low-quality rating by the rating agencies. Commercial Paper (AA) Asset-backed 30 Day: Short-term, secured investment vehicle with a maturity of 30 days. Security itself is issued by a bank or other financial institution and backed by physical assets. AA denotes high-quality rating by rating agencies)

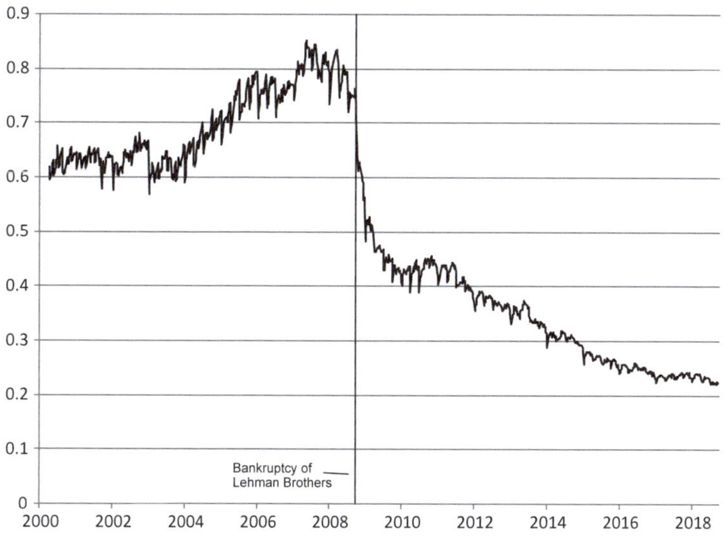

Sources: https://www.newyorkfed.org/markets/gsds/search.html#
https://fred.stlouisfed.org/series/FINCP Datastream

Fig. 8.10 Primary dealer repos + financial commercial paper as a fraction of M2

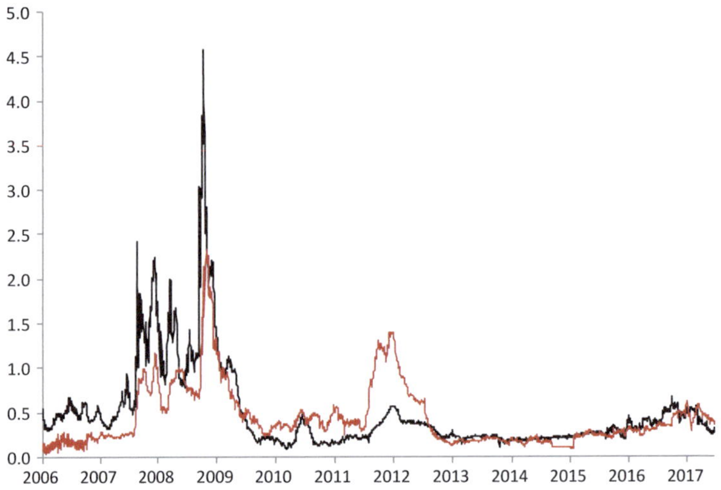

Fig. 8.11 LIBOR-TED spread in the US and Euribor-Eurepo spread in the Euro area

The cost of interbank lending, or, the interest rate R that one bank charges on the loan to another bank, can be decomposed into two parts

$$R = i + \rho$$

in which i is the risk-free rate that can be proxied by the monetary policy rate, and ρ is the risk premium for the loan. The risk premium comes from the lending bank's perception on the counterparty risk, that is, how likely the borrowing bank is going to fail during the maturity of the loan. During normal times, ρ is very small, especially for large banks; however, it can be extremely high during crises. Figure 8.11 shows the risk premium measured by the spread between 3-month LIBOR (London Interbank Offered Rate) and 3-month TED rate (US Treasury bill rate, a proxy for risk-free rate) during the 2007–2009 crisis. It spiked with each market turbulence, especially after the collapse of Lehman Brothers in September 2008. The interbank lending rate became so high that the market was nearly frozen. The Euribor-Eurepo spread, measuring the corresponding risk premium in the Euro area, follows a similar pattern. It spiked again during the Euro crisis from summer 2011 to summer 2012.

The risk premium, or banks' counterparty risk, comes from two sources:

- Solvency risk, that the counterparty may become insolvent.
- Liquidity risk, that the counterparty may not be able to meet its monetary obligations, including
  - Market liquidity risk, that the bank cannot convert its assets to cash to fulfill the demand. The banks hold too much illiquid assets whose conversion to cash incurs large discounts.
  - Funding liquidity risk, that the bank cannot raise funding in the market at reasonable price.

8.3.2 Monetary Policy Response in Financial Crisis

To restart the banking system, monetary policy needs to reduce the interbank funding cost R by targeting i and ρ. The central bank has to choose among a variety of options. For those banks that are already insolvent, orderly closure is the solution to avoid further damage to the system. However, if the insolvent bank is systemically important and the closure generates costly spillovers to the other financial institutions, it may be better for the public to bail it out, take it over and provide necessary guarantees to ensure that it still provides the desired services for the rest of the system. During a crisis, it is hard if not impossible to distinguish between those banks which are truly insolvent and those banks who are illiquid yet solvent, provided policy succeeds in combatting the crisis.

8.3.2.1 Targeted Liquidity Provision

To ease the banks' funding liquidity problem, the central bank commits to be the lender-of-last-resort for the entire banking system, providing unlimited funding sources for the banks. The discount rate can be lowered to reduce banks' funding cost, and the maturity of discount loans can be extended from overnight to several months to reduce banks' funding liquidity risk in debt rollover. In the 2007–2009 crisis, the Federal Reserve offered targeted liquidity aid to systemically important institutions in the USA; it also made currency swap agreements with several central banks, such as the European Central Bank, Bank of England, Norges Bank, etc., to provide stable foreign currency funding for global banks.

8.3.2.2 Qualitative Easing

To ease the banks' market liquidity problem, the central bank needs to extract illiquid assets from banks' balance sheets and replace them with liquid assets. The central bank can thus use its balance sheet as an instrument, buying illiquid assets from and at the same time selling its holdings of government securities to the banks to improve the liquidity in bank assets. Such operation does not increase bank reserves in the system, but instead, only qualitatively changes the composition of bank non-reserve assets. The strategy is thus called "qualitative easing."

The period before September 2009 in Fig. 8.12 shows the qualitative easing period of the Federal Reserve during the crisis. Traditionally, the Fed held mainly safe short-term Treasury securities. In the first phase of the crisis, the Fed sold a large share of these liquid assets without expanding its overall balance sheet and instead bought risky assets from the financial sector (captured by the item "lending to financial institutions," providing liquidity to key credit markets). The stock of traditional Treasuries fell by more than two-third in this period. However, with the collapse of Lehman Brothers, the Fed started to face another limit: The volume of government securities on its balance sheet was too low to conduct necessary market operations in the future. Therefore, the Fed could not improve banks' market liquidity further without affecting bank reserves or significantly expanding its own balance sheet. In other words, monetary policy had to shift from qualitative to quantitative stage.

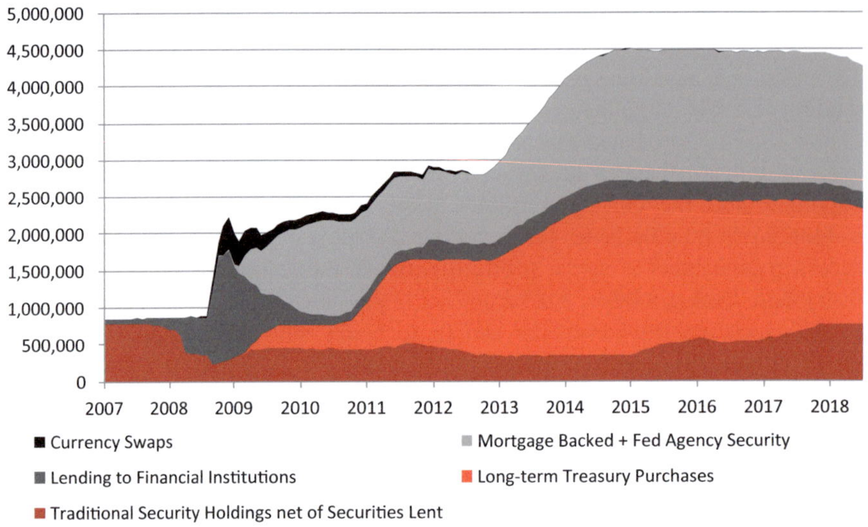

Fig. 8.12 Total assets and the asset components of the Federal Reserve, 01.2007–08.2018 (Source: Cleveland Fed, Data on Credit Easing)

8.3.2.3 Quantitative Easing

In quantitative easing (QE), the central bank purchases financial assets, such as government securities, agency debts, mortgage-backed securities (MBS), directly from banks and nonbank institutions. Quantitative easing leads to a substantial expansion of the central bank's balance sheet, as well as a large quantity of excess reserves in the banking sector which incentivizes the banks to increase lending to the real economy. Figure 8.12 illustrates that the Fed initially expanded its balance sheet with emergency lending to financial institutions and currency swaps to other central banks worldwide, later substituted by purchases of mortgage-backed securities. Later on, the Fed bought long-term treasuries at a large scale.

Table 8.3 shows the different stages of the Fed's quantitative easing after the 2007–2009 crisis. The most noteworthy is the third stage, QE3 or "QE Infinity." By September 2012, the interbank lending rate in the USA was as low as in normal times,

Table 8.3 Quantitative easing of the federal reserve

QE1 (11.2008–10.2009)	• $500 billion MBS, 11.2008–03.2009 • $750 billion MBS, 03.2009–08.2010 • $300 billion Treasury securities, 03.2009–10.2009 • $200 billion agency debt, 11.2008–08.2010
QE2 (11.2010–06.2011)	• $600 billion Treasury securities
QE3 ("QE Infinity") (09.2012–10.2014)	• $40 billion MBS per month, 09.2012–11.2012 • $85 billion MBS and Treasury securities per month, 12.2012–03.2014 • $55 billion MBS and Treasury securities per month, 04.2014–10.2014

the financial system was back to shape and ready to restart, however, the real economy was stuck in a deep recession, especially the unemployment rate reached 10%. To further stimulate the economy at the zero lower bound, the Fed committed to purchasing securities at a large scale with an open end: The Fed announced it would not stop easing unless the employment situation was improved. Such radical measure went on for one and half years until the unemployment returned to the natural rate. Asset purchasing was downscaled from early 2014Q2, and eventually terminated in October 2014. As shown in Fig. 8.12, the assets on the Fed's balance sheet expanded to $4.5 trillion after 6 years of QE, five times as much as the pre-crisis level.

Figure 8.13 illustrates the impact of QE programs on long-term interest rates. In November 2008, long-term rates for risky bonds (such as Baa rated US corporate bonds) spiked despite cuts in the Fed funds target rate. Unconventional policies succeeded in stabilizing long-term rates. The shaded phases mark the different periods of QE programs (QE1, QE2, and QE3). The rate on 10-year US treasuries declined substantially until May 22, 2013. At that time, the Fed started to hint that it may start tapering off (reduce and reverse) the QE program. Tapering was officially announced not before December 18, 2013.

In the recession that followed the crisis, several other central banks switched to a regime of quantitative easing as well, such as the Bank of Japan (BoJ), European Central Bank (ECB), Riksbank of Sweden, with unemployment staying high at the zero lower bound, threatening the danger of deflation. Table 8.4, Figs. 8.14 and 8.15 present the phases of QE conducted by the ECB and the Riksbank, respectively.

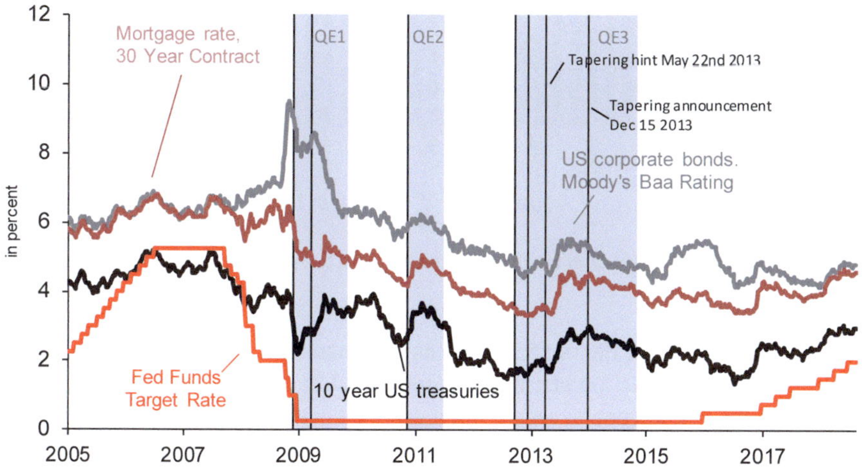

Fig. 8.13 Fed funds target rate vs. long-term rates and phases of QE programs. Since mid of December 2008 till December 2015, the Fed funds target rate was held close to zero. Long-term rates for risky bonds (such as Baa rated US corporate bonds) spiked in November 2008

Table 8.4 Quantitative easing of the European Central Bank (as of October 2018)

Stage 1	• Covered Bond Purchase ProgramsCBPP €60 billion 05.2009–06.2010CBPP2 €16.4 billion 11.2011–10.2012 • Securities Markets Program (SMP) 10.5.2010–6.9.2012€111 billion purchases of government debt securities of distressed countries in the Euro area held to maturity
Stage 2 (03.2015–12.2018)	• Expanded asset purchase program (APP) Purchases in public and private sector securities amounting to €60 billion per month from March 2015 (extended to €80 billion from April 2016 till March 2017). Reduced to €30 billion in January 2018 and further to €15 billion in October 2018. Projected to be terminated in December 2018. Purchases include covered bonds and asset-backed securities, but mainly public sector purchases (PSPP) of Euro area bonds from central governments, agencies, and European institutions, held in the Euro system (see Fig. 8.14)

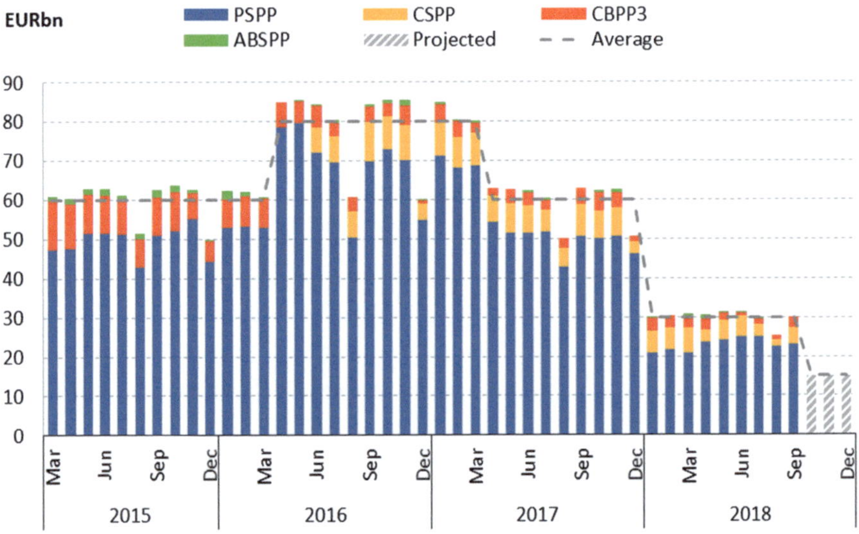

Fig. 8.14 ECB's expanded asset purchase program (APP): Net purchases of assets by the ECB per month

The vertical axis in Fig. 8.15a shows net purchases of government bonds by the Swedish Riksbank. Net purchases were concluded end of year 2017, but principal payments and coupon payments are still reinvested in the government bond portfolio until the middle of 2019. From then on, the Riksbank's holdings of government bonds are expected to decrease (Fig. 8.15b). In August 2018, total Riksbank's government overall bond holdings amounted to around SEK 330 billion. They are projected (as of September 2018) to decrease slowly with the ending of reinvestment policy.

Quantitative easing led to a substantial expansion of the monetary base. Figure 8.16 illustrates the increase in the monetary base in the USA, UK, Euro area,

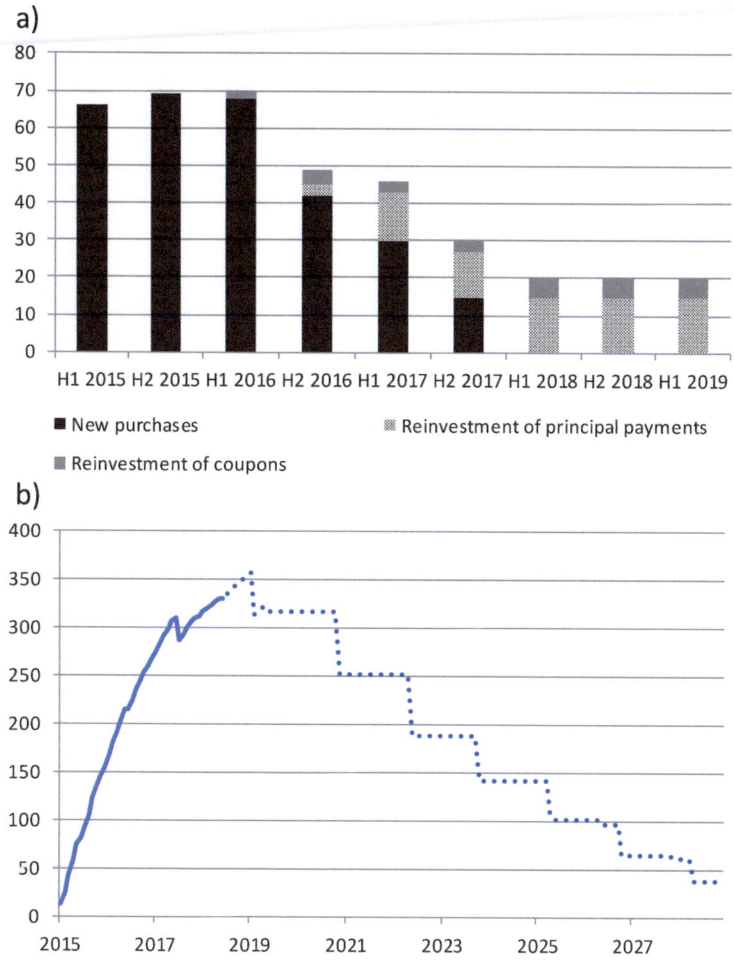

Fig. 8.15 Swedish Riksbank's purchases and reinvestments (**a**) and holdings (**b**) of government bonds (nominal amounts, SEK billion)

Japan and Switzerland, with the level in September 2008 being normalized to 100 in each case. Figure 8.17 shows the evolution of central bank's balance sheet as a share of GDP. In Japan and Switzerland, with the balance sheet having been large relative to GDP already before the crisis, the share reached 75–100% at the end of 2015.

The monetary easing practice of central banks, qualitative or quantitative, is highly controversial. The Wallace Irrelevance Theorem (Wallace, 1981) poses a theoretical challenge doubting the effectiveness of these policies. It is a version of Barro-Ricardian equivalence for monetary policy: With quantitative easing, the central bank swaps long-term against short-term government bonds. With a complete set of futures markets, the maturity of bonds of the same issuer held by private agents should be irrelevant. According to Ricardian equivalence, households should

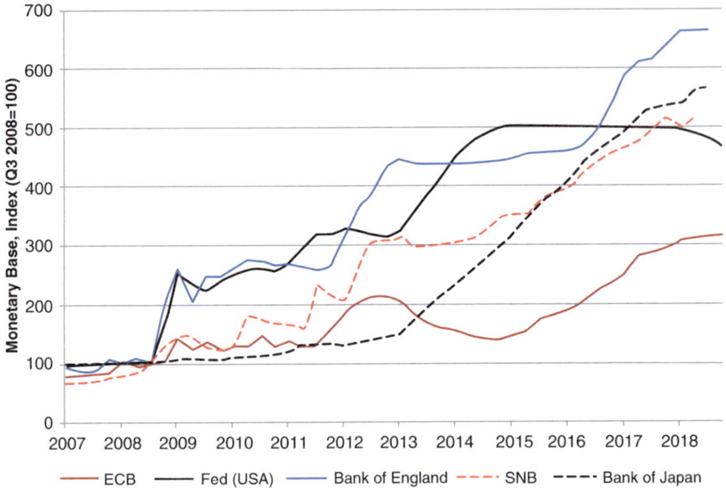

Fig. 8.16 Expansion of monetary base, starting from September 2008

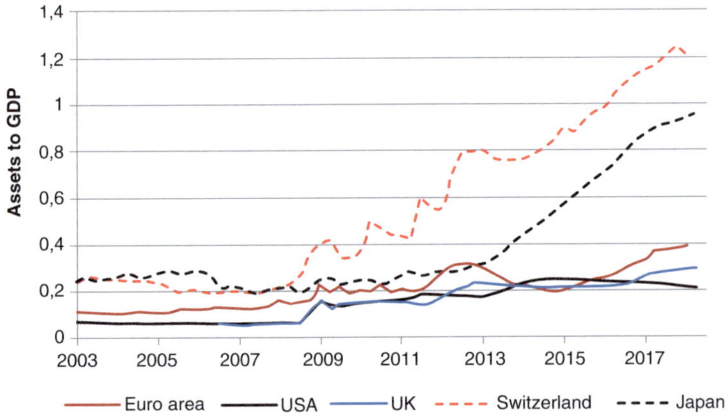

Fig. 8.17 Central bank assets as a percent of gross domestic product

not respond in their intertemporal consumption decisions when holding more short-term rather than long-term bonds of same quality. Similar, with qualitative easing the central bank swaps government securities with banks for risky, illiquid assets. With risks of financial assets transferred from the private sector to the central bank, these risks do not vanish into thin air. Instead, they are taken over by government authorities and thus in the end by the taxpayer. Again, with perfect markets private agent's wealth and so consumption should stay unchanged (see Sect. 9.2.1 for details).

The answer is that the assumptions of the Wallace Irrelevance Theorem do not hold in reality. Heterogeneous agents cannot trade via perfect inter-temporal markets. In the presence of financial frictions, they have to trade via banks or other financial intermediaries. When there is misallocation of assets with different maturity risk such that the interbank market fails during crisis, central bank's provision of liquid assets can help to restore the optimal allocation of liquidity risks. As discussed in Chap. 9, the transmission mechanism of monetary policy has to cope with many financial frictions. These frictions may get the banking sector stuck in the inferior equilibrium, and the central bank's easing policies may push the banks out of the undesirable equilibrium, restoring their normal business. On the other hand, the dramatic expansion of the central banks' balance sheets may encourage excessive risk taking in search of higher yields, creating bubbles in certain asset classes. Chapter 10 analyzes these mechanisms in more detail.

Focus Box: Measuring the Shadow Rate

After 2008, central banks cut policy rates close to zero. For a long time, the usual indicator of monetary policy, the short-term rate, stayed unchanged at low rates close to or in some regions even below zero. Nevertheless, central banks have implemented a huge variety of unconventional monetary policies in order to try to further ease financial conditions. They implemented various unconventional measures, such as large-scale asset purchases and long-maturity lending to banks. More recently, some central banks in Europe like the ECB, the Swiss, Swedish and Danish central banks, and the Bank of Japan cut deposit rates even below zero. If we just look at the key short-term policy rates, the impact of such unconventional measures is not captured.

How can we account for the effect of such unconventional measures? Some researchers try to use information from the term structure of interest rates (the forward rates) aiming to calculate the so-called shadow short-term rate. They interpret this shadow rate as an indicator of the stance of monetary policy, taking unconventional policy measures into account. Wu and Xia (2016) apply a statistical method (an unobserved components model) to forward rates on US Treasuries in order to compute such a "shadow rate" for the periods when the policy rate is constrained at the zero lower bound. They have estimated such a shadow rate also for the UK and the Euro area, making their data are available online at the Atlanta Fed homepage.

Figure 8.18 shows their estimates for the Fed and the ECB. According to their indicator, the Fed succeeded in easing policy substantially until 2015, even though the effective Fed funds rate stayed nearly unchanged at close to zero since 2009. In contrast, the ECB was initially rather restrictive before starting easing aggressively in 2015. These charts seem quite suggestive. But one needs to be aware of the limitations of such calculations. As Bauer and Rudebusch (2016) argue, the estimated shadow short-term rates differ markedly depending on the particular model used and the assumed values of the numerical lower bound for interest rates. Model-implied shadow short rates are highly sensitive to both the specific short-term yields included in the model and the assumption about the minimum rate—the imposed lower bound on

(continued)

yields. Obviously, a key question is how to estimate the anticipated timing of the liftoff of the policy rate from the ZLB. A common approach is to use the horizon at which forward rates cross a given threshold. Wu and Xia (2016) use a rate of 0.25 as the estimate of the expected date of liftoff and so get the line with the steepest fall. As shown in Fig. 8.19 taken from Bauer and Rudebusch (2016), the calculated shadow rate is much higher if lower rates such as 0, 0.05, or 0.1 are imposed as lower bound. As they point out, this lack of robustness raises a warning flag about using shadow short-term rates as a measure of monetary policy.

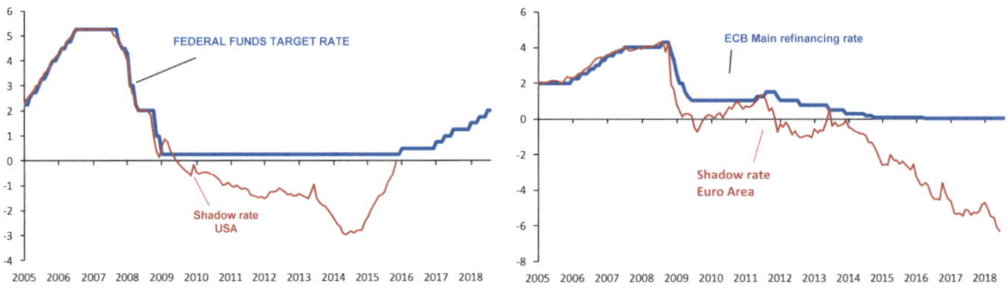

Fig. 8.18 Shadow rates for the USA and the Euro area (source: Wu & Xia, 2016)

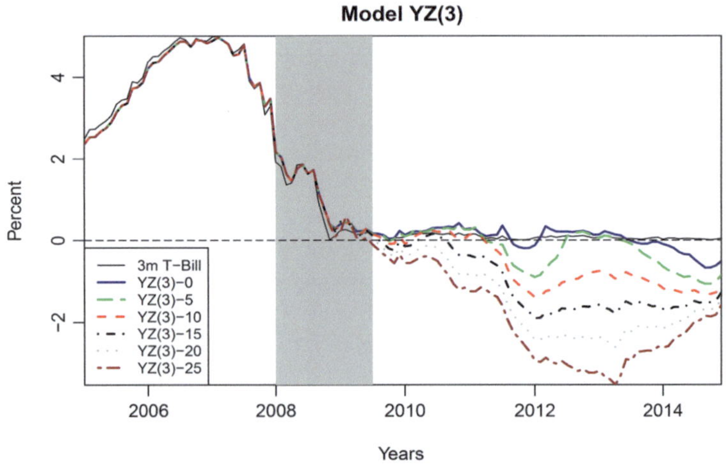

Fig. 8.19 Lack of robustness of shadow rates (Source: Bauer & Rudebusch, 2016; online appendix https://www.frbsf.org/economic-research/economiFsts/glenn-rudebusch/)

Focus Box: Helicopter Money and Wallace Irrelevance

What is the difference between quantitative easing and helicopter money? Both have the same fiscal implications, but QE preserves the traditional separation between monetary and fiscal policy. Under QE, the government (the Treasury) has the authority to decide how to allocate the net present value of the operations. It could make direct transfers to private agents or raise government spending. With helicopter money, the central bank would be directly involved in fiscal policy (such as handing out cash as transfer).

QE increases the monetary base through a purchase of government bonds by the central bank, committed to maintain the monetary base permanently at the higher level. With helicopter money, the central bank prints new base money to finance a transfer to the public and commits never to retire the newly issued money. Both operations lead to the same equilibrium as long as the path of government purchases is the same and taxes are raised to the extent necessary to finance those purchases and to service the outstanding government debt, after transfers of the central bank's seignorage income to the Treasury.

Under QE, the central bank acquires assets, but it rebates the interest paid on the government bonds back to the Treasury, such that the budgets of all parties are the same as if no government bonds were actually bought, as is explicitly the case with helicopter money. So, both QE and helicopter money are a mix of monetary and fiscal policy: Fiscal programs are financed through money creation. The key distinction is that under QE there is a clear separation of assignments: As long as monetary dominance prevails, the central bank's operations aim to restore price stability, whereas the fiscal authority decides about the appropriate path of fiscal policy, taking the fiscal implications of central banks' actions properly into account.

The effects would be different only if the public perceives the consequences for future policy as different. In contrast to the case of QE, people might expect the increase in the monetary base to be permanent with helicopter money. Furthermore, if people get an immediate transfer, they might believe that they can afford to spend more, which may not be the case for QE. With separation between monetary and fiscal policy, the fiscal authority would make the transfers and issue debt to pay for them. It does not need to tax people later to service its debt, as long as the debt service is covered by the revenues generated via QE operations. Under QE, the central bank conducts open market operations, holds assets against the liabilities that it issues, and distributes its earnings to the Treasury. The key difference is the role of assignments of tasks.

When a central bank engages in QE, it exchanges government debt for money. As shown in the chapter on the interaction between fiscal and monetary policy, by issuing money instead of debt, the intertemporal government

(continued)

budget constraint is indeed relaxed as long as the interest rate paid on money is lower than the interest rate on short-term debt generating seigniorage revenue in the government wealth constraint. But at the ZLB, $i_d = i_m = 0$, so no seigniorage revenue arises. The same also applies outside the ZLB as long as the central bank pays interest on money holding (that is if $i_d = i_m$). In that case, money and bonds are equivalent forms of finance. Nevertheless, some claim that even with $i_d = i_m$, printing money can be a cheaper source of finance for the government than issuing bonds. They argue that by creating base money, private agents hold real wealth because money is a non-redeemable liability. Buiter (2014, p. 9) frames that argument as follows:

> Fiat base money is an asset (wealth) to the holder (the owner—households...) but does not constitute in any meaningful sense a liability to the issuer (the "borrower"—the State or the Central Bank as an agent of the State). ... UK currency notes worth £X carry the proud inscription "... promise to pay the bearer the sum of £X" but this merely means that the Bank of England will pay out the face value of any genuine Bank of England note no matter how old. The promise to pay stands good for all time but simply means that the Bank will always be willing to exchange one (old, faded) £10 Bank of England note for one (new, crisp) £ 10 Bank of England note (or even for two £ 5 Bank of England notes). Because it promises only money in exchange for money, this "promise to pay" is, in fact, a statement of the irredeemable nature of Bank of England notes.

Buiter (2014) argues that the government's solvency constraint needs only include the present discounted value of its net nonmonetary liabilities, ignoring net financial liabilities out of base money in the No-Ponzi game condition due to its irredeemability.

$$\frac{M(t)+B(t)}{P(t)} = \int_t^{\infty} \left(T(v) - G(v) + i(v)\frac{M(v)}{P(v)} \right) e^{-\int_t^v r(u)du} dv + \lim_{v \to \infty} \frac{M(v)}{P(v)} e^{-\int_t^v r(u)du}$$

This version of the government's solvency constraint seems to suggest that public spending can be financed without any tax obligations by printing base money which is held permanently by the private sector. This argument, however, neglects the fact that irredeemability of base money crucially depends on the private sector trusting the central bank to implement price stability. Even though at the ZLB, the risk of inflation is negligible, the central bank may be forced later in normal times to redeem part of the base money issued in order ensure price stability. If not, the private sector may lose trust in money holding. The resulting overshooting of inflation might drive down the value of irredeemable base money to zero.

8.4 Channels for Monetary Transmission

By conducting monetary policy, the central bank changes the level of bank reserves and shifts the equilibrium in the market for bank reserves. However, monetary policy only has an impact on the macro economy if the real economy responds to these changes in the banking sector. Hence, the transmission mechanisms from the banking sector to the macro economy are crucial to the efficiency of monetary policy. The interaction between banks and the real economy also affects the exposure of an economy to financial risks, or, its financial stability. In practice, there exist different channels through which the monetary transmission mechanisms work. The experience during recent years has challenged the traditional understanding of the transmission of monetary policy.

8.4.1 The Interest Rate Channel

The classical interest rate channel focuses on the responses in banks' liabilities to monetary policy shocks, which is based on the assumption that the banks' reserve requirement is always close to be binding, since banks minimize excess reserves to reduce the opportunity costs of holding cash. Suppose that the central bank tightens monetary policy by draining bank reserves through security sales, the bank reserves will fall below the required level, and the cost of raising reserves in the interbank market will be higher due to the aggregate shortage in reserves. Therefore, banks will be forced to scale-down their checkable deposits to fulfill the reserve requirement. This restricts their capacity of issuing new loans to firms and households. In order to induce depositors to move away from checkable accounts, banks managing stylized balance sheets as shown in Table 8.2 have to raise the interest rates paid on term deposits, bank bonds, and the other funding sources. The higher interest rates paid on these liabilities of longer maturities imply a higher average long-term interest rate for the economy, which incentivizes households to spend less and save more, reducing aggregate demand today. Overall, lower bank lending together with lower aggregate demand mean a reduction in the real activities—the tightening in monetary policy ends up with a contraction in macro economy.

The interest rate channel is the standard paradigm for presenting the transmission mechanism of monetary policy in many macroeconomic textbooks. It provides valid insights for policy discussions. However, the basic assumption that the banks' reserve requirement should be binding rarely holds in reality in the past decade, when banks often hold large excess reserves. Furthermore, changes in the short-term interest rate are usually rather modest. Empirically, however, they seem to lead to relatively large changes in economic activity. If the impact on the real economy works only through the traditional interest rate channel, aggregate demand must react implausibly strong to interest rate changes. Obviously, monetary policy also generates impact on the real economy via other channels.

The availability of credit plays a crucial role to understand why modest changes in short-term rates can lead to relatively large movements in credit costs and economic activity. We consider two distinct credit channels, the balance sheet channel and the bank lending channel. The balance sheet channel derives financial market imperfections from agency costs. It shows that changes in interest rates are amplified by large changes in credit costs with credit spreads and term premia adjusting. The bank lending channel addresses fragility in the banking sector. It may affect aggregate spending in a way not directly caused by changes in interest rates. Losses of capital on bad loans or a tightening of the regulatory environment may cause a fall in bank lending or even a breakdown of financial intermediation, leading to a credit crunch.

8.4.2 Credit Channel 1: The Balance Sheet Channel

Bernanke and Gertler (1989) have proposed one such channel, the balance sheet channel. It works through frictions on the *borrowers*' side of the economy. The credit channel helps to understand the empirical fact that the impact of monetary policy on the real economy is much larger than implied by the responses in the loan and deposit rates through the standard interest rate channel. Obviously, there must be other factors, so-called "financial accelerators," outside of the banks. They amplify the impact of monetary policy on banks themselves.

These amplifiers come from the frictions that widely exist in the real-world lender–borrower relationships. In a frictionless world, funds will end up in the hands where they are needed most. The borrowers will pay the lenders prices that reflect the scarcity of funds. However, in reality, problems in the lender–borrower relationships often prevent such efficient allocation to be implemented: Borrowers may not be able to find lenders when they need to borrow; borrowers know their own projects better than lenders, such asymmetric information implies that borrowers may cheat on the true returns of the projects, and so on. These frictions create a wedge between lending and funding rate in the banking sector, imposing a constraint on the debtors' borrowing capacity. Depending on the source of friction, monetary policy may help to narrow the wedge and thus push the allocation of funds closer to the efficient level.

Most models motivating the credit channel are exploring one of the following three types of financial frictions:

- Incomplete market. Credit constraints may just come from missing markets, i.e., sometimes borrowers can only borrow from alternative, more expensive sources when funds are needed. This reduces the demand for credit, leaving the real activity below the optimal level.
- Costly state verification. After borrowers get loans and start running projects, it is costly for the lenders to verify the true outcome of the projects. Therefore, this creates an incentive for a borrower to misreport her project's return, i.e., report low return when the true return is high, in order to return less to the lender and pocket some private benefit. The consequence is that the borrower can only borrow less than she actually needs, such that she needs to add her own fund to

start the project. Her wealth, or, "net worth," thus determines her borrowing capacity.

- Principal–agent problems such as moral hazard and adverse selection. As the borrowers' efforts in running the projects cannot be observed by the lenders, borrowers always have the incentive to mismanage the projects, obtaining private benefits and leaving all the bad outcomes to the lenders. Therefore, lenders have to leave some rent to borrowers to induce them to behave well or take borrowers' projects as collateral so that lenders can seize the projects and recover some value once they suspect borrowers to misbehave. Such problems also put constraints on borrowers' borrowing capacity.

All these agency problems between borrowers and lenders create a wedge between external finance cost and the opportunity cost of internal finance. Even though specific models differ on the precise way central bank policy influences credit constraints, a general prediction is that the balance sheet channel magnifies the impact of the interest rate changes on private borrowing rates via the impact on credit spreads. In contrast to a frictionless economy, the borrower's capacity to raise outside funds is limited by her net worth, restricting intertemporal trading.

8.4.3 Credit Channel 2: The Bank Lending Channel

The balance sheet channel focuses on frictions affecting borrowers. Banks as intermediaries are treated as a veil: They are seen as passive actors who merely enable transactions between lenders and borrowers. Financial intermediaries may have superior skills in evaluating borrowers (lower agency costs), so it will be efficient to channel credit through intermediaries. Savers deposit funds with intermediaries and these lend to borrowers. Agency problems will also limit the ability of intermediaries to obtain funds from depositors, again creating a wedge between deposit and loan rates. These spreads widen in bad times, raising the cost of funds to borrowers. Seen in that way, modelling intermediaries explicitly does not provide much additional insight for understanding the dynamic response to shocks.

As impressively illustrated by the recent financial crisis, intermediaries, however, are not just a veil, rather they play a special role in the economy, possibly being a source of trouble themselves. Bank failures can have severe adverse impacts on the economy. When there is the risk of a breakdown of financial intermediation, standard transmission mechanisms of monetary policy are likely to be severely endangered. For many firms, particularly small firms, bank loans represent the principal source of funds for investment. For a long time, the bank lending channel emphasized this special role. Before the crisis, however, many models abstracted from this issue, trusting that in case of a failure of banks, financial markets will easily find other ways to replace them as substitutes. The emergence of less regulated shadow banks seemed to confirm this market view. But in crisis times, highly leveraged shadow banks relying on market liquidity to roll over short-term debt turned out to be among the first to run into trouble themselves, having problems raising funds from other intermediaries. Markets, which appeared to be perfectly liquid, suddenly dried up completely. Disruptions in the interbank market severely affected real activity. Financial markets became segmented, generating an inefficient allocation of funds among intermediaries.

In order to better understand the role of banks, we need to treat banks as active players in the financial market, who manage different components in their balance sheets facing real and monetary shocks. In Chap. 9, we discuss various models of the role of intermediaries. In Sect. 9.5, we look at incentives for liquidity management: Banks face market and funding liquidity risk. Holding excess liquidity above the required reserve level is costly, but helps to avoid shortfalls in reserves after withdrawal shocks. Presenting a simplified version of the model of Bianchi-Bigio (2018), we explicitly characterize the trade-off a bank faces on the liability side when deciding about its loan supply. We show that bank lending is constrained by banks' liquidity management practice even in normal times.

Bank equity is also an important determinant of both the bank's funding cost and its lending growth. Banks as intermediaries combine borrowed funds with their own funds as capital, lending to borrowers. Well capitalized banks enjoy lower funding costs and lend more. The higher the capital of a bank, the more it can lend and the easier it is to borrow more from its creditors on good terms compared to a poorly capitalized bank.

8.5 Summary

Well-functioning monetary policy uses a combination of various tools and relies on a well-functioning banking sector, transmitting monetary policy targets into supply of credits that further affects real activities in the macro economy. This chapter gave a survey of the channels of monetary transmission mechanisms and showed how they work via various tools affecting intermediation in the banking sector. Section 8.2 analyzed traditional transmission mechanisms. We focused on the link between central bank's balance sheet management and the transmission into the banking sector. We discussed repo agreements and the role of collateral and showed that many central banks use a corridor of interest rates with the discount rate as upper bound and the interest rate paid on bank reserves as lower bound.

Financial crises impede the resilience of the banking sector, interrupting standard transmission mechanisms, and triggering huge spikes in credit spreads. Section 8.3 illustrates this failure during the Great Recession and analyzes various unconventional policy responses, in particular the policy of qualitative and quantitative easing. We have seen that these measures can drive the shadow rate (as a measure of the effective stance of monetary policy taking unconventional policies explicitly into account) into negative territory. Finally, Sect. 8.4 emphasized the key role of two important credit channels: The balance sheet channel and the bank lending channel. The following chapters will provide various theoretical foundations for these channels.

References

Adrian, T., & Shin, H. (2009). Financial intermediaries and monetary policy. In *Handbook of monetary economics* (pp. 601–650). Amsterdam: Elsevier.

Bauer, M. D., & Rudebusch, G. D. (2016). Monetary policy expectations at the zero lower bound. *Journal of Money, Credit and Banking, 48*, 1439–1465.

Bech, M. L., & Monnet, C. (2013). The impact of unconventional monetary policy on the overnight interbank market. In A. Heath, M. Lilley, & M. Manning (Eds.), *Liquidity and funding markets* (pp. 147–177). Sydney, NSW: Reserve Bank of Australia.

Bernanke, B., & Gertler, M. (1989). Agency costs, net worth, and business fluctuations. *American Economic Review, 79*(1), 14–31.

Bianchi, J., & Bigio, S. (2018). Banks, liquidity management and monetary policy. *Working Paper*, Federal Reserve Bank of Minneapolis.

Brunnermeier, M. K. (2009). Deciphering the liquidity and credit crunch 2007-2008. *Journal of Economic Perspectives, 23*(1), 77–100.

Buiter, W. (2014). The simple analytics of helicopter money: Why it works – always. *Economics, 8*, 2014–2028.

Wallace, N. (1981). A Modigliani-Miller theorem for open-market operations. *American Economic Review, 71*(3), 267–274.

Wu, C., & Xia, F. D. (2016). Measuring the macroeconomic impact of monetary policy at the zero lower bound. *Journal of Money, Credit, and Banking, 48*(2–3), 253–291.

Financial Frictions and Monetary Policy 9

9.1 Introduction

In practice, the effect of monetary policy work through the transmission mechanism as presented in the last chapter. The central bank announces its monetary policy rate, and the target rate is implemented through open market operation. Banks respond by adjusting the components of their assets, increasing or reducing credit supply to the real economy, which has further real consequence in investment, output, employment, and consumption.

However, what is often missing in standard theories of monetary transmission mechanism is the role of financial sector, or, banks. Banks are treated as black boxes. Indeed, in normal times, banks function as they are supposed to, so policymakers only need to focus on the final outcome in the macro economy without looking at what happens along the way.

Unfortunately, in reality, financial sector is not a static black box, and financial markets are never perfect. Many frictions prevent banks from allocating credit to those agents needing it most. These frictions induce banks to overreact to macroeconomic shocks, increasing output volatility. Such financial frictions, therefore, have redistribution effects in transmitting monetary policy. Monetary policy may have the potential to reduce distortions arising from financial frictions, improving social welfare. Furthermore, conducting monetary policy through open market operation implies that the central bank is an active player in the financial market. So monetary policy implementation changes the risk components in banks' balance sheet. Banks adapt to monetary policy by adjusting their balance sheet—not only the components, but also the risks they take; monetary policy thus has implication for financial stability: it shifts the risk level in the financial system, and changes the likelihood of systemic events such as financial crises.

In this chapter, we mainly focus on the financial frictions that hinder the transmission of monetary policy to the real economy, and leave monetary policy—financial stability linkages to the final chapter. Such financial frictions may come from many sources, including:

J. Cao, G. Illing, *Money: Theory and Practice*, Springer Texts in Business and Economics, https://doi.org/10.1007/978-3-030-19697-4_9

- *Incomplete markets*: In reality, some markets are missing. With markets being segmented market participants cannot trade specific risks with each other. So these risks can no longer be properly priced and insured, creating a risk premium for certain assets. The model of Cúrdia and Woodford (2015) presented in Sect. 9.2 provides a tractable structure to address these issues. In that model, households cannot always insure against the uncertainty in their demand for consumption, forcing them to borrow from banks; this creates a premium in banks' lending rate and distorts consumption. Therefore, optimal monetary policy needs to respond to such lending premium, alongside with inflation and output gap, to bring the economy closer to the first-best outcome.
- *Principal–agent problems*: As lenders and borrowers cannot perfectly monitor each other, typical principal–agent problems arise in financial intermediation. Problems may come from borrower side, for example, borrowers have the incentive to misreport the outcome of their loans and pocket some private benefit (Bernanke & Gertler, 1989, as in Sect. 9.3); problems may also come from bank side, who may divert assets for private consumption and declare bankruptcy (Bernanke–Gertler–Karadi model, as in Sect. 9.4). The consequence is that borrowers/banks need to have their own stakes in financial intermediation to align their interests with their counterparties, imposing constraints on the credit available in the real economy.
- *Maturity mismatch*: A key business model in banking is so-called "maturity transformation," i.e., banks invest in long-term projects by borrowing short-term debts, creating a mismatch of maturities between assets and liabilities. When the short-term debts are due, banks have to renew the debts with creditors, exposing themselves to rollover risks ("funding liquidity risk"). For this reason, in liquidity management, banks have to hold certain assets that can be easily converted to cash ("liquid assets," such as government bonds) to repay creditors if they cannot rollover all the debts. However, if creditors' cash demand is higher than the market value of the liquid assets, banks have to sell the other assets (such as loans to firms and households) that can only be converted to cash at a cost ("market liquidity risk"). This may lead to amplified damage to the real economy. The Bianchi–Bigio model in Sect. 9.5 focuses on this issue.
- *Leverage cycles*: Economic agents are heterogeneous in their preferences. Some are less risk averse/optimistic than the others, so they are natural borrowers to increase their investment opportunities (or, "taking leverage"). The leverage borrowers take is restricted by risk management: They need to hold sufficient equity to absorb losses. When the real economy booms, borrowers' profit becomes higher, raising the value of their equity and allowing them to borrow more (or, "leverage up"), and vice versa ("leverage cycles"), amplifying the initial shocks, and increasing the volatilities in the economy. In this chapter, we present two mechanisms that generate leverage cycles: Through asset prices (the Shin model in Sect. 9.6), or through funding supply of lenders in general equilibrium (the Geanakopolos model in Sect. 9.7).

9.2 Incomplete Markets: The Cúrdia–Woodford Model

9.2.1 Wallace Neutrality as Reference Point

In the New Keynesian framework outlined in previous chapters, the size of the central bank's balance sheet plays no role at all. The short-term nominal interest rate (or better: the expected path of nominal rates from now on till indefinite future) is the only relevant policy tool. Any change in the size or composition of the central bank's balance sheet leaving the expected future path of nominal rates constant will have no impact on the real economy. Such central bank open market operations are simply irrelevant in that framework. Based on that insight, there was strong skepticism about the effectiveness of unconventional policy measures in the academic community. Many argued that such measures will be futile. Others instead warned that expanding the balance sheet is likely to cause hyper inflation; they worried about tax payer's burden when central banks engage in trading risky assets. In contrast, those pushing for unconventional policy hoped that these measures will help to dampen risk premia and to lower yields on long-term bonds. Obviously, these contradictory claims are based on hugely different views about the proper transmission mechanism.

The irrelevance result provides a good reference point for evaluating these inconsistent statements. It is important to understand the conditions driving that result. Essentially it is a variant of the Ricardian equivalence theorem. Ricardian equivalence says that—taking some path for government spending as given—the timing for generating revenue is irrelevant: In a general equilibrium analysis, it does not matter whether expenditures are financed by taxes raised today or by running a deficit, financed by taxes in later periods. The underlying reason is an argument of perfect arbitrage: Since—in present value terms—future tax obligations are the same for a given level of spending, forward-looking private agents would simply increase savings today in order to off set future tax obligations from debt financing. The key assumption behind that theorem is that there are no trading frictions preventing perfect arbitrage: All agents are able to trade any future contingent claims today at the same prices; furthermore, taxes are not distortionary.

Neil Wallace (1981) applied this logic to open market operations. He called his paper "A Modigliani-Miller theorem for open-market operations." In a frictionless world with competitive asset pricing, the market price of any asset is determined simply by the present value of the random payoffs to which it is a claim. The present value of an asset can be calculated using stochastic discount factors (the asset pricing kernel) determined by the representative household's marginal utility of income in different future states of the world. As long as a mere reshuffling of assets between the central bank and the private sector does not change the real quantity of resources available for consumption in each state of the world, the representative household's marginal utility of income in different states of the world should not change. Hence the pricing kernel cannot change, and so the market price of these assets will not change either, provided the risky returns to which the asset represents a claim have not changed.

Assume the central bank takes some risky assets into its own balance sheet, enabling private agents to hold more of less risky securities (safe assets that pay out the same amount during financial turmoil as in calmer states). As long as this operation does not make the risk disappear from the economy, the central bank's earnings on its portfolio will now be lower in the crisis state, resulting in lower revenues distributed to the treasury. If so, the government needs to collect higher taxes from the private sector in that state. But then the household's after-tax income will be just as dependent on the underlying risk as before. The household, anticipating this risk, will take precautions against that event in the same way as if it held the underlying asset directly. So asset prices will be unaffected by such an open market operation.

Just as with Ricardian equivalence, this irrelevance breaks down if frictions in intermediation prevent perfect trading on asset markets. In that case, market prices may not reflect adequately the true risks in the economy. This will be relevant in particular if there are multiple equilibria due to the lack of private insurance contracts. In that case, by intervening in the market a different, superior equilibrium may be reached, affecting overall total risk in the economy. If the risk absorbing capacity of the government is larger than the capacity in the private sector, providing more safe assets may be welfare improving.

When participation in trading in particular markets is limited, changes in the central bank balance sheet can have real effects by relaxing such binding constraints. Private agents seeking to borrow at long maturity frequently face severe and binding collateral requirements, paying much higher interest rates than the government. Liquid assets will then provide a nonpecuniary return—supplying transactions services by relaxing constraints that would otherwise restrict the transactions in which the holders of the asset can engage.

An expansion of the balance sheet will be effective if it helps to satiate private agents with base money, implementing the Friedman rule by setting the nominal rate equal to zero. Any expansion of the supply of base money beyond the satiation level, however, will not work in a world of Wallace neutrality. But note that unconventional measures such as buying additional government bonds may nevertheless be effective if they work as signaling device, that is, if they are seen as a commitment to keep interest rate policy low in the future for an extended period. In that case, however, the impact comes not from these measures themselves but rather from the perceived commitment to change the future interest rate path. Finally, those being concerned about balance sheet risk and hyperinflation may view unconventional measures as signalling an interest rate path inducing high inflation in the future.

9.2.2 Financial Frictions with Heterogeneous Agents

To understand the impact of financial frictions we need to introduce a role for intermediation between heterogeneous agents: Some agents want to save, and others want to borrow, and frictions may impede markets for intertemporal trading.

Obviously, a representative agent framework cannot address this issue. In reality, households are heterogeneous in their endowments, in their abilities and in their preferences for consumption across time. A straightforward way to introduce heterogeneity is to assume (temporary) differences in the individual rate of time preferences.

Nevertheless, in a frictionless world, borrowers and savers still would be able to trade contingent claims with each other at perfectly competitive markets without the need to resort to intermediaries. As long as there are well-functioning markets to diversify risks, they can always trade with each other and so achieve an efficient allocation. However, if some markets are missing or malfunctioning, agents may face divergent inter-temporal prices and may end up in an inferior, distorted equilibrium. This may justify a potential role for monetary policy to partially replace the missing market by taxing or subsidizing households, and so move the economy closer toward the frictionless equilibrium.

Intertemporal trading across agents is limited due to information costs: For a saver, it is costly to assess whether a specific borrower will be able to honor the contract. This is of particular concern if the payout of the contract is state contingent—that is, if repayments are linked to the actual income of the borrower as in equity-like contracts: The investor receiving part of the actual return of the project funded also shares risk in the project, and so needs information about the true outcome.

If the outcome is hard to verify, the borrower always has an incentive to understate the own return in order to cut down on payments. Thus, the lender may need to incur high verification costs in order to check the truth and be able to prove claims to be false in front of the court. It is natural to assume that intermediaries specializing in those activities have a comparative advantage with lower verification costs. To minimize these costs, frequently it will be optimal to use debt contracts: Such contracts specify a fixed repayment independent of actual return; so verification is needed only in those cases the actual return is not sufficient for repayment. In that case, the borrower defaults.

A key challenge for dynamic general equilibrium analysis with heterogeneous agents is to keep the structure simple enough to keep the model tractable. When heterogeneous agents are repeatedly hit by idiosyncratic shocks with time passing, aggregation across agents gets increasingly complex; a careful analysis would need to keep track of the specific states of each agent, so complicating computation enormously. It would be impossible to maintain the simple recursive structure which makes the representative agent framework so tractable, reducing monetary policy analysis to simple log–linear relations. To avoid that problem, Cúrdia and Woodford (2015) use an elegant modelling technique which allows to keep a simple recursive structure. At each point in time, households are either borrowers or lenders (savers). Most of the time, each household can borrow or lend only through intermediaries, at a one-period, riskless nominal rate. This rate is different for savers and borrowers. At some stages, however, all households have intermittent access to an insurance agency. Only on those occasions, state-contingent contracts across all households are enforceable.

This modelling technique allows both for incomplete contracts (frictions in intermediation) during times when the insurance contracts are not feasible and at the same time for simple long-run aggregation: Regardless of their specific history of spending opportunities, the long-run marginal utility of income will be the same for all households.

9.2.3 The Basic Model

Cúrdia and Woodford (2015) model incomplete markets to modify the standard New Keynesian framework. They introduce the following departures from the standard model:

- Households are heterogeneous in their utility functions. All have standard neo-classical preferences $u^{\tau_t(i)}(c_t(i), \xi_t)$, with $c_t(i)$ as the real consumption of household i in period t. ξ_t is an aggregate shock to taste, and $\tau_t(i)$ denotes the type of the household in this period. Type τ may take on two values, b (being impatient or borrower) or s (being patient or saver). Depending on the specific shock, which determines the impatience between today and tomorrow, each household will be either a borrower or a saver. Those who are more impatient want to be borrowers. For all levels of consumption, impatient households (type b) have a higher marginal utility to consume than the patient types—the savers s, as

$$\frac{\partial u^b(c_t, \xi_t)}{\partial c_t} > \frac{\partial u^s(c_t, \xi_t)}{\partial c_t}.$$

  Initially each household belongs to one of the two types. With probability δ the household stays the same type in the next period. But with probability $1 - \delta$ $(0 < \delta < 1)$, a new household type is drawn next period. A change in a household's type changes its impatience to consume today relative to tomorrow. The household will be type b—a borrower—with probability is π_b $(0 < \pi_b < 1)$, and type s—a saver (being more patient and willing to save rather than borrow)—with probability $1 - \pi_b$. Technically, each household's type $\tau_t(i) \in \{b, s\}$ evolves as an independent two-state Markov chain.
- Impatient households are naturally borrowers, patient households savers. But due to financial frictions, savers, and borrowers cannot trade with each other on anonymous markets. Instead, if households want to consume more or less than their current income, they need banks as financial intermediaries to either deposit or borrow. Banks borrow d_t from savers and lend b_t. In Cúrdia and Woodford (2011, 2015), the frictions in intermediation are not modelled explicitly, but rather in a very stylized reduced form: Banks incur an operational cost $\Xi_t(b_t, R_t)$, that is, increasing in the amount of lending b_t and decreasing in the reserves R_t held at the central bank. The identity of balance sheet requires that the funds from deposits cover also operational cost: $d_t = b_t + \Xi_t(b_t, R_t)$.

- At some points in time, all households have access to an insurance agency, to insure themselves against the switch in types. If markets were complete, they would be able to sign a state contingent insurance policy right from the start, making sure that each household receives a compensation when it turns out to be impatient. Thus, the first best allocation of resources could be achieved. However, the friction here is that households can only access the insurance service and get compensated very infrequently; therefore, during periods when a household is not able to access the insurance, it has to rely on the banking service to partially mitigate the friction coming from the missing market. To simplify the analysis, assume that the dates on which a household is able to access the insurance service are exactly the same dates as those on which it draws a new type of preference. In the beginning of each period, with probability δ the household stays with the same type as in the previous period, and has no compensation from the insurance sector; with probability $1-\delta$ the household receives a transfer from the insurance service first, then it draws its type for this period and makes consumption, saving as well as borrowing decisions.

Households are able to sign state contingent contracts to insure against aggregate risks and also against the risk of being either borrower or lender. But transfers from these insurance contracts can be received only occasionally. This way, all households have exactly the same expectations about marginal utility of consumption far enough into the future. But between today and tomorrow, borrowers and lenders are heterogeneous and can trade only via intermediaries. The insurance market is incomplete so that households cannot always get compensation when they are impatient, and insurance compensation arrives before the households' types are drawn so that the insurance policy cannot be contingent on households' types. These frictions generate a wedge between banks' lending rate and saving rate, such that the impatient households are willing to pay a premium to borrow. Since all households of the same type are identical, they will have the same consumption.

Savers can deposit funds at a bank; they may also invest in short-term government bonds. Since bonds and bank deposits are perfect substitutes, they give the same return i_t^d. Borrowers can get funding only via financial intermediaries at the higher borrowing rate $i_t^b > i_t^d$ or $1+i_t^b = \left(1+i_t^d\right)(1+\omega_t)$. There is a spread $\omega_t = \left(i_t^b - i_t^d\right)/\left(1+i_t^d\right)$ between borrowing and savings rate. For each type, we have now a separate Euler condition. A representative household i's marginal utility here, denoted by $\lambda_t(i)$, still satisfies the Euler equation

$$\lambda_t(i) = \beta\left(1+i_t^\tau\right)E_t\left[\frac{\lambda_{t+1}(i)}{\Pi_{t+1}}\right]$$

in which Π_{t+1} denotes the gross inflation rate in $t+1$, and i_t^τ is the interest rate it faces in t, depending on its type τ. A saver receives the deposit rate i_t^d, whereas a borrower has to pay the borrowing rate i_t^b. The household's marginal utility in the future $\lambda_{t+1}(i)$ depends on its type, therefore, the Euler equation, characterizing the evolution of marginal utility for both types of households can be expressed as

$$\lambda_t^b = \beta E_t \left[\frac{1 + i_t^b}{\Pi_{t+1}} \left\{ \delta \, \lambda_{t+1}^b + (1 - \delta) \left[\pi_b \lambda_{t+1}^b + (1 - \pi_b) \lambda_{t+1}^s \right] \right\} \right]$$

for a borrower, and

$$\lambda_t^s = \beta E_t \left[\frac{1 + i_t^d}{\Pi_{t+1}} \left\{ \delta \, \lambda_{t+1}^s + (1 - \delta) \left[\pi_b \lambda_{t+1}^b + (1 - \pi_b) \lambda_{t+1}^s \right] \right\} \right]$$

for a saver.

It can be easily seen that even with heterogeneous households these two equations collapse to the standard Euler equation as long as there is no spread between borrowing and deposit rate, that is, if $i_t^d = i_t^b$ or $\omega_t = 0$. The credit spread $\omega_t = \frac{i_t^b - i_t^d}{1 + i_t^d}$ drives the borrowing rate above the lending rate, creating a wedge between marginal intertemporal utility of borrowers and lenders. The spread imposes a deadweight loss: The marginal rate of substitution is no longer the same across all households. In the presence of the financial frictions impatient households cannot obtain sufficient compensation from insurance and have to apply for costly loans from banks. The gap between λ_t^s and λ_t^b reflects the inefficiency in financial intermediation, denoted by $\Omega_t = \lambda_t^b - \lambda_t^s$. It is a measure of the gap between the marginal utilities of borrowers and savers. The larger the credit spread ω_t in the current period, the larger the distortion between savers and borrowers, and so the larger the gap Ω_t. In a linearized system in which we use that variables for deviations from their steady-state values, it can be shown that

$$\widehat{\Omega}_t = \widehat{\omega}_t + \widehat{\delta} E_t \left[\widehat{\Omega}_{t+1} \right]$$

in which $\widehat{\omega}_t$ captures the spread between lending rate i_t^b and saving rate i_t^d, and $\widehat{\delta}$ contains the transition parameters δ and π_τ. It can be further solved forward as

$$\widehat{\Omega}_t = \sum_{j=0}^{+\infty} \widehat{\delta}^j E_t \left[\widehat{\omega}_{t+j} \right]$$

given that $\widehat{\delta} < 1$. So the inefficiency in resource allocation is captured by the interest rate spread.

Both types of households would be better off with a lower spread: Borrowers would like to consume more at a lower borrowing rate, and lenders would like to save more at a higher savings rate. Of course, in equilibrium the aggregate amount saved by patient households has to be the same as the amount borrowed by impatient households. So what will be the impact on aggregate consumption arising from more severe distortions? A careful analysis shows that under plausible conditions an increase in the spread will reduce aggregate consumption.

Let us consider the following thought experiment: What will be the effect on aggregate demand of an increase in the spread for a constant average interest rate? Since the lending rate will be lower, savers will save less and thus consume more; at the same time, the rate the borrowers have to pay rises. So borrowers can borrow less and thus need to cut down on consumption. It turns out that we can determinate the aggregate effect precisely. Since the marginal utility of consumption for savers is low, their increase in consumption will be relatively small. In contrast, the increase in the borrowing rate triggers a strong reduction in consumption of borrowers, more than offsetting the first effect. Thus, an increase in the spread at constant average rate is bound to dampen current aggregate consumption.

9.2.4 The Modified IS and AS Curves with Credit Spreads

The larger the credit spread in the current period, the larger the distortion between savers and borrowers and so, aggregated across all types, the smaller will be current relative to future consumption. Of course, as long as the spread stays constant across time, apart from the distortion, there will be no intertemporal effect. But an increase in the current spread definitely dampens current consumption. As shown by Cúrdia and Woodford (2015), using this elegant modelling technique, the impact on aggregate demand can be captured by adding the additional term $\Omega_t = \lambda_t^b - \lambda_t^s$ (the gap between the marginal utilities of borrowers and savers) to the standard Euler equation.

So the intertemporal IS relation can simply be modified by an additional term $\chi(\Omega_{t+1} - \Omega_t)$. The sign of χ is determined by the relative intertemporal elasticity of spending across the two types. Since borrowers have a larger intertemporal elasticity than savers, the sign is positive: $\chi > 0$.

$$c_t = E_t(c_{t+1}) + \chi(\Omega_{t+1} - \Omega_t) - \sigma\ (i_t - E(\pi_{t+1})).$$

The New Keynesian IS curve in the presence of financial friction can be characterized as

$$\widehat{Y}_t = -\overline{\sigma}\left(\widehat{\imath}_t^{avg} - E_t[\pi_{t+1}]\right) + E_t\left[\widehat{Y}_{t+1}\right] - \overline{\sigma} s_\Omega \widehat{\Omega}_t + \overline{\sigma}\psi_\Omega E_t\left[\widehat{\Omega}_{t+1}\right]$$

in which $\overline{\sigma}$ is the weighted average of two type households' intertemporal elasticity of substitution, s_Ω , ψ_Ω contain the parameters that reflect the households' heterogeneities on steady-state marginal utility of income as well as transition probability between types, and $\widehat{\imath}_t^{avg}$ is the weighted average of saving rate and lending rate

$$\widehat{\imath}_t^{avg} = \pi_b \widehat{\imath}_t^{b} + \pi_s \widehat{\imath}_t^{d}.$$

An increase in the spread at a constant average interest rate has a similar impact on the labor market, also affecting adversely the Phillips curve and so aggregate supply. As already shown above, the effective lending rate for savers is lower than the borrowing rate. So savers will not only want to consume more, but also work less. For borrowers it is just the other way round: they want to consume less, and work more. What can we say about the aggregate effect for labor supply? As savers work relatively more, they account for a larger share of labor supply. A decrease in the lending rate triggers a stronger negative effect on their labor supply compared to the positive effect for borrowers. So in the aggregate, there will be a net decrease in labor supply, shifting effective labor supply to the left. Just as with the Euler equation, the log–linear New Keynesian Phillips curve (NKPC) relation needs to be modified by introducing the marginal utility gap as well. Thus, the gap between the marginal utilities of borrowers and savers will not only affect the IS but also the AS curve.

The aggregate supply is pinned down by the "real" interest rate $\widehat{i}_t^{avg} - E_t[\pi_{t+1}]$ and output, and in addition, the efficiency gap. The forward looking NKPC now takes the form as

$$\pi_t = \kappa\left(\widehat{Y}_t - \widehat{Y}_t^n\right) + \varsigma\widehat{\Omega}_t + \beta E_t[\pi_{t+1}] + u_t.$$

Besides the standard terms, $\kappa\left(\widehat{Y}_t - \widehat{Y}_t^n\right)$ reflecting the output gap from natural rate of output $\widehat{Y}_t^n$ as well as u_t for demand shock, it also includes the term for financial efficiency gap $\varsigma\widehat{\Omega}_t$, with the parameter $\varsigma > 0$ capturing households' heterogeneities.

Let us summarize: Frictions from financial intermediation affect the key aggregate equations of the New Keynesian macro model, the IS and the AS curve. An increase in the wedge Ω_t leads to an adverse shift both on consumption demand and on labor supply. Such a shock shifts both aggregate demand and aggregate supply adversely. Cúrdia and Woodford show that the familiar log–linear relations can easily be generalized by including an additional variable in both equations which captures the gap in marginal utility between borrowers and savers $\Omega_t = \lambda_t^b - \lambda_t^s$. The modified IS and AS curves are (with positive weights $\chi > 0;\ k_\Omega > 0$):

IS curve: $c_t = E_t(c_{t+1}) + \chi(\Omega_{t+1} - \Omega_t) - \sigma(i_t - E(\pi_{t+1}))$
AS curve: $\pi_t = k(Y_t - Y_t^n) + \beta E_t(\pi_{t+1}) + k_\Omega\Omega_t + u_t$

9.2.5 Monetary Policy in the Presence of Credit Spreads

Cúrdia and Woodford (2015) analyze optimal monetary policy as response to an exogenous and time varying spread term. In their model, the central bank controls the deposit rate i_t^d. This rate is equivalent to the policy rate (the one-period interest rate on government liabilities and at the same time the interbank funding rate). So the central bank can counter the negative effect of an increase in Ω_t on current demand

and supply by reducing the lending rate, thus also lowering the average interest rate. When the financial markup ω_t is an exogenous process and no resources are used in intermediation (so in the steady state there are no credit frictions), optimal policy is characterized by the same target criterion (flexible inflation targeting) as in basic NK model. Monetary policy simply has to offset exogenous fluctuations in the markup of credit spreads in a way similar to markup shocks. Crucial for monetary policy is to stabilize the variation in the marginal utility gap (the deviation of credit spread from its steady-state value). Under the financial friction, the implied Taylor rule type of monetary policy that stabilizes the economy is given by

$$\widehat{i}_t^{avg} = \phi_t \pi_t + \phi_y \widehat{Y}_t + \pi_b \widehat{\omega}_t + \epsilon_t^m.$$

Monetary policy still works in a way similar to the standard NK model. Responses of output, inflation, interest rates to nonfinancial shocks (under a given monetary policy rule, e.g., a Taylor-type rule) are similar to those predicted by basic NK model. From the point of stabilizing in response to such disturbances, standard conclusions about desirability of a given rule stay unchanged. The monetary policy rate should not only respond to inflation and output gap; it should also respond to shocks in the interest rate spread. The reason is straightforward: In the presence of inefficiency in financial intermediation, shocks to the economy widen the interest rate spreads together with output gap and inflation. The welfare loss comes from the dispersion in prices, resulting in an inefficient resource allocation for the two types of households. Therefore, by explicitly addressing the source of financial frictions through targeting the spreads in interest rates, monetary policy can reduce the efficiency gap and move the economy closer to the first best allocation.

Cúrdia and Woodford argue that such a rule is still a fairly good approximation to optimal policy for more general credit frictions if financial markup depends on quantity of (real) loans supplied. The mere existence of a positive average spread makes little quantitative difference for the predicted effects of particular policies. Variations in spreads over time are of greater significance, with consequences both for the equilibrium relation between the policy rate and aggregate expenditure and for the relation between real activity and inflation.

Time varying credit spreads do not require fundamental modification of the view of monetary transmission mechanism. Policy decisions will still be based on a target criterion, relating inflation to the output gap (as is optimal in the absence of credit frictions). Credit frictions are addressed by stabilizing the financial markup. The augmented model incorporates measured spreads and thus improves forecasts (tightened credit conditions are reflected in higher credit spreads). A spread-adjusted Taylor rule (adjusting the intercept of the Taylor rule in proportion to changes in spreads) can improve upon a standard Taylor rule. But even with the correct size of adjustment, such a rule of thumb remains inferior to an optimal targeting rule. The adjustment of the Taylor rule intercept in response to the shock that would best approximate optimal policy is not necessarily the same multiple of the change in the credit spread in all cases. Indeed, the optimal factor of proportionality varies widely in the cases considered above. Thus, simply tracking credit spreads would not provide enough information to make the correct adjustment: A central bank would also need to determine which kind of disturbance is responsible for an observed change in credit spreads.

So a welfare analysis requires a careful study and correct identification of the sources driving the fluctuations in the wedge. If they result solely from resource constraints in financial intermediation, banking equilibrium may be constrained efficient as long as competition among banks makes sure that a zero-profit condition prevails in the banking industry. In that case, the wedge just covers the resource cost of intermediation between borrowers and lenders. Similarly, if lending is risky because some borrowers are likely to default, the spread would just reflect the underlying real risk. As long as lending by government agencies is not more efficient than private banking, there is no reason to intervene in the market.

In contrast, if variations in spreads over time are due to fluctuations in monopoly power, dampening such fluctuations will be welfare improving. This may be the case in particular if the government has a higher risk absorbing capacity (due to taxing capabilities). Furthermore, risk taking of financial intermediaries may be distorted to due externalities, if private banks do not adequately take into account the impact of their own activity on the aggregate economy. Alternatively, externalities may result from the risk of a breakdown of financial intermediation during turmoil. If so, however, it is doubtful whether interest rate policy is the adequate tool to address the underlying problem. So one must be careful in drawing conclusions about welfare implications of credit policy.

As argued in Cúrdia and Woodford (2011), the model provides no role for quantitative easing in the classical sense: In line with Wallace irrelevance, any expansion of the supply of reserves beyond the satiation level will not be effective in stimulating aggregate demand as long as done by buying additional government bonds. At a rate of zero, base money and bonds are perfect substitutes. But an increase in central bank lending to the private sector may be effective if private intermediation is inefficient with the central bank having access to a superior transaction technology or better risk absorbing capacity. If investment requires financial intermediation and there is a breakdown of the financial sector, stopping intermediation between saving and investment, standard monetary policy affecting only the lending rate will not be able to stabilize the economy. Direct provision of liquidity may be lead to a superior outcome. We will analyze these issues closer in the following sections.

Focus: The Spread from Financial Intermediation Technology

Introducing credit market imperfections in the New Keynesian framework creates a wedge between borrowing and lending rates. Because of the credit spread, there is a gap between the marginal utility of borrowers and lenders. Without modelling financial intermediation in detail, Cúrdia and Woodford assume that all intermediation has to be done via loans provided through banks

(continued)

via some lending technology $\Xi_t\left(b_t^{FI}, R_t\right)$. The function $\Xi_t\left(b_t^{FI}, R_t\right)$ represents the real resource cost of financial intermediation for the loans originated in the banking sector. Given central bank reserves R_t, financial intermediaries must spend (real) resources $\Xi_t\left(b_t^{FI}, R_t\right)$ for supplying loans in (real) quantity b_t^{FI}. These costs increase in the amount of lending $\partial \Xi_t^{FI}\left(b_t^{FI}, R_t\right)/\partial\ b_t^{FI} \geq 0$. It is natural to assume that costs decrease with larger holdings of central bank reserves R_t held by the intermediaries $\partial \Xi_t^{FI}\left(b_t^{FI}, R_t\right)/\partial R_t \leq 0$ as long as banks are not satiated with reserves. But for any level of lending b_t^{FI} there is some finite satiation level of reserves $\overline{R}\ \left(b_t^{FI}\right)$ such that $\partial \Xi_t^{FI}\left(b_t^{FI}, R_t\right)/\partial R_t = 0$ for all $R \geq \overline{R}\left(b_t^{FI}\right)$.

Banks collect deposits from savers, hold part of these funds as central bank reserves and provide loans to lenders. Next period, the bank needs to pay back depositors the amount $d_t\left(1 + i_t^d\right) = b_t\left(1 + i_t^b\right) + R_t\left(1 + i_t^m\right)$.

The bank can distribute as profits those funds (deposits) that are not used to finance either loans or the holding of reserve balances. So profits from financial intermediation are: $\Pi_t^{FI} = d_t - b_t - R_t - \Xi_t^{FI}(b_t, R_t)$ (note that the model abstracts from default risk for banks—there is no limited liability for bank equity).

Substituting $d_t = b_t \dfrac{1 + i_t^b}{1 + i_t^d} + R_t \dfrac{1 + i_t^m}{1 + i_t^d}$, profits can be written as a function of lending and bank reserves:

$$\Pi_t^{FI} = b_t\ \frac{i_t^b - i_t^d}{1 + i_t^d} + R_t\ \frac{i_t^m - i_t^d}{1 + i_t^d} - \Xi_t^{FI}(b_t, R_t).$$

The optimal amount of bank reserves held at the central bank is determined by the first-order condition

$$\frac{i_t^d - i_t^m}{1 + i_t^d} = -\frac{\partial \Xi_t^{FI}}{\partial R_t}.$$

For $i_t^d = i_t^m$, intermediaries are satiated in reserves $R_t(b_t) = \overline{R}(b_t)$. For any given level of lending, resource costs of financial intermediation are lowest for $\overline{R}(b_t)$ (Note that the spread will also be lowest for $\overline{R}(b_t)$ as long as $\partial^2 \Xi_t^{FI}\left(b_t^{FI}, R_t\right)/\partial b_t^{FI} \partial R_t \leq 0$). So for monetary policy, it will always be optimal to supply reserves up to the satiation level for banks. Not surprisingly, the Friedman rule derived in Chap. 2 applies in this setting too.

Taking the first derivative with respect to b_t, the profit maximizing condition for optimal loan supply is

(continued)

$$\frac{i_t^b - i_t^d}{1 + i_t^d} = \omega_t = \frac{\partial \Xi_t^{FI}}{\partial b_t}$$

Given that intermediaries must spend (real) resources for supplying loans according to the financial intermediation technology $\Xi_t(b_t^{FI}, R_t)$, equilibrium in a competitive banking sector will be characterized by a credit spread. According to Cúrdia and Woodford (2015), the spread ω_t may be caused by quite different sources. It may reflect (a) resource costs in the banking sector but also (b) a markup due to monopoly power in the financial industry or (c) (more generally) a premium for risky loans. Obviously, the source of the spread has a crucial impact on the question whether monetary policy aimed at reducing the spread may result in a superior outcome. If the spread is due to monopolistic power of banks, dampening the spread will definitely improve the allocation, eliminating inefficiencies from the monopolistic markup. If the spread instead reflects a premium for risky loans, it may just be the outcome of efficient risk pricing. If it reflects resource costs in the banking sector, it is not all obvious that central bank intermediation could lead to a superior outcome. After all, competitive banks may be more efficient in allocating funds to the most productive borrower. A natural starting point would be to assume that the central bank has an inferior intermediation technology, resulting in even higher resource costs.

9.2.6 The Cúrdia–Woodford Model: Evaluation

The main contribution of Cúrdia and Woodford (2015) is to characterize the dynamics of an economy with frictions causing spreads among the prices of heterogeneous households. But in a reduced form analysis, it is hard to do sound policy analysis. Without explicitly modeling the exact nature of the underlying friction, one needs to be careful to draw policy conclusions. A key issue not addressed in this framework is the fragility of the banking sector: The nature of deposit contracts, giving the depositors the right to withdraw at any time, combined with limited liability makes banks subject to the risk of runs. The model, however, abstracts from limited liability and default risk for banks. As long as the aggregate portfolio of a representative bank is well diversified, idiosyncratic risks of individual loans cancel out on the aggregate. In that case, the bank can payout depositors the safe return i_t^d without any risk of default. If inflowing funds are not sufficient to cover liabilities, here losses are assumed to be covered by equity.

In reality, specific features of financial intermediation make banks subject to bankruptcy risk with potentially contagion effects. Even solvent banks may run into trouble if liquidity dries up. In that case, intervention in intermediation aiming to dampen rising spreads may be justified for the following reason: Actions of financial intermediaries may cause externalities, in particular if limited liability gives incentives to risky activities, providing insufficient buffers. If spreads are a signal of solvency problems in the banking sector with the risk of a breakdown of intermediation due to contagion, central bank support may help to prevent such a break down, stabilizing financial intermediation with easier access to funds (such as lender of last resort activities) and superior technologies for providing insurance against aggregate risks. The remaining sections of this chapter look into these issues in more detail. We start with a closer look at how incentive problems for borrowers cause frictions in intermediation and lead to spreads between the rate for borrowers and savers. Following Bernanke and Gertler (1989), we show that such frictions give rise to a financial accelerator, amplifying the impact shocks.

9.3 Costly State Verification: The Bernanke–Gertler Model

The Cúrdia–Woodford model simply restricted the scope of feasible trading contracts across agents. But financial contracts and institutions are determined endogenously, based on underlying frictions. So policy conclusions that hinge on arbitrary restrictions of trading on financial markets may be somewhat suspect. A sound analysis needs to derive the financial frictions from first principles, modelling the incentive problems behind incomplete markets.

The financial accelerator, first explored by Bernanke and Gertler (1989), is among the pioneer ideas that integrate the financial frictions in the standard dynamic macroeconomics models. The credit constraint arises from the problem that the borrowers have the incentive to seek for private rents, so the lenders have to implement a costly auditing technology to monitor the borrowers. If the return of borrower's projects is not publicly observable without incurring costs, it is not feasible to arrange state contingent contracts with repayments dependent on the actual outcome of the investment—contrary to what usually is taken as granted in many standard models. There is a costly state verification problem. As has been well known for a long time since Townsend (1979), under such conditions a standard debt contract may be optimal, minimizing the verification costs. It has the following simple structure: Borrowers have to pay back a fixed amount pre-arranged for repayment, independent of the actual return. Only in case the borrower claims that the actual return is not sufficient to honor repayment the true state needs to be verified. So only if the borrower defaults, verification costs have to be incurred. Thus, no borrower has an incentive to falsely claim bankruptcy in order to renege on repayment, because that claim will be verified at least with some positive probability. Those who declare bankruptcy are monitored by their creditors and lose everything.

Bernanke and Gertler (1989) have been the first to apply this insight into a dynamic general equilibrium macro models. The costly state verification model has now become the most widely used model of financial frictions in macroeconomics. A key insight is that this friction causes a financial accelerator mechanism, so credit market frictions may significantly amplify both real and nominal shocks. Endogenous feedback mechanisms in credit markets work to amplify and propagate shocks to the macro economy: Relatively small shocks (such as modest changes in real interest rates induced by monetary policy) can have large real effects, resulting in widespread economic boom or bust. The intuition behind is fairly straightforward: With financial frictions, the borrower's net worth determines the borrowing capacity. The larger the own stake, the less serious the incentive problem. In good times, a borrower has plenty of own funds, and hence expected agency costs are rather low, reducing effective interest rates. In contrast, the lower the wealth, the more serious the agency problem and so the higher the effective borrowing costs. This accelerator is a general feature of many models with credit frictions.

In this section, we just present a two-period structure in order to illustrate the key mechanism as simple as possible. Many nonstandard assumptions that we introduce in this setting are designed to achieve analytical solutions and to see clearly the working mechanism. Deviating from other parts of the book, in this section we use an overlapping generation model of Samuelson-Diamond type with endogenous capital formation, because capital formation is at the core of the investment problem. In each generation, the population consists of a fraction of depositors with standard intertemporal preferences and by a fraction of entrepreneurs. Only entrepreneurs can build capital, by running specific projects. But entrepreneurs differ in their cost of production. Only low cost types will be able to realize their project. High cost types will get no funding. Each project has a stochastic return. For tractability, the return of capital can take on just two values. It can be either high or low (This is without loss of generality; it would be straightforward but mathematically complex to generalize for continuous stochastic return). To simplify savings decisions, we assume that entrepreneurs want to consume only when they are old, so they invest all their current income as equity in their own project provided they get sufficient funding. But projects are lumpy and need additional outside finance. The return being not verifiable without cost, agency costs and frictions distort the outcome relative to the first best, with capital investment being too low. Furthermore, shocks to equity lead to fluctuations in capital production.

9.3.1 The Model Setup

The Agents, Preferences, and Technology

Consider a Samuelson-Diamond type economy in discrete time $t = 0, 1, \ldots$ populated by overlapping generations. The population of each generation is constant with one unit mass. A new generation is born at each period t—call it generation t— who work to earn labor income at t when they are young using their labor endowment (normalized to be 1), and save for future consumption after they get retired at $t + 1$. In each generation the population is exogenously divided into two groups of agents when they are born:

(1) A fraction η are entrepreneurs who own their specific production technology, which will be explained later in more detail. The entrepreneurs are heterogeneous in the cost of production ω, which is uniformly distributed with support $[0, 1]$. In the rest of this section, the entrepreneurs are ranked by their ω. The

entrepreneurs do not consume when they are young, but consume their lifetime income when old.

(2) The remaining fraction $1 - \eta$ are depositors. These depositors consume in both periods. The utility function of one representative generation t depositor is

$$U_t = u\left(c_t^y\right) + \beta u\left(c_{t+1}^o\right).$$

c_t^y (c_{t+1}^o) is consumption at t ($t + 1$) when being young (old), and β is the discount factor. $u(\cdot)$ is strictly concave and twice differentiable.

There are two goods in the economy:

(1) A consumption good—the output from production using capital and labor. This good can either be consumed, or used as input by entrepreneurs for the production of capital. As explained below, entrepreneurs can convert the consumption good into capital in the next period. The consumption good can also be stored, with gross return rate $r \geq 1$ for one period.
(2) A capital good, which is not consumable, but can be used as input for producing the consumption good. In each period the depreciation rate of capital is 100%.

Technologies

There are different technologies for producing the consumption good and the capital good, respectively:

(1) The consumption good is produced via a neoclassical technology, with labor and capital as inputs, $Y_t = \widetilde{\theta}_t F(K_t, L_t)$ in which Y_t is the aggregate output in period t, K_t the aggregate capital stock, and L_t the labor supply. $\widetilde{\theta}_t$ represents the random exogenous technological shock which is i.i.d. over time with mean θ. The production function is homogeneous of degree 1 so that it can be written in per capita form

$$y_t = \widetilde{\theta}_t f(k_t).$$

(2) The capital good is produced through the entrepreneurs' projects. Each entrepreneur has one unit of project, which transfers y units of consumption good into k units of capital, to be used as the next period's capital input for producing consumption good. For an entrepreneur with type ω, the technology is characterized by

$$k = \begin{cases} 0, & \text{if } y < x(\omega), \\ \kappa_i, & \text{if } y \geq x(\omega). \end{cases}$$

That is, each project needs to incur a fixed cost $x(\omega)$, which is an increasing function of ω. The marginal product of the project is 0 if the input exceeds the threshold $x(\omega)$. The output κ_i can take two values: With probability π the output is high κ_H, and with probability $1 - \pi$ the output is low $\kappa_L < \kappa_H$. Denote the expected value of κ_i as $\pi\kappa_H + (1 - \pi)\kappa_L$.

The Agency Problem

The exact output of each project is private information for the entrepreneur owning the project, it cannot be directly verified by the outsiders. Therefore, the entrepreneur can misreport κ_H as κ_L and pockets the difference $\kappa_H - \kappa_L$ as private benefit. The other agents can learn the true value only by employing auditing. Auditing costs γ units of capital goods; it gives the exact value of output as public information. This agency problem is a classic costly state verification problem. The micro foundation has been provided by Townsend (1979), as well as Gale and Hellwig (1985).

In any period t with i_t projects deployed and a share of h_t audited, the capital intensity expected for $t + 1$ is

$$k_{t+1} = (\kappa - h_t\gamma)i_t. \tag{9.3.1}$$

9.3.2 Market Equilibrium with No Asymmetric Information

As a reference, we first analyze the market equilibrium with perfect information, i.e., the case that there is no auditing cost to learn the true output of one project, $\gamma = 0$. For any period t, denote the next period price of capital as q_{t+1}. Thus, the expected return of a project invested at t is $q_{t+1}\kappa$, and the opportunity cost of investing in a project instead of storage is $rx(\omega)$. An entrepreneur will invest in his project only if expected return exceeds opportunity cost. The profitability constraint for entrepreneur ω—call it $(PC - \omega)$—is

$$q_{t+1}\kappa \geq rx(\omega).\ (PC - \omega) \tag{9.3.2}$$

There is a cutoff value $\overline{\omega} = x^{-1}\left(\frac{q_{t+1}\kappa}{r}\right)$ separating the entrepreneurs: For those with low cost $\omega \leq \overline{\omega}$ it is profitable to undertake the investment, while for those with high costs $\omega > \overline{\omega}$ storage is more profitable. To focus on the interesting case, assume that the aggregate saving in the economy are large enough to finance the entrepreneurs' projects, i.e.,

$$\underbrace{\eta w_t}_{(A)} + \underbrace{(1 - \eta)\left(w_t - c_t^y\right)}_{(B)} > \int_0^{\overline{\omega}} x(\omega)d\omega.$$

Part (A) in the left hand side is the aggregate wage income of the entrepreneurs, and part (B) is the depositors' net income after consumption.

Out of all the entrepreneurs—whose population is η—only a share of $\overline{\omega}$ carry out the projects. As long as $\gamma = 0$, the total number of the projects undertaken at t is

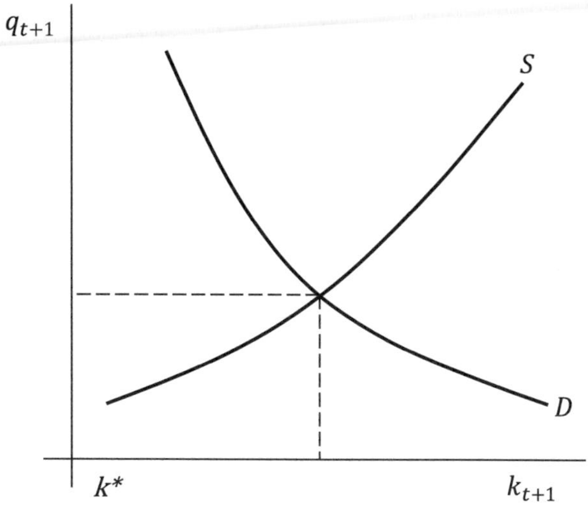

Fig. 9.1 Capital demand and supply

$$i_t = \overline{\omega}\eta. \tag{9.3.3}$$

So the expected capital intensity for $t + 1$ is

$$k_{t+1} = \kappa i_t = \kappa\overline{\omega}\eta. \tag{9.3.4}$$

Combining Equation 9.3.4 with Equation 9.3.2 gives the equilibrium capital price

$$q_{t+1} = \frac{r}{\kappa} x\left(\frac{k_{t+1}}{\kappa\eta}\right). \tag{9.3.5}$$

The larger q_{t+1}, the higher the cutoff value $\overline{\omega}$, so the more entrepreneurs are willing to invest in projects producing capital. Thus, Equation 9.3.5 defines the supply curve (*S*) of capital as shown in Fig. 9.1. The supply curve is upward sloping since

$$\frac{\partial q_{t+1}}{\partial k_{t+1}} = \frac{r}{\kappa^2\eta} x'\left(\frac{k_{t+1}}{\kappa\eta}\right) > 0.$$

On the other hand, in a competitive capital market, the capital price q_{t+1} is determined by productivity. The expected marginal product of capital is:

$$q_{t+1} = E_t[\tilde{\theta}_{t+1}]f'(k_{t+1}) = \theta f'(k_{t+1}). \tag{9.3.6}$$

This defines the demand of capital, curve (*D*) in Fig. 9.1, which is downward sloping since

$$\frac{\partial q_{t+1}}{\partial k_{t+1}} = \theta f''(k_{t+1}) < 0.$$

The equilibrium capital price and intensity are jointly determined by Equation 9.3.5 and Equation 9.3.6. As long as all other parameters are constant, in equilibrium, q and k will be constant over time. The economy builds up its capital stock k^* independent of the initial capital intensity k_0, just as in standard overlapping generation models.

Focus: Limited Liability, Risk Sharing, and Collateralization

With perfect information, all projects will be funded provided expected profitability is positive: $q_{t+1}\kappa - rx(\omega) \geq 0$. The expected return $q_{t+1}\kappa = q_{t+1}(\pi\kappa_H + (1-\pi)\kappa_L)$ and the project's opportunity cost $rx(\omega)$ are the only decisive criteria. The cutoff value $\overline{\omega} = x^{-1}\left(\frac{q_{t+1}\kappa}{r}\right)$ and thus the number of projects funded is independent of the own funds invested by the entrepreneur herself into his project. So the level of debt incurred plays no role at all. Since entrepreneurs consume only in the second period, they are willing to put all their available funds w_t in their own project. Obviously, the burden of repayment $r[x(\omega) - w_t]$ is increasing in the level of debt $[x(\omega) - w_t]$. The higher the cost $x(\omega)$ and the lower the own funds w_t, the larger the debt. Projects with very low costs can easily cover debt obligations even if the project's return turns out to be low (κ_L). Those projects are fully collateralized. That means that the lender will be able to recover the funds lent, including interest payments $r[x(\omega) - w_t]$ safely, independent of the actual return of the project. But for many projects with positive expected profitability, the return in the bad state κ_L will not be high enough to fully pay back the debt obligation: $q_{t+1}\kappa_L - r[x(\omega) - w_t] < 0$, if w_t is low. Obviously, the entrepreneur cannot pay back more than the actual return $q_{t+1}\kappa_L$. There is limited liability, so he will have to declare default in that case with a loss $L(\omega) = r_\omega[x(\omega) - w_t] - q_{t+1}\kappa_L$. To make sure that the borrower receives the market return r despite the default risk, the contract needs to charge a risk premium $r_\omega > 0$ depending on type ω, raising the effective debt burden in the good state κ_H accordingly such that $\{\pi\, r_\omega[x(\omega) - w_t] + (1-\pi)\, q_{t+1}\kappa_L\} = r[x(\omega) - w_t]$.

So there is a spread—the risk premium $r_\omega - r = \frac{(1-\pi)}{\pi} r - \frac{(1-\pi)}{\pi} \frac{q_{t+1}\kappa_L}{[x(\omega) - w_t]}$. The spread $r_\omega - r$ is rising with the cost type ω and decreasing in w_t. It makes sure that the default risk for borrower ω is taken into account efficiently. In an economy with perfect information, this risk spread is part of efficient pricing rather than being a reason to worry about market failure.

In the absence of informational frictions (in a world with a complete set of contingent risk markets), there are many ways to implement such contracts. The borrower could buy insurance against default risk, with the insurance

(continued)

coverage giving him sufficient funds to pay back easily the debt obligations. Alternatively, the lender could insure against default risk, providing him with a safe return independent of the actual realization of project risk. Finally, financial intermediaries may pool lending across different types. Relying on the law of large numbers, the average funds from lending to a pool of entrepreneurs may be sufficient to guarantee a safe return r to depositors in the absence of aggregate risk. As long as there are no information cost, the institutional details of the specific arrangement simply do not matter. Obviously, this is patently unrealistic. In reality, information costs and agency problems play a crucial role in the case of debt. As we will see in the following section, contracts get far more complex when the type κ_i is not observable without verification cost. There is a natural role for banks as intermediaries financing specific types. In that case, the size of available funds w_t (the entrepreneur's own stake) will be a key determinant of agency costs.

In the context of lending, one can easily think of a wide variety of other agency problems as well. The entrepreneur's cost type ω may be private information, giving an incentive to pretend to be a low cost type in order to get cheaper funding. It will be hard to identify good (low cost) investment projects. The return of the project κ_i usually is not just a random number, but also depends on the effort of the entrepreneur, which again is costly to observe. Entrepreneurs may be reluctant to put their own stake w_t into the project, trying to diversify risk and protect own funds against default. All these agency problems create frictions, motivating a natural role for intermediaries to cope with the lack of perfect risk sharing markets. Even though in this section we analyze a very stylized moral hazard problem, most of the results obtained easily generalize to other frictions. In particular, equity and collateral constraints will play a key role in all agency problems.

But note that financial intermediaries themselves are also subject to quite similar agency problems: The effort of banks to identify good investment projects is again costly to observe; bank managers may privately abuse some fraction of the assets they have under management. Given limited liability of banks, the portfolios of some banks may be particular risky if it is costly for depositors to observe and monitor the bank's portfolio. Again, the equity stake in banks will play a key role for alleviating frictions. These issues will be discussed in sequel in the following sections.

9.3.3 Market Equilibrium with Asymmetric Information

Now suppose that because of costly state verification problem the outsiders have to incur an auditing cost to learn the true output value of the projects. This affects those entrepreneurs who need to borrow, i.e., those with small cost ω—the project's net present value is positive—provided the financing cost $x(\omega)$ exceeds the entrepreneur's savings—that is, the wage income in the first period of life, or $x(\omega) > w_t$.

The optimal contract for the borrowers is determined by the revelation principle (the general theorem is explained in Mas-Colell, Whinston and Green, 1995, Chap. 23), which is characterized by:

(1) Participation constraint for depositors $(PC - i)$: The expected return from lending must exceed the return from storage.
(2) The incentive compatibility, or truth telling constraint (*IC*): Entrepreneurs should not lie about the projects' outcomes.
(3) Limited liability (*LL*): Entrepreneurs only have limited liability.

To find the optimal contract, notice that the entrepreneur only gets private benefit if he announces the project's outcome as κ_L while the true one is κ_H. Therefore, there is no need to audit if the entrepreneur announces κ_H. Auditing is only necessary for the announcement κ_L.

Suppose a representative generation t entrepreneur's consumption is c_t^i if he announces κ_i, $i \in \{H, L\}$. When he announces κ_L, he will be audited with probability $p_t \in [0, 1]$. After auditing, a contract specifies the consumption c_t^a if he tells the truth, and c_t^l if he lies. The optimal contract for the entrepreneur is to find

$$\{p_t, c_t^H, c_t^L, c_t^a, c_t^l\} = \text{argmax}(1 - \pi)\left[p_t c_t^a + (1 - p_t) c_t^L\right] + \pi c_t^H, \tag{9.3.7}$$

s.t.

$$(1 - \pi)\left[q_{t+1}\kappa_L - p_t(c_t^a + q_{t+1}\gamma) - (1 - p_t)c_t^L\right] + \pi\left(q_{t+1}\kappa_H - c_t^H\right) \geq r[x(\omega) - w_t],\ (PC - i) \tag{9.3.8}$$

$$c_t^H \geq (1 - p_t)\left[q_{t+1}(\kappa_H - \kappa_L) + c_t^L\right] + p_t c_t^l,\ (IC) \tag{9.3.9}$$

$$c_t^L \geq 0,\ (LL - 1) \tag{9.3.10}$$

$$c_t^a \geq 0.\ (LL - 2) \tag{9.3.11}$$

First of all, we see that in order to meet (*IC*) it is optimal to maximize the punishment for lying, i.e., to make sure that consumption will be minimized in that case: $c_t^l = 0$. Given that the entrepreneur always tells the truth, $(PC - i)$ says that the expected return of the entrepreneur's project must be sufficient to repay the depositors, with the expected capital price being q_{t+1}. Further, expected consumption maximization as in object function (Equation 9.3.7) implies that $(PC - i)$ is always binding. (*IC*) means that when κ_H is realized, the expected consumption from telling the truth must exceed that from telling a lie. $(LL - 1)$ and $(LL - 2)$ mean that there is limited liability for the entrepreneur in the bad state: Even after being audited, consumption cannot be negative.

The optimal contract depends on the value of the entrepreneur's project. In the best case, the value always exceeds the entrepreneur's liability to depositors, even in the bad state. In this case, there is no need to audit, so $p_t = 0$:

$$p_t = 0, \text{ for } q_{t+1}\kappa_L \geq r[x(\omega) - w_t].$$

For given q_{t+1}, $x(\omega)$, define the minimum income level with which the entrepreneur is able to borrow without being audited as

$$w_t^*(\omega) = x(\omega) - \frac{q_{t+1}\kappa_L}{r}. \tag{9.3.12}$$

With $p_t = 0$, $(PC - i)$ implies that under optimal contract

$$(1-\pi)\left[q_{t+1}\kappa_L - c_t^L\right] + \pi\left(q_{t+1}\kappa_H - c_t^H\right) = r[x(\omega) - w_t],$$

$$E[c_t] = q_{t+1}\kappa - r[x(\omega) - w_t]. \tag{9.3.13}$$

The expected consumption of the entrepreneur is the profit from capital production.

Obviously, the problem gets more interesting but also more complicated if $q_{t+1}\kappa_L < r[x(\omega) - w_t]$. Now, the value of the entrepreneur's project is not sufficient to meet the entrepreneur's liability to depositors in the bad state, so the entrepreneur would have to default. The incentive problem for entrepreneurs to misreport is the temptation to get a private benefit from $\kappa_H - \kappa_L$ by claiming κ_L. To make it least attractive to pretend a return κ_L in the good state (if κ_H is realized), the optimal contract will set $c_t^a = 0$ and $c_t^L = 0$, simplifying the IC condition to: $c_t^H \geq (1 - p_t)\left[q_{t+1}(\kappa_H - \kappa_L)\right]$. As long as κ_H is not too large compared to κ_L, misreporting would not be worthwhile even for $p_t = 0$. In the following, we concentrate on the interesting case that there is indeed a moral hazard problem, such that $c_t^H < \left[q_{t+1}(\kappa_H - \kappa_L)\right]$. Should there be no auditing, the entrepreneur would now always have the incentive to misreport κ_H as κ_L and pocket the difference $\kappa_H - \kappa_L$ as private benefit, making the loan contract break down. Therefore, in equilibrium, the probability of auditing, p_t, must be large enough to deter such moral hazard problem. The object function (Equation 9.3.7) implies that all constraints (Equation 9.3.8)–(Equation 9.3.11) are binding. So the equilibrium p_t can be solved as

$$p_t = \frac{r[x(\omega) - w_t] - q_{t+1}\kappa_L}{\pi q_{t+1}(\kappa_H - \kappa_L) - (1-\pi)q_{t+1}\gamma}. \tag{9.3.14}$$

As long as the gain from deterring misreporting, $\pi q_{t+1}(\kappa_H - \kappa_L)$, exceeds the cost of auditing, $(1-\pi)q_{t+1}\gamma$, the probability of auditing, p_t, is always positive. One can further infer from Equation (9.3.14) that p_t decreases with the entrepreneur's own saving, w_t. The intuition behind is fairly straightforward: The higher the own stake the entrepreneur holds in the investment, the less he needs to borrow and hence, the less private benefit he would get from misreporting. So the higher the stake, the less severe the moral hazard problem is. Obviously, with increasing inside funds, there is less need for external finance, reducing the agency cost.

Applying Equation (9.3.14) in $(PC - i)$, the expected consumption of the entrepreneur is

$$E[c_t] = \frac{\pi q_{t+1}(\kappa_H - \kappa_L)}{\pi q_{t+1}(\kappa_H - \kappa_L) - (1-\pi)q_{t+1}\gamma} \{q_{t+1}\kappa - r[x(\omega) - w_t] - (1-\pi)q_{t+1}\gamma\}. \quad (9.3.15)$$

From Equation (9.3.13), we see that $\frac{\partial E[c_t]}{\partial w_t} = r$ when there is no agency problem. In this case, any additional unit of saving will become an additional unit of investment on the project, returning the market rate of investment. In contrast, now we have $\frac{\partial E[c_t]}{\partial w_t} = \frac{\pi q_{t+1}(\kappa_H - \kappa_L)}{\pi q_{t+1}(\kappa_H - \kappa_L) - (1-\pi)q_{t+1}\gamma} r > r$. With costly state verification, having one additional unit of internal funds has two effects: First, as before it returns r from the capital market; second, by having one unit more "inside" funding from own pocket, the entrepreneur needs one unit less "outside" funding from borrowing. Since agency costs are reduced this allows him to create more resources for consumption. Agency costs create a wedge between internal and external funding: The effective cost of external finance exceeds r. For that reason, fewer entrepreneurs will carry out their projects compared to the solution without frictions.

For an arbitrary entrepreneur ω, whether he will be successful in getting sufficient funding to carry out his project depends on his expected profit: The difference between the expected return of the project and its opportunity cost including auditing cost, $E_t[R_{t+1}(\omega)] = q_{t+1}\kappa - rx(\omega) - p(1-\pi)q_{t+1}\gamma$. So expected profit depends on his type ω and the probability of being audited. There are several generic cases:

(1) He is never able to start the project because the expected profit of the project is negative, even when in the absence of auditing cost with $p = 0$, $E_t[R_{t+1}(\omega)] = q_{t+1}\kappa - rx(\omega) < 0$, or $\omega > \overline{\omega} = x^{-1}\left(\frac{q_{t+1}\kappa}{r}\right)$.
(2) He is always able to start the project because the expected profit is always positive, even when there is the maximum auditing cost with $p = 1$, $E_t[R_{t+1}(\omega)] = q_{t+1}\kappa - rx(\omega) - (1-\pi)q_{t+1}\gamma > 0$, or $0 \leq \omega < \underline{\omega} = x^{-1}\left(\frac{q_{t+1}\kappa - (1-\pi)q_{t+1}\gamma}{r}\right)$.
(3) For the intermediate range $\underline{\omega} < \omega < \overline{\omega}$, whether he is successful depends on the auditing probability p.

Those in case (1) will become depositors, lending their income to the successful entrepreneurs instead of running the projects by themselves. Those in case (2) are certainly successful entrepreneurs, but whether their projects will be audited or not depends on their income: There is no auditing only if the wage income exceeds $w_t^*(\omega)$ so that the project is fully collateralized (compare Equation (9.3.12)). There is auditing if the wage income is below $w_t^*(\omega)$, and the auditing probability is given by Equation (9.3.14) as $p_t = \frac{r[x(\omega)-w_t]-q_{t+1}\kappa_L}{\pi q_{t+1}(\kappa_H-\kappa_L)-(1-\pi)q_{t+1}\gamma}$.

Those in case (3) are ambiguous, call them "swinging entrepreneurs." As Equation (9.3.14) shows, the auditing probability p is negatively correlated with w_t. Therefore, if these entrepreneurs contract directly with depositors, when an entrepreneur has efficiently low ω and his w_t is high enough to make $E_t[R_{t+1}(\omega)] > 0$, the entrepreneur will carry out the project. In contrast, when an entrepreneur is not sufficiently efficient and his w_t is not high enough that the auditing probability p and hence the auditing cost is so high to make $E_t[R_{t+1}(\omega)] = q_{t+1}\kappa - rx(\omega) - (1-\pi)q_{t+1}\gamma < 0$, the entrepreneur will be barred from running his project.

However, even for the least efficient swinging entrepreneur, i.e., the entrepreneur whose ω is close to $\overline{\omega}$, his project is still profitable, or, socially beneficial, should there be no auditing. Therefore, there is a need for financial intermediation that allows all swinging entrepreneurs to invest and improve social welfare. Such financial intermediation is introduced in the following way:

- Suppose that all swinging entrepreneurs delegate their projects to the most efficient person among them, i.e., the entrepreneur whose ω is the closest to $\underline{\omega}$—call him a "banker" with efficiency level ω^*.
- The banker pools all wage income w_t from swinging entrepreneurs and invests only in fully collateralized projects that need $w_t^*(\omega^*)$ "inside" funding each. The banker borrows the rest ("outside" funding) from depositors to initiate these projects.
- To focus only on borrowers' problem, assume that the banker is perfectly monitored by other entrepreneurs and works only for the group's interest, i.e., there is no friction in the financial intermediation.
- The profit from the projects is distributed among all swinging entrepreneurs, proportional to the inverse of each one's efficiency level ω.

In the presence of financial intermediation, the entrepreneurs divide themselves into three groups, as Fig. 9.2 shows:

- The most efficient entrepreneurs, or, successful entrepreneurs, contract directly with depositors—call it "direct finance," each of them is able to carry out his own project, even sometimes subject to a small fee of auditing.
- The less efficient entrepreneurs, or, swinging entrepreneurs, delegate their projects to the bank—call it "bank finance." The bank has the expertise in producing fully collateralized projects, or, safe assets, to the depositors. Although the bank can only fund less projects than the population of swinging entrepreneurs (note that the number of collateralized projects that can be funded by one entrepreneur's income, $\frac{w_t}{w_t^*(\omega^*)}$, is less than 1 for this group), it allows all of them—even the less efficient ones—to benefit from the supported projects and

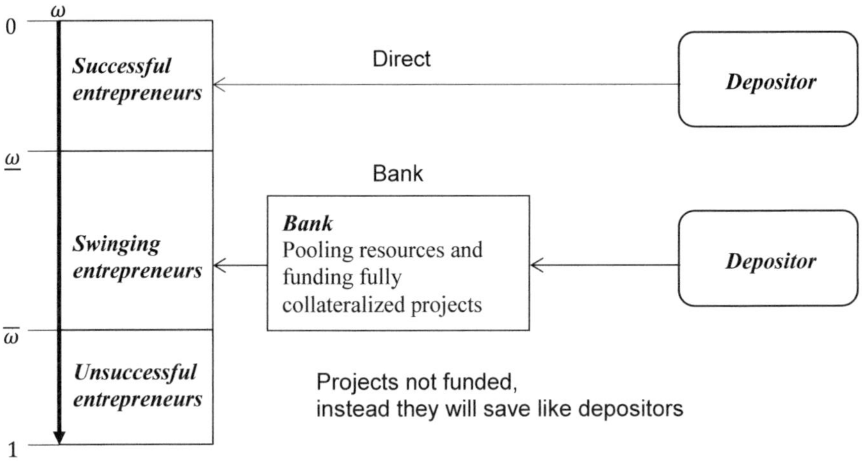

Fig. 9.2 Funding structure of the economy

avoids the high auditing cost which these entrepreneurs would have to incur, should they contract directly with the depositors.

- The least efficient entrepreneurs, or, unsuccessful entrepreneurs, whose projects are too expensive to be profitable for funding. Those entrepreneurs will not get any funding and will instead invest their own funds in other projects just like the depositors.

The funding structure resembles the reality fairly well: Well established, usually big firms, can easily fund themselves directly from investors, for example, on the bond market, subject to small fees charged by bookrunners, credit rating agencies, etc. Less well established, typically small- and medium-size firms, usually cannot access bond market, but they can still apply for bank loans; it is often very hard for the start-up firms with few tangible assets to raise funding. Similar funding structure arises from other agency cost-based models, such as Holmström and Tirole (1998).

Now, under such funding structure in the economy, the production of capital will be carried out by the successful entrepreneurs (possibly with auditing) and the delegated swinging entrepreneurs (without auditing):

$$k_{t+1} = \left[\underbrace{\kappa\underline{\omega} - \pi\gamma \int_0^{\underline{\omega}} p_t(\omega) d\omega}_{(A)} + \underbrace{\kappa \int_{\underline{\omega}}^{\overline{\omega}} \frac{w_t}{w_t^*(\omega^*)} d\omega}_{(B)} \right] \eta, \tag{9.3.16}$$

in which term (A) is the capital production from the (partially) audited directly financed projects deducting the auditing cost, term (B) from the non-audited bank financed projects, and in term (A)

$$p_t(\omega) = \begin{cases} \dfrac{r[x(\omega) - w_t] - q_{t+1}\kappa_L}{\pi q_{t+1}(\kappa_H - \kappa_L) - (1-\pi)q_{t+1}\gamma}, & \text{if } w_t \leq w_t^*(\omega), \\ 0, & \text{otherwise.} \end{cases}$$

In contrast to the market equilibrium without financial friction where q and k are constant over time, here the agency problem generates both short-term (intra-period) and long-term fluctuations through the supply curve of capital, although the demand curve remains the same as before.

First of all, notice that the supply curve of capital with financial friction (such as the dark gray curve S') is always above the supply curve without financial friction (the black curve S) as Fig. 9.3 shows, since the agency problem implies a deadweight loss in capital production (the triangle $\triangle ABE$ in the figure, corresponding to a lower capital production $k' < k^*$). This can be easily seen from Equation (9.3.16)

$$k_{t+1} = \left[\kappa\underline{\omega} - \pi\gamma\int_0^{\omega} p_t(\omega)d\omega + \kappa\int_{\underline{\omega}}^{\overline{\omega}} \frac{w_t}{w_t^*(\omega^*)}d\omega\right]\eta < [\kappa\underline{\omega} + \kappa(\overline{\omega} - \underline{\omega})]\eta = \kappa\overline{\omega}\eta,$$

given that $\int_0^{\omega} p_t(\omega)d\omega \geq 0$ and $\frac{w_t}{w_t^*(\omega^*)} < 1$, that the total capital output is always lower than that in the frictionless economy, $\kappa\overline{\omega}\eta$, as in Equation (9.3.4).

In the short run, notice that the supply of capital k_{t+1} depends on the number of the entrepreneurs who participate the capital production at t, and this depends on the entrepreneurs income w_t. The neoclassical production function $y_t = \widetilde{\theta_t}f(k_t)$ implies that $w_t = \widetilde{\theta_t}[f(k_t) - k_t f'(k_t)]$, which depends on the technological shock $\widetilde{\theta_t}$. When the realized θ_t is high, the entrepreneurs' wage income increases, too. This increases the net worth of the projects from the successful entrepreneurs, making them more likely to face lower probability of being audited, or even completely collateralized so that there is no need for auditing at all. As a result, the agency cost is lower and there

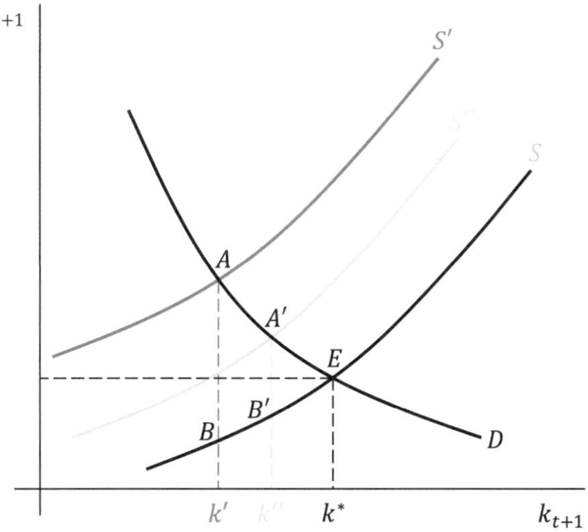

Fig. 9.3 Capital supply with financial friction

will be more resources devoted to capital production. Further, the increase in the entrepreneurs' income makes the bank able to finance more fully collateralized projects, given the number of collateralized projects that can be funded by one entrepreneur's income, $\frac{w_t}{w_t^*(\omega^*)}$, is increasing in w_t. These two effects jointly shift the capital supply curve S'' closer to the frictionless equilibrium supply curve S, leading to a higher level of capital production k'' and reduced deadweight loss in capital production (the triangle $\triangle A'B'E$), as Fig. 9.3 shows. Formally, from Equation (9.3.16) one can see that

$$\frac{\partial k_{t+1}}{\partial w_t} = \left[-\pi\gamma \int_0^{\underline{\omega}} \frac{\partial p_t(\omega)}{\partial w_t} d\omega + \kappa \int_{\underline{\omega}}^{\overline{\omega}} \frac{\partial \left(\frac{w_t}{w_t^*(\omega^*)} \right)}{\partial w_t} d\omega \right] \eta$$

$$= \left[\underbrace{-\pi\gamma \int_0^{\underline{\omega}} \frac{\partial p_t(\omega)}{\partial w_t} d\omega}_{(A)>0} + \underbrace{\kappa \int_{\underline{\omega}}^{\overline{\omega}} \frac{1}{w_t^*(\omega^*)} d\omega}_{(B)>0} \right] \eta,$$

given that $\frac{\partial p_t(\omega)}{\partial w_t} \leq 0$, $\frac{\partial k_{t+1}}{\partial w_t} > 0$. Terms (A) and (B) reflect the effects from reduced auditing cost in the directly financed projects and increased number of bank financed projects, respectively.

The interesting feature here is that the economic boom does not only increase the net worth of the projects which enables the entrepreneurs to expand their balance sheets, but also make more entrepreneurs accessible to outside funding which further increases the capital output—exhibiting a financial accelerator effect.

On the contrary, when the realized $\widetilde{\theta}_t$ is low, the entrepreneurs' wage income declines. The fall in the projects' net worth both increases the auditing costs for the successful entrepreneurs and drives down the number of bank financed projects. These two effects jointly shift the capital supply curve away from the frictionless equilibrium supply curve S, leading to a lower level of capital production and increased deadweight loss in capital production.

Such short-run fluctuations also ripple into the long-run future. Since the impact of fluctuations in the level of capital will persist for some time, the impact on economic activity is likely to be more persistent than the initial shock. A positive technological shock $\widetilde{\theta}_t$ leads to higher capital output from period t projects, or, higher capital input k_{t+1} for period $t+1$ production. This makes the economy more resilient in the next period, i.e., when there is a negative technological shock $\widetilde{\theta}_{t+1}$ the wage income w_{t+1} will not decline as long as the shock is small, so that there is even a persistent economic growth in the mid term.[1]

[1]The long-run implication for such financial accelerator effect is not straightforward. Suppose that an economy starts with very low initial capital intensity k_0, or high marginal product of capital $\widetilde{\theta}_0 f'(k_0)$. The high productivity of capital may outweigh the possible negative technological shock,

How does the economy respond to unexpected monetary shocks? Let us consider a monetary policy shock as follows. Suppose that changes in the nominal interest rate transmit into the real economy by adjusting the risk-free rate r proportionally. So the impact on aggregate output of capital is

$$\frac{\partial k_{t+1}}{\partial r} = \left[\kappa \frac{\partial \underline{\omega}}{\partial r} - \pi\gamma\left(p_t(\underline{\omega})\frac{\partial \underline{\omega}}{\partial r}\right) - \pi\gamma \int_0^{\underline{\omega}} \frac{\partial p_t(\omega)}{\partial r} d\omega + \kappa \frac{w_t}{w_t^*(\omega^*)}\left(\frac{\partial \overline{\omega}}{\partial r} - \frac{\partial \underline{\omega}}{\partial r}\right)\right]\eta.$$

To simplify our analysis, assume that $x(\omega) = a\omega + b$ with $a > 0$, then

$$\frac{\partial k_{t+1}}{\partial r} = \left[\underbrace{(\kappa - \pi\gamma p_t(\underline{\omega}))}_{>0} \underbrace{\frac{\partial \underline{\omega}}{\partial r}}_{(A),<0} \underbrace{-\pi\gamma \int_0^{\underline{\omega}} \frac{\partial p_t(\omega)}{\partial r} d\omega}_{(B),<0} + \kappa \underbrace{\frac{w_t}{w_t^*(\omega^*)}}_{>0} \underbrace{\frac{-(1-\pi)q_{t+1}\gamma}{ar^2}}_{(C),<0}\right]\eta < 0,$$

in which $\kappa - \pi\gamma p_t(\underline{\omega}) > 0$ because the expected output of successful entrepreneurs always exceeds the expected auditing cost. That is, when expansive monetary policy lowers r, the aggregate output of capital increases. This comes from two effects, as can be seen from the derivative above: First, it increases the net worth of entrepreneurs, making more of them successful for direct finance (term (A)) with lower auditing cost (term (B)); second, it enlarges the group of swinging entrepreneurs, allowing more bank financed projects (term (C)). A looser monetary policy thus translates to a higher total number of successfully funded projects as well as lower agency cost, thus raising aggregate output.

9.3.4 The Financial Accelerator: Evaluation

The financial accelerator is a powerful modeling device for introducing the financial friction in the standard macroeconomic model in a tractable way. The idea is heavily explored to uncover the impact of credit constraints on macro economy, following Bernanke, Gertler and Gilchrist (1999) that integrate financial accelerator in a full-fledged dynamic stochastic general equilibrium model. Credit frictions work as

---

and the economy starts accumulating capital although the growth path is stochastic due to the random shocks $\widetilde{\theta}_t$ coming in each period. However, with time going on, the marginal product of capital diminishes when k_t gets higher, a negative shock $\widetilde{\theta}_t$ now may sharply decrease the labor income. With the presence of the financial accelerator, this suffocates many bank financed projects and highly raises the auditing cost; the economic growth may be completely reversed. And, to make it worse, such economic downturn will persist for some periods. Without further restrictions on the parameter values, the economic growth is hardly determinate. See Matsuyama (2008) for more discussion.

accelerator, amplifying both real and nominal shocks. Spreads widen in bad times, raising the cost of external funds. In turn, spreads are lower in good times, encouraging higher production. Thus, monetary policy needs to play a more active role in stabilizing shocks compared to models without frictions. As illustrated in Fig. 9.3, financial frictions lead to an undersupply of capital production, imposing a deadweight loss. But apart from stabilizing shocks, monetary policy cannot eliminate the structural inefficiency caused by such incentive constraints. On average, the outcome may even be constrained efficient, given agency costs. After all, the credit spread reflects real agency problems, creating a wedge between external finance and the opportunity cost of internal finance.

Note, however, that agency costs will be lower on average the stronger the equity buffers. Externalities may prevent markets from building up sufficiently strong buffers as shown by Davila and Korinek (2018). They model endogenous systemic financial risk from the feedback between incomplete financial markets and the real economy. Adverse shocks to the real economy tighten individuals' credit constraints, triggering the contraction of economic activities. This depresses the prices of productive assets, hence the net worth of their owners, and worsens their credit constraints. The financial accelerator amplifies negative shocks to the economy, giving rise to externalities: Atomistic agents take the level of asset prices in the economy as given. In their demand for productive assets, they do not internalize the externalities that arise when aggregate shocks lead to aggregate fluctuations. So decentralized agents undervalue social benefits of having stronger buffers when financial constraints are binding, taking on too much systemic risk in their investment strategies.

So far, we focused only on the borrower side frictions, assuming perfectly functioning financial intermediaries. Nevertheless, the role of the bank in the model is non trivial: It provides an insurance for the depositors, by producing safe assets (fully collateralized projects). So depositors are free from bankruptcy cost in the bad state with κ_L; on the other hand, all less efficient entrepreneurs are able to access external funding and get exempted from costly auditing, improving social welfare—these are exactly what financial intermediaries are doing in the real world, making them socially productive institutions. In the current section, following Bernanke and Gertler, the only friction on the borrower side was that verification of the random return of funded project is costly. In reality, the type ω of the entrepreneur may also be private information. Providing such information can motivate an additional role for banks: Specializing in screening technologies, they may be more efficient in extracting information about which projects are profitable. Screening costs will result in similar effects as in the model presented here, contributing again to a financial accelerator mechanism.

However, one has to be aware that financial intermediaries are prone to incentive problems themselves, resulting in a fragile structure: In reality, they are also subject to many frictions, such as agency problems and moral hazard, as well as many regulatory rules, which also have profound implications for the monetary transmission mechanism, or sometimes even make the transmission fail altogether. In the next sections, we will see how problems arise from the frictions *inside* financial intermediaries.

9.4 Moral Hazard: The Gertler–Karadi–Kiyotaki Model

Consider an economy that is populated by many identical households who live for 2 periods, $t = 1, 2$. Each of the households has an initial wealth N to start with. In each household, some members are workers, while the others are bankers. To focus on the financial friction, we abstract from the production sector in this economy and assume that for a representative household:

- In $t = 1$, the workers work and earn a fixed labor income y. They deposit d in competitive banks and leave the rest for the entire household's current consumption. The bankers establish banks, using the household's initial wealth N. Bankers offer deposits to workers from all households on a competitive market, taking the deposit rate r as given. Using these funds, banks issue loans L to firms (which we do not explicitly model).
- In $t = 2$, the loans yield a fixed gross return R. Workers withdraw deposits from banks with gross return r. Bankers then dissolve their bank, and pay out the banks' profit—call it π to their own household.

We assume that consumption is shared equally across all members within a household. Each household maximizes utility from consumption in both periods, i.e.,

$$\max_{c_1, c_2} u(c_1) + u(c_2).$$

Suppose the utility function takes the form of $u(c) = \frac{c^{1-\gamma}}{1-\gamma}$, $\gamma > 0$. The budget constraint of the household for $t = 1$ is

$$c_1 + d \leq y,$$

and for $t = 2$, the budget constraint is

$$c_2 \leq rd + \pi.$$

In addition $c_1 > 0$, $c_2 > 0$, and $d > 0$. The solution to the household's problem is therefore

$$c_1 = \frac{yr + \pi}{r^{\frac{1}{\gamma}} + r}, d = y - c_1, c_2 = rd + \pi.$$

Let us now endogenize the banks' profit, π, analyzing the bankers' decision problem. Note that bankers use their own household's wealth N as equity. They get deposits d from workers, and issue loans L to firms; this implies the banks' balance sheet as shown in Table 9.1.

Table 9.1 The banks' balance sheet

Assets	*Liabilities*
Loans, L	Equity, N
	Deposits, d

The banks' problem is thus to maximize profits with $L = N + d$:

$$\max_{d} \pi = RL - rd,$$

Without financial friction, the equilibrium is characterized by the conditions: (1) Bankers and households solve their decision problems, and (2) the market for deposits is cleared. In equilibrium, R must be equal to r. Otherwise banks would either accept no deposit if $R < r$, or demand infinite deposits if $R > r$.

Before we introduce financial friction, we compute the planner's problem as a benchmark. A social planner maximizes a representative household's welfare by

$$\max_{c_1, c_2} u(c_1) + u(c_2),$$

$$s.t. c_1 + d \leq y,$$

$$c_2 \leq rd + \pi,$$

$$\pi = RL - rd = R(N + d) - rd,$$

$$c_1 > 0, c_2 > 0, d > 0, R = r.$$

The solution is almost the same as the solution to the household's problem:

$$c_1 = \frac{yr + \pi}{r^{\frac{1}{\gamma}} + r}, d = y - \frac{yr + \pi}{r^{\frac{1}{\gamma}} + r}, c_2 = R(N + d).$$

In the absence of financial frictions, the household's supply of deposits, $S = d = y - \frac{yr + R(N+d) - rd}{r^{\frac{1}{\gamma}} + r}$, is upward sloping with respect to deposit rate r, and banks' demand for deposits is infinitely elastic at the constant deposit rate $r = R$. The equilibrium is characterized in Fig. 9.4.

Now we introduce a financial friction arising from banker's moral hazard problem: Instead of honoring all the claims and paying out the remaining profit, bankers have the opportunity to divert a share θ of banks' total assets for their private consumption and leave only the rest to the depositors. With insufficient funds to honor deposit contracts, they have to default in $t = 2$. The higher the amount of funds d deposited at some bank, the stronger the temptation to the banker to divert assets. Being aware of the moral hazard problem, in $t = 1$, depositors can infer the likelihood of default of a bank. They will only deposit in those banks which will not default. So there is an incentive compatibility constraint: A banker's profit from the no-default option must exceed the private benefit from diverting assets:

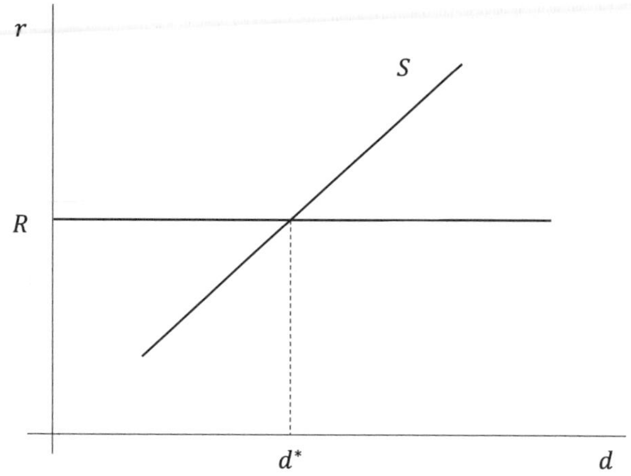

Fig. 9.4 Deposit market equilibrium in the absence of moral hazard

$$\pi = R(N + d) - rd \geq \theta R(N + d).$$

Obviously, this gives an upper bound to the amount of deposits d a bank can collect. It will be limited by the own equity N and meets the following condition:

$$0 \leq d \leq \frac{(1-\theta)RN}{r-(1-\theta)R}. \quad (IC)$$

The banks' problem is thus characterized by maximizing profits subject to the incentive constraint (IC). To find the solution, first note that banks will not take any deposit if $R < r$. They are indifferent if $R = r$ as long as the IC constraint (IC) holds, or, $d < \frac{(1-\theta)N}{\theta}$. For $R > r$, banks are willing to accept deposits, but the actual amount savers are willing to deposit is bounded by the incentive constraint (IC). In addition, since $0 \leq d$ the deposit rate is bounded below, $r > (1-\theta)R$. To summarize, banks' demand for deposits, as a function of r, is

$$D = \begin{cases} \left[0, \frac{(1-\theta)N}{\theta}\right], & \text{if } r = R, \\ \frac{(1-\theta)RN}{r-(1-\theta)R}, & \text{if } (1-\theta)R < r < R. \end{cases}$$

The equilibrium is presented in Fig. 9.5. The supply curve is still upward sloping, while the demand curve for deposits is kinked: It stays horizontal at $r = R$ as long as $d \leq \frac{(1-\theta)N}{\theta}$. Then, it becomes downward sloping with r. To see the implication of moral hazard, suppose banks start with high initial wealth N so that in equilibrium the supply curve crosses the demand curve on the horizontal part, with no interest rate spread, or, $r = R$. In that case, bankers' stakes in their bank is high: They can earn higher profit as stake holders than by diverting some private benefits. When banks' net worth is high enough, there will be no strategic default.

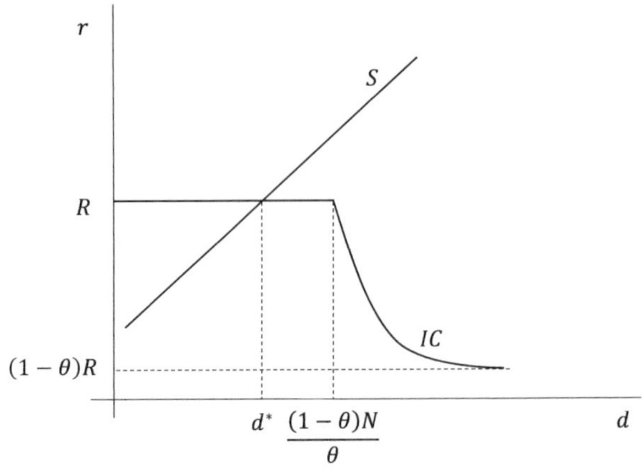

Fig. 9.5 Deposit market equilibrium in the presence of moral hazard with high equity

However, things change if the bankers' stake value is low. Suppose households' initial wealth N is falling. This has an immediate impact on the demand for deposits: Falling N shifts the IC curve to the left. If N is low enough, the supply curve will cross the demand curve on its downward sloping part in equilibrium. The intuition is clear: With low banks' net worth, bankers have less stake in the banks, so strategic default becomes attractive. The gain from private benefit in the default is high, while the loss in losing the stakes is low. With temptation for default being so prominent, in order to maintain the financial intermediation service, bankers need to get paid some information rent in order to stay in business instead of defaulting. So the rate for depositors is now lower than the return R, dampening incentives to save.

As is shown in Fig. 9.6, the new equilibrium in the deposit market is thus characterized by an interest rate spread $R - r > 0$ and lower bank deposits; as a result, bank lending, $L = N + d$, will be inefficiently low.

9.5 Liquidity Management: The Biachi–Bigio Model

9.5.1 Introduction: The Bank Lending Channel

The credit channel outlined in the last two sections shows successfully how small shocks from the real economy or monetary policy can be amplified by the banking sector. These types of models, however, can hardly explain why sometimes these amplifiers fail to work, just as they did in the recent 2007–2009 global financial crisis, unless one has to assume that the initial shock to the economy is extremely huge and unlikely (once in billions of years) to produce a downturn on the same scale as the Great Recession. The reason is that the banking sector typically only works as a passive financial accelerator in these models, like a black box, rather than a trouble maker. This neglects a crucial fact that instabilities may build up from within the banking sector. Under certain conditions the entire banking system may get suddenly melt down, with devastating consequence.

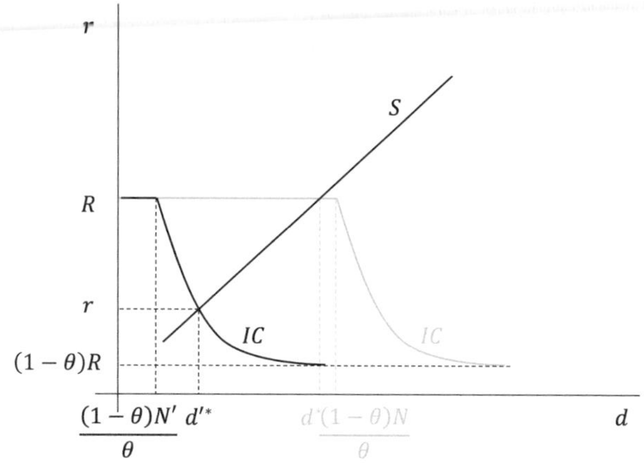

Fig. 9.6 Drop in deposits when moral hazard problem dominates. Black *IC* is the new demand curve under falling households' initial wealth *N*

The most recent global financial crisis reminds us that standard transmission mechanisms focused too much on business-driven credit cycles, i.e., bank lending is the output that amplifies business cycle and monetary policy shocks. They pay too little attention to credit-driven business cycles, i.e., the way how fragilities within banking sector have been accumulated as the result of banks' strategic, active responses to monetary policy, which eventually blow up the real economy. Thus, monetary policy is not only a stabilizer of the real economy, but may also be a cause of financial instabilities that destabilize the real economy.

Briefly speaking, in order to understand the role of banks in both types of cycles better, one has to treat banks as active players in the financial market, who manage different components in their balance sheets under real and monetary shocks. The balance sheet management leads to changes in lending, which is desirable as a transmission mechanism for monetary policy; however, it also changes the systemic financial risks within the banking sector, which may someday destroy the transmission mechanism.

We call this mechanism the "bank lending channel." As it is often associated with banks' risk-taking behavior, it is sometimes called "risk-taking channel" (proposed by Borio & Zhu, 2012). Generally speaking, after banks incur real or monetary shocks on the asset side of their balance sheets, they need to adjust their liabilities; however, due to some of the real-world frictions or restrictions—be it agency problem or regulatory requirement—the adjustment in the liabilities cannot perfectly accommodate the shock on the asset side. In the end, assets need to be adjusted, too. After such feedback between both sides of banks' balance sheets, the components in the balance sheets change, including banks' loan supply and financial risk exposure.

In the following sections, we present two approaches to modelling the bank lending channel. They focus on different perspectives of banking. The first one is motivated by banks' liquidity management practice: Liquidity can be described as the capability of banks to meet monetary obligations when they come due. To fulfill such obligations in the daily business, for example, cash withdrawals from checkable deposit accounts, banks need to hold a certain amount of reserves. However, as the return to bank reserves, or, the interest paid on reserve accounts in the central bank, is usually very low, banks prefer to hold less reserves, invest more in high yield loans, and borrow from other banks (or the central bank) if they fall short of reserve. When banks expand lending, they earn profit from the new loans, but also take higher exposure to liquidity risks—because more liabilities become checkable so that banks are more likely rely on costly interbank borrowings. In the end, total bank lending is determined by the balance between the marginal profit from issuing an additional loan and the expected cost for liquidity due to increased exposure to liquidity risks.

Suppose a bank incurs a negative shock to the assets, after the central bank conducts a tightening monetary policy and drains some of bank reserves by open market sales. This raises the interest rate in the market for reserves. From liquidity management perspective, the cost of funding liquidity gets higher. As long as banks cannot find cheaper substitutes for funding, and cannot raise new reserves by converting some of the assets to cash, they have to reduce their loan supply—a transmission of monetary policy. In this section, we present a model set up by Biachi–Bigio capturing this transmission mechanism.

The second approach focuses on banks' risk management practice: To cushion the financial risks on the balance sheets, banks build capital buffers as required by regulation. A shock to banks' assets initially reduces (raises) the riskiness of bank assets, relaxes (tightens) the constraint from capital requirement as a result of risk management, allowing them to take more (cut) debts and expand (shrink) the supply of risky loans on the asset side. This mechanism has been coined as "leverage cycle," as it works through the bank leverage (capital to asset ratio). Sections 9.6 and 9.7 present models of the leverage cycle.

9.5.2 Reserves and Liquidity Risk

In reality, liquidity management is one key issue in the core of banks' daily business. It also plays a crucial role in the monetary transmission mechanism. To understand the concept of liquidity, liquidity risks, and liquidity management, suppose a stylized bank is managing a balance sheet as shown in the left chart of Fig. 9.7. The asset side contains loans to firms and households, holdings of liquid assets, as well as central bank reserves. On the liability side, the funding comes from the bank's own equity, and demand deposits from depositors.

When the bank decides to issue a new loan, it does not necessarily need to raise loanable funds before the loan issuance, but rather, it just issues the loan that becomes part of the assets, and creates a credit line, or, a deposit account for the debtor, as shown in the right chart of Fig. 9.7. The debtor can withdraw from the credit line, and in the future will repay the bank the loan with interest. The interest income will become the bank's profit, increasing its net worth, or, equity.

In this way, banks can expand loan supply, or, create money at a stroke of a pen. However, they cannot do this without limit. Although banks earn profit from loan issuance, they also expose themselves to several risks. The most obvious risk from the loan issuance is credit risk, i.e., the likelihood that the debtor cannot repay when the loan is due. When the loan is non-performing and the value of the loan cannot be fully recovered, the bank will incur a loss in its equity. If total losses exceed equity, the bank will go bankrupt.

The less obvious risk is liquidity risk, or, the likelihood that banks cannot meet their monetary obligations when they come due. There are many sources of liquidity risks. We can see how they emerge after a new loan has been issued as follows: The debtor receiving the loan may withdraw from her deposit account at any time; for example, after a household receives a mortgage loan, a deposit account is created simultaneously, and the household may need cash out of the account to pay the home developer. Such withdrawal leads to an equivalent fall in the bank's reserves, as Fig. 9.8 shows.

If the decline in reserves is so large that the level of bank reserves falls below the required reserve ratio, new reserves need to be raised immediately to fulfill the reserve requirement. The bank may directly sell some of its assets to raise cash, but mostly, it borrows from the central bank's discount window or from other banks (as shown in Fig. 9.9), using eligible liquid assets, such as government securities, as collateral. However, the bank needs to pay interest on such loans, and this erodes some of its equity.

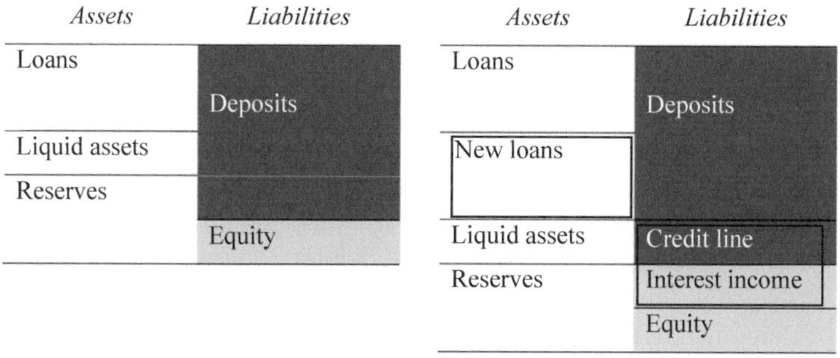

Fig. 9.7 Loan expansion

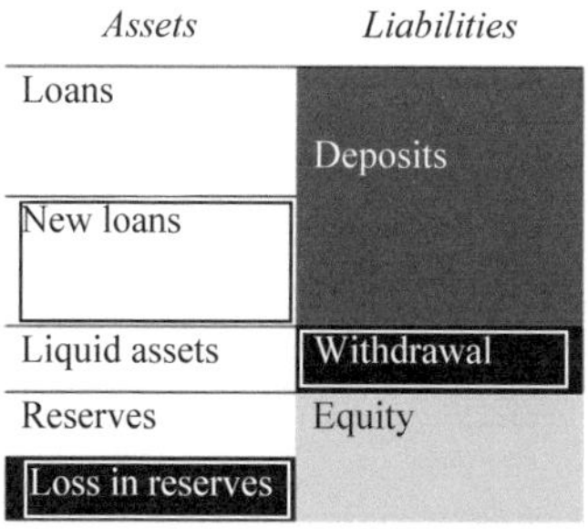

Fig. 9.8 Deposit withdrawal and fall in bank reserves

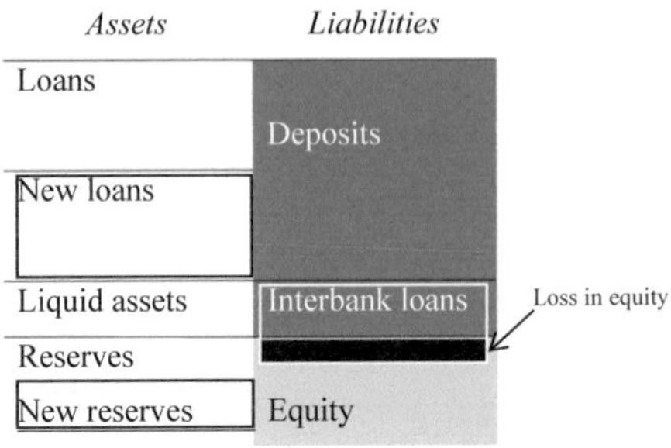

Fig. 9.9 Raising reserves through interbank loans

From the bank's point of view, holding reserves is costly, as the interest paid to reserves held at the central bank usually is much lower, compared to the returns on other types of assets. Therefore, apart from required reserves, banks typically have the incentive to minimize the excess reserves. They would rather borrow from the interbank market/central bank's discount window when reserves fall below the required level, as long as the interbank lending rate/discount rate is not too high.

This simple example illustrates that the bank exposes itself to two types of liquidity risks, when it provides lending to the real economy: Market liquidity risk and funding liquidity risk (see also Brunnermeier & Pederson, 2009).

9.5.3 Market Liquidity Risk

A bank faces risks in the market's valuation on its assets. The market value of bank assets is usually below the face value: When bank assets are sold in the market, the price is subject to a discount bank. If these discounts are too high, banks will not be able to raise sufficient resources in interbank lending or asset market sales, causing further problems in liquidity management.

Market liquidity is an indicator of the ease of converting assets to cash when needed without incurring a large discount on such assets; it is asset-specific. The market liquidity of assets affects the extent to which banks can raise funding through asset sales or liquidation. Highly liquid assets can be sold quickly without any discount, whereas illiquid assets may take a long time to sell and/or have to be sold at a discount.

The market liquidity of assets also affects the banks' ability for borrowing on the interbank market when these assets are used for collateral. The value of collateral is also subject to a discount, called "haircut." The haircut incurred on assets used as collateral will be larger the larger the discount when sold on the market.

Market liquidity of bank assets vary from time to time because of many frictions in the financial market, including:

(1) Moral hazard problems. Bank assets are often backed by ongoing projects. Since project managers cannot be perfectly monitored, they may act in a manner that

promotes their private benefit instead the depositors' best interests. Hence investors may be willing to buy such assets only at a discount on their face value.

(2) Adverse selection problems. As buyers have less knowledge than sellers about asset quality, buyers cannot tell whether they are being sold bad assets. The fear of buying lemons can lead to discounts in asset prices.

(3) Complexity in financial product design can also reduce market liquidity, especially during the crises. When a market is under stress, some financial products are too complicated and/or customized to be priced in short time; for example, it can be extremely challenging to identify the risks and reprice an entire asset pool that backs a structured product. Although only a few assets may be under water, price can still crash for all assets in the same asset class (see Brunnermeier & Oehmke, 2009).

9.5.4 Funding Liquidity Risk

A bank also faces the risk in the feasibility of funding liabilities, i.e., it may not be able to access funding sources at reasonable cost when it needs. We use the term funding liquidity to refer to the ease with which banks can raise funds by rolling over or taking on more debt. While the concept of market liquidity is asset-specific, the concept of funding liquidity reflects several institution-specific factors. A bank's funding liquidity depends on many factors, including:

(1) The availability of liquidity suppliers in the market, which may change over the business cycles. For example, in normal times there are many active participants in interbank markets so that one bank can easily borrow from others for a short term at fairly low costs; in contrast, when markets are under stress there may be few lenders in the market and borrowing costs become very high.

(2) Funding liquidity is affected by corporate governance: Investors are more willing to lend to better managed banks.

(3) Raising new debt implies that claims of existing creditors are diluted, which may impede banks' funding capability. Such conflict among investors, called debt overhang, reduces banks' funding liquidity.

(4) The bank's funding structure. On the asset side, it usually takes considerably long time for bank loans to mature, while on the liability side, the bank often needs to fund itself via debt claims that repay creditors in a short time. Such maturity mismatch implies that the bank needs to replace old creditors with new ones, or, to roll over the debt, to keep the long-term loans going. The higher degree of maturity mismatch there is between the bank's assets and liabilities, the more frequently the bank needs to roll over the debts, hence the more uncertainty on the availability of new funding creditors, or, the lower the bank's funding liquidity is.

Liquidity Spiral

Market liquidity and funding liquidity are interconnected. Given that assets are often used as collateral when banks borrow, market liquidity and funding liquidity can reinforce each other, destabilizing banking systems under market stress and leading to liquidity spirals: In normal times, banks, by participating in asset markets, provide market liquidity to the system. If some asset is mispriced at excessive discount, offering arbitrage opportunities, banks—acting as highly specialized arbitrageurs—buy the undervalued asset and so help to bring prices in line with fundamentals. They take large leveraged positions, using other people's money. Leaning against the wind usually helps to correct the mispricing of financial assets, fundamentally stabilizing the economy. So in normal times, arbitrageurs make illiquid markets more liquid, reducing market volatility.

But banks' capability to do so depends on their ability to obtain funding. Leveraged investors rely on market liquidity being available to perform arbitrage; they do not provide liquidity themselves. Professional arbitrageurs may clearly spot an arbitrage opportunity to buy the undervalued assets, but they need outside funds from non-informed investors—they face funding constraint. Under extreme conditions, when prices diverge far from fundamental values, non-informed investors, judging investment skills from past performance and fearing a further decline, may not be willing to provide the funds needed to make arbitrage effective.

When markets dry up, assets have to be sold at large discounts. For instance, in a financial crisis, many financial institutions need to raise cash by selling assets, but at the same time, they are all under stress so that buyers can hardly be found. This can create a limit of arbitrage. Outside investors are likely to withdraw their funds at precisely the time as prices move further away from fundamental values and arbitrage opportunities improve. Thus, arbitrage becomes ineffective exactly at those times when most urgently needed, triggering fire sales. When a bank needs to sell assets in a fire sale during a crisis, the market price of assets can be depressed persistently due to a lack of buyers. This mechanism has been modelled already by Shleifer and Vishny (1997).

When things go wrong, liquidity dries up completely, making things much worse. If there is stress in markets for liquidity, banks cannot get enough funding via borrowing and they will need to sell illiquid assets instead. With many banks attempting to sell illiquid assets, a situation can arise where there are far fewer buyers relative to sellers of such assets. This generates downward pressure on asset prices, worsens market liquidity in the system, and increases haircut levels. This situation further reduces bank asset value as collateral, aggravates banks' funding liquidity, forcing banks to liquidate more assets which makes asset prices plummet even further... the entire banking system falls into a downward liquidity spiral (Brunnermeier & Pederson, 2009).

As shown by Brunnermeier and Pederson (2009), when arbitrageurs have large existing positions, there can be multiple equilibria and liquidity can be fragile. In one equilibrium, markets are liquid, leading to favorable margin requirements for speculators, which in turn helps speculators make markets liquid. In another equilibrium, markets are illiquid, resulting in larger margin requirements (or arbitrageur losses), thus restricting arbitrageurs from providing market liquidity. Any equilibrium selection has the property that small speculator losses can lead to a discontinuous drop of market liquidity. This "sudden dry-up" or fragility of market liquidity is due to the fact that with high levels of arbitrageur capital, markets must be in a liquid equilibrium, and, if arbitrageur capital is reduced enough, the market must eventually switch to a low-liquidity/high-margin equilibrium. Just as the famous saying states:

> A banker is a fellow who lends you his umbrella when the sun is shining, but wants it back the minute it begins to rain—Mark Twain (1835–1910)

Monetary Policy, Liquidity Management, and Bank Lending

How does monetary policy affect banks' lending decisions through liquidity management? In reality, from the liquidity management point of view, one bank's total lending comes from the balance between the profit earned from the loans and the exposure to both liquidity and credit risks. Credit risks mostly comes from banks' screening and monitoring of the loans, while liquidity risks are directly affected by the feasibility of liquidity as well as the interest rates the banks are charged in interbank market, which are regulated by monetary policy. In other words, banks' loan supply reacts to monetary policy through their liquidity management practice:

- When the central bank conducts expansionary monetary policy through security purchases in open market operation, bank reserves increase. This reduces banks' liquidity risk as the likelihood of raising external funding falls, and encourages banks to issue new loans. The opposite applies if the central bank conducts contractionary monetary policy through security sales.
- When the central bank adjusts its discount rate, say, setting a lower interest rate for discount window, the funding cost through central bank falls. Because the discount window is a (imperfect) substitute to interbank lending, as a result of (imperfect) competition, the interbank lending rate is most likely to fall, too. This reduces banks' overall external funding cost when they need to raise new reserves, and thus encourages banks to increase loan supply.
- When the central bank changes required reserve ratio, banks' liquidity risk is also affected. For example, when the required reserve ratio gets higher, banks are more likely to hit the constraint and get forced to raise new reserves; therefore, banks will reduce their lending.

The central bank's lender-of-last-resort policy provides emergency lending to banks, especially in the market under stress where banks are reluctant to lend to each other and interbank lending rate is too high. This reduces banks' liquidity risk in the downturn and stabilizes bank lending.

9.5.5 A Simple Model of Liquidity Management, Based on Bianchi and Bigio (2018)

The monetary transmission mechanism through banks' liquidity management can be seen through a simple model, based on Bianchi and Bigio (2018). Consider a banking sector that banks maximize their dividends that are paid to the shareholders after three periods, $t = 0, 1, 2$. There are infinite number of competitive banks, and the banks are indexed by $i \in [0, 1]$. Table 9.2 shows a representative bank's balance sheet in period t, similar to Fig. 9.7: On the liability side it funds itself by issuing equity E_t to shareholders, and raising demand deposits (deposits that can be withdrawn any time on demand) D_t from depositors at the gross deposit rate R^D; on the asset side it holds reserves C_t and issue loans B_t. Assume that reserves are denominated in nominal terms, while loans, equity, and deposits are in real terms. Deposits are a numeraire good.

A bank enters period $t = 0$ with its balance sheet $\{B_0, C_0, E_0, D_0\}$. We call the period between $t = 0$ and $t = 1$ "lending stage," in which the bank decides new loan issuance. During the lending stage, the bank issues new loans I_0—denote the market price of the bank loans as q_0—and raises new reserves φ_0 at price p_0. At the same time, the existing loans B_0 are repaid—note that bank deposits fall by B_0 after the repayment. The laws of motion, or, the intertemporal resource constraints, for the balance sheet during the lending stage is characterized by

$$\frac{D_1}{R^D} = D_0 + q_0 I_0 + p_0 \varphi_0 - B_0,$$

$$B_1 = I_0,$$

$$C_1 = C_0 + \varphi_0.$$

Banks are subject to capital requirement, i.e., the ratio of equity to total assets must be above a certain threshold. This is equivalent to require that

$$\frac{D_1}{R^D} \leq \kappa \underbrace{\left(q_1 B_1 + p_1 C_1 - \frac{D_1}{R^D} \right)}_{\text{equity value}}$$

in which κ is a constant number, and the bank's equity value can be computed through balance sheet identity. The inequality simply says that the bank's debt liabilities should not exceed κ times of its equity value.

Now, in period $t = 1$, a random share ω_1 of bank deposits are withdrawn by the depositors. Assume that the cumulative distribution function of ω_1 follows $F(\omega_1)$

Table 9.2 The banks' balance sheet in period t

Assets	*Liabilities*
Loans B_t	Equity E_t
Reserves C_t	Reserves C_t

with the support $(-\infty, 1)$. The value $\omega_1 > 0$ means that there is an outflow of bank deposits, while $\omega_1 < 0$ implies that the bank receives deposits.

There is a reserve requirement imposed by the central bank, i.e., the ratio of bank reserves to demand deposits shall not fall below a constant value ρ, $0 \leq \rho \leq 1$, at any time t

$$p_t C_t \geq \frac{\rho D_t (1 - \omega_t)}{R^D}.$$

After the withdrawal shock in $t = 1$, the bank's reserves may fall below the required level. The shortfall is

$$x = \underbrace{\frac{\rho D_1 (1 - \omega_1)}{R^D}}_{(A)} - \underbrace{\left(p_1 C_1 - \frac{\omega_1 D_1}{R^D} \right)}_{(B)}.$$

In the equation, term (A) is the required reserve level, and term (B) is the actual reserve level after withdrawal—note that when deposits are withdrawn, there is an equal amount fall in bank reserves. To fulfill the reserve requirement, from now on the bank needs to close the gap x. We call the period between $t = 1$ and $t = 2$ "balancing stage." In this stage:

- If $x > 0$, the bank needs to borrow reserves from other banks at interest rate χ_b.
- If $x < 0$, it implies that the bank holds excess reserves. In such circumstance, the bank can lend its excess reserves x at the market interbank lending rate χ_l.

Whether the bank is a borrowing or a lending bank depends on the level of the withdrawal shock it experiences. Suppose there is a $\underline{\omega}_1$ that makes

$$x = 0 = \frac{\rho D_1 (1 - \underline{\omega}_1)}{R^D} - \left(p_1 C_1 - \frac{\underline{\omega}_1 D_1}{R^D} \right),$$

or,

$$\underline{\omega}_1 = \frac{R^D p_1 C_1 - \rho D_1}{(1 - \rho) D_1},$$

then the bank is a lending bank if $\omega_1 < \underline{\omega}_1$, and it is a borrowing bank if $\underline{\omega}_1 < \omega_1 \leq 1$.

The laws of motion for the balance sheet during the balancing stage is characterized by

$$C_2 = C_1 - \frac{\omega_1 D_1}{p_1},$$

$$B_2 = B_1,$$

$$D_2 = D_1(1 - \omega_1) + \chi(x),$$

in which

$$\chi(x) = \begin{cases} \chi_l x, & \text{if } x \leq 0, \\ \chi_b x, & \text{if } x > 0. \end{cases}$$

After $t = 2$, the bank is dissolved. All bank loans are repaid, remaining depositors withdraw, and the rest is distributed to the shareholders as dividends, DIV

$$DIV = p_2 C_2 + q_2 B_2 - \frac{D_2}{R^D}.$$

Assume that the price for loans and bank reserves are invariant over time, so that we can drop the time subscript for p and q as follows (it is left as an exercise for the readers to discuss the role of p and q if they are time varying). Note that once the bank fixes its loan supply I_0 and new reserves φ_0 in the lending stage $t = 0$, it just reacts passively to meet all the constraints in the balancing stage after the withdrawal shock is materialized. Therefore, the bank's problem to maximize expected DIV is to choosing its loan supply I_0 and new reserves φ_0 in the lending stage

$$\max_{I_0, \varphi_0} E_0[DIV]$$

with the intertemporal resource constraints as well as regulatory requirements

$$C_2 = C_1 - \frac{\omega_1 D_1}{p},$$

$$B_2 = B_1,$$

$$D_2 = D_1(1 - \omega_1) + \chi(x),$$

$$\frac{D_1}{R^D} = D_0 + qI_0 + p\varphi_0 - B_0,$$

$$B_1 = I_0,$$

$$C_1 = C_0 + \varphi_0,$$

$$x = \frac{\rho D_1(1 - \omega_1)}{R^D} - \left(pC_1 - \frac{\omega_1 D_1}{R^D}\right),$$

$$\frac{D_1}{R^D} \leq \kappa\left(qB_1 + pC_1 - \frac{D_1}{R^D}\right).$$

Using the intertemporal resource constraints, the bank's dividends can be rewritten as

$$DIV = pC_2 + qB_2 - \frac{D_2}{R^D} = p\left(C_0 + \varphi_0 - \frac{\omega_1 D_1}{p}\right) + qI_0 - \frac{D_1(1-\omega_1) + \chi(x)}{R^D},$$

and D_1 is given by $\frac{D_1}{R^D} = D_0 + qI_0 + p\varphi_0 - B_0$. To simplify the analysis, assume that the capital requirement is not binding—the requirement is specified here for a complete picture of the bank's problem, however, exploring the role of capital requirement further is left as an exercise for the readers.

Note that the expected rebalancing cost $\chi(x)$ can be computed as

$$E_0[\chi(x)] = \underbrace{\int_{-\infty}^{\underline{\omega}_1} \chi_l x dF(\omega_1)}_{(A)} + \underbrace{\int_{\underline{\omega}_1}^{1} \chi_b x dF(\omega_1)}_{(B)}$$

in which term (A) is the return on lending if the bank is a lending bank in the balancing stage, while term (B) is the cost on borrowing if the bank is a borrowing bank.

The bank's optimal decision is determined by the first-order conditions with respect to I_0 and φ_0.

$$\begin{aligned}
\frac{\partial E_0[DIV]}{\partial I_0} &= 0 \\
&= (1-R^D)\overline{\omega}_1 q - \frac{1}{R^D} \\
&\times \left[\int_{-\infty}^{\underline{\omega}_1} \chi_l f(\omega_1)\frac{\partial x}{\partial I_0} d\omega_1 + \chi_l x f(\underline{\omega}_1)\frac{\partial \underline{\omega}_1}{\partial I_0} + \int_{\underline{\omega}_1}^{1} \chi_b f(\omega_1)\frac{\partial x}{\partial I_0} d\omega_1 - \chi_b x f(\underline{\omega}_1)\frac{\partial \underline{\omega}_1}{\partial I_0}\right] \\
&= (1-R^D)\overline{\omega}_1 q - \frac{1}{R^D} \\
&\times \{(\chi_b - \chi_l) x f(\underline{\omega}_1)\frac{R^{D2} pC_1}{1-\rho} D_1^{-2} q + \chi_l q E[\rho(1-\omega_1) + \omega_1 | \omega_1 \le \underline{\omega}_1] \\
&+ \chi_b q E[\rho(1-\omega_1) + \omega_1 | \underline{\omega}_1 < \omega_1 \le 1]\},
\end{aligned}$$

Here $\overline{\omega}_1$ denotes the unconditional mean of ω_1, or, $\overline{\omega}_1 = \int_{-\infty}^{1} \omega_1 f(\omega_1) d\omega_1$, the term $E[\rho(1-\omega_1) + \omega_1 | \omega_1 \le \underline{\omega}_1]$ is the conditional expectation of $\rho(1-\omega_1) + \omega_1$ for all $\omega_1 \le \underline{\omega}_1$, and the term $E[\rho(1-\omega_1) + \omega_1 | \underline{\omega}_1 < \omega_1 \le 1]$ is the conditional expectation of $\rho(1-\omega_1) + \omega_1$ for all $\underline{\omega}_1 < \omega_1 \le 1$. Rearrange the equations to get

$$(R^D - 1)\overline{\omega}_1 = \frac{1}{R^D}\left\{\underbrace{(\chi_l - \chi_b)xf(\underline{\omega}_1)\frac{R^{D2}pC_1}{1-\rho}D_1^{-2}}_{(A)}\right.$$

$$\left. \underbrace{-\chi_b E[\rho(1-\omega_1)+\omega_1|\underline{\omega}_1 < \omega_1 \leq 1]}_{(B)} - \underbrace{\chi_l E[\rho(1-\omega_1)+\omega_1|\omega_1 \leq \underline{\omega}_1]}_{(C)}\right\}.$$

This equation shows clearly the tradeoff on the liability side the bank faces when it decides to change its loan supply on the margin. Suppose that the bank increases its loan supply by one unit, the left hand side of the equation is the net contribution to *DIV* before balancing—note that $(R^D - 1)\overline{\omega}_1$ comes from the derivative of $E_0[DIV]$, excluding $\chi(x)$ term, with respect to I_0. The right hand side of the equation comes from the marginal cost to *DIV* in rebalancing, as the result of marginal increase in loan supply:

- Term (A) captures the marginal cost coming directly from shifting the threshold $\underline{\omega}_1$. Suppose a bank with ω_1 slightly lower than $\underline{\omega}_1$, and it would have been a lending bank and could have lent to other banks for interest profit χ_l; however, by increasing one unit of loan supply, $\underline{\omega}_1$ gets lower, the bank becomes a borrowing bank and instead has to borrow at the interest cost χ_b. Term (A) thus shows the opportunity cost directly associated with the shifting threshold.
- Higher loan supply corresponds to an equal rise in demand deposits. After the withdrawal shock, the bank becomes more likely to have a shortfall in reserves and need to borrow. Term (B) is thus the expected marginal increase in the borrowing cost for new reserves.
- The bank also becomes less likely to have excess reserves before the balancing stage, therefore, Term (C) reflects the expected marginal fall in the profit in interbank lending.

The second first-order condition for the bank's problem determines the level of new reserves φ_0

$$\begin{aligned}
\frac{\partial E_0[DIV]}{\partial \varphi_0} &= 0 \\
&= (1-R^D)\overline{\omega}_1 p - \frac{1}{R^D} \\
&\times \left[\int_{-\infty}^{\underline{\omega}_1} \chi_l f(\omega_1)\frac{\partial x}{\partial \varphi_0}d\omega_1 + \chi_l x f(\underline{\omega}_1)\frac{\partial \underline{\omega}_1}{\partial \varphi_0} + \int_{\underline{\omega}_1}^{1} \chi_b f(\omega_1)\frac{\partial x}{\partial \varphi_0}d\omega_1 - \chi_b x f(\underline{\omega}_1)\frac{\partial \underline{\omega}_1}{\partial \varphi_0}\right] \\
&= (1-R^D)\overline{\omega}_1 p - \frac{1}{R^D}\left\{(\chi_l - \chi_b)xf(\underline{\omega}_1)\frac{R^D p(1-\rho)D_1 - R^{D2}p^2(C_0+\varphi_0)(1-\rho)}{(1-\rho)^2 D_1^2}\right.
\end{aligned}$$

$$\left. + \chi_l E[\rho(1-\omega_1)q + \omega_1 q - p|\omega_1 \leq \underline{\omega}_1] + \chi_b E[\rho(1-\omega_1)q + \omega_1 q - p|\underline{\omega}_1 < \omega_1 \leq 1]\right\},$$

Here the term $E[\rho(1-\omega_1)q+\omega_1 q-p|\omega_1\leq\underline{\omega}_1]$ is the conditional expectation of $\rho(1-\omega_1)q+\omega_1 q-p$ for all $\omega_1\leq\underline{\omega}_1$, and the term $E[\rho(1-\omega_1)q+\omega_1 q-p|\underline{\omega}_1<\omega_1\leq 1]$ is the conditional expectation of $\rho(1-\omega_1)+\omega_1$ for all $\underline{\omega}_1<\omega_1\leq 1$. Rearrange the equation to get

$$(R^D-1)\overline{\omega}_1 q=\frac{1}{R^D}\Bigg\{\underbrace{(\chi_l-\chi_b)xf(\underline{\omega}_1)\frac{R^{D2}p^2(C_0+\varphi_0)(1-\rho)-R^D p(1-\rho)D_1}{(1-\rho)^2D_1^2}}_{(A)}$$
$$\underbrace{-\chi_b E[\rho(1-\omega_1)q+\omega_1 q-p|\underline{\omega}_1<\omega_1\leq 1]}_{(B)}$$
$$-\underbrace{\chi_l E[\rho(1-\omega_1)q+\omega_1 q-p|\omega_1\leq\underline{\omega}_1]}_{(C)}\Bigg\}.$$

This equation shows clearly the tradeoff on the asset side the bank faces when it decides to change its reserves level on the margin during the lending stage. Suppose that the bank increases its reserves by one unit, the left hand side of the equation is the net contribution to *DIV* before balancing—note that $(R^D-1)\overline{\omega}_1 q$ comes from the derivative of $E_0[DIV]$, excluding $\chi(x)$ term, with respect to φ_0. The right hand side of the equation comes from the marginal cost to *DIV* in rebalancing, as the result of marginal increase in reserves: Term (A) reflects the shift in the cost on the threshold, while term (B) captures the marginal reduction in the borrowing cost due to reduced exposure to funding liquidity risk during the balance stage, and term (C) is the marginal benefit from interbank lending due to the increased likelihood of holding excess reserves after the withdrawal shock.

In brief, the model implies that bank lending is constrained by banks' liquidity management practice. When a new loan is issued, a demandable deposit account is simultaneously created for the borrower, and the bank has an increased exposure to funding liquidity risk, i.e., it becomes more likely that the bank needs to borrow from the market if reserves fall below the required level after withdrawals from the deposit accounts. The equilibrium bank lending is therefore determined by the marginal return from loan supply and the marginal cost from liquidity management.

In this framework, monetary policy affects bank lending, and further real economy activities, via shifting interbank market rates. In the model, χ_l and χ_b resemble the interest rate paid on reserves and the discount rate, respectively: Assume that banks do not trade reserves with each other, but rather, the central bank serves as an intermediary between banks. Banks with excess reserves deposit in the central bank with interest rate χ_l, and the central bank lends to banks with deficits in reserve through the discount window at the rate χ_b. The banks reacts in their loan supply I_0 when the central bank conducts its monetary policy through χ_l and χ_b. For example, when the central bank implements an expansionary monetary policy by setting lower χ_b, it reduces the cost of financing reserve deficits in the future, the balancing stage. Knowing this, banks will choose higher I_0 in the lending stage.

It is also worth noting that for simplicity in this model we focused only on funding liquidity risk, i.e., banks only face uncertainties in their liabilities. However, in reality, market liquidity risk and credit risk are also other major concerns in liquidity management, i.e., banks need to hold liquid assets as collateral for borrowing from other banks and loans may be non-performing; they both affect bank lending, and monetary transmission mechanism may have a farther reaching impacts to other dimensions. For example, when the central bank relaxes monetary policy by setting lower χ_b, banks' funding liquidity risk is reduced. This does not only allow banks to issue more loans, but also provides more headroom for banks to provide more loans for high yield, but riskier projects, increasing credit risk. In reality, lax monetary policies such as policy rate cuts or lending guarantees for banks are often introduced to stimulate the real economy; however, one has to keep in mind that credit risk may rise in the banking system, and such "risk-taking channel"—if not contained—can eventually result in excess risk taking leading to financial instabilities or even financial crises. We will explore such link between monetary policy and financial stability in the next chapter.

9.6 Risk Management and the Leverage Cycle (Shin Model)

Hyun Song Shin argues that the financial cycle is at least in part the product of the behavior of financial intermediaries such as investment banks. In a number of papers, Shin jointly with several coauthors (Adrian & Shin, 2014; Bruno & Shin, 2015a, 2015b) shows empirically that the size of the balance sheets of investment banks and the amount they borrow is pro-cyclical. In particular, during "quiet" periods these intermediaries borrow aggressively, build up leverage and load up on risk. This behavior raises the demand for risky assets during the boom. When risk and volatility increase, these institutions reverse this process. They shrink their balance sheets and deleverage. This reduces the supply of credit and the demand for risky assets, creating very powerful pro-cyclicality that may threaten financial stability: If the process of deleveraging is sharp enough, failures and financial instability can follow. Risky borrowers who received credit in the boom period cannot finance themselves any longer. The highly leveraged positions put on in good times become a downward accelerant.

In this section, we show how leverage cycle that amplifies real and monetary policy shocks emerges as a result of bank's risk management practice, using the model from Cao (2012) which is based on Shin (2010). The risk management practice in the financial institutions is widely based on the Value-at-Risk (VaR) assessments. The VaR of a portfolio of a bank's assets defines the worst loss over a certain time horizon such that with a pre-specified probability the realized loss is larger. Quantitatively, the VaR of a portfolio of assets at confidence level α means that the event that the realized loss L exceeds VaR happens at a probability no higher than $1 - \alpha$, i.e., $Prob(L > VaR) \leq 1 - \alpha$, or equivalently $Prob(L < VaR) \geq \alpha$.

For example, the VaR of a portfolio over 1 month at confidence level 99% means that the probability of having a loss larger than VaR does not exceed 1%, or with

99% probability the realized loss is below VaR within the next month. Since VaR gives a clear assessment on a financial firm's potential loss during a certain period and a reference about the buffer the firm needs to hold to avoid bankruptcy, it is widely adopted as a key indicator in risk management.

9.6.1 Market Equilibrium and Asset Price

Banks' active management of their balance sheets using VaR brings extra volatility to asset prices and amplifies the market turbulence in the crises. The mechanism can be seen from the following model. Consider an economy that extends to two periods, $t = 0, 1$. There are two types of assets in this economy:

(1) The risky assets. They are securities issued by a fix number of entrepreneurs, traded in the initial period, $t = 0$, at the price level P, and the holders of the assets get the return from the assets at $t = 1$. The stochastic return from one unit of risky asset holding, R, follows a uniform distribution over the interval $[\overline{R} - z, \overline{R} + z]$, with $z > 0$. The expected value of R, $E[R]$ is $\overline{R}$, and the variance of R is therefore $\text{Var}[R] = \frac{z^2}{3}$.
(2) The riskless assets in the form of bank deposits, which pay a fixed gross return $r \geq 1$ for the holders.

There are also two groups of agents, with a unit of population for each group, in the economy:

(1) The risk-neutral leveraged ("active") investors, call them banks, who manage their portfolios using VaR.
(2) The risk averse non-leveraged ("passive") depositors, or, consumers, who do not actively adjust their balance sheets. To capture the risk aversion, assume that the non-leveraged depositors have a mean–variance preference with utility function of consumption c being $E[U] = E[c] - \frac{1}{2\tau}\text{Var}[c]$, in which $E[U]$ denotes the expected utility at $t = 0$, and τ indicates the degree of consumers' tolerance on risks: The higher τ is, ceteris paribus, the more the consumers are tolerant on taking risks.

Both types of agents own an endowment e at the start of $t = 0$.

For a representative consumer, as she does not like volatility in consumption, to reduce such volatility, she keeps some of her endowment as safe deposits in the banks in $t = 0$, and invests the rest in risky assets, i.e., by purchasing q_p of risky assets at market price P. Her balance sheet in $t = 0$ is characterized in Fig. 9.10. Her realized return at $t = 1$ is therefore

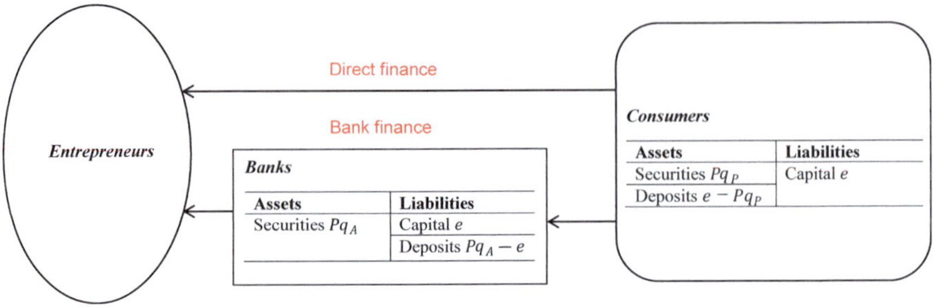

Fig. 9.10 The balance sheets of banks and consumers in $t = 0$

$$c = Rq_p - r\left(Pq_p - e\right).$$

Therefore, her investment decision at $t = 0$ is defined by maximizing her expected utility

$$\begin{aligned} \max_{q_p} E[U] &= E[Rq_p - r(Pq_p - e)] - \frac{1}{2\tau}\mathrm{Var}[Rq_p - r(Pq_p - e)] \\ &= \overline{R}q_p - r(Pq_p - e) - \frac{1}{2\tau}\frac{z^2}{3}q_P^2. \end{aligned}$$

The first-order condition $\frac{\partial E[U]}{\partial q_p} = 0$ gives the unleveraged depositor's optimal level of holding risky assets, $q_P(P)$

$$q_P(P) = \begin{cases} \frac{3\tau}{z^2}\left(\overline{R} - rP\right), & \overline{R} > P, \\ 0, & \text{otherwise.} \end{cases}$$

A representative bank, being risk neutral, always wants to maximize profits by investing in risky assets as much as possible. Therefore, it takes debts (or, it leverages) by borrowing from consumers to expand the balance sheet, which is characterized in Fig. 9.10. The investment decision at $t = 0$ is to maximize expected return in $t = 1$ by purchasing q_A of risky assets at market price P, borrowing $Pq_A - e$ from consumers, given the *VaR* constraint in risk management

$$\max_{q_A} E[Rq_A - r(Pq_A - e)] = \left(\overline{R} - rP\right)q_A + re,$$

$$s.t.\ e \geq VaR.$$

Since the expected return is linear in q_A and e, the bank will maximize q_A as long as $\overline{R} > rP$, until the *VaR* constraint becomes binding.

For simplicity, assume that the *VaR* constraint requires that the bank should be able to stay solvent even in the worst state, i.e., be able to repay the depositors even

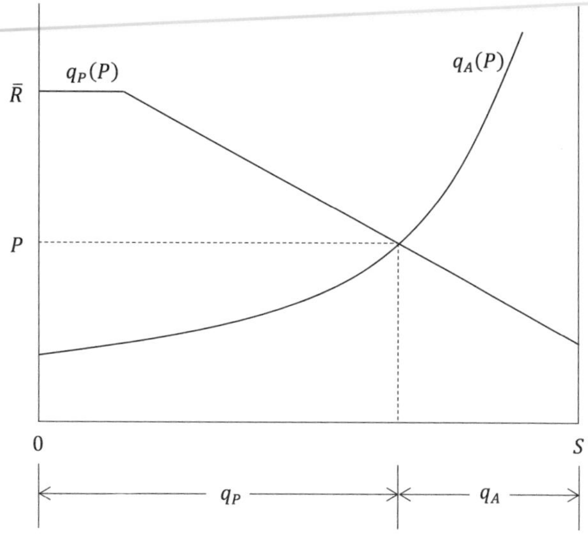

Fig. 9.11 The equilibrium asset price and demand for risky assets

the payoff from the risky asset is the lowest, $\overline{R} - z$. This implies $(\overline{R} - z)q_A \geq r(Pq_A - e)$. When the *VaR* constraint is binding, $e = \left(P - \frac{\overline{R}}{r} + \frac{z}{r}\right)q_A$. Rewrite it as

$$q_A(P) = \frac{re}{rP - \overline{R} + z} \tag{9.6.1}$$

for the demand of risky assets from the leveraged banks.

To focus on the key mechanism, assume that in the short run the aggregate supply of risky assets is fixed at S—because the number of entrepreneurs are fixed, or equivalently, assume that the asset price adjustment is much faster than asset quantity. Therefore, we have $q_A + q_P = S$. Depict $q_A(P)$ and $q_P(P)$ in the same space, as Fig. 9.11 shows, the equilibrium asset price P and the demand of risky assets from both types of agents can be determined simultaneously.

9.6.2 VaR, Asset Price, and the Leverage Cycle

To produce leverage cycles by the feedback between asset price and leverage in boom-bust cycles, suppose there is an unexpected shock to the risky assets' return at an intermediate period, call it $t = 0.5$, so that both banks and consumers have the chance to adjust their balance sheets. Assume that at $t = 0.5$, it turns out that the true distribution of the risky assets' return is $\left[\overline{R'} - z, \overline{R'} + z\right]$, $\overline{R'} > \overline{R}$, i.e., the economy is in a boom.

The impact of such positive shock to asset return, or economic fundamentals, on asset price is visualized in Fig. 9.12. Both demand curves are shifted upwards,

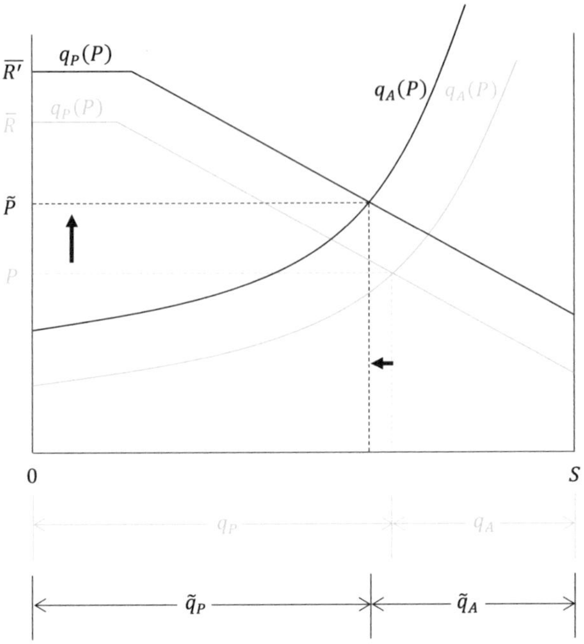

Fig. 9.12 Asset price rises in the boom phase

leading to a higher price level. This fits perfectly the observed fact that the asset price increases in the economic boom.

Although the equilibrium price P is simultaneously determined by the demand curves of banks and consumers once the shock to the fundamental value of the risky assets gets realized, we may break the entire process in several steps to see how the shock to $\overline{R}$ propagates through the leverage channel:

(1) The rising $\overline{R}$ increases the banks' demand of the risky assets, which is characterized by $q_P = \frac{3\tau}{z^2}\left(\overline{R} - rP\right)$. With all other things equal, an upward shifted $q_P(P)$ line has a positive impact on the price level P.

(2) With a higher price level, call it $\widetilde{P}$, the value of banks' risky assets, $\widetilde{P}q_A$, increases. From its balance sheet, this implies a higher level of equity value

$$\widetilde{e} = \widetilde{P}q_A - \left(\frac{\overline{R} - z}{r}\right)q_A, \tag{9.6.2}$$

given its starting debt level $\left(\frac{\overline{R}-z}{r}\right)q_A$.

(3) With a higher equity value, a bank's VaR constraint becomes relaxed as $\widetilde{e} > e = VaR$. This allows the bank to expand its balance sheet, take in more debts and purchase more risky assets to $\widetilde{q}_A > q_A$ in order to catch up with the improved fundamental value $\overline{R'}$. The expanded balance sheet is then featured by

$$\widetilde{e} = \widetilde{P}\widetilde{q}_A - \left(\frac{\overline{R'} - z}{r}\right)\widetilde{q}_A. \tag{9.6.3}$$

Comparing Equation 9.6.2 with Equation 9.6.3, we can express the new demand of risky assets from the banks, using the old demand level

$$\widetilde{q}_A = \frac{r\widetilde{P} + z - \overline{R}}{r\widetilde{P} + z - \overline{R'}} q_A = \left(1 + \frac{\overline{R'} - \overline{R}}{r\widetilde{P} + z - \overline{R'}}\right) q_A; \tag{9.6.4}$$

(4) Under the new circumstance, the demand level of risky assets from the consumers is

$$\widetilde{q}_P = \frac{3\tau}{z^2}\left(\overline{R'} - r\widetilde{P}\right) = S - \widetilde{q}_A. \tag{9.6.5}$$

Both Equations 9.6.4 and 9.6.5 determine the equilibrium demand for both types of agents,

$$\widetilde{q}_A = \left[1 + \frac{\overline{R'} - \overline{R}}{z + (\widetilde{q}_A - S)\frac{z}{3\tau}}\right] q_A. \tag{9.6.6}$$

Denote the right hand side of Equation 9.6.6 by $f(\widetilde{q}_A)$. Note that its denominator part, $z + (\widetilde{q}_A - S)\frac{z^2}{3\tau}$, comes from $r\widetilde{P} + z - \overline{R'}$ of Equation 9.6.1 which is positive. Therefore $f(\widetilde{q}_A)$ is a downward sloping curve of $\widetilde{q}_A$ and the solution to 9.6.6 is the intersection between $f(\widetilde{q}_A)$ and $\widetilde{q}_A$, as Fig. 9.13 shows.

As in the figure, with a higher $\overline{R'}$ the $f(\widetilde{q}_A)$ curve is shifted upwards, leading to a higher demand $\widetilde{q}_A$ for risky assets. As a mirror case, $\widetilde{q}_A$ falls if $\overline{R'} - \overline{R} < 0$.

Figure 9.14 summarizes the working mechanism of leverage channel in the boom. An initial positive shock to the bank's asset value leads to the increased value of bank capital; as a result of risk management through *VaR*, this allows the bank to expand its balance sheet by taking more debts to issue credits for purchasing risky securities, pushing up asset price in the market. This further strengthens bank's balance sheet, further increases the value of bank capital and incentivizes the bank to take more debts... Through such virtuous cycle, the initial small shock to bank assets ends up in a much more expanded supply of credits and higher asset price, as the left chart of Fig. 9.14 shows.

Furthermore, note from Equation 9.6.6 that $\widetilde{q}_A$ becomes more sensitive to the fundamental shock $\overline{R'} - \overline{R}$ when z is smaller, as in this case, the banks get more leveraged, and the asset price becomes more volatile. The leverage in banks' balance sheets generates higher flying asset price in the boom phase, while more devastating

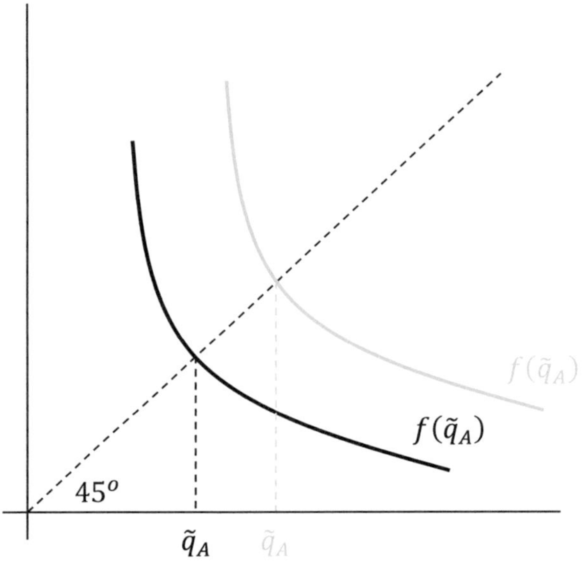

Fig. 9.13 Equilibrium demand for risky assets

Assets	**Liabilities**
Securities $\tilde{P}q_A$	Capital $\tilde{e}$
	Deposits $\left(\frac{\overline{R}-z}{r}\right)q_A$

→

Assets	**Liabilities**
Securities $\tilde{P}\tilde{q}_A$	Capital $\tilde{e}$
	Deposits $\left(\frac{\overline{R'}-z}{r}\right)\tilde{q}_A$

Fig. 9.14 Balance sheet expansion through bank leverage

collapse when the economy comes to the downturn (the vicious cycle, as the right chart in Fig. 9.15 shows).

In the transmission mechanism of monetary policy, the leverage cycle plays an important role in translating small changes of monetary policy rate into big reactions in banks' credit supply. In the model above, suppose that, instead of an unexpected shock to security return from $\overline{R}$ to $\overline{R'}$, there comes an unexpected monetary policy shock that raises the deposit rate r. This leads to an immediate rise in the bank's deposit liabilities and a fall in the value of bank capital. The risk management through VaR requires the bank to deleverage, or, to reduce its investments in risky securities. This triggers a vicious cycle: Falling demand of securities leads to falling asset price, further weakening the bank's balance sheet and forcing the bank into further deleverage.

The leverage channel increases the volatility in banks' credit supply, hence the volatility in the real economy; this is often not desirable. Even worse, beyond the excess volatility, it is worth noting that banks' risk taking combined with the

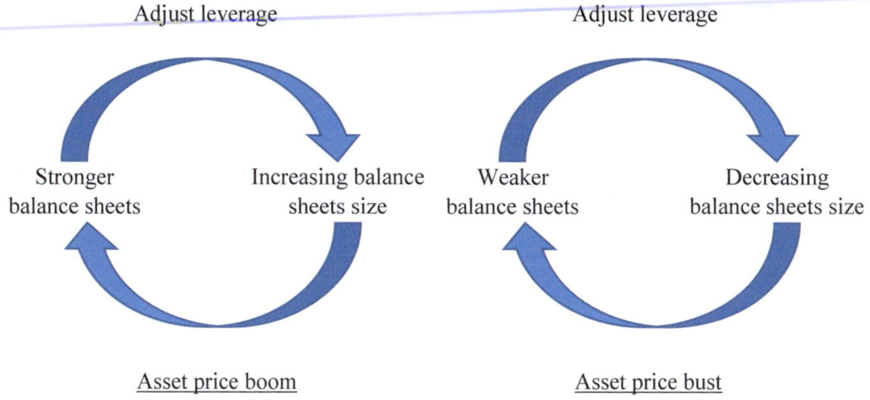

Fig. 9.15 The virtuous and vicious cycles through bank leverage

leverage cycle may bring damaging consequences, even though this mechanism is not modeled here. Rising asset prices in the boom phase of leverage cycles often build up bubbles, while in the bust phase, plummeting asset prices are often accompanied by panics and fire sales that further destroy values in the financial market. A rising number of recent studies on the long human history of bubbles and bursts, such as Reinhart and Rogoff (2009), Schularick and Taylor (2012), almost unanimously show that fast credit growth together with asset price boom is the single best leading indicator for financial crises.

In Shin's model, the supply of assets as well as the population of investors (both active and passive) is assumed to be fixed. Leverage cycle arises out of active investors' risk management through VaR. Shin argues that—given this mechanism—monetary policy is likely to trigger shifts the risk taking, contributing to global financial cycles. Changes in short-term policy rates will have an impact on the feedback loop between leverage and measures of risk. Easy credit conditions inducing lower volatility increases the risk appetite, resulting in higher leverage and rapid expansion of credit. When policy eventually tightens, the process is suddenly reversed, possibly violently. This mechanism reflects long-run buildups of financial risk rather than short-run swings in risk appetite.

As pointed out by Bernanke (2015), the pro-cyclicality in leverage and risk-taking is due to myopia of both risk managers and suppliers of funds to intermediaries. Using value at Risk risk-management methodologies, investment banks, their funders, and their regulators judge the riskiness of assets mainly by past experience. So they tend to underestimate underlying risks during quiet times and overestimate them in periods of high volatility. This myopic behavior leads to excessive swings in lending and risk seeking. A natural way to address this problem is to strengthen financial regulation such as to limit excessive cyclicality in lending standards, and to focus stress tests on the ability of institutions to bear tail risks.

9.7 The General Equilibrium Effect and the Leverage Cycle (Geanakoplos Model)

The leverage cycle can arise even without the explicit *VaR* constraint, as Geanakoplos (2010a) demonstrates. He develops a general equilibrium model of asset pricing in which collateral, leverage and default play a central role. In this model, the price of an asset at any point in time is not simply determined by the expected future stream of revenues but also by access to leverage for different agents with varying beliefs about the probability of high returns. For many assets there is a class of buyer for whom the asset is more valuable than it is for the rest of the public. These buyers are willing to pay more, either because they know better how to hedge their exposure to the assets, or because they are more risk tolerant. Geanakoplos shows that endogenous variations in leverage can have a huge impact on the price of assets, contributing to economic booms and busts. If the collateral requirement for a loan gets looser, buyers can get more outside funds through higher leveraged borrowing. They will spend it on the assets and drive those prices up. If they lose wealth, or lose the ability to borrow, they will buy less, so the asset will fall into more pessimistic hands and be valued less.

A fairly small decline in expectations about future revenues can result in a crash of asset prices because of two amplifying mechanisms: changes in the degree of equilibrium leverage, and the default of those who hold the most optimistic beliefs. So leverage gets too high in boom times, and too low in bad times. As a result, in boom times asset prices are too high, and in crisis times they are too low: the leverage cycle.

To illustrate the key idea, we consider a simple model with a single asset, two periods, and two future states in which the asset value will be either high or low. Beliefs about the relative likelihood of the two states vary across individuals. Borrowers and lenders can choose to enter or exit market when their expected returns on assets shift. Suppose initially that there is no borrowing. Then the price of the asset will be such that those who wish to sell their holdings at that price collectively own precisely the amount that those who wish to buy can collectively afford. Specifically, the price will partition the public into two groups: Those who are more pessimistic about the future price sell to those who are more optimistic.

In a next step, we allow for borrowing, with the asset itself as collateral (as in mortgage contracts). Suppose that the amount of lending is constrained by the lowest possible future value of the collateral, so lenders are fully protected against loss. Even in this case, the asset price will be higher than it would be without borrowing: The most optimistic individuals will buy the asset on margin, while the others sell their holdings and lend money to the buyers. So the price is higher when margin purchases are possible even if there is no change in beliefs about the future value of the asset. The looser the collateral requirement, the higher are the prices of assets. The extent of leverage is determined jointly with the interest rate in the market for loans. Aggregate demand for and supply of credit nail down the equilibrium asset price. The leverage cycle is thus endogenously determined through the general equilibrium effect. Finally, we extend the baseline model to explain the impact of new information on leverage and asset prices. We show how leverage is built up after good news and how bad news can cause an asset price crash after excessive deleveraging. Endogenous leverage is an important part for understanding the financial crisis.

9.7.1 Model Setup

The Agents, Time Preferences, and Technology

As Geanakoplos (2003, 2010a, 2010b), consider an economy that extends to two periods, $t = 0, 1$. The only commodity in the economy is a consumption good C, which can be consumed at any time, stored, or used for investment. There are two states of the world, $S \in \{U, D\}$, as in Fig. 9.16, namely "up" or "down," for t = 1. The only asset in this economy is a risky asset Y, at $t = 1$ each unit of Y returns R_U (R_D) units of consumption good in the state $U(D)$. As a regularity condition, it is assumed that $R_U \geq 1 > R_D > 0$.

There is a continuum of investors, each of which is endowed with one unit of the asset Y and one unit of consumption good C at $t = 0$. The investors are indifferent in the timing of consumption. The investors are heterogeneous in their belief at $t = 0$ of the probability π that the economy goes up at $t = 1$. For simplicity, suppose π is uniformly distributed and $\pi_i = i$ for a investor indexed by $i \in [0, 1]$. The more the index gets close to 1(0), the more optimistic (pessimistic) the investor becomes.

Assume that the short selling is not allowed in this economy. When the price of the asset Y is P at $t = 0$, the investor i is (weakly) willing to buy the asset as long as she believes that P is (weakly) below the asset's expected value, i.e., $iR_U + (1 - i)R_D \geq P$, otherwise she wants to sell the asset. Therefore, the more optimistic investors tend to buy the assets and hence are natural buyers of the risky assets, and the more pessimistic ones tend to be natural sellers. Here we have the first novelty of this model: The types of investors are endogenously determined by their subjective expectation on the risky asset's return.

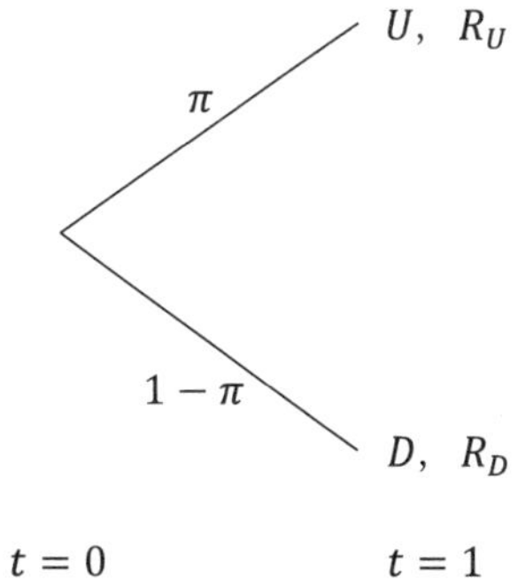

Fig. 9.16 The payoff of the risky assets

9.7.2 Market Equilibrium Without Borrowing

To get some flavor about the market equilibrium, we start from the reference case in which no borrowing is allowed, i.e., the buyers can only buy with their own endowments. For a representative investor i, let c_0^i denote her consumption at $t = 0$, and c_U^i (c_D^i) denote her consumption at $t = 1$ if the state of the world is $U(D)$. Then at $t = 0$ her subjective expected utility is

$$u^i = c_0^i + ic_U^i + (1 - i)c_D^i. \tag{9.7.1}$$

Besides consuming c_0^i at $t = 0$, the investor can also invest w_0^i as storage which can be consumed at $t = 1$. Let y_0^i denote the investor's holding of risky assets for $t = 1$. Given some risky assets are traded between the two types of the investors at price P, the investor's budget constraint at $t = 0$ is therefore

$$c_0^i + w_0^i + P\left(y_0^i - 1\right) = 1. \tag{9.7.2}$$

With the payoff structure of the risky assets, the expected consumption at $t = 1$ for each state is

$$c_U^i = w_0^i + R_U y_0^i, \tag{9.7.3}$$

$$c_D^i = w_0^i + R_D y_0^i. \tag{9.7.4}$$

The market clearing conditions must hold:

(1) The aggregate $t = 0$ consumption and storage is equal to the aggregate endowment of consumption good,

$$\int_0^1 \left(c_0^i + w_0^i\right) di = 1. \tag{9.7.5}$$

(2) The aggregate $t = 0$ holdings of risky assets should be equal to the aggregate endowment of risky assets,

$$\int_0^1 y_0^i di = 1. \tag{9.7.6}$$

(3) The expected aggregate $t = 1$ consumption in each state is equal to the expected return from all the risky assets plus the aggregate storage made at $t = 0$,

$$\int_0^1 c_U^i di = R_U + \int_0^1 w_0^i di, \tag{9.7.7}$$

$$\int_0^1 c_D^i di = R_D + \int_0^1 w_0^i di. \tag{9.7.8}$$

The investor's problem is to choose the optimal $\left(c_0^i, w_0^i, y_0^i, c_U^i, c_D^i\right)$ to maximize the object function (Equation 9.7.1) with the budget constraints (Equation 9.7.2)–(Equation 9.7.4) and market clearing conditions (Equation 9.7.5)–(Equation 9.7.8).

Remember that the equilibrium price P divides the investors into two groups: With the boundary i^*, buyers are those with indices $i \in (i^*, 1]$, and seller are those with $i \in [0, i^*)$. Therefore, the equilibrium price P can be solved from the boundary buyer who is indifferent between buying and selling:

$$i^* R_U + (1 - i^*) R_D = P. \tag{9.7.9}$$

Further, note that without borrowing the buyers, whose measure is $1 - i^*$, spend all their endowment of consumption good, to purchase the endowment of risky assets from the sellers, whose measure is i^*. The equilibrium price of the risky asset is therefore denoted by the ratio between the total expenditure and the purchased quantity, i.e.,

$$P = \frac{1 - i^*}{i^*}. \tag{9.7.10}$$

The equilibrium price and the boundary buyer are jointly determined by Equation (9.7.9) and Equation (9.7.10), as Fig. 9.17 shows.

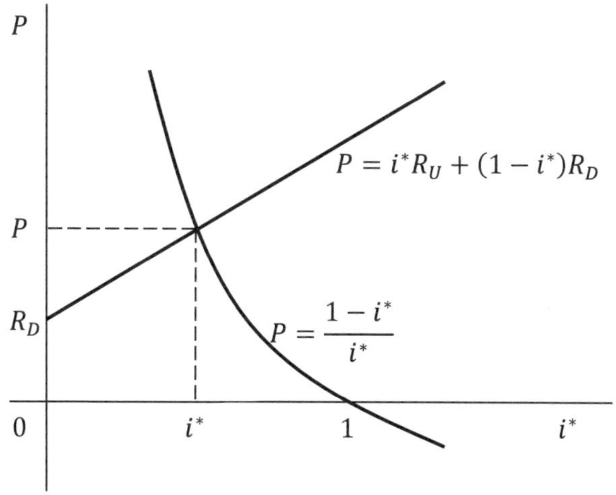

Fig. 9.17 The equilibrium price and the boundary buyer

9.7.3 Market Equilibrium with Borrowing

In our reference case, the buyers' demand of risky assets is limited by their endowments of consumption goods, given that borrowing is not allowed.

What will happen if borrowing is allowed in this economy? Obviously buyers tend to become borrowers to purchase more of the risky assets—so long as their subjective expected return is higher than the asset price (resembling the active leveraged investors, or banks, in Shin model). Sellers tend to become lenders (resembling the passive non-leveraged investors, or depositors, in Shin model) so long as the market interest rate is weakly higher than one. The extreme case is the buyer $i = 1$: Since the subjective expected return is $R_U > P$, the buyer is willing to borrow infinite amount with interest rate R_U. However, the lenders, those $0 \le i < i^*$, will not offer the lending because they believe that the probability of the state D at $t = 1$ is strictly positive in which the borrower will have to default. Therefore, in order to avoid default, the lenders must require collateral from the borrowers as a commitment device.

Assume now that buyers can borrow from the sellers at $t = 0$ and the loan contract between the borrowers and lenders is featured by:

(1) The contract is non-contingent, i.e., the lenders get the same return in the both states, U and D.
(2) In order to guarantee the safe return in both states, the lenders take the borrowers' risky assets as collateral.

To find the market equilibrium, suppose that borrower i borrows $\frac{\varphi_0^i}{1+r}$ at $t = 0$ with interest rate r and promises to repay φ_0^i at $t = 1$. The collateral requirement guarantees that the collateral value is sufficient to repay the loan even when the borrower has to default in the D state, i.e.,

$$R_D y_0^i \ge \varphi_0^i. \tag{9.7.11}$$

This gives the limit of the buyer's borrowing capacity. Now the buyer's budget constraint at $t = 0$ becomes

$$c_0^i + w_0^i + P\left(y_0^i - 1\right) = 1 + \frac{\varphi_0^i}{1+r}. \tag{9.7.12}$$

The expected consumption at $t = 1$ for each state is now

$$c_U^i = w_0^i + R_U y_0^i - \varphi_0^i, \tag{9.7.13}$$

$$c_D^i = w_0^i + R_D y_0^i - \varphi_0^i. \tag{9.7.14}$$

The market clearing conditions must hold:

(1) For the aggregate $t = 0$ consumption and storage,

$$\int_0^1 \left(c_0^i + w_0^i\right) di = 1. \tag{9.7.15}$$

(2) For the aggregate $t = 0$ holdings of risky assets,

$$\int_0^1 y_0^i di = 1. \tag{9.7.16}$$

(3) For the expected aggregate $t = 1$ consumption in each state,

$$\int_0^1 c_U^i di = R_U + \int_0^1 w_0^i di, \tag{9.7.17}$$

$$\int_0^1 c_D^i di = R_D + \int_0^1 w_0^i di. \tag{9.7.18}$$

(4) Any investor i, is a borrower if $\varphi_0^i > 0$ and a lender if $\varphi_0^i < 0$. The lending and borrowing cancel out in aggregate, which makes

$$\int_0^1 \varphi_0^i di = 0. \tag{9.7.19}$$

Now the investor's problem is to choose the optimal $\left(c_0^i, w_0^i, \varphi_0^i, y_0^i, c_U^i, c_D^i\right)$ to maximize the object function (Equation 9.7.1) with the borrowing constraint (Equation 9.7.11), budget constraints (Equation 9.7.12)–(Equation 9.7.14) and market clearing conditions (Equation 9.7.15)–(Equation 9.7.19).

Similar as the reference case, the market equilibrium price P can be solved by the boundary buyer i^* with

$$i^* R_U + (1 - i^*) R_D = P. \tag{9.7.20}$$

In equilibrium, the buyers will hold the risky asset of the entire economy, which means a collateral value R_D. This allows all the buyers to borrow up to $\frac{R_D}{1+r}$ in total from the sellers to finance their purchase of risky asset, i^*, besides their endowment of consumption good, $1 - i^*$. Suppose that R_D is so low that the total collateral value of the economy is below the lenders' aggregate endowment of consumption good,

$R_D \leq i^*$. The competition among the lenders will drive the equilibrium interest rate r down to 0. The equilibrium price of the risky asset is therefore

$$P = \frac{1 - i^* + R_D}{i^*}. \tag{9.7.21}$$

The equilibrium price and the boundary buyer are jointly determined by Equation (9.7.20) and Equation (9.7.21), as Fig. 9.18 shows.

Comparing with the reference market equilibrium without borrowing (depicted in gray), as Fig. 9.18 shows, the access to tapping the credit from the lenders enables the borrowers to increase their expenditure on risky assets. This shifts the asset price to a higher level, given the aggregate supply of risky assets is inelastic. Facing a higher asset price, only those investors who are more optimistic are still willing to purchase, and this crowds out those who are less optimistic and raises the bar for one investor becoming a natural buyer.

One may suspect that the market equilibrium derived here is due to the assumption imposed that the loan contract is non-contingent, i.e., we have assumed that lenders must get the same return in the both states, so that one buyer's borrowing is upper bounded by $R_D y_0^i$ and the aggregate borrowing is limited to R_D. One might conjecture that optimistic investors would be able to borrow more if we relax this noncontingency restriction on the loan contract. For example, the most optimistic investor $i = 1$ may promise a higher payoff $\widetilde{R} y_0^1$, $R_D < \widetilde{R} < R_U$, as $t = 1$ return, to attract more loans from the lenders. However, this will not happen in equilibrium because of the heterogeneous beliefs of the investors. A natural seller, or a lender, believes that the collateral is worth $\widetilde{R} y_0^1$ only with a low probability $i < i^*$ being convinced that it is worth just $R_D y_0^1$ with a fairly high probability $1 - i$. Therefore, if the lender agrees to lend, she must take into account that with probability $1 - i$ her loan is not fully pledgeable. Therefore, the lender will ask for a higher interest rate to

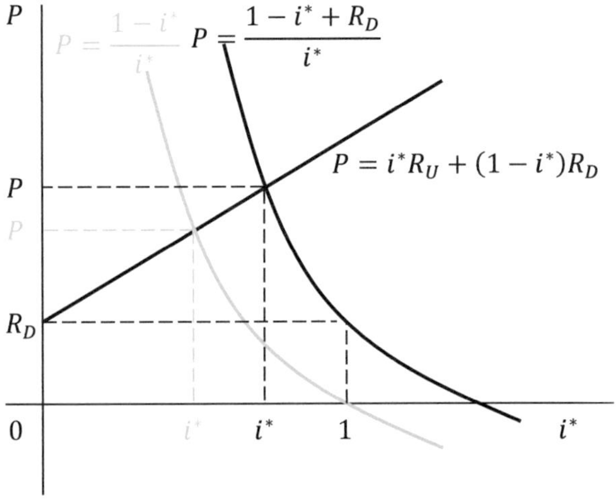

Fig. 9.18 The impact of borrowing

insure against the high probability of default. However, the borrower $i = 1$ believes that she will come up with state U with certainty so that she always has to pay the high interest rate to the lender. This is obviously dominated by just promising $R_D y_0^1$ and paying zero interest rate.

Note that in the market equilibrium with borrowing, the total value of risky assets is P, which is financed by the borrowers' endowment and the debt R_D raised from the lenders. The leverage ratio of the economy is therefore

$$L = \frac{P}{P - R_D}. \tag{9.7.22}$$

Now we have the second novelty of this model: In the market equilibrium, not only the asset price, but also the leverage of the economy is endogenized.

Using the simplest framework constructed by Equation (9.7.20), Equation (9.7.21), and Equation (9.7.22), we are able to analyze the impact of economic fundamentals on the equilibrium leverage. For example, suppose that the investors becomes more optimistic such that at $t = 0$ investor i believes that the economy goes down at $t = 1$ with a lower probability $\pi = (1 - i)^2 < 1 - i$, and the chance that the economy goes up gets higher since $1 - \pi = 1 - (1 - i)^2 > i$. As a result, the boundary investor becomes the one with $\left[1 - (1 - i^*)^2\right] R_U + (1 - i^*)^2 R_D = P$. Given that the borrowing constraint $P = \frac{1 - i^* + R_D}{i^*}$ remains the same as before, it is easily seen that the equilibrium price P goes up and the boundary i^* goes down. Intuitively, when the investors get more optimistic, those who were previously marginally below the boundary i^* now realize the expected payoff gets higher so that they will switch to be buyers. This increases the total expenditure on risky assets and imposes a positive pressure on asset price through Equation (9.7.21). But when asset price gets higher, it makes the risky asset less appealing for the marginal buyers which prevents more sellers from joining the buyers. The equilibrium P and i^* thus reflect the balance between these two diverting effects.

Instead of a shock on π, now suppose the expected return of the risky asset in the upside, R_U, gets improved. As Fig. 9.19 shows, this means a higher slope for $P = i^* R_U + (1 - i^*) R_D$, leading unambiguously to a higher asset price P and lower equilibrium boundary i^*. That is, a higher R_U means a higher fundamental value of risky assets, implying a higher asset price. On the other hand, with higher R_U even previously less optimistic investors will find it worthwhile to hold risky assets since the expected return gets higher. Therefore, some of the natural sellers will be converted to buyers. The leverage $L = \frac{P}{P - R_D}$ becomes lower because of the higher asset price. The equilibrium price would have been higher, should there be no shift in boundary i^*. In other words, the impact of higher R_U on asset price has been dampened by the fall in leverage.

Now suppose the expected return of the risky asset in the downside, R_D, gets improved. This means that both $P = \frac{1 - i^* + R_D}{i^*}$ and $P = i^* R_U + (1 - i^*) R_D$ are shifted upwards in Fig. 9.20, and $P = i^* R_U + (1 - i^*) R_D$ gets flatter, implying a higher asset price P. To see impact on the equilibrium boundary i^*, combine Equation (9.7.20) and Equation (9.7.21) to get the implicit function $i^*(R_D)$

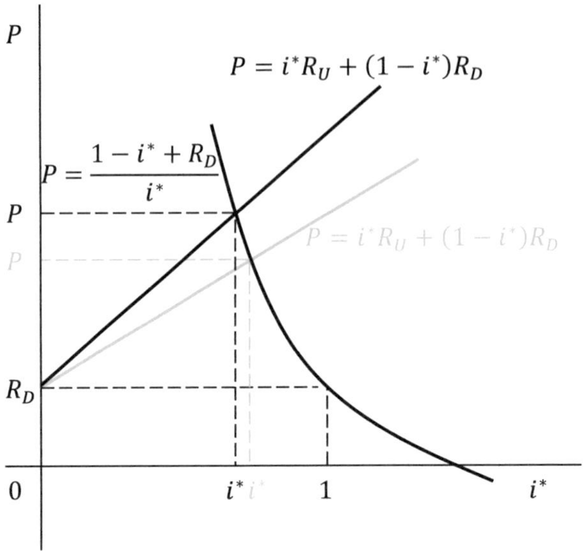

Fig. 9.19 The impact of improving fundamentals (I)

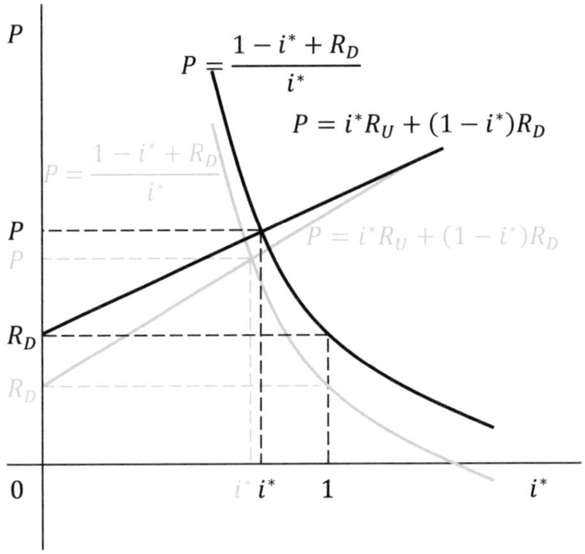

Fig. 9.20 The impact of improving fundamentals (II)

$$\frac{1 - i^* + R_D}{i^*} = i^* R_U + (1 - i^*) R_D.$$

Differentiating with respect to R_D yields

$$\frac{\partial i^*}{\partial R_D} = \frac{1 - i^* + i^{*2}}{1 + R_D + 2i^*(R_U - R_D)} > 0. \tag{9.7.23}$$

This means the equilibrium boundary i^* gets higher, too.

Here the rising boundary i^* comes as a result of the general equilibrium effect, which amplifies the impact of R_D through the feedback mechanism between the asset price and the leveraged investors' balance sheet. The improvement of the expected return on the downside relaxes the buyers' borrowing constraint through the improved collateral value, and this is immediately translated to a higher asset price through the multiplier—$P = \frac{1-i^*+R_D}{i^*}$ implies that the shock to R_D is amplified by $\frac{1}{i^*} > 1$. However, the sharp rise in asset price also makes the buyers' feasibility constraint, $iR_U + (1 - i)R_D \geq P$, less likely to hold. In the end, the marginal buyers who were previously just above the boundary i^*, are now crowded out, and only the more optimistic investors will stay as buyers. But when i^* rises, the total endowment of consumption good from the buyers falls, which brakes the rising trend in asset price through $P = \frac{1-i^*+R_D}{i^*}$ as a feedback. Finally, Equation (9.7.22) suggests that in equilibrium the amplification effect outweighs the dampening effect.

9.7.4 The Business Cycle and the Leverage Cycle

As the simple general equilibrium model shows, by comparative analysis one can see the impact of fundamental value on asset prices through the lenders' balance sheet. One interesting extension to this baseline model is to analyze the impact of new information affecting investors' expectation on the fundamental value. We will show how leverage cycles may be amplified: Leverage will be built up after good news; bad news can cause an asset price crash after excessive deleveraging.

To capture such leverage cycle, the model needs to be extended to introduce additional periods with new information arriving. Keeping the settings almost the same as in the baseline model, there is one additional intermediate date, $t = 0.5$, in which investors can observe a signal regarding the risky asset's payoff in the future. For investor i with subjective probability π $(1 - \pi)$ the signal is $U(D)$. At $t = 1$ the investors observe another signal, which is independent on, but of the same distribution of the previous one, as Fig. 9.21 shows. The $t = 1$ payoff of the risky asset is R_D only of both signals are D. Again, suppose π is uniformly distributed and $\pi_i = i$ for a investor indexed by $i \in [0, 1]$.

With an additional intermediate date, the investors will have a chance to reconsider their investments. Therefore, assume that all the loans only last for one period. At $t = 0$, based on their expected payoff, the investors will be endogenously separated

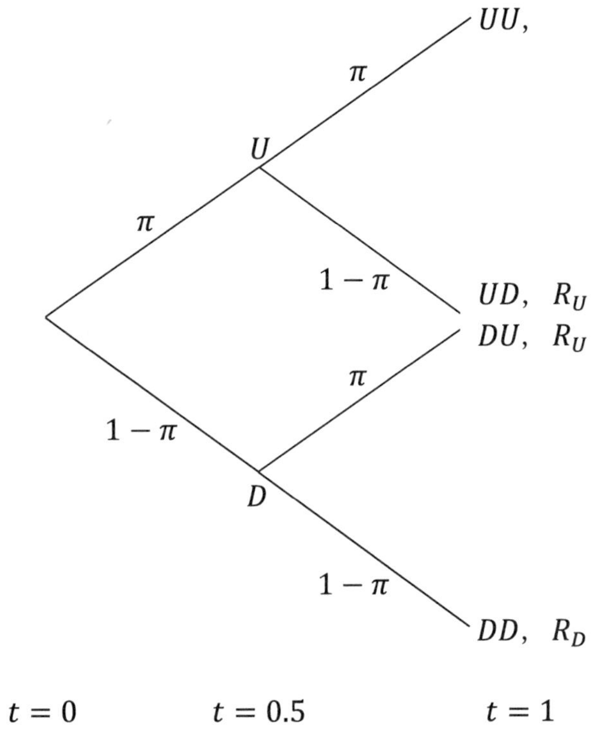

Fig. 9.21 The 3-date extension

into buyers (or, borrowers) and sellers (or, lenders), and the equilibrium is characterized by the asset price P_0 and the boundary investor i_0^*. The borrowers get their loans from the lenders, using their assets as collateral. When it comes to $t = 0.5$, conditional on the signal they receive, the investors have to adjust their expectation on $t = 1$ payoff and reconsider their holdings of risky asset, i.e., the borrowers may want to increase or have to deplete their asset stocks, the lenders may want to liquidate the collateral or roll over their loans into the next period (we will explain the details later). The equilibrium depends on the observed signal: asset price $P_{0.5,S}$ and the boundary investor $i_{0.5,S}^*$ under signal $S \in \{U, D\}$.

In the current 3-date model, the investors are more optimistic at $t = 0$ than in the baseline model, since the investor i's subjective probability of having a low return R_D now is $(1 - i)^2 < 1 - i$. Therefore, similar as the in the comparative analysis of last section, the equilibrium price P_0 and the boundary investor i_0^* are connected by $\left[1 - \left(1 - i_0^*\right)^2\right] R_U + \left(1 - i_0^*\right)^2 R_D = P_0$. As argued before, the equilibrium price P_0 tends to be higher than the baseline model, given that the investors are more optimistic.

The difference here is the buyer's borrowing capacity. Note that all the loans are short term so that for the loans made at $t = 0$, the collateral value is the value from liquidating the risky asset at $t = 0.5$, i.e., the asset price $P_{0.5,S}$ which further depends on the signal observed at $t = 0.5$. When $S = U$, it is easily seen that $P_{0.5,U} = R_U$

because R_U will be realized at $t = 1$ with certainty; when $S = D$, $P_{0.5,D}$ is yet to be determined, but should be above R_D because there is still a positive probability of ending up with DU at $t = 1$. In the end, the buyers' total borrowing capacity at $t = 0$ should be larger than that in the baseline model. As is argued before, the equilibrium price P_0 tends to be higher, along with the buyers' higher borrowing capacity.

Suppose that with equilibrium P_0 and i_0^* the time goes on from $t = 0$ to $t = 0.5$, when the first signal gets revealed. If $S = U$, the high return R_U is guaranteed with certainty, and the asset price will be bid up to R_U. The economy booms before the high return is materialized.

In contrast, if $S = D$, the economy incurs a crash. To make it worse, the downward spiral will be fueled by the general equilibrium effect. To see this, note that when signal D is observed:

(1) For investor i the probability of having a low return becomes $1 - i > (1 - i)^2$, i.e., the investors become more pessimistic, implying a lower asset price $P_{0.5,D}$.
(2) Therefore, the initial buyers at $t = 0$ go bankrupted as Fig. 9.22 shows, and all their asset holdings as collateral are seized by the initial sellers.
(3) Now only the less optimistic investors $i \in [0, i_0^*)$ are still in the market. Given that all the investors are more pessimistic, the equilibrium price of the risky assets $P_{0.5,D}$ has to fall even further.
(4) With a sufficiently low $P_{0.5,D}$, the investors on the top of $[0, i_0^*)$ are willing to buy the asset. However, the collateral value is only R_D in this case, implying that the borrowing capacity has been also contracted. Such deleveraging imposes more downside pressure on $P_{0.5,D}$.

In the end, the equilibrium ends up with a low $P_{0.5,D}$, and the boundary investor $i_{0.5,D}^*$ for the surviving investors.

Such vicious spiral makes a perfectly analogy to fire sale, and the key mechanism in the model explains how economic downturn triggers the disastrous fire sale. In contrast to the standard models with representative investors, i.e., all the investors

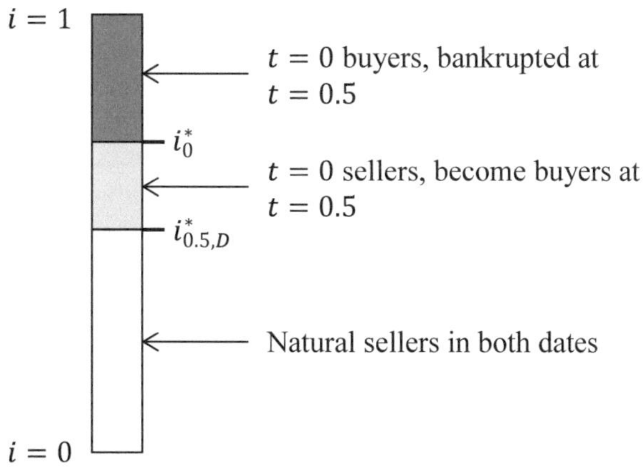

Fig. 9.22 The leverage cycle and the marginal buyer

are (at least ex ante) homogeneous in all dimensions, here from the beginning investors are heterogeneous in their subjective expectation of the future payoff from holding risky asset. Thus, by the simple "buy low, sell high" principle, all investors are endogenously separated into natural buyers and sellers: Those more optimistic investors hold the asset, which they buy from the pessimistic ones using the funds borrowed from the sellers. Since borrowers need to post their asset as collateral, their leverage ratio is endogenously determined in equilibrium, too.

Certainly the asset price in equilibrium is determined by the law of demand and supply, however, what becomes more important here is who serves as a buyer or a seller when the shock gets revealed. When the market becomes more optimistic about the fundamentals, the asset price is bid up, and the trend is then dampened by the leverage of the economy. But when a negative shock hits and the market becomes more pessimistic, after the first wave of asset price decline caused by the deteriorating fundamentals, the initial natural buyers, or the optimistic investors, get bankrupted and driven out of the market. This further aggravates the market outcome: Now the buyers are less optimistic and their willingness to pay is low, and their borrowing capacity gets contracted because of the deterioration in the fundamentals. These two factors jointly depress the asset price even further into a full collapse, and the effect is amplified by deleveraging. Finally, it is not surprising that asset has to be sold at the fire sale price simply—because the optimistic buyers are all gone.

The endogenous leverage cycle through general equilibrium sheds much light on many asset price puzzles both in the economic boom and in the financial crisis. One such puzzle is why during financial crises financial assets have to be sold at the fire sale prices—quite often such prices are much lower than the assets' fundamental values—as this is obviously an arbitrage opportunity such that investors should buy assets at depressed prices and profit from selling them in the future once asset prices recover. But here such "limits to arbitrage" (as coined by Shleifer & Vishny, 1997) arise quite naturally from Geanakoplos model: There is a lack of demand for assets even at depressed prices, because the potential, most optimistic buyers are all bankrupted after the financial shock, and this allows fire sale prices to persist. We will return to the issue of fire sale later in Sect. 10.2.

The leverage cycle framework, such as Shin model and Geanakoplos model, exhibits a distinct contrast to the standard dynamic stochastic general equilibrium models, even those models with financial accelerator type of financial frictions. In the standard models, exogenous shock triggered price fluctuations cause (amplified) real volatilities, generating a distributional effect; while in the leverage cycle framework, price fluctuations are both cause and consequence of real volatilities—the feedback between asset prices and real volatilities leads to far larger and devastating boom-bust cycles.

One also has to keep in mind that even in the current simplest model with only one-dimension heterogeneity, the equilibrium is hard to compute—calculating the quantitative solution needs to go through the complicated equilibrium conditions—and it is often not obvious to make comparative statics analysis. This may limit the model's applicability. But, on the other hand, with powerful computers getting universally available, it becomes easier to allow for more heterogeneities and agents at play. A more agent-based, computer-aided, general equilibrium framework is currently rising and seems promising to help us find out more equilibrium patterns which are missed by the homogeneous, representative agent models.

9.8 Empirical Evidence for the Monetary Transmission Mechanism

The negative correlation between monetary policy and bank lending has been well accepted and documented at least on aggregate level, for example, Romer and Romer (1990), that banks cut their lending under tightening monetary policy. However, two key empirical questions still remained unsolved for studies based on aggregate level data. First, the correlation does not mean that the transmission mechanism through banking sector exists because of causality problem—such transmission mechanism only exists if changes in banks' loan supply to the real economy are caused by monetary policy shocks; however, the causality may also be reversed such that monetary policy and bank lending are just reacting to changes in aggregate demand. Monetary policy is not completely exogenous to bank lending. Second, even if such transmission mechanism does exist, evidence from aggregate data cannot tell through which channels the mechanism actually works.

Answering these questions needs microlevel data on individual banks' balance sheet and their loans, which has not been available until very recently. The ground-breaking research started from Kashyap and Stein (2000), based on quarterly observations of every insured US commercial bank from 1976 to 1993. In order to directly address the endogeneity and causality problems, they take a two-step regression approach. In step one, they run the following cross-sectional regression for banks grouped by their asset size

$$\Delta \ln L_{i,t} = \sum_{j=1}^{m} \alpha_{t,j} \Delta \ln L_{i,t-j} + \beta_t B_{i,t-1} + \psi_t L.CONTROLS_{i,t} + \epsilon_{i,t}$$

in which $\Delta \ln L_{i,t}$ is the growth rate in lending for bank i in quarter t, $B_{i,t}$ is the ratio of non-required holdings of liquid assets (excess reserves and government securities, required reserves are not included) to total assets, $L.CONTROLS_{i,t}$ contains lagged control variables reflecting features of the bank's balance sheet, such as capitalization ratio, asset size, and value of nonperforming loans. The key variable here, "balance sheet strength" variable $B_{i,t}$, reflects the bank's capability in absorbing asset side shocks by converting liquid assets to cash.

Take the time series β_t generated from the first step for the second-step regression

$$\beta_t = \eta + \sum_{k=1}^{n} \phi_k r_{t-k} + \delta controls_t + \mu_t$$

in which r_t is the monetary policy rate in quarter t, $controls_t$ contains (lagged) macro variables such as GDP growth rate to capture the demand side effect from the business cycles.

Note that the endogeneity problem still exists in the two-step regression: Banks' holdings of liquid assets ($B_{i,t}$) may vary along business cycles ($controls_t$). To address this issue, they regress $B_{i,t}$ on the ratio of commercial/industrial lending to total lending and the ratio of nonperforming loans to total loans—the impacts of business cycles on bank liquidity are captured by these two regressors—and use the residual of the regression to instrument $B_{i,t}$.

In the first regression, the coefficient β_t reflects the sensitivity of bank lending to balance sheet liquidity. When monetary policy is tightened and the policy rate rises, bank lending should be more sensitive to liquidity strength indicator $B_{i,t}$, as the bank is less likely to fully absorb the monetary shock by using its liquidity buffer without adjusting its loan supply, should the monetary transmission mechanism exist and work through the bank's liquidity management. Therefore, in the second-step regression, the sum of coefficients for lagged monetary policy rate r_t, $\sum_{k=1}^{n} \phi_k$, which reflects the accumulated impacts of monetary policy over n quarters on the sensitivity parameter β_t, should be positive. The authors find it indeed significant and positive, i.e., the monetary transmission through banks' liquidity management is supported. Furthermore, they find that lending from small banks reacts more to monetary policy than lending from large banks, as the smaller ones' lending are more sensitive to liquidity buffers.

More supportive evidences emerged as more microlevel data became available. Ashcraft (2006) finds that the lending from small American banks that are affiliated with large banks is less affected by monetary shocks than the lending from stand-alone small banks, because the former have better access to federal funds market so that they are less liquidity constrained. Campello (2002) shows that the small American banks that are members of big financial conglomerates react less to monetary policy in their lending supplies, comparing with the stand-alone ones, as the former have the access to the internal liquidity market of the conglomerates, making them more easily to obtain funding and better shielded from the monetary shocks. Adrian and Shin (2014) document how leverage cycles arise from banks' responses to *VaR* in their risk management practice, while Jiménez, Ongena, Peydró and Saurina (2014) present some strong evidence on how banks' risk taking varies in the monetary transmission mechanism. Using credit registry in Spain that contains bank-firm level data on both loan applications and outcomes in 2002–2009, Jiménez et al. (2014) start with a two-stage regression: The first one explains banks' decisions on granting loans to firms by the ex ante credit risk of the firms and monetary policy rate, and the second one explains the performance of granted loans by the same explanatory variables. They find that lax monetary policy encourages riskier (poorly capitalized) banks to issue loans to ex ante risky firms, with lower lending standard (more lenient requirements on collateral), and these loans are more likely to be non-performing in the future. A clear evidence for risk-taking channel.

Krogstrup and Tille (2015) investigate how European multinational banks react to monetary shocks by changing the composition of their funding currencies, through the Swiss franc lending monitor operated by the Swiss National Bank. They find the changes in funding currency composition very much depend on the funding costs of the currencies, which is in line with the liquidity management approach. Such international liquidity management practice is also documented by Cetorelli and Goldberg (2012a) using a similar two-step identification model as in Kashyap and Stein (2000), who show that the lending from American owned multinational banks reacts less to the monetary policy in the USA, as these banks are able to obtain cheaper funding from their foreign affiliates, if the domestic monetary policy is tightened. Such cross-country funding flows through the monetary transmission inside global banks may benefit "home" and "guest" countries alike. Cetorelli and Goldberg (2012b) show that global banks manage liquidity on a global scale. During the Great Recession when liquidity in the interbank market became more scarce, global banks can allocate liquidity in the intrabank market between parent banks and affiliates, so that those affiliates that are more important for the parent banks' revenue streams are favored in the internal liquidity allocation so that their lending is less affected. Similarly, out of all loan applications from the affiliates of a foreign owned multinational bank in Azerbaijan during the 2007–2009 crisis, Berg and Kirchenman (2015) find that when the parent bank experienced negative monetary shocks from the "home" market while the economy of the "guest" country was still performing well, the falling number of loan applications in the guest country that followed are mainly explained by reduced prospecting instead of tightening lending standards; the quality of the loans was in fact improved, due to the falling number of risky borrowers that were attracted by prospecting.

However, there is also a dark side in the global banks' international liquidity management practice. It has been frequently warned that crises may spread from one country to another through global banks (Bank for International Settlement, 2010a, 2010b; Brunnermaier et al., 2012)—for example, when a parent bank is severely hit by a crisis in the home country, it may reshuffle funds from foreign affiliates back home, and trigger another crisis in the guest country—and the monetary policy in the home country has a spillover effect on the guest country (Temesvary, Ongena, & Owen, 2018). Furthermore, global liquidity management also creates a new channel for banks' risk taking, weakening the transmission of domestic monetary policy. Using country-level data, Bruno and Shin (2015a, 2015b) find that when a country is booming and its currency is appreciating, banks' holdings of the debts dominated in foreign currencies become cheaper; this increases banks' equity and encourages them to expand their balance sheets as a result of risk management. At the same time, the appreciating domestic currency and falling risk premium imply that the cost of foreign funding declines. In banks' liquidity management, this allows them to borrow more from abroad and take more risk on the balance sheets. As a consequence, the global liquidity channel increases both domestic financial risks and the country's exposure to global liquidity risks. Using Norwegian bank level data from 1994 to 2015, Cao and Dinger (2018) find that banks take foreign currency funding to arbitrage against domestic monetary policy; they borrow more from abroad when domestic monetary policy is tightened, leaving the monetary transmission mechanism less effective. Indeed, with banking sector becoming more globalized, it has been more challenging for central banks to implement monetary policy without taking controls on cross-border funding flows (Avdjiev, McCauley, & Shin, 2016; Hofmann, Shim, & Shin, 2016; Rey, 2015).

9.9 Summary

In this chapter, we looked models focusing on the role of financial sector, in particular on banks for the monetary transmission mechanism. We have seen how frictions prevent banks from allocating credit to those agents needing it most, and that such frictions induce banks to overreact to macroeconomic shocks, increasing volatilities in output. So they have redistribution effects in transmitting monetary policy. We characterized conditions under which monetary policy can help to dampen the distortions arising from financial frictions, improving social welfare. In this chapter, we focused on financial frictions that impede the transmission of monetary policy to the real economy. We considered various sources for such financial frictions. In particular, we focused on the following issues:

Markets May Be Incomplete With some markets missing, there will be segmented trading. So certain risks will no longer be properly priced and insured. This creates a premium for specific assets. As example, we discussed the model of Cúrdia and Woodford (2015) in Sect. 9.2. In that model, households cannot always insure against the uncertainty in their demand for consumption, forcing them to borrow from banks. This creates a premium in banks' lending rate and distorts consumption. Therefore, optimal monetary policy needs to respond to such lending premium, alongside with inflation and output gap, to bring the economy closer to the first-best outcome. As shown, in that model monetary policy works in a way very similar to the standard NK model, except that optimal monetary policy need to respond also to an exogenous and time varying spread term (the interest rate spread). But one needs to be careful to draw policy conclusions as long as the exact nature of the underlying friction in intermediation is not explicitly modeled. In the following sections, we looked at various ways to model such frictions explicitly.

Principal–Agent Problems As lenders and borrowers cannot perfectly monitor each other, typical principal–agent problems arise in financial intermediation. Some problems come from the borrower side as discussed in the Bernanke and Gertler (1989) model presented in Sect. 9.3: Borrowers have the incentive to misreport the outcome of their loans and pocket some private benefit, limiting the availability of credit. Problems may also come from financial intermediation sector itself—the banking side as in the Bernanke–Gertler–Karadi model analyzed in Sect. 9.4. To prevent bankers from diverting assets for private consumption and declaring bankruptcy, again the set of feasible contracts will be restricted. We have seen that, as result of principal–agent frictions, borrowers and banks need to have their own stakes in financial intermediation to align their interests with their counterparties, imposing constraints on the credit available in the real economy.

Maturity Mismatch A key business model in banking is so-called "maturity transformation," i.e., banks invest in long-term projects by borrowing short-term debts, creating a mismatch of maturities between assets and liabilities. When short-term debt is due, banks have to renew the debts with creditors, exposing themselves to rollover risks ("funding liquidity risk"). For this reason, in liquidity management, banks have to hold certain assets that can be easily converted to cash ("liquid assets," such as government bonds) to repay creditors if they cannot roll over all the debts. The Bianchi–Bigio approach presented in Sect. 9.5 provides a tractable model for handling liquidity management. We have seen that, if creditors' cash demand is higher than the market value of the liquid assets, banks may have to sell other assets (such as loans to firms and households) that can only be converted to cash at a cost ("market liquidity risk"). This mechanism may amplify damages to the real economy.

Leverage Cycle Economic agents are heterogeneous in their preferences. Some are less risk averse/optimistic than the others, so they are natural borrowers to increase their investment opportunities (or, "taking leverage"). The leverage borrowers take is restricted by risk management: They need to hold sufficient equity to absorb losses. When the real economy booms, borrowers' profit becomes higher, raising the value of their equity and allowing them to borrow more (or, "leverage up"), and vice versa ("leverage cycles"), amplifying the initial shocks and increasing the volatilities in the economy. In this chapter, we present two mechanisms that generate leverage cycles: In the Shin model (Sect. 9.6) it works through asset prices, in the Geanakopolos model (Sect. 9.7) it works through funding supply of lenders in general equilibrium. Finally, we examined recent empirical evidence on the role of bank lending for the monetary transmission mechanism.

We have seen that monetary policy implementation has a direct impact on the risk components in banks' balance sheet. Since banks adapt to monetary policy by adjusting the risks they take, monetary policy thus has implication for financial stability: It shifts the risk level in the financial system, and changes the likelihood of systemic events such as financial crises. We will focus on the monetary policy—financial stability linkages in the final chapter.

References

Adrian, T., & Shin, H. S. (2014). Procyclical leverage and value-at-risk. *Review of Financial Studies, 27*(2), 373–403.

Ashcraft, A. B. (2006). New evidence on the lending channel. *Journal of Money, Credit, and Banking, 38*(3), 751–775.

Avdjiev, S., McCauley, R. N., & Shin, H. S. (2016). Breaking free of the triple coincidence in international finance. *Economic Policy, 31*, 409–451.

Bank for International Settlement. (2010a). Funding patterns and liquidity management of internationally active banks. *CGFS Publications*, No. 39.

Bank for International Settlement. (2010b). Long-term issues in international banking. *CGFS Publications*, No. 41.
Berg, G., & Kirschenmann, K. (2015). Funding versus real economy shock: The impact of the 2007-09 crisis on small firms' credit availability. *Review of Finance, 19*(3), 951–990.
Bernanke, B. (2015). The Taylor rule: A benchmark for monetary policy? *Brookings Blog*. http://www.brookings.edu/blogs/ben-bernanke/posts/2015/04/28-taylor-rule-monetary-policy.
Bernanke, B., & Gertler, M. (1989). Agency costs, net worth, and business fluctuations. *American Economic Review, 79*(1), 14–31.
Bernanke, B., Gertler, M., & Gilchrist, S. (1999). The financial accelerator in a quantitative business cycle framework. In J. B. Taylor & M. Woodford (Eds.), *Handbook of macroeconomics* (Vol. 1, pp. 1341–1393). Amsterdam: Elsevier.
Bianchi, J., & Bigio, S. (2018). Banks, liquidity management and monetary policy. *Working Paper*, Federal Reserve Bank of Minneapolis.
Borio, C., & Zhu, H. (2012). Capital regulation, risk-taking and monetary policy: A missing link in the transmission mechanism? *Journal of Financial Stability, 8*(4), 236–251.
Brunnermaier, M. K., et al. (2012). Banks and cross-border capital flows: Policy challenges and regulatory responses. *Committee on International Economic Policy and Reform.*
Brunnermeier, M. K., & Oehmke, M. (2009). *Complexity in financial market.* Unpublished working paper.
Brunnermeier, M. K., & Pedersen, L. H. (2009). Market liquidity and funding liquidity. *Review of Financial Studies, 22*(6), 2201–2238.
Bruno, V., & Shin, H. S. (2015a). Cross-border banking and global liquidity. *Review of Economic Studies, 82*(2), 535–564.
Bruno, V., & Shin, H. S. (2015b). Capital flows and the risk-taking channel of monetary policy. *Journal of Monetary Economics, 71*, 119–132.
Campello, M. (2002). Internal capital markets in financial conglomerates: Evidence from small bank responses to monetary policy. *Journal of Finance, 57*(6), 2773–2805.
Cao, J. (2012). *Banking regulation and the financial crisis.* Abingdon, UK: Routledge.
Cao, J., & Dinger, V. (2018). *Financial globalization and bank lending: The limits of domestic monetary policy?* Unpublished working paper.
Cetorelli, N., & Goldberg, L. S. (2012a). Banking globalization and monetary transmission. *Journal of Finance, 67*(5), 1811–1843.
Cetorelli, N., & Goldberg, L. S. (2012b). Liquidity management of U.S. global banks: Internal capital markets in the great recession. *Journal of International Economics, 88*(2), 299–311.
Cúrdia, V., & Woodford, M. (2011). The central-bank balance sheet as an instrument of monetarypolicy. *Journal of Monetary Economics, 58*(1), 54–79.
Cúrdia, V., & Woodford, M. (2015). Credit frictions and optimal monetary policy. *Federal Reserve Bank of San Francisco Working Paper Series, 2015-20.*
Davila, E., & Korinek, A. (2018). Pecuniary externalities in economies with financial frictions. *Review of Economic Studies, 85*, 352–395.
Gale, D., & Hellwig, M. (1985). Incentive-compatible debt contracts I: The one-period problem. *Review of Economic Studies, 52*, 647–664.
Geanakoplos, J. (2003). Liquidity, default, and crashes: Endogenous contracts in general equilibrium. In *Advances in economics and econometrics: Theory and applications*, Econometric Society Monographs. Eighth World Conference (Vol. 2, pp. 170–205). New York: Cambridge University Press.
Geanakoplos, J. (2010a). The leverage cycle. In D. Acemoglu, K. Rogoff, & M. Woodford (Eds.), *NBER macroeconomic annual 2009* (Vol. 24, pp. 1–65). Chicago: University of Chicago Press.
Geanakoplos, J. (2010b). Solving the present crisis and managing the leverage cycle. *Federal Reserve Bank of New York Economic Policy Review*, August 2010, pp. 101–131.
Hofmann, B., Shim, I., & Shin, H. S. (2016). Sovereign yields and the risk-taking channel of currency appreciation, *BIS Working Papers*, No. 538.

Holmström, B., & Tirole, J. (1998). Private and public supply of liquidity. *Journal of Political Economy, 106*(1), 1–40.

Jiménez, G., Ongena, S., Peydró, J.-L., & Saurina, J. (2014). Hazardous times for monetary policy: What do twenty-three million bank loans say about the effects of monetary policy on credit risk? *Econometrica, 82*(2), 463–505.

Kashyap, A. K., & Stein, J. C. (2000). What do a million observations on banks say about the transmission of monetary policy? *American Economic Review, 90*(3), 407–428.

Krogstrup, S., & Tille, C. (2015). What drives the funding currency mix of banks? *Working Paper*.

Mas-Colell, A., Whinston, M. D., & Green, J. R. (1995). *Microeconomic theory*. Oxford: Oxford University Press.

Matsuyama, K. (2008). Aggregate implications of credit market imperfections. Notes for the lectures at the University of Tokyo.

Reinhart, C. M., & Rogoff, K. S. (2009). This time is different: Eight centuries of financial. In *Folly*. Princeton: Princeton University Press.

Rey, H. (2015). Dilemma not trilemma: The global financial cycle and monetary policy independence, *NBER Working Paper*, No. 21162.

Romer, C. D., & Romer, D. H. (1990). New evidence on the monetary transmission mechanism. *Brookings Papers on Economic Activity, 1*, 149–213.

Schularick, M., & Taylor, A. M. (2012). Credit booms gone bust: Monetary policy, leverage cycles, and financial crises, 1870-2008. *American Economic Review, 102*(2), 1029–1061.

Shin, H. (2010). *Risk and liquidity* (Clarendon Lectures). New York: Oxford University Press.

Shleifer, A., & Vishny, R. W. (1997). The limits of arbitrage. *Journal of Finance, 52*(1), 35–55.

Temesvary, J., Ongena, S., & Owen, A. L. (2018). A global lending channel unplugged? Does U.S. monetary policy affect cross-border and affiliate lending by global U.S. banks? *Journal of International Economics, 112*, 50–69.

Townsend, R. (1979). Optimal contracts and competitive markets with costly state verification. *Journal of Economic Theory, 21*(2), 265–293.

Wallace, N. (1981). A Modigliani-Miller theorem for open-market operations. *American Economic Review, 71*(3), 267–274.

Monetary Policy and Financial Stability 10

10.1 Introduction

It is well accepted that the financial sector plays a key role in the transmission mechanism of monetary policy, i.e., banks react to monetary policy by changing the level of their credit supply, and this further affects aggregate output of the real economy. A more subtle point is that at the same time banks also strategically adapt to monetary policy by changing their risk-taking on the balance sheets. As has been shown in the Bianchi–Bigio model in the last chapter, when monetary policy is lax, banks' refinancing cost and funding liquidity risk are reduced. This encourages them to load up more credit and liquidity risks for higher yields. Thus the risk level in the banking system rises.

On the other hand, banks are very special institutions. One of their key roles in the financial system is maturity transformation: They finance long-term, risky, yet high yield projects with short-term debts. The need to roll over these short-term debts exposes themselves to maturity mismatch with the risk of bank runs: Once creditors have doubt about profitability of the long-term projects, they may immediately demand their money back, refusing to roll over the debts; thus banks may be forced to sell ("liquidate") half-finished projects at high cost, until they declare bankruptcy. If a large share of banks stop functioning, the real economy will soon run out of funding, triggering a systemic crisis.

Obviously, rising risk level in the banking system increases the likelihood of systemic bank failure, therefore, monetary policy has a profound implication for financial stability. The most recent episode of the 2007–2009 global financial crisis is just another evidence of such linkage: Encouraged by the Fed's low policy rate since 2001, banks created enormous exposure to credit and liquidity risks, especially through expanding credit lines to low quality, subprime mortgage loan borrowers. Once the accumulated systemic risk scared creditors away from funding the banks, the entire global financial system came to a full stop.

In this chapter, we present two main approaches to analyzing the feedback between monetary policy and financial stability. One approach is macro approach,

J. Cao, G. Illing, *Money: Theory and Practice*, Springer Texts in Business and Economics, https://doi.org/10.1007/978-3-030-19697-4_10

integrating banking sector in standard DSGE models, such as Gertler–Kiyotaki model in Sect. 10.2. This approach works best to show how financial instability evolves over time, how it propagates to the real economy, and how monetary policy helps the economy recover from the crisis, while the drawback is that the behavior of banks has to be much simplified—sometimes even ad hoc—to get tractable solutions in such a complicated framework so that one has to abstract much from the sources of systemic risks. The banking approach tries to fill that gap, integrating central bank and a simplified real economy in (usually, partial equilibrium and static) banking models. This approach is best at modelling the rich strategic responses of banks to monetary policy and capturing the sources of financial instabilities. Section 10.3 considers the Cao–Illing model, analyzing the feedback central bank actions and banks incentives to expose to systemic risk. The downside of the banking approach is that it is often technically difficult to make such models dynamic. Therefore, this approach is less capable to replicate those business cycle features as in the DSGE models, or, to demonstrate both short-run and long-run impact of financial shocks on the real economy. Section 10.4 draws lessons for macroprudential regulation.

10.2 Bank Failure in Macro Dynamics: Gertler–Kiyotaki Model

10.2.1 Introduction

When introducing financial frictions, the traditional "macroeconomic" approach focuses on financial accelerator effects as outlined in Sects. 9.3 and 9.4. In contrast, the finance or "microeconomic" approach stresses the relation between bank liquidity mismatch and bank runs. Banks hold long-term assets and issue short-term debt. As a consequence they are potentially subject to runs. If we take the risk of bank runs seriously, the feedback effects between banking distress and the state of the real economy are far more complex than standard financial accelerator models suggest. Economic downturns adversely affect a bank's ability to intermediate funds. But a recession that constrains bank lending due to conventional financial accelerator effects also opens up the possibility of runs: The associated weakening of balance sheets and reduced liquidity of secondary markets for bank assets increase the risk of runs.

Extending the framework discussed in Sect. 9.4, Gertler and Kiyotaki (2015) develop a macroeconomic model of banking instability that integrates both of these mechanisms. In the model discussed in this section, they emphasize the complementary nature of financial accelerator effects and bank runs. Balance sheet conditions not only affect the cost of bank credit, but they also affect whether runs are possible. Whether runs may occur depends on macroeconomic conditions: Runs are likely to be triggered in bad times. In turn, runs feed back into the macro economy, aggravating the downturn. This gives rise to the possibility of multiple, self-fulfilling equilibria.

As in Gertler–Karadi–Kiyotaki model, the bank's portfolio is constrained by its net worth. Fluctuations in net worth induce fluctuations in bank lending, leading to conventional financial accelerator effects. Endogenous pro-cyclical movements in bank balance sheets lead to countercyclical movements in the cost of bank credit. If incentive constraints are not binding, banks can perform unlimited arbitrage and will be able to intermediate all the capital. The economy resembles one with frictionless financial markets, where financial structure in banking is irrelevant to the real activity. But incentive constraints impose limits to arbitrage, with leverage restrictions constraining the amount of lending by bank net worth. In bad times, tightened bank balance sheets raise the cost of bank credit. This induces the kind of financial accelerator mechanism prevalent in Bernanke and Gertler (1989) and other macroeconomic models of financial distress. But that is not all: Due to liquidity mismatch, now bank runs may be triggered, because a bank cannot operate with negative net worth. Whether or not a bank run equilibrium exists depends on two key factors: the condition of bank balance sheets and an endogenously determined asset liquidation price. Thus, a situation can arise where a bank run cannot occur in normal times, but where a severe recession opens up the possibility of runs.

A severe recession induces financial distress that amplifies the fall in assets prices and raises the cost of bank credit. An unanticipated negative productivity shock reduces net worth, which tightens bank balance sheets. If depositors have doubts about getting back their funds, this may lead to a contraction of bank deposits with fire sales of bank assets, which in turn magnifies the asset price decline. Banks being in trouble, they will be forced to liquidate, transferring assets to agents with less expertise in screening and monitoring investment projects relative to banks. Gertler and Kiyotaki model this process such that in that case intermediation will be taken over by households. Because of their lack of expertise, doing this is costly for them, so the amount households acquire is limited, absorbing only part of the assets. The net effect is a substantial increase in the cost of bank credit, raising the spread between the expected return to bank assets and the riskless rate even more.

10.2.2 Agents, Technology, and Timing

Consider an augmented Gertler–Karadi–Kiyotaki model as follows. There are two groups of agents in the economy: Risk averse households and risk neutral bankers, and each group has a fixed population of unity. Assume that the economy extends for infinite time horizon, $t = 0, 1, \ldots, +\infty$, although the key mechanism of the model can be easily seen in just two periods. Households live forever; while in each period a banker has the probability $1 - \sigma$ to exit the economy. The exit probability being a Poisson distribution with parameter $1 - \sigma$, the expected lifetime of a banker (the waiting time for exit to happen) is therefore $\frac{1}{1-\sigma}$. Exiting bankers are assumed to be replaced by new bankers entering the economy in the next period so that the population of bankers stays constant over time.

There are two types of goods in the economy: One perishable consumption good that cannot be stored for more than one period, and one nonperishable capital good that is used as input for production. Each period, every household receives an endowment of perishable consumption good, $Z_t W^h$. Here, W^h is constant, while the stochastic variable Z is the *aggregate* serial correlated shock to all households' endowment in each period t. Each banker only receives an endowment w^b (From now on, we follow the convention of using lower case letters for "per capita" variables and capital letters for aggregate variables) in perishable consumption good when she enters the economy.

Both households and bankers can hold nonperishable, zero-depreciating capital. This capital is in fixed total supply, normalized to be unity, i.e.,

$$K_t^b + K_t^h = 1.$$

K_t^b and K_t^h denote total capital held by bankers and households, respectively, in period t. Capital can be used to produce the perishable good for consumption in each period using a technology of constant return to scale. Bankers are more efficient in utilizing capital. Precisely, after investing in K_t^b units of capital in period t, a banker receives $Z_{t+1}K_t^b$ units of consumption good as output in the next period, $t+1$, with the same amount of capital K_t^b being carried over to period $t+1$, as Fig. 10.1 shows. The stochastic variable Z reflects an aggregate shock to productivity in each period, which is assumed to be public information. So everyone in the economy observes the true value of Z once it is revealed.

If instead a household invests herself in K_t^h units of capital in period t, she also receives $Z_{t+1}K_t^h$ units of consumption good as output in the next period, $t+1$, with the same amount of capital K_t^h being carried over to period $t+1$. But on top of that, she has to incur an additional capital management cost $f(K_t^h)$ in period t, as shown in Fig. 10.2.

The capital management cost $f(K_t^h)$ is convex in K_t^h,

$$f(K_t^h) = \frac{\alpha}{2}(K_t^h)^2, \quad \alpha > 0.$$

In a frictionless economy, all investments should be delegated to bankers—being more efficient, they should hold the entire capital stock in the economy. Households save all their endowment as bank deposits, with bankers investing more efficiently in productive capital. However, just as in the Gertler–Karadi–Kiyotaki model, a financial friction arises from a moral hazard problem: Each banker can divert a share θ of assets under her management as private benefit, leading to the bankruptcy of her bank. As a result, in the equilibrium with financial friction, bankers face borrowing constraints. They cannot acquire the entire capital stock; some of the capital stock will be held by households, despite being less efficient because of positive capital management cost $f(K_t^h)$.

In each period t, bankers offer one-period deposit contracts to households, promising a noncontingent fixed gross return $\overline{R}_{t+1}$. Such deposit contracts create a

Period t	*Period t* + 1
Capital input K_t^b	Output of consumption good $Z_{t+1}K_t^b$
	Capital K_t^b

Fig. 10.1 Bankers' production technology

Period t	*Period t* + 1
Capital input K_t^h	Output of consumption good $Z_{t+1}K_t^h$
Capital management cost $f(K_t^h)$	Capital K_t^h

Fig. 10.2 Households' production technology

maturity mismatch: The productive assets are of infinite maturity, but they are funded by short-term deposit contracts that need be renewed every period.[1] As demonstrated by Bianchi–Bigio model, the maturity mismatch exposes banks to funding liquidity risk. If households suspect that they will not be fully repaid by the banks, they are entitled to demand immediate repayment and will refuse to renew their deposits contracts; as a result, a bank run gets started. Being under the pressure of withdrawals from depositors and unable to roll over their debts, banks are forced to liquidate all assets in a fire sale at depressed price, similar to the process modeled by Geanakoplos in Sect. 9.7. On average, depositors will only receive a lower return than what has been promised. The payoff structure of the deposit contracts can be written as

$$R_{t+1} = \begin{cases} \overline{R}_{t+1}, & \text{without bank run}, \\ x_{t+1}\overline{R}_{t+1}, & \text{with bank run}, \end{cases}$$

with $0 \leq x_{t+1} < 1$ being endogenized later. More details on bank run will be explained later.

Should there be no bank run, the timing of events in the economy is as follows (Fig. 10.3):

(1) In the beginning of period t, the aggregate technological shock Z_t is revealed and consumption good is produced out of the capital input from period $t-1$. The deposit contracts issued by a banker from the past period d_{t-1} are repaid, and households receive their endowment;

[1] Deposit contracts can provide efficient insurance against idiosyncratic household liquidity risks (which is not modelled here explicitly), but they induce fragility due to the risk of bank runs in case of adverse aggregate shocks. In Diamond and Dybvig (1983) the risk of runs is the result of a sequential service constraint (leaving those late in the queue empty-handed). But bank runs can occur even if all depositors are treated equally (receiving the same haircut) provided they anticipate that the bank will be left with zero net worth in the event of a run such that $x_{t+1} < 1$.

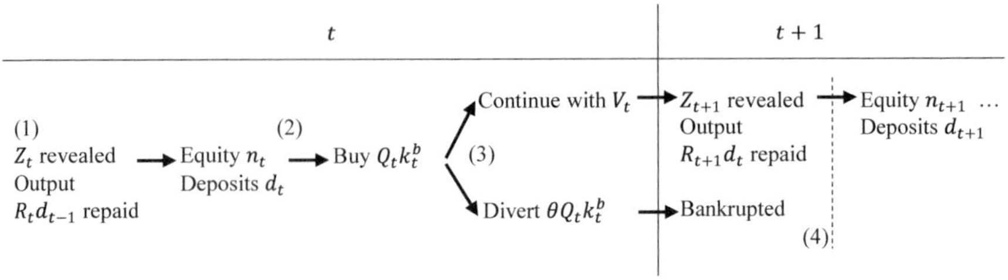

Fig. 10.3 Timing of events without bank run

(2) A banker then gets funding, partially from her own pocket—call it equity n_t—and partially from collecting deposits d_t from the households. Using the funds, she buys capital input k_t^b in the competitive capital market at price Q_t.

(3) Now the banker has two options
   (a) To carry on the capital stock into next period, which gives her a "franchise value V_t"—the benefit for her to continue her business, will be explained in more details later. Then in the beginning of period $t+1$, the aggregate technological shock Z_{t+1} is revealed and consumption good is produced out of the capital input from period t. The bank continues its business, similar as in step (1).
   (b) To divert a share θ of her assets for her private benefit and declare bankruptcy. Then she stays out of business until she exits the economy.

(4) Independent on bankers' choices, after all the debts are cleared, a share $1-\sigma$ of the bankers exit, and they are replaced by the same population of new bankers, entering with an endowment w^b each. The banking service in period $t+1$ is provided by the surviving bankers, jointly with the new bankers.

However, should there be a bank run, the timing of events in the economy follows Fig. 10.4:

(1) Suppose, after Z_t is revealed in period t, households run on banks for some reason (to be explained later). They demand their deposit repayment and refuse to make new deposits in period t. As a result, banks cannot roll over their debts and have to liquidate all assets in a fire sale. Households on average receive a poor return $x_t \overline{R}_t$ on their deposits. The bankers remain bankrupted for the rest of their lives.

(2) A population of $1-\sigma$ new bankers enters the economy with endowment of w^b each; however, they cannot do anything during the bank run and have to stay idle, and a share σ of them will survive for the next period;

(3) In period $t+1$ the surviving bankers will join the new bankers of population $1-\sigma$ to restart the banking business; therefore, $t+1$ is a rebalancing period: They will inject equity into the new banks and take deposits from households. Afterward, the business continues as usual, following Fig. 10.3 if there is no new bank run.

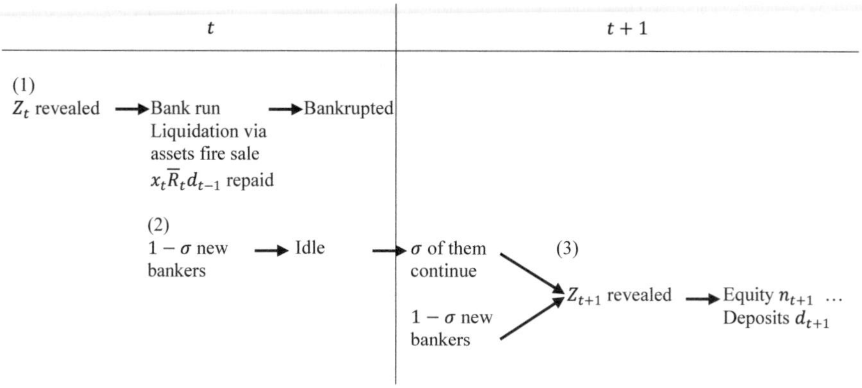

Fig. 10.4 Timing of events with bank run

10.2.3 Baseline Case with Unanticipated Bank Runs

To better understand the implication of bank runs, we consider a simple baseline case. Here all agents consider the probability of a bank run to be zero, i.e., bank runs are completely unanticipated, they arise as exogenous shocks. In this case, households optimize their decisions, assuming that the return from deposits is always $\overline{R}_t$. Precisely, they maximize their lifetime utility from consumption stream C_t^h,

$$\max_{\{C_t^h, D_t, K_t^h\}} U_t = E_t\left(\sum_{i=0}^{+\infty} \beta^i \ln C_{t+i}^h\right),$$

by choosing consumption C_t^h, deposits D_t, and capital stock K_t^h after receiving the endowment $Z_t W^h$, repayment from the past deposit contracts $R_t D_{t-1}$ and output of productive capital $Z_t K_{t-1}^h$ in each period, subject to the budget constraint

$$C_t^h + D_t + Q_t K_t^h + f\left(K_t^h\right) = Z_t W^h + R_t D_{t-1} + (Z_t + Q_t) K_{t-1}^h.$$

The productive capital is valued at price Q_t in the capital market. The first-order condition for deposits implies

$$E_t(\Lambda_{t,t+1} R_{t+1}) = 1 \tag{10.2.1}$$

in which the stochastic discount factor $\Lambda_{t,t+1}$ is defined by

$$\Lambda_{t,t+1} = \beta^i \frac{C_t^h}{C_{t+i}^h}.$$

This is the familiar first-order condition for holding riskless bonds in standard models. The first-order condition for holding productive capital is

$$E_t\left(\Lambda_{t,t+1}R^h_{t+1}\right) = 1 \tag{10.2.2}$$

in which

$$R^h_{t+1} = \frac{Z_{t+1} + Q_{t+1}}{Q_t + f'\left(K^h_t\right)} = \frac{Z_{t+1} + Q_{t+1}}{Q_t + \alpha K^h_t}. \tag{10.2.3}$$

R^h_{t+1} is the gross marginal return to holding capital by households, because $Z_{t+1} + Q_{t+1}$ is the return from carrying on one unit capital to period $t + 1$, and $Q_t + f'\left(K^h_t\right)$ is the marginal cost of investing in productive capital in period t.

Combining (Equation 10.2.2) with (Equation 10.2.3) and solving forward for Q_t, we can calculate the price for capital

$$Q_t = E_t\left[\sum_{i=1}^{+\infty} \Lambda_{t,t+i}\left(Z_{t+i} - \alpha K^h_{t+i}\right)\right] - \alpha K^h_t. \tag{10.2.4}$$

Quite intuitively, the price for the productive capital held by households is determined by the future discounted flow of capital output Z_{t+i} minus the marginal capital management cost αK^h_{t+i}. Equation 10.2.4 is the key equation driving all the dynamics; we will come back to it later from time to time.

Different from households, bankers are risk neutral. Since bankers are constrained by their net worth, it will be optimal to defer all consumption until the exit period. So as long as banking is profitable, they will accumulate wealth to consume only in the period they exit. This gives the "franchise value" V_t of a bank in period t, i.e., the implied future consumption for the banker if she continues with her business. Her problem is therefore to maximize the franchise value, as long as she is in business

$$\max_{\left\{d_t, k^b_t\right\}} V_t = E_t\left[\sum_{i=1}^{+\infty} \beta^i(1-\sigma)\sigma^{i-1}c^b_{t+i}\right]$$

in which c^b_{t+i} is her consumption if she exits in period $t + i$, by choosing the deposit she takes, d_t, and the productive capital she invests in, k^b_t. Further, as the terminal consumption c^b_{t+i} comes from the banker's equity n_{t+i}, the banker's decision problem can be rewritten in the recursive form

$$\max_{\left\{d_t, k^b_t\right\}} V_t = E_t[\beta(1-\sigma)n_{t+1} + \beta\sigma V_{t+1}],$$

which states that a banker's current franchise value depends on her fate in the next period: She may exit at probability $1 - \sigma$ with her equity n_{t+1} for consumption, or continue at probability σ with the franchise value V_{t+1}.

Following Fig. 10.3, at the beginning of period t, when a new banker enters, she can use her endowment w^b as equity for her new bank

$$n_t = w^b.$$

For an existing banker, her bank equity comes from accumulating net worth via retained earnings after all past deposit contracts have been cleared, i.e.,

$$n_t = (Z_t + Q_t)k_{t-1}^b - R_t d_{t-1}.$$

For both types of bankers, they collect deposits to fund their investments in productive capital. For a representative banker, her budget constraint comes from the balance sheet identity

$$Q_t k_t^b = d_t + n_t.$$

In the absence of financial frictions, bankers would want to borrow as much as possible and hold the entire capital stock in the economy. Given that bankers always have the incentive to divert assets for private benefit and leave all the losses to depositors, households, however, are only willing to provide limited supply of funding to avoid the moral hazard of bankers. Precisely, households are only willing to deposit d_t in each bank if bankers' benefit from diverting assets is below their franchise value so that bankers will not misbehave

$$\theta Q_t k_t^b = \theta(d_t + n_t) \le V_t. \quad (IC)$$

This is the incentive compatibility constraint (IC) for deposit funding. The growth path of a bank's net worth is

$$\frac{n_{t+1}}{n_t} = \frac{(Z_{t+1} + Q_{t+1})k_t^b - R_{t+1}\left(Q_t k_t^b - n_t\right)}{n_t} = \left(R_{t+1}^b - R_{t+1}\right)\phi_t + R_{t+1} \quad (10.2.5)$$

with

$$R_{t+1}^b = \frac{Z_{t+1} + Q_{t+1}}{Q_t}$$

as the banker's marginal gross return from holding capital for one period, and

$$\phi_t = \frac{Q_t k_t^b}{n_t}$$

as the bank's total assets to equity ratio, or, leverage ratio. The bank's net worth growth increases with its leverage, as long as its profit margin, $R^b_{t+1} - R_{t+1}$, is positive.

Because the bank's optimization problem is linear and the investment technology has constant return to scale, we can rewrite the bank's problem in "per equity" form to better reveal the mechanisms at work. Denote $\frac{V_t}{n_t}$ by ψ_t as the franchise value per equity, then the bank's problem becomes

$$\max_{\phi_t} \frac{V_t}{n_t} = E_t\left[\beta(1-\sigma)\frac{n_{t+1}}{n_t} + \beta\sigma\frac{n_{t+1}}{n_t}\frac{V_{t+1}}{n_{t+1}}\right],$$

or

$$\max_{\phi_t} \psi_t = \beta E_t\left\{\left(1-\sigma+\sigma\psi_{t+1}\right)\left[\left(R^b_{t+1} - R_{t+1}\right)\phi_t + R_{t+1}\right]\right\}$$

using equation (Equation 10.2.5). It can be further simplified as

$$\max_{\left\{d_t, k^b_t\right\}} \psi_t = \mu_t\phi_t + \nu_t$$

in which

$$\mu_t = \beta E_t\left[\left(1-\sigma+\sigma\psi_{t+1}\right)\left(R^b_{t+1} - R_{t+1}\right)\right] = \beta E_t\left[\Omega_{t+1}\left(R^b_{t+1} - R_{t+1}\right)\right] \quad (10.2.6)$$

reflects the marginal profit of the bank assets, and

$$\nu_t = \beta E_t(\Omega_{t+1}R_{t+1})$$

is the marginal worth of bank deposits.

Note that the term $1-\sigma+\sigma\psi_{t+1}$, denoted by Ω_{t+1}, is the weighted average of the bank's marginal return of one unit equity from exiting (one, with probability $1-\sigma$) and surviving (ψ_{t+1}, with probability σ). Using the same set of notations, the incentive compatibility constraint can be rewritten as

$$\theta\frac{Q_t k^b_t}{n_t} = \theta\phi_t \leq \frac{V_t}{n_t},$$

or

$$\theta\phi_t \leq \frac{V_t}{n_t} = \psi_t = \mu_t\phi_t + \nu_t. \quad (IC)$$

Given that $\nu_t > 0$, (IC) requires that $0 < \mu_t < \theta$. Because the bank's net worth growth increases with leverage ϕ_t, the banker will always choose the highest leverage that makes (IC) binding. As a result, the bank's leverage ratio in the equilibrium is determined by

$$\phi_t = \frac{\psi_t}{\theta} = \frac{\nu_t}{\theta - \mu_t}.$$

The agency problem imposes an endogenous capital constraint on the size of the bank's portfolio. As in Gertler–Karadi–Kiyotaki model, banks face a borrowing constraint. The size of their portfolio is limited by the condition that the bank's gain from diverting funds (per unit of net worth $\theta\,\phi_t$) is exactly balanced by the cost of losing the franchise value, measured by $\psi_t = \nu_t + \psi_t\,\mu_t$. The limits to arbitrage lead to positive expected excess returns in equilibrium: $R^b_{t+1} - R_{t+1} > 0$, or $\mu_t > 0$.

Now, what happens if an unanticipated bank run occurs in period t? First of all, note that such bank runs happen only—even if unanticipated—if the households fear that they may not be fully repaid on average once the run starts. Otherwise there is no need to run on the banks at all. Because of the first-come-first-served rule in banking, given such expectation, every depositor tries to stand in front of the queues and get full repayment from her bank, triggering a full-blown bank run—although funds in the banks will soon get exhausted and those who arrive late may receive nothing. So expected recovered value from liquidating bank assets must be below banks' liabilities from deposits, or, the recovery ratio x_t is less than one:

$$x_t = \frac{(Z_t + Q^*_t)K^b_{t-1}}{R_t D_{t-1}} < 1$$

with Q^*_t as the fire sale price of capital. Using the fact that in aggregate

$$Q_{t-1}K^b_{t-1} = D_{t-1} + N_{t-1},$$

x_t can be further rearranged as

$$x_t = \frac{R^{b*}_t}{R_t}\frac{\phi_{t-1}}{\phi_{t-1} - 1} < 1,$$

with $\phi_{t-1} = \frac{Q_{t-1}K^b_{t-1}}{N_{t-1}}$ on aggregate and $R^{b*}_t = \frac{Z_t + Q^*_t}{Q_{t-1}}$ as the return on fire sale assets in the bank run. As explained, in order to make a bank run happen, R^{b*}_t must be low enough. Given that the distribution of Z_t is public information, Z_t cannot be too low—otherwise the bank run would have been anticipated. Therefore, an unanticipated bank run can only happen if Q^*_t is too low.

So what determines the fire sale price of capital Q^*_t? When banks are forced to liquidate all assets in a fire sale, the only buyers left are households. Thus, the entire capital stock ends up in the hands of households, i.e., $K^{h*}_t = 1$. To keep track of bankers' resources, following Fig. 10.4, after the idle period t, total equity that bankers start with in the balancing period $t + 1$ includes those endowments carried over by the surviving generation t new bankers, plus those which arrive with generation $t+1$ new bankers, i.e.,

$$N_{t+1} = \sigma(1-\sigma)w^b + (1-\sigma)w^b = \sigma W^b + W^b$$

in which $W^b = (1-\sigma)w^b$ denotes the total endowment that arrives with new bankers in each period. In later periods, banking business returns to normal, i.e., surviving bankers retain equity after repaying depositors, and new bankers start their business using endowment as equity:

$$N_{t+i} = \sigma\left[(Z_{t+i} + Q_{t+i})K^b_{t+i-1} - R_{t+i}D_{t+i-1}\right] + W^b$$

for $i \geq 2$.

By equation (Equation 10.2.4), the price of capital during the bank run is now

$$Q^*_t = E_t\left[\sum_{i=1}^{+\infty} \Lambda_{t,t+i}\left(Z_{t+i} - \alpha K^{h*}_{t+i}\right)\right] - \alpha K^{h*}_t. \tag{10.2.7}$$

It can be easily seen that the fire sale price Q^*_t is lower, because all productive capital will now be held in total by the households, $K^{h*}_t = 1$, who value capital less; moreover, even when banks recover from the devastating bank run, it will take time for bankers to build up capital again by buying from households. So households' holdings of capital during the recovery, K^{h*}_{t+i}, are persistently too high, further depressing the fire sale price Q^*_t.

This bank run equilibrium resembles very closely the sunspot equilibrium proposed by Diamond and Dybvig (1983). Here banks have sound fundamentals, as long as the asset price Q_t defined by equation (Equation 10.2.4) is sufficiently high to ensure full repayment of all deposits. In that case, households have no incentive to run on the bank. That is, as long as Q_t stays at the non-run equilibrium price, a bank run is a zero probability event. However, once a bank run sets in, with households coordinated by some signal that may not even be correlated with fundamentals in the banks—say, a sunspot,—the run will be self-fulfilling. Now all households will join, because the asset price falls to Q^*_t which is too low to support the full repayment of all deposits. Given that such non-predictable sunspot equilibria may occur, banking is intrinsically fragile.

The insight into such runs may occur as sunspot equilibria suggests a pessimistic message for policy makers: After all, sunspots are not predictable. However, there are instruments and devices to induce households to coordinate on the non-run equilibrium, which we will discuss later.

10.2.4 Equilibrium with Anticipated Bank Runs

The more interesting case is the bank run that is triggered by fundamentals. As can be seen in equation (Equation 10.2.4), when there is a large, negative, and serial correlated shock in Z_t, the output will drop as well as the fundamental value of the productive capital. This will also lead to a drop in Q_t and so may trigger a bank run. However, as the distribution of Z_t is public information, all agents will anticipate that such bank runs may be triggered by negative fundamental shocks. This leads to a more complex decision problem both by households and bankers. Next, we will explore the outcome from their decision problems, given that bank runs are triggered by fundamentals and are anticipated.

Unfortunately, computation is very much complicated by the fact that whether a run happens depends on the realized time-varying serial correlated shock Z_t. To focus more on the key mechanisms and to avoid too much complication, we assume that households assign some probability p_t in each period, as the likelihood of bank run in $t+1$. Obviously p_t is related with household's expectation on the recovery ratio of their deposits in $t+1$, $E_t[x_{t+1}]$, in which

$$x_{t+1} = \min\left[1, \frac{(Z_{t+1} + Q^*_{t+1})K^b_t}{R_{t+1}D_t}\right] = \min\left[1, \frac{R^{b*}_{t+1}}{R_{t+1}}\frac{\phi_t}{\phi_t - 1}\right].$$

Intuitively, the probability is $p_t = 0$ if $E_t[x_{t+1}] = 1$ and increases when $E_t[x_{t+1}]$ falls from 1.

Similar first-order condition applies for a household's decision on deposits in period t,

$$E_t[(1 - p_t)\Lambda_{t,t+1}R_{t+1} + p_t\Lambda^*_{t,t+1}x_{t+1}R_{t+1}] = 1.$$

Here the stochastic discount factor $\Lambda^*_{t,t+1}$ under bank run in $t+1$ is defined by

$$\Lambda^*_{t,t+1} = \beta^i \frac{C^h_t}{C^{h*}_{t+i}},$$

with C^{h*}_{t+i} being the household's consumption in a bank run period. Compared with the no-run first-order condition (Equation 10.2.1), as long as $\Lambda^*_{t,t+1}x_{t+1} < \Lambda_{t,t+1}$, here R_{t+1} needs to be higher to compensate depositors' loss in the bank run and it increases with the likelihood of bank run p_t. R_{t+1} can be solved as

$$R_{t+1} = \frac{1 - p_t E_t\left(\Lambda^*_{t,t+1}R^{b*}_{t+1}\right)\frac{\phi}{\phi_t - 1}}{(1 - p_t)E_t(\Lambda_{t,t+1})}.$$

Note that R_{t+1} increases with bank leverage ϕ_t: Because of limited liability of banks, the higher a bank leverages up, the lower is the banker's own stake in the bank, the higher the loss that has to be shouldered by the depositors. This leads to a higher risk premium in R_{t+1}.

Following the "per equity" form, a bank's problem is

$$\max_{\phi_t} \psi_t = E_t\left[\beta\left(1-\sigma+\sigma\psi_{t+1}\right)\frac{n_{t+1}}{n_t}\right]$$
$$= \beta E_t\{(1-\iota_{t+1})\Omega_{t+1}\left[\left(R^b_{t+1}-R_{t+1}\right)\phi_t+R_{t+1}\right]$$
$$+\iota_{t+1}\Omega^*_{t+1}\max\left[0,\left(R^{b*}_{t+1}-R_{t+1}\right)\phi_t+R_{t+1}\right]\},$$
$$s.t.\ \theta\phi_t \le \psi_t\ (IC)$$

in which

$$\iota_{t+1} = \begin{cases} 1, & \text{if a bank run occurs,} \\ 0, & \text{otherwise,} \end{cases}$$

and $\Omega^*_{t+1} = \left(1-\sigma+\sigma\psi^*_{t+1}\right)$ is the expected value of one unit equity in a bank run. Given that all banks are symmetric, it can easily be seen that in the bank run—which happens at the probability p_t—all bankrupted bankers receive zero equity; therefore, the bank's problem can be rewritten as

$$\max_{\phi_t} \psi_t = \beta(1-p_t)E_t\{\Omega_{t+1}\left[\left(R^b_{t+1}-R_{t+1}\right)\phi_t+R_{t+1}\right]\}$$
$$= \beta(1-p_t)E_t\left\{\Omega_{t+1}\left[\phi_t R^b_{t+1}-\frac{\phi_t-1-\phi_t p_t E_t\left(\Lambda^*_{t,t+1}R^{b*}_{t+1}\right)}{(1-p_t)E_t(\Lambda_{t,t+1})}\right]\right\}.$$

Define $R^0_{t+1}=\frac{1}{E_t(\Lambda_{t,t+1})}$ as the risk-free rate in the absence of bank runs, then ψ_t can be rewritten in the similar form as in the baseline case:

$$\psi_t = \beta E_t\{\Omega_{t+1}[\phi_t(1-p_t)R^b_{t+1}-R^0_{t+1}\phi_t+R^0_{t+1}+\phi_t p_t R^0_{t+1}E_t(\Lambda^*_{t,t+1}R^{b*}_{t+1})]\}$$
$$= \beta E_t\{\Omega_{t+1}[(R^b_{t+1}-R^0_{t+1}-p_t(R^b_{t+1}-R^0_{t+1}E_t(\Lambda^*_{t,t+1}R^{b*}_{t+1})))\phi_t+R^0_{t+1}]\}$$
$$= \mu_t\phi_t+\nu_t$$

in which

$$\mu_t = \beta E_t\{\Omega_{t+1}\left[R^b_{t+1}-R^0_{t+1}-p_t\left(R^b_{t+1}-R^0_{t+1}E_t\left(\Lambda^*_{t,t+1}R^{b*}_{t+1}\right)\right)\right]\},$$
$$\nu_t = \beta E_t\left[\Omega_{t+1}R^0_{t+1}\right].$$

Again, μ_t reflects the marginal profit of the bank assets.

What can we say about the bank's decision problem? First of all, as long as $\mu_t > 1$, the bank always has the incentive to be fully leveraged, i.e., to set ϕ_t such that (*IC*) is binding; second, compared with equation (Equation 10.2.6) in the baseline case, now the marginal profit of the bank assets μ_t obviously depends on the probability of bank run p_t. The higher that probability, the more value of assets is likely to be destroyed in a bank run. This lowers the bank's marginal profit of holding assets. Further, a lower μ_t reduces the bank's franchise value ψ_t, which forces the bank to reduce leverage by (*IC*).

What happens to asset prices in an anticipated bank run, when it happens in $t+1$? Quite similar as (Equation 10.2.4), now the price for the productive capital is

$$Q^*_{t+1} = E_{t+1}\left[\sum_{i=1}^{+\infty} \Lambda^{**}_{t+1,t+1+i}\left(Z_{t+1+i} - \alpha K^{h*}_{t+1+i}\right)\right] - \alpha K^{h*}_{t+1} \tag{10.2.8}$$

in which $\Lambda^{**}_{t+1,t+1+i}$ is the "post-run" stochastic discount factor. Note that Q^*_{t+1} is depressed not only by the limit of arbitrage—the fact that the entire capital stock has to be held by the less efficient households during the run and efficient bankers need to gradually buy back the capital during the recovery—but also by the large negative serial correlated shock Z_{t+1+i} which reduces the fundamental value of the capital; this will be anticipated in period t by the households and determines their perceived probability of bank run, p_t.

10.2.5 Policy Implications

Gertler–Kiyotaki model integrates financial fragility in a dynamic stochastic general equilibrium framework, making them capable to generate financial crisis in an otherwise standard model. Both types of bank runs, "sunspot" type and fundamental driven type, arise naturally from the model. One can further simulate the model numerically and generate collapses and recessions that fit observed regularities nicely.

The model policy has clear policy implications. Bank runs lead to an efficiency loss in the economy, because productive capital is transferred to nonspecialists (in the stylized framework here to households) who have less expertise in asset management. So social welfare would improve if runs could be eliminated. In the Diamond Dybvig framework, a simple way to achieve this is to introduce deposit insurance: In normal times banks pay a premium to the insurance scheme, and deposits will be recovered by the insurance if banks' deposit recovery ratio falls below 1. Such a scheme helps to eliminate sunspot runs completely: Knowing that their deposits are guaranteed by the insurance, households will collectively stay in the non-run equilibrium and never run; the insurance scheme thus provides a device for households to coordinate beliefs.

In the current model, deposit insurance would not work because of the impact on banks incentive constraints: With deposits being fully protected, banks would increase leverage and divert funds. The banks in this model correspond best to the lightly regulated shadow banking sector which was at the center of the instability during the recent financial crisis. Aggregate shocks decreased the perceived value of collateral in the economy. With the price of collateral falling, creditors became increasingly reluctant to roll over short-term loans to shadow banks, raising haircuts rapidly for highly leveraged institutions. Eventually, this triggered a run on financial institutions in the shadow banking sector (for details see Gorton & Metrick, 2012).

The model illustrates that the distinction between a liquidity shortage and insolvency is fairly subtle. If a bank run equilibrium occurs, banks become insolvent, i.e., their liabilities exceed their assets if assets are valued at the fire-sale prices. But if assets would be valued at the price in the no-run equilibrium, all banks would be considered to be solvent. Thus, whether banks are insolvent or not depends on equilibrium asset prices which in turn depend on the liquidity in the banking system. This liquidity can change abruptly in the event of a run. The collapse of the banking system during the Great Depression impressively illustrates this phenomenon. As already pointed out by Friedman and Schwartz (1963), what was initially a liquidity problem in the banking system (due in part by inaction of the central bank), turned into a solvency problem as runs on banks led to a collapse in long-term security prices and in the banking system along with it.

This insight motivates a role for ex post lender of the last resort policies in reducing vulnerability to runs. Whenever private intermediaries are finance constrained, there is scope for interventions in credit markets. In the downturn, the central bank can support asset prices by purchasing the productive capital. This prevents asset prices from falling further and triggering costly bank runs, and avoid the bank assets from ending up in the hands of inefficient households. Later, when the economy recovers, the central bank can sell the capital back to banks, without increasing the burden of tax payers.

There will be no efficiency loss provided the central bank has the same expertise of asset management as private banks. But even if the central bank is less efficient at intermediating credit than private banks, it has the advantage that the government is not balance sheet constrained in the same way as private banks. The central bank can issue interest-bearing reserves or sell other short-term government debt to provide credit. It can do so either directly by purchasing assets or indirectly by lending funds to banks and taking loans made by these banks as collateral (such as the commercial paper funding facility the Fed set up in the wake of the collapse of this market in October 2008). Not being constrained by limits of arbitrage, central bank interventions in a financial crisis can support asset prices and reduce credit spreads, thereby stimulating the economy.

More generally, such interventions can be done via quite different channels with possibly rather diverse distributional impact: Rather than interventions done by the central bank, banks may be supported via public equity injection (diluting existing shareholder rights) or alternatively via government credit, in each case financed by taxes. Each intervention needs to take into account the impact on incentive constraints. So government lending will have an advantage relative to private credit only if it is harder for banks to cheat the government agency.

Focus Box: Brunnermeier and Sannikov—A Continuous-Time Approach

Brunnermeier and Sannikov (2014) develop a macroeconomic model of banking instability with a structure very close to Gertler and Kiyotaki (2015), but they use a continuous-time approach. They also consider an economy populated by two types of agents: bankers (called productive "experts") and households. Both types of agents can own capital, but experts are able to manage it more productively. Without frictions, experts would manage all capital forever. In their model, experts are less patient than households, and so would consume their net worth early by issuing equity to households. But due to agency problems, experts can issue only risk-free short-term debt, exposing them to liquidity risk. If the net worth of an expert ever reaches zero, he cannot absorb any more risk, so he has to liquidate his assets and gets zero utility from then on.

Brunnermeier and Sannikov (2014) solve for full dynamics of the model using continuous-time methods. They find a sharp distinction between normal times and crisis episodes and focus on measures such as the length, severity, and frequency of crises. The system's reaction to shocks is highly nonlinear. The system is resilient to minor financial shocks near the steady state since experts can rely on their existing wealth. Unusually large shocks off the steady state will instead be strongly amplified. They trigger capital sales which further depress asset prices and lead to further fire sales. The system's reaction to shocks is asymmetric. Positive shocks at the steady state lead to larger payouts for experts and little amplification, while large negative shocks are amplified into crisis episodes resulting in significant disinvestment and slow recovery.

If exogenous risk is low—if the economy experienced a sequence of low volatility—precautionary savings are low. Thus a large shock that hits the economy will cause major harmful deleveraging creating endogenous risk. So the period of great moderation may have made the financial crisis in 2008 worse as a result of endogenous choice of low precautionary cash holdings. Financial innovation may also have contributed: When experts can hedge idiosyncratic risks better among each another, they will take on more leverage, making the system less stable.

The model of Brunnermeier and Sannikov (2014) provides a strong case in favor of macroprudential regulation. Capital requirements may actually be harmful if they are not cyclically adjusted. Following shocks, strict capital requirements—if not relaxed in downturns—will force banks to deleverage, accelerating the downturn triggered by the shock. Further, regulation that restricts payouts (such as dividends and bonus payments) should depend primarily on aggregate net worth of all intermediaries. Even if some of the intermediaries are well capitalized, allowing them to pay out dividends can destabilize the system if others are undercapitalized.

10.2.6 The Need for a Risk-Taking Channel

In the Gertler–Kiyotaki model, central bank intervention helps to prevent socially costly fire-sale mechanisms. Such actions, however, when anticipated, may encourage bankers to engage in more risky activities. Such risk-taking behavior of banks is still missing in that model. To keep the model tractable, there is only one type of asset, therefore, the risk from asset investments is no choice variable, but instead exogenously given. The only remaining problem is moral hazard—the incentive for bankers to divert assets from households. Banks have less incentive to divert if they have more own stakes, or, equity, on the balance sheets. In this model, banks will always choose the highest possible leverage. Because depositors would never put funds into a bank that violates the incentive constraint, there will be no default in equilibrium other than triggered by runs.

In reality, banks conduct active risk management, and banks' incentives on taking risks are very much affected by monetary policy. As the Bianchi–Bigio model illustrates, when the central bank conducts an expansionary monetary policy, banks' funding liquidity risk is reduced which allows them to take more risks elsewhere, for example, by investing in riskier, high-yield assets, and reduce the safety buffer such as liquid assets on their balance sheets. Such risk-taking channel links monetary policy closely to financial stability, which previously had been mainly neglected, but contributed much to building up the 2007–2009 global financial crisis. To better understand this linkage, we need a framework that contains a richer asset structure and captures banks' strategic behavior. In the following section, we analyze the endogenous supply of aggregate liquidity in a stylized setting, modelling explicitly the interaction between central bank lender of last resort activity and risk-taking of financial intermediaries.

Focus Box: Multiple Equilibria

The Gertler–Kiyotaki model considers runs on the entire banking system. Following intuition, the probability of a run is assumed to increase with worsening fundamentals—a lower recovery rate x_{t+1}, following a negative aggregate productivity shock on Z_t. Nevertheless, all runs are pure sunspot events: If there were no run, banks would always be able to fully payout their depositors. In more realistic settings banks may no longer be solvent when fundamentals get bad enough, even if depositors would not run at all. So in general, facing uncertainty about the true state of fundamentals, it is not at all evident that deposit insurance or central bank intervention will always be able to recover the funds used to stabilize the economy without imposing a burden on tax payers.

The model demonstrates that there is a range of indeterminacy, the distinction between illiquidity and insolvency being blurred. Knowing the state of fundamentals alone is not sufficient; there may be self-fulfilling equilibria. As

(continued)

Fig. 10.5 illustrates, the probability of a run will depend both on fundamentals and beliefs. If fundamentals are really strong ($Z_t > Z_H$), it will never be rational to trigger a bank run. In contrast if fundamentals are really bad ($Z_t < Z_L$), a default cannot be avoided so the unique equilibrium is to trigger a bank run. For an intermediate range of fundamental values $Z_L < Z < Z_H$, however, there is indeterminacy. As long as all agents believe that no bank run occurs, banks will always be able to pay out, so it is rational not to withdraw. In contrast, if all agents believe that there is a bank run, there will be fire sales with low prices, resulting in low payoffs. Both outcomes are self-fulfilling rational expectations equilibria.

Which of these equilibria will be realized may depend purely on sunspot events. But with good fundamentals—Z_t being slightly below, but close to Z_H—the equilibrium with a run seems quite unlikely to occur. More in line with intuition, the worse the negative shock to fundamentals, the higher usually the probability of a run. Policy interventions (such as lender of last resort activities) may help to select the good outcome and prevent triggering fire sales for $Z_t > Z_L$. In reality, however, it is hard to identify the true fundamental value. Policy makers may mistakenly believe to be in the intermediate range even if $Z_t < Z_L$. Reversely, private agents may perceive default being inevitable even though $Z_t > Z_L$.

This indeterminacy poses serious challenges for policy makers. With information being distributed heterogeneously, any decision taken is bound to be controversial. For example, there were strong doubts during the subprime crisis whether the collateral value of the assets held by investment banks in trouble would be of sufficient quality to protect against potential losses. When setting up various funding facilities, the Fed was accused to buy toxic assets at above market prices aiming to bail out insolvent unscrupulous bankers at taxpayer's risk. When market prices are not uniquely determined, but instead strongly depend on the specific policy actions taken, such actions are likely to stir controversy—the more so since each option may have quite different distributional impact.

Figure 10.6 illustrates the challenges involved in the context of fire-sale models for mortgage backed securities. As emphasized by Brunnermeier and Pedersen (2009), liquidity spirals may lead to discontinuous jumps in demand such that overall demand decreases with falling prices for some price range. With forced deleveraging triggering fire sales of financial intermediaries, projects may have to be liquidated early, lowering their productive value. For some range of fundamentals, such as with demand curve *DD* in Fig. 10.6,

(continued)

there are multiple equilibria: In the absence of fire-sales equilibrium A prevails with a high price P_A. Otherwise, forced deleveraging leads to equilibrium C with low price P_C (we ignore the third equilibrium, being unstable). If central bank interventions put a lower bound P_B on the asset price, effective support can prevent fire sales so ruling out the bad equilibrium C. But if fundamentals get really bad (shifting demand to curve D_2), liquidation with price P_D is the unique equilibrium, resulting in substantial losses from intervention.

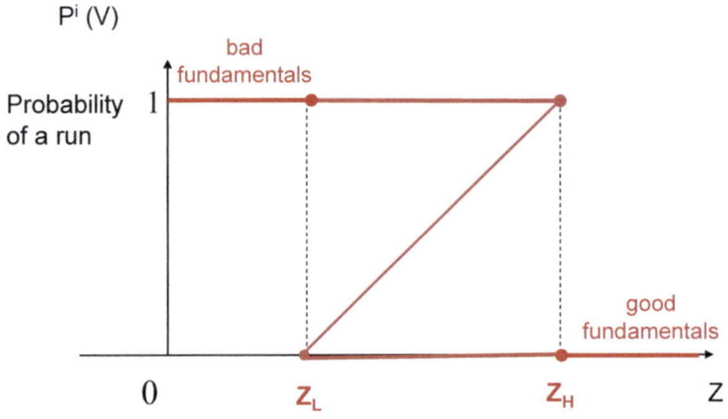

Fig. 10.5 Indeterminacy with self-fulfilling equilibria

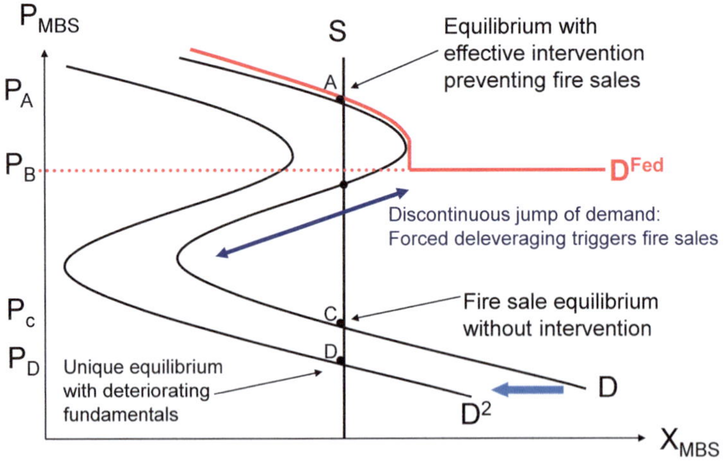

Fig. 10.6 Discontinuities with liquidity spirals

Focus Box: Self-Fulfilling Equilibria for Default Risk in a Currency Union
Similar as deposit contracts make the banking system fragile, a government having issued bonds in foreign currency may also suffer from a loss of confidence in a liquidity crisis. If sovereign debt is issued in its own currency instead, public debt issued by the central government can be considered as safe asset because there is no nominal default risk. In the event of a crisis, a credible central bank can generate an unlimited amount of the currency in which bonds are indebted, acting as a backstop for government funding. Variations in the price level can cushion the impact of unexpected fiscal shocks (see Sims, 2013).[2] In contrast, in a monetary union without central fiscal agency, government debt is like debt issued in a foreign currency, making it vulnerable to contagion effects and self-fulfilling expectations.

Following De Grauwe (2013), Fig. 10.7 illustrates the basic idea: Line C represents the costs of a sovereign default. Default costs C represent costs from collapsing economic activity when access to the international capital market is restricted after a debt moratorium (For simplicity these costs are assumed to be constant). The other lines in Fig. 10.7 represent potential benefits of a default. Resources can be spent on other purposes if outstanding debt is no longer honored. These benefits increase with a rising debt ratio. There is an incentive to default whenever these benefits exceed costs.

As long as interest rates stay low, benefits of default increase only slowly with a rising debt ratio (as the curve passing through point Y at debt ratio b_1). With high interest rates, however, benefits of default rise rapidly (the curve passing through point X). If the debt ratio is sufficiently low (for $b < b_L$), default never pays off even with high interest rates. So in that case, low rates on debt are the unique equilibrium. Conversely, for debt being high enough (for $b > b_H$), default will always be the preferred option, making high rates the unique equilibrium. But again, there is an intermediate range of debt ratios $b_L < b < b_H$ where fundamentals do not determine uniquely the outcome. Both X and Y are rational expectations equilibria for b_1. With the same fundamental data, either the "good" or the "bad" equilibrium may occur, depending on the expectations prevailing in financial markets. In that case, a central bank acting as backstop for public debt may ensure that financial markets focus on the "good" equilibrium with low interest rates.

The absence of such a backstop in a currency area may create destabilizing dynamics: After a fiscal shock, once investors start to doubt the solvency of

(continued)

[2]If the central bank lacks credibility in implementing price stability in the long run, sovereign countries may also suffer from self-fulfilling inflationary expectations. Inspired by the experience in the Latin American debt crisis, Calvo (1988) showed that with nominal bonds multiple, self-fulfilling equilibria with either low or high expected inflation may prevail. See also Corsetti and Dedola (2016).

one participating country, they will reallocate their funds in a flight to other, safer areas. Rising spreads trigger a potentially dangerous spiral with financial fragmentation risking a breakup of the whole system. With spreads for periphery countries like Spain and Italy rising dramatically in the euro area, ECB president Mario Draghi announced that the ECB would be "ready to do whatever it takes to preserve the euro" within its mandate. In August 2012 the ECB launched the so-called Outright Monetary Transactions (OMT) program to intervene potentially limitless in secondary markets for sovereign bond, issued by Euro area member-states, conditional on these countries participating in a standard financial assistance program. The aim was "to restore the functioning of monetary policy transmission channels" by reducing liquidity premiums and the risk premium for "redenomination" (i.e., the risk related to concerns about a breakup of the euro area).

At that time the pure verbal announcement of the OMT program helped to reduce spreads on government bonds within the euro area substantially (see Fig. 10.8), without the need to actually intervene. Nevertheless, the ECB came under heavy attack when it launched these measures. There were strong debates to what extent the sharp rise in the interest rate spreads during the euro crisis was indeed due to the redenomination risk or instead rather reflected country specific fundamental factors. The ECB was accused to distort market prices by its intervention, redistributing fundamental risks from the periphery to the core states. Nevertheless, long-term interest rates for German government bonds, for example, remained significantly lower than those of the US and the UK (see Fig. 10.8) after the introduction of OMT. The persistent fall in interest rates suggests that rising spreads before intervention may indeed have been caused by self-fulfilling expectations associated with multiple equilibria.

10.3 Banks Risk-Taking: Endogenous Exposure to Systemic Liquidity Risk

10.3.1 Introduction

Monetary policy is implemented through the central bank's market operations, which affect banks' lending decisions to firms and households, hence real activities. However, in this process, the conduct of monetary policy also enters banks' decision problems in their risk management and liquidity management practice. This has twofold implications on the stability of financial system.

First, it generates extra volatilities, or, pro-cyclicality, in the system, as is shown in the leverage cycle model. That is, the credit cycle, as a response to the initial shocks from the business cycle, generates more volatile feedback to the business cycle. Of course the boom–bust cycle itself in the model does not say anything about

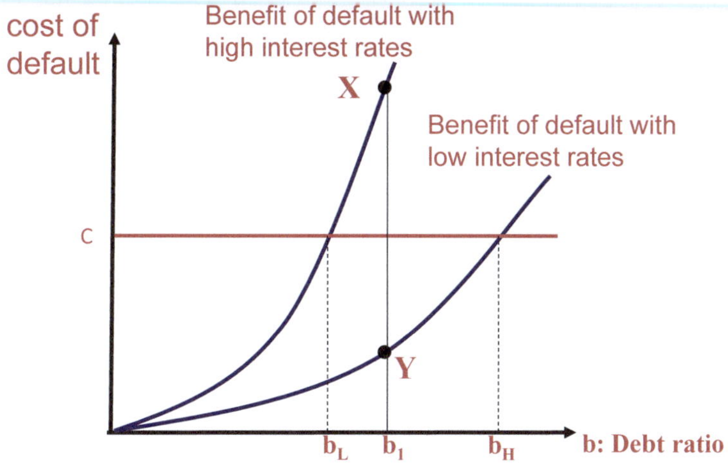

Fig. 10.7 Self-fulfilling equilibria for default risk in a currency union

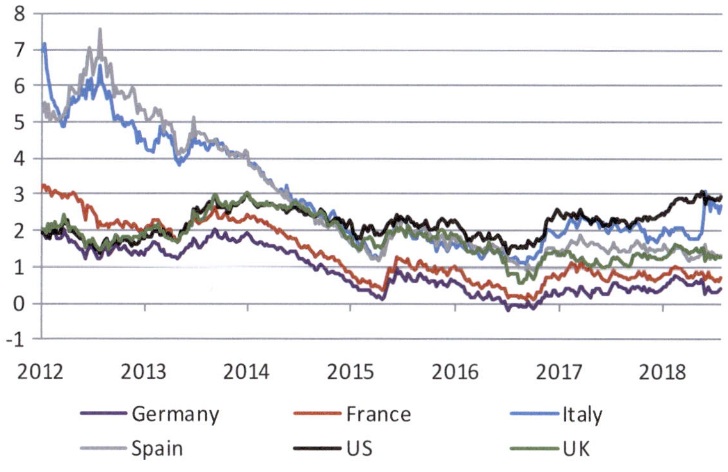

Fig. 10.8 Yields on 10 year government bonds 2012–2018

financial stability, it is systemic risk—which will be analyzed in the next paragraphs—that may generate devastating consequences along the cycle.

Second, monetary policy changes banks' perception of financial risks, hence the risks they take on their balance sheets. As long as the central bank remains an important player in the banking system, it affects banks' incentive on risk-taking. The so-called "risk-taking channel" is a natural by-product of monetary transmission mechanism.

Banking is all about risk-taking and risk sharing. As financial intermediaries, banks improve the matching efficiency between creditors and debtors; they screen and monitor debtors to reduce credit risks and charge the debtors proper credit spreads to reflect such risks; they collect funding via short-term deposit contracts to support profitable, long-term risky projects, and hold liquidity buffers against refinancing risks. As a result, banking improves risk and resource allocation in the economy, making banks socially desirable institutions.

However, banks' incentive in risk-taking and risk sharing may be distorted by the central bank's implementation of monetary policy. This can be easily seen from the Bianchi–Bigio model: When the central bank relaxes its monetary policy by open market purchases, increasing bank reserves in the system, banks' funding liquidity risk is reduced as they become less likely to borrow from the market for reserves; this allows banks to take in more risks, for example, by providing loans to high-yield, riskier projects (although this is not modelled there). Without proper regulation, such distortion may be further amplified by other frictions inside the banking sector, leading to a suboptimal high level of systemic risk that destabilizes the entire financial system.

In this section, we explore the link between monetary policy and financial stability through systemic liquidity risk, based on the model developed in Cao and Illing (2011). Different from Bianchi–Bigio model (Sect. 9.4) which deals with banks' funding liquidity risk, here we mainly focus on the market liquidity risk: As in reality, banks' main business model is maturity transformation, i.e., they borrow through short-term contracts with depositors whose time preferences of consumption are short and lend to long-term risky projects. On the one hand, such financial intermediation improves social welfare: Depositors benefit from the high yields out of the long-term projects, and the long-term projects receive funding from the "impatient" depositors—as this would never happen, should entrepreneurs contract directly with depositors; on the other hand, banks also expose themselves to liquidity risk, making the banking system fragile: Banks must hold sufficient market liquidity, or, liquid assets that can be easily converted to cash without deep discount, to repay depositors when the short-term deposit contracts are due, otherwise panic depositors would run on the bank and destroy the value of bank assets. The model presented in the following sections shows that private provision of liquidity by banks relying on public support will be insufficiently low. To focus on liquidity risk, the model abstracts from solvency risk.

10.3.2 A Basic Model

Consider the following baseline economy with three types of risk-neutral agents: depositors, banks (operated by bank managers), and entrepreneurs. There is no central bank or money at this stage, so all contracts are written in real terms. The economy extends over three periods, $t = 0, 1, 2$, and the details of timing will be explained later. We assume that:

(1) There are depositors of one-unit population, each being endowed with one unit of resources at $t = 0$. They will be willing to deposit in banks as long as the real return is (weakly) larger than 1. Depositors are impatient: They want to withdraw and consume at $t = 1$; in contrast, banks and entrepreneurs are indifferent between consuming at $t = 1$ and $t = 2$.

(2) There is a finite number N of active banks participating in Bertrand competition, competing for depositors' deposits at $t = 0$. Using these deposits, banks as financial intermediaries can fund the projects of entrepreneurs.
(3) There are infinite number of entrepreneurs, and there are sufficiently many entrepreneurs competing for funds so that bank deposits are scarce. Each of the entrepreneurs runs one of two types of projects starting from $t = 0$:
   - Safe projects, which are realized early at $t = 1$ with a safe return $R_1 > 1$.
   - Risky projects, which give a higher return R_2, with $R_2 > R_1 > 1$. With probability p, these projects will be realized at $t = 1$, but the return may be delayed with probability $1 - p$ until $t = 2$. Therefore, in the aggregate, a share p of risky projects will be realized early. The value of p, however, is not known at $t = 0$. It will only be revealed between period 0 and 1 at some intermediate period, call it $t = \frac{1}{2}$.

In the following, we are interested in the case of aggregate shocks to all risky projects: The value of p can be either p_H or p_L with $p_H > p_L$. The "good" state with a high share $p = p_H$ of risky projects realized early at $t = 1$ will occur with probability π. Since the "bad" state with p_L, or, the "crisis" state, is rare, we assume that π is almost 1. We further assume that $1 < p_S R_2 < R_1$ $(s = H, L)$ to focus on the relevant case.

We analyze the private and public provision of liquidity. Banks as financial intermediaries offer liquid deposit contracts redeemable at any time after $t = 0$. Instead of simply imposing this structure, we derive it as optimal contracts in the presence of incentive constraints. Since there is a market demand for liquidity only if depositors' funds are the limiting factor, we assume that these funds are scarce in the sense that there are more projects of each type of entrepreneurs available than the aggregate endowment of depositors. If there were no financial friction, depositors would contract directly with entrepreneurs, receiving the total surplus of all realized projects. Being impatient, they would simply invest all their funds in safe projects and capture the full return at $t = 1$. This frictionless market outcome is our reference point when analyzing the role of liquidity.

In reality, incentive problems prevent the realization of the frictionless market outcome, creating a demand for liquidity. Following Hart and Moore (1994), we introduce a holdup problem: Entrepreneurs have the expertise, or, the necessary human capital, on running projects: Only they can ensure the success of the projects. If depositors run the projects by themselves, they can only receive an inferior return of γR_s $(0 \leq \gamma < 1)$. We assume that $\gamma R_s > 1$, $s = 1, 2$. As a result, if depositors ask for more than γR_s, entrepreneurs would walk away from their project. So entrepreneurs can only commit to pay a fraction γ of their return to depositors. Banks, as financial intermediaries, are assumed to have better collection skills (higher γ) than depositors. Thus depositors are better off by depositing their endowment at banks instead of contracting directly with entrepreneurs.

However, at $t = 1$, after collecting returns from early entrepreneurs, banks would then have themselves an incentive to abuse their collection skills, forcing depositors to renegotiate and accept a lower repayment. Such threat of renegotiation would prevent depositors from funding projects at $t = 0$. Douglas and Rajan (2001) have shown that standard deposit contracts—a common feature in banking in reality—can be an efficient commitment mechanism to cope with that holdup problem. Deposit contracts provide banks with a credible disciplinary mechanism to gain the trust from depositors not to abuse their superior collection skills: Banks offer deposit contracts with a fixed payment d_0 payable at any time after $t = 0$, not contingent on the state of the world. Depositors are entitled to run on the bank once they perceive that banks cannot honor the contracts, leaving all banks' assets liquidated, giving only the inferior return $c < 1$. The threat of a bank run thus disciplines banks to respect deposit contracts.

Deposit contracts work as a credible commitment device not to abuse banks' collection skills. To maximize depositors return, it will be optimal to invest part of the funds in risky high return projects. However, this introduces a fragile structure into the economy. The larger the share invested in risky projects, the more vulnerable banks are to aggregate shocks. If the "crisis" state occurs and banks do not hold enough liquid assets, depositors will run, forcing banks to liquidate all projects. To prevent such inefficient liquidation, the central bank as lender of last resort can provide public liquidity. But anticipating that reaction, banks are likely to underinvest in the provision of private liquidity.

At $t = 0$ banks compete for depositors by offering them fixed deposit contracts that promise a return d_0 at $t = 1$. At the same time, banks decide the proportion α of deposits to be invested in the safe projects. Depositors have rational expectations: They deposit in banks that offer them the highest expected return, after they get to know banks' plans on the investment portfolios.

At $t = \frac{1}{2}$ the value of p is revealed, and this is public information. Given the value of p, if one bank will not be able to meet its depositors' claims at $t = 1$, the depositors will run on the bank at $t = \frac{1}{2}$ because of the first-come-first-served rule in banking. If a bank experiences a run at this date, it has to liquidate all unmatured assets, i.e., both safe and risky projects. Each unit of liquidated asset (project) yields a poor return $c < 1$.

If there is no bank run, at $t = 1$ banks collect a proportion $0 < \gamma < 1$ from the return of early projects (safe projects plus those risky projects that return early). Early entrepreneurs retain the rest (The implication of γ will be explained later). To maximize depositors' return, banks can raise additional funds from early entrepreneurs in the liquidity market: Banks borrow from early entrepreneurs, promising a borrowing rate r and using their delayed projects as collateral. Since entrepreneurs are indifferent between consuming at $t = 1$ and $t = 2$, they will be willing to lend to banks as long as $r \geq 1$. Banks make payouts to depositors using the return collected from early projects and the liquidity borrowed from the liquidity market.

At $t = 2$ banks collect return from late projects and pay back early entrepreneurs. The timing of events is shown as Fig. 10.9.

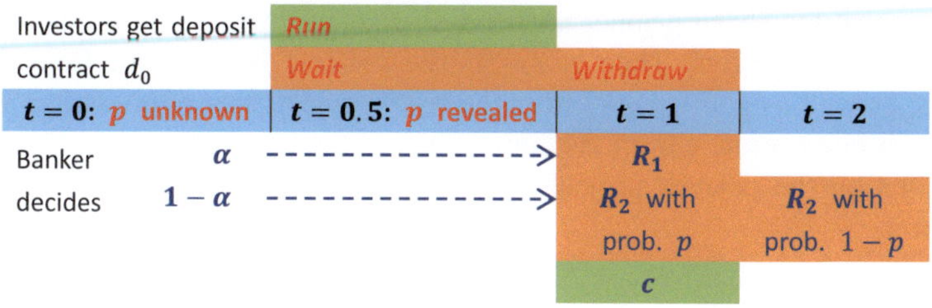

Fig. 10.9 The timing of events

10.3.3 Constrained Efficiency

To see the best possible outcome from the model, we first analyze the problem of a social planner maximizing the depositors' payoff. This provides the reference point for the market equilibrium in which banks serve as financial intermediaries. Depositors being impatient, the social planner would choose the share invested in illiquid, risky projects so as to maximize the resources available to depositors at period 1. Since $p_S R_2 < R_1$, in the absence of holdup problems, the planner would invest only in liquid, safe projects, this way maximizing resources available at period 1. But due to the holdup problem caused by entrepreneurs, the social planner can implement only a constrained efficient solution. If the planner had unlimited taxation authority, she could eliminate the holdup problem completely by taxing the entrepreneurs' rent and redistributing the resources to the depositors. Again, all resources would be invested only in liquid, safe, projects, and the entrepreneurs' rents would be transferred to the depositors in period 1.

Obviously, allowing for non-distortionary taxation biases the comparison between the market and the planner's solution, giving the planner an unfair advantage. Effectively, redistribution via lump-sum taxation would make both holdup and liquidity constraints nonbinding, assuming the relevant issues away. To make the planner's constrained optimization problem interesting, we assume that non-distortionary taxation is not feasible in period 1. In order to impose sensible restrictions, we take private endowments as a binding constraint and assume that the entrepreneur has to receive an equivalent compensation when she is asked to give up resources in period 1. Being indifferent between consuming at $t = 1$ and $t = 2$, the entrepreneur needs to be compensated by an appropriate transfer in period 2. In order not to distort the comparison in favor of banks, we furthermore assume that the planner has the same collection skills (the same γ) as financial intermediaries.

To find the optimal solution for the planner, first assume that there is no uncertainty on p; then the social planner maximizes the depositors' return by choosing its investment portfolio at $t = 0$ such that

$$\alpha = \arg\max_{\alpha} \gamma\left\{\alpha R_1 + (1-\alpha)\left[pR_2 + \frac{(1-p)R_2}{r}\right]\right\}, s.t.\ r \geq 1.$$

It says that the social planner invests a share α of its assets in safe projects and $1-\alpha$ on risky projects. Then at $t=1$, she collects $\gamma\alpha R_1$ return from the safe projects, as well as $\gamma(1-\alpha)pR_2$ from the risky projects that return early. She also borrows at interest rate r from the entrepreneurs who obtain returns at $t=1$, using her claims on the delayed projects $\gamma(1-\alpha)(1-p)R_2$ as collateral. The optimal solution is

$$\alpha = \frac{\gamma - p}{\gamma - p + (1-\gamma)\frac{R}{R_2}}.$$

The optimal α is decreasing in p, i.e., the less delay that comes from the risky projects, it becomes less necessary for the planner to hold safe projects to guarantee depositors' return at $t=1$.

Now, what happens if the social planner faces the uncertainty on p at $t=0$? She can reap the high return from the risky projects by setting lower α, if p turns out to be p_H ("normal state") at at $t=1$; however, depositors will be worse off if p turns out to be p_L ("crisis state") at at $t=1$, as the optimal α implied by p_L should be higher. Because we have assumed that the probability of crisis state is low, the incentive of getting higher return in the normal state dominates. The optimal solution for the planner is thus to set

$$\alpha_H = \frac{\gamma - p_H}{\gamma - p_H + (1-\gamma)\frac{R}{R_2}},$$

call it α^*. The expected depositors' return at $t=0$ is thus

$$E[R(p_H, p_L)] = \pi \underbrace{[\alpha_H R_1 + (1-\alpha_H)p_H R_2]}_{\text{total collected returns under } p_H} + (1-\pi)\underbrace{[\alpha_H R_1 + (1-\alpha_H)p_L R_2]}_{\text{total collected returns under } p_L}.$$

In both states, the planner is able to collect all returns, from both safe and non-delayed risky projects, at $t=1$ and forward them to the depositors.

10.3.4 Social Cost of Bank Runs

What is the outcome if there is no such social planner in this economy? The banks compete in the deposit market with each other by choosing a portfolio of investment at $t=0$ and only those providing the highest return to depositors get deposits. To find the optimal strategy of the banks, first assume that there is no uncertainty on p, so that banks choose

$$\alpha = \arg\max_{\alpha} \gamma \left\{ \alpha R_1 + (1-\alpha)\left[pR_2 + \frac{(1-p)R_2}{r} \right] \right\}, s.t.\ r$$
$$= \frac{\gamma(1-\alpha)(1-p)R_2}{(1-\gamma)[\alpha R_1 + (1-\alpha)pR_2]} \geq 1.$$

The gross interest rate r at which banks borrow from entrepreneurs at $t = 1$ is determined by the funding available from the entrepreneurs $(1-\gamma)[\alpha R_1 + (1-\alpha)p R_2]$, and the value of collateral that banks can pledge, $\gamma(1-\alpha)(1-p)R_2$. As banks' choice on α determines both collateral value and available funding at $t = 1$, the optimal α must ensure that at $t = 1$ banks can borrow to refinance themselves at the lowest cost, i.e., $r = 1$. As a result, the optimal solution for banks' problem is the same as that in the planner's problem

$$\alpha = \frac{\gamma - p}{\gamma - p + (1-\gamma)\frac{R}{R_2}}.$$

Now with uncertainty in p, the banks face a trade-off: If they set lower α and provide corresponding deposit contract d_0 to depositors, they will indeed maximize depositors' return if p turns out to be p_H ("normal state") at at $t = 1$; however, if p turns out to be p_L ("crisis state"), depositors will expect at $t = \frac{1}{2}$ that they are not able to get fully repaid, they will run on the banks, forcing them to liquidate all assets at a low return $c < 1$. As the probability of crisis state is low, and the cost from bank run is small, the optimal choice of banks is to simply choose

$$\alpha_H = \frac{\gamma - p_H}{\gamma - p_H + (1-\gamma)\frac{R}{R_2}} = \alpha^*,$$

at $t = 0$, offering contract $d_0 = \alpha_H R_1 + (1-\alpha_H)p_H R_2$ to depositors to benefit from high returns in the normal state.

What happens if p turns out to be p_L in the crisis state? At $t = \frac{1}{2}$, after the true state is revealed, depositors know that their expected return will be $\alpha_H R_1 + (1-\alpha_H)p_L R_2 < d_0$. By the first-come-first-served rule, all depositors will immediately run to banks and demand d_0, which exceeds resources available for banks. This forces banks to convert all projects to cash at a huge cost.

Compared with the solution to the planner's problem, depositors' expected return at $t = 0$ is now

$$E[R(p_H, c)] = \pi[\alpha_H R_1 + (1-\alpha_H)p_H R_2] + (1-\pi)c < E[R(p_H, p_L)].$$

The costly bank run incurs a loss in social welfare.

10.3.5 Money Provision as Lender of Last Resort

What we can see so far is that, without aggregate risk, banks can fully hedge against liquidity risk by holding liquid assets as buffers and achieve the constrained efficiency. This is true even if there is idiosyncratic liquidity risk, as long as the market for liquidity is well functioning: Suppose that at $t = 1$ each bank faces an idiosyncratic, random p drawn from a probabilistic distribution $f(p)$ over $[0, \gamma]$; at $t = 0$, banks just need to offer the contract $d_0 = \alpha(\overline{p})R_1 + [1 - \alpha(\overline{p})]\overline{p}R_2$ to depositors, with $\overline{p} = \int_0^{\gamma} f(p)dp$, and all banks will be able to meet depositors' demand by borrowing from early entrepreneurs at $t = 1$—as by the Law of Large Numbers, the total return from all early projects is exactly $\alpha(\overline{p})R_1 + [1 - \alpha(\overline{p})]\overline{p}R_2$.

Problem arises only when the liquidity shock is aggregate: As banks cannot offer state contingent contracts to depositors, when the crisis state occurs, there will be liquidity shortage across the entire banking system, leading to a systemic banking crisis. In reality, deposit contracts are defined in nominal terms, i.e., all contracts and transactions are denominated by fiat money, with central banks as monetary authorities. Using monetary tools and instruments, central banks do not only implement monetary policy, but also provide liquidity insurance to the banking system, thus reduce fragilities in banking through risk sharing between the central bank and banking sector and improve social welfare.

From now on, we introduce the money system in the model, based on Cao and Illing (2015a). As in reality, money is issued for the following two main purposes:

- As medium of transaction. From now on, all the transactions are committed via exchanges of cash versus goods. Fiat money is issued by the central bank to facilitate the transactions ("monetizing the economy"), and the quantity of money in circulation is equal to the transaction demand for money. For simplicity, we assume that the quantity of money issued for transaction in each period is equal to the quantity of real goods in transaction, thus normalizing the price level in the absence of additional liquidity provision to 1.
- As the most liquid asset. Banks can borrow additional fiat money from the central bank to meet their demand for liquidity subject to the central bank's policy rate, using their illiquid assets as collateral.

Now we add a central bank as the monetary authority in the model. Resembling the reality, we assume that money provision and monetary policy of the central bank are conducted through the following two types of operations:

- Money, as medium of transaction, is issued through *intraday* loans to banks during the period. Its quantity is equal to the quantity of real goods in transaction, and banks have to pay back the loans in the end of the period.
- Banks can borrow money as liquidity from the central bank via *interday* loans which resemble the discount loans, using banks' illiquid assets as collateral. The loans are paid back one period later, after the return of illiquid assets materializes.

The model economy is thus transformed into a monetary economy, in which all contracts are written in nominal terms, and money is used for transactions between banks and nonbanks. The following charts, Fig. 10.10, show how money facilitates exchanges through central bank operations, how the aggregate liquidity risk is reduced, and how the constrained efficiency is restored.

At $t = 0$

1. Banks get 1 unit of intraday money loans from the central bank, which is equal to the entrepreneurs' demand for buying the endowments of the depositors.
2. Banks issue loans to the entrepreneurs, a share of α for the entrepreneurs running safe projects (short term loans), $1 - \alpha$ for those running risky projects (long term loans).
3. Entrepreneurs use the loans to purchase the depositors' endowments, as capital input to their projects.
4. Depositors deposit the money in banks. Banks offer depositors the nominal demand deposit contracts that promise $d_0 = \alpha_H R_1 + (1 - \alpha_H) p_H R_2$ *nominal* return at $t = 1$ for each unit of deposit.
5. At the end of the period, banks pay back the loans to the central bank.

At $t = 1$ (good state)

Suppose at $t = \frac{1}{2}$ it is revealed that the economy will be in the good state, Fig. 10.11 shows the flows of money throughout the period $t = 1$:

1. Banks get d_0 unit of intraday money loans from the central bank, which is equal to the depositors' demand for buying the consumption goods from the entrepreneurs whose projects return early.
2. Banks repay d_0 to the depositors.
3. The depositors purchase $d_0 = \alpha_H R_1 + (1 - \alpha_H) p_H R_2$ consumption goods from the early entrepreneurs.

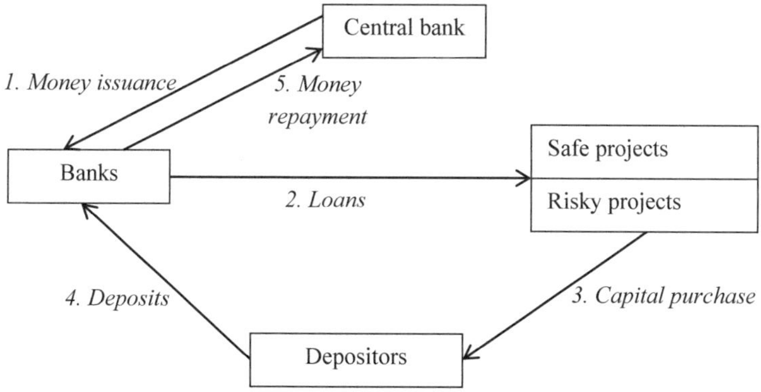

Fig. 10.10 Monetizing the economy at $t = 0$. The arrows show the direction of money flows, and the numbers indicate the sequence of money flows

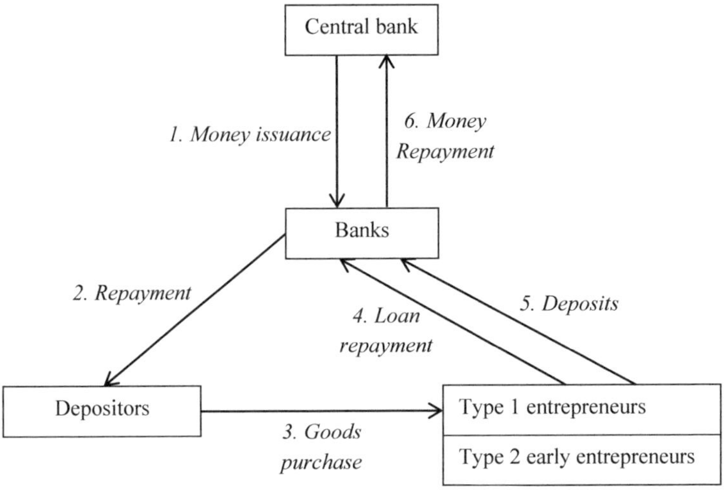

Fig. 10.11 Money flows at $t = 1$ in the good state

4. Early entrepreneurs repay their loans, $\gamma[\alpha_H R_1 + (1 - \alpha_H)p_H R_2]$, to banks, and
5. Deposit $(1 - \gamma)[\alpha_H R_1 + (1 - \alpha_H)p_H R_2]$ in banks.
6. At the end of the period, banks pay back the loans to the central bank.

At $t = 2$ (after the good state)

After the good state in period $t = 1$, Fig. 10.12 shows the flows of money throughout the subsequent period $t = 2$:

1. Banks get $(1 - \gamma)[\alpha_H R_1 + (1 - \alpha_H)p_H R_2]$ unit of intraday money loans from the central bank, which is equal to early entrepreneurs' demand for buying the consumption goods from late entrepreneurs.
2. Banks repay $(1 - \gamma)[\alpha_H R_1 + (1 - \alpha_H)p_H R_2]$ to early entrepreneurs.
3. Early entrepreneurs purchase $(1 - \gamma)[\alpha_H R_1 + (1 - \alpha_H)p_H R_2] = \gamma(1 - \alpha_H) \times (1 - p_H)R_2$ consumption goods from the late entrepreneurs.
4. Late entrepreneurs repay their loans, $\gamma(1 - \alpha_H)(1 - p_H)R_2$, to banks.
5. At the end of the period, banks pay back all the loans to the central bank.

So far, in the absence of aggregate liquidity risk, the monetary economy achieves the same constrained efficiency as in the real, baseline model. Money only changes denomination and the central bank is rather "passive": The capital transaction in $t = 0$ and aggregate output in $t = 1/t = 2$ determine aggregate money demand in the economy. However, this will be changed if there is aggregate liquidity risk: When the state of the world turns out to be bad, there is a systemic liquidity shortage at $t = 1$, as the aggregate output is lower than depositors' withdrawal demand. If the central bank stayed with its "passive" money provision, money supply at $t = 1$ would be lower than depositors' cash demand, leading to a market liquidity problem for the banks. However, in this case, banks have more illiquid assets (delayed

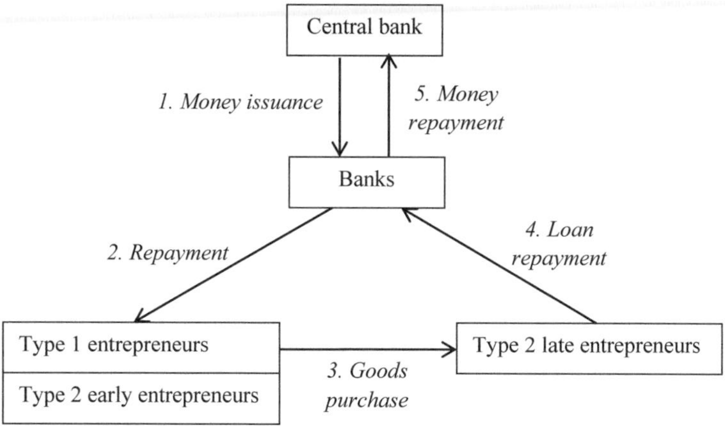

Fig. 10.12 Sequence of money flows at $t = 2$ following the good state

projects) on their balance sheets, this provides an opportunity for the central bank to play an "active" role on injecting liquidity into the banking sector, via its market operation: The central bank can take banks' illiquid assets as collateral and lend them money via the interday loans; in this way, banks are able to meet depositors demand, making them free from runs, and the central bank can safely get repaid after the delayed projects return at $t = 2$. The following charts show how this mechanism works.

At $t = 1$ (bad state)

As in Fig. 10.13:

1. When it comes to the repayment to the depositors, banks can only get a total of $\alpha_H R_1 + (1 - \alpha_H)p_L R_2 < d_0$ intraday loans from the central bank. Therefore

   1.5 Banks get $(1 - \alpha_H)(p_H - p_L)R_2$ liquidity through interday loans from the central bank using $(1 - \alpha_H)(p_H - p_L)R_2$ illiquid assets as collateral, given the policy rate $r^m = 1$.
2. Banks thus repay d_0 to the depositors.
3. The depositors purchase $\alpha_H R_1 + (1 - \alpha_H)p_L R_2$ consumption goods from the early entrepreneurs. Suppose that there is no price stickiness, then the equilibrium price is determined by the ratio of money in circulation to the real goods purchased, i.e., $\frac{d_0}{\alpha_H R_1 + (1 - \alpha_H)p_L R_2} > 1$.
4. Early entrepreneurs repay their loans, $\gamma[\alpha_H R_1 + (1 - \alpha_H)p_L R_2]$, to banks, and
5. Deposit $\gamma(1 - \alpha_H)(1 - p_L)R_2$ in banks with gross interest rate 1.

The final step 5 is similar to Fig. 10.12, except that banks only repay $\alpha_H R_1 + (1 - \alpha_H)p_L R_2$ intraday loans to the central bank, retaining $(1 - \alpha_H)(p_H - p_L)R_2$ as liabilities to the central bank backed by the collateral.

At $t = 2$ (after the bad state)

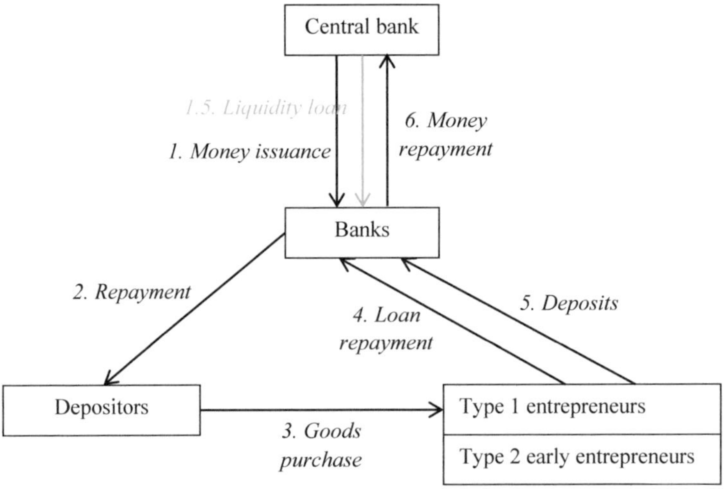

Fig. 10.13 Sequence of money flows at $t = 1$ in the bad state

In the subsequent period $t = 2$, banks need to repay the interday loans when the return of illiquid collateral is realized. As Fig. 10.14 shows,

1. Banks get $(1 - \alpha_H)(1 - p_L)R_2 - (1 - \alpha_H)(p_H - p_L)R_2$ unit of money loans from the central bank, which is equal to early entrepreneurs' demand for buying the consumption goods from late entrepreneurs less the collateral.
2. Banks repay $\gamma(1 - \alpha_H)(1 - p_L)R_2$ to early entrepreneurs.
3. Early entrepreneurs purchase $\gamma(1 - \alpha_H)(1 - p_L)R_2$ consumption goods from late entrepreneurs.
4. Late entrepreneurs repay their loans, $\gamma(1 - \alpha_H)(1 - p_L)R_2$, to banks.

Since at that stage return of the collateral is realized, banks

4.5 Repay $(1 - \alpha_H)(p_H - p_L)R_2$ interday loans to the central bank.

And in the last step 5, the intraday loan is repaid, too.

Abstracting from business cycles, the optimal monetary policy rule implied by the model is straightforward:

- In the good state, as the outcome of market equilibrium is constrained efficient, the central bank should stay away from the market for liquidity; therefore, the monetary policy rate in the good state should be so high, say, $r^m > \overline{r} = R_2$, as to deter banks from borrowing through interday loans and encourage them to borrow directly from the market;
- In the bad state, the central bank should commit as the lender of last resort, providing interday loans at low interest rate. In this model, the central bank

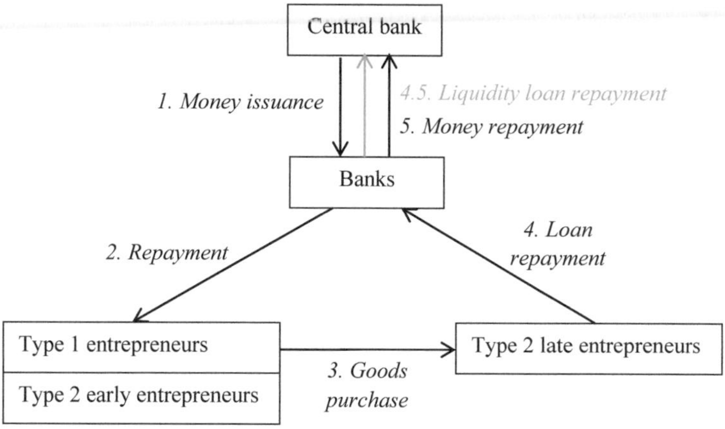

Fig. 10.14 Sequence of money flows at $t = 2$ following the bad state

should cut its policy rate directly down to $r^m = 1$ once p_L is revealed, enabling banks to meet their nominal contracts with depositors and avoiding bank runs.

Compared with the baseline model with real economy, the constrained efficient allocation is restored in the monetary economy. The reason is that in a crisis state banks can obtain liquidity from the central bank, using the delayed projects as collateral; therefore, they are able to fulfill the nominal deposit contract d_0 and there will be no costly bank run any more. Instead of the poor real return c, now depositors receive $\alpha_H R_1 + (1 - \alpha_H) p_L R_2$ real return. Although depositors' *nominal* return is d_0 in both states, the expected *real* return at $t = 0$ is now

$$E[R(p_H, p_L)] = \pi[\alpha_H R_1 + (1 - \alpha_H) p_H R_2] + (1 - \pi)[\alpha_H R_1 + (1 - \alpha_H) p_L R_2],$$

exactly the same as in the planner's problem, higher than that in the baseline model in which the real return is

$$E[R(p_H, c)] = \pi[\alpha_H R_1 + (1 - \alpha_H) p_H R_2] + (1 - \pi)c < E[R(p_H, p_L)],$$

as shown in Fig. 10.15.

10.3.6 The Risk-Taking Channel

However, without further restrictions on banks' behavior, new problems emerge out of such monetary economy with an active central bank. Note that the constrained efficient result in the previous section depends on the optimal risk sharing between the central bank and the banking sector, but it may fail to be achieved given that now the central bank is participating maturity transformation in the banking sector. Similar as in Bianchi–Bigio model, the conduct of monetary policy changes liquidity

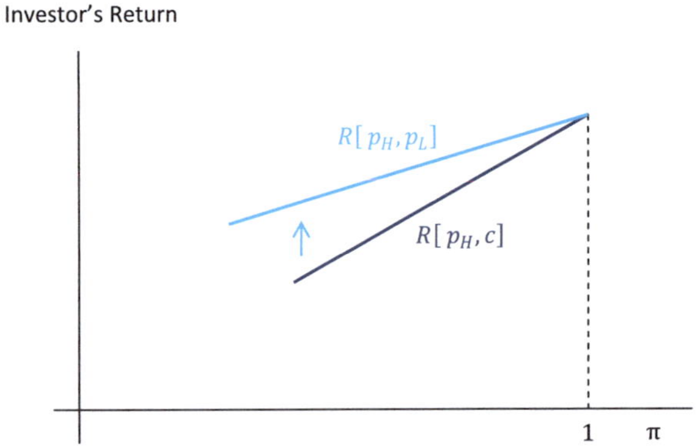

Fig. 10.15 Constrained efficiency in the monetary economy

risks in the banking system, and this incentivizes the banks to adjust the risks taken in their investment portfolios. It creates two types of problems in monetary economy in general:

First, monetary policy that is designed to stabilize the real economy may have side effects on banks' risk-taking and financial stability. For example, the central bank is obliged to conduct expansionary monetary policy when the output gap is negative and the inflation is low, however, as we have already seen from Bianchi–Bigio model, this also lowers banks' liquidity risk and encourages them to expand their credit supply, generating a boom in the asset market, for example, the market for real estates. Without further restrictions in the banking sector, such imbalance may fuel a boom to a bubble and many more troubles in the future;

Second, even in the current model which is abstract from business cycles, the central bank's conduct of monetary policy distorts banks' incentive on building liquidity buffers: By accepting illiquid assets as collateral in the interday loans, banks are encouraged to invest more in illiquid, risky assets, leaving the economy in an inferior equilibrium with excess systemic liquidity risk, low monetary policy rate, and low real return for the depositors.

To see what comes out in the model, taken into account the banks' response to the monetary policy rule, consider the banks' decision at $t = 0$:

- If banks choose α^* and $d_0 = \alpha^* R_1 + (1 - \alpha^*) p_H R_2$
  - Banks' *nominal* return is always $d_0 = \alpha^* R_1 + (1 - \alpha^*) p_H R_2 = \gamma[\alpha^* R_1 + (1 - \alpha^*) R_2]$ if the central bank sets $r^m = 1$ at $t = 1$, call the return $R(\alpha^*, 1)$, because banks can survive on their own under p_H and survive on the interday loans from the central bank under p_L. However, depositors' *real* return differs across states: It is higher under p_H—$\alpha^* R_1 + (1 - \alpha^*) p_H R_2$, but lower under p_L—$\alpha^* R_1 + (1 - \alpha^*) p_L R_2$.
  - If the central bank sets $r^m > \bar{r}$ at $t = 1$, banks will survive on their own under p_H but have to go bankrupted under p_L, because in the latter case they cannot

get enough liquidity from the interday loans at such high policy rate. Given that the likelihood of p_L is low, banks' expected nominal return should be close to $R(\alpha^*, 1)$. Depositors' real return is $\alpha^* R_1 + (1 - \alpha^*) p_H R_2$ under p_H, and c under p_L.

- However, if banks choose $\alpha = 0$ instead and nominal deposit contracts $d_0' = \gamma R_2 > d_0$
  - If the central bank sets $r^m = 1$ at $t = 1$, banks will survive on the interday loans and achieve the nominal return d_0', call it $R(0, 1)$, for the depositors. Note that $R(0, 1) > R(\alpha^*, 1)$. However, the real return of depositors is only $p_s R_2$, $s = H, L$, which is lower than $\alpha^* R_1 + (1 - \alpha^*) p_s R_2$, because of too many delays.
  - If the central bank sets $r^m > \bar{r}$ at $t = 1$, banks will not survive, as there is a systemic liquidity shortage in either state and banks cannot get enough liquidity from the interday loans at such high policy rate. Banks will go bankrupted and depositors' real return is c.

All the outcomes under various circumstances are shown in Fig. 10.16. It can be easily seen that the unique Nash equilibrium is given by the thick black lines:

- In order to compete for deposits, banks offer the highest possible nominal deposit contract d_0' at $t = 0$ and invest everything in the illiquid, risky projects.
- In order to avoid any costly bank failure at $t = 1$, the central bank is forced to set $r^m = 1$ independent on the state of the world.

In other words, taken into account banks' best response to the central bank, the "optimal" monetary policy rule that attempts to achieve the constrained efficiency is actually not implementable! To make it worse, although depositors are promised higher nominal return d_0' at $t = 0$ (and they will indeed get it at $t = 1$), their real consumption is only $p_s R_2$, $s = H, L$, inferior to that in the constrained efficient allocation.

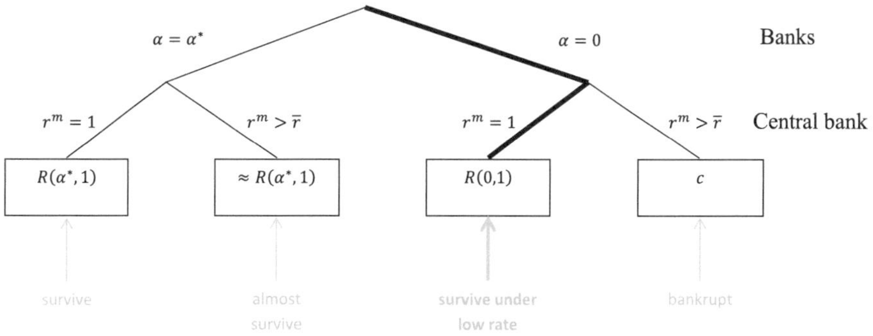

Fig. 10.16 "Interest rate trap" as the inferior equilibrium outcome

Such inferior equilibrium does not only arise in the static model, in reality, it may persist for a long time horizon, especially after a recession, when the central bank tries to stimulate the economy by cutting down its policy rate and promising keeping the low interest rate for an extended period via forward guidance. Persistent low interest rates induce high-risk activities in the financial sector, aggravating imbalances in the economy. Low interest rates, particularly in combination with an explicit, transparent announcement to keep them low in the future, might increase incentives for financial intermediaries to invest in fragile activities, tying the hands of the central bank, making it harder to reverse the path of policy rate after the economy recovers. Held hostage by the financial industry, central banks might thus end up in a "low interest rate trap"—the economy remains stuck in a long-lasting period of suboptimal, low interest rate equilibrium with excess systemic risk (Cao & Illing, 2015b).

Focus Box: Fragile Deposit Contracts and the Search for Run Proof Financial Systems

The structure of the model discussed in this section is based on Douglas and Rajan (2001). They derive deposit contracts as market response to frictions preventing state contingent contracts and show that deposits can be an efficient commitment mechanism to cope with holdup problems of financial intermediaries: The threat of runs prevents banks to renege on contracts. In the absence of aggregate risk, deposit contracts offered by banks provide efficient insurance against idiosyncratic liquidity shocks. However, bank runs introduce a fragile structure into the economy, making it vulnerable to aggregate shocks. To prevent inefficient liquidation, the central bank has to provide public liquidity as lender of last resort. But public insurance introduces a moral hazard problem: Anticipating central banks reaction, banks will underinvest in the provision of private liquidity in the absence of macroprudential regulation imposing some minimum liquidity requirements.

In economic history, there have been long and heated debates about the adequate design of robust institution to cope with the trade-off between stability and efficiency. Sargent (2011) provides an instructive historical overview of this debate. The financial crisis has again stimulated the search for how to make financial systems run proof without the persistent need of regulatory intervention. During the Great Depression the Chicago Plan proposed the separation of the monetary and credit functions of the banking system. It suggests a radical monetary reform requiring 100% reserve backing for deposits (see Fisher, 1936). This proposal have been revived recently (see Benes & Kumhof, 2012).

Various proposals call for limiting the creation of money and run prone deposit contracts by restricting banks to narrow or equity financed banking (see Chari & Kehoe, 2016; Cochrane, 2016). For instance, instead of contracts

(continued)

with fixed payments (promising to pay out a dollar for a dollar's nominal value), money market funds could offer equity type contracts with floating net asset value, paying out just the depositor's share of the current market value of that funds accounts. Sudden withdrawals from mutual funds holding illiquid loans will simply trigger a fall in the market value.

To evaluate these proposals, it is crucial to be aware of the role of debt contracts offering fixed payments at any time in an environment of financial frictions. In the model of Cao and Illing (2011), both narrow banking and pure equity financed contracts yield an inferior outcome compared to the mix of deposit contracts, lender of last resort policy and macroprudential regulation. Narrow banking requires banks to hold sufficient liquid funds to pay out in all contingencies. Here, it is equivalent to forcing banks to invest only in low risk projects, preventing any maturity transformation. In contrast to deposits, equity is subject to the holdup problem, making equity financing a renegotiable claim. So equity holders can only get some share of the surplus collected by banks. This imposes costs and is likely to be inferior even to the outcome with bank runs. The model of Cao and Illing (2011) focuses purely on liquidity risk.[3] In the presence of solvency risk, there is also a need for capital requirements (see Cao, 2012).

Narrow banking basically amounts to eliminating any scope for leverage in financial intermediation. However, as illustrated by the models of Shin and Geanakoplos (Sects. 9.5 and 9.6), leverage can arise as a funding structure to improve risk sharing and social welfare in an economy with heterogeneous agents (such as risk averse versus risk neutral, pessimistic versus optimistic agents). This suggests that instead of eliminating leverage completely, the focus should rather be on designing robust mechanisms to curtail excessive leverage arising from market failures such as limited liability and market externalities. Various macroprudential policies discussed in Sect. 10.4 aim to restrict excessive leverage—such as imposing leverage ratios or *Loan To Value Ratios* (LTV). A key challenge is how to cope with the pro-cyclicality inherent with leverage that amplifies volatilities in the economy. Policies designing countercyclical capital buffers seem to be a promising route for making financial systems more robust.

[3]Holmström and Tirole (1998) provide an alternative micro-foundation to evaluate private and public liquidity provision. In their model, private firms suffer from liquidity shocks, struggling to get external funds to finance valuable projects. They show that credit lines from financial intermediaries can implement the socially efficient (second-best) allocation in the absence of aggregate shocks (firms' liquidity shocks being independent). With aggregate uncertainty, private provision of liquidity is insufficient, so government-provided liquidity can improve the allocation by committing future tax income to back up the reimbursements. Holmström and Tirole (1998) consider a real model with public finance interventions via lump-sum taxation. They assume that the government has unlimited power to tax real resources and so is always able to redistribute resources ex post.

10.3.7 Risk-Taking Channel, Lender-of-Last-Resort Policy, and Macroprudential Regulation

What lessons can we learn from this simple model? Obviously, the transmission mechanism of monetary policy is neither static nor passive; as monetary policy is implemented by the central bank's market operation, the central bank is an active participant in the banking sector and affects the entire financial market. Banks react to monetary policy by adjusting their credit supply to the households and firms, affecting real economy activities, but on the other hand, monetary policy also changes banks' risk-taking incentives and leads to adjustments in banks' balance sheets through their liquidity and risk management practice, which has further implication for financial stability. Such risk-taking channel goes hand in hand with the transmission of monetary policy.

To stabilize the monetary economy, conventional wisdom generally focuses on eliminating the devastating bank runs during financial crises. In order to provide banks liquidity insurance against aggregate shocks, a central bank today usually serves as the lender of last resort for the banking sector, largely following the "Bagehot Rules," proposed by Bagehot (1873):

1. The central bank should lend freely against good collateral.
2. The central bank should lend at a "very high rate."
3. The lender-of-last-resort-policy needs to be credible such that the central bank should announce its readiness to lend without limits.

Unfortunately, the cause of the risk-taking channel—the feedback between monetary policy and banks' risk-taking incentives—cannot be properly addressed by these rules. In practice, implementing these rules can hardly solve the underlying issues. Bagehot's rules have frequently been misinterpreted in the sense that he claimed central banks should only lend to solvent institutions at a penalty rate. But the criterion for Bagehot was not the solvency of the bank but instead the quality of the collateral in normal times (not in crisis times). He clearly stated that the central bank should lend against collateral "*on what in ordinary times is reckoned a good security—on what is then commonly pledged and easily convertible*," Bagehot never used the word "penalty," but instead suggested to lend at a "*very high rate*"—relative to the rate prevailing in the precrisis period. During panics, financial markets tend to become dysfunctional, with no one being prepared to lend at reasonable rates (See Goodhart & Illing, 2009).

During crises, it is extremely difficult if not impossible to distinguish between illiquid and insolvent banks. Sometimes the central bank even has to bail out some obviously insolvent banks if these banks are systemically important, in order to prevent further contagion to the rest of financial market. Bagehot suggested that the central bank should lend at a very high rate, in order to avoid banks from abusing the rules and encourage them to build buffers in the normal time. But it does not help banks that are already in the crisis—charging high rates makes these weak banks even more fragile.

As the simple model without solvency problems shows, rules that are contingent on banks' being illiquid but solvent cannot reduce the fragility in banking sector, if not making it worse. No matter whether monetary policy rules are ex ante contingent on banks' liquidity risk, ex post, it is always optimal for the central bank to lend to banks in trouble at zero interest rate to avoid costly bank runs, and troubled banks can always borrow from the central bank since they have sufficient illiquid assets as collateral; in other words, such contingent rules are not time consistent. Knowing that they will always get support from the central bank, unconditional on their liquid asset positions, banks have no incentive at all to build buffers against liquidity risk. Thus, the economy gets stuck in the inferior, fragile equilibrium with excess liquidity risk.

For all these reasons, financial fragility that arises from the risk-taking channel of monetary policy can hardly be addressed by monetary policy itself. Especially, when the credit cycle does not coincide with the business cycle, maintaining financial stability via monetary policy may conflict with other mandates of the central bank, such as price stability. To solve financial stability problems, financial regulation is a necessary complement for monetary policy. For example, in the model of this section, the constrained efficient solution can easily be implemented in a dynamic consistent way by the mix of two instruments: (1) ex ante macroprudential regulation combined with (2) ex post lender of last resort policy.

The regulatory agency needs to impose ex ante a minimum liquidity coverage ratio α^* on banks, i.e., banks have to hold at least a share of α^* liquid assets on their balance sheet in normal times. Then once the market is under the stress of liquidity shortage, the central bank is able to implement its lender-of-last-resort policy without inducing banks to take excess liquidity risks.

10.4 Monetary Policy and Financial Stability: A Resume

10.4.1 The Linkages Between Macro and Finance

Along with the great success of the New Keynesian dynamic stochastic general equilibrium framework in the past two decades, what had been largely overlooked before the 2007–2009 global financial crisis in monetary theory and policy practice was the macro-finance linkages, i.e., how fluctuations in macro economy are amplified by the financial sector, as well as how monetary policy affects risk-taking in the banking system that leads to booms and busts. The former has been attracting people's attention since the mechanism of financial accelerator was proposed in late 1980s, while the latter still remains a big challenge for research economists and policy makers today. For quite long time there had been almost no role for the banking sector in the workhorse models for monetary policy analysis, therefore, the most recent financial crisis came almost as a great surprise for many in the central banks worldwide.

There are several reasons why the macro-finance linkages have not been paid sufficient attention to in monetary theory and practice. First, all theories are much simplified reality; and as during a natural development of a theory, people need first focus on the questions that are both crucial for monetary policy and tractable in computation, therefore, in the early stage of developing the dynamic stochastic general equilibrium (DSGE) framework which is based on real business cycle models, priorities have been given to central issues such as consumption, investment, unemployment, and inflation that naturally arise from these models. Although monetary policy transmission mechanism is also a key issue by itself, it would have been extremely cumbersome to address the details of banking in the already complicated DSGE models. Therefore, as long as the transmission mechanism works for the most of the time, it would be fairly safe to take the static view on banking as a good approximation of reality, i.e., by assuming that all sectors in the economy react directly to monetary policy, as a result, one can talk about the transmission mechanism in the models without explicitly modelling the banks, just like that in some of these models one can talk about monetary policy in a cashless economy even without money.

Second, from the empirical point of view, monetary policy transmission mechanism mostly breaks down during the crises, which are rare events; therefore, for DSGE models estimated over long time series, there is hardly much impact of these events on the transmission mechanism, or, again, the static view on banking seemed like a good approximation and reversely, there would have been not much paid off to take the pains in modelling the complicated banking structure in the DSGE framework, had there been no crisis. However, even during the normal times, standard models based on aggregate data level estimation neglected much of the structural change in the banking sector, where banks arbitrage against monetary policy by taking more risks, and the storm of the next crisis is already accumulating its strength underneath the tranquility.

Third, integrating banking sectors and financial fragility in the DSGE framework is also technically challenging. Banking, as financial intermediation, involves interactions among banks, creditors and debtors, is difficult to be modelled in the prototype DSGE world where all agents can be treated as representative. Modelling heterogeneous agents in DSGE models became tractable only in recent years, for example, in Gertler and Kiyotaki (2010) consumers and bankers can swap their identities randomly such that in each period agents can still be treated as representative with mixed identities. More challenging is to capture bank failure and crisis, which lead to discontinuities in payoff functions generating possibly multiple, Pareto -ranked steady state equilibria. These problems have been gradually solved very recently by the progress in computational techniques, for example, Boissay, Collard, and Smets (2014).

Last, but not least, macro and finance are usually studied separately in economic research, and in practice, there are separate institutions governing monetary policy and financial stability (either by having separate divisions within a central bank, or by having both the central bank as the monetary authority and the financial supervisory authority for financial stability). Such division of labor in both economic research and policy institutions also makes it difficult for people to explore the linkage between monetary policy and financial stability. Fortunately, the situation has been slowly changing after the most recent global financial crisis. Joint task forces are established by monetary authorities and financial supervisory agencies, and more research is booming to close the gap between macro and finance.

Now, if the risk-taking channel of monetary policy has crucial implication for financial stability, the next question is: What should people do about it in monetary policy practice?

As we have already seen from the models capturing the risk-taking channel, when monetary policy is implemented through the central bank's market operation with the banking sector, banks adjust the risks in their investment portfolios which affect the degree of fragility in the banking system. Therefore, the risk-taking channel, as a by-product of monetary policy implementation, cannot be fully addressed by monetary policy itself. Such impossibility also holds in practice, as the business cycles, which are indicated by inflation and output gaps, and the credit cycles, which often herald financial volatilities and instabilities, are not always driven by the same set of factors and do not necessarily coincide with each other; therefore, it is hardly possible to pin down both inflation target and financial stability at the same time with only one instrument, i.e., monetary policy.

This implies that we need additional tools to address the causes of financial instabilities alongside with monetary policy. In practice, these tools come from financial regulatory policies. Financial regulation itself is a huge topic, which has been going through a long way before and after the current crisis and deserves a separate book; but with respect to the risk-taking channel of monetary policy, people can borrow at least two sets of instruments from there:

The first set of instruments aims at reducing excess volatilities from the pro-cyclicality of credit cycles, with which excess risk-taking often accompanies. Currently, rules of countercyclical capital buffer are designed for this purpose, which require the banks to build up capital buffer in the boom and allow them to use the buffer to cushion the shocks to their balance sheets in the bust. Take Shin (2010) model as an example: In Sect. 9.5, when the economy starts to boom and banks' capital level rises to $\widetilde{e} > e$, if at this moment banks are required to build up capital buffer equal to $\widetilde{e} - e$, there will be no further expansion in banks' balance sheets, thus containing the credit boom is. In the same vein, when the economy comes to a bust and banks' capital level falls to $e < \widetilde{e}$, if at this moment banks are allowed to use the capital buffer $\widetilde{e} - e$ and the required capital ratio falls to e, there will be no further contraction in banks' balance sheets, preventing the vicious deleveraging cycle. Another impact of raising capital requirement during the boom is that this increases banks' stakes in their portfolio, which encourages them to take due diligence and reduces the incentive on excess risk-taking. Furthermore, the capital buffer established in the boom increases banks' loss absorbing capabilities, making them more likely to survive during the bust.

The second set of instruments aims at optimal sharing of liquidity risks between the central bank and the banking sector. The key business model of banking is maturity transformation, i.e., to "borrow short and lend long." It provides the necessary liquidity service and liquidity insurance in the economy, as Cao–Illing model shows, improving social welfare. On the other hand, as a consequence of maturity transformation, the maturity mismatch between assets and liabilities also exposes banks to market liquidity risk and funding liquidity risk, making the banking sector fragile; this requires banks to build buffers and cushions to insure against liquidity risks, through active liquidity management practice, as both Bianchi–Bigio model and Cao–Illing model demonstrate. However, banks' liquidity management is complicated by the fact that monetary policy is implemented by the central bank's market operations, which actively shift banks' liquidity positions and liquidity risk in the banking sector. Therefore, complementary liquidity rules are necessary to achieve optimal sharing of liquidity risks between the central bank and the banking sector: Under aggregate liquidity shocks, the central bank should credibly commit to providing liquidity to illiquid banks without limit, acting as the lender of last resort and keeping the banks in the solvent equilibrium free from devastating bank runs; however, in order to avoid the time inconsistency problem that banks may abuse the lender-of-last-resort policy by taking excess liquidity risks, as illustrated by Fig. 10.16, requirements are needed to make sure that banks take sufficient due diligence in liquidity management, in the absence of aggregate liquidity risks. Currently, two types of liquidity requirements are considered by regulators:

- Liquidity Coverage Ratio (LCR) requirement, targeting on banks' market liquidity risk. LCR is the ratio between a bank's holding of liquid assets—unencumbered, high-quality liquid assets that can be converted to cash to meet liquidity demand—and the assumed outflow of funding for the bank during a 30-day stressed funding scenario, i.e.,

$$LCR = \frac{Stock\ of\ high\ quality\ assets}{Net\ cash\ outflows\ over\ 30\ days} \times 100\%.$$

Usually LCR is required to be no lower than 100%. In the stylized Cao–Illing model, this is equivalent to requiring banks to hold a share of α^* liquid assets on their balance sheet at $t = 0$.

- Net Stable Funding Ratio (NSFR) requirement, targeting on banks' funding liquidity risk. NSFR is the proportion of long-term assets which are funded by long-term, stable funding—such as customer long-term deposits, long-term wholesale funding, equity, etc. Usually NSFR is required to be no lower than 100%. In the stylized Bianchi–Bigio model, this is equivalent to restricting banks' liabilities from demand deposits D_t.

After all, the relationship between monetary policy and financial stability is by far not yet thoroughly understood. Monetary authorities need to take into account the impact of monetary policy on banks' risk-taking incentives, as well as the evolution of financial institutions; on the other hand, how banking regulation interacts with monetary policy and whether regulatory rules conflict with monetary policy largely remain as open questions.

10.4.2 Macroprudential Regulation

Global regulatory framework for financial institutions, the so-called "Basel Accords," has been established since late 1980s, and now financial regulatory authorities worldwide are implementing its third edition, "Basel III." The framework is designed for a more resilient global financial system and covers a wide varieties of regulatory instruments targeting extensive classes of financial risks. However, all the huge effort people invested in financial regulation failed to prevent the 2007–2009 global financial crisis, which evolved to the Great Recession; many developed countries, such as Italy, lost a decade of economic growth.

The crisis provided a unique opportunity for people to rethink about what has gone wrong in the existing regulatory practice. One of the main lessons people have learned is that, to maintain financial stability and reduce its contribution to macroeconomic volatility, it is not sufficient to implement microprudential regulation, i.e., the regulatory policies targeting individual financial institution's viability. On top of that, macroprudential regulation is needed to maintain the stability of the entire financial system.

Conventional wisdom, or, the microprudential view, holds that, if the regulatory authority is able to properly supervise each individual bank and ensure their health, the entire financial system is safe. However, such view largely overlooks those risk factors that each individual institutions tends to neglect—so that such factors are hardly possible to be identified only on bank level—while have the potential to destabilize the entire financial system: the systemic risks on the system level.

There are many sources of systemic risks in a financial system. One large share of them arise from various externalities: One institution's behavior affects other institutions, however, this is not internalized in individual institution's decision-making, leading to excess risks in the system. One example is the impact of fire sale on asset price: When a troubled institution sells its risky assets, it generates a downward pressure on asset price, increasing the credit risks of other institutions who hold the same type of assets, i.e., one institution's asset fire sale has a *negative* externality on the rest of the system. However, ex ante, when a financial institution makes decisions on its investment portfolio, it does not take into account this externality; therefore, everyone tends to over invest in risky assets in order to benefit from all the high yields in the good time while the cost in asset fire sale is mostly shouldered by the others. In equilibrium, there is excess investment in risky assets across all financial institutions, increasing the fragility of the entire financial system. Another example is holding liquid assets, say, reserves: The yields of liquid assets are typically very low compared with illiquid assets, therefore, holding liquid assets implies an opportunity cost for a bank; on the other hand, besides infrequently providing the holder liquidity buffer when being under stress, the liquid assets benefit other banks via being lent to those with liquidity shortages, i.e., one bank's holding liquid assets has a *positive* externality on the rest of the system, as it has to bear all the opportunity cost while others enjoy most of the benefit. Therefore, as Cao and Illing (2011) show, individual banks thus have a strong incentive to free ride on liquidity provision by others, holding low liquid assets individually. As shown in Fig. 10.17, the share of liquid assets in banks' total assets fells almost to zero before the crisis in both the USA and UK. Such systemic liquidity shortage increases the vulnerability of financial system under market stress: Liquidity buffer in the system can be easily exhausted, leading to a system wide liquidity crunch.

Another important source of systemic risk arises from the network effect. Modern financial institutions are heavily connected to each other via lending and borrowing, forming a huge "web of claims;" therefore, the failure of one bank may bring down its immediate counterparties, and the bank failure can quickly spread over the entire network—in this sense, banks are "too connected to fail." Such mechanism can be easily seen from Fig. 10.18, as proposed by Allen and Gale (2000): The arrow means the flow of funding, i.e., bank A borrows from bank D, bank B borrows from bank A, etc. Now suppose that bank A fails, this incurs a loss to its immediate creditor, bank D, and bank D may fail if the loss is large enough... in the end, such domino effect may make all the connected banks in the network go bust. If a regulator only focuses on individual banks' operational risks, it will miss the systemic risk from the financial contagion over the banking network.

To address the systemic risks, regulators need to go one step beyond the microprudential view and adopt the macroprudential perspective. Borio (2003) compares the differences between these perspectives, as in Table 10.1.

Precisely, macroprudential regulation aims to address those systemic risks that cannot be contained on the level of individual financial institutions and reduce the likelihood of systemic events. The ultimate goal is to provide financial stability as a public good and avoid the macroeconomic costs from systemic failure, one step beyond the conventional regulatory objective that often focuses exclusively on limiting market power of individual institutions. The financial institutions should not be treated as passive financial accelerators, but rather, they may be troublemakers so financial crises can arise from inside of the financial system. Special attentions are needed for the interconnections between financial institutions, as well as their common exposures to certain risks, excess correlation of their investment portfolios, etc., that make them particularly vulnerable to financial contagions.

In order to achieve the macroprudential objectives, tools and instruments are needed to fix well-articulated problems through well-understood mechanisms; at the same time, these tools and instruments should be compatible with incentives and waterproof for arbitrage. This is still a big challenge, as the research on systemic risk has just taken off. Recent discussions include introducing taxes/subsidies against externalities—for example, levying an additional financial transaction tax to curb banks' excess appetite for risky assets, and surcharges on capital requirements for systemically important financial institutions (SIFIs)—to improve the resilience of these institutions and prevent financial contagion from these institutions to the rest of the financial network. However, many questions still remain to be answered.

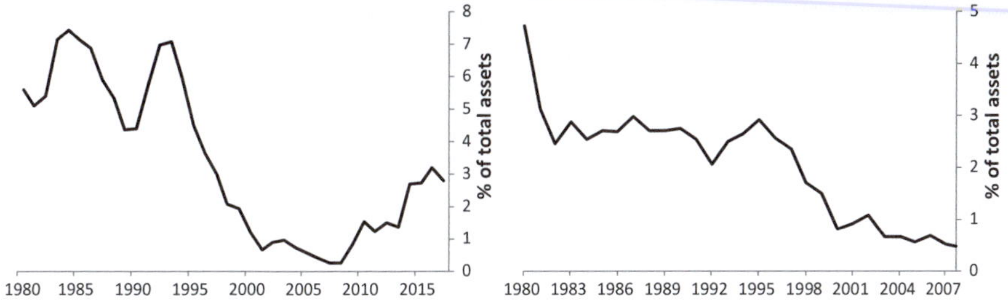

Fig. 10.17 Liquid assets as share of banks' balance sheets: US (left) and UK (right). Source: Ahnert and Nelson (2012)

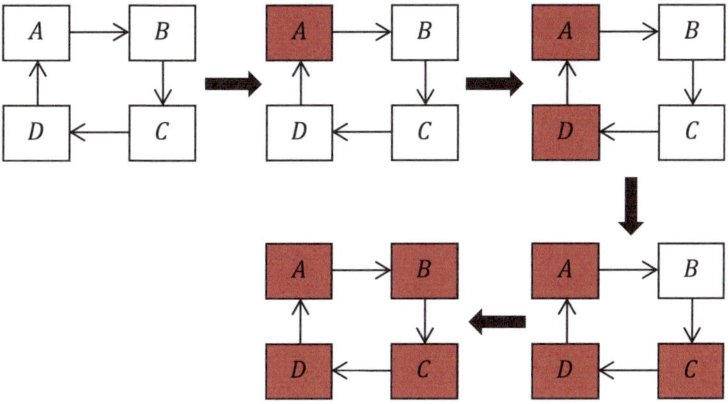

Fig. 10.18 Financial contagion

Table 10.1 The macro- and microprudential perspectives compared

	Macroprudential	Microprudential
Proximate objective	Limit financial system-wide distress	Limit distress of individual institutions
Ultimate objective	Avoid output (GDP) costs	Consumer (investor/depositor) protection
Model of risk	(In part) endogenous	Exogenous
Correlations and common exposures across institutions	Important	Irrelevant
Calibration of prudential controls	In terms of system-wide distress; top-down	In terms of risks of individual institutions; bottom-up

Any regulation trying to prevent financial crises has to rely on past experience; it may be slow to change in response to new challenges. For intermediaries, there are strong incentives to move into corners of the market outside of the current focus of regulation and supervision. It is technically almost impossible to implement the right requirements at the right time. So regulation always runs the risk of "fighting the last war." There are good reasons to opt for simple yet effective rules, "getting in all of the cracks." According to Admati and Hellwig (2013), imposing sufficiently high capital requirements could be key for implementing robust rules. The larger the capital requirements imposed on intermediaries, the weaker is the pro-cyclicality of the financial system and so less the need for macroprudential interventions.

10.5 Summary

In the final chapter, we analyzed the feedback between monetary policy and financial stability. We considered two main approaches. The first one in Sect. 10.2 was a macro approach, integrating the banking sector in a standard DSGE model. We presented a simplified version of the Gertler–Kiyotaki model which shows how financial instability evolves over time, how it propagates to the real economy, and how monetary policy can help the economy to recover from the crisis. That model integrates both financial accelerator effects and bank runs. Banks hold long-term assets and issue short-term debt, making them subject to the risk of runs. So the feedback effects between banking distress and the state of the real economy are far more complex than standard financial accelerator models suggest: The weakening of balance sheets and reduced liquidity of secondary markets for bank assets during recessions not only trigger financial accelerator mechanisms but also increase the risk of runs. Whether runs may occur depends on macroeconomic conditions: Runs are likely to be triggered in bad times when bank balance sheets are tightened. In turn, runs feed back into the macro economy, aggravating the downturn. This gives rise to the possibility of multiple, self-fulfilling equilibria, introducing nonlinearity in the system; A severe recession induces financial distress that amplifies falls in assets prices and raises the cost of bank credit. Banks will be forced to liquidate, transferring assets to agents with less expertise in screening and monitoring investment projects relative to banks. The net effect is a substantial increase in the cost of bank credit, raising the spread between the expected return to bank assets and the riskless rate even more.

The model illustrates that the distinction between a liquidity shortage and insolvency is fairly subtle. If a bank run equilibrium occurs, banks become insolvent, i.e., their liabilities exceed their assets if assets are valued at the fire-sale prices. But if assets would be valued at the price in the no-run equilibrium, all banks would be considered to be solvent. Thus, whether banks are insolvent or not depends on equilibrium asset prices which in turn depend on the liquidity in the banking system. This liquidity can change abruptly in the event of a run, motivating a role for ex post lender of the last resort policies in reducing vulnerability to runs.

Recently, quite a few models have been addressing issues of multiple equilibria and the resulting nonlinearity in the macro economy. To get tractable solutions, the behavior of banks has to be very much simplified in most of these models, abstracting from some key sources of systemic risks. The banking approach presented in Sect. 10.3 tries to fill that gap. It integrates central bank actions and a simplified real economy in partial equilibrium banking models in order to model the strategic responses of banks to monetary policy, so capturing key sources of financial instabilities. We analyzed a simplified version of the Cao–Illing model of a risk-taking channel. Monetary policy changes banks' risk-taking incentives and leads to adjustments in banks' balance sheets through their liquidity and risk management practice, affecting financial stability. We showed that the central bank's conduct of monetary policy distorts banks' incentive on building liquidity buffers: By accepting illiquid assets as collateral in the interday loans, banks are encouraged to invest more in illiquid, risky assets, leaving the economy in an inferior equilibrium with excessive exposure to systemic liquidity risk, low monetary policy rate and low real return for the depositors. We learned that a mix between ex ante macroprudential liquidity regulation and ex post lender of last resort policy can implement the constrained efficient solution in a dynamic consistent way. In Sect. 10.4 we analyzed the link between monetary policy and macroprudential regulation in more detail.

References

Admati, A., & Hellwig, M. (2013). *The bankers' new clothes*. Princeton, NJ: Princeton University Press.

Allen, F., & Gale, D. (2000). Financial contagion. *Journal of Political Economy, 108*(1), 1–33.

Bagehot, W. (1873). *Lombard street: A description of the money market*. London: Henry S. King & Co.

Benes, J., & Kumhof, M. (2012). The Chicago plan revisited. *IMF Working Paper* 12/202.

Bernanke, B., & Gertler, M. (1989). Agency costs, net worth, and business fluctuations. *American Economic Review, 79*(1), 14–31.

Boissay, F., Collard, F., & Smets, F. (2014). *Booms and banking crises*. https://papers.ssrn.com/sol3/papers.cfm?abstract_id=2131075

Borio, C. (2003). Towards a macroprudential framework for financial supervision and regulation? *BIS Working Papers* No. 128.

Brunnermeier, M. K., & Pedersen, L. H. (2009). Market liquidity and funding liquidity. *Review of Financial Studies, 22*(6), 2201–2238.

Brunnermeier, M. K., & Sannikov, Y. (2014). A macroeconomic model with a financial sector. *American Economic Review, 104*(2), 379–421.

Calvo, G. (1988). Servicing the public debt: The role of expectations. *American Economic Review, 78*(4), 647–661.

Cao, J. (2012). *Banking regulation and the financial crisis*. Abingdon, UK: Routledge.

Cao, J., & Illing, G. (2011). Endogenous exposure to systemic liquidity risk. *International Journal of Central Banking, 7*(2), 173–216.

Cao, J., & Illing, G. (2015a). Money in the equilibrium of banking. *Norges Bank Working Paper* 22/2015.

Cao, J., & Illing, G. (2015b). 'Interest rate trap', or: Why does the central bank keep the policy rate too low for too long? *Scandinavian Journal of Economics, 117*(4), 1256–1280.

Chari, V., & Kehoe, P. (2016). Bailouts, time inconsistency, and optimal regulation: A macroeconomic view. *American Economic Review, 106*, 2458–2493.

Cochrane, J. H. (2016). Equity-financed banking. *The Grumpy Economist*. https://johnhcochrane.blogspot.com/2016/05/equity-financed-banking.html

Corsetti, G., & Dedola, L. (2016). The "mystery of the printing press" monetary policy and self-fulfilling debt crises. *Journal of European Economic Association, 14*, 1329–1371.

De Grauwe, P. (2013). The European Central Bank as lender of last resort in the government bond markets. *CESifo Economic Studies, 59*(3), 520–535.

Diamond, D. W., & Dybvig, P. H. (1983). Bank runs, deposit insurance, and liquidity. *Journal of Political Economy, 91*(3), 401–419.

Douglas, W. D., & Rajan, R. G. (2001). Banks and liquidity. *American Economic Review, 91*(2), 422–425.

Fisher, I. (1936). 100% Money and the public debt. *Economic Forum, Spring Number*, April–June 1936, pp. 406–420.

Friedman, M., & Schwartz, A. (1963). *A monetary history of the United States, 1867–1960.* Princeton, NJ: Princeton University Press.

Gertler, M., & Kiyotaki, N. (2010). Financial intermediation and credit policy in business cycle analysis. In B. M. Friedman & M. Woodford (Eds.), *Handbook of monetary economics* (Vol. 3, pp. 547–599). Amsterdam: Elsevier.

Gertler, M., & Kiyotaki, N. (2015). Banking, liquidity, and bank runs in an infinite horizon economy. *American Economic Review, 105*(7), 2011–2043.

Goodhart, C., & Illing, G. (2009). *Financial crises, contagion, and the lender of last resort.* Oxford: Oxford University Press.

Gorton, G., & Metrick, A. (2012). Securitized banking and the run on repo. *Journal of Financial Economics, 104*(3), 425–451.

Hart, O., & Moore, J. (1994). A theory of debt based on the inalienability of human capital. *Quarterly Journal of Economics, 109*(4), 841–879.

Holmström, B., & Tirole, J. (1998). Private and public supply of liquidity. *Journal of Political Economy, 106*(1), 1–40.

Sargent, T. (2011). Where to draw lines: Stability versus efficiency. *Economica, 78*(310), 197–214, 2011.

Shin, H. (2010). *Risk and liquidity* (Clarendon Lectures). New York: Oxford University Press.

Sims, C. (2013). Paper money. *American Economic Review, 103*(2), 563–584.

MIX
Papier aus verantwortungsvollen Quellen
Paper from responsible sources
FSC® C105338
FSC
www.fsc.org

If you have any concerns about our products,
you can contact us on
ProductSafety@springernature.com

In case Publisher is established outside the EU,
the EU authorized representative is:
Springer Nature Customer Service Center GmbH
Europaplatz 3, 69115 Heidelberg, Germany

Printed by Libri Plureos GmbH
in Hamburg, Germany